THIRD EDITION

INTERNATIONAL MANAGEMENT

A Cultural Approach

In memory of my parents, Maria and Cesaro, and my brother, Antonio

THIRD EDITION

INTERNATIONAL MANAGEMENT

A Cultural Approach

CARL RODRIGUES

Montclair State University

Los Angeles • London • New Delhi • Singapore

For information:

SAGE Publications, Inc.
2455 Teller Road
Thousand Oaks, California 91320
E-mail: order@sagepub.com

SAGE Publications India Pvt. Ltd.
B 1/I 1 Mohan Cooperative Industrial Area
Mathura Road, New Delhi 110 044
India

SAGE Publications Ltd.
1 Oliver's Yard
55 City Road
London EC1Y 1SP
United Kingdom

SAGE Publications Asia-Pacific Pte. Ltd.
33 Pekin Street #02-01
Far East Square
Singapore 048763

Printed in the United States of America

Library of Congress Cataloging-in-Publication Data

Rodrigues, Carl.
International management: A cultural approach / Carl Rodrigues. — 3rd ed.
     p. cm.
Includes bibliographical references and index.
ISBN 978-1-4129-5141-8 (pbk.: acid-free paper)
    1. International business enterprises—Management—Social aspects. 2. Strategic planning—Social aspects. 3. International business enterprises—Management—Case studies. 4. Intercultural communication. I. Title.

HD62.4.R645 2009
658′.049—dc22   2008008498

This book is printed on acid-free paper.

08   09   10   11   12   11   10   9   8   7   6   5   4   3   2   1

Acquisitions Editor:	Al Bruckner
Associate Editor:	Deya Saoud
Editorial Assistant:	MaryAnn Vail
Copy Editor:	QuADS Prepress (P) Ltd.
Typesetter:	C&M Digitals (P) Ltd.
Cover Designer:	Edgar Abarca
Marketing Manager:	Jennifer Reed Banando

BRIEF CONTENTS

DETAILED CONTENTS

PART VIII   COURSE INTEGRATIVE ASSIGNMENT

This section presents instructions for preparing a project aiming to integrate the entire textbook—a sort of mini course thesis.

PREFACE

To the Student

Why Study International Management?

In the past, in some nations, the United States, for example, most business enterprises were able to maintain a steady growth rate—or at least survive—in their home-country market. However, since costs have steadily increased in those nations and foreign competitors with lower costs of production have rapidly emerged, many of those businesses lost that market stability and have been or are now being forced to compete in the international market arena. And as technologies continue to transfer across countries, businesses in more and more nations are becoming active and competitive participants in the global economy. These developments will continue to generate not only new global competitors but also new business opportunities in foreign markets. This means that more firms will have to, or choose to, become involved in international business. It also means that more companies will need managers with the ability to apply the managerial process across countries and cultures with differing characteristics. A good starting point toward the development of such managers is at the college/university level (and even at the precollege level).

Therefore, the transfer of business activities across nations is growing at a rapid rate. Furthermore, the collapse of communism in the Soviet Union and Eastern Europe, the emergence of market economies in Latin America and Asia, and emerging democracy in Africa has led to placing a nation's economic destiny in the hands of its people. To set the stage for the economic boom, these countries are making themselves attractive places for foreign enterprises to invest. This means that in the years ahead, the globalization of business activities is likely to increase enormously, and global competition is likely to intensify even more than in recent years. It also means that to remain competitive in the global marketplace, firms must employ people who possess international management skills. Thus, there is a need for a college/university text of this nature.

Text Objective

The purpose of *International Management: A Cultural Approach* is to teach, in a comprehensive, "user friendly" style, the managerial process (planning, organizing, staffing, coordinating, and controlling) in a global context to upper undergraduate and

M.B.A. students, who will take a course on international management. Ideally, students who enroll in this course will have completed a generic management course, such as Introduction to Management, Principles of Management, Management Process, Organizational Behavior, and Introduction to International Business.

Text Organization

The text describes how varying national cultures affect the application of the managerial process. The following are some examples:

- Individuals in some cultures commit to plans more readily than individuals in others.
- Strategies are affected by the varying cross-cultural preference for products and services and marketing techniques.
- People in some cultures require more organizational structure than people in others.
- Executives sent abroad to manage a firm's foreign subsidiary adapt more readily to some cultures than to others. Many executives have great difficulty adapting to any foreign culture.
- Individuals in some cultures want to participate more in the decision-making process and have a lower tolerance for authoritarian managers than individuals in other cultures.
- Business practices and negotiation styles that work in one culture usually do not succeed in another culture.
- Most nations have their own unique language, both verbal and nonverbal, which affects the application of the communication process across cultures.
- Employee motivation and work values vary from country to country. Thus, the motivational technique that works in one culture might not necessarily work in another culture.
- Managers in some cultures want more control over an international corporation's local subsidiary than do managers in other cultures.
- The practice of business ethics is affected by the country's culture, as is a corporation's social responsibility.

Chapter 1 gives an overview of how culture affects the managerial process. Chapter 2 discusses cross-cultural business ethics and corporate social responsibility. Chapter 3 describes how other country factors, such as the legal, political/governmental, economic, and technological systems, affect the managerial process. Chapters 4 and 5 discuss strategies for internationalizing business operations. Chapter 6 presents various international organizational structures. Chapters 7 and 8 discuss options for staffing international operations and training and developing global managers. Chapters 9 and 10 discuss cross-cultural communication, business practices, and negotiations. Chapters 11 and 12 discuss cross-cultural decision making, leadership, and motivation. Chapter 13 discusses control of global organizations. In addition, each chapter contains at least one section describing how current information technology affects the international management process.

To the Instructor

Text Flexibility

Some of the chapters in *International Management: A Cultural Approach* can be adapted to an instructor's preference for sequencing topics. For example, an instructor may prefer to cover certain topics, such as cross-cultural business ethics and corporate social responsibility (Chapter 2) later in the course. Some instructors may prefer to cover international organizational structures (Chapter 6) and international controls (Chapter 13) sequentially. And others may see fit to cover parts of chapters out of sequence.

Pedagogy

The text provides the following features.

Practical Chapter-Opening Quotation

Each chapter begins with an opening quotation on practical international management intended to pique students' interest in the material contained in the chapter.

Learning Objectives of the Chapter

Following the opening quotation, all chapters offer a brief background of the substance of the chapter and its objectives.

Practical Perspectives and Anecdotes

All chapters contain numerous practical perspectives inserted in toned form. (Two practical perspectives in Chapter 10 are long and are thus presented as appendices at the end of the chapter.) The chapters also contain short practical anecdotes throughout the text. The aim of these practical perspectives and anecdotes is to help students understand the theoretical aspects of the chapter.

Figures, Tables, and Graphs

To make reading the chapters more interesting, many of the processes, concepts, and theories are presented in figure, table, or graphic form. For classroom discussion, these can generally be displayed via overhead transparencies and/or through a PowerPoint presentation.

Key Terms and Concepts, Discussion Questions and Exercises, Chapter Assignment, and Case Studies

At the end of each chapter there is a set of key terms and concepts, followed by discussion questions and exercises, an assignment, and case studies. All these tie to the body of the chapter and help students develop an integrative understanding of the essence of the chapter.

Index

An index is provided at the end of the text.

Instructor's Resources

An Instructor's Manual and Test Bank (on CD-ROM) provides lecture assistance and includes PowerPoint slides, a test bank, suggested class and Internet exercises, and a special feature titled *Learning from SAGE Journal Articles* that provides original research and discussion questions to give students additional information about the material.

New to This Edition

The third edition of *International Management: A Cultural Approach* has been updated and revised to reflect the most recent research, laws, cases, and examples. Specific changes and new material include the following.

Organizational Changes

We have cut some topics in various chapters and pasted them in other chapters, and we have eliminated various topics to develop a smoother flow for the reader. Chapter 14 has been eliminated, but key points have been transferred to Chapter 1.

We have also eliminated the integrative cases at the end of the textbook. In its place, we have included step-by-step instructions for students on how to prepare a timetable project (a business plan) for internationalizing a business enterprise. The students are given the choice of selecting a domestic enterprise and developing a business plan for internationalizing it or starting a new business enterprise and developing a business plan for internationalizing it, or they can research an existing international enterprise and describe, using the timetable, how it internationalized itself. This is a sort of course thesis. It works best when the project is assigned to three or four students, and at the end of the semester, each group presents its project to the class.

Additional Material

Each chapter includes updated research findings, new textual examples, and practical perspectives where appropriate. In addition, each chapter uses a more varied representation of countries and regions as examples to more accurately reflect the global focus of the book. Furthermore, current information technology, such as the Internet, e-mail, videoconferencing, and cellular phones, is a new topic added to each chapter of this edition of the textbook. Each chapter now contains a section describing how current information technology affects the chapter's focus, such as international planning, organizing, staffing, coordinating, and controlling. These comprehensive revisions and expansions were designed to allow greater depth into specific issues in international management and to enhance chapter readability and relevance for all students.

Other

This textbook is designed to accomplish many goals, including, but not limited to, a multidimensional approach designed to enhance and fortify student comprehension and retention of the information. Thus, the text and ancillaries are a complete package, with a balance of concepts, examples, and practical applications. To promote understanding of international management, the following changes have been made to the text and ancillaries:

Practical Perspectives has been modified to reflect the most up-to-date perspectives on international management issues and concepts. It is our belief that these practical perspectives reflect the most cutting-edge information available in international management today.

Key Terms has been expanded to include key terms and concepts to accurately reflect and draw attention to the most important points in the text.

Many chapter integrative cases have been updated and replaced with informative, thought-provoking, and current cases to accurately reveal to students the issues and challenges facing international business and managers today. These cases were selected with the 21st-century student in mind.

This edition also includes a PowerPoint presentation with an abundance of full-color slides. The presentation is varied and is designed to hold students' interest while reinforcing each of the chapters' main points.

Acknowledgments

I owe a deep debt of gratitude to the reviewers for their expert assistance with all three editions. Each comment and suggestion was thoroughly evaluated, and served to improve the final product. To each of the reviewers below, I give my most sincere thanks:

Ron Abernathy, *UNCG Bryan School of Business*

Sheila A. Adams, *University of North Carolina at Wilmington*

Douglas Allen, *University of Denver*

Fritz E. Bachli, *Lesley College*

Richard Baldwin, *Cedarville College*

B. R. Baliga, *Wake Forest University*

Charles Byles, *Virginia Commonwealth University*

Shari Carpenter, *Eastern Oregon University*

Warnock Davies, *Golden Gate University*

Raffaele DeVito, *Emporia State University*

Meredith Downes, *Illinois State University*

Richard E. Dutton, *University of South Florida*

David Flynn, *Hofstra University*

Franco Gandolfi, *Regent University*

Manton C. Gibbs, Jr., *Indiana University of Pennsylvania*

George Gore, *University of Cincinnati*

Jian Gu, *Salem State College*

Santiago Ibarreche, *University of Texas at El Paso*

Sara L. Keck, *Pace University*

Weixing Li, *University of Nebraska-Lincoln*

Franz T. Lohrke, *Louisiana State University*

Robert C. Losik, *New Hampshire College*

Lauryn A. Migenes, *University of Central Florida*

Ray Montagno, *Ball State University*

Francine Newth, *Providence College*

John N. Orife, *Indiana University of Pennsylvania*

Eren Ozgen, *Troy University, Dothan Campus*

Steven K. Paulson, *University of North Florida*

Joseph A. Petrick, *Wright State University*

S. Benjamin Prasad, *Central Michigan University*

Gerald W. Ramey, *Eastern Oregon University*

Abdul Rasheed, *University of Texas at Arlington*

Rajib N. Sanyal, *Trenton State College*

C. Richard Scott, *Metropolitan State College of Denver*

John A. C. Stanbury, *Indiana University at Kokomo*

Gregory K. Stephens, *Texas Christian University*

Jeffrey D. Stone, *California State University, Northridge*

Arthur Whatley, *New Mexico State University*

I especially wish to thank Nailin Bu, a colleague at Queen's University, Canada, for providing me with numerous materials that were very useful in the development of the first edition, as well as for her willingness to help whenever needed. For the second edition, I wish to thank the reviewers for their valuable suggestions on how to improve on the first edition. And I want to thank the reviewers for their valuable suggestions on how to improve on the second edition. I also wish to thank Theresa and Kelly Curtis of Ohlinger Publishing Services for their very valuable ideas on how to improve the first edition and for their skillful management of the project. Many thanks also to Libby Shipp, the production editor, and Debbie Cress, the project manager for the second edition. And I wish to thank John R. Szilagyi, Executive Editor, South-Western/Thomson, for having faith in the second edition project.

I wish to thank Deya Saoud, Associate Editor at Sage Publications, for her extraordinary input and coordination with the reviewers for the third edition project. I also want to thank, again, John R. Szilagyi (now Executive Editor of Sage Publications), who moved from South-Western to Sage and took the book with him; Al Bruckner, the current editor, for believing in the third edition project; as well as Sheri Gilbert for her assistance with the permissions. I also wish to thank Diane Foster, the production editor; Nichole Angress, the marketing editor; and Shamila Swamy and her copyediting team from Quads Prepress (P) Ltd.

Part I INTRODUCTION TO INTERNATIONAL MANAGEMENT

The term *management* is defined in many Western, and particularly U.S., textbooks as the process of completing activities efficiently with and through other individuals. The process consists of the functions or main activities engaged in by managers. These functions or activities are usually labeled *planning, organizing, staffing, coordinating* (leading and motivating), and *controlling*. The management process is affected by the organization's home country environment, which includes the shareholders, creditors, customers, employees, government, and community, as well as economic, technological, demographic, and geographic factors.

International management is applied by managers of enterprises, who attain their goals and objectives across unique multicultural, multinational boundaries. These business enterprises are generally referred to as international corporations, multinational corporations (MNCs), or global corporations, which are discussed in Chapter 4. This means that the process is affected by the environment where the organization is based, as well as by the unique culture, including views on ethics and social responsibility, existing in the country or countries where it conducts its business activities. Chapter 1 discusses the impact of culture on the managerial process, and Chapter 2 describes the views on business ethics and social responsibility that have an impact on international management.

THE INTERNATIONAL MANAGEMENT PROCESS

An Overview

"Why do some international managers succeed while nearly half their counterparts fail? The answer is culture shock—the failure to adjust to people with different motivations, behaviors, and ways of making decisions."[1] In other words, too many companies assume that they can do things abroad the same way they do them at home.[2] For example, Wal-Mart, the international giant retailer, recently (August 2006) announced that it would pull out of Germany after more than a decade of trying in vain to succeed there. Wal-Mart discovered that its formula doesn't fit every culture.[3]

Learning Objectives of the Chapter

Since the environment differs across countries, the managerial approach that works in one country does not necessarily work in another. This suggests that to manage effectively across cultures, managers require skills beyond those required to manage in the home country. For example, managers would know that in the United States it is the individual who counts. In Japan, it is the group—things get done not by nonconforming lone rangers but by group consensus. The consensus is possible only through cultivation of relationships. Relationships help define the essence of Japanese society, including the conduct of business. Thus, to be effective in managing international business enterprises, managers must develop cross-cultural competence.[4] After studying this chapter, you should be able to describe the following:

1. Culture

2. The impact of culture on international planning, international organization, international staffing, international coordinating, and international controlling

3. The impact of religion on international management

4. Other factors that affect the management process

5. Global management, as a future perspective

6. Cross-cultural convergence and the impact of information technologies on cultural change

7. The skills international/global managers require

The International Management Process

The international management process is heavily affected by the culture (as well as other factors) of the country where enterprises pursue their goals and objectives. (For a description of how culture affects the international management process in Asia, read Practical Perspective 1.1.)

PRACTICAL PERSPECTIVE 1-1

Managing Cultural Diversity in Asia

Cultural elements can affect business behavior in Asia in several ways. Western companies may find that differences occur in areas such as commitment to the organization, work ethic, the drive to achieve and succeed, acceptance of responsibility; the relationship with seniors, the way in which subordinates are motivated, or handling discipline and control. The Confucian cultures hold a secret to success. [The author cites Gordon Redding, a professor at Hong Kong University.]

From the huge monolithic networks of Japan (*keiretsu*) and Korea (*chaebol*) to the small family-owned businesses of overseas Chinese that dominate Taiwan, Hong Kong, and Southeast Asia, "patterns replicate like successful recipes," he [Professor Redding] said. The common denominator is paternalism. It is difficult to generalize, but it has been argued that the hierarchical, vertical, familial, highly status-differentiated structures that permeate Asia show marked contrast to the more egalitarian, horizontal institutions of the West.

Social relationships tend to be more authoritarian, paternalistic, and personal in Asia, nurturing autocratic or unilateral decision-making processes and interpersonal relationships that are based on collectivism and group welfare. Corresponding parameters in the West include more consultative decision making but an emphasis on individualism, self-interest, and impersonal or aggressive relations. Words such as loyalty, trust, and cooperation enjoy high rating in motivating and controlling Asian employees, whereas competency and individual performance are strong motivators in the West.

Western multinationals planning to gear up their businesses in Asia may have to adapt their corporate cultures to embrace elements more familiar to Asian businesses. This could include profit sharing, a highly disciplined structure, a more humanistic corporate culture, increased non-individualistic reward, a greater sense of corporate pride, or a stronger cementing in of workers by use of fringe benefits.

SOURCE: Excerpted from Lyn Tattum, "Managing Cultural Diversity in Asia," *Chemical Week* (February 3, 1993), p. 14. Reprinted with permission.

Culture

Culture comprises an entire set of social norms and responses that condition people's behavior; it is acquired and inculcated, a set of rules and behavior patterns that an individual learns but does not inherit at birth.[5] It enables people to make sense of their world, and it is foreign only to those outside. Knowledge of the concept of culture is imperative for understanding human behavior throughout the world, including in one's own country. Fundamentally, groups of individuals develop a social environment as an adaptation to their physical environment, and they pass down their customs, practices, and traditions from generation to generation.[6]

For a brief account of how cultures differ across countries, see Practical Perspective 1.2. For an illustration of how culture affects international business practices, read Practical Perspective 1.3.

PRACTICAL PERSPECTIVE 1-2

Different Cultures, Different Meanings

Never touch the head of a Thai or pass an object over it, as the head is considered sacred in Thailand. Likewise, never point the bottoms of the feet in the direction of another person in Thailand or cross your legs while sitting, especially in the presence of an older person. Avoid using triangular shapes in Hong Kong, Korea, or Taiwan, as a triangle is considered a negative shape in those countries. Remember that the number 7 is considered bad luck in Kenya, good luck in Czechoslovakia [now Czech Republic and Slovakia Republic], and has magical connotations in Benin. Red is a positive color in Denmark but represents witchcraft and death in many African countries. A nod means "no" in Bulgaria, and shaking the head side-to-side means "yes."

SOURCE: Excerpted from M. Katharine Glover, "Do's and Taboos: Cultural Aspects of International Business," *Business America* (August 13, 1990), p. 2. Reprinted with permission.

PRACTICAL PERSPECTIVE 1-3

Culture in the Arab World

Most managers in the U.S. and other Western countries say that culture consists of beliefs, values, ways of thinking, and language. But most Arab managers—like their Japanese counterparts—think of culture as history, tradition, and a way of life. Clearly, culture is a behavioral norm that a group of people have agreed upon in order to survive. These norms vary by time and place and are constantly adapted to the changing environment.

Within each culture, there are many subcultures of which we are simultaneously members. An Egyptian-born executive of a Cairo computer company belongs to the subcultures of Egypt, his company, his sales department, product group, family, and so forth. Every sort of normal, day-to-day business activity is affected by these cultural identities—including personal introductions, meetings, presentations, training, motivation, and written communication.

One way of looking at culture is to consider what values are most important: competition, formality, group harmony, risk-taking, or authority. Among Americans, emphasis is usually placed on independence, competition, and individual success. In the Arab world, however, primacy is given to family security, compromise, and personal reputation. Let's consider a few situations in which dramatic differences in behavior can generate conflict, or at least misunderstanding:

An American attending a business conference is likely to introduce himself to an Arab businessman then quickly walk off to talk to other Arab executives, declining invitations to have some coffee during the break. The American doesn't have enough time for more than a brief chat with anyone; his objective is to make as many contacts as possible. The Arab businessmen are put off by this behavior because Arabs place a high value on building personal relationships; they want to get to know someone fairly well before discussing business matters.... Like the Japanese, Arabs hold a much longer-term view of time; they don't shun spending months or years building personal relationships and trust....

Friction is likely to occur when there is disagreement in the workplace since Arabs take a very different view of how to manage conflict than do Americans. If an American worker disagrees with his [her] manager, he [or she] is most likely to discuss the matter directly with the manager. This is because Americans value social equality and believe that frank discussion can solve many difficult problems. In the Arab countries, however, an employee who has a disagreement with his or her immediate supervisor (American or otherwise) may well decide to appeal to a higher authority—the manager's boss. If the immediate supervisor is American, this surprise can generate even greater ill will.

Even the "simple" subject of physical distance can create misunderstandings. An Arab executive may well stand closer to you than would an American or Japanese. While this is a way of expressing personal warmth and hospitality most Westerners—and Japanese—will retreat, because they feel their comfort zone of personal space has been invaded.

SOURCE: Excerpted from Farid Elashmawi, "Managing Culture in the Arab World," *Trade & Culture* (September–October, 1994), pp. 48–49. Farid Elashmawi, Ph.D., a native of Cairo, Egypt, is the president of Tech-Trans/Global Success, a consultancy that specializes in issues of global cultural diversity. Copyright © 1994, Trade and Culture Inc. Reprinted with permission. All rights reserved.

Practice and Value Aspects of Culture

Corporate Culture. Some cross-cultural researchers have broken down the meaning of corporate culture into symbols, heroes, and rituals, which they defined as organizational practices, also often referred to as corporate culture, and into values, such as good/evil, beautiful/ugly, normal/abnormal, and rational/irrational. As you will learn in this book, what is good and evil, beautiful and ugly, normal and abnormal, and rational or irrational varies from culture to culture—for example, bribery is unethical in the United States but quite acceptable in many parts of the world.

Values. These researchers contend that corporate cultures "reflect nationality, demographics of employees and managers, industry, and market; they are related to organization structure and control systems; but all of these leave room for unique and idiosyncratic elements."[7] Among national cultures, comparing "otherwise similar people," these researchers found "considerable differences in values." Among corporate cultures (practices), the opposite was the case; they found "considerable differences in practices for people who held about the same values."[8]

Therefore, according to these researchers, the value aspects of corporate culture are attributed to nationality, but the practice aspects (symbols, heroes, and rituals) are attributed to the corporation, and the corporation changes practices in response to environmental demands. Since the environment changes at different times for different organizations, the practice aspects will differ from corporation to corporation, even when the values remain relatively similar. This means that individuals in the same national culture may possess broad behavioral similarities but different organizational practices depending on the organization they work for.[9]

As a case illustration, from 1975 to 1980, this writer worked for a South Florida Native American Indian tribe, whose reservation is located in the Everglades, about 40 miles west of downtown Miami. Until the 1960s, the tribe lived by its traditional way, a culture and values that are the complete opposite of U.S./Western culture and values. Historically, to survive, tribal members hunted and fished in the Everglades. But the huge influx of the northern Westerners to South Florida (poachers, hunters, and the draining of everglades water to build houses for the northerners) depleted their means of surviving.

The tribal leaders employed this writer and several other Westerners to help them modernize the tribe to an extent that they could develop programs that would help them survive. The head of the tribe made it clear that the tribal members despise the Western values and ways and would rather die than be like the Westerners. This meant changing their practices while maintaining their traditional values, which are about 10,000 years old—a monumental challenge, indeed, because many of the practices we wanted to change were totally unacceptable by their traditional values. And the Medicine Man, the tribe's religious leader and the keeper of the Tribe's traditional medicines, made the decisions as to which Western-like positions a trial member could practice or could not practice.

The change efforts were hindered by the existence of three tribal groups: the left, the middle, and the right. The left pushed for the change, and the right strongly opposed it. Furthermore, there were various clans within the tribe. Tribal members claimed that their way was egalitarian, but the ruling clan was in power and its members were given the better jobs, and the members of the less powerful clans were given the less important jobs. We developed numerous income-generating programs so that they could earn money to buy the things they needed to survive. We tried farming programs, but their culture didn't permit it; we tried oil exploration on the reservation, but none turned up. Ultimately, a tourist trade; relatively inexpensive alcohol and cigarette shops, because Tribes are exempt from taxes on such items; and gambling casinos, because Tribes are not subject to U.S. gambling laws, turned out to be the most lucrative sources of income for them—at the same time, under treaty stipulations, the U.S. government still has certain heavy financial treaty obligations to them.

A visit by the writer to the reservation in 2008 was a culture shock to him. Much modernization was there; numerous of their practices had changed dramatically, but it also became clear to him that their values had not changed at all, and neither had many of the practices as many were being carried out by non-Indians for the tribe—just as the writer had done nearly 30 years earlier.[10]

How Culture Is Learned

According to the well-known anthropologist Edward T. Hall, culture is learned through formal, informal, and technical means.

Formal Learning

In formal learning, "formal activities are taught by precept and admonition. The adult mentor molds the young according to patterns he [or she] himself [herself] has never questioned."[11]

Informal Learning

In informal learning, "the principal agent is a model used for imitations. Whole clusters of related activities are learned at a time, in many cases without the knowledge that they are being learned at all or that there are patterns or rules governing them."[12]

Technical Learning

Technical learning, in its pure form, "is close to being a one-way street. It is usually transmitted in explicit terms from the teacher to the student, either orally or in writing."[13]

Sources of Cultural Learning

Sources of cultural learning include the family, educational institutions, and religion.[14]

The Family

The most fundamental unit to the development of culture is the family.[15] The construction of family households varies across cultures. For example, in the United States, the nuclear family has been a fairly independent unit. However, in many cultures, such as that of Italy, the family unit is made up of the mother, father, children, grandparents, aunts, and uncles.

Educational Institutions

Another fundamental source of cultural development is educational institutions, which differ from society to society. Some societies, such as Germany, heavily emphasize organized, structured forms of learning that stress logic, while others, including Great Britain and the United States, take a more abstract, conceptual approach.[16]

Religion

Different societies develop different religions, which are the major causes of cultural differences in many societies. Basically, religious systems "provide a means of motivation and meaning beyond the material aspects of life."[17] For example, the United States, to a great extent, reflects the Protestant work ethic. Protestantism, as does Catholicism, derives from Christianity. On the other hand, many Asian cultures, such as Japan and China, are heavily influenced by Buddhism and the practical aspects of Confucianism. (It should be noted that, as will be discussed below, Confucianism is not a religion; it is a practical philosophy.) There are many religions throughout the world, including Christianity, Islam, Hinduism, and Buddhism.

Christianity. Most Christians live in Europe and the Americas, but Christianity is growing rapidly in Africa. The founder of Christianity, which emerged from Judaism, is Jesus Christ. Like Judaism, Christianity is a monotheistic (belief in one god) religion. The two major Christian organizations are the Roman Catholic Church and the Eastern Orthodox Church. The Roman Catholic Church is dominant in Southern Europe and Latin America, and the Eastern Orthodox Church is dominant in numerous countries, including Greece and Russia.

The Reformation in the 16th century led to a split in the Catholic Church and to the formation of Protestantism by Martin Luther. Subsequently, numerous denominations, including Baptist, Methodist, and Calvinist, emerged under the umbrella of

Protestantism. The famous German sociologist, Max Weber, once noted that, in Western Europe, "business leaders and owners of capital, as well as the higher grades of skilled labor, and even more the higher technically trained personnel of modern enterprises, are overwhelmingly Protestant."[18]

Islam. Islam, which dates back to about 600 AD, was started by the prophet Muhammad. Those who adhere to Islam are referred to as Muslims. It is the major religion of many African and Middle Eastern countries and in some parts of China, Malaysia, as well as some other Far East countries. Islam has some roots in both Judaism and Christianity and accepts Jesus Christ as one of God's prophets. However, Islam, also a monotheistic religion, is based on the belief that the supreme deity is Allah and the chief prophet and founder is Mohammed. The major principles of Islam (similar to Judaism and Christianity) are to honor and respect one's parents, respect the rights of others, not commit adultery, be just and equitable with others, have a pure heart and mind, safeguard the possessions of orphans, and be humble and unpretentious.[19] Religion is paramount in all aspects of Muslims' lives—for example, Muslim ritual necessitates prayer five times a day, and women dress in a certain way and must be subordinate to men.

Hinduism. Hinduism is dominant in the Indian subcontinent, where it began about 4,000 years ago. Hindus adhere to the belief that there exists a moral force in society that requires the acceptance of certain responsibilities, referred to as dharma. They believe in reincarnation and karma—the spiritual progression of each individual's soul. One's karma is affected by the way one lives, and it determines the challenges the individual will be confronted with in his or her next life. Hindus believe that by making their soul more perfect in each new life, they can eventually attain nirvana—a state of total spiritual perfection, which makes reincarnation no longer necessary. They also believe that nirvana is attained through a lifestyle of material and physical self-denial—by devoting one's life to spiritual, rather than material, attainment.

Buddhism. Buddhism also has its roots in India. It was founded in about 600 BCE by Siddhartha Gautama. Gautama, who later became known as Buddha ("the awakened one"), was an Indian prince who renounced his wealth to pursue an austere lifestyle and spiritual perfection. He believed that he had achieved nirvana but decided to stay on earth to teach his followers. According to Buddhism, misery and suffering derives from people's desires for pleasure. These desires can be repressed by following the Noble Eightfold Path: right views, right intention, right speech, right action, right livelihood, right effort, right awareness, and right concentration. Hinduism supports the caste system; Buddhism does not. And Buddhism does not advocate the type of extreme ascetic behavior that is encouraged by Hinduism. Most of the world's followers of Buddhism reside in Central and Southeast Asia, China, Korea, and Japan.

The Effects of Religion on International Management. It is apparent that religion is closely associated with the development of cultural values and that it affects people's day-to-day activities, such as a business's opening and closing times, employees' days off, ceremonies, work habits, and foods. For example, most businesses in Christian-dominated societies close on Christmas Day and often during the week before Christmas Day because of festivities; output slows down enormously. Muslim ritual requires prayer five times a day; work is often interrupted. For instance, Muslim workers at Whirlpool Corporation's Nashville, Tennessee, plant demand time off from the assembly line for daily prayers.[20] Managers of international corporations must therefore be sensitive to employees' religious needs, and corporate policies must be flexible and accommodating to the varying needs existing around the globe—otherwise, there may be high employee absenteeism and many disappearances from work to satisfy these needs.

Religion also affects international management with respect to employee motivation. For example, the principles of Hinduism and Buddhism do not focus on the practice of working to accumulate wealth; Hindus value spiritual achievements more than they value material achievements.

The Impact of Culture on International Planning

Planning entails defining the organization's mission and establishing goals and objectives, and an overall strategy to achieve them. It means being more proactive than reactive. Instead of just responding to a situation, planning allows an organization to create and influence its environment, to exert some degree of control over its destiny. International planning is affected by the various ideas on which normative cultural concepts are based, including the master-of-destiny versus the fatalistic viewpoint and the never-ending quest for improvement viewpoint.[21]

The **master-of-destiny** viewpoint is prominent in numerous cultures, including those of the United States, Britain, and Australia. Individuals holding this viewpoint believe that they can substantially influence the future, that they can control their destiny, and that through work they can make things happen. Planning in such cultures is feasible because individuals are willing to work to achieve objectives.[22]

In contrast, in many societies, including numerous Middle Eastern cultures, and those of the Muslim faith in Malaysia and Indonesia, the **fatalistic** viewpoint, or "determinism,"[23] is part of the cultural fabric. Individuals influenced by this viewpoint believe that they cannot control their destiny, that God has predetermined their existence and willed what they are to do during their lives. International managers are therefore likely to encounter more difficulty in obtaining a commitment to their plans in fatalistic cultures than they would in master-of-destiny cultures.

Furthermore, some societies, such as those of Native Americans, are dominated by **antiplanning** beliefs. Antiplanners believe that "any attempt to lay out specific and 'rational' plans is either foolish or dangerous or downright evil. The correct approach is to live in them [existing systems], react in terms of one's experience, and not to try to change them by means of some grandiose scheme or mathematical model."[24] Implementing managerial plans in these cultures is therefore difficult.

The international planning function is also affected by the concept of **never-ending quest for improvement**. Managers in some cultures, such as the United States, adhere to this view, which is a belief that change is normal and necessary and that no aspects of an enterprise are above improvement. Organizations' current practices, therefore, are constantly evaluated in the hope that improvements can be made. In contrast, in many other cultures, managers' power arises not from change but from the maintenance of stability in the status quo. These managers will interpret a suggestion for improvement as a threat and an implication that they have failed.[25] Planned change may be difficult to implement in these cultures as well.

The Impact of Culture on International Organizing

Organizing involves designing an organizational structure that best enables the enterprise to attain its goals and objectives. This includes determining what tasks need to be done and by whom, how tasks should be grouped, who is responsible for what, and how authority should be delegated. Organizing across countries is affected by the cultural views held by the society, such as the cultural viewpoint of the independent enterprise as an instrument of social action.

The concept of **independent enterprise as an instrument of social action** is widely accepted in some cultures such as the United States. Here, a corporation is viewed as an entity that has rules and a continuous existence, a separate and important social institution that must be protected and developed. As a result, individuals develop strong feelings of obligation to serve the company, and the enterprise can take priority over their personal preferences and social obligations, including family, friends, and other activities. Managers in the United States, for example, assume that each member of the organization will make a primary effort to carry out assigned tasks in the interests of the firm, that he or she will be loyal and conform to the enterprise's managerial systems. In contrast, individuals in many cultures, including some South American cultures, consider personal relationships more important than the enterprise.[26] The organizing approach applied in the two cultures would thus be different—for example, there is likely to be less delegation of authority in the personal relationships culture than in the independent enterprise culture.

The Impact of Culture on International Staffing

Staffing means finding, training, and developing the people needed to accomplish the organization's tasks. It is obvious from the previous discussion that the cultural views held by a society have an enormous impact on international staffing strategies and policies. One cultural viewpoint is the concept of personnel selection based on merit.

That **personnel selection** is based on merit is a managerial view dominant in some cultures, including that of the United States. Managers holding this view select or promote the best-qualified people for jobs and keep them as long as their performance standards meet the firm's expectations. In contrast, in many cultures, including some South American cultures, friends and family are considered more important than the enterprise's vitality; organizations expand to accommodate the maximum number of friends and relatives. For example, a Mexican's first priority is often his family, and since employers view it as an obligation that they take care of the people who work for them, nepotism is a natural part of the working world in Mexico. In Venezuela, most companies are family owned, and decisions are made to please family members more than to increase productivity.[27] Individuals who are not members of the family or in the circle of friends may therefore be less motivated to work hard or may work harder to make themselves indispensable, and family members may not work as hard since their jobs are guaranteed.[28]

The staffing function is also affected by individuals' views of wealth. In most cultures, such as Australia, wealth is generally considered desirable, and the prospect of tangible gains serves as a substantial motivator. However, the practice in some cultures, such as Mexico and Malaysia, is to work only until one earns a desired amount of money and then not return to work until the money has been spent.[29] Offering rewards in these cultures will thus not obtain high commitment to organizational goals.

The Impact of Culture on International Coordinating

Coordinating refers to the function of directing the people in the organization. It includes inspiring, appealing to individual motivations, communicating, and resolving conflicts. In their leading roles, some managers make all the decisions, and some managers allow their subordinates to make decisions. Culture also affects this managerial function. For example, the cultural viewpoint of wide sharing in decision making has an impact on the coordination of organizations across cultures.

In some cultures, such as the United States, managers adhere to the viewpoint of **wide sharing in decision making.** They believe that personnel in an organization need the responsibility of making decisions for ongoing development, and they give employees the opportunity to grow and to prove their ability, decentralizing decision making as they grow. On the other hand, managers in many cultures, such as France, believe that only a few people in the organization have the right to make decisions, and they offer no such opportunities; they centralize decision making.[30]

Culture also impairs international communication. As was suggested earlier, societies possess unique social norms and responses that condition their members' behavior. The behavior includes the tendency to block out practices that are not congruent with one's own cultural beliefs. Therefore, many groups reject prospective change, and dissimilar groups tend to misjudge one another. When an individual from one group interacts with an individual from another group, there is the tendency to make certain assumptions about the precepts, judgments, and thought processes of the other person. When these assumptions are inaccurate, misunderstanding and miscommunication occur.[31]

This means that international managers must be aware of countries' local practices with respect to leadership style and communication approaches and adapt accordingly to them. For example, an international manager from a culture in which employee participation or consultation in decision making is the norm would not do well applying the same practice in cultures in which employees expect authoritarian leadership, and vice versa. And an international manager who is frank in communicating with people because it is a valued practice in his or her culture (e.g., the United States) would not be respected by people in a culture in which frankness is unacceptable and face-saving is valued (e.g., Japan). Also, in some cultures, including the United States, an individual feels uneasy when the person with whom he or she is communicating becomes silent (pauses to think). Americans find silence clumsy and like to plug any conversational pauses, and they measure people who respond directly as being trustworthy. On the other hand, the Japanese distrust a person who responds directly; they value a person who pauses (becomes silent) to give careful thought to a question before responding.[32]

The Impact of Culture on International Controlling

Controlling is the act of evaluating performance; it is monitoring the results of the goals and objectives previously established and implemented, including measuring individual and organizational performance and taking corrective action when required. Establishing controlling mechanisms across countries is also affected by the cultural views held by the society's members, such as making decisions based on objective analysis.

A belief in **making decisions based on objective analysis** is widely held by managers in numerous cultures, including U.S. culture. Managers who practice this belief make decisions based on accurate and relevant information, and they are prompt in reporting accurate data to all levels in the organization. On the other hand, in many cultures, managers do not place much value on factual and rational support for decisions, and the reporting of details is unimportant. These decision makers do not seek out facts; they often rely on emotional and mystical considerations rather than on objective analysis; when they are asked to explain the rationale for their decisions, they will interpret the question as a lack of respect or confidence in their judgment.[33] The international manager has to address this problem when establishing controls.

Hofstede's Cultural Dimensions Model

Currently, one of the most popular theories addressing the impact of culture on the management process was that developed by Geert Hofstede, a researcher from the Netherlands.[34] He proposed a paradigm to study the impact of national culture on individual behavior and examined the values and beliefs of 116,000 IBM employees based in 40 nations throughout the world. He subsequently conducted the study in 10 other countries, raising the total number of respondents to about 145,000. Hofstede developed a typology consisting of four national cultural dimensions by which a society can be classified: power distance, uncertainty avoidance, individualism, and masculinity. The characteristics of these cultural dimensions are depicted in Tables 1.1, 1.2, 1.3, and 1.4. Professor Hofstede's framework was published in 1980, but since then an abundance of studies using his framework have been published.[35]

The Confucian Dynamism Dimension

Subsequent to his study that identified the cultural dimensions of power distance, individualism, masculinity, and uncertainty avoidance, Hofstede, in collaboration with Michael Bond, a professor and researcher at the Chinese University of Hong Kong, identified an additional cultural dimension by which nations can be classified, the *Confucian Dynamism*. This fifth dimension was identified through a questionnaire (named the Chinese Value Survey) developed on the basis of traditional Confucian values that are believed to influence East Asian countries (including the People's Republic of China, South Korea, Japan, Hong Kong [now part of China], and Singapore).[36]

This survey included 22 countries. Eighteen of these countries and two regions were included in Hofstede's earlier study. The scores for Confucian Dynamism for the 18 countries and two regions are listed in the last column of Tables 1.5 and 1.6. As shown in Table 1.5, Hong Kong, with an index score of 96, ranked Number 1 on the Confucian Dynamism dimension, and Pakistan, with an index score of 0, ranked Number 20. As Table 1.5 also depicts, East Asian countries measure high on the Confucian Dynamism dimension, while non–East Asian countries, with the exception of Brazil, tend to measure low.

| TABLE 1.1 | The Power Distance Dimension |

Small Power Distance	Large Power Distance
Inequality in society should be minimized.	There should be an order of inequality in this world in which everybody has a rightful place; high and low are protected by this order.
All people should be independent.	A few people should be independent; most should be dependent.
Hierarchy means inequality of the roles, established for convenience.	Hierarchy means existential inequality.
Superiors consider subordinates to be "people like me."	Superiors consider subordinates to be a different kind of people.
Superiors are accessible.	Superiors are accessible.
The use of power should be legitimate and is subject to the judgment as to whether it is good or evil.	Power is a basic fact of society that antedates good or evil. Its legitimacy is irrelevant.
All should have equal rights.	Power holders are entitled to privileges.
Those in power should try to look less powerful than they are.	Those in power should try to look as powerful as possible.
The system is to blame.	The underdog is to blame.
The way to change a social system is to distribute power.	The way to change a social system is to dethrone those in power.
People at various power levels feel less threatened and more prepared to trust.	Other people are a potential threat to one's power and can rarely be trusted.
Latent harmony exists between the powerful and the powerless.	Latent conflict exists between the powerful and the powerless.
Cooperation among the powerless can be based on solidarity.	Cooperation among the powerless is difficult to attain because of their low-faith-in-people norm.

SOURCE: Geert Hofstede, "Motivation, Leadership, and Organization: Do American Theories Apply Abroad?" *Organizational Dynamics* (Summer 1980), p. 46. Copyright © Geert Hofstede. Reprinted with permission.

Confucianism. Confucianism is not a religion but a system of practical ethics; it is based on a set of pragmatic rules for daily life derived from experience. The key tenet of Confucian teachings is that unequal relationships between people create stability in society. The five basic relationships are ruler-subject, father-son, older brother–younger brother, husband-wife, and older friend–younger friend. The junior owes the senior respect, and the senior owes the junior protection and consideration.

The prototype for all social institutions is the family. A person is mainly a member of a family, as opposed to being just an individual. Harmony in the family must be preserved, and harmony is the maintenance of one's face—that is, one's dignity, self-respect, and prestige; and treating others as one would like to be treated oneself is virtuous behavior.

TABLE 1.2	The Uncertainty Avoidance Dimension
Weak Uncertainty Avoidance	**Strong Uncertainty Avoidance**
The uncertainty inherent in life is more easily accepted and each day is taken as it comes.	The uncertainty inherent in life is felt as a continuous threat that must be fought.
Ease and lower stress are experienced.	Higher anxiety and stress are experienced.
Time is free.	Time is money.
Hard work, as such, is not a virtue.	There is an inner urge to work hard.
Aggressive behavior is frowned upon.	Aggressive behavior of self and others is accepted.
Less showing of emotions is preferred.	More showing of emotions is preferred.
Conflict and competition can be contained on the level of fair play and can be used constructively.	Conflict and competition can unleash aggression and should therefore be avoided.
More acceptance of dissent is entailed.	A strong need for consensus is involved.
Deviation is not considered threatening; greater tolerance is shown.	Deviant persons and ideas are dangerous; intolerance holds sway.
The ambience is one of less nationalism.	Nationalism is pervasive.
More positive feelings toward younger people are seen.	Younger people are suspect.
There is more willingness to take risks in life.	There is great concern with security in life.
The accent is on relativism, empiricism.	The search is for ultimate, absolute truths and values.
There should be as few rules as possible.	There is a need for written rules and regulations.
If rules cannot be kept, we should change them.	If rules cannot be kept, we are sinners and should repent.
Belief is placed in generalists and common sense.	Belief is placed in experts and their knowledge.
The authorities are there to serve the citizens.	Ordinary citizens are incompetent compared with the authorities.

SOURCE: Geert Hofstede, "Motivation, Leadership, and Organization: Do American Theories Apply Abroad?" *Organizational Dynamics* (Summer 1980), p. 47. Copyright © Geert Hofstede. Reprinted with permission.

Virtue with respect to one's tasks consists of attempting to obtain skills and education, working hard, not spending more than necessary, being patient, and persevering.

It should be noted that individuals may have inner thoughts that differ from the group's norms and values; however, individuals may not act on those thoughts because group harmony and not shaming the group are of paramount importance.[37] (For an illustration of how Confucianism affects international management, refer again to

Text Continued on Page 19

TABLE 1.3	The Individualism Dimension
Collectivist	**Individualist**
In society, people are born into extended families or clans who protect them in exchange for loyalty.	In society, everybody is supposed to take care of himself/herself and his/her immediate family.
"We" consciousness holds sway.	"I" consciousness holds sway.
Identity is based on the social system.	Identity is based in the individual.
There is emotional dependence of the individual on organizations or institutions.	There is emotional independence of the individual from organizations or institutions.
The involvement with organizations is moral.	The involvement with organizations is calculative.
The emphasis is on belonging to organizations; membership is ideal.	The emphasis is on individual initiative and achievement; leadership is ideal.
Private life is invaded by organizations and clans to which one belongs; opinions are predetermined.	Everybody has the right to a private life and opinion.
Expertise, order, duty, and security are provided by the organization clan.	Autonomy, variety, pleasure, and individual financial security are sought in the system.
Friendships are predetermined by stable social relationships, but there is need for prestige within these relationships.	The need is for specific friendships.
Belief is placed in group decisions.	Belief is placed in individual decisions.
Value standards differ for in-groups and out-groups (particularism).	Value standards should apply to all (universalism).

SOURCE: Geert Hofstede, "Motivation, Leadership, and Organization: Do American Theories Apply Abroad?" *Organizational Dynamics* (Summer 1980), p. 48. Copyright © Geert Hofstede. Reprinted with permission.

TABLE 1.4	The Masculine Dimension
Feminine	**Masculine**
Men needn't be assertive but can also assume nurturing roles.	Men should be assertive. Women should be nurturing.
Sex roles in society are more fluid.	Sex roles in society are clearly differential.
There should be equality between the sexes.	Men should dominate in society.
Quality of life is important.	Performance is what counts.
You work in order to live.	You live in order to work.
People and environment are important.	Money and things are important.
Interdependence is the ideal.	Independence is the ideal.
One sympathizes with the unfortunate.	One admires the successful achiever.
Small and slow are beautiful.	Big and fast are beautiful.
Unisex and androgyny are ideal.	Ostentatious manliness ("machismo") is appreciated.

SOURCE: Geert Hofstede, "Motivation, Leadership, and Organization: Do American Theories Apply Abroad?" *Organizational Dynamics* (Summer 1980), p. 49. Copyright © Geert Hofstede. Reprinted with permission.

TABLE 1.5 Scores on Five Dimensions for 50 Countries and Three Regions in IBM's International Employee Attitude Survey

Country	Power Distance		Individualism		Masculinity		Uncertainty Avoidance		Confucian Dynamism	
	Index	Rank	Index	Rank	Index	Rank	Index	Rank	Index	Rank
Argentina	49	35–36	46	22–23	56	20–21	86	10–15		
Australia	36	41	90	2	61	16	51	37	31	11–12
Austria	11	53	55	18	79	2	10	24–25		
Belgium	65	20	75	8	54	22	94	5–6		
Brazil	69	14	38	26–27	49	27	76	21–22	65	5
Canada	39	39	80	4–5	52	24	48	41–42	23	17
Chile	63	24–25	23	38	28	46	86	10–15		
Colombia	67	17	13	49	64	11–12	80	20		
Costa Rica	35	42–44	15	46	21	48–49	86	10–15		
Denmark	18	51	74	9	16	50	23	51		
Ecuador	78	8–9	8	52	63	13–14	67	28		
Finland	33	46	63	17	26	47	59	31–32		
France	68	15–16	71	10–11	43	35–36	86	10–15		
Germany	35	42–44	67	15	66	9–10	65	29	31	11–12
Great Britain	35	42–44	89	3	66	9–10	35	47–48	25	15–16
Greece	60	27–28	35	30	57	18–19	112	1		
Guatemala	95	2–3	6	53	37	43	101	3		
Hong Kong	68	15–16	24	37	57	18–19	29	49–50	96	1
Indonesia	78	8–9	14	47–48	46	30–31	48	41–42		
India	77	10–11	48	21	56	20–21	40	45	61	6
Iran	58	19–20	41	24	43	35–36	59	31–32		
Ireland	28	49	70	12	68	7–8	35	47–48		
Israel	13	52	54	19	47	29	81	19		
Italy	50	34	76	7	70	4–5	75	23		
Jamaica	45	37	39	25	68	7–8	13	52		
Japan	54	33	46	22–23	95	1	92	7	80	3
South Korea	60	27–28	18	43	39	41	85	16–17	75	4
Malaysia	104	1	26	36	50	25–26	36	46		
Mexico	81	5–6	30	32	69	6	82	18		

TABLE 1.5	(Continued)									
	Power Distance		Individualism		Masculinity		Uncertainty Avoidance		Confucian Dynamism	
Country	Index	Rank	Index	Rank	Index	Rank	Index	Rank	Index	Rank
Netherlands	38	40	80	4–5	14	51	53	35	44	9
Norway	31	47–48	69	13	8	52	50	38		
New Zealand	22	50	79	6	58	17	49	39–40	30	13
Pakistan	55	32	14	47–48	50	25–26	70	24–25	0	20
Panama	95	2–3	11	51	44	34	86	10–15		
Peru	64	21–23	16	45	42	37–38	87	9		
Philippines	94	4	32	31	64	11–12	44	44	19	18
Portugal	63	24–25	27	33–35	31	45	104	2		
South Africa	49	35–36	65	16	63	13–14	49	39–40		
Salvador	66	18–19	19	42	40	40	94	5–6		
Singapore	74	13	20	39–41	48	28	8	53	48	8
Spain	57	31	51	20	42	37–38	86	10–15		
Sweden	31	47–48	71	10–11	5	53	29	49–50	33	10
Switzerland	34	45	68	14	70	4–5	58	33		
Taiwan	58	29–30	17	44	45	32–33	69	26	87	2
Thailand	64	21–23	20	39–41	34	44	64	30	56	7
Turkey	66	18–19	37	28	45	32–33	85	16–17		
Uruguay	61	26	36	29	38	42	100	4		
United States	40	38	91	1	62	15	46	43	29	14
Venezuela	81	5–6	12	50	73	3	76	21–22		
Yugoslavia	76	12	27	33–35	21	48–49	88	8		
Regions										
East Africa	64	21–23	27	33–35	41	39	52	36	25	15–16
West Africa	77	10–11	20	39–41	46	30–31	54	34	16	19
Arab countries	80	7	38	26–27	53	23	68	27		

SOURCE: Geert Hofstede and Michael H. Bond, "The Confucius Connection: From Cultural Roots to Economic Growth," *Organizational Dynamics* (Spring 1988), pp. 12–13. Copyright © Geert Hofstede. Reprinted with permission.

NOTE: The distance between the lowest- and the highest-scoring country is about 100 points. Rank numbers: 1 = *highest*, 53 = *lowest* (for Confucian Dynamism: 20 = *lowest*).

TABLE 1.6 Cultural Profile of 50 Countries

Country	PD	IN	MA	UA	CF
Argentina	LG*	LO	ST	ST	—
Australia	SM	HI	ST	WK*	LO
Austria	SM	HI	ST	ST	—
Belgium	LG	HI	ST*	ST	—
Brazil	LG	LO	ST*	ST	HI
Canada	SM	HI	ST*	WK	LO
Chile	LG	LO	WK	ST	—
Colombia	LG	LO	ST	ST	—
Costa Rica	SM	LO	WK	ST	—
Denmark	SM	HI	WK	WK	—
Ecuador	LG	LO	ST	ST	—
Finland	SM	HI	WK	ST*	—
France	LG	HI	WK*	ST	—
Germany	SM	HI	ST	ST	LO
Great Britain	SM	HI	ST	WK	LO
Greece	LG	LO	ST	ST	—
Guatemala	LG	LO	WK*	ST	—
Hong Kong	LG	LO	ST	WK	HI
Indonesia	LG	LO	WK*	WK	—
India	LG	LO	ST	WK	HI
Iran	LG	LO	WK*	ST*	—
Ireland	SM	HI	ST	WK	—
Israel	SM	HI	ST*	ST	—
Italy	LG*	HI	WK*	ST	—
Jamaica	LG*	LO	ST	WK	—
Japan	LG	LO	ST	ST	HI
South Korea	LG	LO	WK*	ST	HI
Malaysia	LG	LO	ST*	WK	—
Mexico	LG	LO	ST	ST	—
Netherlands	SM*	HI	WK	WK*	HI*

TABLE 1.6 (Continued)

Country	PD	IN	MA	UA	CF
Norway	SM	HI	WK	WK	—
New Zealand	SM	HI	ST	WK	LO
Pakistan	LG	LO	ST*	ST	LO
Panama	LG	LO	WK*	ST	—
Peru	LG	LO	WK*	ST	—
Philippines	LG	LO	WK	WK	LO
Portugal	LG	LO	WK*	ST	—
South Africa	LG*	HI	ST	WK	—
Salvador	LG	LO	WK*	ST	—
Singapore	LG	LO	WK*	WK	HI
Spain	LG	HI	WK*	ST	—
Sweden	SM	HI	WK	WK	LO
Switzerland	SM	HI	ST	ST*	—
Taiwan	LG	LO	WK*	ST	HI
Thailand	LG	LO	WK	ST*	HI
Turkey	LG	LO	WK*	ST	—
Uruguay	LG	LO	WK*	ST	—
United States	SM*	HI	ST	WK	LO
Venezuela	LG	LO	ST	ST	—
Yugoslavia	LG	LO	WK	ST	—

SOURCE: The PD, IN, MA, and UA dimensions are adapted from Geert Hofstede, "The Cultural Relativity of the Quality of Life Concept," *Academy of Management Review*, 9, no. 3 (1984), pp. 391–393. The CF dimension is adapted from Geert Hofstede and Michael H. Bond, "The Confucius Connection: From Cultural Roots to Economic Growth," *Organizational Dynamics* (Spring 1988), pp. 12–13. This study categorized only 18 countries.

NOTE: PD = power distance; IN = individualism; MA = masculinity; UA = uncertainty avoidance; CF = Confucianism; LG = large; SM = small; HI = high; LO = low; ST = strong; WK = weak. * = But near the line that divides the two extremes.

Practical Perspective 1.1. Practical Perspective 1.4 illustrates the self versus group orientation. It should be pointed out that in the not distant future, estimated by 2020, Confucian values will bring China's economy on a par with the U.S. economy, and it will perhaps even surpass it.

Table 1.5 shows the index and the ranking for the 50 countries and the three regions, as well as the Confucian Dynamism. Table 1.6 lists the 50 countries included in Hofstede's study and their cultural classifications as well as the Confucian measure for 18 of the 50 countries.

PRACTICAL PERSPECTIVE 1-4

The Self Versus The Group

Upon leaving the United States for several months of study at a Japanese university, Leo got a crash course in culture shock. Activities that the undergraduate had enjoyed in his native land, such as playing a match of volleyball with friends, suddenly felt strange and unnatural. Casual volleyball games back at home featured a relaxed, cheerful atmosphere and good-humored competitiveness. In Japan, players adopted a grim, no-nonsense manner suited to the application of *ganbaru*, a dogged determination to persevere and keep trying until the end of a task.

Leo's Japanese volleyball experience was, to use a culinary analogy, like biting into a cheeseburger and getting a mouthful of sushi. Something about Japanese life changed the flavor of even the most innocuous items on his menu of customary pursuits. Leo quickly learned to put on a Japanese-style "game face" when he played volleyball, but he did not feel like himself.

Culture clashes such as this accentuate the fact that largely unspoken, collective assumptions about appropriate social behavior vary greatly from one country or geographic region to another, says Japanese psychologist Shinobu Kitayama of Kyoto University. Moreover, the goals, values, ideas, and behaviors that a person learns and uses as a member of a cultural group have far-reaching effects on mental life, Kitayama argues.

The cherished Western concept of a sovereign self provides a case in point. Consider Leo, whose passport to Japan probably should have been stamped with this brief warning: Bearer comes from a culture that treats individuals as independent operators, each of whom must emphasize personal strengths and pump up self-esteem to succeed in life. In contrast, Japanese culture views individuals as part of an interconnected social web, Kitayama contends. A sense of self develops as a person discerns the expectations of others concerning right and wrong behavior in particular situations. Self-improvement requires an unflagging commitment to confronting one's shortcomings and mistakes; their correction fosters harmony in one's family, at work, and in other pivotal social groups. This cultural perspective appears in various forms throughout East Asia. Its adherents tend to write off the European-American pursuit of self-esteem as an immature disregard for the relationships that nurture self-identity, Kitayama says.

SOURCE: Excerpted from Bruce Bower, "My Culture, My Self," *Science News*, 152 (October 18, 1997), p. 248. Reprinted with permission from Science News, the weekly newsmagazine of science. Copyright © 1997 by Science Service Inc.

High- and Low-Context Cultures

Some cultures are high context and some are low context. When conducting business, people in high-context cultures, including the Chinese, Korean, Japanese, Vietnamese, Saudi Arabian, Syrian, Greek, Egyptian, Italian, French, Lebanese, and Spanish cultures, (1) establish social trust first, (2) value personal relations and goodwill, (3) make agreements on the basis of general trust, and (4) like to conduct slow and ritualistic negotiations.[38] People in these cultures prefer that messages not be structured directly, that they do not get right to the point and state conclusions or bottom lines first. Instead, they prefer that a message be indirect, building up to the point and stating conclusions or bottom lines last.[39]

On the other hand, individuals in low-context cultures, including the Australian, English, North American, Scandinavian, Swiss, and German cultures, (1) get down to business first; (2) value expertise and performance; (3) like agreement by specific, legalistic contract; and (4) like to conduct negotiations as efficiently as possible.[40] Individuals in these cultures prefer that messages be structured directly, that they get immediately to the point and state conclusions or bottom lines first.[41]

The African Thought System (*Ubuntu*)[42]

Just as there is no totally homogeneous thought in other regions of the world, such as Europe and South America, there is no totally homogeneous thought in Africa. There is in fact a diverse sociocultural, linguistic, and historical composition among the African nations. However, as is the case in the other regions throughout the globe, there is an underlying pan-African character that results from a unique geographical, historical, cultural, and political experience. Therefore, Africans can be identified by certain common characteristics in their daily lives. Just as there is an Asian thought system—Confucianism, for example, there is an African thought system—*Ubuntu*. One important characteristic of *Ubuntu* is a high degree of harmony—unity of the whole rather than its distinct parts is emphasized. Thus, similar to Confucianism, the individual is strongly connected to the group. Hence, *Ubuntu*, too, emphasizes suppression of self-interest for the sake of the group's needs. Table 1.7 presents a comparison of African and Western systems. Therefore, in general, managing people in organizations in Africa is likely to require a substantially different managerial approach from the one used in many of the organizations in the United States, Sweden, and Denmark, for example. This means that, in many organizational situations in Africa, a reward system emphasizing group achievement is often more effective than a reward system emphasizing individual achievement.

TABLE 1.7   A Comparison of African and Western Systems

Element	African	Western
Other people	Treat others as human beings; your child is my child is the community's child. Strangers are regarded as part of extended family.	Relations are instrumental, contractual. Strangers are kept at a distance. Children are taught "Don't talk to strangers."
Focus of benefits	Center of focus is the collective community or society at large. Individual drives are subjugated to the collective.	Individual is the center of focus.
Decision making	Decisions arrived at by consensus. The process is circular. Vision tends to be polyocular. Dissenters compensated for at some future time.	Usually by majority. The process is linear. Unity of vision is typical. Monocular.
Time	Not a finite commodity, it is the healer. Allow enough time of it for important issues before arriving at a decision.	Time is money. It is a strategic commodity to be used frugally.
Age	An ongoing process of maturing and acquiring wisdom. Gray hairs are respected.	Age beyond a certain point becomes a negative. Senior citizens regarded as "dead wood."
Familial ties	Extended family ties are central. Family connectedness is important.	Nuclear.
Dispute resolution	Aims to restore harmony rather than justice. Good of the collective is preeminent.	Justice takes precedence over harmony. Individual rights are preeminent.

SOURCE: M. P. Mangaliso, N. A. Mangaliso, and J. H. Bruton, "Management in Africa, or Africa in Management? The African Philosophical Thought in Organizational Discourse." Paper presented at the International Management Division, Academy of Management Meetings, San Diego, CA (August 6, 1998), p. 27. Reprinted with permission. Permission conveyed through Copyright Clearance Center, Inc.

It should be emphasized again that Africa is not a country; it is a continent that consists of many tribal systems. The countries' borders in Africa, as was the case in the United States and in Middle East, were created by the European colonists, such as Portugal, Spain, and England.[43] Actually, Africa consists of 54 countries, 4 racial groups, and more than 2,000 ethnic communities.[44] Different tribes may have some differences in their cultural values and different practices. Nevertheless, the concept of *Ubuntu*, as are all the other cultural concepts discussed in this chapter, is a broad stereotype that serves well as a starting point for studying and learning about a country's culture.

And it should be further emphasized that communication between nations, and in the age of superhighways of information flowing across nations, is now extensive; cultural convergence has taken place—thus, while there are many cultural differences among nations, there are also many similarities in organizational practices, especially in large MNCs.[45] That is why international decisions must not be made solely on the basis of national stereotypes, even though they tend to be applicable, but on the basis of individual situations. For example, not every American is individualistic, and not every German is strong on uncertainty avoidance.

Impact of the Above Cultural Dimensions on Management[46]

These cultural dimensions have an impact on international management in many ways (as will be demonstrated throughout the book). For example, people in large-power-distance cultures prefer stronger leadership than do people in small-power-distance cultures, and people in strong uncertainty avoidance cultures take fewer risks than individuals in weak uncertainty avoidance cultures. This would affect international coordinating and planning functions. For instance, the current buzzword in management is empowerment—higher levels transferring responsibilities to lower levels. However, people in large-power-distance and strong uncertainty avoidance cultures may not be able to cope with the increased responsibility that empowerment brings. An example is Wal-Mart in Germany. Wal-Mart has traditionally been union-free, but in Germany, a strong uncertainty avoidance culture, Wal-Mart learned the hard way that there is a strong connection between the enterprise and the union (Wal-Mart is currently closing down its operations in Germany).[47] On the other hand, France's Carrefour, Wal-Mart's chief global competitor, is doing very well in China because it adapted to China's culture.[48] The international business adage is "Think global, act local."

Other Factors That Affect the Management Process

The above shows how the management process is affected across cultures. Table 1.8 provides a broad outline. However, besides culture, different societies also develop distinct economic and technological systems by which they produce and distribute goods and wealth; distinct political systems, such as tribal, democratic, or communistic systems; and distinct legal systems.[49] Societies also develop distinct written, verbal, and nonverbal means of communication and are at differing stages of economic development.

These factors affect international management in many ways. For example, differences in language make cross-country business negotiations difficult to conduct. And the stage of the country's economic development affects product/service strategies. For instance,

TABLE 1.8 Cultural Classifications and Some of Their Influences on Management

Cultural Classifications	Managerial Influences
Master of destiny	With the right rewards, there is likely to be high employee commitment to plans.
Fatalism	There is likely to be low commitment to plans; strong formal controls may be required; greater use of expatriates may be needed.
Quest for improvement	Planning and implementing change may be feasible.
Maintaining status quo	Planning and implementing change may not be feasible, and strong motivational incentives and control mechanisms may be required.
Enterprise is important	Managers may be able to delegate a high degree of authority to subordinates.
Relationships are important	Managers may be able to delegate only a low degree of authority to subordinates, and strong control mechanisms may be required; greater use of expatriates may be required.
Selection based on merit	Employees may be highly motivated to work.
Selection based on relationships	Employees in the outer circle may be less motivated to work, and so may family members and members of the inner circle; strong work incentives and controls may be needed; greater use of expatriates may be required.
Accumulation of wealth	A higher commitment to the organization's goals and objectives may be obtained.
"Just enough"	There may be a lower commitment to the organization's goals and objectives; strong controls may be needed; greater use of expatriates may be needed.
Sharing in decision making	Participative decision-making and leadership styles may work best, and substantial authority may have to be delegated to subordinates.
Few people make decisions	Authoritative decision-making and leadership styles may work best.
Decisions based on data	Looser control mechanisms can be applied.
Decisions based on emotions	Stronger control mechanisms may have to be applied; greater use of expatriates may be required.
High-context cultures	Business transactions and negotiations may have to be slow paced.
Low-context cultures	Business transactions and negotiations may have to be fast paced.
Large power distance	Authoritative decision-making and leadership styles may work best.
Small power distance	Participative/consultative decision-making and leadership styles may work best.
Collectivism	There is heavy reliance on informal controls; team approach is highly applicable.
Individualism	Heavy reliance on formal controls; team approach not very applicable.
Strong uncertainty avoidance	Mechanistic organization may work best.
Weak uncertainty avoidance	Organic organizational structures may work best.
Masculinity	Equal employment opportunity programs may be resisted by males.
Femininity	Equal employment opportunity programs may be resisted relatively less by males.
Confucianism	Organizations may rely more on informal than on formal controls; individuals prefer authoritative decision making and leadership.

SOURCE: Carl Rodrigues, "Cultural Classifications of Societies and How They Affect Cross-Cultural Management," *Cross-Cultural Management: An International Journal,* 5, no. 3 (1998), pp. 31–41.

economically poor countries usually cannot afford the expensive products manufactured in economically richer countries. The quality of the product may have to be reduced to make it affordable in poorer countries. Or the enterprise may have to move manufacturing to a country where labor is cheaper as a means of making the product affordable in poorer countries. These factors will be discussed more thoroughly in Chapter 3 and in subsequent chapters. Table 1.8 provides a broad overview of how culture affects the management process. Table 1.9 presents an overview of the book's content.

TABLE 1.9 **International Management**

The Management Process	Varying Country Factors That Affect the Management Process
Planning (Chapters 4 and 5)	Culture (discussed throughout the book)
Product/service	
Price	**Other factors**
Promotion	Business practices (Chapter 10)
Distribution/entry mode	Negotiating styles (Chapter 10)
Organizing (Chapter 6)	Conflict resolution (Chapter 10)
Organizational structures	Business ethics (Chapter 2)
Centralization	Communication (Chapter 9)
Decentralization	
Staffing (Chapters 7 and 8)	Factors discussed in (Chapter 3)
Expatriate	Domestic environment
Host country	International environment
Training/development	Foreign environment
Compensation	Legal systems
Coordinating	Labor relations
Leadership/motivation style (Chapter 12)	Political systems
Decision-making style (Chapter 11)	Government policies
Communication (Chapter 9)	Competitive forces
Control (Chapter 13)	Economic forces
Formal/informal	Trade barriers
Loose/tight	Exchange rates
	Geography
	Mother Nature

Global Management: A Future Perspective

New markets, rapid advances in communications, and new sources of brainpower and skilled labor are forcing businesses into their most fundamental reorganization since the multidivision (discussed in Chapter 6) corporation became standard in the 1950s. "We're talking about a new order, a sea of change, that will go on for the rest of my career," says Richard J. Callahan, CEO of U.S. West International. "It's almost like Halley's comet arriving unannounced." Senior managers are struggling to adapt themselves and their organizations to the 21st-century business world that's rapidly taking shape. Boundaries will be even less important than they are today.

The rate of technological progress will accelerate, with breakthroughs in biotechnology or digital electronics coming from unexpected places such as Israel, Malaysia, or China. At the same time, the huge demands of the new middle classes and their governments will revive supposedly mature businesses such as household appliances and power-plant construction. All this means that business opportunities will explode—but so will competition as technology and management know-how spread beyond brand-name companies to new players in Asia and Latin America. Thriving in this fast-paced environment requires a new kind of company and a new kind of CEO. Just as much of the world is embracing a liberalized economic model, so businesses of all stripes seem to be converging on a common management model to run their far-flung operations.

Although that model is still a work in progress, the outlines of what is likely to be the early-21st-century's world standard are beginning to take shape—the notion of "globalization," where countries throughout the globe are becoming economically interdependent, is constantly being mentioned in practical and academic writings. This model will rely on Western-style accounting and financial controls yet stress Japanese-style teamwork. It will value ethnic diversity, though less from high-mindedness than from pragmatism. It will be centrally directed by multicultural, or at least cosmopolitan, executives who will set the overall tone and strategy but give entrepreneurial local managers a long leash.[50]

Cross-Cultural Conversion and Technological Advancements

Historically, the practices in cultures have transcended across nations, although in most cases with customization. For example, in the 1980s, cross-cultural theorists theorized that American and Japanese cultural organizational management practices would converge—the United States and the West would adopt many of the Japanese practices—such as organizations using groups more in decision making, and Japanese organizations would adopt many of the managerial practices of the United States and the West—for instance, becoming more individualistic and competitive. Japanese organizations, however, have not, it seems, adopted the U.S. "cutthroat" competitiveness; their competitiveness seems to involve managing better rather than indulging in cutthroat behavior, nor do they seem to be managing by individualism, and U.S. organizations have not so far been highly successful in managing by "use of groups."

Nevertheless, large corporations the world over tend to have adopted many similar corporate practices, while small local businesses tend to maintain their unique corporate culture.

Technological advances, such as the Internet, satellite television, and video-conferencing, along with the globalization of business, are today spreading the practice of cultural traits across cultures at a very rapid rate. Historically, countries have attempted to slow cultural conversion or attempted to keep their culture intact by filtering out foreign ideas through walls, such as distance, national borders, and the likes of the Iron Curtain and the Berlin Wall. But advancements in information technologies have destroyed or are destroying these culture-preserving filters.[51] As traits are absorbed by a culture, the practice aspects of the culture are likely to change more rapidly than ever before. For example, the notion of McDonald's food restaurants in France was absurd not very long ago. Critics in some cultures—France, for instance—have accused U.S. companies of cultural imperialism (as an illustration, read Practical Perspective 1.5). This suggests that there may be a growing uniformity of practice aspects of culture throughout the globe. Uniformity, however, will evolve at a very slow pace. International managers may thus deal with the accusation of cultural imperialism by being more adaptable to the needs of cultures where they are conducting business.[52]

PRACTICAL PERSPECTIVE 1-5

A Battle Against Globalization

Fist raised, mustache bristling, José Bové looked defiant as he handed himself in to French police in the southern town on Montpellier a few days ago. "My struggle remains the same," this farmer declared to an appreciative crowd, "the battle against globalization and for the right of people to feed themselves as they choose."

A Parisian-turned-sheep-farmer who moved to southwest France 20 years ago, Mr. Bové emerged this month as a sort of Subcomandante Marcos of the French countryside, the leader of a self-styled, anti-imperialist revolt over food. His crime, committed on August 12 [1999], was to lead the ransacking and demolition of a McDonald's restaurant nearing completion in the southwestern town of Millau.

It was only the most conspicuous of a rash of recent protests against McDonald's, targeted not so much for anything the company has done but as a symbol of the United States and of what Mr. Bové has called "the multinationals of foul food." His efforts have struck a chord. French labor unions, ecologists, communists, and farmers have joined to demand his immediate release, burying other differences in a shared politico-gastronomic outcry.

An army, Napoleon noted, marches on its stomach, and the European forces gathering this summer in protest against what is seen as American-led globalization have abruptly focused on food. Where it was once the deployment of American nuclear missiles that caused alarm, it is now McDonald's, Coca-Cola, genetically modified American corn, and American beef fattened with growth hormones that have Europeans up in arms.

"Behind all this lies a rejection of cultural and culinary dispossession," said Alain Duhamel, a French political analyst. "There is a certain allergy in Europe to the extent of American power accumulated since the cold war's end, and the most virulent expression of that allergy today seems to be food."

SOURCE: Excerpted from Roger Cohen, "Fearful Over the Future, Europe Seizes on Food," *The New York Times* (August 29, 1999), Section 4, p. 1. Copyright © 1999 by The New York Times Company. Reprinted by permission.

Of course, these advancements are also revolutionizing international management. The Internet and electronic commerce are reshaping how business thinks about managing its employees. Distance—geographic, political, and cultural—has been a factor that shaped how companies organized and managed their global operations. The Internet's compression of time and distance has forced multinational organizations to rethink these patterns. For example, employees located throughout the globe can now work in teams.

Characteristics of the Global Manager

Globalization trends mean that more and more business firms must now develop managers with global management and multicultural capabilities. (Refer to Practical Perspective 1.6.) The managerial skills that are effective in managing enterprises at home will not be effective in managing enterprises across the globe. What type of skills do global managers need? According to Ed Dunn, the corporate vice president of Whirlpool Corporation, "The top twenty-first-century manager should have multi-environment, multi-country, multifunctional, multi-company, and multi-industry experience."[53]

PRACTICAL PERSPECTIVE 1-6

The Multicultural Manager

You cannot motivate anyone, especially someone of another culture, until you have been accepted by that person. A multilingual salesperson can explain the advantages of a product in other languages, but a multicultural salesperson can motivate foreigners to buy it. That's a critical difference.

A buyer will not like a foreigner who is arrogant about his own culture. He will find reasons not to buy from such monocultural salesperson. The trouble is most people are arrogantly monocultural without being aware of it. Even those who have become aware of it cannot hide it. Foreigners sense this at once and set up their own cultural barrier, effectively blocking any attempt by the monocultural person to motivate them.

Ironically, that multicultural requirement has been neglected too often in hiring managers for international positions. Worse, it has mostly been neglected when sending fast-track managers on international assignments, pointing to almost certain failure. And it is affecting every industry. Even if you do not work for a multinational company, you may be in touch with foreign customers, distributors, suppliers, licensers or licensees. Do you have the right employee forging these relations?

For more than 20 years, I [Gunnar Beeth] have run a PanEuropean executive-search firm from Brussels. When clients ask us to find the right person for a sales or management position, they usually ask for the same qualities as for a domestic position but in addition require the new manager to speak English, German, and French. After discussion, we usually specify something like:

The new manager must be able to motivate throughout Europe, which requires an ability to be accepted throughout Europe. Thus, the new manager should be multicultural.

SOURCE: Excerpted from Gunnar Beeth, "Multicultural Managers Wanted," *Management Review* (May 1997), pp. 17, 19. Copyright © 1997, American Management Association International. Reprinted by permission of American Management Association International, New York. All rights reserved.

Cecil G. Howard, a consultant and professor of management at Howard University, Washington, D.C., has proposed that the 21st-century global managers will possess multidimensional skills and knowledge. He grouped the skills and knowledge into two categories: core skills and augmented skills. These are depicted in Table 1.10. According to Howard, the core skills are a must for the expatriate manager (discussed in Chapter 7) to succeed in the foreign assignment, but the augmented skills help facilitate managing in a foreign country.[54]

TABLE 1.10 Characteristics of the 21st-Century Expatriate Manager

Core Skills	Managerial Implications
Multidimensional perspective	Extensive multi-product, multi-industry, multifunctional, multi-company, multi-country, and multi-environment experience.
Proficiency in line	Track record in successfully operating a strategic management business unit(s) and/or a series of major overseas projects.
Prudent decision making skills	Competence and proven track record in making the right strategic decisions.
Resourcefulness	Skillful in getting himself or herself known and accepted in the host country's political hierarchy.
Cultural sensitivity	Quick and easy adaptability into the foreign culture. An individual with as much cultural mix, diversity, and experience as possible.
Ability as a team builder	Effective people skills in dealing with a variety of cultures, races, nationalities, genders, religions. Also, sensitive to cultural differences.
Physical fitness and mental maturity	Endurance for the rigorous demands of an overseas assignment.
Augmented Skills	**Managerial Implications**
Computer literacy	Comfortable exchanging strategic information electronically.
Prudent negotiating skills	Proven track record in conducting successful strategic business negotiations in multicultural environment.
Ability as a change agent	Proven track record in successfully initiating and implementing strategic organizational changes.
Visionary skills	Quick to recognize and respond to strategic business opportunities and potential political and economic upheavals in the host country.
Effective delegating skills	Proven track record in participative management style and ability to delegate.

SOURCE: Cecil G. Howard, "Profile of the 21st-Century Expatriate Manager," *HR Magazine* (June 1992), p. 96. Reprinted with the permission of *HR Magazine*; published by the Society for Human Resource Management, Alexandria, VA. All rights reserved.

Summary

A major thrust of this chapter has been to point out that the managerial approach that works in one country may be ineffective in another. This is because the managerial process is affected by unique national factors, including culture and religion. Some cultures view change positively; others view it negatively. Organizations are viewed in some cultures as entities to be protected and developed; but in many cultures, they are viewed simply as a place to socialize. In some cultures, employees are selected and promoted on the basis of merit; but in others, promotion is on the basis of friendship and family affiliations. Managers in some cultures make decisions in a participative manner, but in many cultures decisions are made authoritatively. Organizational controls in some cultures are based on objective data and information; in others they are based on subjective means. People in some cultures, such as weak uncertainty avoidance cultures, take higher risks than people in other cultures, such as strong uncertainty avoidance cultures.

Another major thrust has been to point out that because business opportunities in foreign nations are increasing rapidly and because enterprises from foreign countries are increasingly presenting threats to many businesses, more and more domestic firms will enter the international business arena. This suggests that in the future more and more managers with the ability to manage multinational, multicultural environments will be required.

KEY TERMS AND CONCEPTS

1. The international management process
2. Culture, practice, values, organizational culture, corporate culture
3. Formal, informal, and technical cultural learning
4. Religion
5. Master of destiny; fatalistic; never-ending quest for improvement; independent enterprise as an instrument of social action; personal selection based on merit; wide sharing of decision making; the concepts of decisions based on objective analysis
6. Antiplanning
7. The cultural dimensions of power distance; uncertainty avoidance; individualism; masculinity; and Confucian dynamism
8. *Ubuntu*
9. Cultural imperialism
10. The global manager

DISCUSSION QUESTIONS

1. Differentiate between management and international management.
2. What is culture? How is it learned? What are the sources of learning it?
3. Discuss how the following cultural viewpoints affect international planning, international organization, international staffing, international coordinating, and international controlling: decisions based on objective analysis; independent enterprise as an instrument of social action; master of destiny, fatalistic, and never-ending quest for improvement viewpoints; personnel selection based on merit; and wide sharing of decision making.
4. How does religion affect international management?
5. How do the large power distance and strong uncertainty avoidance cultural dimensions affect international management?
6. What is Confucianism? What is the key tenet of Confucianism? What are the five basic relationships of Confucianism? In Confucianism, what does virtue mean?
7. What is *Ubuntu?* What is its key tenet?
8. Besides culture, what are some of the other factors that affect international management?
9. What are some of the characteristics of the effective global manager?
10. Why is it important to train global managers?

11. How are technological advancements affecting international management?

12. Why is it important to study international management?

EXERCISES

1. You are the personnel director of a U.S. international corporation and are interviewing an American executive for an assignment in the firm's subsidiary in Japan. You notice that the executive is quite frank and direct in communication. What will you advise the executive to do?

2. You are the cross-cultural trainer for a U.S. global corporation. You are preparing a group of American executives for assignment in China. What will you point out to these executives?

3. You are the cross-cultural trainer for a Chinese global corporation. You are preparing a group of Chinese executives for assignment in the United States. What will you point out to these executives?

4. You are the cross-cultural trainer for a Japanese global corporation. You are preparing a group of Japanese executives for assignment in Germany. What will you point out to these executives?

5. You are the cross-cultural trainer for a U.S. global corporation. You are preparing a group of American executives for assignment in a South American country. What will you point out to these executives?

ASSIGNMENT

Go to the library. Peruse business periodicals such as *The Wall Street Journal*, *Business Week*, and *Fortune*. Select an article that discusses an international management topic, and prepare a short summary to be shared with your peers.

CASE 1-1

Globalizing Yourself

Kelly O'Dea used to think of himself as a Lone Ranger, living and working in countries where only a select breed of American businesspeople had gone before. As president of worldwide client services for Ogilvy & Mather Advertising, O'Dea commuted between London and New York. He was outside the United States about 70 percent of the time; for the past 15 years he had handled assignments in dozens of countries on five continents.

On a layover in the Bangkok airport, O'Dea realized that the Lone Ranger wasn't alone. He struck up a conversation with the woman sitting next to him, an investment banker who was also making the 25-hour flight from Sydney to London. As the two of them talked about their companies' urgent emphasis on global operations, two others chimed in with similar stories. The four of them soon realized that they represented a completely new kind of business leader: one who is multicultural and multiskilled, who doesn't regard an overseas assignment as either exotic or traumatic. It occurred to O'Dea that people, just like brands must be "globalized" if they're to compete successfully in rapidly changing international markets.

"International work experience is no longer just an option—it's mandatory for anyone in business," said O'Dea . . . "So it's no longer adequate to think about only your domestic market. You need to have a firm understanding of how business gets done in different countries." Before you rush off for parts unknown, a few words of caution: an overseas assignment helps only if you do it right.

Questions

1. Discuss what O'Dea means by "an overseas assignment helps only if you do it right."

2. Describe some of the key determinants of the effective international manager.

SOURCE: Excerpted from Eric Matson, "How to Globalize Yourself." Reprinted from the April–May 1997 issue of *Fast Company Magazine.* All rights reserved.

CASE 1-2

Managing in the Constantly Changing Global Environment

How do we manage in this constantly changing global and regional environment? Change is certainly not new. But I [Paul Allaire, Chairman and CEO of Xerox Corporation] think there are two aspects of change that are different and worth focusing on. First is the speed of change. It is clearly faster and, in my view, it is accelerating. And that acceleration is going to continue. The second difference is that change is much less predictable. And in addition to global and regional issues, there

(Continued)

are a number of other changes that complicate our jobs of managing global enterprises in this environment. I'll just mention a couple of those.

The first is that our traditional sources of competitive advantage are now short-lived. Capital is becoming a global commodity moving very easily across borders. Technology also is being very quickly dispersed. And in almost all of the markets in which we operate, we're also finding very fine skills that previously existed only in the developed countries, generally our home markets. . . .

So, the question is: How do we manage in this new environment? Rather than trying to give you a prescription, let me briefly tell you about some principles that Xerox has used to change our corporation in order to manage in this new environment that we foresee. . . .

The first principle in which I believe very strongly is that the old command-and-control system of management will no longer work. It is too slow and cumbersome, our environment is too complex, and our customers are too demanding. As we move away from this command-and-control approach, we must focus on speed. Our organizations must have the capability of making decisions much more quickly, and, more importantly, implementing those decisions much more quickly. So what we are trying to do is to maintain the advantages of a large global enterprise and still have the speed of a small local company.

Another key principle around which we've organized is empowerment: pushing responsibility and accountability down to the people who really have the knowledge—first, to do what is right for the customer and second, to bring capabilities to the customer in a value-added manner. This includes allowing the individuals down in the organizations to define the management process that they will use to best achieve that.

Questions

1. CEO Allaire's ideas certainly have substance. However, there are bound to be cultural barriers. Discuss some of the barriers culture may present.

2. What are the technological changes that have taken place in the past few decades that have helped improve international organizations' capability of making decisions more quickly than was the case prior to these changes?

3. How is the implementation of empowerment programs hindered by culture? Give some examples.

NOTES

1. Elizabeth Marx, *Breaking Through Culture Shock: What You Need to Succeed in International Business* (London: Nicholas Brealey Publishing, 1999).

2. Glenn Rifkin, "Building Better Global Managers," *Harvard Management Update* (March 2006).

3. Mark Landler and Michael Barbaro, "No, Not Always: Wal-Mart Discovers That Its Formula Doesn't Fit Every Culture," *The New York Times* (August 2, 2006), pp. C1, C4.

4. James P. Johnson, Tomasz Lenartowicz, and Salvador Apud, "Cross-Cultural Competence in International Business: Toward a Definition and a Model," *Journal of International Business Studies*, 37 (2006), pp. 525–541.

5. A. L. Roeber and C. Kluckhohn, "Culture: A Critical Review of Concepts and Definitions," *Papers of the Peabody Museum of American Archaeology and Ethnology* (Cambridge, MA: Harvard University, 1952), no. 1.

6. P. H. Harris and R. T. Moran, *Managing Cultural Differences* (Houston, TX: Gulf Publishing, 1979).

7. G. Hofstede, B. Neuijen, D. Ohayv, and G. Sanders, "Measuring Organizational Cultures: A Qualitative and Quantitative Study Across Twenty Cases," *Administrative Science Quarterly,* 35 (1990), pp. 286–316, 311.

8. Ibid., p. 312.

9. This contention is supported by Ping Ping Fu, Jeff Kennedy, Jasmine Tata, Gary Yukl, Michael Harris Bond, Tai-Kuang Peng, et al., "The Impact of Societal Social Cultural Values and Individual Social Beliefs on the Perceived Effectiveness of Managerial Influence Strategies: A Meso Approach," *Journal of International Business Studies,* 35 (2004), pp. 284–305.

10. For some further information about the above experience, see C. A. Rodrigues, "When Cross-Cultural Equals Double Cross: How Developmental Aid Can Backfire, *Administration & Society,* 22, no. 3 (1990), pp. 608–623.

11. E. T. Hall, *The Silent Language* (Garden City, NY: Anchor Press/Doubleday, 1973), p. 68.

12. Ibid., p. 69.

13. Ibid., p. 71.

14. Harris and Moran, *Managing Cultural Differences,* op cit.

15. Ibid.

16. Ibid., p. 63.

17. Ibid., p. 63.

18. Max Weber, *The Protestant Ethic and the Spirit of Capitalism* (New York: Scribner's Sons, 1958, originally 1904–1905).

19. S. M. Abbasi, K. W. Hollman, and J. H. Murray, "Islamic Economics: Foundations and Practices," *International Journal of Social Economics,* 16, no. 5 (1990), pp. 5–17.

20. Glenn Burkins, "Work Week," *The Wall Street Journal* (March 24, 1998), p. A1.

21. A descriptive discussion of these concepts appears in W. H. Newman, C. E. Summer, and E. K. Warren, *The Process of Management* (Englewood Cliffs, NJ: Prentice-Hall, 1977).

22. N. J. Adler, *International Dimensions of Organizational Behavior* (Cincinnati, OH: South-Western College Publishing, 1997).

23. G. Renwick and E. J. Witham, *Managing in Malaysia: Cultural Insights and Guidelines for Americans* (unpublished manuscript, 1997).

24. C. West Churchman, *The System's Approach* (New York: Dell Books, 1968), p. 14.

25. Newman, Summer, and Warren, *Process of Management,* op cit.

26. Ibid.

27. Valerie Frazee, "Getting Started in Mexico," *Workforce,* 2, no. 1 (January 1997), pp. 16–17; Mike Johnson, "Untrapped in Latin America," *Management Review* (July 1996), p. 32.

28. Newman, Summer, and Warren, *Process of Management,* op cit.

29. R. N. Farmer and B. M. Richman, *Comparative Management and Economic Progress* (Homewood, IL: Richard D. Irwin, 1965), pp. 177–189; Adler, op cit., p. 14.

30. Newman, Summer, and Warren, *Process of Management,* op cit.

31. Harris and Moran, *Managing Cultural Differences,* op cit., p. 63.

32. "Go Along and Get Along," *The Economist* (November 24, 1990), p. 76.

33. Newman, Summer, and Warren, *Process of Management,* op cit.

34. Geert Hofstede, "The Cultural Relativity of the Quality of Life Concept," *Academy of Management Review,* 9, no. 3 (1984), pp. 389–398; Geert Hofstede, "Motivation, Leadership, and Organization: Do American Theories Apply Abroad?" *Organizational Dynamics* (Summer 1980), pp. 42–63.

35. See B. L. Kirkman, K. B. Lowe, and C. B. Gibson, "A Quarter Century of *Culture's Consequences:* A Review of Empirical Research Incorporating Hofstede's Cultural Values Framework," *Journal of International Business Studies,* 37 (2006), pp. 285–320.

36. G. Hofstede and Michael H. Bond, "The Confucius Connection: From Cultural Roots to Economic Growth," *Organizational Dynamics* (Spring 1988), pp. 5–21.

37. Ibid.

38. Edward T. Hall, "How Cultures Collide," *Psychology Today* (July 1976), pp. 67–74.

39. Ibid.

40. Ibid., p. 74.

41. Ibid.

42. This discussion draws from M. P. Mangaliso, N. A. Mangaliso, and J. M. Bruton, "Management in Africa, or Africa in Management? The African Philosophical Thought in Organizational Discourse," Paper presented at the International Management Division, Academy of Management Annual Meetings, San Diego, CA (August 6, 1998).

43. See T. Lenartowicz and J. P. Johnson, "A Cross-National Assessment of the Values of Latin America Managers: Contrasting Hues or Shades of Gray," *Journal of International Business Studies,* 34 (2003), pp. 266–281.

44. Kon Akosha-Sarpong, *African Journalism Within the Ethos of African Renaissance,* Master of Journalism (MJ) Thesis, Carleton University, Ottawa, Canada (2001).

45. Kwok Leung, Rabi S Bhagat, Nancy R Buchan, Miriam Erez, and Cristina B Gibson, "Culture and International Business: Recent Advances and Their Implications for Future Research," *Journal of International Business Studies,* 36 (2005), pp. 357–378.

46. For a deeper understanding of this discussion, see *Handbook of Cross-Cultural Management,* a collection of invited chapters edited by M. J. Martin and K. Newman (Oxford, UK: Blackwell, 2002).

47. Mark Landler and Michael Barbaro, "No, Not Always: Wal-Mart Discovers That Its Formula Doesn't Fit Every Culture, op cit., p. C4.

48. SOURCE: "Carrefour's Sales Secret," *World News* (July 26, 2006). http://article.wn.com/view/2006/07/26/Carrefour's-sales-secret/

49. Hofstede and Bond, "The Confucius Connection," op cit.

50. SOURCE: B. Dwyer, P. Engardio, Z. Schiller, and S. Reed, "Tearing Up Today's Organizational Chart," *Business Week: 21st Century Capitalism* (Special Issue 1994), p. 81.

51. See Thomas L. Friedman, "It's a Flat World, After All," *The New York Times* (April 3, 2005).

52. William B. Werther Jr., "Toward Global Convergence," *Business Horizons* (January–February 1996), pp. 3–9.

53. Cecil G. Howard, "Profile of the 21st-Century Expatriate Manager," *HR Magazine* (June 1992), p. 96.

54. Ibid.

2

CROSS-NATIONAL ETHICS AND SOCIAL RESPONSIBILITY

*I*n the Third World, many nations—and their bribe takers—have never known life *without bribery. Countries such as Indonesia, Malaysia, China, India, Nigeria, and Thailand are known for having government officials who are easily bribable. "In the U.S., the social lubricant is alcohol," says A. Rushdi Siddiqui, an international trade lawyer. "In many Third World nations, it's gifts." Sometimes, these gifts can be as much as 10% of the cost of the project.[1] Corruption can hurt a firm's competitive position in the market.[2] Relative to social responsibility, Global Alliance once reported that workers at nine of Nike's contract factories in Indonesia had witnessed verbal and physical abuse by supervisors against coworkers and that female employees were being coerced into sex.[3]*

Learning Objectives of the Chapter

When managers of corporations begin to formulate strategy to conduct business across nations, they must possess a thorough understanding of their firms' views on business ethics and social responsibility, as well as the views of each nation in which the firm wishes to transact business. Therefore, multinational corporations (MNCs) have a responsibility to adhere to the specific ethical codes of each country or region in business dealings.

Views on what is ethical or unethical in business transactions vary from company to company, as well as from country to country. For example, the practice of bribery in business transactions is overtly acceptable in many countries, and in many situations it is expected and needed to supplement a low-wage structure, such as among customs workers, while in other countries it is overtly unacceptable but covertly practiced. And in the United States, managers must understand that under the U.S. Foreign Corrupt Practices Act (FCPA) of 1977, it is illegal to practice the act of bribery not only in the

United States but in other countries as well, even if it is an acceptable and expected business practice there.

Views on what actions denote corporate social responsibility (CSR) also vary from company to company, as well as from country to country. For example, some executives believe that they must not be judgmental and should adhere to countries' varying views. Following this view, an executive of a U.S. international corporation—corporations that conduct business in more than one nation—would hire female managers at home because it is the right thing to do but would not do so for the firm's operations in Saudi Arabia. This is because it is not an acceptable practice in Saudi Arabia to hire female managers for most jobs.[4]

Others believe that there should be a universal guideline, that international corporations should apply one view on social responsibility in all nations. Therefore, adhering to this view, the executive of the U.S. international corporation would hire female managers in Saudi Arabia—which conflicts with Saudi Arabia's views. Dealing with conflicting ethical norms between home and host country, as well as defining and applying social responsibility in cross-national settings, is thus a huge problem confronting the managers of international companies. After studying this chapter, you should be able to do the following:

1. Describe what ethics are, including legality and social acceptability

2. Examine the considerations and complications in complying with foreign ethical practices

3. Examine some of the events leading to the passage of the FCPA

4. Examine the impact of the FCPA on U.S. international corporations

5. Discuss social responsibility in a cross-national context

Cross-National Ethics

Basically, ethics is the study of morality and standards of conduct. Some businesspeople believe that what is ethical or unethical is governed by the legality of the situation and by the social aspects of the situation (what members of the society generally accept as being "right" or "wrong"). For example, if it is illegal to practice the act of bribery in a country and a firm's manager bribes someone there to obtain a favor, it would be unethical, and the violator could be prosecuted under the law. However, if bribery is illegal but not enforced and practiced in a society, there is no violation—bribery is not unethical. And if bribery is not illegal in a country but is known to be generally socially unacceptable, it would be unethical to practice it; the violator would be punished not by formal law but by informal means, such as by negative publicity and/or by customers boycotting the firm's product or service.

Regarding the social aspects of the situation, many cultures establish informal ethical principles or moral standards that define "right" and "wrong" conduct. However, what is right or wrong is difficult to define conclusively and agree on in any culture. For example, in the United States, some Americans believe that legal abortion is right; others think it is wrong. And what is right or wrong is far more difficult to define conclusively and agree on among the different cultural environments around the globe. For example, many people throughout the globe resent Western ways and often call Westerners evil, and many Westerners call them evil—who is right or wrong depends on one's views.

This is because different societies are confronted with different opportunities and constraints, and to cope, each society develops a unique culture and standard of ethics. As a result, what is right and wrong may differ dramatically from one culture to another. This means that managers of international corporations will often find themselves with conflicting ethical responsibilities; that is, one's own nation's standard of ethics often collides with those of other nations. For example, the practice of bribery in business transactions is acceptable in Brazil and many other nations but not in the United States. An American executive transacting business in Brazil would thus be confronted with conflicting ethical responsibilities.

In part, because of these conflicting ethical responsibilities, the actions of many international corporations have been subjected to considerable criticism, which in turn has led to a wide range of negative consequences, such as negative publicity, consumer boycotts, lawsuits, and government intervention, such as the passage of the FCPA (discussed later in this chapter). Practical Perspective 2.1 presents the case of Lockheed's involvement in bribery in Egypt and its negative consequences.

PRACTICAL PERSPECTIVE 2-1

A Violation of the Foreign Corrupt Practices Act

Several years ago, Lockheed hired a consultant and promised her a sizable commission for each plane sold to the Egyptian government. The consultant was later elected to the Egyptian Parliament, becoming—under the U.S. Foreign Corrupt Practices Act—a foreign government official. Before taking office, she turned over the consulting responsibilities to a company her husband headed. Two years later Lockheed sold three C-130 transport aircraft to the Egyptian government, and Lockheed allegedly paid the local consulting company a termination fee in lieu of the commissions, keeping the payment confidential through code names and other means.

A federal grand jury in Georgia subsequently indicted Lockheed and two of its officers for conspiracy to violate the Foreign Corrupt Practices Act, even though there was no factual allegation that the Parliament member had taken a single step to misuse her official position on Lockheed's behalf. The prosecutors successfully argued that it was Lockheed's intent, not the recipient's actions, that mattered, and that one indication of corrupt intent was the secrecy surrounding the commission payment.

Lockheed pleaded guilty to a negotiated single count and agreed to pay the maximum fine of $24.8 million. The Lockheed executives pleaded guilty to false information charges or bribery charges and were fined $20,000 and $125,000, respectively, and sentenced to three years' probation in one case and eighteen months in prison in the other.

SOURCE: Excerpted from Margaret M. Ayres, "Staying Above Board Overseas," *Financial Executive* (March–April 1996), p. 38.

Bribery and Payoffs Abroad

An investigation in the early 1970s by the U.S. Securities and Exchange Commission (SEC) into illegal corporate contributions to President Nixon's campaign fund discovered that many corporations had made substantial illegal contributions during the 1972 presidential election campaign. Subsequent investigations in 1976 and 1977 by the SEC revealed that instances of undisclosed, questionable, or illegal corporate payments, both domestic and foreign, were widespread—major international corporations regularly made "payoffs" abroad to foreign government officials and politicians in the course of conducting business.[5] The SEC investigation generated other investigations by the Senate Foreign Relations Committee, the Internal Revenue Service, and the departments of Defense and State. (Department of Defense corporations had been a major source of payoffs abroad.) These investigations, too, revealed that many U.S. international corporations regularly made questionable or illegal payments to foreign government officials and politicians to secure business.

The difficulties and pressures international corporations face in conducting business with foreign government officials and politicians were presented in testimony before a U.S. Senate Foreign Relations Subcommittee by the then chairman of Gulf Oil Corporation, Bob R. Dorsey. Dorsey described his dealings with the then finance chairman of South Korea's Democratic Republican Party, S. K. Kim: "He [S. K. Kim] happens to be as tough a man as I've ever met. I have never been subjected to that kind of abuse."[6] When Kim first approached Dorsey, his demand was $1 million. Later, Kim demanded $10 million from Dorsey in the form of a campaign contribution to his political party. Dorsey said, "He [Kim] left little to the imagination as to what would happen to Gulf's $300 million investment, most of it in refining and petrochemicals, if the company would choose to turn its back on the request."[7] Dorsey haggled the $10 million extortion demand by Kim down to $3 million, making it a total of $4 million to save $300 million in assets in South Korea.[8]

Another case that helps illustrate the difficulties and pressures international corporations—henceforth referred to as MNCs—face in transacting with officials and politicians involved Exxon in Italy. Italy is noted for a government and political system in which approvals, permits, and licenses are issued extremely slowly, and perhaps disapproved, when payments (called *bustarella*) are not made to the proper officials. Exxon had large refineries in Italy producing oil products for sale in Italy and in the entire European Union. Between 1963 and 1972, Exxon admitted making payments of more than $29 million to Italian political parties. In the wake of the ongoing SEC investigation into such foreign payments, Exxon suspended any further payments to Italian political parties. Subsequently, rate increases requested by Exxon during the period when OPEC (Organization of Petroleum Exporting Countries) was drastically raising the price of crude oil were ignored. As a result, the once profitable Exxon subsidiaries in Italy generated large losses.[9]

The investigations caused many board members of MNCs to become concerned about their exposure and liability to lawsuits brought by stockholders. U.S. Internal Revenue Service officials were concerned about the apparent laxity of independent auditing firms in pointing out such questionable and often sizable payments. And the SEC believed that "when a company receives substantial benefits as a result of a payoff or, if its continued operations are subject to extortion, investors are entitled to know."[10]

Assertions were made at the time that "the SEC had embarked on a typical American exercise in ethnocentrism—imposing its own moral judgments on foreign governments and U.S. international corporations."[11]

Forms of Bribery

Basically, a bribe can be defined as a payment in any form (cash or gift) for the purpose of influencing action by a government official to obtain or retain business. Bribes can be classified as "whitemail bribes" or as "lubrication bribes."

Whitemail Bribes

Whitemail bribery refers to payments made to induce an official in a position of power to give favorable treatment where such treatment is either illegal or not warranted on an efficiency, economic benefit scale. Fundamentally, a key point in this type of bribery is that the payment be intended to induce the official "to do or omit doing something in violation of his lawful duty, or to exercise his [or her] discretion in favor of the payer's request for a contract, concession, or privilege on some basis other than merit."[12] These payments, when exposed, can lead to scandals, fines, and so on. Payments of this nature have historically been "buried" in the books of MNCs or concealed in some other way. (Practical Perspective 2.2 presents some illustrations of whitemail bribes.)

PRACTICAL PERSPECTIVE 2-2

Wandering Into Ethical No-Man's Land

When American businesspeople venture abroad, a common view is that they're wandering into an ethical no-man's land, where each encounter holds forth a fresh demand for a "gratuity," or baksheesh. William C. Norris, who founded and for many years headed Control Data Corporation, says, "No question about it. We were constantly in the position of saying how much we were willing to pay" to have a routine service performed overseas. Norris recalls frequently facing situations such as this: "The computer is on the dock, it's raining, and you have to pay $100 to get it picked up. . . . "

In South America, firms often face a "closed bidding system" when dealing with that region's large, nationalized companies, says John Swanson, a senior consultant of communications and business conduct at Dow Corning Corporation. He said that his company had been locked out of the South American market at times because it refused to pay the bribes necessary to get that business.

In Japan, bids for government construction jobs are routinely rigged—a result of Japanese firms purchasing "influence" from politicians, according to one former U.S. government official who asked to remain anonymous. Donald E. Peterson, former chairman and chief executive officer of the Ford Motor Company, cites ethical challenges in much of the developing world. "Give me a military dictator with absolute power, and it doesn't matter if he's South American or African or Asian—you've got problems."

SOURCE: Excerpted from Andrew W. Singer, "Ethics: Are Standards Lower Overseas?" *Across the Board* (September 1991), p. 31. Copyright © 1991, Conference Board, Inc., New York. Reprinted with permission. All rights reserved.

Lubrication Bribes

This type of bribe is typically described as payment to facilitate, expedite, or speed up routine government approvals or other actions to which the firm would legally be entitled. Such payments are generally made to minor officials such as custom agents or licensing clerks. Another trait of lubrication bribes is that the amounts are generally smaller than whitemail bribes, although there have been cases where large lubrication-type payments were made. The number and acceptability of the practice of lubrication bribes is much greater than that of whitemail bribes. Officials in many Third World countries, countries that lag behind the developed nations, such as the United States, Japan, and Western Europe, are especially noted for requiring "grease" to make their political and administrative wheels turn. Somewhat similar to waiters or waitresses in U.S. restaurants, who receive a salary that is much lower than the United States' legal minimum wage and rely on customers' tips to supplement their income, in many countries, numerous officials receive a low salary and rely on "grease" payments to supplement their income.

Extortion

A distinction can be made between bribery and extortion. Bribery is offered by an individual or a corporation seeking an unlawful advantage, while extortion is force exerted in the other direction—an official seeking payment from an individual or corporation for an action to which the individual or corporation may lawfully be entitled. Gulf Oil's dilemma in South Korea is an example of extortion. Also, organized groups existing in numerous countries sometimes kidnap international executives and hold them for ransom—see Practical Perspective 2.3, the case of Chiquita Bananas in Colombia.

PRACTICAL PERSPECTIVE 2-3

Chiquita Bananas in Colombia: Terrorism Gone Bananas

In March (2007) the Cincinnati-based Chiquita Brands International, Inc., paid a $25 million settlement to the U.S. Justice Department for paying off right-wing paramilitary groups in Colombia, groups that Washington classifies as "terrorist organizations." Chiquita is one of the biggest and most powerful food marketing and distribution companies in the world and one of the world's largest banana producers. The company shows annual revenues of approximately $4.5 billion and about 25,000 employees operating in more than 70 countries. The banana market, worth about $5 billion a year in 2001, is the most important global fruit export. The majority of the 14 million tons of bananas exported every year come from Latin America.

The charges state that from 1997 to 2004 several unnamed high-ranking corporate officers from Chiquita and its Colombian Banadex subsidiary made monthly payments, totaling $1.7 million, to the United Self-Defense Forces of Colombia (AUC). Even though Chiquita's outside lawyers insisted that payments stop in 2001, Banadex continued to write checks to the AUC, though Chiquita executives later decided that cash was a better idea. The AUC, often described as a "death squad," was incorporated as one of 28 "Foreign Terrorist Organizations" on the U.S. Department of State Web site in September 2001. Not without reason, even *Forbes Magazine* describes the AUC as "responsible for some of the worst massacres in Colombia's civil conflict and for a sizable percentage of the country's cocaine exports." With approximately 15,000 to 20,000 armed troops, the AUC uses "kidnapping, torture, disappearance, rape, murder, beatings, extortion and drug trafficking" among its standard techniques...

Chiquita's involvement with the paramilitaries developed at a time when the right-wing groups were growing quickly and deepening their ties with politicians, security forces and businesses across Colombia. In the state of Antioquia, Chiquita's business boomed as the group took over banana-growing lands and were blamed for the killing of human rights workers and trade unionists... The U.S. complaint noted that "by 2003, Banadex was Chiquita's most profitable banana-producing operation." Chiquita sold its wholly owned subsidiary Banadex to the local company Banacol in June 2004 for between $43.5 and $52 million...

In May 1998, *The Cincinnati Enquirer* published a series of articles that exposed Chiquita's still questionable business practices. The articles, written by Mike Gallagher and Cameron McWhirter, reported cases in which the company used tactics including "bribery, abusive corporate control in Honduras and Columbia, the use of harmful pesticides, and repressive actions against workers" to bolster profits. Bribery proved to be the least of it. The investigation found Chiquita to be the secret owner of "dozens of supposedly independent banana companies." The authors found cases of worker and union suppression on Chiquita-controlled farms, though the "employee pamphlet" assures workers that they have the right to unionize. In one case, the company used the Honduran military to "evict residents of a farm village; the soldiers forced the farmers out at gunpoint and the village was bulldozed."

When Chiquita does face competition, they prove to be similarly ruthless. A federal lawsuit filed by a competitor's employee filed charges that Chiquita-hired thugs attempted to abduct him in Honduras. The investigation also found that Chiquita was aerial spraying workers, despite its pact with Rainforest Alliance since November 2000, which forbids aerial spaying... Despite probably well-founded articles and a book greenwashing Chiquita's transformation in 2004, it is questionable if Chiquita has really changed its practices.

Chiquita didn't take the criticism kindly, however, and when their shareholders sued the company, Chiquita sued the newspaper, claiming that its reporter Mike Gallagher obtained voice-mail tapers illegally. "*The Cincinnati Enquirer* published an apology across the top of its front page and said it agreed to pay Chiquita Brands International Inc. more than $10 million to avoid being sued for the series of articles that exposed the fruit company's criminal practices." ... While the company claims that it was strong-armed into making the recent payments to paramilitaries in Colombia to protect its employees, human rights groups accuse the company of paying the paramilitaries not only to "protect" workers "but also to target union leaders and agitators perceived as going against the company's interests" and to force communities off farming land.

SOURCE: Abstracted from April Howard, "Chiquita in Colombia: Terrorism Goes Bananas" (April 3, 2007), http://upsidedownworld .org/main/content/view/684/1/. The entire article cites 44 references.

To Bribe or Not to Bribe?

Bribery and corruption top the list of global ethics issues. According to former U.S. Commerce Secretary Mickey Cantor, bribery and corruption cost U.S. firms $64 billion in lost business in 1996.[13] Thus, when a manager crosses a nation's borders to conduct or negotiate business, he or she will sometimes be confronted with the need to decide whether or not to practice the act of bribery. Box 2.1 presents some questions whose answers can help international business executives make such a decision. Box 2.2 presents a perspective on how to conduct business legally in foreign countries.

Box 2.1   Questions to Determine Whether to Bribe

Legal Questions

1. What are the legal consequences in the parent country?
2. How comprehensive is the law of the host country? What is the enforceability of its law?
3. Will the corporation be liable to its competitors for financial damages (such as unfair practice or restraint of trade)?
4. Will the company be held liable by stockholders in the host or parent country?

Moral Questions

5. What is the company's policy regarding overseas payoffs? Will it cause any deviation from standard practice?
6. If the questionable payment is disclosed, will it damage the public image of the company in the parent country?
7. Will the payoff activity affect employee morale of the company at home or overseas?
8. What is the custom in the host country?
9. Does the public opinion of the host country carry the same weight as it does in the parent country?

Economic Questions

10. How does the expected gain compare with the company's total earnings?
11. What is the cost of payoff as a percentage of total revenue? Is it a one-time payment or a periodic contribution?
12. Is the company diversified in many countries?
13. Will the payoff trigger other host countries to make the same demand?
14. Will the payoff action cause retaliation from competitors?

Personal Questions

15. Will top management find out about the payoff? If so, am I subject to censure?
16. Am I likely to be held personally liable for such action?
17. Does the company carry insurance to pay my legal fees if I am found guilty of violating a law?
18. Will disclosure of payoff harm my reputation and make it difficult to obtain or retain a management position in the future?
19. How would my family and friends react to disclosure of such activity?

SOURCE: G. W. Gruenberg and Y. Kugel, "Criteria and Guidelines for Decision Making: The Special Case of International Payoffs," *Columbia Journal of World Business* (Fall 1977), p. 120. Copyright © 1977, JAI Press Inc. Used with permission of JAI Press Inc. All rights reserved.

Box 2.2   Conducting International Business Legally

● Rigorously learn about the culture, the business practices, and the laws of your host country—not just the customs and niceties. Talk with others who have done business there and with local lawyers. Contact the area group that represents American and indigenous interests, often a local chamber of commerce with a joint agreement with the U.S. Chamber of Commerce. Seek out the commercial attaché in the U.S. embassy.

● Hire a local journalist to do a comprehensive local media search. Do not rely solely on the U.S. business press. You need to know how much attention is being paid to corruption and whether criminal charges have ever been brought—in short, how seriously bribery and corruption are regarded in your host country.

● Perform a due diligence investigation of everyone who will work for the company as an agent, representative, distributor, licensee, or joint venture partner. Examine the reputation, especially with regard to honesty. Enter into a specific contract delineating the person's responsibilities as they pertain to company policies and the Foreign Corrupt Practices Act. The person must sign a detailed statement promising not to engage in bribery. This prudent step could lessen both your company's liability and your personal liability.

● For all managers: Clearly, enunciate your corporate policies regarding bribery and U.S. law to your employees with direct and indirect sales responsibilities overseas. Restate them often—annually, at least. Each time, employees should complete and sign a detailed worksheet and a declaration that they have read and understood the policies; they know these papers go into their dossiers.

SOURCE: Barbara Ettorre, "Why Overseas Bribery Won't Last," *Management Review* (June 1994), p. 24. Copyright © 1994 American Management Association International. Reprinted by permission of American Management Association International, New York. All rights reserved.

The U.S. Foreign Corrupt Practices Act of 1977

The revelations by the SEC and Senate Foreign Relations subcommittee investigations of U.S. MNCs' "whitemail bribery" practices abroad, and the concern for the negative image such practices generated for the United States, helped plant the seed that eventually produced U.S. Senate Bill 305, the Foreign Corrupt Practices Act (FCPA). (See Practical Perspective 2.4.) The FCPA was passed and signed into law in 1977. Its purpose was twofold:

1. To establish a worldwide code of conduct for any kind of payment by U.S. businesses to foreign government officials, political parties, and political candidates

2. To require appropriate accounting controls for full disclosure of firms' transactions

The law applies even if such payments are common practice (viewed as an ethical practice) in the country where they are made. Some of the basic provisions of the FCPA are as follows:

- It is a criminal offense for a firm to make payments to a foreign government official, political party, party official, or candidate for political office in order to secure or retain business in another nation.
- Sales commissions to independent agents are illegal if the business has knowledge that any part of the commission is being passed to foreign officials.
- Government employees whose duties are essentially ministerial or clerical are excluded, so expediting payments to persons such as customs agents and bureaucrats are permitted. (Thus, the FCPA does not apply to small "lubrication" bribes.)
- In addition to the antibribery provisions that apply to all businesses, all publicly held corporations that are subject to the SEC are required to establish internal accounting controls to ensure that all payments abroad are authorized and properly recorded.[14]

PRACTICAL PERSPECTIVE 2-4

The Murky Land of the FCPA

The Foreign Corrupt Practices Act (FCPA) became law in 1977, in the wake of foreign bribery scandals involving U.S. companies that shook the governments of Belgium, the Netherlands, Honduras, Italy, and Japan. One of the most notorious incidents involved an estimated $25 million in concealed payments made overseas by Lockheed Corporation in connection with sales of its Tristar L-1011 aircraft in Japan. This culminated in the resignation and subsequent criminal conviction of Japanese Prime Minister Kankuie Tanaka.

The FCPA, which makes it a crime for U.S. corporations to bribe officials of foreign governments to obtain or increase business, is controversial, in part, because it seeks to forge a distinction between "bribes" (which it deems illegal) and "gratuities" (which the FCPA permits). The difference is murky, according to the FCPA's critics.

"The law marked the difference between gratuities paid to low-level officials and payments made to authorities," writes Duane Windsor in his book, *The Foreign Corrupt Practices Act: Anatomy of a Statute*. "In many countries a payment to a customs official is a matter of course and a matter of economic necessity. A customs official may backlog an order or hinder a shipment by elaborately checking each imported item. The detrimental effect to the shipment is obvious. In response, lawmakers sought to delineate gratuities and bribes very clearly. But in reality the delineation of gratuities was so vague that some people felt it had a chilling effect [on business]."

SOURCE: Excerpted from Andrew W. Singer, "Ethics: Are Standards Lower Overseas?" *Across the Board* (September 1991), p. 33. Copyright © 1991, Conference Board, Inc., New York. Reprinted with permission. All rights reserved.

The penalty levied on the business enterprise for not complying with the FCPA was set at $1 million for each count. The penalty levied on individual members of the corporation found guilty of making the illegal payment is a fine of up to $10,000 and/or five years' imprisonment, with the added provision that the firm may not pay or reimburse the employees for the fines levied on them. Thus, the FCPA calls for both civil and criminal penalties.

Enforcement of the FCPA was assigned to two federal agencies: the SEC and the Department of Justice. The SEC's responsibility included enforcement of the record keeping and accounting control provisions of the FCPA and civil authority to enforce the prohibitions against foreign bribery by U.S. publicly held corporations. The U.S. Department of Justice was given the responsibility to enforce criminal penalties for corporate bribery of foreign officials and the authority to bring civil actions against domestic concerns whose securities are not registered with the SEC.

Over the years, numerous companies have been fined. For example, in the late 1980s, Young & Rubicam Inc., the New York–based advertising agency, and three of its executives were indicted on a conspiracy charge under the FCPA. The U.S. government contended that the firm had "reason to know" that one of its Jamaican agents was paying off that country's Minister of Tourism to obtain advertising business. "In order to avert a lengthy trial, the corporation paid a $500,000 penalty," said R. John Cooper, the executive vice president and general counsel of Young & Rubicam. And in the 1970s, Control Data Corporation was prosecuted by the U.S. government under the FCPA for making payments in Iran. In 1978, Control Data Corporation pleaded guilty to three criminal charges that it had made improper payments to unnamed foreign officials. It was fined $1,381,000 by the U.S. Customs Services.[15] In 2005, Titan Corporation settled a federal overseas bribery probe in the West African nation of Benin for $28 million—the San Diego–based defense contractor pleaded guilty to violating federal antibribery laws, as it sought to influence elections in Benin in exchange for higher management fees on a telecommunications project.[16] Practical Perspective 2.1 describes the fines imposed on Lockheed.

Complaints Made by MNCs Concerning the FCPA

The major areas of concern communicated by U.S. MNCs over the FCPA were as follows:

- The FCPA placed them at a competitive disadvantage because companies from other countries, as well as from the host country, were not bound by the FCPA laws and could continue making whitemail payments to secure business, thus putting them at a competitive advantage. (See Practical Perspective 2.5.)
- The accounting burden of internal controls, along with the vagueness of this section of the law, makes the MNCs' duty and liability difficult to assess.
- MNCs complain that the FCPA forces them to become political tools of the U.S. government because they have to exert its will in the world through their economic power.

Furthermore, a report issued in 1978 by the Export Disincentives Task Force, created by the White House to find ways of improving the negative balance of trade between the United States and other nations, pointed to the FCPA as being potentially harmful. This statement, which was made one year after passage of the FCPA, was based on interviews with executives of U.S. MNCs who claimed that their firms lost export business because of compliance with the FCPA.

PRACTICAL PERSPECTIVE 2-5

Can We Litigate Morality?

Passed in the late '70s in the wake of Watergate [the investigation that led to President Richard M. Nixon's resignation] and the overseas bribery scandals, the Foreign Corrupt Practices Act (FCPA) made it a felony for U.S. companies to obtain business by paying off foreign government officials. From its inception, the FCPA has been controversial. "Managers in other countries often chuckle at the United States hoping to export its morality in the form of the Foreign Corrupt Practices Act," said Gene Laczniak, management professor at Marquette University in Milwaukee.

"It's anachronistic in today's world," said William Norris, the former Control Data [Corporation] chief. "It's like the antitrust laws in many ways. The world has passed it by. [The antitrust laws] worked fine as long as the U.S. economy was an isolated system," said critics. But now antitrust laws may be inhibiting large U.S. firms from competing in the international arena. "In any case," said Norris, "most U.S. companies don't want to become involved in activities such as bribing foreign officials."

R. John Cooper, executive vice president and general counsel of Young & Rubicam Inc., made a similar argument. The FCPA was enacted at a time when the competitive position of U.S. companies in the world was stronger than it is today, Cooper pointed out. In 1970, the United States was the source of 60 percent of the world's direct foreign investment. By 1984, according to the United Nations, that figure dropped to 12 percent. Japanese, European, and East Asian firms picked up much of the slack, launching economic forays even into America's own backyard. The United States risks becoming economically hamstrung by statutes such as the Foreign Corrupt Practices Act, suggested Cooper.

"We have to reexamine some of these high-toned notions." According to Cooper, with increasingly heated international competition, the act is out of date. It puts too much of a burden on U.S. corporations to know everything about their foreign agents—a burden not shouldered by foreign competitors.

SOURCE: Excerpted from Andrew W. Singer, "Ethics: Are Standards Lower Overseas?" *Across the Board* (September 1991), p. 33. Copyright © 1991, Conference Board, Inc., New York. Reprinted with permission. All rights reserved.

Yet another problem with the FCPA was that it was not clear enough with respect to the use of foreign subsidiaries to transact business. For example, Boeing Corporation sold its planes abroad through a distributorship, Overseas International Distributors Company, which was registered as a Netherlands company but doing business out of Geneva. Overseas International Distributors bought planes from Boeing after obtaining orders for the aircraft from officials in the Middle East. Finally, many MNCs saw the FCPA as landmark legislation that could beget more legislation, thus hindering the ability of the U.S. MNCs to deal effectively in the global marketplace. Overall, many U.S. MNCs saw the FCPA as another stumbling block to an already complex challenge of competing in the global arena.

1988 Amendments to the FCPA

In early 1981 and again in early 1983, the U.S. Senate attempted to repair some of the uncertainties associated with the FCPA. The Senate's proposed amendments were rejected by the House of Representatives. The amendment was finally passed as a section of the Omnibus Trade and Competitiveness Act of 1988. The amendment clarifies various provisions of the FCPA, consolidates most of the enforcement responsibilities for bribery violations into the U.S. Department of Justice, and increases the civil and criminal penalties for violating the FCPA. Relative to the accounting aspects of the FCPA, the amendment limits future criminal liability to intentional actions to circumvent the internal accounting control system or falsify the corporation's books. With respect to payments made through third parties, the amendment eliminates the "reason to know" standard and modifies the "knowing" standard. Under the act, "knowing" is defined to entail the substantial certainty or conscious disregard of a high probability that the third-party payment will become a bribe.[17]

Relative to enforcement of the FCPA, the amendment increased the civil and criminal penalties for violations. Criminal penalties were increased from $1 million to $2 million for corporations and from $10,000 to $100,000 for individuals. The maximum imprisonment remained five years. A civil penalty of $10,000 for individuals was established and may not be paid by the corporation. All jurisdictions for enforcing the antibribery provisions of the FCPA were consolidated within the Department of Justice. The SEC remained responsible for civil enforcement of the records and internal accounting control provisions of the FCPA.[18]

An Alternative Payoff Approach

Many international executives do not view the FCPA as hindering their competitiveness in the global marketplace. (See Practical Perspective 2.6.) These executives enhance their competitiveness by improving their enterprises' technical expertise, their customer service, and their responsibility to the customer through quality. Furthermore, there are indications that the practice of bribery is not as widespread as it once was; it seems to be waning. (Refer to Practical Perspective 2.10.) And when these executives must make some sort of payment to obtain a favor, they do not pay "private individuals"; instead, they make payments to institutions, such as contributions to build schools, hospitals, medical clinics, or agricultural projects.[19] Payments of this nature obtain favors and goodwill for the MNC; they also improve the local situation, such as by increasing local employment. This payment approach, thus, does not improve only one person's bank account; instead, the payment is shared with the community.

PRACTICAL PERSPECTIVE 2-6

Keeping the Cutting Edge Sharp

Because the Foreign Corrupt Practices Act has been such an entrenched influence, many U.S. companies have ceased to regard it as a stumbling block. "I've never had a manager say, 'We can't do business because we're limited by the Foreign Corrupt Practices Act,'" said Raymond V. Gilmartin, [former] chairman, president, and CEO of Becton Dickinson and Company and board chairman of the Ethics Resource Center. "We are not at a competitive disadvantage at all." . . .

Gilmartin said foreign sales were growing twice as fast as domestic. But Gilmartin was the first to say that any company doing business beyond U.S. borders has to keep sharply focused on doing the lawful thing.

PRACTICAL PERSPECTIVE 2-6 (Continued)

Before, echoing the thoughts of many U.S. companies, Becton Dickinson thought it was "an ethical company with ethical employees," Gilmartin said. "We said we wanted to do the right thing, but it became clear that we must use training and reinforcement." Accordingly, Becton Dickinson used interactive workshops for the first time—small group exercises and case studies that train employees to recognize ethical dilemmas and to work them through. The company also revised its written code of conduct, making it more "understandable, readable, and practical," said Gilmartin. "I've also made it clear in speeches that in no way do we want you, the employee, to compromise your personal integrity. But we are going beyond that. We are serious. We are giving recognizable managerial support."

"When doing business abroad," Gilmartin said, "an aggressive approach works best." A company should "make it clear right upfront" to any prospective foreign client that it doesn't give payoffs. "If our principles seem to preclude us from certain business, we'll forego this opportunity—but we won't give up," he states. "We will try other avenues."

SOURCE: Excerpted from Barbara Ettorre, "Why Overseas Bribery Won't Last," *Management Review* (June 1994), p. 22. Copyright © 1994, American Management Association International. Reprinted by permission of American Management Association International, New York. All rights reserved.

Cross-National Social Responsibility

Social responsibility has been defined as "the notion that corporations have an obligation to constituent groups in society other than stockholders and beyond that prescribed by law or union contract."[20] CSR therefore means that a firm's actions must take into account not only the well-being of the stockholders but also the well-being of the community, the employees, and the customers. Box 2.3 presents the ten commandments of CSR, and Box 2.4 presents United Nations Global Compact's Ten Principles. With respect to MNCs' cross-national social responsibility, many international business executives condone the concept of cultural relativism, while others condone the concept of universalism.

Box 2.3 The Ten Commandments of Social Responsibility

I. Thou Shall Take Corrective Action Before It Is Required.

II. Thou Shall Work With Affected Constituents to Resolve Mutual Problems.

III. Thou Shall Work to Establish Industry-Wide Standards and Self-Regulation.

IV. Thou Shall Publicly Admit Thy Mistakes.

V. Thou Shall Get Involved in Appropriate Social Programs.

VI. Thou Shall Help Correct Environmental Problems.

VII. Thou Shall Monitor the Changing Social Environment.

VIII. Thou Shall Establish and Enforce a Corporate Code of Conduct.

IX. Thou Shall Take Needed Public Stands on Social Issues.

X. Thou Shall Strive to Make Profits on an Ongoing Basis.

SOURCE: Larry D. Alexander and William F. Matthews, "The Ten Commandments of Corporate Social Responsibility," *Business and Society Review*, 50 (Summer 1984), pp. 62–66.

Box 2.4   United Nations Global Compact's Ten Principles

Human Rights

Principle 1: Business should support and respect the protection of internationally proclaimed human rights and

Principle 2: make sure that they are not complicated in human rights abuses.

Labor Standards

Principle 3: Business should respect the freedom of association and the effective recognition of the right to collective bargaining;

Principle 4: the elimination of all forms of forced and compulsory labor;

Principle 5: the effective abolition of child labor; and

Principle 6: the elimination of discrimination in respect of employment and occupation.

Environment

Principle 7: Business should support a precautionary approach to environmental challenges;

Principle 8: undertake initiatives to promote greater environmental responsibility; and

Principle 9: encourage the development and diffusion of environmentally friendly technologies.

Anticorruption

Principle 10: Business should work against corruption in all forms, including extortion and bribery.

SOURCE: www.unglobalcompact.org

Cultural Relativism

Cultural relativism holds that *no culture's ethics are any better than any other's.*[21] Under this standard, there are no international "rights" or "wrongs." Thus, if Thailand tolerates the bribery of public officials, then Thai tolerance is no worse than U.S. or German intolerance. If Switzerland is liberal with respect to insider trading, then Swiss liberalism is no worse than U.S. restrictiveness.[22] These executives would therefore not support the FCPA.

But the concept of cultural relativism can backfire. For example, suppose a U.S. corporation invents a product and patents it. Patent piracy is wrong (and illegal) in the United States, but it is not wrong in some nations (and if it is illegal, it is not enforced because it is culturally acceptable). What if a company in one of these countries pirated the patent? Would the executives in the company from which the patent was pirated simply write the loss off as "Oh well, that's culture"? As an illustration, some enterprises in China readily pirate U.S. firms' copyrighted computer software, movies, and music and put phony U.S. labels on consumer products. (See Practical Perspective 2.7.) If the U.S. pirated firms' executives adhered to the cultural relativism concept, they would not complain about the Chinese firms' pirating practices because they are not viewed as being unethical in China; in fact, there, "copying is the biggest form of flattery." However, U.S. trade representatives continue applying strong pressure on Chinese government officials to implement and enforce policies that preclude Chinese enterprises from undertaking such activities.[23] Suppose also that a U.S. MNC is manufacturing in Bangladesh using cheap child labor. Use of child labor in such a way is not tolerable in the United States, but it is tolerable in Bangladesh. What happens to the MNC when the U.S. press gets hold of the information and promulgates it among the U.S. public that the MNC is exploiting child labor in a country? Will it result in a boycott? (Practical Perspective 2.8 illustrates this problem.) It therefore seems that the concept of cultural relativism is sometimes not very practical.

PRACTICAL PERSPECTIVE 2-7

The Risks Are Rising in China

China's flagrant piracy of American pop music, movies, and computer software is more than the biggest rip-off in global commerce. It's also the latest evidence of the growing and increasingly visible risks confronting Western and Asian companies doing business in the People's Republic.... Nowhere are the stakes bigger—or less amenable to a quick, lasting solution—than the current U.S.-China dispute over heisted copyrights. More than a trade war, think of this fight as a clash of civilizations. The new U.S. economy, with its edge in handling information technology, confronts an ambitious Asian giant with a voracious appetite for capital, know-how, and export markets—and a primitive legal system that lacks almost any concept of the Western notion of intellectual property. Said Kenneth DeWoskin, a University of Michigan business school professor and China specialist, "Most Chinese do not understand the notion of intangible assets like brands or copyrighted material. We're in for a long siege on these issues."

Beijing would have a hard time fixing the situation if it wanted to: It has devolved economic power on the provinces, which control the pirate factories and the courts. Further complicating matters, senior politicians, military men, and their families are often involved in the pirating industries. Said Howard Lincoln, chairman of Nintendo of America, "We have evidence that government officials have ownership stakes in companies doing the counterfeiting. . . . "

Showbiz products such as Madonna recordings and Mickey Mouse films grab the spotlight, but intellectual property of corporations with manufacturing plants in China is equally at risk. To get into the PRC, companies must disclose to authorities details of their products and processes. Said DeWoskin, "Chinese research and design institutes look for the best technology in the country and spread it around. They also examine plans and specifications of new ventures, so there's bound to be some leakage."

Protecting a brand name in the China market often resembles a mission impossible. A bogus Chinese breakfast cereal product called Kongalu Cornstrips has a trademark and packaging identical to that of Kellogg's cornflakes. A small Chinese computer manufacturer, Mr. Sun, has appropriated the trademark of Sun Microsystems for its machines. And mineral water drinkers in China can enjoy Pabst Blue Ribbon Water. As for videos, movies, compact discs, and computer software, virtually the entire Chinese market is a pirate's den because Beijing denies market access to most of the legal products. Nor is there much shame about the grand larceny. . . . According to a report issued by the U.S. Trade Representative's office, "Anyone can walk into a store in Beijing and buy a pirated copy of Microsoft's popular Windows software package. The store simply copies it onto a few blank floppy disks while you wait."

The crisis atmosphere has at least sent everyone back to the bargaining table. . . . Can a solution emerge? Optimists point to Taiwan. Only a dozen years ago that island nation harbored a vigorous underground export industry that skillfully copied leading global brands. A visitor could buy good-looking knockoffs of Rolex watches in the back streets of Taipei. The counterfeiting abated once Taiwanese companies developed their own intellectual property and thus a deeper appreciation of its value. Given time and a few more knocks in the game of global trade, the Chinese too should eventually come to see piracy as more expensive than it's worth. Until then, expect it to remain one more reason to cast a cautious eye on China's red-hot but risky market.

SOURCE: Louis Kraar, "The Risks Are Rising in China," *Fortune* (March 6, 1995), pp. 179–180. Copyright © 1995, Times, Inc., New York. Reprinted with permission. All rights reserved.

NOTE: As of 2007, this is still an issue confronting multinational corporations entering China. See, for example, Charles W. Hill, "Digital Piracy: Causes, Consequences, and Strategic Responses," *Asia Pacific Journal of Management*, 24, no. 1 (March 2007), pp. 9–25.

PRACTICAL PERSPECTIVE 2-8

How Multinational Corporations Export Human Rights

In 1996 Kathie Lee Gifford made front-page news. The well-liked television personality had lent her name to a discount line of women's clothing that, it was discovered, had been made by underage Central American workers. That same year the Walt Disney Company was exposed contracting with Haitian suppliers who paid their workers less than Haiti's minimum wage of $2.40 a day. Nike and Reebok, makers of perhaps the world's most popular athletic footwear were similarly and repeatedly exposed.

PRACTICAL PERSPECTIVE 2-8 *(Continued)*

In all these cases, the companies accused were U.S. manufacturers of consumer products. They were being targeted for human rights violations committed abroad not by their own managers or in their own plants but by the subcontractors who produced their products in overseas facilities. Traditionally, the corporate response to this subcontractor problem has been predictable, if unfortunate. U.S. firms have argued that they cannot realistically or financially be held responsible for the labor practices of their foreign suppliers. "The problem is, we don't own the factories," a Disney spokesperson protested. "We are dealing with a licensee."

Recently, though, this attitude has started to change. As a direct result of heightened human rights activism, sharper media scrutiny, and the increased communication facilitated by the Internet, U.S. corporations are finding it difficult to sustain their old hands-off policy. Under pressure, they are beginning to accept responsibility for the labor practices and human rights abuses of their foreign subcontractors.

SOURCE: Excerpted from Debora L. Spar, "The Spotlight and the Bottom Line," *Foreign Affairs*, 77, no. 2 (March–April 1998), p. 7. Reprinted with permission.

Universalism

On the other hand, the concept of universalism, *a rigid global yardstick by which to measure all moral issues* (e.g., the U.S. FCPA), is often not very practical either. This is because its application would show disrespect for valid cultural differences and different economic needs. For example, people in the United States do not tolerate manufacturing facilities that disperse health-damaging smog. Under the concept of universalism, it would be unethical to transfer such manufacturing facilities to another country. But in countries where people are starving, economic development may be more important than health, and such manufacturing facilities would thus be welcome. A manager guided by the cultural relativism view would export such manufacturing facilities to the starving country. But, as mentioned above, it is likely to backfire.

For example, many years ago, U.S.-based Union Carbide established gas production facilities in Bhopal, India. In its U.S. plants, Union Carbide was required by the U.S. government to install expensive accident prevention systems. The Government of India did not require such systems. In the 1980s, an accident at the Bhopal plant killed more than 3,000 people and injured thousands of others.[24] The press coverage of the Union Carbide incident was very negative. Many Americans felt that Union Carbide, knowing the dangers of not taking preventive measures, had a moral obligation to have taken them in India, even if India did not require them and could not afford them.

These Americans thus adhere to the concept of universalism. On the other hand, many Americans adopted the concept of cultural relativism—they believed that Union Carbide did not have the right to interfere with Indian government matters; they believed that it is the responsibility of India's government to make such decisions.

Thus, developing, implementing, and controlling cross-cultural business ethics and social responsibility programs is an enormous challenge confronting the managers of MNCs. The problem is enlarged by the press sometimes persuading MNCs to impose their social responsibility on their manufacturing subcontractors. For example, Starbucks Coffee has agreed to adopt a "code of conduct" that must be adhered to by its coffee suppliers and may help workers in Guatemala and other Third World nations. Starbucks' management made the decision after stores in British Columbia, Canada, and the United States were targeted in a February 1995 leafletting blitz. The protesters were concerned about "harsh working conditions, paltry pay, and human rights violations on Guatemalan coffee plantations."[25] (As an illustration, read Practical Perspectives 2.8 and 2.9.) The press, therefore, often asks MNCs to reject the concept of cultural relativism and apply the concept of universalism.[26]

PRACTICAL PERSPECTIVE 2-9

The Supply Police

The Christmas-week NBC show asserting that Wal-Mart's "Buy American" program misleads consumers also leveled a more sinister charge: that children as young as nine churn out clothes for the nation's largest retailer in Bangladeshi sweatshops. Other big-name U.S importers aren't waiting to see whether the public buys Wal-Mart's denials. Instead they're making sure their own suppliers are free of environmental, human rights, or other potential embarrassments. The supplier police had better hurry. Jeff Fiedler, the AFL-CIO official who helped NBC mug Wal-Mart, says that he's drawing beads on a dozen new targets, including apparel and dress-shoe companies.

Suddenly, "going global" invites a hazard nobody mentioned back in B-school. Activists pushing a variety of causes have discovered that exposing corporate exploitation will accomplish what tamer strategies, such as leafletting annual meetings, have not. Scrutiny by labor unions, activists, and socially conscious investors is forcing importers to monitor not just their foreign subsidiaries but their far-flung network of independent suppliers—and their suppliers' as well. Says Donna Katzin of the Interfaith Center on Corporate Responsibility, "Just because companies don't make a product themselves doesn't relieve them of all obligations. . . . "

Is it fair to hold Third World suppliers to U.S. standards of conduct? Even many of those who say it is admit to ambivalence about imposing their values on countries and companies halfway around the world. "It's easy to take cynical views of American corporations," says Northwestern University business ethicist David Messick. "But what gives us the right to decide at what age people in Bangladesh should work?" . . . To which image-conscious executives might respond: Why take risks? As the Wal-Mart case demonstrates, even perceived transgressions can lead to big embarrassment . . . .

Several companies have made pre-emptive strikes to avoid similar pratfalls. Last March, Sears said it wouldn't import forced-labor products from China. Phillips-Van Heusen explicitly threatens to terminate orders to apparel suppliers that violate its broad ethical, environmental, and human rights code. And Dow Chemical asks suppliers to conform not just to local pollution and safety laws but to the often tougher U.S. standards. At least one major U.S. company acted merely to stamp out falsehoods: Persistent rumors that McDonald's suppliers grazed their cattle on cleared rainforest land finally led it to ban the practice in writing. . . .

Separating right from wrong overseas doesn't guarantee a company high praise at home. Just ask Nike, which ran afoul of cultural relativism late in 1992. *Harper's Magazine* printed a U.S. labor activist's dissection of a pay stub for an Indonesian woman; she netted the equivalent of $37.46 a month for making sneakers. Later, an article in the *Far Eastern Economic Review* reported that Indonesians who make Nikes earn far more than most workers lucky enough to get jobs in the impoverished country. "Americans focus on wages paid, not what standard of living those wages relate to," said Nike's Dusty Kidd. But such arguments miss the point. When it comes to social responsibility, it's not enough for a company to be right. It also has to convince its increasingly touchy customers.

SOURCE: Excerpted from John McCormick and Marc Levinson, "The Supply Police," *Newsweek* (February 15, 1993), pp. 48–49. Copyright © 1993, Newsweek, Inc. All rights reserved. Reprinted with permission.

The Normative and the Instrumental Views

Similar to the notion of universalism is the notion of the normative view, which believes that "MNCs have a moral responsibility to their stakeholders . . . Thus, moral standards are independent of profits . . . , and the instrumental view, whose proponents argue that firms should pursue high labor standards if it is good for profitability to do so."[27]

In essence, certain ethical principles are appropriate for some but not all cultures, which creates a "moral free space." For example, abuse of child labor or slavery may be inappropriate in most cultures, thus universal standards in this respect might be acceptable, but other issues such as pollution or employees' rights to annual leave vary from country to country, thus cultural relativism may be more appropriate in internationalization decisions.[28] Therefore, we need to learn much more about these issues than we now know. For example, some countries only require citizens to go through four years of education, therefore people by age 11 are ready for the workforce; and some countries don't even enforce mandatory education. Thus, an MNC accused by the media or the ethics police of child abuse in such a country and calling for a boycott may actually be doing that country a disservice.

Human Rights

As discussed above, the topic of human rights is a cross-cultural sensitive issue. People in rich countries, such as the United States, will interpret human rights quite differently from people in poor countries. For example, Levi's once pulled its operations out of China because China was viewed as being in violation of human rights. Some academics have accused Levi's of pulling out for the purpose of marketing promotion for building goodwill in other countries. In protest against human rights violations, some companies pulled out of South Africa during its apartheid years. Some academics accused those companies of pulling out only to avert a backlash or boycott in other markets. But some companies, such as Ford, remained, claiming that more good can be accomplished by staying. The U.S. media readily reports such human rights violations in developing nations and calls for action against such violations. Of course, one needs to examine specific situations. In many cases, as proposed above, what Americans perceive to be child labor abuse in a country may actually be better than no child abuse in that country at that point of economic development. The U.S. media sometimes overlooks the fact that child labor abuse was highly practiced in the United States when it began shifting from an agriculture economy to an industrial economy. This is not to suggest that the media should stop reporting such activities, but Ford's staying to correct the situation might sometimes be a better option than pulling out or boycotting in protest.

Communicating Corporate Social Responsibility

Isabelle Maignan and David A. Ralston, using the Internet's Web pages (CSR on the Web), compared the extent businesses in France, the Netherlands, the United Kingdom, and the United States communicated CSR.[29] They randomly selected 100 of the nations' top 500 corporations and found that the "businesses in these countries do not display the same eagerness to appear socially responsible and employ diverse means to convey social responsibility images."[30] Table 2.1 presents their results.

TABLE 2.1 Corporate Social Responsibility (CSR): Europe and U.S. CSR Principles, Processes, and Stakeholder Issues Presented in Web Pages

Companies Mentioning:	FR	NL	UK	US
Principles motivating CSR				
1. Value-driven CSR	5	4	8	31
2. Performance-driven CSR	10	10	37	11
3. Stakeholder-driven CSR	14	10	16	6
a. Community	2	2	9	5
b. Customers	12	8	10	3
c. Regulations	9	6	4	3
CSR progress				
1. Philanthropic programs	6	10	48	52
2. Sponsorships	4	7	34	11
3. Volunteerism	0	0	23	25
4. Code of Ethics	2	3	11	10
5. Quality programs	9	2	12	3
6. Health and safety programs	1	4	14	6
7. Management of environmental programs	12	13	25	15
Stakeholder issues				
1. Community stakeholders				
a. Arts and culture	2	7	16	22
b. Education	2	7	28	31
c. Quality of life	4	2	18	37
d. Safety	0	2	14	2
e. Protection of environment	18	17	52	25
2. Customer stakeholders				
a. Productivity/service quality	12	2	14	6
b. Safety	2	5	4	3
3. Employee stakeholders				
a. Equal opportunity	2	1	1	6
b. Health and safety	1	6	17	7
4. Shareholders	1	4	5	5
5. Suppliers	1	5	6	2

SOURCE: I. Maignan and D. A. Ralston, "Corporate Social Responsibility in Europe and the U.S.: Insights From Business' Self-Presentations," *Journal of International Business Studies*, 33, no. 3 (2002), p. 506.

NOTE: FR = France, NL = The Netherlands, UK = United Kingdom, US = United States.

Toward the Globalization of Business Ethics

The U.S. approach to business ethics is unique. In comparison with other capitalistic societies, it is more individualistic, legalistic, and universalistic.[31] In other words, issues of business ethics are far more visible in the United States than they are in other capitalistic societies. This may be because there are far more laws regulating business in the United States than there are in other capitalistic countries. Therefore, the U.S. public reads and hears far more about business misconduct than do people in other countries. Hence, the "ethics gap" between the United States (but perhaps only in an ideological sense and not as much in covert practice) and the rest of the developed world is considerably large.[32]

Minor strides toward closing the ethics gap had been made in Europe and, on a much smaller scale, in Japan. In November 1987, a group of 75 European business executives and academics established the European Business Ethics Network (EBEN) in Brussels. Its mission is to promote business ethics in European private industry, public sector, voluntary organizations, and academia. The EBEN network, as of 2007, has close to 800 members in more than 34 countries. Each year, EBEN organizes a Research Conference in spring and an Annual Conference in the fall, normally hosted by an academic institution in a European country. The first European business ethics journal, *Ethica Degli Affari*, was established in 1987 in Italy. Since the mid-1980s, ethics research centers have been established in Britain, Belgium, Spain, Germany, Poland, the Netherlands, and Switzerland, and as of 2007, they are being developed in Estonia, Turkey, and France. In 1989 and 1991, the Institute of Morality sponsored international ethics conferences in Kashiwa City, Chiba Ken, Japan.[33] The International Business Ethics Institute (IBEA), with centers in Washington, D.C., and London was established to foster global business practices that promote equitable economic development, resource sustainability, and just forms of government. The IBEA publishes the *International Business Ethics Journal.*

Also, chief executives of Newmont Mining Corporation of Denver, Rio Tinto PLC of London, and Bechtel Group Incorporated of San Francisco, global leaders of their industries, signed onto a "zero-tolerance" pact against paying bribes being sponsored by a coalition of groups working with the World Economic Forum, according to company executives and forum organizers. Altogether, 47 large MNCs committed to the pact, representing at least $300 billion in annual revenue. "The momentum is building," said Fluor Corporation Chief Executive Alan Boeckmann, an organizer of the project. The world's five largest oil companies also are being pressed to sign the agreement, but none have yet agreed. Officials of Royal Dutch/Shell Group and Total SA said that they were considering the idea but already had their own zero-tolerance policies. A spokesman for the London-based BP PLC said that the company declined to sign for that reason.[34]

Notwithstanding, as pointed out above, a considerable ethics gap between the United States and other advanced nations still exists. However, as discussed above and in Practical Perspective 2.10, major strides were recently made to close the ethics gap. It has been pointed out that bribery is perceived as endemic in business and government in parts of Africa and East Asia; that while efforts at reform are under way, there is skepticism about how successful these will be; and that corruption and bribery are a part of the culture and environment of certain markets and will not simply go away.[35]

PRACTICAL PERSPECTIVE 2-10

A Tough Act to Follow

For most major multinationals, bribery has long ceased to be good business practice. There's never been any guarantee it would work. And now, thanks to years of international negotiation, it will no longer be legal either. Last November [1997], 36 nations signed the first Convention on Combating Bribery of Foreign Public Officials in International Business Transactions in Paris. The signatories comprised the 29 member-nations of the Organization for Economic Cooperation and Development (OECD), in addition to seven non-members . . . Each nation participating in the convention pledged to submit an act criminalizing bribery in that country to its legislature by April 1 [1998]. The treaty will enter into force once five of the ten largest of the OECD exporting countries have ratified it. . . . To the treaty's negotiators, this is a mere technicality. They believe the concept of banning international bribery as a means of doing business is one whose time has finally come.

In fact, the pressure for change is coming from all quarters. From the sellers' perspective, bribery has become an increasingly expensive and dangerous way to do business. From the buyers' side, it has added more costs to expensive international acquisitions at a time when a country's scarce resources should be used to develop its economy and infrastructure, not to pad the foreign bank accounts of bureaucrats and officials. As for international financial institutions and distributors of development assistance, bribes divert desperately needed resources from their intended purposes.

"In the last few years, countries have begun to wake up and say the costs of this kind of corruption are unacceptably high," says Thomas White, deputy director of the State Department's office of investment affairs and the chief U.S. negotiator of the treaty. "That's what has enabled us to take this out of the arena of being a simple competitive issue and place it in the area of good governance and economic efficiency. That's the argument that has won over other governments; we can no longer devote scarce resources to development while at the same time permitting governments to distort and pervert the development process. We can't undermine our own efforts to promote more stable governments while at the same time permitting our companies to undertake the kinds of bribery that destabilize political systems and discourage the development of democratic institutions."

For more than 20 years, the United States has held the moral high ground almost single-handedly in this area in the form of the Foreign Corrupt Practices Act. Over time, U.S. companies have come to grips with this law and learned to live with its constraints. "I don't think we can expect things to change overnight," says GE's Heimann. "I would expect it would take a five- to ten-year time frame for things really to change."

SOURCE: Excerpted from David A. Andelman, "Bribery: The New Global Outlaw," *Management Review* (April 1998), p. 49. Copyright © 1998 American Management Association International. Reprinted by permission of American Management Association International, New York. All rights reserved.

NOTE: Currently, in 2007, bribing public officials is a crime in the 36 countries that ratified the Convention. OECD is currently attempting to expand membership in the Convention.

The Impact of Culture on the Business Ethics Visibility Gap

The United States is one of the most individualistic cultures in the world. As indicated in Chapter 1, people's decisions in individualistic cultures tend to be guided by self-interest, as opposed to group interest. On the other hand, managers in group-oriented cultures tend to reflect less their personal moral guidance and more their shared understanding of the nature and scope of the corporation's responsibilities—and the enterprise's moral expectations are shaped by the norms of the community, not the personal values and reflections of the individual.[36] This helps explain why there are many more laws regulating business in the United States than there are in other advanced nations, and it helps explain why there is such a large business ethics gap between the United States and other nations.

This suggests that globalization of business ethics (application of the concept of universalism) is distant and that the concept of cultural relativism still prevails. Thus, as the integration of the global economy increases, effective international managers develop a "better appreciation of the differences in the legal and cultural context of business ethics between the USA and other capitalist nations and between Western and Asian economies as well."[37]

Business Ethics and the Internet

The World Wide Web, an area of the Internet, is a virtual, global, open-ended organization of interconnected information sources. It is now a quick way for companies, large or small, to market products or services globally to people who access the Internet. However, managers of such a global network are faced with the challenge of addressing the concerns of its constituents with respect to confidentiality, authenticity, and integrity, balancing security against responsiveness and performance. The system needs to be secure against malicious use, misuse, and data corruption while protecting the privacy of its users and the intellectual property of the vendors.[38] For example, providing copyright protection for knowledge providers on the Internet is quite different from providing it to their counterparts in hard copy publication. However, as was demonstrated in this chapter, hard copy publications do not have much protection in numerous countries. The Internet may thus be a great challenge in this respect.[39]

The U.S. intelligence community uses electronic eavesdropping to maintain and update a top secret database of international bribery cases. The information is being used extensively as a leverage to help U.S. firms compete abroad. And currently, there are issues of business ethics pertaining to bloggers on the Internet. Practical Perspective 2.11 presents the story of how Wal-Mart is addressing this issue. Whatsnextblog.com provides many stories, including Practical Perspective 2.11, relating to this issue.

PRACTICAL PERSPECTIVE 2-11

Wal-Mart: Desperately Seeking Ethics

Wal-Mart's ethical issues extended way beyond its relationship with bloggers, reported in the *New York Times* and in scores of blogs this week. As part of its massive "multi-pronged PR offense," Mathew Boyle at *Fortune* said that Wal-Mart has headhunters Martha Montag Brown & Associates seeking Wal-Mart's new director of global ethics.

"The world's largest retailer," *Fortune* says, "is trying to get out in front of critics and project a reputable image." . . . That Wal-Mart needs to beef up its ethics organization is not too surprising. "The Bentonville, Ark. Behemoth has been bloodied on several fronts lately—an $11 billion class-action discrimination lawsuit, employee pay and health benefits, and former chairman Tom Coughlin's alleged expense accounting padding have all provided ample fodder for the retailer's growing chorus of critics."

"But whom should Wal-Mart hire? The headhunters aren't talking, but retail and ethics experts contacted by *Fortune* suggested everyone from former Federal Reserve chairman Alan Greenspan to Sherron Watkins, the Enron whistleblower."

How Wal-Mart will give the ethics director, who oversees a department of 12, teeth, will be the question. Half of Fortune 500 have ethics directors, but there hasn't exactly been an avalanche of ethical behavior in corporate America.

I hope the new ethics director tells Wal-Mart that it should be ethical to start a corporate blog and engage in conversation with its public, including its critics.

SOURCE: BL Ochman's whatsnextblog.com. 2006. www.whatsnextblog.com/archives/businessethics/

Summary

This chapter has discussed cross-national ethics and social responsibility. It has proposed that certain business practices, such as bribery, are viewed as unethical in some cultures but ethical in others. The practice of bribery and "payoffs" by numerous U.S. MNCs led to the passage of the FCPA of 1977. Managers of many MNCs have complained that the Act, because it precluded them from bribing or "paying off" officials in foreign countries to obtain "favors," even if it was an acceptable practice in the country, put them at a competitive disadvantage with foreign competitors, who were not bound by the Act. The chapter has also discussed cross-national CSR. It has proposed that some international executives condone the concept of "cultural relativism," which holds that no culture's ethics are any better than any other's, that there are no international "rights" or "wrongs." It was suggested that the practice of cultural relativism often backfires. Some international executives condone the concept of "universalism," which holds that there should be a global yardstick by which to measure all moral issues. This approach often leads to a show of disrespect for valid cultural differences. The media often influence MNCs to reject cultural relativism and apply the concept of universalism. There is a large visible business ethics gap between the United States and other advanced nations; Americans are exposed to far more business misconduct issues than are people in other economically advanced countries.

KEY TERMS AND CONCEPTS

1. Ethical or unethical
2. Bribery
3. Socially acceptable or unacceptable
4. Conflicting ethical responsibilities
5. Payoffs
6. *Bustarella*
7. Whitemail bribes; lubrication bribes
8. Extortion
9. The Foreign Corrupt Practices Act
10. The ten commandments of corporate social responsibility
11. Cross-cultural social responsibility
12. Cultural relativism; universalism
13. The normative and the instrumental views
14. Human rights
15. Communicating social responsibility
16. Business ethics gap
17. Business ethics visibility gap
18. World Wide Web

DISCUSSION QUESTIONS

1. How do some businesspeople determine what is ethical or unethical?
2. Why is it difficult to define what is ethical or unethical across cultures?
3. What is meant by "conflicting responsibilities"?
4. Differentiate between "whitemail" and "lubrication" bribes, and extortion.
5. Why do so many international businesspeople pay lubrication bribes?
6. What was the major purpose of the U.S. Foreign Corrupt Practices Act?
7. What were some of the major complaints from U.S. international executives against the U.S. Foreign Corrupt Practices Act?
8. With respect to cross-national social responsibility, what are the potential negative consequences of the practice of cultural relativism and universalism?
9. From a social responsibility perspective, what are the potential negative consequences associated with home-country corporations using manufacturing subcontractors abroad?
10. Why is there a relatively large visible business ethics gap between the United States and other advanced nations?
11. Discuss human rights.
12. Discuss the challenges with which managers of the World Wide Web are confronted.

EXERCISES/BUSINESS ETHICS CASES

1. The top management of a U.S. MNC has decided to build a manufacturing facility in a city in country X. A city bureaucrat in country X has approached the executive responsible for implementing top management's decision. The bureaucrat has informed the executive that a permit to build in the city is extremely difficult to obtain and it is a very lengthy process; that he has "a friend" on the city council who, for U.S. $200,000, would be able to get the council to issue the permit immediately. It is important to the top management that the permit be issued and, for competitive reasons, that it be issued as fast as possible. Time is thus very important to the MNC. You are the executive. What will you do?

2. You are in charge of trying to secure a contract for the sale of U.S. telecommunications equipment worth about $40 million to the communications and transport ministry of a Latin American country with a military government. European firms are also eager for the contract. Quality differences in the products of the various suppliers are not important. A local accountant, who has helped you with government negotiations in the past, suggests to you that the company might receive the contract if it were willing to deposit $2 million in the Swiss bank account of the general in charge of the ministry.

3. You are responsible for negotiating with an African government the terms under which your company would build and operate a battery plant in the country. You have a U.S. counsel and know a local law firm with two Harvard-trained principals. However, other Americans who have successful investments in the country suggest that you hire the local Speaker of the House, who is a lawyer, to help represent you in the negotiations. You are aware that the House must eventually approve the agreement you negotiate.

4. Your U.S. company has a major petroleum investment in a non-Arab oil country. All foreign investors have been notified that their contracts (covering taxes, royalties, etc.) will be reviewed in light of events in other countries. A lawyer, who is the brother of the vice president, offers his services to your firm in the upcoming renegotiations. The proposed fees are about 25% higher than those that might be asked by a U.S. law firm.

5. You have just been put in charge of a U.S. subsidiary in a developing country and have discovered that the previous manager has been paying $40 to immigration officials each time the residence permit of U.S. employees is to be extended. There is no official basis for the charge, and it has been paid each time in cash. You are told that other foreign companies and even private U.S. foundations pay similar fees.

6. You are the vice president for international operations of a U.S. company. One of your new managers of a rapidly expanding subsidiary in a developing country reports the following experience. A tax collector visited the firm with a bill for the firm's annual income tax. Although the bill seemed a bit high, based on the accounts earlier submitted to the government, the manager told the collector that he would authorize a check to the Treasury. The collector pointed out that the total due could be discussed and he was sure that some less costly arrangement could be worked out. The manager replied that he preferred to accept the Treasury's calculation and had a check made out. Two weeks later, the manager received a registered letter from the collector saying that an error had been made and that the company owed about 35% more. A bill was enclosed, but the letter mentioned that the tax collector would be happy to discuss the matter further.

7. You are the U.S. manager of a local subsidiary in a developing country. As you are leaving the country for a brief visit to headquarters, the clerk at the counter for the local airline you are using points out that you have overweight luggage. (This was not a surprise to you, since you are carrying home Christmas presents for your and your wife's families, but you know some international airlines have dropped the weight limit or would simply overlook the small amount of excess weight.) You ask the charge and hear that it is $75. When you look hesitant, the clerk suggests that $5 might actually take care of the matter.

8. You are on a consulting trip to a Latin American country and discover a very fine suit in a smart downtown shop. You ask about the price and discover that it is 9,000 pesos. The clerk explains that that would be $75 if you will pay in dollars. You realize that it is $300 at the official rate of exchange that you encountered at the airport and at banks.

9. The American manager of one of your Latin American subsidiaries has been kidnapped by a leftist political group. You are informed that he will be released unharmed if you will have your company run an ad in the local newspaper presenting the group's criticism of the government in power, provide $100,000 of food for distribution to the poor, and pay $1 million in ransom to the group. You discover that the ransom payment would be illegal in that country.

Questions

1. What would you do in each of the above cases?

2. Why?

SOURCE: Exercise 1: Self. Exercises 2–9: Louis T. Wells Jr., Harvard Business School, Harvard University. Used with permission of Professor Wells. Taken from a typed handout that he gave at the International Business workshop in 1995 held at the University of Connecticut.

ASSIGNMENT

Contact an international executive in an MNC, and ask him or her to describe the company's policy pertaining to cross-national ethics and social responsibility. Prepare a short report to be shared with the class.

CASE 2-1

Merchants of Death

In many countries, such as China and Germany, women in very short sexy skirts set up a display table alongside an expensive American automobile. In exchange for an empty pack of local cigarettes, they offer people passing by a pack of U.S. cigarettes and a leaflet that reads, "You just got hold of a nice piece of America." Says German physician Bernhard Humberger, who monitors youth smoking, "Young kids time and again receive cigarettes at such promotions." A Jeep decorated with the yellow Camel logo pulls up in front of a high school in Buenos Aires. The driver, a blond woman, begins handing out free cigarettes to 15- and 16-year-olds in their lunch recess.

At a video arcade in Taipei, free American cigarettes are placed on top of each game. "As long as they're here, I may as well try one," says a high school girl in a Chicago Bears T-shirt. Before the U.S. tobacco companies entered the Taiwanese cigarette market, such giveaways were not common at places frequented by young people.

A Reader's Digest investigation covering 20 countries on four continents revealed that millions of young people were being lured into nicotine addiction by U.S. cigarette makers. In several nations, U.S. tobacco companies have been lobbying against legislation that curtails cigarette use by minors and are cleverly violating the spirit of curbs on advertising. Their activities clearly show a cynical disregard for public health. But the most shocking finding is that children are being seduced into smoking in the name of America itself. In some countries, tobacco companies never would have gained a foothold without the help of a powerful ally: the U.S. government. "Many African children have two hopes," says Paul Wangai, a physician in Nairobi, Kenya. "One is to go to heaven, the other to America." U.S. tobacco companies capitalize on this by associating smoking with affluence.

Questions

1. Are the cigarette companies behaving ethically?

2. Would you consider the free samples of cigarettes these companies give to teenagers in foreign countries a form of bribery? Please explain your answer.

3. Based on what you have learned in this chapter regarding cross-national social responsibility, are these MNCs behaving in a socially responsible fashion?

4. Do you believe that this problem can be solved? What are your thoughts?

SOURCE: Adapted from William Ecenbarger, "America's New Merchants of Death," *Reader's Digest* (Canadian version) (April 1993), pp. 85–92. Used with permission.

CASE 2-2

Union Carbide's Entry Into India

As was pointed out in the chapter, many years ago U.S.-based Union Carbide established gas production facilities in Bhopal, India. In its U.S. plants, Union Carbide was required by the U.S. government to install expensive accident prevention systems. The Government of India did not require such systems. In the 1980s, an accident at the Bhopal plant killed more than 3,000 people and injured thousands of others. The press coverage of the Union Carbide incident was very negative. Many Americans felt that Union Carbide, knowing the dangers of not taking preventive measures, had a moral obligation to have taken them in India, even if India did not require them and could not afford them.

Questions

1. Was Union Carbide socially irresponsible? Why or why not?

2. What are the key issues one must consider to determine if Union Carbide was or was not socially irresponsible?

3. What was the Indian government's responsibility in this matter?

4. Did the Indian government act irresponsibly?

SOURCE: R. C. Trotter, S. G. Day, and A. E. Love, "Bhopal, India and Union Carbide: The Second Tragedy," *Journal of Business Ethics*, 8 (1989), pp. 439–454.

CASE 2-3

Chiquita Bananas in Colombia

Refer to Practical Perspective 2.3, the case of Chiquita Bananas in Colombia.

Questions

1. In the contexts of cultural relativism and universalism, did Chiquita Bananas act ethically or unethically? Did it act socially responsible or socially irresponsible? Bear in mind that the company provides food for 70 countries or more.

NOTES

1. John Kimelman, "The Lonely Boy Scout," *Financial World* (Fall 1994), p. 50.

2. Yadong Luo, "An Organizational Perspective of Corruption," *Management and Organization Review,* 1, no. 1 (March 2005), p. 142.

3. "Report Says Nike Plant Workers Abused by Bosses in Indonesia," *The New York Times* (February 22, 2001). http://search.nytimes.com/plweb-cgi/fastweb?state_id=1005665257&view=site&docrank=7d

4. Thomas Donaldson, "Global Business Must Mind Its Morals," *The New York Times* (February 13, 1994), p. F11.

5. O. Ronald Gray, "The Foreign Corrupt Practices Act: Revisited and Amended," *Business and Society* (Spring 1990), p. 11.

6. P. Nehemkis, "Business Payoffs Abroad: Rhetoric or Reality?" *California Management Review* (Winter 1975), p. 13.

7. Ibid.

8. Ibid.

9. Ibid.

10. Ibid., p. 6.

11. Ibid.

12. W. A. Label and J. Kaikati, "Foreign Antibribery Law: Friend or Foe?" *Columbia Journal of World Business* (Spring 1980), p. 46.

13. Patricia Digh, "Shades of Gray in the Global Marketplace," *HR Magazine* (April 1997), p. 93.

14. Gray, "The Foreign Corrupt Practices Act," op cit., p. 14.

15. Andrew W. Singer, "Ethics: Are Standards Lower Overseas?" *Across the Board* (September 1991), p. 33.

16. Seth Hettena, "Titan Settles Federal Overseas Bribery," *Yahoo! Finance, Financial News* (March 1, 2005). http://biz.yahoo.com/ap/050301/titan_investigation_2.html17. Ibid., pp. 15–16.

18. Ibid, p. 16.

19. Kent Hodgson, "Adapting Ethical Decisions to a Marketplace," *Management Review* (May 1992), pp. 56–57. See also Morgen Witzel, "Business Life Management," *Financial Times* (July 11, 2005), p. 14.

20. Donna J. Wood, "Corporate Social Performance Revisited," *Academy of Management Review,* 16 (October 1991), pp. 691–718.

21. Donaldson, "Global Business Must Mind Its Morals"; Thomas Donaldson, "Values in Tension: Ethics Away from Home," *Harvard Business Review* (September–October 1996), pp. 48–62.

22. Ibid.

23. David E. Rosenbaum, "China Trade Rift With U.S. Deepens," *The New York Times* (January 29), 1995, p. 1.

24. R. C. Trotter, S. G. Day, and A. E. Love, "Bhopal, India and Union Carbide: The Second Tragedy," *Journal of Business Ethics,* 8 (1989), pp. 439–454.

25. Sarah Cox, "Starbucks Pours One for Coffee Workers," *Monday Magazine* (Victoria, British Columbia, Canada) (March 16–22, 1995), p. 6.

26. See D. Spar, "The Spotlight and the Bottom Line," *Foreign Affairs,* 77, no. 2 (1998), pp. 7–12.

27. See Klaus E. Meyer, "Perspective on Multinational Enterprises in Emerging Economies," *Journal of International Business Studies,* 35 (2004), pp. 271–273.

28. Ibid.

29. I. Maignan and D. A. Ralston, "Corporate Social Responsibility in Europe and the U.S.: Insights From Business' Self-presentations," *Journal of International Business Studies,* 33, no. (2002), pp. 497–514.

30. Ibid., p. 497.

31. David Vogel, "The Globalization of Business Ethics: Why America Remains Distinctive," *California Management Review,* 35, no. 1 (Fall 1992), p. 30.

32. Ibid., pp. 35–37.

33. Ibid., p. 35.

34. Adapted from Glenn R. Simpson, "Multinational Companies Unite to Fight Bribery," *The Wall Street Journal,* Eastern Edition (January 27), 2005, p. A.2.

35. Morgen Witzel, "Combating Corruption," *Financial Times,* London Edition (July 11, 2005), p. 14. http://web.lexis-nexis.com

36. Ibid., pp. 46–47.

37. Ibid., p. 49.

38. See Jeanette Slepian, "Corporate Social Responsibility" (August 5, 2006). www.bettermanagement.com/library/library.aspx?1=12791; M. Dickie and S. Kirchgaessner, "Technology and Society," *Financial Times*, London Edition 1, Comment and Analysis (February 15, 2006), p. 15. http://web.lexis-nexis.com.ezproxy.montclair.edu:2048/ university/document?_m=4be0a45b

39. N. A. Adam, B. Slonim, J. Wagner, P. Yesha Yelena, "Globalizing Business, Education, Culture, Through the Internet," *Communications of the ACM,* 40, no. 2 (February 1997), pp. 115–121.

Part II THE INTERNATIONAL PLANNING PROCESS

Planning means monitoring the enterprise's external environment to ascertain where there are business opportunities and/or threats and to become familiar with the internal aspects of the organization, including knowledge of its resources and business strengths. When the external environment presents opportunities and/or threats, planning involves preparing a strategy to mobilize the firm's resources and strengths to seize the opportunities or combat the threats. This process is called SWOT (strengths, weaknesses, opportunities, and threats) analysis. The global environment is discussed in Chapter 3. The reasons why firms establish strategy to penetrate the international business arena, as well as the types of international strategies and objectives, are discussed in Chapter 4. International product/service, place/entry, price, and promotion strategies are discussed in Chapter 5.

3

THE GLOBAL ENVIRONMENT

Every company is looking to reduce its costs, raise its market share or generate more value for the money it spends. When contemplating a project, you can't afford to look only at your home market. Instead, you evaluate the whole world. You look at what countries offer in terms of infrastructure, tax structure, intellectual property protection, technical capabilities, and markets, and you evaluate the trade-offs.[1]

Learning Objectives of the Chapter

Effective managers are constantly aware of the changes taking place at home and around the globe; they scan their environment on an ongoing basis, and when they detect opportunities and/or threats, they transform their organization to seize the opportunities and/or combat the threats.[2] This means that to make effective decisions, managers must gather information from their domestic (home country) environment, as well as from the international and foreign environments. After studying this chapter, you should be able to do the following:

1. Briefly discuss the nature of the firm's home country environment

2. Describe the international environment, such as groupings of nations— the European Union (EU), for example, and its impact on international management

3. Discuss the nature of countries' cultural, economic, legal and political, and competitive environments, as well as trade barriers, exchange rates, and labor relations, and their impact on international management

4. Point out some of the sources of this information.

The Domestic Environment

At the domestic (home country) level, international business enterprises are affected by numerous factors, including the political, competitive, economic, legal, and governmental climates.

Domestic Political Climate

International managers must remain informed about the political climate in their home country, and based on the information, they must ascertain whether the climate can now or in the future have an impact on their enterprises' business. For example, for economic and other reasons, interest groups sometimes persuade their government to attach tariffs (taxes) or place quotas (number limits) on certain imports. Tariffs and quotas (discussed later in the chapter) can have a direct, as well as an indirect, effect on businesses.

Embargos, where a country's government, for political reasons, prohibits its businesses to trade with another country—the U.S. embargos on Cuba and North Korea, for example—also have a direct impact on businesses. If a company needs to do business in a country on which its country's government has imposed an embargo, it will find a way to do it, thus increasing costs. For instance, if a company in the United States needs a certain resource available in Cuba, it can get it by Cuba selling it to a company in another country, which subsequently sells it to the company in the United States, thus increasing the costs. The company in the United States can itself set up a subsidiary in the foreign country (discussed more thoroughly in Chapters 4 and 5), again increasing costs in the sense that jobs are lost in the home country.

For illustration purposes, suppose that the managers of a corporation manufacturing tractors in Country X are considering exporting to Country Y, that companies in Country Y export wheat to Country X, and that wheat growers at home (Country X) are attempting to persuade their government to apply a quota or a tariff on wheat imports. It is possible that if a tariff or a quota is imposed, Country Y's wheat exporters, in retaliation, might persuade their government to attach a tariff or quota on tractor imports. (As discussed later in the chapter, history shows that one tariff usually begets another.) The tariff or quota would affect the tractor exporters' business.

International business managers thus need to be thoroughly familiar with nations' tariff and quota practices, as well as with the embargos. In the United States, an aid is The National Trade Estimate Report on Foreign Trade Barriers, generated by the Office of the U.S. Trade Representatives (USTR), which had a new purpose bestowed on it by the 1988 Trade Act. The Act requires the USTR to submit the report to Congress by the end of April and point out the trade barriers that cost the United States the most exports. A recalcitrant will be open to retaliatory tariffs or bans.[3] The USTR (www.ustr.gov), a part of the Executive Office of the President, is involved in trade agreements, in trade and development, in trade sectors, and with World Trade Organization (WTO) (discussed later in the chapter) issues. (For illustration purposes, read Practical Perspective 3.1.)

September 11, 2001. Of course, the September 11, 2001, attack on the United States has changed the U.S. political climate dramatically, as well as the global political climate.

PRACTICAL PERSPECTIVE 3-1

U.S. Hikes Tariffs on Imports

WASHINGTON—A bitter trade battle between the United States and Europe over bananas turned even nastier yesterday as the United States began notifying importers that they are now liable for hefty penalty tariffs on $520 million worth of European goods. If allowed to stand, the tariffs of 100 percent on items such as German coffee makers and French handbags effectively would double their price, putting them out of reach for most U.S. consumers. The administration is seeking to penalize European producers by an amount equal to the damages U.S.-based banana companies say they are suffering in lost sales because of unfair European trade barriers.

The U.S. action, which caught European officials by surprise, was immediately denounced by the [then] 15-nation European Union. The move came only a day after the World Trade Organization asked for more information before ruling on the legality of the U.S. trade sanctions. The WTO had requested both sides to provide that information by March 15 [1999]. "The United States decided to defy the WTO system by introducing a form of sanctions that has no WTO authorization whatsoever," said Leon Brittan, EU's trade minister, in a statement issued in Brussels. "What the United States has done is therefore unacceptable and unlawful."

The United States said it would not collect any punitive tariffs until the WTO rules on the appropriate size of the sanctions. But starting yesterday, importers of those products must post bonds and assume liability for paying the higher tariffs if the WTO rules in the U.S.'s favor. The United States contends that American banana companies are losing $520 million annually in lost sales to Europe because of illegal trade barriers that favor bananas imported from former European colonies in the Caribbean and Africa. Chiquita Brands, Inc. and Dole Food Company, Inc., the major American companies involved, grow their bananas on plantations in South America. While the United States won a WTO case on this issue, the EU argued that the matter needed further review because it has changed some banana import rules. The U.S. side says the changes do not satisfy American objections.

SOURCE: Excerpted from Martin Crutsinger, "U.S. Hikes Tariffs on Imports," *The Star Ledger* (March 4, 1999), p. 43. Reprinted with permission. Copyright by the Associated Press.

These changes have affected business practices in the United States (e.g., the airline and security industries), as well as business practices throughout the globe. In July 2006, extremists were getting ready to carry out a clever plan to blow up numerous passenger airplanes scheduled to fly from London to various cities in the United States, but those extremists were caught by U.K. security authorities before they could execute their plan.

September 11, 2001, has created higher security costs in the airline industry, which in turn had negative economic consequences on many other industries—for instance, delaying executives at the United States' airport security checks is costly, and so are the additional security people and additional technologies needed to do the checking. Importing goods into the United States is now more costly because of the additional security requirements at the nation's ports. And the creation of the U.S. Homeland Security Agency, resulting from the 9/11 incident, is very costly, and so is the cost of insurance, other transport costs, the costs of investments and security, as well as the costs in the tourism industries. These are just a few of the many political consequences brought on the United States' and other nations' political atmosphere by the September 11, 2001, incident.

Domestic Competitive Climate

Managers also need information about domestic competitors' objectives. Domestic competitors may be developing similar strategies to penetrate the same foreign markets, and they may be introducing a newer product that would give them a competitive edge. Or they may be planning to manufacture their products in a foreign country where labor is cheaper, which would also give them a competitive edge. This would have an impact on the enterprise's promotional, product, pricing, and place (channels of distribution) strategies and may force it to internationalize its operations, to leave home and go produce in a foreign country (discussed more thoroughly in Chapters 4 and 5).

Domestic Economic Climate

Information is also needed about the domestic economic climate. If it is deteriorating, the government may place constraints on foreign investments to strengthen the domestic economy. On the other hand, if a firm's sales are declining because the local economy is in recession and there are no governmental constraints, entering prosperous foreign countries may be a viable survival strategy for the firm (discussed more thoroughly in Chapter 4).

Domestic Legal System and Government Policies

Managers must be thoroughly familiar with their home country's legal system and government policies. For political and security reasons, as well as other reasons, the U.S. government sometimes prohibits the export of certain technologies—for example, the United States' high-tech industries, such as machine tools, telecommunications, military-oriented technologies, and supercomputers. Executives in such industries have complained about contradictions in such U.S. government policies. They claim that while the government helped them develop technology for military reasons, it used the same national security concerns to impose export controls on high technology, hence keeping United States' most dynamic corporations from competing in global commercial markets. Nevertheless, the United States is the leading exporter of military goods in the world to developed countries, and Russia is the leading exporter of military goods in the world to less developed countries.

U.S. machine tool manufacturers, for instance, were once deterred from exporting advanced machines for producing soda cans to Hungary. U.S. West was prohibited from assisting the former U.S.S.R. in laying modern optical fiber cable. And Cray Research Corporation, a maker of supercomputers subsidized by the military, once had difficulty getting the U.S. government's clearance to sell products in India and Brazil.[4] For sure, one would think, after the September 11, 2001, incident, that the U.S. government would very strongly prohibit U.S. weapons manufacturers from selling their products to the United States' enemies, those who say they want to kill Americans.

The International Environment

Managers must remain informed about the international environment, which consists of groupings of nations such as the EU; of worldwide bodies such as the World

Bank, the International Monetary Fund (IMF), the WTO; and of organizations of nations by industry agreements, such as the Organization of the Petroleum Exporting Countries (OPEC). For example, the 1970s' manipulation of oil prices by OPEC had a tremendous negative economic and business impact on many nations, and many nations are today (2007) still trying to recover from the setbacks. It seems as if the consolidation of nations into free-trade blocks is going to continue. (For illustration purposes, read Practical Perspective 3.2.) Such organizations have an impact on firms' international strategies, and effective international business managers must carefully and continuously monitor their policy and program changes, because changes present both threats and opportunities for businesses.

PRACTICAL PERSPECTIVE 3-2

The Road to Santiago

When in December 1994 Bill Clinton welcomed to Miami the leaders of 33 other countries in the Americas, their meeting was widely seen as the start of a new chapter in the often troubled relations between the United States and Latin America. With the Cold War over, with elected governments in power except (uninvited) Cuba, and with market reforms and freer trade supplanting protectionism, many old sources of tension seemed to have been replaced by shared ideas and new opportunities for cooperation.

Chief among these was the notion, mooted earlier by President George Bush in 1990, of a "free-trade area of the Americas" (FTAA), stretching from Alaska to Cape Horn. In Miami, Latin America's leaders embraced the idea with surprising enthusiasm. A target date of 2005 was set for its achievement, with "concrete progress" to be made by 2000. Alongside this, the 34 summiteers put their names to a long list of collective virtues, 150 "action items" concerned with topics ranging from health services through women's rights to the environment.

On April 18 and 19 [1998] in the Chilean capital, Santiago, the 34 countries' leaders [were scheduled to] meet again . . . [to] formally launch the FTAA negotiations. After three years of hard talking, at a final preparatory meeting in Costa Rica last month, their trade ministers agreed to a detailed agenda of what to negotiate, how, where, and when. Their ambitious dream might seem, at first glance, to be steadily becoming a reality.

True, the FTAA concept faces criticism. Some economists argue that regional preferences divert more trade than they create. Some Latin Americans fear that the cost of adjusting to free trade with the world's most powerful economy will far outweigh the benefits, especially in smaller and less developed countries.

SOURCE: Excerpted from "The Road to Santiago," *The Economist* (April 11, 1998), p. 25. Reprinted with permission.

The European Union[5]

The economic unification of the EU had a strong impact on international business. The unification, which officially took place on December 31, 1992, and the foundation on November 1, 1993, is the result of the Single European Act of July 1, 1987. The Act aimed to commit the then 12-member EU nations to an economically standardized/harmonized single market of about 320 million people—which was expected to be the industrialized world's largest single market.[6] The 12 nations were Belgium, Denmark, France, Germany, Great Britain, Greece, Ireland, Italy,

Luxembourg, the Netherlands, Portugal, and Spain. In January 1995, Austria, Finland, and Sweden also became members. And on May 1, 2004, Cyprus (the Greek part), the Czech Republic, Estonia, Hungary, Latvia, Lithuania, Malta, Poland, Slovakia, and Slovenia also became EU members. Thus, the EU is now a union of 25 independent states based on the European Communities and founded to enhance political, economic, and social cooperation.

Oops! The world changes so fast! The EU now consists of 27 nations—Bulgaria and Romania became members on January 1, 2007. It used to be that residents traveling outside Europe would identify themselves as being from their specific country (I'm from France, or Germany, or Spain, and so on), but now people in the EU countries are starting to identify themselves as being from Europe (I'm European). This is similar to the United States, where people traveling within the U.S. states identify themselves as being from their state of residency (I'm from Kentucky, and so on), but when traveling in another country, they say they are from America (the United States), or Americans. So the EU is becoming very similar to the United States—of course, there is no European language yet, but many Europeans learn several European languages, including English. Hence, the EU's MNCs are likely to become even more powerful competitors than they already are in the global marketplace.

Opportunities Presented by the EU[7]

The original EU generated many opportunities and threats for external firms (discussed more thoroughly in Chapter 4), both small and large firms. The harmonization aimed to replace the then existing patchwork of standards, which varied from country to country, region to region within countries, and even city to city within regions. This means that external firms can now realize greater profits because they will need to produce only one version of a product as opposed to their then practice of producing dozens. Furthermore, the EU intended to establish mutual recognition among member countries. Under the mutual recognition directive, goods and services legitimately produced in one member country can be marketed without hindrance anywhere in the EU.[8] This helped firms attain greater economies of scale, as they no longer needed to make expensive modifications and prepare the 100 or so customs forms then required to meet different EU members' regulations.[9]

The EU also aimed to establish the means for capital, including cash and bank transfers, to move freely between member countries. On January 1, 2002, most of the member countries adopted a single currency unit—the euro. This, too, provided new opportunities to many external firms, as did the EU's deregulation of transportation. Previously, trucks entering one EU country could make only one stop in the nation. Now trucks are permitted to make several stops and are not required to stop for border checks.[10] This decreased transportation costs and made transportation more efficient. For example, the United States' Federal Express benefited from this change, and it purchased companies in the EU that held national trucking licenses.[11]

The EU also proposed a directive permitting cross-border transmission of television signals. This enables firms to advertise more efficiently. As a result, many new cable and satellite stations were started. 3M Corporation, for example, took a pan-European approach to advertising and expected to reach a vast audience at far less cost.[12] The EU is committed to fair competition. The cartels that monopolize certain EU industries were to be dismantled to provide competition and opportunities to new businesses.[13] And it also created the European Research Corporation Agency, which provides financial assistance to EU-based firms in the fields of energy, IT, robotics, lasers, and biotechnology.

Threats Presented by the EU

The objective of the EU was to make its members' firms more competitive in the global marketplace, not to offer external enterprises a large market to exploit. This threatened many external firms. For example, some external firms that had planned to start operating in the EU feared that they would not have direct contact with the EU's standard-setting body. To combat this, some U.S. companies already in the EU tried to secure fair treatment in tenders for public contracts and to avert being handicapped when the EU sets product and safety standards. In order to have input, IBM joined JESSI, a government-backed European research project on semiconductors.[14]

External companies also feared that a "Fortress Europe," which allows protectionism and preferential treatment, may evolve. For example, the EU indicated that it may continue imposing quantitative restrictions on some imported products—such as automobiles—to enable EU companies to adjust to their internal market. Its directive on telecommunications proposed that bids must be rejected unless 50% or more of their value is derived from EU sources and that EU companies be preferred even when the 50% is met. Furthermore, the harmonization of the EU was expected to lead to the fall of prices across Europe.[15] This was likely to provide a threat to many external firms that depended on the prices they were then charging in the EU but may have had to lower them to compete with EU enterprises. Well, that's what competition is for, isn't it?

North American Free Trade Agreement (NAFTA)

It should be noted that the North American Free Trade Agreement (NAFTA), a union consisting of Canada, Mexico, and the United States, was started in January 1994 to combat the EU's threats. But NAFTA is relatively new, and its mission is quite different from the EU's mission. As of 2007, NAFTA's three members are not quite as cooperative as are the EU's members—although, it has generated a number of economic developments, such as the reduction of tariffs, removal of restriction on certain products, and more investment opportunities. But reports indicate that NAFTA has failed so far.[16] Will the United States build the 700-mile-long fence on Mexico's border? Will the United States build an even longer one? It's very difficult getting though the U.S./Canada border customs. There are no border customs among the EU's countries.

The notion of a unified Europe actually started about 1,000 years ago, and it still has a long way to go. On the other hand, NAFTA and other similar unions existing throughout the globe are in their early starting stages, but they can accelerate development if they can learn from the EU's experience. Some U.S. opinion leaders have proposed that NAFTA should reorganize itself along the EU model.

The World Bank

The World Bank (http://web.worldbank.org) describes itself as a vital source of financial and technical assistance to developing countries around the world but not a bank in the common sense. It is made up of two unique development institutions owned by 184 member countries—the International Bank for Reconstruction and Development (IBRD) and the International Development Association (IDA). Each institution plays different but supportive roles in the Bank's mission of global poverty reduction and improvement of living standards. The IBRD focuses on middle-income and creditworthy poor countries, and the IDA focuses on the poorest countries in the world. Together, they provide low-interest loans, interest-free credit, and grants to developing countries for education, health, infrastructure, communications, and many other purposes. Thus, the programs the World Bank funds provide many opportunities for international businesses.

International Monetary Fund (IMF)

The IMF is an international organization that oversees the global financial system by monitoring exchange rates and balance of payments, as well as offering technical and financial assistance when asked. Its headquarters is in Washington, D.C. The IMF describes itself as an organization of 184 countries, working to foster global monetary cooperation, secure financial stability, facilitate international trade, promote high employment and sustainable economic growth, and reduce poverty.

The World Trade Organization (WTO)

The WTO, located in Geneva, established on January 1, 1995, and created by the Uruguay Round negotiations between 1986 and 1994, is the only international organization dealing with the rules of trade between nations. At its heart are two agreements, negotiated and signed by the bulk of the world's trading nations and ratified in their parliaments. The goal is to help producers of goods and services, exporters, and importers conduct their business, including providing intellectual property protection and subsidies. As of December 11, 2005, its membership consisted of 149 countries. Vietnam became a member on January 1, 2007, increasing the membership to 150 countries.

Organization of the Petroleum Exporting Countries (OPEC)

As January 1, 2008, OPEC is made up of 13 developing nations whose economies rely on oil export revenues. The nations are Algeria, Angola, Ecuador, Indonesia, Iran, Iraq, Kuwait, Libya, Nigeria, Qatar, Saudi Arabia, the United Arab Emirates, and Venezuela. It was created at the Baghdad Conference, September 10–14, 1960. One of OPEC's primary missions is to achieve stable oil prices that are fair and reasonable for producers and consumers. OPEC member countries coordinate their oil production to help stabilize the oil market and help achieve a reasonable rate of return on their investments. This policy is also designed to ensure that oil consumers continue to receive stable supplies of oil.

Just as blood sustains our physical being, oil sustains the economic, political, and social being of nations and organizations within them. In the 1970s, OPEC's policies created global instability and devastation in many nations. Brazil, for example, on track to becoming a super economic power, became paralyzed. Currently (2008), OPEC, by increasing the cost of oil (in March 2008, a barrel of oil rose to U.S.$105), is creating problems for many nations. The inflation of oil costs has hurt many corporations throughout the globe. For example, in 2006, Wal-Mart's profits fell by 26%, its first drop in 10 years. They attribute this to the rise in the cost of gasoline, leaving consumers with less money to spend at retail stores.[17]

In the 1970s, the United States combated the problem created by OPEC by implementing many austerity programs to conserve oil usage, such as importing small, fuel-efficient automobiles; imposing the 55-miles-per-hour speed limit, which was found to be the most fuel-efficient highway speed; encouraging people to walk more and use cars less; and many other programs.

Currently, Americans drive large, gas-guzzling automobiles. George Bush, the current (2007) president of the United States, has informed the American public that "we have become foreign oil addicted." Heroin drug addicts become dependent on their suppliers and would steal/and or even kill to get the money they need to purchase the heroin their body craves the cost of heroin goes up when the supply becomes scarcer, and the supply becomes scarcer because of the producers and/or governments' actions or because of the greater number of customers.

New entrants into the industrialized world—for example, China, with its 1.3 billion people—are likely to make the costs of oil go higher and higher and, like the United States, are likely to become foreign oil addicted. On the other hand, Brazil, in the 1970s, took a different route; it invented ethanol, which is made out of sugarcane, as an alternative to oil fuel. Thus, currently, Brazil is almost totally independent of foreign oil—it is not addicted to foreign oil. But it did take Brazil many years to develop and implement its ethanol program. Visit Japan, and you will see hundreds of thousands of people getting around via a bicycle. Visit Taiwan, and you will see hundreds of thousands of people getting around via a scooter or a bicycle.

The Foreign Environment

Foreign (individual nations) environmental factors can have a dramatic impact on international business and management. The factors include the cultural environment, the economic environment, the legal and political environment, as well as the competition, trade barriers, fluctuating monetary exchange rates, labor relations, and geography. These factors differ in many respects from country to country, and in some cases from region to region within each nation. To develop an effective strategic plan for doing business in a foreign country, enterprises' managers must first become thoroughly familiar with the foreign factors and how they differ from their home country factors.[18] And they must make the necessary adaptations—otherwise, failure is almost inevitable. The ensuing sections briefly explain the above factors.

Culture

Culture, as discussed in Chapter 1, is the total of humankind's knowledge, beliefs, arts, morals, laws, customs, and other capabilities and habits adopted by individuals as members of society.[19] As pointed out in Chapter 1, societies around the globe develop differing cultures. To develop an effective international business strategy, the critical aspects of culture must be identified. (As an illustration of how culture affects international strategies, read Practical Perspective 3.3.)

Practical Perspective 3.4 suggests that Japanese international business managers tend to make greater efforts to study foreign cultures than do U.S. international managers.

The cultural environment, as demonstrated in Chapter 1, affects the international management process in many ways. For example, for many managers of U.S. organizations, the highest priority is profit maximization. However, for many managers of Japanese organizations, the highest priority has always been, and remains, increasing the market share and keeping people employed.[20] Therefore, American

PRACTICAL PERSPECTIVE 3-3

The Case of the Sacred Ground

A civil engineer in a U.S. construction firm was given the responsibility of selecting a site for, designing, and constructing a fish-processing plant in a West African nation. The engineer identified viable sites on the basis of availability of reliable power, closeness to transportation means and to the river which accesses fishing boats from the Atlantic Ocean, nearness to major markets, and the availability of housing and human resources. Following the analysis of the viable sites, the optimum site was selected. Just before obtaining bids from contractors for site preparation, the engineer happened to learn that the site was located on ground considered by local people to be sacred—where their gods resided. The local people on whom the engineer was counting to "man" the operation would thus not work there. The engineer therefore chose another site.

SOURCE: Excerpted from H. W. Lane and J. J. DiStefano, *International Management Behavior,* 2nd ed. (Boston: PWS-Kent, 1992), p. 27. Reproduced with permission of South-Western College Publishing, a division of Thomson Learning. Fax 800-730-2215.

PRACTICAL PERSPECTIVE 3-4

The Impatient North Americans

Numerous North American government officials and businesspeople were sent on a trade mission to Brazil. They returned two weeks later after having toured several Brazilian cities. Upon their return, one of the businesspeople commented that the trip had been a flop since no orders had been obtained during the entire trip. In contrast, a Japanese firm sent a business manager to Rio de Janeiro with instructions to "Get to know the people and learn Portuguese during your first year there, and then concern yourself with conducting business."

SOURCE: Excerpted from H. W. Lane and J. J. DiStefano, *International Management Behavior,* 2nd ed. (Boston: PWS-Kent, 1992), p. 27. Reproduced with permission of South-Western College Publishing, a division of Thomson Learning. Fax 800-730-2215.

managers' practices would not fit well in Japanese organizations. The cultural environment also dictates what a product or service should look like or be able to do, what people will consume, as well as promotional strategies (these are discussed in Chapter 5).

For example, the British like dry cakes with their tea, but Americans tend to favor fancy, iced cakes, and Brazilians eat pizza and other foods with a knife and fork, but Americans eat pizza and many other foods with their hands. Not knowing these things, America's General Mills[21] and KFC[22] failed miserably when they entered these markets because they did not make the necessary adaptations required by their cultures.[23] And Wal-Mart, like many other entrants into foreign markets, is learning through "the school-of-hard-knocks."[24] Similar issues were at stake when United

Airlines entered the Pacific market. During the inauguration of its concierge services for first-class passengers from Hong Kong, each concierge proudly wore a white carnation. This was not well received by the Chinese, for whom the white carnation is a symbol of death.[25] Many Hong Kong Chinese businesspeople believe that their business office must have a view of the water for it to prosper; otherwise the business will do poorly. Buildings in Hong Kong tend to have a view of the bay. As a matter of fact, several years ago, a huge convention center was built by Hong Kong's bay, blocking the water view of several offices in the building across the street from it. The companies that occupied those offices then moved out, leaving the offices vacant for quite some time—certainly presenting an opportunity for a Western company to rent an office there at a cheap cost.

Culture also affects how business and negotiations are conducted. For instance, in Mexico and most of South America as well as in many other cultures, personal relationships must be established before business negotiations can begin. Furthermore, culture affects a country's human resources management practices. For example, in China, employees expect their enterprises to watch out for their welfare, ranging from the provision of pay and bonuses to housing, health care, child education, meal services, and recreation. Chinese managers are expected to become involved in their employees' personal family matters. And although divorce is rare in China, when a couple divorces, the enterprise is often expected to provide housing for the departing spouse. However, as China heads toward a market-like economy, these practices are likely to become less and less common.

As was also pointed out in Chapter 1, closely related to culture is religion. The religious aspects of culture are of great importance in consumption patterns. For example, Judaism and Islam prohibit the consumption of pork. In essence, religion influences people's habits, the products they buy, and their perception of life. Sex in advertising, for example, which is widely used in the United States and Brazil, may not be acceptable in some cultures—Honduras, for instance—as a result of religious beliefs; it may be viewed as immoral or demeaning. And some religions have a negative view of profits earned by investors who do not work for the business (Practical Perspective 3.5 presents an illustration of how religion affects the banking system in the Muslim world).

PRACTICAL PERSPECTIVE 3-5

Turning the Prophet's Profits

According to Islamic tradition, overturned wine jars stained the streets of Medina red when Allah revealed to the prophet Muhammad that Muslims should be forbidden alcohol. He banned interest payments too, but bankers have had better luck than vintners. Most banks across the Muslim world still earn their money in the time-honored way, rewarding savers with some interest and charging borrowers a little more. Some, however, claim to offer a truly "Islamic" alternative. These are proving popular as well as pious. But in order to keep growing, they are having to explore more adventurous ways to invest their depositors' cash.

There are now more than 100 specialized institutions that invest money according to strict Islamic principles, ranging from mass-market savings banks in Jordan to *pukka* private banks in Geneva. Even some western banks are embracing the concept: the U.S.'s Citibank opened the first western-owned Islamic bank. Based in Bahrain, Citi Islamic Investment Bank has a start-up capital of $20 million.

Islamic banks are [1996] still puny by international standards. Taken together, their assets of somewhere between $25 billion and $100 billion (depending on whom you believe) are equal only to those of a middling American or European bank. But they are growing fast. Some of the biggest, such as Kuwait Finance House and Pakistan's Muslim Commercial Bank, are growing their assets by about 10 percent a year. The potential market—one billion or so Muslims—is huge.

Islam's religious revival is the industry's motor. True believers obey *sharia*, Islam's holy law. This places several demands on Muslim savers. They must not finance activities prohibited by the Koran, such as gambling and the consumption of alcohol. Nor are they allowed to receive interest. ("Those who benefit from interest," warns the Koran, "shall be raised like those driven mad by the touch of the devil.")

To abide by these strictures, Islamic banks have developed alternative financial contracts. The most common of these is *murabaha*, a form of so-called "cost-plus" financing. This works as follows: Say a company wants to purchase $100 million of equipment. Instead of lending it the money for three months at 2 percent interest, an Islamic bank will buy the equipment itself. It will then sell it to the firm for $102 million, with payment deferred for three months. The bank can then claim that it is charging a profit mark-up rather than an interest rate.

SOURCE: Excerpted from "Turning the Prophet's Profits," *The Economist* (September 9, 1996), p. 32. Reprinted with permission.

Economic Environment

Economics is the way people manage their material wealth and the results of their management. The economic environment includes the production of goods and services, their distribution and consumption, the means of exchange, and the income derived from them. In the search for new markets, international business managers will find that nations differ in their stage of economic development. A nation's stage of economic development will have a great impact on the types of products and services it needs, the price, the promotional strategies, and the distribution system. It will also have an enormous impact on the type of financial concessions a foreign government is willing to make to attract technologies that will aid the country in its economic development efforts. Nations in earlier stages of development tend to subsidize foreign investments more than countries in a later stage of development. (For illustration purposes, read Practical Perspective 3.6.)

PRACTICAL PERSPECTIVE 3-6

Singer's Internationalization Strategy

The Singer Company developed itself into an international enterprise, conducting business in more than 30 countries, including the U.S., soon after it was founded in Europe in the late 1800s by Sir Isaac Singer. The firm primarily produced sewing machines. Early in the twentieth century, Singer applied techniques for assessing entry into foreign markets that are widely applied by many corporations today. It analyzed foreign country variables, such as geography, labor costs, economic environment, financial stability, market support for the product, export potential, and the country's repatriation of profits policies. Singer considered foreign government subsidies, such as tax breaks and land and factories

PRACTICAL PERSPECTIVE 3-6 (Continued)

provided for free or at reduced rates, as important factors in deciding whether or not to start operations in a foreign nation. Foreign governments were willing to make many concessions to Singer because they needed the technology for economic development and other reasons. Singer thus became a pioneer in entering markets in less-developed countries and developed excellent skills in negotiating foreign government subsidies.

SOURCE: Excerpted from an unpublished term paper by William Werner, M.B.A. student, for the course Issues in International Management, Montclair State University (Spring 1992).

Nations' Technological Needs as They Develop

Walt W. Rostow, formerly a professor in the United States, developed a theory that can aid managers in assessing a foreign country's technological needs.[26] The theory concludes that societies pass through five stages of economic development, described in Box 3.1.

Box 3.1   The Stages of Economic Development of Nations

Stage One   In the first stage, agriculture usually comprises the largest part of the country's resources. The society operates on past societal precepts, technology is essentially static, occupations are passed down from one generation to the next, and the social and economic systems remain essentially closed to change.

Stage Two   In the second stage, government and entrepreneurs establish the preconditions for take-off. The government must be dedicated to modernization and must be willing to spend public monies on education and infrastructure to service industry (roads, communication, electricity, etc.). A leading sector, such as agriculture, mining, petroleum, etc., is essential.

Stage Three   In Stage three, takeoff begins. Investment rises; manufacturing becomes a leading growth sector; political, social, and institutional structures are transformed to help maintain a steady rate of growth. This period lasts 20 to 30 years.

Stage Four   Stage four is the drive to maturity. The most advanced technology available is used. This period lasts about 60 years.

Stage Five   In Stage five, high mass consumption occurs. Emphasis is given to consumer durables and services that allow the majority of a country's population to attain a relatively high standard of living.

SOURCE: Excerpted from Walt W. Rostow, *The Stages of Economic Development* (New York: Cambridge University Press, 1971).

In general, the goods and services required by a country in an earlier stage of economic development are different from the goods and services required in a later stage. For example, residents in a country where electricity is scarce would have little use for electric refrigerators. A less developed country may need to import industrial machinery and equipment to exploit its raw materials and to produce agricultural products, as well as specialized construction equipment to develop a transportation system.[27] It may need management consulting, accounting systems, and training and development services. These services are needed because nations seldom possess the systems and skilled personnel required to manage the new technologies (e.g., refer to this author's experience with an American Indian tribe, described in Chapter 1).

When a country begins to process its raw materials and resources for export, the demand may be for other kinds of machinery and industrialized goods—for example, British and American companies, such as Halliburton, provided for these demands in the Middle East, in Africa, as well as in other parts of the world.

When entering the stage in which investment and manufacturing become the leading growth sector, a country may need products necessary to operate entire manufacturing facilities. When the country becomes fairly well industrialized, producing capital and consumer goods such as machinery, automobiles, and refrigerators, it may need more specialized and heavy capital equipment not yet manufactured there. For example, a country producing automobiles may need more modern equipment, such as wheel alignment indicators. In the fifth stage, a country reaches complete industrialization and usually assumes world leadership in the production of a variety of goods. Even though a country may be totally industrialized, a demand for goods from another country still exists, because highly industrialized countries tend to specialize in the production of certain goods. For example, U.S. enterprises are highly skilled in producing communications and sophisticated computer technologies, and Japanese enterprises are highly skilled in producing process technologies.[28]

It should be noted that there have been several objections to Rostow's theory. First, in practice, the stages are not clearly distinguishable from each other. Second, they do not display characteristics that can be tested empirically. Third, the characteristics that tend to cause movement from one stage to another are not identifiable. Fourth, the time periods Rostow suggests do not apply to all industrialized nations—for instance, China is currently industrializing at a very rapid pace. And fifth, the model is more applicable to some nations than others.[29] Nevertheless, the theory can be useful as a concept or framework for strategic analysis. For example, the theory tells the international manager that people in countries in an earlier stage of development may possess a different perspective from those in countries in a later stage with respect to the aesthetic values of a product/service and preference for managerial styles. For instance, people in less developed countries may place relatively little value on electric toothbrushes, and they may not value participative management as much as do people in the more developed nations. As demonstrated in Chapter 1, most of the less developed countries tend to be governed by the large power distance cultural dimension, thus people in these cultures expect a more directive approach to leadership.

Legal and Political Systems

A nation's legal and political systems have an enormous impact on international business management. As Joseph Conner, former chairman of Price Waterhouse World

Firm, indicated, "Multinational corporations start by looking at the stability of government, the legal structure regarding expropriation and how strongly private property is protected, and they look at how easy it is to move capital in and out of the country."[30] (Practical Perspective 3.7 discusses the instability in Mexico.) And, of course, the September 11, 2001, incident has helped create enormous instabilities that currently exist throughout the globe.

PRACTICAL PERSPECTIVE 3-7

Troubles in Mexico

In Mexico, the path to progress has some enormous obstacles along its way. True, the economic reforms of the 1980s and 1990s were impressive, even if the government badly mismanaged its currency devaluation at the end of 1994. By 1997 the country appeared to be on the road to recovery from the peso crisis: forecasters estimated growth in the range of 4 to 5 percent for 1997, and the nation's export economy was flourishing. But the current-account deficit started rising again. Mexico's external debt had grown from 35 percent of GDP in 1992 to more than 60 percent in 1996. High interest rates and taxes were strangling the middle class. The banking system bordered on insolvency. In the recession of the past two years, 5 million Mexicans had been added to the 22 million citizens (one-fourth of the population) who already lived in extreme poverty. And the government estimated that an annual growth rate of 6 percent was necessary to absorb the 1 million new entrants into the labor force each year—a rate that did not appear to be attainable anytime soon.

Mexico's ability to deal with those daunting problems depended on an effective government. The country had been ruled by the iron fist of the Institutional Revolutionary Party for more than 60 years, but the party had become arthritic and corrupt. It was incapable of acting as a safety valve for the wellspring of popular discontent in Mexico, let alone as a vehicle for implementing critical new policies necessary for a rapidly changing economy. The party was in fact resisting change, having recently overturned President Ernesto Zedillio's far-reaching proposal to open and modernize Mexico's political process.

Nevertheless, political change will come—if not peacefully then violently. Already, crime, kidnapping, assassinations, and guerilla activity were [and in 2007, still are] on the rise, signaling both a mounting level of dissatisfaction and the inability of the public sector to maintain order. But even if a more open and representative government emerges, it will lack the experience and the underlying institutions—such as honest courts—to govern effectively in the short run. Initially, that government may be besieged by the accumulated demands of tens of millions of Mexican citizens who have felt disenfranchised. It also will have its hands full cleaning up the old system—getting a grip on widespread criminality and creating a rule of law that all segments of the population can respect.

In light of those pressures, future governments may put off liberalizing the economy and instead concentrate on the immediate welfare of ordinary citizens. A democratic administration could become more nationalistic and more protectionist than the existing oligarchy. It could take many years before Mexico restores its current trajectory, at least in the eyes of foreign companies and governments.

SOURCE: Excerpted from Jeffrey E. Garten, "Troubles Ahead in Emerging Markets," *Harvard Business Review* (May–June 1997), pp. 39–40. Reprinted with permission.

Legal Systems

Laws vary widely in the world's societies. The following are some common issues of the legal environment that must be given special attention when planning to transact business in a foreign country:

- Rules of competition on (a) collusion, (b) discrimination against certain buyers, (c) promotional methods, (d) variable pricing, and (e) exclusive territory agreements
- Retail price maintenance laws
- Cancellation of distributor or wholesaler agreements
- Product quality regulations and controls
- Packaging laws
- Warranty and after-sales exposure
- Price controls, limitations on markups or markdowns
- Patents, trademarks, and copyright laws and practices[31]

Labor laws, foreign investment, contract enforcement, and other issues must also be given special attention. For example, foreign moviemakers are not allowed to distribute movies in mainland China or even own copyrights. They can, however, share in the profits by setting up coproductions with Chinese companies, provided they give the government the final cut.[32] Besides imposing steep taxes on cars, the Thai government unofficially controls their price. Car manufacturers must file the prices of new cars three weeks before they go on sale. In 1996, government officials decreed that the $15,000 Honda City was overpriced by 16,000 baht ($625) because of too much corporate overhead. In addition to lowering prices, Honda was required to pay rebates to 150 customers.[33] Wal-Mart, which is pulling its operations out of Germany, was frustrated by the legal charges for the way it does business. In November 2002, Germany's highest court ruled that Wal-Mart and other retailers could not sell milk and butter below the wholesale prices, because doing so was damaging competition.[34]

Labor Laws. Wages may be low in a nation, but its legal authority may require that high fringe benefits, such as profit sharing, health and dental, and retirement benefits be given to workers. Labor laws in many countries provide extensive security for workers and make it extremely expensive to terminate an employee. For instance, Germany fiercely holds on to its "cradle-to-grave" benefits and job projections at the expense of job creation and vigorous growth, and its slow economic growth combined with its generous social welfare benefits has created a problem for the country.[35] China had a 100% employment policy. Some companies in China were therefore overstaffed. Furthermore, the laws in many countries mandate long vacations—for example, there was a six-week mandatory vacation in Germany, and firing an employee in France is almost impossible (see Chapter 8). Wal-Mart also had cultural issues with workers in Germany. Wal-Mart has historically operated union-free, but about 2,000 workers from several dozen of its stores went on strike in a bid to pressure Wal-Mart to join the employers association.[36] Wal-Mart has encountered similar problems in Canada as well.

Foreign Investment. Many countries' laws often dictate that foreign investments in their nation must be in the form of a joint venture with local partners and that the local partners must be majority owners. For example, in the past, IBM's policy was that its foreign subsidiaries had to be wholly owned (100% ownership). IBM became confronted with a problem when many countries' governments began to mandate joint ventures with local partners. For instance, IBM was operating in India on a wholly owned basis. The Indian government subsequently issued a mandate requiring that foreign investments in India be on a joint-venture basis, with the local partners owning 70%. Not wanting to take on partners, IBM elected to pull its operations out of India. India has since substantially reduced the 70% local ownership requirement. China once mandated more than 50% local ownership (see Case 3.1 at the end of the chapter). China now allows fully owned operations, but it's different from fully owned foreign operations in other countries, as the Chinese communist government still maintains substantial control through land ownership and ownership in companies' stock.

Also, the legal systems in some countries mandate that top management of foreign-owned enterprises must consist of locals. This can lead to problems when capable managers are not available in the foreign country. For example, when Russia began to shift from a communist to a market-like economy in the mid-1980s and began to draw foreign investments, its laws required that top management of foreign-owned enterprises be Russian. However, since Russians lacked experience in managing market-like enterprises, they were not very effective. By the late 1980s, the Russian government repealed the law, allowing foreigners to manage foreign-owned operations.

Contract Enforcement. Contract enforcement can sometimes be a problem. For example, if there is a default in a contract entered into by firms from different nations, which nation's law is applied? Usually, the contract stipulates whose law is applied in the event of default. However, some countries' legal systems mandate that the laws of the nation where the contract was signed shall be applied. Other legal systems mandate that the laws of the country where the contract was executed shall be applied. In some parts of the world, enforcing contracts is difficult. For example, what happens if Iraq defaults on its contract with Halliburton or Halliburton defaults on its contract with Iraq? How would the dispute be settled?

Other Issues. These include the issues of sovereignty and sovereign immunity, international jurisdiction, doctrine of comity, and act of state of doctrine, as well as "bureaucratization" and "privatization" facing MNCs (discussed in Chapters 4 and 5).

Political Systems

Awareness of the foreign country's political thinking and activities is absolutely essential. Before investing in a foreign country, a manager must learn about the country's type of government and what effect it could have on business operations. A manager must learn if the political system is primarily a democracy, a dictatorship, a monarchy, or a socialist or communist system, or if it seems to be moving in any of these directions. The political environment, if it is extreme or headed toward extremes, would greatly influence an investment decision. If a country's radical party is likely to be dominant, investment may be too risky. International companies have had their foreign subsidiaries confiscated when a radical political party in the country suddenly assumed power. Extreme social and economic turbulence are sometimes omens that foreshadow the emergence of extremist parties.

Types of Political Systems. Some nations, such as the United States and the United Kingdom, function with a two-party system. Change from one party to another does not cause great changes in the business realm. Other nations, such as Germany and France, are not dominated by any one party; theirs is a multiparty system, and the government may be controlled by a coalition of parties. Still other nations, such as Mexico, for many decades had a multiparty system, but only the candidates of one party had a real chance of being elected and controlling the government. This one-party control provided some degree of stability in Mexico's governmental policies. The most extreme type is the one-party political system, such as in China, Cuba, and the former USSR, where opposition is repressed. The one-party system can, however, also provide stability.

Regardless of the political system, firms can generally do business in any nation and with any party as long as there is stability in policy. For example, some U.S. firms, such as Pepsi Cola, conducted business effectively in the former USSR, and many foreign firms are currently conducting business effectively in Communist China. If policies change gradually, as they do in most nations, the firm has time to adjust its business strategies accordingly. The danger occurs when a country's dominant party makes radical changes in its policy. In this case, the firm would not have sufficient time to adapt, thus placing it in a difficult situation.

Government Policies. Extreme social and economic conditions may some times force a political party into radical policy changes. Generally, however, government policies change gradually; governments implement new policies to attract the foreign investments needed by the nation to attain its economic development objectives. William Stoever, a professor of international business at Seton Hall University, developed a schema linking the stages of a country's economic development described in Rostow's theory to the country's policy changes toward foreign investment.[37] This model can be helpful to international managers in predicting and understanding a nation's policy changes.

According to Stoever, countries at Stage 1 of economic development are usually unattractive to foreign investment, though government subsidies may attract some "show" factories. Stage 2 countries tend to attract low-technology investments; they attract labor-intensive technology for assembling or producing for the local market or for assembling for export. In moving to Stage 3, Stoever proposed, policymakers begin to be more selective in the type of investments they import, and their policies aim to take over part or full ownership of foreign-owned facilities. To move to Stage 4, the country's economy must strengthen and diversify to the point where it can rely more on market mechanisms. The country's policies are therefore those that guide the nation to a "free market" system. The more productive capabilities now existing in these countries make it an attractive investment for MNCs, and firms are usually more willing to supply their advanced technologies to these countries.

The Government's Attitude Toward the Product. International business managers also need to learn about the foreign government's attitude toward investment and products. Some investments and products are more politically vulnerable than others. Some receive favorable consideration by a nation, such as lower tariffs and higher quotas, while others receive unfavorable impositions. Product vulnerability is influenced by political philosophies, economic variations, and cultural differences. For example, China, as of 2005, allowed only 20 foreign films to be shown in the country.[38]

By obtaining accurate answers to the questions in Box 3.2, an international manager may discover whether a product will face a favorable or a hostile environment. Generally, a firm may expect to receive favorable consideration if its product/service contributes to the achievement of the import nation's goals, and it will receive unfavorable attention if, in view of the nation's current needs, the product/service is nonessential. Box 3.3 presents a framework that helps international firms improve the political considerations they will receive in a foreign country.

As a case illustration, Honda Motor Company of Japan applies a strategy of localizing profits and production.[39] Honda reinvests as much of its profits as possible in the local market. It regards itself as a local company and aims to prosper together with the host nation. For example, in 1959, Honda established a wholly owned marketing subsidiary, American Honda, in California with a capital investment of $250,000. By 1999, this sum had grown to $200 million through reinvestment of American Honda's profits. Honda has invested in the construction and expansion of motorcycle, automobile, and engine manufacturing plants in Ohio and Canada.

Box 3.2   A Process for Assessing the Political Vulnerability of a Product

1. Is the availability of the product ever going to be subject to political debate? (Sugar, salt, gasoline, public utilities, medicines, foodstuffs)

2. Do other industries depend on the production of the product? (Cement, power machine tools, construction machinery, steel)

3. Is the product considered socially or economically essential? (Key drugs, laboratory equipment, medicines)

4. Is the product essential to agricultural industries? (Farm tools and machinery, crops, fertilizers, seed)

5. Does the product affect national defense capabilities?

6. Does the product require important resources that are available from local sources? (Labor, skills, materials)

7. Is there local competition or potential local competition from manufacturers in the near future? (Small, low-investment manufacturing)

8. Does the product relate to channels of mass communication media? (Newsprint, radio equipment)

9. Is the product primarily a service?

10. Does the use of this product or its design depend on legal requirements?

11. Is the product potentially dangerous to the user? (Explosives, drugs)

12. Does the product induce a net drain on scarce foreign exchange?

SOURCE: Adapted from Richard D. Robinson, "The Challenge of the Underdeveloped National Market," *The Journal of Marketing* (October 1961), pp. 24–25. Used with permission of publisher. © 1961 American Marketing Association, Chicago, IL. All rights reserved.

Box 3.3.   How to Make Friends in Foreign Countries

Remember that

1. the company is a guest in the country and its managers should act accordingly;

2. the profits of an enterprise do not belong solely to the company—the local "national" employees and the economy of the purchasing country should also benefit;

3. it is not wise to try to win over new customers by trying to completely "Americanize" them;

4. although English is an accepted language overseas, fluency in the language of the international customer goes further in making sales and cementing good public relations;

5. the international company should try to contribute to the host country's economy and culture with worthwhile public projects;

6. it should train its executives, and their families, to act appropriately overseas; and

7. it is best not to conduct business from headquarters but to staff foreign offices with competent foreign nationals and supervise the operation from headquarters.

SOURCE: Adapted from "Making Friends and Customers in Foreign Lands," *Printer's Ink* (June 3, 1960), p. 59. Reprinted with permission.

Relative to localization of production, Honda does not merely make profits by exporting completed products to a foreign market; it produces where major markets exist, therefore contributing to the development of the host country and achieving mutual prosperity. For example, in 1990 Honda produced about 470,000 automobiles in its North American plants, in 1994 it produced about 520,000, and it planned to produce 610,000 in 1995—an indication that Honda continues to invest locally. As of October 1999, Honda's investment was $2.562 billion in the United States, $800 million in Canada, and $92 million in Mexico.[40] Practical Perspective 3.8 represents a time line of some of Honda's expansion activities in the United States through 2007.

PRACTICAL PERSPECTIVE 3-8

American Honda: Time Line

1959   American Honda Motor Co. was established with a small motorcycle store in Los Angeles.

1970   Honda introduced its first car, the N600 Sedan, to the United States

1979   Production began at the Honda Motorcycle Plant in Marysville, Ohio.

1982   A new auto plant began producing the Accord, making Honda the first Japanese automobile company to manufacture in the United States.

1985   Honda began production at an engine plant in Anna, Ohio, to manufacture both motorcycle and automobile engines.

1988   The first American-made Accord was exported to Japan.

1989   Honda began production of the Civic Sedan and Coupe at its new plant in East Liberty, Ohio.

1991   Honda began exporting the Accord Wagon to Europe and Japan. It was designed, engineered, and produced exclusively in the United States.

1994   Honda sold its 10 millionth car in the United States.

1999   In September, Honda sold 91,054 units, and for the nine-month period, it sold 1,067,468 units in the United States.

2001   Honda Accord is the best-selling car in America.

        Honda introduces the redesigned 2002 CR-V.

2006   Honda Aircraft Company was established. It produces and markets HondaJet in the United States.
        • Honda is to build a new automobile manufacturing plant in Indiana, scheduled to begin production in 2008, employing 2,000 people.
        • Honda America directly employs more than 25,000 Americans. And it employs more than 100,000 workers at authorized Honda automobile, motorcycle, and power equipment dealerships in the United States. Tens of thousands of additional Americans are employed by more than 600 U.S. suppliers, from which it purchases its parts and equipment.

2007   Honda Aircraft Company announces that it will establish its world headquarters in Greensboro, North Carolina. HondaJet is to be produced at the new plant for delivery to customers in 2010.

SOURCE: www.honda.com

Scarce Foreign Exchange. International managers must understand the dynamics of hard versus soft currencies. Hard currencies are those readily accepted as payment in international business transactions. The currencies of most of the industrialized nations, such as Japan, the United States, and the EU, are hard currencies. The currencies of most less developed countries and of countries with government-controlled economies (e.g., Cuba and China), are generally classified as soft currencies. These are normally not accepted as payment in international business transactions.

The governments of countries whose money is classified as soft currency usually accumulate hard currencies. These countries' governments use the hard currencies to pay for foreign goods and services, which in their view are needed to accomplish national goals. If the product or service is viewed as needed, the government may authorize payment in hard currency; if not, the government usually will not authorize such payment. (Box 3.2 aids the international manager in assessing the situation.) Payment in hard currency usually must be negotiated with authorized government officials. If the officials do not authorize payment in hard currency, international managers who have decided to do business in the country must seek alternative ways, such as barter trade (discussed in Chapter 5); payment is made in goods or services that can be sold for a profit in another market. For example, in the former USSR, the United States' Pepsi Cola sold its product to Russia for vodka, which it then sold in other markets for money. A current (2007) practice is the Middle East trading oil for food and the buying high technology for oil.

Political Risk Insurance. Many industrial nations offer some form of political risk insurance when investments are made in foreign countries. The United States, for example, provides coverage through the Overseas Private Investment Corporation (OPIC). OPIC insures new investments in qualified projects, in less developed but friendly countries, against losses owing to certain political risks. OPIC is authorized to provide insurance against three specific types of risks:

1. Inability to convert into dollars currencies received by the investor as profits of earnings or return on the original investment

2. Loss of investments resulting from expropriation, nationalization, or confiscation by the action of a foreign government

3. Loss due to war, revolution, civil strife, or insurrection (civil strife, coverage for which is optional, would encompass damage resulting from politically motivated violent acts, including terrorism and sabotage)[41]

The Multilateral Investment Guarantee Agency, an affiliate of the World Bank, offers similar insurance.[42]

Expropriation, Nationalization, Confiscation

Expropriation is the seizure by a government of foreign-owned assets. This does not violate international law if it is followed by prompt, adequate, and effective compensation.

Nationalization occurs when a government takes over private property. Reasonable compensation is usually paid by the government. For example, in May 2007, Hugo Chavez, Venezuela's president, announced that his government will nationalize the country's energy and telecommunications industries where there is substantial foreign ownership.

Confiscation occurs when a government seizes foreign-owned assets and does not make prompt, effective, and adequate compensation.

Competition

Throughout the 20th century, most nations tried to avoid competition; competition was viewed as a wasteful practice. The major exception has been the United States, where its citizens are taught to be competitive, as opposed to harmonious, at an early age. However, as the world heads toward a single marketplace, a more aggressive international competitive environment seems to be evolving. Japanese culture considers competition a wasteful practice, but Japanese MNCs behave very competitively in the global market arena. Numerous factors restrict international competition, including cartels, bribery, economic conditions, government-owned enterprises, and a short-range versus long-range managerial orientation.

Cartels

Cartels consist of groups of private businesses that agree to set prices, share markets, and control production. (OPEC is a prime example.) Cartels restrict competition. In Japan, *keiretsu* links[43] (giant industrial groups linked by cross-ownership, such as Mitsubishi or Sumitomo), bidding cartels, and old-boy networks present external firms with formidable obstacles that Japanese corporations do not face in some markets, such as the U.S. market.[44]

Bribery

Bribery as a means of obtaining a competitive edge is an accepted business practice in many nations. As pointed out in Chapter 2, the U.S. Foreign Corrupt Practices Act of 1977 makes it illegal for U.S. businesspeople to engage in bribery in any country, even if it is an accepted practice there. Many U.S. businesspeople have complained that this law has made their firms less competitive, because competitors from other nations are not bound by such laws. Numerous U.S. businesspeople, however, have said that the law has not impeded their competitive position, and what really make many U.S. firms less competitive in the international arena is the high-cost, low-quality products they are trying to market.

Economic Conditions

Competition can also be weakened by a nation's economic conditions.[45] During difficult economic times, many governments apply protectionist policies, such as tariffs and quotas, to restrict or diminish foreign competition. And many governments manipulate their currency exchange rates up or down to deter foreign competition during difficult economic times.

Government-Owned Enterprises

Competition is further weakened by government-owned enterprises competing with private firms. Governments do not necessarily have to realize profits and therefore can afford to cut prices. These government-owned enterprises can also get cheaper financing, can easily win government contracts, and, with government assistance, can even hold down wages in their country. Government-owned firms thus have a competitive advantage over private enterprises. The Japanese, for example, through the

Ministry of International Trade and Industry, target certain industries, help them reduce the risk of developing new technologies, and assist them in achieving large-scale production to reduce costs. These practices enable Japanese firms to compete more effectively in international markets.[46] By conducting research, which is made available to businesses for commercialization, the U.S. government also aids firms in reducing risk and obtaining a competitive edge. The NASA program, for example, has generated many ideas that were subsequently commercialized by business entrepreneurs. Furthermore, the U.S. government awards grants to less developed nations to aid them in their development objectives. Some of these grants stipulate that certain goods and services necessary to carry out the program must be procured from U.S.-based enterprises. Such practices also restrict competition.

Long-Range Versus Short-Range Orientation

Firms holding a short-range managerial orientation (e.g., many U.S. firms) often find it difficult to compete with firms holding a long-range managerial orientation (e.g., Japanese firms tend to hold a long-range orientation). For instance, one of Japan's top computer manufacturers won a contract over a U.S. firm to design a computer system in Hiroshima by bidding $1. Its strategy was to give away the design job in order to gain the inside advantage for the city's equipment purchase. This exemplifies a common Japanese strategy of forgoing short-range profits for long-term profits. Japanese firms project that once they have established a business relationship, they will obtain lifetime orders. Firms that cannot wait for possible profits down the road, such as many U.S. firms, which are usually evaluated on the basis of quarterly profits, will therefore encounter difficulties in competing with Japanese companies.

In this respect, it should be noted that some Japanese MNCs have been accused of "dumping," which under the 124-nation General Agreement on Tariffs and Trade (GATT) is illegal. (GATT will be discussed further in the section Trade Barriers.) Dumping is practiced when an MNC sells a product in a foreign market at a price lower than the one it sells the product for in its own market and/or at below production cost. For example, it was reported in 1998 that the U.S. Department of Commerce had issued a preliminary finding that the South Korean chip makers Hyundai Electronics Company and LG Semicon Company (now merged and known as Hyundai Electronics Industries Company, Ltd.) dumped memory chips, or sold them below costs, in the U.S. market from May 1, 1996, to April 30, 1997.[47]

The intent of dumping is to sell the product at a price much lower than the competitors' price, thus putting the competition out of business. Once the competition is out of the way, the MNC raises the price. These accusations are debatable, and Japanese managers refute them. Many international business managers and scholars view managers of Japanese MNCs not as "dumpers" but as effective customer- and quality-oriented strategists.

A Theory That Aids in Predicting Foreign Competition

Raymond Vernon and Louis T. Wells Jr., professors at Harvard Business School, developed a theory labeled *the international product life cycle* (IPLC), which can be used to assess which products are in danger of international competition.[48] According to this theory, many products pass through four phases.

Phase 1. *As a result of competition, large market size, strong market expertise, and the society's openness to innovation, firms in economically advanced countries, such as the United States, through research and development (R&D), create new products. In this phase, many firms eventually start selling the product in foreign markets. In the 20th century, U.S. firms were the leaders in this phase—about 80% of the world's innovations were first commercialized in the U.S. market.*

Phase 2. *Demand in some of these foreign markets grows large enough to justify local production, and many firms make direct investment in manufacturing facilities in those markets. Eventually, local firms in some of the overseas markets learn the manufacturing process and gain control of domestic production. Subsequently, the original manufacturers' sales in those countries, because of competition from the locals, begin to decline.*

Phase 3. *Eventually, some of the early foreign producers become highly experienced in marketing and manufacturing the product, and their costs lessen. As their markets become saturated, they look for customers in foreign markets. At this point, according to the IPLC theory, foreign producers are competing in the original producers' foreign markets. The original producers' sales continue to decline.*

For example, in the 1960s, Japan and West Germany (now Germany) began competing with U.S. firms in many industries, including the automobile industry. Japan, for instance, had only one industrial corporation in the top 50 of the world's largest industrial corporations in 1970; by 1980, it had six.[49] As of 1993, Japan had 128 companies on Fortune's Global 500 list; the United States, 161; Great Britain, 40; Germany, 32; and France, 30. U.S. firms held 10 of the 15 major industries in 1960; the number was reduced to 9 in 1970 and 3 in 1980.[50] Of the top 50 corporations listed on the 1999 Fortune 500 list (www.fortune.com), 16 were U.S. based, 16 Japanese based, and 7 German based. The German car manufacturer Daimler-Benz acquired the U.S. car manufacturer Chrysler several years ago—the headquarters is in Germany. And as indicated in Practical Perspective 3.10, Honda, a Japanese car manufacturer, now builds cars in the United States, sells them locally, and exports them to Europe and Japan as well. And in 2006, Toyota's U.S. sales edged past Ford's (being second only to General Motors [GM]), and it was expected that Toyota would become No. 1 by the end of the year.[51]

Phase 4. *Production to meet the wants of both domestic and foreign consumers may be large enough to allow the foreign manufacturers to reach economies of scale similar to those of the original producers. Since foreign producers started later, they possess newer plants, which results in a cost advantage over the original producers. At this point, the original manufacturers' exports dwindle, and sales in their domestic market by the foreign producers accelerate. Such competition may become so severe that the original manufacturers close production completely.*

For example, in the late 1960s, there were as many as 18 American television set manufacturers; by the 1990s, just about all brands (e.g., RCA, General Electric, Magnavox) were made by foreign companies.[52] German steel and Japanese radios and automobiles compete with U.S. industries in the domestic market. By the 1980s, a great many of the automobiles sold in the U.S. market were imported from Japan. In 2005, GM, the world's largest auto producer, announced that it will cut 30,000 jobs in North America and close all or some of a dozen plants over a three-year period. This action was triggered by Toyota's and Honda's as well as other auto producers' lower costs and reputation for building more reliable cars.[53] In 2006, Toyota became the world's number two automaker after GM, bypassing Ford. In 2007, Toyota became the world's No. 1 automaker. By 1979, the Japanese, unchallenged, were flooding the U.S. market with videocassette recorders.[54] (For a case illustration of the automobile industry, read Practical Perspective 3.10.)

The U.S. television, steel, and automobile industries are cases that help substantiate the IPLC theory. These industries seem to be in Phase 4, and to remain "alive," they, in the early 1980s, tried to push the U.S. government to take protective measures;[55] that is, through tariffs and quotas (discussed in the next section), the government keeps out or limits foreign competition. It should be noted that it is not a necessary condition that the original producers go out of business. They often, as will be discussed in Chapter 4, make direct investment in foreign markets to enjoy the same advantages foreign producers enjoy. The large increases in U.S. direct foreign investment and the huge U.S. trade deficits in recent decades indicate that many U.S. firms are doing this. Many U.S. firms are producing goods in foreign markets and shipping them back to the U.S. domestic market. However, many foreign firms, such as the automobile manufacturers Honda and Toyota, have found it more profitable to establish assembling plants in the United States. Currently, with the advent of the Web, even many of the United States' service jobs are being sent to foreign countries.

Trade Barriers

In an effort to limit or restrict competition, nations often take protective measures by imposing trade barriers. (As an illustration, read Practical Perspective 3.9.) Some of the reasons for protectionist activities are as follows:

- Protection of an infant industry
- Protection of the home market
- The need to keep money at home
- Encouragement of capital accumulation
- Maintenance of the standard of living and real wages
- Conservation of natural resources
- Industrialization of a low-wage nation
- Maintenance of employment and reduction of unemployment
- National defense
- Increase of business size
- Retaliation and bargaining[56]

In the 2000s, there have been a great many complaints reported in the media about U.S. companies outsourcing American jobs to foreign countries, and many media reporters, such as CNN's Lou Dobbs, have been crusading against such outsourcing. And the U.S. government is now (in 2008) taking extensive action to keep out illegal immigrants to preserve Americans' jobs—but this action may not be wise in the sense that these immigrants are needed to do the jobs Americans won't do or are unwilling to do for low pay.

PRACTICAL PERSPECTIVE 3-9

WTO's Kodak Ruling Heightens Trade Tensions

The World Trade Organization's [1997] resounding rejection of U.S. claims of Japanese protectionism in photographic film promised to heighten trade tensions and increase competitive pressures on Eastman Kodak Company. The WTO's verdict brought calls by Kodak for consideration of new tariffs or other unilateral sanctions against Japan. Set against the backdrop of a widening trade deficit with Japan and a strong dollar that was fettering U.S. exports and making imports from Japan cheaper, it also stands to set back efforts by the Clinton administration to convince congressional skeptics and voters that the international trade system is fair and open.

The WTO ruling "raises serious questions about the credibility of this international body and of the U.S. trade representatives' capacity to secure and defend free-trade agreements," said Sen. John Ashcroft, a Missouri Republican, in a statement. While the U.S. does have the right to challenge the decision, it could be awkward. The U.S. doesn't want to be seen as undercutting an organization it worked hard to create. Also, it doesn't want to turn up the heat too high on Japan while Tokyo is trying to deal with its economic problems. But the U.S. believes Japan can only deal with economic stagnation if it opens up its economy—exactly what it was calling for in its complaint.

SOURCE: Excerpted from K. S. Greenberger, L. Johannes, and R. Kerber, "WTO's Kodak Ruling Heightens Trade Tensions," *The Wall Street Journal* (December 8, 1997), pp. A3, A14. Permission conveyed through Copyright Clearance Center.

Tariffs and Quotas

Tariffs and quotas are often employed by governments to restrict trade. Tariffs are a form of tax imposed on incoming products. Quotas specify the number of foreign units allowed to enter the country. The tax added to the incoming products will increase prices on imported goods, thus reducing competition for domestic manufacturers. Quotas also tend to reduce competition and increase the price domestic manufacturers charge their home-country customers.

For example, for a period of three years in the early 1980s, Japanese car manufacturers could export only an established number of cars to the United States per year. The quota was established by the Japanese government—which was encouraged by the U.S. government. This measure was taken so that U.S. car manufacturers could earn higher profits, which they would then use to invest in retooling strategies. GM, for instance, diversified into other manufacturing fields, such as robotics, space travel, and artificial intelligence. Toyota, the Japanese car manufacturer, reacted to the embargo by attacking the high-end U.S. car market, and it moved its plant to assemble cars for the low-end U.S. market to U.S. soil. (As an illustration, refer to Practical Perspective 3.10.)

Tariffs tend to

- *increase* inflationary pressures, special interests' privileges, government control and political considerations in economic matters, and the number of tariffs—because tariffs beget other tariffs (as an illustration, refer again to Practical Perspective 3.1);

PRACTICAL PERSPECTIVE 3-10

United States Steel Tariff 2002

The Section 201 steel tariff is a political issue in the United States regarding a tariff that President George W. Bush placed on imported steel on March 5, 2002 (which took effect from March 20). The tariffs were lifted by Bush on December 4, 2003. The temporary tariffs of 8% to 30% were originally scheduled to remain in effect until 2005. They were imposed to give U.S. steel makers protection from what a U.S. probe determined was a detrimental surge in steel imports. More than 30 steel makers had declared bankruptcy in recent years. Steel industries had originally sought up to a 40% tariff. Canada and Mexico were exempt from the tariff because of the penalties the U.S. would face under the free-trade agreement. Additionally, developing countries such as Argentina, Thailand, and Turkey were also exempt . . . For some of the President's conservative allies, imposing the tariff was a step away from Bush's commitment to free trade. Critics also contended that the tariffs would harm consumers and U.S. businesses that relied on steel imports and would cut more jobs than it would save in the steel industry. . . .

The tariffs ignited international controversy as well. Immediately after they were filed, the European Union announced that it would impose retaliatory tariffs on the United States, thus risking the start of a major trade war. To decide whether or not the steel tariffs were fair, a case was filed at the Dispute Settlement Body of the World Trade Organization (WTO). In late autumn of 2003, the WTO came out against the steel tariffs. After receiving the verdict, Bush declared that he would preserve the tariffs; in retaliation and under WTO rules, the European Union threatened to counter with tariffs of its own on products ranging from Florida oranges to cars produced in Michigan. . . . Faced with this threat, the United States backed down and withdrew the tariffs early.

SOURCE: Adapted from http://en.wikipedia.org/wiki/United_States_steel tariff_2002 (February 27, 2007).

- *weaken* balance-of-payment positions, supply and demand patterns, and international understanding—they can start trade wars; and
- *restrict* manufacturers' supply sources, the choices available to consumers, and competition.[57]

GATT/WTO

The imposition of tariffs has in the past been governed (although not very effectively) by GATT. GATT provided the conditions under which a nation could impose tariffs—for example, a nation could impose a tariff to protect its infant industry. GATT also prohibited a nation from imposing tariffs on selected countries; that is, if the tariff was legally imposed, it had to be applicable to all nations.

There is a current movement among nations to make GATT a more forceful regulatory organization. To accomplish this, a new organization (discussed earlier in the chapter), the WTO, was established to replace the old GATT organization. The three main goals of the WTO are to aid in the free flow of trade, to help negotiate further opening of the markets, and to settle trade disputes between its members. In 1999, the WTO recognized 133 member nations and 35 observer members, of which 31 have applied for membership—as pointed out earlier, the WTO, as of December 11, 2005, consists of 149 country members. The new organization intends to slash tariffs by an average of 38% worldwide, and for some products, such as beer, tariffs are eliminated altogether. The WTO, based in Geneva, Switzerland, also settles trade disputes. (Refer again to Practical Perspectives 3.1 and 3.8.)

Monetary Barriers

Monetary barriers are another form of protection imposed by governments. Using this approach, the government creates a trade barrier by imposing exchange restrictions. Three methods used are blocked currency, differential exchange rate, and governmental approval requirements.

Blocked currency is a method used for cutting off all importing above a certain level. In using this approach, a government refuses to redeem national currencies in the world financial marketplace for specified imports or above specified amounts on certain imports.

With differential exchange rates, a government encourages the importation of certain goods and discourages the importation of others. The government accomplishes this by requiring the importer to pay a higher amount of domestic currency for the foreign currency needed to pay for the imported product being discouraged and a lower amount for the foreign currency needed to pay for the imported product being encouraged.

Using governmental approval requirements for securing foreign exchange, a government can create a barrier by not approving the acquisition of foreign exchange needed by importers for the purchase of specific foreign products.

Nontariff Protection

Nontariff barriers are used by many governments. Using this approach, a government can discourage imports by creating administrative barriers, such as by making importing a complex, frustrating, and expensive process. Japan offers a prime example. Because of administrative barriers, many foreign firms have in the past refused to export to Japan. There are also cultural barriers. For example, Americans with an individualistic cultural perspective (discussed in Chapter 1) often do not transact business well in Japan's collectivistic culture. In other words, Americans' "spirit of competitiveness" culture does not integrate well into the Japanese "spirit of cooperation" culture, and many Americans thus have difficulty when attempting to penetrate Japan's market.

Consequences of Trade Barriers

The added costs that result from trade barriers have an impact on a product's price as well as on the channels of distribution. The higher the tariffs or the smaller the quotas, the higher the costs and, therefore, the higher the prices to the final consumer.

To avoid tariffs, instead of exporting, a firm may decide to manufacture or at least assemble the product in the foreign market. Many countries have a much higher tariff rate on products brought in assembled than on products brought in unassembled because assembling the products locally helps create jobs, which in turn helps the nation's economy—for example, Toyota and Honda establishing car assembling plants on U.S. soil. On the other hand, the exporting country will encounter loss of jobs. Furthermore, tariffs keep out competition, and the lack of competition leads to higher prices being charged to consumers; for instance, when the U.S. car quota was imposed in the early 1980s, prices rose quickly. As another example, in 1989, Japan's virtual ban on rice imports was costing Japanese consumers an estimated $28 billion a year. The U.S. Rice Millers' Association claimed that "if even 10 percent of the Japanese market were opened to imports, the resulting lower prices would have saved the Japanese $6 billion annually."[58]

Fluctuating Exchange Rates

Countries' currency exchange rates, just like the selling value of a company's stock, can and do fluctuate on a daily basis. For example, U.S.$1 can equal 100 Japanese yen today and change to 95 yen or to 105 yen tomorrow. Fluctuations can be "dirty" or "clean."

Dirty fluctuations are the result of a government, for economic and/or other reasons, adjusting the exchange rate up or down.

Clean fluctuations are the result of supply and demand, just like a company's stock. If there is an abundance of a nation's currency for sale in international financial markets, its sale value is likely to decline, and if it is scarce and there is a demand for it, it is likely to appreciate. Nations tend to apply the "dirty" approach. One of the United States' current objectives (in 2007) is to convince China to increase currency flexibility, to let the yuan's value be set more freely by market forces.[59]

The fluctuation can have an enormous impact on international business transactions. And the impact can be positive or negative depending on the direction of the fluctuation. International business managers must thus be skilled, or employ skilled people, in this area.

The case of Laker Airways serves as a good example of what can happen to an international enterprise when exchange rates fluctuate and its managers have not taken that possibility into account. Laker Airways, a British firm, was gravely affected by fluctuating exchange and interest rates and by fixed prices.[60] In 1980, Laker borrowed $240 million from banks in the United States to finance its growing fleet of airplanes. At the time it seemed like a wise transaction because British interest rates were far above the U.S. levels. Laker sold advance tickets to British travelers with fares fixed in British pounds. Subsequently, U.S. interest rates rose and the value of the U.S. dollar also began rising rapidly. The fares had been fixed late in 1980, when £1 equaled U.S.$2.40. Laker's U.S. bank loans had to be repaid in dollars in August 1981, when £1 equaled U.S.$1.93.

When Laker borrowed the $240 million, it was the equivalent of £100 million ($240 million divided by $2.40). When the loans were to be paid, however, Laker had to pay back approximately £124 million ($240 million divided by $1.93). In other words, to purchase the $240 million it had to pay the U.S. banks, Laker Airways now had to spend £124 million, which is far more than the £100 million it would have spent had the exchange rate remained stable. Since Laker had sold tickets at a fixed rate, it could not adjust its prices to compensate for the change in the exchange rates. As a result of this, and the refusal of the banks to postpone payment or grant more loans, Laker went bankrupt in early 1982. Another illustration is the case of Coca-Cola. In 1998, Coca-Cola reported a 13.2% drop in its first-quarter earnings, sending its stock down. The company attributed the decline to devalued currencies in many countries where it was doing business.[61]

Of course, if the fluctuation had gone the other way, the firms would have realized unexpected profits. There are businesses that realize profits solely by buying and selling foreign currencies. At more than $1 trillion in trading volume, the foreign exchange market is by far the largest capital market in the world—its volume is several times over the New York Stock Exchange. The market participants include governments, banks, nonbank financial institutions, and corporations.[62] But Laker Airways, like most companies, are in the business of realizing profits from sales of goods and/or services—not from buying and selling foreign currencies.[63] As a result, such businesses often attempt to protect against negative fluctuations by contracting for a fixed exchange rate; by contracting for payment with a nation's currency that has a history of being relatively stable—for example, the U.S. dollar; or by contracting for a choice of payment by one of several nations' currencies—for instance, EU euros, U.S. dollars, or Japanese yens (whichever is the most advantageous at the time of payment is selected).

At the national level, in the 1990s, a financial collapse took place in Japan. Exchange rates were partially responsible for the collapse. Around 1980, U.S.$1 cost about 300 Japanese yen. The U.S. dollar gradually became cheaper during the 1980s, to the point where the U.S.$1 cost only 89 Japanese yen (the term used is *weak dollar* or *weakening of the U.S. dollar*). As the U.S. dollar gradually weakened in the 1980s, many Japanese businesses began to invest in the United States—"Japan's buying America," as it was then said. But the value of the investments in the United States did not inflate at the rate the U.S. dollar cheapened; the value of the Japanese investments in the United States, when translated into yen, declined dramatically. Of course, the value of the investments U.S. businesses had made in Japan also declined dramatically when the yen was translated into the dollar. The dollar has remained relatively weak, but the dramatic inflation of many properties in the United States in the 2000s has helped Japan stabilize its financial status. It should be noted that the weakening of the dollar did help increase exports to Japan—instead of producing certain products in Japan, it became cheaper to buy them from the United States. And the weak dollar made it very expensive for Americans to go on vacation to Japan, but it made it cheaper for the Japanese to go on vacation to the United States, thus helping the U.S. economy. Currently (2008), it costs U.S.$1.50 to purchase 1 euro, whereas in 2002 it cost 98 U.S. cents to purchase 1 euro, which has created the same dynamic as the weakening of the dollar against the yen. (The Appendix describes trade theory and the impact of fluctuating exchange rates on international trade.)

Labor Relations

Labor relations, also referred to as industrial relations, have been defined as the "totality of the interactions between an organization's management and organized labor."[64] The term *international labor relations* can be misleading when applied within the context of the MNC. Webster's New Collegiate Dictionary defines *international* as "1. of, relating to, or constituting a group or association having members in two or more nations. 2. affecting or involving two or more nations. 3. of or relating to one whose activities extend across national boundaries." Even though some labor unions contain the word *international* in their title, they are not really international. This is because their domain does not really cut across multiple nations. International labor relations, in the context of the MNC, thus means management interacting with organized labor units in each country.

Unions in some nations, such as in the United States, are very hostile toward management—for this reason (and other reasons, such as cheaper labor), when Toyota established its car-assembling plants in the United States, it did so in the rural parts of the United States, where, in comparison with Detroit, labor unions tend to be less hostile (and land and labor tend to be cheaper).

It should be noted, however, that in the early 1980s, some U.S. unions began seeking transnational bargaining and standardization of labor conditions among MNC operations.[65] Andy Stern, who leads the largest and fastest-growing union in the United States, in 2005, was providing leadership in forming a global union.[66]

Furthermore, it is difficult to compare labor (or industrial) relations systems and behavior across nations. For example, collective bargaining in the United States means negotiations between the firm's management and the labor union local, but in Germany and Sweden it means negotiations between an employer's organization and a trade union at the industry level. Also, the objective of collective bargaining is viewed differently across nations. For instance, in the United States it is viewed mostly in economic terms, but in Europe it is viewed as a form of "class struggle." And workers' actions also differ across countries. For instance, dissatisfied workers in U.S. unionized firms may totally disrupt output as a way of protesting against management's actions, but in Japan, dissatisfied workers protest during their work breaks, thus not disrupting output.

Differences in Labor Relations Across Nations

Labor relations across nations have their roots in two fundamental ideological themes: the pluralist/systems approach and the class approach.[67] The pluralist/systems approach, which is the prevalent ideology in the United States and the United Kingdom, tends to focus on procedural and institutional methods in labor relations problem solving. The class (Marxist) approach places greater emphasis on politics, political action, and the tensions between employers and employees than it does on procedures and practices related to labor relations. This type of system is dominant in Italy. Japan melds the two approaches. Different societies have thus developed their labor relations systems differently. It should be noted that governments also play an increasingly significant role in collective bargaining. In "varying ways, countries have developed income policies, or wage and price guidelines, for the purpose of controlling the outcomes of the collective bargaining process."[68]

Labor Unions' Impact on MNCs' Strategies

Labor unions affect MNCs' strategies in three ways: (1) by influencing wage levels, (2) by limiting MNCs' employment-level variation, and (3) by hindering global integration.[69]

Influencing Wage Levels. Unions can influence wages to a cost level that puts companies at a disadvantage, making them less competitive in the global economy. This has forced many U.S. companies to flee overseas—for example, the U.S. bicycle manufacturer, Schwinn Bicycle Company (discussed in Chapter 4), was having problems with its union workers, so it transferred manufacturing to Asia.

Limiting Employment-Level Variation. Redundancy legislation in many nations often specifies that enterprises must compensate involuntarily terminated employees on the basis of a specified formula, such as one week's pay for each year of service, and in some countries it may even be more. For example, if an employer in Mexico decides to terminate an employee who has been with the company for six months, the employee could create a back pay issue of as much as an additional six weeks, plus prorated vacation and bonuses.70 Labor unions influence this process by lobbying for such legislation. In France, it is almost impossible to dismiss an employee. And, as discussed earlier, Wal-Mart has learned its lesson about unions in Germany, from where it is pulling out its operations, and it is having its problems in Canada, where it has 260 stores and where unionization is strong. Wal-Mart closed its store in Quebec after it was certified by the Quebec government as the only unionized Wal-Mart store in North America.71

Hindering Global Integration. As discussed in Chapter 5, many MNCs rationalize production and pricing across a number of nations to optimize their investments. Powerful unions, however, can force MNCs not to undertake such activities or force them to make suboptimal investments in their nation. As mentioned above, Japanese car makers, who do import car parts from many parts of the world and outsource many functions, stay away from Detroit, where unions are powerful, and locate where unions are traditionally less powerful, such as in the United States' rural South.

Geography

There is not much businesses can do about geography. Bananas do not grow in Alaska, or in Russia or Europe, thus they must be imported from South and Central America, where they do grow. Coffee does not grow in the United States and in many parts of the world, so it must be imported from where it does grow, such as Brazil, Colombia, and some Central American countries. Rubber plants needed to build tires for automobiles, as well as other products, do not grow on the soil of many countries, such as the United States, and must be obtained from where it does grow, such as in Southeast Asia—Malaysia, for example.

In the early 1900s, Henry Ford, the efficient car manufacturer, attempted to bring his source of rubber closer to home by contracting with the Brazilian government to be allowed to grow rubber trees in the Amazons. It was a huge failure. First, the diseases workers encountered were overwhelming, and second, Ford's managers, against the Brazilian engineers' strong advice, planted the trees too close together for efficiency reasons. The trees rotted, and the soil was spoiled. It seems as if the "American way is O.K. everywhere" mentality was present then and is still present today.[72]

Oil is not available in many countries, thus it must be purchased from countries where it is available, such as the Middle East. And historically, nations have conquered and gone to war with other nations to obtain vital resources needed at home or to obtain resources to make a profit at home or elsewhere.

Mother Nature

There is nothing very much businesses can do about natural disasters, such as hurricanes (e.g., Hurricane Katrina), tornados, tsunamis, earthquakes, and so on. However, like wars, natural disasters provide businesses both threats and opportunities (discussed in Chapter 4).

Sources of Information

The above discussion of the global environment suggests that effective international business managers require an abundance of information. How is the information obtained? Information can be obtained through primary research and/or secondary research. Primary research is carried out to obtain first-hand information about the environment. Generally, only larger, wealthier corporations can afford to gather primary information, and only a few can afford to establish information sources around the globe. General Electric Corporation, for example, a huge multinational corporation, has established its own global scanning system.

Less wealthy enterprises usually depend on information obtained through secondary research, which is less costly. Basically, secondary research means obtaining information that was gathered through primary research by other organizations. There are many sources of secondary data, including the following:

Corporations: Some large multinational enterprises, such as GE, and banks, such as Citicorp, gather primary information. These corporations make much of the information available to other organizations.

Governments: Many governments have established agencies to gather and compile information to aid managers in making international business decisions. For instance, the U.S. Department of Commerce has established agencies that gather information relative to worldwide economic, social, political, and technological developments. This information is available at a nominal cost.

The United Nations: The UN also gathers and disseminates an abundance of information about global economic, political, social, and technological developments.

International organizations: Organizations such as the Organization for Economic Cooperation and Development, the EU, the Pan American Union, the World Bank, and the IMF gather and compile information that is useful in international business decisions.

Chambers of commerce and trade organizations: National and international chambers of commerce and foreign trade associations also gather and disseminate useful information.

Research universities: Many professors at universities conduct empirical research relevant to global economic, social, political, and technological developments. Their findings are made available in published practical (and academic) journals, books, and professional conference papers.

Business periodicals: There is an abundance of business periodicals. In the United States, to mention just a few, there are *The Wall Street Journal, Business Week, Fortune, Forbes, The Financial Times, Business International,* and *Business America.*

Cable television: Many television channels, such as CNN, Fox, and NBC, provide information 24 hours a day, 7 days a week, and 12 months a year.

Certain religious institutions: The Mormon religion, for expansionary reasons, studies and documents the culture of many countries throughout the world. This information is available to business managers who want to learn about a certain country's culture.

The Internet: Of course, the Internet, discussed below, is now a valuable source of information.

The Internet as a Source of Information

The Internet is generating rapid changes in homes, businesses, and organizations of all kinds. Using the Internet on a laptop computer, it is possible, while sipping coffee in bed, to order products from anywhere in the world. Technologies of this nature have within the past decade generated rising expectations in consumers and business for value, choice, and innovation. These expectations have encouraged governments, regulatory agencies, and industry-leading companies to provide more diversity, openness, and competition in the marketplace.[73] (Practical Perspective 3.11 presents the views of C. Michael Armstrong, AT&T's Chairman and CEO, on the new technology.)

Such changes are likely to force governments and international organizations to change their policies toward international trade, investment, intellectual property, and financial transactions. They will have to find ways to deal with the new issues of privacy, consumer protection, taxation, and the like. For example, a company publishing a magazine in Country A exports it to Country B and pays a tax for crossing the border. What if the publisher decides to transmit the magazine via electronic means to Country B for production and sale there? For example, the American magazine *Business Week*, which paid a high tariff to sell its magazine in Canada several years ago, started transmitting the information via the Internet to its subsidiary in Canada, and the magazine was produced there. *Business Week* claimed that it did not have to pay tariffs to Canada. Canada disputed this and tried to collect the tariffs. Such issues are being dealt with by the World Trade Organization.

PRACTICAL PERSPECTIVE 3-11

It's All Coming Together

Now technology and competition will redefine communications between countries. They will slip the constraints of national borders to make the very concept of "place" irrelevant. That, in essence, is what multinational businesses have long wanted: seamless communications services that operate the same way in New York, New Delhi, and New Zealand. Multimedia capabilities that make it possible to hold virtual meetings wherever an executive finds herself. Toll-free calling that crosses borders ... Use of global communications by the world's largest companies is growing, and use by small and medium-sized companies is growing even faster. And consumer demand for international voice and data services is increasing. In fact, traffic between countries is increasing almost twice as fast as traffic within the countries themselves. ...

Communications companies are racing to make the Internet a reliable business tool. They are using wireless technology to extend advanced services to less-developed nations. They are increasing networking intelligence to give their customers greater control over communications, making them reachable whenever and wherever they want, on their own terms ... data have overtaken voice traffic on the majority of the world's communication networks. In fact, global communications traffic is rapidly becoming global data transfer. Technology's ability to digitalize and transmit every form of information, combined with the ubiquity of the Internet, is redefining what the industry delivers to customers ... These [giant mergers] reflect the fact that technology could remove the boundaries between markets: wired and wireless services, local and long distance, cable television and telephone, information and entertainment. Technology could bring these services together and so the market is bringing together companies that want to make customers an expanded offer.

SOURCE: Excerpted from C. Michael Armstrong, Chairman and CEO, AT&T, "It's All Coming Together," in *The World in 1999* (London: The Economist Publications), p. 90. Reprinted with permission.

Therefore, to be effective, international managers must continuously scan their environment for changes taking place around the globe. The Internet, a global web of many thousands of computer networks,[74] such as Google, now provides a quick and inexpensive means of global communication and access to information about the external environment.[75]

Most organizations around the globe now offer information about their activities on the Web—for example, Nike (www.nike.com), Reebok (www.reebok.com), Adidas (www.adidas.com), Toyota (www.toyota.co.jp), and Sony (www.sony.com).

Caveat

Caveat About the Sources of Information. Before managers use information, they first must analyze carefully its sources and its age. They must obtain answers to the following questions:

- Who collected the information? Would there be any reason for deliberately misrepresenting the facts? (National pride and politics sometimes persuade the gatherers of information to inflate or deflate the data. For example, around election time, politicians like to create optimism or establish a positive image of their past performance; they sometimes do this by manipulating economic data.)
- For what purpose were the data collected?
- How were they collected (methodology)?
- Are the data internally consistent and logical in light of known data sources or market factors?[76]

The age of the data must also be considered. Information about nations now changes very rapidly. For example, not too long ago, the idea of McDonald's in Paris was absurd, but today they are popular there. Also, many countries are rapidly growing economically. The national totals of income and income distribution are therefore quickly invalidated. And while primary and secondary data are of vital importance to international managers for decision-making purposes, it is also very important that they make on-site visits to intuitively assess the situation before they make their final decisions. And, of course, managers must be very careful about the way they interpret statistics because statistics can lie, and liars can use statistics.

Caveat on the Anecdotal Examples, Practical Perspectives, and Cases Appearing in This Textbook. In the above context, it should be emphasized that the anecdotal examples, practical perspectives, and cases appearing in this textbook are not provided with the intention that they be used as information for managers in making actual business decisions. The intent is simply to exemplify in an interesting way the academic ideas presented in the textbook. It is the reader's responsibility to keep abreast of global activities currently taking place by using the sources outlined above as well as other sources that may be available.

Summary

The major thrust of this chapter was that managers of effective international businesses must be aware of the changes taking place in their home country and throughout the globe. At home, they should remain informed about changes that can affect their organization, including legal, political, economic, and competitive changes. They must also remain informed about changes taking place in international organizations, such as the EU, and in individual foreign nations. When the changes present opportunities and/or threats, managers must develop strategies to seize the opportunities and/or combat the threats (discussed in Chapter 4). They should also recognize that different countries present different cultural, economic, legal, political, and competitive environments, as well as trade barriers, monetary exchanges, and labor relations. When they develop international strategies, these managers should consider the differing factors and make the necessary adaptations. Therefore, effective international business managers do their "homework"; they gather the information needed to make effective decisions.

KEY TERMS AND CONCEPTS

1. Domestic environment
2. International environment
3. Foreign environment
4. Cultural environment
5. Economic, legal, and political environments
6. The five stages of economic development
7. A less developed country
8. Labor laws; foreign investment; contract enforcement
9. Political systems; government policies
10. Government's attitudes toward products/services
11. Hard and soft currencies
12. Expropriation, nationalization, and confiscation
13. Competitive environment
14. Cartels, keiretsu
15. Dumping
16. The international product life cycle (IPLC)
17. Trade barriers; tariffs and quotas
18. GATT/WTO
19. Monetary barriers
20. Nontariff barriers
21. Currency exchange rates
22. International labor relations
23. Primary and secondary research
24. The Internet as a source of information

DISCUSSION QUESTIONS

1. Discuss how the domestic environment affects international business strategies.

2. What is meant by the term *international environment*? How does the international environment affect international business strategies?

3. What is meant by the term *foreign environment*?

4. How does culture affect international business?

5. How does a nation's economic environment affect international business?

6. The theory of the stages of economic development has been criticized. What are the criticisms? Notwithstanding the criticisms, how is the theory useful to international business managers?

7. How do labor laws, foreign investment laws, and contract enforcement laws affect international business management?

8. Political systems differ from country to country. Should a nation's political system be a factor in an international corporation's decision on whether or not to do business there? Why or why not?

9. How can an international firm reduce its political vulnerability?

10. In what ways do cartels, bribery practices, a nation's economic condition, government-owned enterprises, and long-range versus short-range managerial orientations affect competition?

11. Discuss the IPLC theory. How is it useful to international business managers?

13. Discuss the reasons for a nation's protectionist activities (tariffs and quotas).

14. What is nontariff protection?

15. What are the negative aspects of tariffs?

16. What is the role of GATT/WTO in international business?

17. What are monetary barriers?

18. How do fluctuating monetary exchange rates affect international business?

19. What are "clean" and "dirty" exchange fluctuations?

20. Discuss how labor relations differ across nations.

21. How do labor relations affect international business strategies?

22. Discuss the major sources of information available to international managers.

23. What are the major concerns about information?

EXERCISES

1. You are an international business consultant who has been employed by a domestic company involved in selling beef and pork products. The firm wants to expand its business activities into foreign markets. What would be the primary advice you would give your client?

2. You are an international business consultant employed by a domestic firm seeking to conduct business in a less developed country. The chapter discusses hard and soft currencies. In this context, what advice would you give your client?

3. You are an international consultant employed by a firm seeking to establish a subsidiary in China. What would you tell your client to expect?

4. You are an international business consultant who has been employed by a domestic company that wants to expand its business into a foreign market and wants to remain there for the long term. What would be the primary advice you would give your client?

5. You are an international business consultant who has been employed by a domestic company that wants to move its manufacturing activities into a foreign country because it has discovered that labor there is much cheaper than at home. What would be the primary advice you would give your client?

ASSIGNMENT

Interview a student or an acquaintance who is from another country. Ask him or her to describe how some of the factors discussed in this chapter differ between his or her country and your country.

CASE 3-1

Protecting the Pepsi Taste

When PepsiCo, Inc. was obliged to begin producing concentrate within China for its Chinese bottling plants, the company decided a wholly owned venture would be the only viable option. Only a WFOE [wholly foreign-owned enterprise] could adequately protect patented soft-drink formulas—but Chinese central government officials drove a hard bargain before approving the project.

While PepsiCo chose the WFOE option to protect formulas, there was another compelling reason for opening a new plant—pressure from the Chinese government to reduce imports of soft-drink concentrates. The company currently imports concentrates and sells them in hard currency to four joint-venture bottling plants—producing Pepsi Cola, 7 Up, and Mirinda Orange—in which it has equity stakes of up to 15–20 percent. PepsiCo balances foreign exchange through various countertrade and production ventures, such as its joint venture with McCormick & Co. Inc. in Shanghai, which processes spices sourced in China and sells them to the United States. Even though PepsiCo was not a net user of foreign exchange, China expressed dissatisfaction with the use of scarce hard currency to buy soft-drink concentrate. China views soda as a luxury item and refuses to let PepsiCo open any new bottling facilities before localizing concentrate production. Thus, PepsiCo agreed it would produce concentrate within China, selling in renminbi (RMB) to domestic factories and exporting part of the production—expected to average 20–50 percent—to bottling plants in Asia to balance foreign exchange. "This puts the monkey on our back to balance our foreign-exchange requirements," says Peter M.R. Kendall, regional vice president for PepsiCo/North Asia. PepsiCo hopes eventually to source most of the citrus extracts, essential oils, caramel, and other ingredients within China, but finding suppliers that meet international standards is expected to be a problem. Negotiations for the 20-year, $10 million venture began in 1988, and construction was to be completed in June 1990.

"What's in It for China?"

PepsiCo chose the WFOE site in the Huangpu Economic and Technological Development Zone (ETDZ), about 20 miles from the center of Guangzhou. Near Hong Kong, the site offers proximity to shipping lines and convenience for expatriate staff. Perhaps more important, PepsiCo had developed good working relationships with local Guangzhou and Guangdong authorities through its bottling plants in Guangzhou and Shenzhen, and that local support proved important in selling the project in Beijing. As "very visible signs of foreign presence," soft drink production ventures must receive central approval regardless of the size of investment, says Kendall. Huangpu ETDZ authorities acted, in effect, as consultants to PepsiCo in shepherding the project through the approval process involving the central Ministry of Light Industry (MLI), the Ministry of Foreign Economic Relations and Trade (MOFERT), and the State Planning Commission.

MLI proved to be the toughest sell. "The ministry was saying, 'What's in it for China?'" Kendall says. "They put pressure on PepsiCo to give a better deal," in part by initially refusing permission for a WFOE that would sell its products domestically on grounds that WFOEs must produce exclusively for export.

In order to win WFOE approval and demonstrate their long-term commitment to China, PepsiCo agreed to build a neighboring joint-venture plant in partnership with the Chinese soda giant Asia Soft Drinks, which will produce concentrate for new, local soft-drink brands and a product-development lab and training facility to help China develop high-quality soft drinks. The two facilities, which will together employ around 40 people (the same number as planned to staff the WFOE), will also provide training in water treatment, packaging, and the development of new flavors.

Government authorities stipulated that the joint-venture plant use the most modern equipment and made specific demands about staffing, management, expatriate compensation, and training. At the WFOE, however, PepsiCo will have a free hand in staffing and compensation. In the later stages of negotiation, government authorities concerned themselves only with holding PepsiCo to a capital-commitment schedule and negotiating foreign-exchange arrangements. Authorities have promised PepsiCo the WFOE plant will receive "high-technology enterprise" status, providing lower land-use fees and possibly some reduction in taxes. Under Chinese law, PepsiCo would not receive notification of its legal status until the plant's opening in fall 1990.

Soda Market Going Flat

Construction was already under way at the WFOE plant in June 1989, when political upheaval devastated China's tourist trade. Not only were tourists avoiding China, but the domestic austerity campaign had reduced spending power and helped discourage official banquets, which formerly provided much business to companies selling international-name beverages. In addition, tightening restrictions on the import and production of aluminum cans had severe impact on PepsiCo's domestic can business, which accounted for 20 percent of total volume. With plastic-bottle (PET) sales also reduced by austerity, the plants saw a rising volume of returnable-bottle sales, necessitating a bigger truck fleet and glass investment by PepsiCo and associated bottlers. And while before austerity PepsiCo's joint venture plants made some of their sales in foreign-exchange certificates (FEC), sales became almost exclusively in RMB.

Since its initial feasibility study for the WFOE, PepsiCo has lowered sales projections by about 20 percent and is keeping a cautious eye on China's political situation. However, in China's enormous market, PepsiCo believes that even severe constrictions in the short term leave ample room for sales. One sign of encouragement may be the strong support PepsiCo has continued to receive from local Guangzhou officials, despite attempts by Beijing to curtail Guangdong's authority over foreign investment. PepsiCo is confident China will continue to support its sales, Kendall says. "A bottle of Pepsi produced in the PRC is almost entirely a Chinese product. It contributes to the country's economic development."

Questions

1. Based on what you have learned in this chapter, do you believe that PepsiCo's managers effectively analyzed China's environment? Why?

2. Based on what you have learned in the chapter, discuss the problems China's systems present for foreign companies planning to invest in China.

3. What did PepsiCo do to establish a more positive relationship with the Chinese government?

4. What draws foreign investors to China?

5. This case is from 1990. The third edition of this textbook was written in 2006–2007. Thus, for discussion in class, using your Internet, obtain information about PepsiCo's current position in China.

SOURCE: Excerpted from Anne Stevenson-Yany, "Protecting the Pepsi Taste," *The China Business Review* (January–February 1990), pp. 32–33. Reprinted with the permission of The U.S.-China Business Council, Washington, DC.

APPENDIX

An Explanation of the Theory of Comparative Advantage and Currency Exchange Rates

The term *international business* is defined as

> *business whose activities involve the crossing of national borders. This definition includes not only international trade and foreign manufacturing but also encompasses the growing service industry in areas such as transportation, tourism, banking, advertising, construction, retailing, wholesaling, and mass communications.*[77]

International business/trade has taken place for many centuries. Effective international business managers possess a thorough command of the impact of international trade theory and fluctuating currency exchange rates on their organization. The classical theory of comparative advantage attempts to explain why international business/trade occurs. It should be noted, however, that the theory is useful only as framework for analysis. Other factors, such as a company being able to earn more profits by penetrating a foreign market, provide practical explanations for why firms internationalize their operations. (The other factors are explained in Chapter 4.)

The Theory of Comparative Advantage

When countries such as the United States, the world's largest economy, run a (trade) deficit year after year that is chronically at very high levels with little hope of rapid reduction, there is a serious problem (Table A3.1 presents the U.S. trade deficit from 1970 to 1989, 1997, 2002, 2003, and 2007). Among the consequences are excessively high interest rates and a reduction in the funds available to other borrowers. The impact is felt by borrowers as diverse as home buyers, manufacturing corporations, and third-world debtors, all of whom pay higher interest rates because of the enormous borrowing demand. Other adverse consequences include a weak currency that encourages exports but is inflationary for the nation and causes major disruptions in many industries and communities. For example, construction in the United States was once adversely affected by high interest rates, and both automobiles and textiles are industries where domestic employment fell significantly in the face of foreign competition.[78]

Classical trade theory proposes that trade among nations exists because of their factor endowment: land, labor, and capital. If each nation concentrates on producing the goods that require a large amount of its relative abundant factor, those goods will have lower production costs and can therefore be sold for less in the international market. One nation may have superiority over another in producing two or more products. However, according to David Ricardo's classical theory of comparative advantage, that nation may still find it advantageous to concentrate on production of a product that it can produce more efficiently than another country and trade it for other products it needs. As an illustration, assume that the following quantities can be produced per man-day in the United States and Mexico:

Commodity	Output per man-day	
	United States	Mexico
Capital-intensive units	2	1
Labor-intensive units	4	3

TABLE A3.1	The U.S. balance of trade: 1970–1989, 1997, 2002–2003, and 2007 ($ billion)		
Year	Exports	Imports	Balance of Trade
1970	42.7	40.0	2.7
1972	49.2	55.6	−6.4
1974	98.1	102.6	−4.5
1976	115.2	123.5	−8.3
1978	143.7	174.8	−31.1
1980	220.6	244.8	−24.2
1982	212.3	244.1	−31.8
1984	217.9	325.7	−107.9
1986	217.3	370.0	−152.7
1988	322.4	441.0	−118.5
1989	349.7	473.0	−123.3
1997	688.7	899.0	−210.3
2002			−418.0
2003			−489.4
2007	1.62 trillion	2.33 trillion	−711.61

SOURCES: 1970–1989: *Statistical Abstract of the United States: 1989,* p. 786; 1997: Michael M. Weinstein, "Limits of Economic Diplomacy," *The New York Times* (April 8, 1999), p. C1; 2002, 2003: www.cbsnews.com/2004/02/13/national/main600034.shtml; 2007: Alan Tonelson (February 20, 2008), www.americaneconomicalert.org./view_art.asp?prod_ID=2945

Production of capital-intensive units requires more advanced machinery and less labor, while production of labor-intensive units requires more labor and less advanced machinery. Note that the United States has superiority in producing both capital-intensive and labor-intensive units. In the United States, one individual can produce 2 capital-intensive or 4 labor-intensive units, while in Mexico an individual can produce only 1 capital-intensive or 3 labor-intensive units. Prior to the development of the theory of comparative advantage, it was believed that because of its superiority in producing both commodities, there would be no need for the United States to trade with Mexico. Based on the theory of comparative advantage, however, it would be advantageous for the United States to concentrate on the production of capital-intensive goods and trade with Mexico for the labor-intensive units; Mexico would benefit by concentrating on the production of labor-intensive goods and trading with the United States for the capital-intensive goods.

The theory is based on the concept that if the United States and Mexico did not trade—that is, if they both produced the capital- and the labor-intensive units, individuals in the United States would have to spend the equivalent of 1 capital-intensive unit to purchase 2 labor-intensive units (4:2), and individuals in Mexico would have to spend the equivalent of 3 labor-intensive units to purchase 1 capital-intensive unit (3:1). If the United States and Mexico concentrated production (and all other factors, such as transportation costs, were equal), the two nations would benefit if they arranged a trade agreement of approximately 2½ labor-intensive units for 1 capital intensive unit. The United

States would get the equivalent of 2½ labor-intensive units for 1 capital-intensive unit, which is greater than the 2 units it would get if no trade existed, and Mexico would only have to spend the equivalent of 2½ labor-intensive units for 1 capital intensive unit, as opposed to 3 units if no trade existed.

We have explained the theory in terms of units of production. However, money and the fluctuating monetary exchange rates existing among nations must be considered in describing the theory. Monetary exchange rates shift rapidly. For example, on February 3, 1984, U.S.$1 equaled 234 Japanese yen (Japan's dollar-equivalent unit). By March 30, 1986, the exchange rate was U.S.$1 to 180 Japanese yen, and as of March 3, 1991, the exchange rate was U.S.$1 to 135 Japanese yen. At one point, U.S.$1 equaled 89 yen. As of April 27, 2007, U.S.$1 was equal to 119.3 Japanese yen and 0.82 euros. As of March 20, 2008, U.S.$1 equals 99.0 Japanese yen and 0.65 euros—a dramatic drop in its value. When the euro was adopted on January 1, 2002, the U.S. dollar and the euro were just about 1:1 (nearly at par). Fluctuating exchange changes, as will be shown shortly, have a dramatic impact on international business transactions.

To illustrate the impact of fluctuating exchange rates on international business transactions, assume that in the United States it costs $40 to produce the 2 capital-intensive units or the 4 labor-intensive units, and that in Mexico it costs 600 Mexican pesos (MP), Mexico's dollar-equivalent unit, to produce the 1 capital-intensive unit or the 3 labor-intensive units. The cost per unit would therefore be as follows:

	Output per man-day	
Commodity	United States	Mexico
Capital-intensive units	$20 per unit (40/2)	600 MP per unit (600/1)
Labor-intensive units	$10 per unit (40/4)	200 MP per unit (600/3)

Suppose that the monetary exchange rate between the two countries is U.S.$1 to 25 MP. The price per unit translated into U.S. dollars is therefore as follows:

	Output per man-day	
Commodity	United States	Mexico
Capital-intensive units	$20	$24 (600 MP/$25)
Labor-intensive units	$10	$8 (200 MP/$25)

Note that if there were no trade between the two nations, the United States would pay $10 per labor-intensive unit as opposed to (other factors, such as transportation, being equal) $8 if it purchased the unit from Mexico, and Mexico would pay $24 per capital-intensive unit, as opposed to $20 if it purchased the unit from the United States. The concentration of production and the trade between these two countries is therefore ideal, in the sense that both benefit.

Suppose, however, that for political, economic, market, or other reasons, the exchange rate between the two nations fluctuated to U.S.$1 equals 30 MP. The impact on trade would therefore be as follows:

| | Output per man-day | |
Commodity	United States	Mexico
Capital-intensive units	$20	$20 (600 MP/$30)
Labor-intensive units	$10	$6.7 (200 MP/$30)

In this situation, the cost of capital-intensive goods would be the same in both countries. Therefore, both nations would produce capital-intensive units. But it would be advantageous cost-wise for the United States not to produce the labor-intensive units and instead import them from Mexico, where the cost is only $6.7, as opposed to $10 in the United States. The result of this trade scenario between the two countries is that Mexico would eventually attain a surplus trade balance and the United States a deficit. The United States is currently confronted with a huge overall trade deficit, which worries many U.S. politicians and economists. As of 2007, the United States has a huge trade deficit with China, and U.S. politicians have in recent years been trying to reduce the deficit by trying to persuade the Chinese government to strengthen its currency (the yuan) against the U.S. dollar (similar to what they did to Japan in the 1980s).

Suppose that the exchange rate between the two nations fluctuates to U.S.$1 equals 20 MP. Again, assuming all other factors, such as inflation and deflation, being equal, the price per unit would be as follows:

| | Output per man-day | |
Commodity	United States	Mexico
Capital-intensive units	$20	$30 (600 MP/$20)
Labor-intensive units	$10	$10 (200 MP/$20)

In this situation, the cost of the labor-intensive units is the same in both countries, and the cost of the capital-intensive units is less in the United States. In this scenario, it would benefit the United States if it produced both the capital-intensive and the labor-intensive units. On the other hand, cost-wise it would benefit Mexico to produce the labor-intensive units and to import the capital-intensive units from the United States, where the cost is $10 less. In this scenario, the United States would eventually attain a trade surplus and Mexico a trade deficit. It should be pointed out that the U.S. dollar has been weak for several years, but, as shown in Table A3.1, the U.S. trade deficit has kept steadily increasing since 1970.

Limitations of the Trade Theory

It should be pointed out that there are limitations to this trade theory.[79] The theory is based on several incorrect assumptions:

- It assumes that factors of production, land, labor, and capital cannot be moved between nations. But labor and capital can be moved. For example, throughout its industrial era, the United States manipulated its immigration policies, importing relatively inexpensive labor from less developed countries to "man" its industries when a shortage of labor existed. And in early 2007, the media reported that there were about 15 million "cheap" labor immigrants in the United States.

- It assumes that complete information about international trade opportunities exists. With the recent vast advancements in the communications technologies, the world is only now beginning to head in that direction, and nations' political forces that control information flow are still very much dominant.

- It assumes that trading firms in different countries are independent entities. The fact is that multinational corporations establish subsidiaries in many nations.

- It assumes that there is perfect competition. In reality, governments interfere in commerce, and there are monopolies, oligopolies, and cartels. which curb competition.

- It does not recognize technology, know-how, and management and marketing skills as significant factors of production.

- It does not recognize the social aspects of consumers. For example, many U.S. consumers pay $75 for an ounce of imported French perfume rather than $10 an ounce for the same perfume produced locally, simply because of the cachet of French perfume.

- It assumes that goods/commodities are globally standardized. This, of course, is not true; not all goods/commodities are transferable.

Nevertheless, the theory does help one understand the impact of fluctuating exchange rates on nations' trade deficits and surpluses and the risks imposed on enterprises conducting international transactions. Table A3.2 illustrates national concerns.

TABLE A3.2	Impact of Fluctuating Exchange Rates on National Economies
The dollar's ascent 1983 to 1985	Investors funnel funds into the United States attracted by strong growth and high interest rates. As the dollar increases in value, U.S. products become more expensive overseas. Exports plunge. The Reagan administration does nothing.
Plaza Agreement 1985	The United States decides that the dollar is too strong, and the other major economic powers agree. The central banks intervene, helping push the dollar down rapidly and bring the yen and German mark up (currently the euro).
Yen shock Late 1985 to early 1987	The strong yen makes Japanese products more costly in foreign markets, including sales abroad. To soften the impact on its economy, Tokyo eases monetary policy. But the easy-money situation means that more funds are chasing assets at home, starting the sharp run-up in the Japanese stock market and in property taxes.
Tokyo's spending spree Late 1980s	The more muscular yen makes foreign investment cheaper for Japanese companies and investors. In the United States, the Japanese buy everything, from U.S. Treasury bonds to the Pebble Beach golf course. Japanese corporations buy several companies and build dozens of factories in the United States.
Resurgence of American manufacturing Late 1980s[a]	With the weaker dollar, U.S. manufacturers that survived the tough times begin to find that they are competitive again in export markets. The growth in exports helps cushion the economic shock waves from the 1987 stock market crash.
1990s to 2007	The huge U.S. trade deficit has increased steadily over the years (see Table A3.1), especially with China. Due to efforts to reduce the U.S. trade deficit, the U.S. dollar has weakened. U.S. politicians have been prodding the Chinese government to strengthen its yuan in an effort to reduce the huge trade deficit with China. And the U.S. dollar has for a couple decades remained weak against the Japanese yen.

SOURCE: a. "The Week in Review," *The New York Times*, sec. 4 (Sunday, April 26, 1992), p. 1; current media reports.

Relative to the impact of fluctuating exchange rates on international business transactions, the case of Laker Airways (cited in the chapter) serves as an example.

Exercise

a. Suppose that the "per-man-day" cost of producing four pairs of shoes or eight razor blades is 60 yen (y) in Japan and in Portugal it costs 360 escudos (e) to produce two pairs of shoes or six razor blades. (Note: *Portugal's currency is as of January 1, 2002, the euro.*) Suppose that the monetary exchange rate is 1 y equals 8 e: (1) Will production be concentrated in any of the two countries, and will trade take place between the two countries? (2) If production is concentrated, what would be the general impact on the two nations' balance of trade if free trade existed and all other factors remained equal? (You must explain your answer and show the computations.)

b. If you find in (a) that there is no concentration of production in both countries, determine the nearest exchange rate required to generate concentration of production in both countries. (You must explain your answer and show the computations.)

The answers are contained in the *Instructor's Manual.*

● ●

NOTES

1. Robert Ackerman, an advisor to Mitsubishi International, cited in Stephen Kindel, "Staying Competitive in a Shrinking World," *FinancialWorld*, 160, no. 21 (October 15, 1991), p. 22.

2. E. J. Miller and A. K. Rice, *Systems of Organizations* (London: Tavistock, 1967).

3. Rahul Jacob, "Export Barriers the U.S. Hates Most," *Fortune* (February 27, 1989), p. 88.

4. R. Kuttner, "Facing Up to Industrial Policy," *The New York Times Magazine* (April 19, 1992), pp. 22, 26, 27, 42.

5. For a current discussion on the economic integration of nations, see G. R. G. Benito, B. Grogaard, and R. Narula, "Environmental Influences on MNE Subsidiary Roles: Economic Integration and the Nordic Countries, *Journal of International Business Studies*, 34 (2003), pp. 443–456.

6. State of New Jersey Department of Commerce and Economic Development, *Europe in the 1990s* (KPMG Peat Marwick, 1990).

7. For a deeper discussion on this topic, see L. Oxelheim and P. Ghauri, Editors, *European Union and the Race for Foreign Direct Investment in Europe*, International Business and Management Series (Oxford, UK: Elsevier, 2004).

8. R. E. Gut, "The Impact of the European Community's 1992 Project," *Vital Speeches of the Day* (November 1988), pp. 34–37.

9. *Europe in the 1990s*, op. cit.

10. R. Straetz, "U.S. Exporters Should Find the Benefits of Europe 1992: Program Will Outweigh Problems," *Business America* (May 1989), pp. 10–11.

11. L. C. White, "Bold Strategies for a Brave New Market: Federal Express," *Business Month* (August 1989), pp. 32–34.

12. T. Murray, "Bold Strategies for a Brave New Market: 3M," *Business Month* (August 1989), pp. 35–37.

13. *Europe in the 1990s*, op cit.

14. "American Firms in Europe," *The Economist*, 311 (May 13, 1989), pp. 70–71.

15. Ibid.

16. "NAFTA AT SEVEN: Its Impact on Workers in All Three Nations" (Washington, DC: Economic Policy Institute, 2007). www.epinet.org/content.cfm/briefingpapers nafta 01 index

17. Michael Barbaro, "Wal-Mart Profit Falls 26%: Its First Drop in 10 Years," *The New York Times* (August 16, 2006), p. C3.

18. P. R. Cateora and J. M Hess, *International Marketing*, 4th ed. (Homewood, IL: Richard D. Irwin, 1979), p. 262.

19. P. H. Harris and R. T. Moran, *Managing Cultural Differences* (Houston, TX: Gulf Publishing, 1979).

20. "Japan on the Brink," *The Economist* (April 11, 1998), p. 16.

21. See Len Lewis, "Growing Global," *Progressive Grocer,* 78, no. 9 (September 1999), pp. 22–28.

22. See Whitaker Penteado, "Fast-Food Franshices Fight for Brazilian Aficionados." Used with permission of publisher from *Brandweek* (June 7, 1993), p. 20.

23. See Lewis, "Growing Global," op. cit; Penteado, "Fast-Food Franchises Fight for Brazilian Aficionados," op cit.

24. M. Landler and M. Barbaro, "No, Not Always: Wal-Mart Discovers That Its Formula Doesn't Fit Every Culture, *The New York Times* (August 2, 2006), pp. C1, C4.

25. J. R. Zeeman, "Service—The Cutting Edge of Global Competition: What United Airlines Is Learning in the Pacific," Remarks before the annual meeting of the Academy of International Business, Chicago (November 14, 1987).

26. W. W. Rostow, *The Stages of Economic Development* (New York: Cambridge University Press, 1971).

27. This discussion draws on Cateora and Hess, *International Marketing,* op cit., pp. 263–266.

28. For a more current discussion on the above topic, see J. P. Doh, H. Teegen, and R. Mudambi, "Balancing Private and State Ownership in Emerging Markets' Telecommunications Infrastructure: Country, Industry, and Firm Influences," Journal of International Business Studies, 35 (2004), pp. 233–250.

29. W. A. Stoever, "The Stages of Developing Country Policy Toward Foreign Investment," *The Columbia Journal of World Business,* 20, no. 3 (Fall 1985), pp. 6–8.

30. Cited by Kindel, "Staying Competitive in a Shrinking World," op cit., pp. 22–24.

31. "151 Checklists: Decision Making in International Operations," *Business International* (1974), p. 84.

32. Frank Rose, "Think Globally, Script Locally," *Fortune* (November 8, 1999), p. 160.

33. Alex Taylor III, "Danger: Rough Road Ahead," *Fortune* (March 17, 1997), p. 116.

34. "The Culture Is a Challenge (Geographic Expansion) (Wal-Mart's Difficulties in Germany Partly Result From Cultural Differences)," *MMR, HighBeam Research* (December 9, 2002). www.highbeam.com/library/docfreeprint.asp?DOCID=1G1:96071354&key=0C177A

35. See Daniel Gross, "Delphi Inc., Meet Germany Inc.," *The New York Times* (October 16, 2005). www.nytimes.com/2005/10/16/weekinterview/16gross.html?pagewanted=print

36. See Gross, "Delphi Inc., Meet Germany Inc.," op cit.

37. Stoever, "The Stages of Developing Country Policy," op cit.

38. See M. Schuman and M. Ressner, "Disney's Great Leap Into China," *Time,* 166, no. 3 (2006).

39. This case illustration draws from Hideo Sugiura, "How Honda Localizes Its Global Strategy," *Sloan Management Review,* 32, no. 1 (Fall 1990), pp. 77–82.

40. SOURCE: *Honda Motor Corp. Ltd. Annual Report* (March 31, 1995), p. 13. www.honda.com

41. Overseas Private Investment Corporation, *Investment Insurance Handbook,* p. 4, cited in M. C. Schnitzer, M. L. Liebrenz, and K. W. Kubin, *International Business* (Cincinnati, OH: South-Western Publishing, 1985), p. 253.

42. L. T. Wells and E. S. Gleason, "Is Infrastructure Investment Still Risky?" *Harvard Business Review* (September/October 1995), p. 54.

43. For a current discussion on *keiretsu,* see J. NcGuire and S. Dow, "The Persistence and Implications of Japanese Keiretsu Organization," *Journal of International Business Studies,* 34 (2003), pp. 374–388.

44. Edmund Faltermayer, "Does Japan Play Fair?" *Fortune* (September 7, 1992), p. 41.

45. See again Gross, "Delphi Inc., Meet Germany Inc.," op cit.

46. Lionel H. Olmer, "Japan Trip Report: Japan's Drive for Technological Preeminence Challenges U.S.," *Business America* (January, 24, 1983), pp. 6–10.

47. Dan Takahashi, "U.S. in a Preliminary Ruling, Finds South Korea Companies Dumped Chips," *The Wall Street Journal* (April 16, 1998), p. A1.

48. R. Vernon and L. T. Wells Jr., *Manager in the International Economy* (Englewood Cliffs, NJ: Prentice Hall, 1976).

49. U.S. Congress, Office of Technology Assessment, *U.S. Industrial Competitiveness: A Comparison of Steel, Electronics, and Automobiles* (Washington, DC: Government Printing Office, 1981), pp. 11–17.

50. M. A. Hitt, R. E. Hoskisson, and J. S. Harrison, "Strategic Competitiveness in the 1990s: Challenges and Opportunities," *Academy of Management Executive,* 5, no. 2 (May 1991), p. 8.

51. M. Maynard and F. Warner, "Toyota's U.S. Sales Edge Past Ford's," *The New York Times* (August 2, 2006), p. C1.

52. Hitt, Hoskisson, and Harrison, "Strategic Competitiveness in the 1990s: Challenges and Opportunities," op cit.

53. SOURCE: Micheline Maynard, "GM Cutting 30,000 Jobs and Closing Plants," *The New York Times* (November 21, 2005). www.iht.com/articles/2005/11/21/news/gm.php

54. C. Christopher, *The Japanese Mind* (New York: Linden Press, 1983).

55. See R. B. Reich, *The Next American Frontier* (New York: Times Books, 1983).

56. Cateora and Hess, *International Marketing*, op cit., p. 63.

57. Ibid., p. 64.

58. Jacob, "Export Barriers the U.S. Hates the Most," op cit. p. 88.

59. "Snow: China Must Prepare for Shocks," *CNN Money* (October 16, 2005).

60. The information on Laker Airways is drawn from Frederick Gluck, "Global Competition in the 1980's," *Journal of Business Strategy* (Spring 1983), pp. 223–227.

61. Constance L. Hays, "13% Fall in Coca-Cola's Net Tied to Devalued Currencies," *The Wall Street Journal* (April 16, 1998), p. A1.

62. See Darren J. Blakely, "Foreign Exchange Strategies," *MeetingsNet* (June 1, 1998). http://am.meetings net.com/ar/meetings

63. For further study on this subject matter, see R. W. Faff and A. Marshall, "International Evidence on the Determinants of Foreign Exchange Rate Exposure of Multinational Corporations," *Journal of International Business Studies,* 36 (2005), pp. 539–558.

64. Jay Shafriz, *Directory of Personnel Management and Labor Relations* (Oak Park, IL: Moore Publishing, 1980), p. 188.

65. Roy B. Helfgott, "American Unions and Multinational Companies: A Case of Misplaced Emphasis," *Columbia Journal of World Business,* 18, no. 2 (1983), pp. 81–86.

66. See Matt Bai, "The New Boss," *The New York Times Magazine* (January 30, 2005), pp. 38–45.

67. The source of this discussion is Peter Doeringer, *Industrial Relations in International Perspective* (New York: Holmes and Meier, 1981).

68. Albert Blum, *International Handbook of Industrial Relations Contemporary Developments and Research* (Westport, CT: Greenwood Press, 1981), p. 674.

69. This discussion draws from P. J. Dowling and R. S. Schuler, *International Dimensions of Human Resource Management* (Boston: PWS-Kent Publishing, 1990), pp.145–147.

70. Jeff Stinson, "Maquiladoras Challenge Human Resources," *Personnel Journal* (November 1989), p. 92.

71. See Anthony Bianco, "No Union, Please, We're Wal-Mart," *BusinessWeek* (February 13, 2006), pp. 78, 80–81.

72. This case illustration is from the author's memory of a program featured on cable TV's History Channel.

73. *Northern Telecom's Transformation 1985–1995,* pp. 7–8.

74. M. A. Hitt, R. D. Ireland, and R. E. Hoskisson, *Strategic Management* (Cincinnati, OH: South-Western College Publishing, 1999), p. 57.

75. For an in-depth discussion on this topic matter, refer to Cynthia B. Leshin, *Management on the World Wide Web* (Upper Saddle River, NJ: Prentice Hall, 1997).

76. Cateora and Hess, *International Marketing*, op cit., p. 255.

77. D. A. Ball and W. H. McCulloch Jr., *International Business* (Plano, TX: Business Publications, 1985), p. 15.

78. C. M. Korth, "Managerial Barriers to U.S. Exports," *Business Horizons* (March–April 1991), p. 20.

79. Part of this discussion is adopted from S. H. Robock and K. Simmonds, *International Business and Multinational Enterprises,* 3rd ed. (Homewood, IL: Richard D. Irwin, 1983), pp. 39–40.

4

International SWOT Analysis

To U.S. automakers, Asia looks like . . . a place to strike it rich. Weary of competing in the slow-growing, overcrowded markets of North America and Western Europe, they cheer at the thought of millions of potential customers who have yet to buy their first Cavalier, Explorer, or Jeep. General Motors, Ford, and Chrysler [now Daimler Chrysler] executives are streaming into cities like Shanghai, Manila, and Kuala Lumpur to negotiate with government officials, meet with potential dealers, and scout locations for parts depots and assembly plants. "There will be ten million units of worldwide automotive growth in the next ten years," says Ford's international boss, W. Wayne Booker, "and the vast majority of that growth will be in Asia." . . . U.S. automakers are planning a huge sales offensive and their first local production in half a century. Each company is pursuing a separate strategy. GM, the most ambitious, is setting up an integrated Asian production system that utilizes its vast parts-making operations as well as its affiliation with Japanese automakers Isuzu and Suzuki. Ford, meanwhile, is pursuing what it calls a "reasoned approach" that relies on alliances with local partners in select markets like Vietnam and India. Chrysler [now Daimler Chrysler] wants to manufacture in only a few countries; its primary focus is exporting vehicles built in North America.[1] And changes that have taken place in China have presented many opportunities—as well as many threats—for international businesses.[2]

Learning Objectives of the Chapter

The changes taking place throughout the globe are creating many opportunities and threats for business enterprises. These opportunities and threats will lure many domestic enterprises into the international business arena; they will entice those firms that rely only slightly on revenues derived from international business into expanding and relying more on their international operations. This means that more and more corporations will have to develop strategies and establish objectives to internationalize their domestic business operations or to expand their current international business operations. This means that these businesses will have to be aware of their internal strengths and weaknesses with respect to their ability to cease the international opportunities and/or combat the international threats, thus requiring a SWOT (strengths, weaknesses, opportunities, and threats) analysis. After studying this chapter, you should be able to discuss the following:

1. Assessing the opportunities and threats that cause domestic firms to internationalize their operations

2. Assessing the firm's strengths and weaknesses

3. Global corporations

4. The strategic approaches used by international corporations

5. The internal organizational factors managers must understand before they attempt to internationalize their enterprises' business operations

6. International strategic and tactical objectives

7. The areas in which international objectives should be established

8. The impact of the Internet on international business

Why Firms Internationalize Their Operations

Historically, domestic enterprises have internationalized their business operations either to seize opportunities or to deal with threats, or both.[3] For example, as was pointed out in Chapter 3, the European Union's (EU) efforts to become more unified presented both opportunities and threats for non-EU business enterprises. Practical Perspective 4.1 lists some of the corporations that in the past developed strategies to seize the opportunities and/or combat the threats anticipated by the EU unification. The advent of the Internet as a means of conducting international business also presents opportunities and threats. The ensuing sections discuss the opportunities and threats that cause domestic enterprises to internationalize their operations.

PRACTICAL PERSPECTIVE 4-1

Examples of Firms That
Reacted to the EU's Unification Aims

The popular press reported many cases of external firms acting to take advantage of the opportunities and/or to combat the threats presented by the EC-92 (when the EC [now the EU] member nations were to become officially unified). The Whirlpool Corporation entered into a $2 billion joint venture to penetrate the European appliance market. The International Paper Company made a $350 million bid for a French paper maker. Shearson Lehman Hutton Inc. expanded its investment banking offices in Milan and Madrid. Coca-Cola started construction of one of the world's largest canning plants in France and has revamped its organizational chart to put greater emphasis on the EC. Citicorp (now Citygroup), already the most prominent non-European bank in Europe, purchased banks in Belgium, Italy, and Spain.

AT&T built a $220 million semiconductor plant in Spain. Connecticut Mutual set up a Luxembourg-based company, CM Transnational, to sell life insurance. American International Group restructured its $500 million European property and casualty insurance operations. AIG has merged most of its operations into one new company, UNAT Europe, replacing 13 different national companies. The U.S.-based Scott Paper Company started planning for EC-92 because it expected to benefit from simplified border restrictions and the deregulation of trucking, grocery distribution, and retailing. Federal Express established regional counsels in Belgium and the United Kingdom to stay close to political developments in the EC at all times. To adapt to the anticipated fierce competition in the EC, 3M formed European Management Action Teams consisting of representatives from management, R&D, sales and marketing, and finance. These teams aimed to integrate individual units' business plans and blend them into a Europe-wide strategy in order to compete on a pan-European basis.

SOURCE: Adapted from S. Greenhouse, "U.S. Corporations Expand in Europe for '92 Prospects," *The New York Times* (March 13, 1989), pp. 1, 6; R. W. King, S. J. Dryden, and J. Kapstein, "Who Is That Knocking on Foreign Doors? U.S. Insurance Salesmen," *Business Week* (March 6, 1989), pp. 84–85; H. Lampert, "Bold Strategies for a Brave New Market: Scott Paper Company," *Business Month* (August 1989), pp. 39–41; L. C. White, "Bold Strategies for a Brave New Market: Federal Express," *Business Month* (August 1989), pp. 32–34; T. Murray, "Bold New Strategies for a Brave New Market: 3M," *Business Month* (August 1989), pp. 35–37. For a more current discussion on this topic, see L. Oxelheim and P. Ghauri, Editors, *European Union and the Race for Foreign Direct Investment in Europe*, International Business and Management Series (Oxford, UK: Elsevier, 2004).

Opportunities and Threats

Opportunity Reasons

The opportunity reasons for internationalizing operations include greater profits, appearance of new markets, faster growth in new markets, obtaining new products for the domestic market, and globalization of financial markets.

Greater Profits

Many domestic firms have internationalized their operations because their managers saw the opportunity to earn greater profits by charging higher prices in a higher-per-capita-income foreign country where a high demand for the product or service existed or where there was less competition. Enterprises have also internationalized their operations because their managers determined that they could earn higher profits by attaining greater economies of scale with foreign expansion. Additionally, many enterprises have been able to earn greater profits by producing in a country where labor was cheaper and/or where materials cost less than at home.

Selling the Product at Higher Prices. Companies in many countries, especially in less developed countries (LDCs), can often sell their products at a higher price in the more advanced countries. For example, in China one can purchase a bottle of Tsingtao beer for about U.S. $0.50. The same bottle of beer sells for about U.S. $1.50 in the United States. Thus, it is more profitable for the Chinese producer to sell its beer in the United States as well as in other richer countries. Today (2007), a great many products made in China are sold in the United States. And many U.S. businesses, such as Levi's, actually sell their products in foreign markets—both rich and poor—at a much higher price than they do at home because of the American mystique. Many young people throughout the globe are attracted to U.S. products and are willing to pay even beyond their economic means just because of the American mystique. Numerous retailers from poor countries, such as the Dominican Republic, come to the United States to buy products, which they sell at a high price back home because they are from the United States. In Honduras, where labor is relatively low cost, a U.S. company manufactures shirts, exports them back to the United States, and then exports them back to Honduras, where they are sold at a much higher price because of the U.S. label.

For illustration purposes, imagine the following scenario: A company's annual domestic market share is 110,000 units, its sales price per unit is $100, its variable costs per unit amount to $70, and its fixed costs total $3 million annually. This enterprise's before-tax earnings would be $300,000, computed as follows:

Number of units sold, 110,000

Profit margin per unit ($100–$70), $30

Income before fixed costs and taxes, $3,300,000

Fixed costs, $3,000,000

Earnings before taxes, $300,000

Assume that the firm determined that if it exported to a certain foreign market, it could increase the unit sales price there to $110; that the foreign market share would be 20,000 units; and that it would incur additional costs of $20 per unit to modify those units to fit the specific market's needs and to ship them overseas. In this situation, the company would earn, before taxes, an additional $400,000, computed as follows:

Additional units sold, 20,000

Before tax profit margin ($110 – $70 – $20), $20

Additional earnings before taxes, $400,000

Greater Economies of Scale. To demonstrate the case in which the firm can obtain larger profits by attaining greater economies of scale, assume that the company determined that due to market and/or other conditions (such as foreign government restrictions), it could not increase the price to $110 as illustrated above, that it could sell the unit in the foreign market for only the same $100 domestic price. In this situation, due to the attainment of greater economies of scale, the company would still realize an additional $200,000 before tax earnings, computed as follows:

Additional units sold, 20,000

Profit margin ($100 – $70 – $20), $10

Additional earnings before taxes, $200,000

For example, Korea's five automobile manufacturers in 1997 had plans to increase their worldwide vehicle-making capacity by 60% by 2002. Their aim was to develop additional capacity to gain the economies of scale required to become more competitive in the global marketplace.[4] Today (2007), Korea's car manufacturers, especially Hyundai, are powerful competitors in the U.S. market.

Cheaper Labor and/or Materials. The cost of labor and materials varies among countries. Many less developed nations, to attract foreign investments, have developed a capable workforce. The cheaper costs and the capable workforce in a country will sometimes enable foreign firms to realize greater profits if they transfer their manufacturing operations there.

To illustrate the instance where cheaper labor and/or cheaper materials in foreign markets contribute to greater profits, suppose a corporation determined that if it established operations in a foreign country, it would incur an additional $800,000 in fixed costs, but the variable costs for the units produced abroad would be reduced by 50% to $35 per unit, and the $20 per unit exporting costs would be reduced to $2. In this scenario, the firm would earn, before tax, an additional $460,000, computed as follows:

Additional units sold, 20,000

Before-tax profit margin ($100 – $35 – $2), $63

Earnings before fixed costs/taxes, $1,260,000

Less additional fixed costs, $800,000

Additional earnings before taxes, $460,000

For example, U.S. clothing, electronics, watch-making, and numerous other industries have transferred some or most of their operations to foreign locations in pursuit of lower costs. For instance, to help enhance its competitiveness in the 1990s, General Electric (GE) shifted some of its appliance manufacturing operations to various parts of the world where labor was cheaper—its gas ranges were made in Mexico.[5] Asia's low-cost labor, especially in China, continuously draws investment from the rich countries, such as the United States and Japan. For example, Delphi Corporation once paid its U.S. unionized workers $27 an hour, and when it computed the workers' benefits, it came to more like $65. In China, Delphi paid its workers about $3 an hour, and about a third of it went to medical and pension benefits.[6]

As another example, a U.S. corporation (name omitted) owns a multitude of companies worldwide. One company it owns manufactures jewelry for global sales. The company itself is divided into several subcompanies. One is located in New York City, and its objective is to design the jewelry. The designers regularly travel to the major world's markets to assess current trends and to obtain ideas for designing new products. The cost of living in New York City is high, but that is where creative people want to live. The design is then sent to an engineering company in Providence, Rhode Island, where engineers design the manufacturing process. The cost of living in Providence is substantially lower than in New York City, and because there are a few technology universities in the region, there are ample personnel available there. The engineering company then sends its manufacturing designs to another company in Southeast China, where labor is very cheap, for manufacturing. From there, it goes to sales companies throughout the globe. The designers in New York City keep a very close watch on the engineers in Providence and on the manufacturers in China. The performance evaluation of these three companies by the parent corporation is based on how well the jewelry sells worldwide.

The positive aspect of this is that transferring production to lower-cost countries results in consumer products at a much lower price. Of course, there is always a negative to this—the loss of jobs at home.

Emerging Markets

Population expansion, income growth, and technological advancements around the globe have created new markets and demands and, thus, new business opportunities. Many domestic firms have internationalized their operations to meet those new demands. For example, Motorola, Inc. reorganized its operations to tap into the huge market for chips used by Japanese companies to manufacture consumer goods.[7] Xircom, Inc., which manufactured pocket-size adapters for portable notebook computers, targeted the EU in 1991 because of the increased popularity of portable computers there.[8] Kobs & Draft, a U.S. direct marketer, expanded into foreign markets at a rapid pace because common U.S. technologies had been reaching the rest of the world, therefore creating a demand for its services.[9]

Automobile executives around the globe have for many years been drooling at the vision of hundreds of millions of potential drivers in China. For example, W. Wayne Booker, who was the executive vice president for international operations of Ford Motor Company (and who became the vice chairman in 1996) once indicated that his first priority for the 1990s was China.[10] As of 2007, Ford Motor Company was selling Fords, Volvos, Jaguars, and Land Rovers in China. For the better part of the past decade, Cisco's India unit has been developing the means to serve the group's largest customers around the world. Now (2005), with strong domestic demand driving a resurgent Indian economy, the U.S. technology products company has set its sights on the subcontinent itself.[11] Saks Fifth Avenue announced on April 18, 2006, that it planned to open its luxury stores in China because it is the world's fastest-growing market in the world, starting in Shanghai in 2008.[12] In 2006, GE Real Estate planned a launch fund to invest in China markets.[13] Sheldon Adelson, the shrewdest investor in Las Vegas, plans to turn Macau, the gambling capital of China, into "the biggest, glitziest gambling Mecca the world has ever seen."[14] In 2006, Las Vegas' Sands Hotel and gambling casino planned to open up operations in Macau in the near future.

In the 1990s, Microsoft made plans to roll out its new PC technology, known as the Venus project (the box), by the end of October 1999. The box, with TV-customized software, lets users read e-mail, surf the Internet, and do simple word processing while sitting in front of a television with a remote keyboard. Microsoft planned to sell the box in China, where then more than 300 million households owned a television but only 2 million owned PCs.[15] For manufacturers such as Emerson Electric, China offered enormous potential. Rural villages in China needed and could afford Emerson's small electric generators. Emerson also had opportunities in the rest of Asia, where newly affluent populations have been demanding increasing numbers of air conditioners and refrigerators.[16]

Faster Growth in Emerging Markets

Many domestic organizations have a strong growth orientation. These firms often enter foreign markets because they can grow at a faster rate there than they can in the established domestic market.[17] For instance, Asian and European computer markets were once stronger than the U.S. market partly because they lagged behind the United States in computer installations. This enabled U.S. computer companies to grow much faster in Asia and Europe than at home. As an example, in 1989, Intel Corporation's European sales were growing twice as fast as they were in the U.S. market.[18] Fusion Systems, in 1999 a division of Eaton Corporation of Maryland, which made sophisticated industrial equipment, began penetrating foreign markets in 1975. At that time, Fusion had 15 employees and $450,000 in annual sales; in 1989, it had 320 employees and $33 million in annual sales—35% from overseas; and from 1985 to 1990, it grew at the rate of 25%.[19] In 1996, Guess Inc., the U.S. jeans maker, targeted expansion into Europe for aggressive growth.[20] Frito-Lay planned to continue its rapid growth by seizing international business opportunities; for example, to improve its European market position, it purchased United Biscuits Holdings PLC (headquartered in the United Kingdom).[21] Companies such as McDonald's, Coca-Cola, and other chains continue entering nearly all markets—both rich and poor.

Obtaining New Products/Services for the Home Market

Many individuals from the home market travel abroad and develop a desire for a product or service that they would like to have available in their home market. For example, English ales, German beers, and French wines are exports/imports that sell well in the U.S. market; Disney's service theme park was imported by Japanese companies, and the service sold well there. Domestic enterprises therefore internationalize their operations to obtain products or services for domestic consumers. If they do not and their competitors do, their competitors will eventually have a competitive advantage over them.

Furthermore, many food products needed at home but grown in another country, such as bananas, must be imported. And many food products grown at home in one season, when the demand for them is year-round, must be imported from countries where they grow during a different season. Rubber tree plants do not grow on U.S. soil, so the product must be imported to meet market demands.

Globalization of Financial Markets

In recent decades, there has been an expansion in the ways in which international business can be financed. This growth in financial options has been the catalyst for the expansion of international business. These new tools include the International Monetary Fund, as discussed in Chapter 3, created in 1945 by the United Nations to encourage and aid world trade, and the World Bank, created by the United Nations for the purpose of encouraging the extension of loans to LDCs. Banks such as Dai-ichi Kangyo Bank and Bank Nationale de Paris have grown into international organizations that draw on a variety of investors from many parts of the world.[22] And South Korea is quietly becoming a large investor in foreign countries—it has become the world's largest investor in China, for example.[23] Citigroup, one of the world's largest banks, has been reaching out to foreign markets where the growth rate is much higher than at home.[24]

Threat Reasons

The threat reasons for internationalizing operations include protection from declining demand in the home market, acquisition of raw materials, acquisition of managerial know-how and capital, protection of the home market, and protection from imports.

Protection From Declining Demand in the Home Market

Demand for a firm's product or service may be low in the home market due to recessionary conditions, a saturated market, or a declining product life cycle. Many firms have been able to hedge against recessions at home and maintain their growth by expanding into foreign markets. For example, in the late 1980s, many U.S. technology corporations found themselves headed for a slump in domestic sales. To offset the slump, many of these companies entered the European and Asian markets. For instance, the market for chips in the United States went flat in the 1980s, but U.S. firms such as International CMOS Technology Inc. and Microsoft Corporation did well as a result of booming sales in Europe and Asia. Microsoft's senior vice president for international operations, Jeremy Butler (now retired), once said that a firm with overseas sales has a much better chance of surviving because it does not put all its eggs in one basket.[25]

By 1989, several U.S. semiconductor equipment makers, such as PerkinElmer Corporation, were dropping out of business. Applied Materials, Inc., however, was making 40% of its sales in Japan. Applied Materials was doing well partly because it got its foot in the door early; it established its own subsidiaries in Japan in the 1970s. It gained experience in dealing with Japanese customers, therefore eliminating its dependence on Japanese representatives, third parties that increase costs.[26]

Because the U.S. market was saturated, dozens of U.S. insurance companies, including Prudential, Equitable Life, and Connecticut Mutual Life, aggressively penetrated new global markets, including China.[27] Philip Morris Company realized that the domestic cigarette market would shrink because of Americans' evolving health consciousness. It thus expanded into foreign markets[28] (refer again to Case 2.1 in Chapter 2). Even though Anheuser-Busch, the beer-brewing company, controlled 43% of the U.S. beer market, its domestic sales growth was slowing dramatically. The analyst Emanuel Goldman of PaineWebber Inc. had estimated that Busch's profits would grow less than 1% in 1993, to $1 billion, as sales had risen by a mere 2%, to $11.6 billion. "That forced the brewer to tap into thirstier regions abroad."[29] (Anheuser-Busch's recent globalization strategies are discussed in subsequent chapters.) And recognizing that the U.S. market was close to saturation point, Merrill Lynch, a U.S. financial services provider, looked outside its own borders to capture more customers. According to its CEO, David Komansky, it aimed to make non-U.S. revenues account for 50% of its business within five years.[30] By the end of 2006, Merrill Lynch had offices in 37 countries and territories and total client assets of approximately U.S. $1.6 trillion (www.ml.com).

Furthermore, emerging markets such as Argentina, Brazil, India, Mexico, Poland, South Africa, South Korea, Turkey, the ASEAN region (Indonesia, Malaysia, Singapore,

Thailand, and Vietnam), and the Chinese Economic Area (China, Hong Kong, and Taiwan) have opened up to foreign investment and trade, thus providing many commercial opportunities for foreign businesses.[31]

To illustrate this aspect mathematically, assume the same conditions used to demonstrate the attainment of greater profits. Suppose that the company's market share declined from 110,000 units annually to 104,000. If this happened, the enterprise's before-tax earnings would decline from $300,000 to $120,000, computed as follows:

Number of units sold, 104,000

Profit margin, $30

Income before fixed costs and taxes, $3,120,000

Fixed costs, $3,000,000

Earnings before taxes, $120,000

If the corporation internationalized its operations, as illustrated in the above discussion on greater profits, it could maintain its profit margin or even increase it. Yet numerous U.S. companies, rather than going abroad, to survive, cut their selling prices by cutting on the quality of the materials they use to produce their products. Hence, where U.S.-made products were once known the world over as high-quality products, today they are known the world over as expensive, low-quality products. And some U.S. companies, to survive, appealed to Americans' patriotism: Buy our product, even if it costs more and is of lower quality than foreign-made products, because it was made in the United States.

Acquisition of Raw Materials

Many domestic manufacturers depend on and import raw materials available in foreign countries. To be assured of the necessary raw materials, numerous enterprises have set up operations overseas. For example, rubber, which is required by numerous U.S. manufacturers, is not available in the continental United States, thus tire-producing firms must acquire rubber from other countries—those in Southeast Asia, for instance. Likewise, U.S. oil companies, in part because of the expectation that availability of oil on U.S. land will diminish, search the world over for new petroleum reserves. It's a form of "stockpiling"; that is, "save yours for the future and use someone else's in the interim." In the case of China, it depends on foreign oil, and oil trade between Saudi Arabia and China exceeded U.S. $15 billion in 2005.[32]

Acquisition of Managerial Know-How and Capital

Enterprises sometimes must go abroad to obtain the managerial know-how and capital that they lack but need to improve their operations. For example, in recent years, there has been a booming demand for travel in Russia. The Russian airline, Aeroflot, was once one of the least efficient airlines in the world. To deal with this problem, the Russian carrier's management shopped around for Western partners who could bring the managerial know-how and capital it needed to meet its expansion demands.[33] As of summer 2006, Aeroflot served 87 destinations in 47 countries and had extensive growth plans.[34] Another example is the shortage of people with IT skills in the United States. But countries such as India, China, and

Russia have an abundance of experienced IT people, forcing many U.S. corporations to outsource these functions.[35] In the case of MNCs in Japan, by the 1980s they had acquired manufacturing and engineering know-how at home but lacked creative research and development (R&D) personnel, thus they established numerous research centers in the United States, where ample creative R&D personnel existed.

Protection of the Home Market

Many firms have internationalized their operations to protect their home market. For example, a firm services a domestic manufacturer that, for its own reasons, decides to set up subsidiary operations abroad. The service enterprise would be wise to follow and provide the services required by the manufacturer's foreign subsidiaries. Otherwise, an aggressive competitor that gets its "foot in the door" through the manufacturer's foreign subsidiary may soon take over the service activities in the domestic market as well. For example, insurance, financial, and accounting enterprises that provide services to other enterprises would fit this mode. Furthermore, numerous U.S. companies are currently (2007) outsourcing many of their service jobs to areas with cheaper labor areas as a way to remain competitive at home.[36]

Protection From Imports

Foreign competitors often hold an advantage over domestic firms because they have access to cheaper labor and/or materials in a foreign country. To remain competitive, domestic firms must often transfer their production activities to a foreign country to obtain the same cost advantages the foreign competitors enjoy. For example, many of the parts used to manufacture U.S.-produced automobiles are actually manufactured abroad, especially in China. Practical Perspective 4.2 presents the case of Applied Digital Data Services, which transferred its manufacturing operations from the United States abroad because its chief competitors who had already gone abroad had access to much cheaper material costs.

PRACTICAL PERSPECTIVE 4-2

Applied Digital Data Systems Transfers Manufacturing Abroad

Applied Digital Data Systems (ADDS) was a wholly owned subsidiary of NCR Corporation [NCR sold ADDS in the mid-1990s], which produced terminals for both its parent company and for other computer OEMs. Founded in 1969 and acquired by NCR in 1981, the firm put heavy emphasis on a flexible assembly operation that offered quick response—and reliable just-in-time (JIT) delivery—to its customers. The "flex" system was devised as part of ADDS' overall strategy for achieving competitive advantage in returning to U.S. soil. Not many years before, however, that notion might have seemed a bit paradoxical. In the early 1980s, the company found itself at a distinct cost disadvantage with respect to its chief competitors. Most of them had already shifted manufacturing operations to the Far East—which was already dominating many of the core technologies for producing TV and display-terminal components.

It wasn't so much a question of labor costs. "The thing that defeated us in those days was material costs," said David G. Laws, then president and CEO of ADDS. "We were buying materials in the USA at USA prices; and our competitors

Why Do Firms Internationalize?

It is not always clear whether firms' internationalization strategies are to seize opportunities or to combat threats. For example, a few years ago, PepsiCo's management recognized that its U.S. markets were mature and that it was unlikely to realize profits attempting to capture a market share in cola drinks from the formidable Coca-Cola Company. To deal with the situation, PepsiCo's management developed a strategy to cash in on changing eating and drinking habits in the rapidly industrializing parts of the world.[37] Was PepsiCo's strategy stimulated by the threatening situation in its home market or by its desire to seize the new opportunities that arose in foreign markets? In other words, if there had been no threats in its home market, would PepsiCo's management still have developed a strategy to seize the new opportunities in the foreign markets? Probably yes.

Furthermore, as pointed out above, many U.S. MNCs are currently (2007) outsourcing many of their IT functions to India. Executives in some of these companies claim that they are outsourcing these U.S. service jobs abroad because they can't find ample qualified personnel at home, but many U.S. residents are accusing these companies of outsourcing these jobs simply to obtain cheaper labor. Thus, are these companies seizing opportunities presented by offshore cheaper labor or combating threats because there is a shortage of skilled IT labor at home?

Strengths and Weaknesses

As suggested above, environmental changes, which are detected by managers being aware of changes taking place in the home and in the global market, often require that firms develop strategies to internationalize their businesses or to expand their foreign operations. To help them develop effective international strategies, along with total familiarity with the external environment, managers must be aware of their enterprises' internal conditions; they must know the firm's strengths and weaknesses. Knowledge of their firm's internal factors will help managers develop wise strategies for penetrating a foreign market or for coping with environmental changes. Basically, managers need to determine how much money the firm has access to, including cash on hand, borrowing power, and ability to sell stock, which can be used to finance the strategy; the nature of its physical assets; and its personnel's capabilities and strengths.

Foreign Sources of Finance

Even if an enterprise has access to the funds required to finance the expansion, managers can inquire about the availability of financial assistance in the foreign market. The governments of many foreign countries make special concessions to foreign firms that bring them the technologies they believe will aid in their nations' development efforts. For example, the government of Morocco was once actively seeking foreign investment in its tourism sector. To attract investment, it offered several incentives, such as the possibility of 100% foreign ownership; tax exemptions of up to 10 years, depending on the location of investment; and the availability of long-term, low-interest financing.[38] (For another illustration, read Practical Perspective 4.3.)

PRACTICAL PERSPECTIVE 4-3

Bangkok's Strategies to Draw Foreign Investments

Bangkok, famed for its tourist attractions and warm hospitality, was attracting more businesspeople than sightseers.... Thailand was wavering on the brink of becoming an important international business hub and opportunity knocked for those who understood this country's native culture and its business and economic climate.... One of the reasons why many multinationals decided to do business in Thailand is that the Thai government was favorable to foreign trade.... Thai government development policies, stated under the Sixth Five-Year Development Plan (1987–92), restricted the public sector to a supporting, coordinating, and advisory role, while fostering activity and growth in the private sector.

The Office of the Board of Investments (OBI) encouraged development in key industrial segments such as telecommunications, building supplies, medical supplies, and electronics and other technologies by offering privileges and incentives for businesses that supported governmental policy.... Encouragement was offered in a number of forms, including holidays or reductions in corporate income taxes, exemptions or reductions on import duty, and exclusion of dividends from taxation.... The Thai government also offered guarantees against price controls, state competition, nationalization, the formation of state monopolies, or the granting of special privileges to government agencies or enterprises.

SOURCE: Excerpted from Bill Bruce, "Thailand: The Next NIC?" *The International Executive* (November–December 1990), pp. 35–37. Copyright © 1990. John Wiley & Sons, Inc., New York. All rights reserved. Reprinted by permission of publisher.

Nature of the Firm's Physical Assets and Personnel Competencies

Managers also need to obtain information about the enterprise's physical assets and their current state. Is their manufacturing capacity capable of producing for the foreign market? Or are new manufacturing means needed? Furthermore, managers must obtain information about their firm's personnel competencies in relation to the company's international strategy. Does the enterprise have the personnel capable of producing for the foreign market(s)? Does it have personnel with the ability to manage the international operations? (This issue is discussed in Chapters 7 and 8.) Again, the governments of many foreign countries will help foreign firms finance machinery and factories and will provide trained personnel, or assist in training personnel, as a means of attracting technologies to aid in accomplishing their nation's developmental objectives.

The firm's internal conditions also affect how it enters a foreign market. Two fundamental approaches to conducting business in a foreign country are by exporting to it or by manufacturing in it (discussed more thoroughly in Chapter 5). Exporting involves manufacturing at home and shipping the goods to the foreign market. Exporting generally requires less investment than manufacturing abroad. If the firm is cash-strapped, it has idle equipment, and its personnel are not highly competent in international business, the firm may prefer to export. However, by producing abroad, the company can often save on the costs of transportation, labor, and materials, as well as on tariffs. Therefore, if an enterprise has adequate cash to invest, it has international managerial know-how, the foreign demand justifies the investment, and the foreign environment is conducive to the investment, it may want to produce abroad. (The approaches to entering a foreign market are discussed in Chapter 5.)

Lead From Strength

Management needs to know what the strengths of the enterprise are. A business should always "lead from strength"; that is, it should focus on doing what it can do better than its competitors. For example, a firm's strength may be engineering and design, so it may be more efficient for the firm to farm its manufacturing out to a company whose strength is manufacturing. For instance, Apple's (former) vice president Al Eisenstat once said, "If I can loop off one area of activity and say, 'Gee, I can join with such and such company,' then I can focus my resources on what I do best."[39] Firms such as Apple, Nike, and IBM have established themselves as design, engineering, and marketing companies, farming out much of their manufacturing to those who are able to do it cheaper and better. Maatschappij Van Berkel's Patent N.V., a Dutch-based multinational supplier of weighing and food processing equipment, met competitive cost pressures by outsourcing its manufacturing and engineering activities and transforming itself into a sales and service company.[40]

Furthermore, a firm may be strong in production but weak in conducting foreign business. This firm may therefore have to form a joint venture or enter into an alliance with an enterprise that is strong in conducting foreign business.[41] (Joint ventures and strategic alliances are discussed more thoroughly in Chapter 5.) Basically, organizations enter into a joint venture or an alliance to

share costs and risks,

gain additional technical and market knowledge,

complement each other,

serve an international market,

strengthen themselves against other competitors, and

develop industry standards together.[42]

As Jack Welch (former CEO) of GE once put it, "Tomorrow's organization will be boundaryless. It will work with outsiders as closely as if they were insiders."[43] Managers should be aware that joint ventures and alliances can backfire, especially when one of the partners becomes stronger by learning more than the other(s). The stronger partner may break up the alliance and go on its own, which may harm the weaker partner. (For an illustration, read Practical Perspective 4.4, the classic case of Schwinn Bicycle Co.)

PRACTICAL PERSPECTIVE 4-4

Bury Thy Teacher

In October 1992, Chicago's 97-year-old Schwinn Bicycle Co., the grand name in American bicycles, filed for bankruptcy. On the other side of the world, Antony Lo took a breather from promoting his high-priced mountain bikes at the Tokyo International Cycle Show to deliver an eloquent eulogy for Schwinn, the company that Lo helped bury. "Without Schwinn, we never would have grown to where we are today," said Lo, the polished president of Taiwan's Giant Manufacturing Co.... "We learned many basic things from them: quality, value, service." Down in Hong Kong, in his office in a converted factory near the colony's mammoth container port, Jerome Sze, the managing director and a large shareholder of Shenzhen, China's publicly traded China Bicycles Co., also paid his respects to the American company that helped him grow. "Schwinn," said Sze, "helped to promote our products in the U.S." ...

[The] great American company lost its way and, through management blunders, created powerful competitors that ultimately did it in. Said Scott Montgomery, president of Cannondale Japan, a wholly owned unit of the successful Georgetown, Connecticut high-end bike company: "After Schwinn built them up (Giant and China Bicycles), they ate Schwinn." ...

Going overseas in the 1970s, Schwinn was more concerned with moving production out of the USA than with selling abroad. "Schwinn was obsessed with cutting costs," says Cannondale Japan's Montgomery, "instead of innovation." It also panicked when its workers went on strike, and instead of negotiating a settlement with the workers, Schwinn closed the plant and sent its equipment and engineers to Giant's factory in Taichung ... Schwinn began its foreign campaign by sourcing many of its bicycles from Japan ... As part of its new partnership with Giant, Schwinn handed over everything—technology, engineering, volume—that Giant needed to become a dominant bikemaker ... Says an executive of a U.S. competitor, "Schwinn gave the franchise to Giant on a silver platter." ...

Dazed by Giant's aggressive brand-name push, Schwinn tried to protect itself by forging a new alliance, this time with Jerome Sze's China Bicycle Co. It began buying CBC's bikes and selling them under the Schwinn name. ... Until Schwinn went into business with China Bicycles, CBC's main business in the U.S. was supplying commodity house-brand bikes to Sears and other mass merchandisers from its low-cost factory in Shenzhen, in the heart of southern China's capitalist revolution. ... But Schwinn taught CBC about the U.S. specialty dealer market, raised the Chinese factory's quality standards and lent it credibility. "CBC came light-years in a short period of time because of a lot of technology transfer from Schwinn," said Bicycling's [editor and publisher, J. C.] McCullagh. Sze subsequently used all the knowledge he gleaned from Schwinn to help bolster his business supplying bicycles to the European operations of bike companies such as Scott and France's MBK (owned by Japan's Yamaha).

Burned once by Giant, Schwinn tried to dissuade China Bicycles from developing its own brand-name business in the USA. But that didn't stop Sze. In 1990, despite Schwinn's opposition, Sze and his Shenzhen partner together acquired a medium-size USA bicycle importer and distributor, which owned the Diamond Back name. That gave CBC its own U.S. brand name and distribution channels. Diamond Back competed directly with Schwinn and was particularly strong on the West Coast. With Giant, China Bicycles, and other competitors taking big bites out of its market share, Schwinn was finally forced to file for bankruptcy in October. It still imports bikes from its two former students and sells them under the Schwinn name. But production of its own bikes in the USA was down to under 10,000 units a year, sold under the Paramount name of high-priced racing bikes.[a]

In 2001, Schwinn was purchased at a bankruptcy auction by Pacific Cycle, a company known for mass-market brands. In 2004, Pacific Cycle was itself, in turn, acquired by Dorel Industries.[b]

SOURCES:

a. Excerpted from Andrew Tanzer, "Bury Thy Teacher," Forbes (December 21, 1992), pp. 90–95. Reprinted by permission of Forbes Magazine © 1999.

b. www.answers.com/topic/schwinn bicycle company

It should be noted that foreign countries' environments generally have an effect on a firm's strengths and weaknesses. For example, an organization may possess a strong ability to distribute a product in one nation because it is capable of dealing with that country's distribution laws and practices. At the same time, it may possess a weak capability to distribute in another country because it lacks the ability to deal with that nation's distribution laws and practices. For instance, international business transactions are either in cash or in barter trade (discussed in Chapter 5). Many enterprises have experience in cash transactions but not in barter trade transactions. In the latter case, if the enterprise wishes to penetrate a foreign market where barter trade is required, it may have to form a partnership with a firm that has experience in barter trade; for example, many Brazilian companies have over the years developed strong skills in barter trade.

Also, an enterprise may possess the ability to differentiate a product in order to fit the needs of a specific country's culture and at the same time lack the ability to differentiate in order to fit another country's cultural needs. U.S. car manufacturers, for example, have historically possessed the capability to differentiate their automobiles to fit the needs of some countries but not the needs of others, such as England, where the steering wheel is located on the right-hand side of the automobile. In this case, if a U.S. car manufacturer wanted to penetrate the British car market, it might have to form a partnership with a car manufacturer that has the capability of producing cars with the steering wheel on the right-hand side.

Firms also form strategies to acquire knowledge. That is, each partner has to learn about the other's strengths. But some firms learn more and faster than others—as in the case of Schwinn Bicycle Company, presented in Practical Perspective 4.4. It seems as if Schwinn's partners learned faster and much more than it did. Furthermore, learning through alliances can be a difficult, frustrating, and often misunderstood process, and, it has been argued on the basis of observation, creating a successful alliance learning environment is the exception rather than the rule.[44] The reasons for failure include the following:

- The alliance knowledge was undervalued.
- The necessary "connections" were not put into place.
- The nature of the knowledge made learning difficult.
- The present corporate culture did not support learning.[45]

It has been found that alliances do not appear to be highly successful, but they do remain popular.[46]

Types of Corporations

In conducting SWOT analysis, international managers must ascertain the type of corporation that best helps their firm attain its international objectives. The three types are international corporations, multinational corporations (MNCs), and global corporations.

Some people use term *the international corporation* to mean firms that produce in the home country and export their products to other countries and term *the multinational corporation* to mean companies that establish subsidiaries in foreign countries. Other people use the two terms interchangeably; both terms refer to companies that have expanded their business activities beyond their home-country market—for example, Japanese, U.S., German, or Dutch companies that do business in multiple nations, usually their own and at least one other.

Global Corporations. An increasing trend is the emergence of *the global corporation.* Global corporations view themselves as "world corporations" (sometimes referred to as *stateless corporations*); they view the world as their marketplace. In other words, these corporations do not promote any overall national label; instead, they integrate themselves into the environment in which they happen to be doing business. For example, Honda, a Japanese global corporation, established operations in the United States. Through the media, Honda has tried to convince the American public that it is, in reality, an American company, not a Japanese company. Other global corporations include Bertelsmann, Coca-Cola, Pepsi Cola, McDonald's, Ford, Citicorp, and Asea Brown Boveri.

A distinct difference between the international and the MNC corporations and global corporations is that global corporations, because of their size, scope, and power are able to make decisions with little regard to national boundaries, and they are able to move factories and laboratories around the world freely. On the other hand, MNCs make decisions with much regard to national boundaries. Some observers believe that the power of global corporations transcends the power of national governments. Some observers also believe that global corporations are forming even more powerful strategic alliances in response to the threats presented by the emergence of regional trading blocks in Europe, North America, and East Asia.[47] And some observers believe that the regional trading blocks are being formed to offset the power of the global corporations.

Although global corporations view themselves as stateless, at this time, many of them, like the MNCs, still maintain their corporate headquarters in the nation where they were first established. Furthermore, it should be noted that it was found that few global corporations are fully global. Researchers found that of the 500 largest MNCs, very few were successful globally; and the data on 320 of 380 firms studied revealed that an average of 80.3% of their total sales were regional.[48]

Anyway, whether an international business enterprise is an international corporation, an MNC, or a global corporation is a matter of perception and definition. For the most part, this book uses the three terms interchangeably.

Types of International Strategies

In conducting SWOT analyses, international firms need to ascertain the type of international strategy to adopt to best pursue their internationalization objectives.

Typically, companies develop their core strategy for the home country first. Subsequently, after they have learned to manage growth in their home country, they internationalize their core strategy through international expansion of activities and through adaptation. Eventually, they globalize their strategy by integrating operations across nations.[49] These steps translate into four distinct types of strategies applied by international enterprises: ethnocentric, multidomestic, global, and transnational.

Ethnocentric Strategy

Following World War II, U.S. enterprises operated mainly from an ethnocentric perspective. These companies produced unique goods and services, which they offered primarily to the domestic market. The lack of international competition offset their need to be sensitive to cultural differences. When these firms exported goods, they did not alter them for foreign consumption—the costs of alterations for cultural differences were assumed by the foreign buyers. In effect, this type of company has one strategy for all markets.

Dean Foods, a dairy and vegetable-processing company based in Illinois, used this strategy. It exported non–dairy powdered creamer and canned and frozen vegetables to Europe and Asia. Its strategy did not provide for operating production facilities abroad. The firm's managers decided that they did not want to take on the problems of setting up complicated distribution systems in LDCs.[50]

However, today, this strategy exists more in theory than in practice—the ensuing three strategies are the main ones used by MNCs.

Multidomestic Strategy

The multidomestic firm (MNC) has a different strategy for each of its foreign markets. In this type of strategy,

a company's management tries to operate effectively across a series of worldwide positions with diverse product requirements, growth rates, competitive environments, and political risks. The company prefers that local managers do what is necessary to succeed in R&D, production, marketing, and distribution, but holds them responsible for results.[51]

In essence, this type of corporation competes with local competitors on a market-by-market basis. A multitude of U.S. corporations have used this strategy— for example, Procter & Gamble in household products, Honeywell in controls, Alcoa in aluminum, and General Foods in consumer goods. The Japanese car manufacturer Toyota also followed this strategy. (Practical Perspective 4.5 presents Aldus's international localization strategy.)

PRACTICAL PERSPECTIVE 4-5

Aldus's International Strategy

At Aldus [established in 1984 and now known as Adobe], entering foreign markets was not a strategy pursued after its products had been successfully marketed in the USA. Aldus President Paul Brainerd set out from the beginning to build products that could be quickly adapted to local markets. . . . The firm's major product was a computer program known as PageMaker which allowed individuals to design, edit, and produce printed documents using microcomputer systems available to most businesses. The firm's potential market included both businesses that generate documents and the publishing industry itself. . . .

The first USA version of Aldus PageMaker was shipped in July 1985. But even before the end of 1984, Brainerd had made a trip to Europe to set up channels of distribution. He was determined to introduce Aldus products almost simultaneously in the USA and Europe. But the firm was small and had very little capital at the time. (An initial public offering of common stock raised approximately $30 million in June 1987.) "We had to build a step-by-step progression of just what we could afford to do at any given point in the development of the company," Brainerd said. So Aldus developed a strategy to penetrate foreign markets quickly and at minimal cost.... The first phase of the plan was to engineer PageMaker in such a way that the computer program could be readily and quickly adapted to different national markets. "Localization" was the term employed by Aldus executives. Since PageMaker and similar programs were oriented to text and design considerations, the same program could hardly be sold in different countries. Software must be modified to conform to local languages and design idioms....

Localization projects have ranged from international English (distinct from American usage) to European languages with their different hyphenation requirements, to Asian languages with thousands of characters as well as vertical headlines and right to left orientation.... Although PageMaker was designed to be adapted to foreign requirements, the capital constraints remained. Brainerd described the Aldus solution: "We worked out a strategy where the distributors who wished to carry our products would essentially do the work for us. They would front end the investment for localization, and we would pay them back on a per-unit basis as they sold the software."[a] By now (August 22, 2006), Adobe has revolutionized how the world engages with ideas and information. Its award-winning software and technologies have redefined business, entertainment, and personal communications by setting standards for producing and delivering content that engages people virtually everywhere at anytime... Adobe is the leader in serving customers worldwide. Its customers include publishing, government, financial services, telecommunications, and education, and it provides its services worldwide to thousands of the world's leading organizations.[b]

SOURCES:

a. Excerpted from Warren Kalbacker, "At Aldus, Globalization Wasn't an Afterthought," *The International Executive* (January–February 1990), pp. 8–9. Copyright © 1990, John Wiley & Sons, Inc., New York. All rights reserved. Reprinted with permission.

b. www.adobe.com

Global Strategy

The global corporation uses all its resources against its competition in a very integrated fashion. All its foreign subsidiaries and divisions are highly interdependent in both operations and strategy. As Thomas Hout, Porter, and Rudden have said

> In a global business, management competes worldwide against a small number of other multinationals in the world market. Strategy is centralized, and various aspects of operations are decentralized or centralized as economics and effectiveness dictate. The company seeks to respond to particular local market needs, while avoiding a compromise of efficiency of the overall global system.[52]

Therefore, whereas in a multidomestic strategy the managers in each country react to competition without considering what is taking place in other countries, in a global strategy, competitive moves are integrated across nations. The same kind of move is made in different countries at the same time or in a systematic fashion. For example, a competitor is attacked in one nation to exhaust its resources for another country, or a competitive attack in one nation is countered in a different country—for instance, the counterattack in a competitor's home market as a parry to an attack on one's home market.[53] (For an illustration, read Practical Perspective 4.6, the case of Wal-Mart and Carrefour.)

PRACTICAL PERSPECTIVE 4-6

Retail Rival Carrefour Bulks Up

The French, dispirited after months of fruitless haggling to create Europe's largest bank, have bounced back by creating Europe's No. 1 retailer with the merger of homegrown chains Carrefour and Promodès Group. Carrefour's $16.5 billion acquisition of Promodès, announced on August 30 [1999], did far more than give France a national champion, though: The merger created a much tougher playing field for Wal-Mart Stores Inc. in its drive to expand internationally... Carrefour was set to challenge Wal-Mart around the globe. As Europe's new top dog, Carrefour used its buying clout to extract deeper discounts from suppliers, undercutting rivals and accelerating a push toward consolidation in the industry. The Promodès deal also widened Carrefour's impressive lead in several Latin American and Asian countries. What's more, Promodès brought to the union a reputation for solid inventory and distribution systems, an area where Carrefour had long lagged behind Wal-Mart. "We're creating a worldwide retail leader," said Carrefour Chief Executive Daniel Bernard...

In Europe, the deal put pressure on Wal-Mart to make another acquisition. The retailer already had holdings in Britain and Germany. But if it didn't grab another partner soon, it could be left without the critical mass to become a major European player. Its biggest European holding, Britain's Asda Group PLC, was only one-fifth the size of the bulked-up Carrefour. Likewise, Wal-Mart needed to counter Carrefour's expansion in emerging markets. Only hours after unveiling the Promodès deal, Carrefour announced the acquisition of three Brazilian chains, boosting its market share there above 20 percent, vs. 1.4 percent for Wal-Mart.[a]

In 2005, the company completed a buyout of French low-cost supermarket Penny Market from Germany's Rewe... and it has acquired hypermarkets in Brazil and Poland, and acquired majority stakes of chains in Cyprus, Turkey, Italy, and Romania. As of 2005, the company had 11,432 stores under its aegis. And on the European Retail Index Score, Carrefour scored an 88 and Wal-Mart scored a 44.[b] By adapting to local culture, [Carrefour] the biggest foreign retailer in China has beaten its rivals, writes Don Lee, July 26, 2006... What about Wal-Mart? "I can't imagine they will come here," said Christian Ruquigni, who manages Carrefour's Uygur store.[c]

SOURCES:

a. Excerpted from C. Matlack, I. Resch, and W. Zellner, "En Garde, Wal-Mart," *Business Week* (September 13, 1999), p. 54. Copyright © 1999, McGraw-Hill. All rights reserved. Used with permission.

b. www.nutraingredients.com/news/ng.asp?n=61524-carrefour-france-strategy (July 26, 2005).

c. "Carrefour's Sales Secret," *Los Angeles Times* (July 26, 2006).

Numerous MNCs have applied the global strategy—including IBM in computers; Caterpillar in large construction equipment; Timex, Seiko, and Citizen in watches; and General Electric, Siemens, and Mitsubishi in heavy electrical equipment. The reasons this strategy can work include the

growing similarity of what citizens of different countries want to buy, the reduction of tariff and nontariff barriers, technology investments that are becoming too expensive to amortize in one market only, and competitors that are globalizing the rules of the game.[54]

Whirlpool, which was mainly a North American corporation, applied a global strategy. It manufactured its products in many nations, with facilities in the United States, Europe, and Latin America, and marketed them in more than 100 locations as diverse as Thailand, Hungary, and Argentina.[55] (Practical Perspective 4.7 describes Whirlpool's global strategy.)

PRACTICAL PERSPECTIVE 4-7

Whirlpool's Views on Global Strategy

The only way to gain lasting competitive advantage is to leverage your capabilities around the world so that the company as a whole is greater than the sum of its parts. Being an international company—selling globally, having global brands or operations in different countries—isn't enough. In fact, most international manufacturers aren't truly global. They're what I [Whirlpool CEO, David R. Whitwam] call flag planters. They may have acquired or established businesses all over the world, but their regional and national divisions still operate as autonomous entities. In this day and age, you can't run a business that way and expect to gain a long-range competitive advantage.

To me, "competitive advantage" means having the best technologies and processes for designing, manufacturing, selling, and servicing your products at the lowest possible costs. Our vision at Whirlpool is to integrate our geographical businesses wherever possible, so that our most advanced expertise in any given area—whether it's refrigeration technology, financial reporting systems, or distribution strategy—isn't confined to one location or division. We want to be able to take the best capabilities we have and leverage them in all our operations worldwide.

In the major-appliance industry, both the size of our products and varying consumer preferences require us to have regional manufacturing centers. But even though the features, dimensions, and configurations of machines like refrigerators, washing machines, and ovens vary from market to market, much of the technology and manufacturing processes involved are similar. In other words, while a company may need plants in Europe, the United States, Latin America, and Asia to make products that meet the special needs of local markets, it's still possible and desirable for those plants to share the best available product technologies and manufacturing processes.... [Before you can develop common technologies and processes,] you must create an organization whose people are adept at exchanging ideas, processes, and systems across borders, people who are absolutely free of the "not-invented-here" syndrome, people who are constantly working together to identify the best global opportunities and the biggest global problems facing the organization. If you're going to ask people to work together in pursuing global ends across organizational and geographic boundaries, you have to give them a vision of what they're striving to achieve as well as a unifying philosophy to guide their efforts.

That's why we've worked so hard at Whirlpool to define and communicate our vision, objectives, and the market philosophy that represents our unifying focus. Our vision is to be one company worldwide. Our overarching objective is to drive this company to world-class performance in terms of delivering shareholder value.... Our market philosophy suggests that the only way to deliver this value over a long term is by focusing on the customer. Only prolonged, intensive effort to understand and respond to genuine customer needs can lead to the breakthrough products and services that earn long-term customer loyalty....

Before 1987, we didn't see the potential power our existing capabilities could give us in the global market because we had been limiting our definition of the appliance market to the United States. Obviously, this also limited our definition of the industry itself and the opportunity it offered. Our eight months of analysis turned up a great deal of evidence that, over time, our industry could become global, whether we chose to become global or not. With that said, we had three choices. We could ignore the inevitable—a decision that would have condemned Whirlpool to a slow death. We could wait for globalization to begin and then try to react, which would have put us in the catch-up mode, technologically and organizationally. Or we could control our own destiny and try to shape the very nature of globalization in our industry. In short, we could force our competition to respond to us.

Before we began making moves on the global stage, Electrolux was out in front of us. It had bought White Consolidated and had acquired several appliance makers in Europe. But Electrolux appeared to be taking advantage of individual opportunities rather than following a coordinated plan. After our Philips acquisition, we also saw General Electric take some opportunistic steps. Today, however, Whirlpool is the front-runner when it comes to implementing a pan-European strategy and leveraging global resources. By expanding our strategic horizon, not just our geographic reach, we've been able to build global management capability that provides us with what we feel is a distinct competitive advantage. Clearly, this should enable us to improve returns to our shareholders significantly.

Advantages and Disadvantages of the Global Strategy

Outlined below are the advantages and disadvantages of the global strategy.[56] The advantages of the global strategy would negate the disadvantages of the multidomestic strategy, and the disadvantages of the global strategy would be negated by the advantages of the multidomestic strategy.

Advantages (Multidomestic Strategy Does Not Provide These Advantages)

- By pooling production or other activities for two or more nations, a firm can increase the benefits derived from economies of scale.
- A company can cut costs by moving manufacturing or other activities to low-cost countries.
- A firm that is able to switch production among different nations can reduce costs by increasing its bargaining power over suppliers, workers, and host governments.
- By focusing on a smaller number of products and programs than under a multidomestic strategy, a corporation is able to improve both product and program quality.
- Worldwide availability, serviceability, and recognition can increase preference through reinforcement.
- The company is provided with more points from which to attack and counterattack competition.

Disadvantages (Multidomestic Strategy Can Reduce These Disadvantages)

- Through increased coordination, reporting requirements, and added staff, substantial management costs can be incurred.
- Overcentralization can harm local motivation and morale, thereby reducing the firm's effectiveness.
- Standardization can result in a product that does not totally satisfy any customers.
- Incurring costs and revenues in multiple countries increases currency risk.
- Integrated competitive moves can lead to the sacrificing of revenues, profits, or competitive positions in individual countries—especially when the subsidiary in one country is told to attack a global competitor in order to convey a signal or divert that competitor's resources from another nation.

Transnational Strategy

The transnational strategy is basically a blend of the multidomestic and the global strategies. It provides for global coordination (like the global strategy), and at the same time it allows local autonomy (like the multidomestic strategy). Nestlé, the world's largest food company, headquartered in Switzerland, followed this strategy.[57] The challenges managers of transnational corporations face are to identify and exploit cross-border synergies and to balance local demands with the global vision for the corporation. Building an effective transnational organization requires a corporate culture that values global dissimilarities across cultures and markets.[58] This type of company does not look solely at countries as a potential market; it also looks at potential markets within a country.

For example, as pointed out in Chapter 3, KFC failed miserably when it entered the Brazilian market without studying Brazilian culture.[59] In the United States, everyone, except the Native Americans, have two nationalities (Irish American, Polish American, etc.), and thus a couple of hundred distinct cultural differences exist in the United States. These cultures usually group in specific areas (an Italian neighborhood, an Irish neighborhood, etc.). Brazil also has many distinct nationalities and cultures, but they are not recognized–all citizens consider themselves as Brazilian and are insulted when they are asked their foreign origin because they don't know there is one.

As pointed out in Chapter 1, culture is passed on from one generation to another. The point here is that like in the United States, Brazilians' distinct foreign cultural lineage is passed on from one generation to another, but in Brazil it's done without them knowing it. In Brazil, there are no St. Patrick's Day parades symbolizing Irish Americans, Columbus Day parades symbolizing Italian Americans, and so on; soccer events symbolize Brazilian culture. Thus, if KFC had studied Brazilian culture before going there, it would have found areas consisting of subcultures—such as Italian Brazilians—that are receptive to its product. The transnational corporation would do this. As another example, teenagers in most countries tend to be receptive to the same product worldwide, especially clothing styles; hence, the transnational corporation would focus on finding these groups in countries.

International Strategic and Tactical Objectives

In conducting international SWOT analyses, firms need to establish two kinds of measurable objectives: strategic and tactical.

Strategic objectives, which are guided by the enterprise's mission or purpose and deal with long-term issues, associate the enterprise with its external environment and provide management with a basis for comparing performance with that of its competitors and in relation to environmental demands. (Refer again to the Whirlpool case, Practical Perspective 4.7.) Examples of strategic objectives include to increase sales, to increase market share, to increase profits, and to lower prices by becoming an international firm. Tactical objectives, which are guided by the enterprise's strategic objectives and deal with shorter-term issues, identify the key result areas in which specific performance is essential for the success of the enterprise and aim to attain internal efficiency. They identify specifically how, for example, to lower costs, to lower prices, to increase output, to capture a larger portion of the market, and to penetrate an international market.

Areas in Which Objectives Should be Established

Peter Drucker, the globally known management authority, has indicated that objectives should be established in at least eight areas of organizational performance: (1) market standing, (2) innovations, (3) productivity, (4) physical and financial resources, (5) profitability, (6) manager performance and responsibility, (7) worker performance and attitude, and (8) social responsibility.[60]

Market Standing

In general, market-standing objectives measure a firm's performance relative to products/services, markets, distribution, and customer service. In an international context, a firm's strategic objective may be to increase market share by entering foreign markets. Tactical objectives established to enter foreign markets may include refocusing advertising, product/service, and pricing to fit each foreign market's environment. (As indicated in Practical Perspective 4.8, Whirlpool Corporation did not attain its objectives.) Performance measures must therefore be developed for each foreign market. Overall, international firms need to measure performance relating to worldwide, region, and country sales volume.

Innovations

A strategic innovation objective may be to lead the industry in introducing new products; a tactical objective may be to spend a specific percentage of revenues from sales for R&D. Innovation objectives are based on a clear vision of where a firm wants

PRACTICAL PERSPECTIVE 4-8

Tough Target

[In 1989,] Whirlpool Corporation came to Europe in a big way, believing that the Continent's appliance business, then a $20 billion market with dozens of marginally profitable companies, was becoming more American. The industry had no choice, Whirlpool thought, but to consolidate into a handful of companies. And America's biggest appliance maker wanted to be one of them.

But the market didn't change; only the competition did. It got tougher. Whirlpool's two biggest rivals, Sweden's AB Electrolux and Germany's Bosch-Siemens Hausgeraete GmbH, improved efficiency step-for-step with Whirlpool. And smaller competitors managed to hold on.

The result for Whirlpool, which earlier had had only a minor presence in Europe, was disappointment. Instead of winning an anticipated 20 percent of the market, it had about 12 percent. Its European profits also were less than expected. In the USA, the Benton Harbor, Michigan, company made $10 on every $100 of sales; in Europe, it earned about $2.30 on that amount of revenue. Whirlpool thus struggled through its second European restructuring [refer to Practical Perspective 4.7]. The goals remained the same, but the company conceded it will take longer to reach them. "We see Europe as being in the fifth year of a 10-year restructuring," said Jeff Fettig, who ran Whirlpool's European operation from his Comerio headquarters. He acknowledged that the company "underestimated the competition."[a]

Today [March 8, 2007], Whirlpool Corporation is the world's leading manufacturer and marketer of major home appliances, with annual sales of more than $18 billion, 73,000 employees, and nearly 60 manufacturing and technology centers around the globe. The company markets Whirlpool, Maytag, KitchenAid, Jenn-Air, Amana, Brastemp, Bauknecht, Consul, and other major brands to consumers in more than 170 countries. In Europe, it continues to design its products in a way that appeals to European consumers and has expanded into Central Europe by acquiring Polar S.A., a leading appliance manufacturer with the No. 1 brand name in Poland. The acquisition provides Whirlpool Europe with a low-cost manufacturing source to serve the entire region.[b]

SOURCES:

a. Excerpted from G. Steinmetz and C. Quintanilla, "Whirlpool Expected Easy Going in Europe and It Got a Big Shock," *The Wall Street Journal* (April 10, 1998), pp. A1, A6. Permission conveyed through Copyright Clearance Center, Inc.

b. www.whirlpoolcorp.com

to be 10, 15, and 20 years from now. R&D may aim at innovation of patentable products and/or production technology—U.S. firms tend to focus on the former and Japanese firms on the latter. It is generally believed that the global and competitive battles of the 2000s will be won by enterprises that are able to get out of the traditional and declining product markets by building and dominating basically new markets. Many believe that Japanese firms' superiority in production technology, coupled with the fact that they are rapidly catching up with the United States in their ability to innovate in new products, will put them at a competitive advantage in the global market. (Practical Perspective 4.9 presents Honda's efforts to attain a competitive advantage through innovation.)

In past years, to obtain R&D innovation know-how, Japanese firms have set up R&D centers in the United States and asked U.S. companies to set up R&D centers in Japan. R&D executives in China say its Confucian education system doesn't produce the creative thinking that leads to cutting-edge innovation. But China's top universities have quickly gained a reputation for churning out capable scientists and engineers who are fuelling the nation's technological revolution.[61]

Managers must also establish tactical objectives concerning the redesigning of products and/or services to fit the needs of each specific foreign market their firms wish to penetrate. (Practical Perspective 4.10 discusses Sony's TV-programming adaptations in China and India.) And they must develop strategies related to the type of technology to be transferred abroad.

PRACTICAL PERSPECTIVE 4-9

Accord's Flexible Design

Honda President Nobuhiko Kawamoto realized years ago that Honda's long-term success was threatened if the automaker couldn't make the company's most important car more successful outside the USA. At the same time, to keep up with the needs of its aging baby-boomer buyers, Honda executives said they needed to substantially enlarge the new USA version. The obvious solution to the Accord's woes—designing a different model for each market—was out of the question. Honda may have had big brand presence in the USA, but it ranked only 13th among the world's automakers. That meant it couldn't afford to spend as much as its bigger rivals—not even on the all-important Accord. While General Motors budgeted a generous $9 billion a year for research and development, Honda got by with a mere $2.1 billion . . . however, Honda may have found a way to customize the Accord for world markets without breaking the bank. The completely overhauled 1998 Honda Accord that hit USA showrooms on September 25 [1997] looked and felt nothing like the Accord being simultaneously introduced in Japan or the one that debuted in Europe the next spring. The USA Accord was a big, staid family car, matching the Ford Taurus in interior roominess. The European version was shorter and narrower and featured the stiff and sporty ride Old World drivers prefer.

Honda's secret lied in an ingenious frame that allows the automaker to shrink or expand the overlying car without starting from the ground up. By coming up with a platform—by far the most expensive part of a new car—that can be bent and stretched into markedly different vehicles, Honda has saved hundreds of millions of dollars in development costs. Analysts estimate that Honda developed the Accord for a relatively modest $600 million. In comparison, Ford Motor Company spent $2.8 billion redesigning the 1996 Taurus.

PRACTICAL PERSPECTIVE 4-10

Think Globally, Script Locally

[In 1999], William Pfeiffer [the executive who launched a Hindi-language channel for Sony] could remember when there was no McDonald's in Kathmandu. That was 16 years earlier, when he'd just moved to Tokyo after B-school at Stanford. He was working for Disney at the time; then, in 1992, Sony hired him to scout business opportunities for Columbia Tri-Star, its then-floundering Hollywood studio. The biggest opportunity was in India, where there was little competition and a newly liberalized foreign investment policy. From modest beginnings—a dirt-floored Bombay office lit by a single bulb that went dark whenever a monsoon hit—Sony became a powerhouse, producing 33 hours of Hindi-language programming a week and beaming it not just to India but also to Africa, Britain, North America, and the Middle East. Reif Cohen notwithstanding, Pfeiffer maintained that Sony Entertainment Television, the Hindi-language television channel he launched in 1995, actually makes money.

After getting established in India, Sony launched the mostly English-language AXN Action satellite channel across Asia. In winter [1998] it became sole owner of Super TV, a Mandarin-language channel that reaches 77 percent of the 5.1 million homes in Taiwan. Sony also produced or co-produced some 35 hours of Mandarin-language programming a week, much of it for Super TV—from City of Love, a prime-time Taiwan soap, to a revivified Charlie's Angels starring a trio of willowy Chinese babes who chopsocked it to bad guys from Shanghai to Kuala Lumpur . . . But the real news was that Super TV gave Sony the potential to go after the mainland's 305 million television households via satellite, instead of just selling shows like Chinese Restaurant to existing terrestrial stations. "China is a market we're very respectful of," said Pfeiffer. "We're certainly interested, if we're allowed in, in entertaining the people."

SOURCE: Excerpted from Frank Rose, "Think Globally, Script Locally," Fortune (November 8, 1999), p. 158. Reprinted with permission.

Classification of Technology

The term *technology* has been defined as machinery, blueprints, process designs, equipments, products, patents, licenses, trademarks, and other techniques such as marketing and advertising, accounting, personnel management, and general management.[62] It should be noted that old technology in the home market may sometimes be innovative technology in a foreign market. Technology has been classified as hard and soft, proprietary and nonproprietary, bundled and unbundled, and front-end and obsolete technology.[63]

Hard technology includes hard goods, blueprints, technical specifications, and the knowledge and assistance necessary for the efficient use of such hardware. Soft technology includes management, marketing, financial organization, and administrative techniques. Proprietary technology is technology that is owned by particular individuals or organizations. Nonproprietary technology includes knowledge that can be imitated or reproduced by observation or reverse engineering without infringement on proprietary rights. Reverse engineering means learning to reproduce technology by taking it apart to determine how it works and then copying it. Bundled technology is controlled technology that the owner is willing to transfer as part of a package. The owner maintains an ownership interest in the overseas affiliate using the technology. Unbundled technology is technology that is transferred independent of the supplier's total package of resources. Front-end technology is the most advanced technology available. Obsolete technology is usually older technology.

Export/Import Older or Advanced Technology?

Historically, some LDCs have sought to import advanced technologies from developed countries, and others have pursued the importation of older technology. A survey has addressed the question of whether LDCs should import the most advanced technology available or older technology that may be obsolete in the more developed countries.[64] Some international executives feel that LDCs with low capital and an abundance of labor should import older technology. They believe that many LDCs in this situation lack the infrastructure, both material and human resources, "to support, feed, operate, and gainfully exploit advanced technology."[65] Other international executives suggest that LDCs should import technology that promotes employment; that is, they should import labor-intensive older technology, especially in those countries where unemployment or underemployment is a severe problem.

A number of executives disagree. They feel that in most situations, LDCs should import the most advanced technology available. One reason for this perspective is that in the long run, older technology produces inferior products and the country thus becomes less competitive in world markets. Another reason is that, regardless of social effects on employment, the most modern technology will contribute more to a country's national income. It is also felt that if countries import the obsolete technology of advanced countries, they will always remain LDCs. Some international executives feel that sophistication of technology should be based on the destination of the product. If the product manufactured by the imported technology is for local consumption, then older technology would be more appropriate; if, however, the product is for exporting, advanced technology would work better.[66] Another view is that the approach a country uses is contingent on factors such as its economic situation, its leaders, and its people. For example, an oil-rich LDC may be able to afford the acquisition of advanced technology. On the other hand, a very poor LDC may be better off importing older, labor-intensive technology, which is often obsolete in the advanced countries and thus less costly. Some leaders have greater ability than others in implementing new technologies, and people in some cultures are more open to innovation than people in others (discussed in Chapter 5). China, for instance, when changing from a communist economy to a market-like economy imported the most advanced technology because it sought to immediately become a global business player, and it has been projected that by 2020 China will be economically as powerful as the United States or even more powerful. And India, with over a billion people, is the second most populated country, next to China. It has developed a sophisticated info-tech industry, but this industry employs fewer than a million people, 200 million Indians subsist on $1 a day or less. Developing its export manufacturing is India's best hope of generating millions of new jobs. Thus, as in the case of China, it would need to import the more advanced manufacturing technology to produce for export. However, the question is "Can India do what China did?"[67] China has always been a very entrepreneurial culture, even during its hardcore communist regime, when its entrepreneurial spirit was carried on in an "underground" manner.

Tactical objectives are relative to the type of technology—old or new; firm transfers are therefore influenced by nations' perceived needs as well as by the extent to which the enterprise's management protects its intellectual property rights. High-technology industries are generally very concerned with intellectual property rights. The laws protecting such rights, however, vary considerably around the globe. For example, it was estimated by the U.S. International Trade Commission that in 1984, infringement of intellectual property throughout the world cost $8 billion in lost U.S. sales. It was reported in 1997 that $1.409 billion illegal copies of entertainment software were sold in China in 1996, and the total in 10 countries in the report (including China) amounted to $5.190 billion (including $2.780 billion in the United States); illegal sales of CDs and cassettes in 10 countries (not including the United States) amounted to $924 million; and illegal sales of copies of videos in 10 countries (not including the United States) amounted to $1.034 billion.[68]

These types of activities remained rampant in many parts of the globe in 2007. The World Trade Organization created The Agreement on Trade-Related Aspects of Intellectual Property Rights (TRIPS) in 1994. But since TRIPS came into force, it has received a growing level of criticism from developing countries, academics, and nongovernmental organizations. Some of this criticism is against the WTO as a whole, but many advocates of trade liberalism also regard TRIPS as bad policy. TRIPS' wealth redistribution effects (moving money from people in developing countries to copyright and patent owners in developing countries) and its imposition of artificial scarcity on the citizens of countries that would otherwise have had weaker intellectual property laws are a common basis for such criticisms.[69]

Furthermore, it is alleged that U.S. enterprises have suffered from a "lack of rigorous and uniform international standards for intellectual property rights."[70] U.S. Senator John J. Rockefeller once communicated some concerns in this respect. He stated, "Once the technology is developed and the resulting product is commercialized, it is vital that patent rights be protected. If a company cannot sell its products and recoup its development costs, the next product will not be developed."[71] The problem is now enlarged by the advent of Internet commerce.[72] As was pointed out in Chapter 2, providing copyright protection for knowledge sources on the Internet is largely different from providing it to their counterparts in hard copy publication.

Productivity

Productivity is usually measured by the ratio of output to input—for example, ratio of output to labor costs, ratio of output to capital costs, ratio of value added to sales, and ratio of value added to profit. In an international context, the manager is concerned with the ratio of foreign to domestic production volume and the economies of scale by means of international production integration. A strategic objective may be to reduce production costs. Tactical objectives based on this strategic objective may include replacing equipment, enhancing plant utilization rates, improving quality control, and transferring production overseas where labor and/or material costs are lower. (Refer again to Practical Perspective 4.2.) Tactical objectives may also include the development of a system for forecasting, monitoring, and interpreting costs. Japan's cost management system is much more sophisticated than that of the United States.

For example, U.S. enterprises developing a new product normally design it first and then compute the cost. If it is too much, the product is returned to the drawing board or the firm accepts a lower profit. On the other hand, the Japanese begin with a target cost estimated on the price the market is likely to accept. Subsequently, they instruct designers and engineers to meet the target. The Japanese system also encourages managers to be concerned less about a product's cost than about the role it could play in gaining market share. This approach is a good reason why Japanese firms often generate winning products that accountants would have killed in a U.S. firm.[73]

Physical and Financial Resources

Physical and financial measures include current ratio, working-capital turnover, acid test ratio, debt to equity ratio, accounts receivable, and inventory turnover. In an international dimension, managers are concerned with how foreign affiliates are to be financed (e.g., by retained earnings, franchising, borrowing, or forming joint ventures), with minimizing the tax burden globally, and with foreign exchange management that seeks to minimize losses from monetary exchange fluctuations (discussed in Chapter 3).

Profitability

Profitability measures include the ratios of profits to sales, profits to total assets, and profits to net worth. A strategic objective may be to increase profits. Tactical objectives may be to reduce costs by consolidating functions or, as discussed earlier in this chapter, by transferring operations overseas where costs and/or materials are lower.

Manager Performance and Responsibility

Managers' international performance and responsibility are based on their skills. A strategic objective may be to identify and upgrade critical areas of international management skills. A tactical objective may be to establish programs aimed at developing managers with a global outlook (refer again to Chapters 1 and 8), at developing residents in the host country for managerial positions, and at initiating programs that prepare employees for foreign assignments. (This is discussed more thoroughly in Chapters 7 and 8.)

Worker Performance and Attitude

A strategic objective to improve worker performance and attitude may be to maintain levels of employee satisfaction consistent with the firm's industry and with similar industries since this is part of an organization's stability and durability. Tactical objectives in this aspect may include bonus plans, pay increases, and application of participative management. In an international context, equipment transfers to a foreign country, in comparison with transferring technical skills, are relatively easy. The problem occurs when there is a shortage of trained personnel in the country and/or workers do not maintain the proper attitude and are low producers. When this is the case, the firm must develop and implement training programs (discussed in Chapter 8).

For example, after nearly half a century of communism, China has begun to shift to a market-like economy. The vastness of China's market potential and low labor costs makes it attractive for foreign corporations to invest there. Under the communist regime, a system evolved of paying employees the same whether they worked hard or not. Therefore, the skills and efficiency of China's workforce did not at first compare with those of the advanced nations' workforces. Thus, foreign corporations establishing subsidiaries in China needed to implement appropriate training programs. For instance, Motorola, Inc. sponsored a technical university and provided hundreds of scholarships to support its new plant in China established to produce paging devices. Panasonic implemented a military-like boot camp for workers at its Beijing television tube plant. Xian-Jenssen Pharmaceutical Ltd., a Chinese-U.S. joint venture spent several thousand dollars to train each local employee; it offered in-house courses in sales, accounting, English, and computer usage.[74]

Other strategic objectives may be to control excessive absenteeism and lateness. It should be noted that individuals in some cultures object to too much control. They believe that it is none of the corporation's business as to why an employee is absent, and any attempt to control absenteeism is viewed as corporate exploitation of individuals. Therefore, rather than attempting to control absenteeism in some cultures, a flexible work system may sometimes be more appropriate.

Social Responsibility

A social responsibility objective would be to respond appropriately everywhere possible to societal expectations and environmental needs. For example, Canon Corporation's "spiritual" basis for its activities and the behavioral norms for employees are based on the following managerial philosophy:

1. To manufacture the best products in the world and thereby contribute to advancement of international development

2. To build an ideal corporation that will enjoy continuous prosperity[75]

Corporate social responsibility is built into the Japanese system—more and more Japanese enterprises are giving a percentage of their profits to promote education, social welfare, and culture in their foreign markets.

Furthermore, all businesses have the responsibility to correct the environmental problems that they create in attaining their goals and objectives. Most nations are concerned with environmental problems and have laws mandating corrective and/or preventive action. (In the United States, the Environmental Protection Agency enforces these laws.) Also, companies that employ child labor are viewed as socially irresponsible in many nations. International corporations must develop objectives in this respect, otherwise there can be negative consequences. (This topic is discussed more thoroughly in Chapter 2.) Chiquita bananas (refer again to Practical Perspective 2.3) were once imported from Honduras through a U.S.-German joint venture. The chemicals that the joint venture used to protect the bananas killed over a thousand Honduran workers. The Honduran government was eventually forced by its citizens to close down the joint venture. Of course, this action harmed Honduras' economy.[76]

Technology and Global Strategy

International SWOT analyses should include current technology. Technology has been the root of the most dramatic changes occurring in commerce today. It now enables organizations to integrate their systems, where changes in one part ripple throughout the system, causing shifts in the other parts. Therefore, no strategy has been left untouched. It has leveled the playing field for small firms, allowing them to compete successfully with large corporations in the same markets. With e-mail, videoconferencing, teleconferencing, multimedia CD-ROMs, and networked databases, small businesses can emulate the marketing tactics of much larger companies—they can set up a home page on the World Wide Web right next door to Wal-Mart. And electronic networks and the Internet have enabled organizations to decentralize business activities and to outsource activities to other organizations.

Brazil, Russia, India, and China, usually referred to as BRIC, consumed $65 billion of information technology in 2005, and combined IT spending in BRIC is expected to reach nearly $110 billion by 2009. However, these economies, today, account for 6% of global IT consumption, but the percentage is expected to soon reach 8%.[77]

From a strategic viewpoint, technology affected international strategy in several ways:[78]

- Emphasis has moved from products to information and solutions.
- Products can be launched from commercialization tactics based on identifying specific customer needs.
- Relationships with customers have been made easier, which enhances product acceptance and minimizes costs due to redesign.
- Firms can now target specific products and services to specific customers.
- Technology supports the integration of engineering and commercialization to get the product to the customer in the least amount of time.
- Technology helps prevent midcourse corrections in product design, which usually result in higher costs and a longer time to commercialize.

From a tactical viewpoint, current technology aids businesses in the commercialization of their products and services in numerous ways:

- E-mail enables firms to communicate rapidly and easily with customers, strategic partners, suppliers, distributors, and others around the globe. This lowers the costs of travel and speeds up response time.
- Teleconferencing and videoconferencing allow enterprises to hold international strategic meetings without getting on an airplane.
- Networked databases provide organizations with online access to research and development information existing around the globe.
- Modems and laptop computers let employees work from virtually anywhere in the world, increasing efficiency and bringing the organization closer to the customer.
- Voice mail lets organizations record telephone messages when no one is available to receive them.
- Satellite systems, which a firm can lease from a provider, allow organizations to receive broadcast messages from chain manufacturers that help move the product.
- Laser color printers let enterprises quickly produce signs, banners, cards, price tags, and so on that look as good as those printed by a professional.
- Some industries have CD-ROM services that businesses can tie into on a regular basis to receive updated information of things such as equipment and supplies. This also makes it easier for a firm to quickly locate customer items that it normally does not carry in stock.
- The World Wide Web as a commercial tool is enabling smaller businesses to be on the same playing field as larger businesses.
- Online databases have put information at the hands of anyone who chooses to access them.[79]

One must bear in mind that technology is a tool used by strategists to improve business activities. It is not intended to replace personal contact with the customer, nor is it intended to replace a manager's unique ability to take vast amounts of information and make sense of it in terms of strategy for the organization. It does make it easier for the manager to integrate all activities of the firm, to automate routine tasks, and generally to free up more time to focus on the firm's strategy.

Some Examples of Business Opportunities Seized via the Internet

- International Development Corporation's online study revealed that India's gaming market was still at a nascent stage, where online gaming service providers were still learning and adjusting to this emerging industry. Telecommunications service providers, online game developers, and even traditional and information communication technology vendors were showing increasing interest in this fast-emerging market.[80]

- Buy wine online? One of the first and most successful enterprises in this market is Virtual Vineyards. The company positioned itself for a growth spurt owing to a fresh infusion of venture capital funding secured in June 1999. Peter Granoff and Robert Olson founded the company in 1994 and opened its Web site (Virtual Vineyard.com) the following January. By 1999, the firm was operating in 40 U.S. states and internationally.[81] As of March 2007, Virtual Vineyards continues to grow rapidly, but Olson won't release numbers (Inc.com/magazine).

- Sea-Land Service, a global ocean transportation provider based in Charlotte, North Carolina, and a subsidiary of CSX Corporation, enhanced its logistics capabilities by using Web-based technology to manage customer information throughout the supply chain and throughout the customer service process. In conjunction with RockPort Trade Systems, a software vendor that specialized in supply chain management on a global scale, Sea-Land and CSX Corporation developed a comprehensive global supply chain management system for Buyers and Shippers Enterprises, the logistics arm of their business. The custom-designed system was used to track goods from the time they were ordered all the way through to delivery at retail sites.[82]

- Deere & Company, the parent company for John Deere equipment and a host of related manufacturing and financial services companies with headquarters in Moline, Illinois, in 1999, had operations in 160 countries. The corporation made a strong push to expand its overseas business activities. Like other global companies, Deere faced the challenges of global information storage requiring support for various languages and databases, uneven network services and technology implementations from one country to another, and a corporate culture of diverse and generally autonomous business units. Deere managed to balance the conflicting demands of central data control and business autonomy by employing a single, worldwide database created from individual databases maintained by local business units. The corporation's DataJoiner project, implemented with IBM technologies, linked these worldwide databases into a logical warehouse, allowing business units to access information throughout the Deere corporate network and across companies as easily and seamlessly as they accessed data on a local server. Deere was moving toward a completely borderless environment in terms of data access.[83]

Outsourcing IT Functions

Outsourcing IT functions has become quite popular worldwide.[84] Currently (2007), many U.S. corporations are outsourcing some of their IT functions to lower-labor-cost nations and where there is an abundance of IT workers available, such as India. Managers of some U.S. corporations, as indicated earlier, claim that they are outsourcing these IT functions because IT workers at home are scarce. As discussed in Chapter 5, outsourcing has both pros and cons—cheaper labor abroad but loss of jobs at home.

Shortcomings of the Internet

Today, most electronic commerce transactions are done via dedicated lines and value-added networks. The Internet supports open access, involves a great many million users worldwide, and is, as the above examples demonstrate, experiencing an enormous growth rate. And it does generate many opportunities for international businesses. However, the Internet in its current state also has some shortcomings, including insecure transactions, though secure protocols are being considered; protocols that provide minimal or nonexistent guarantees of service; no mechanisms for protecting intellectual property; and no support for interoperation or data interchange standards.[85] In 2006, The International Data Corporation was offering its IT Security Road Show, Secure Your Business in an Uncertain World seminars in many parts of the world.

Summary

This chapter has proposed that domestic business enterprises internationalize their operations in response to opportunities and threats generated by changes that have taken place in foreign markets. They develop international strategies to seize the opportunities or to combat the threats. To develop effective international strategies, managers must be totally familiar with the firm's external environment as well as with its internal resources and capabilities. If a firm does not possess the ability to manage international operations, it may have to form a partnership with a firm that does. The chapter has also described four types of international strategies: ethnocentric, multidomestic, global, and transnational, and it has presented the advantages and disadvantages of the multidomestic and the global strategies. It has concluded that the international enterprise must establish strategic and tactical objectives in at least eight areas of organizational performance: market standing, innovations, productivity, physical and financial resources, profitability, manager performance and responsibility, worker performance and attitude, and social responsibility. The chapter has also discussed how IT and the Internet are affecting global commerce.

KEY TERMS AND CONCEPTS

1. Internationalization of operations

2. Opportunities and threats

3. Capable workforce in foreign country

4. Cheaper labor and/or materials

5. Appearance of new markets

6. Globalization of financial systems; financial options

7. Declining demand in home market

8. Acquisition of managerial know-how and capital

9. External and internal audit

10. Foreign sources of finance

11. Personnel competencies

12. Lead from strength

13. Joint venture; strategic alliance

14. Global corporations

15. International strategies: ethnocentric, multidomestic, global, and transnational strategy

16. International strategic and tactical objectives

17. Production technology superiority

18. Classification of technology

19. Reverse engineering

20. Older and advanced technology

21. A global outlook

22. Shortage of trained personnel in foreign country

23. Corporate social responsibility

24. The Internet as a tool for improving global business

DISCUSSION QUESTIONS

1. Why do domestic enterprises internationalize their business operations?

2. How are greater profits realized in the global market?

3. Discuss the "globalization of financial systems" opportunity.

4. List some of the U.S. insurance companies that have internationalized their operations. Why did they do so?

5. Discuss some of the major ideas contained in Practical Perspectives 4.1 to 4.10.

6. Discuss the four types of international strategy.

7. What are the advantages and disadvantages of multidomestic strategy and global strategy? What is the major difficulty in applying the transnational strategy?

8. Differentiate between international strategic and tactical objectives.

9. Briefly describe the areas in which international objectives should be established.

10. Describe the classification of technology.

11. Discuss the major concern of international corporations that transfer technology to a foreign country.

12. Discuss how, from a strategic viewpoint, current technology affects international strategy.

13. Discuss how, from a tactical viewpoint, current technology affects international strategy.

EXERCISES

1. You are an international management consultant hired by a firm that sells computers only in the U.S. market. The firm's growth rate has been steadily declining over the past few years. The firm's management is seeking a solution to the problem. What will you advise the management to do? Why? Where?

2. You are an international management consultant hired by a firm that manufactures and sells textiles in the United States. Competition from Hong Kong is rapidly taking away the firm's market share. The firm's management is seeking a solution. What will you advise the management to do? Why? Where?

3. You are an international management consultant hired by a domestic firm that has decided to internationalize its operations. An internal examination reveals that the firm has strong production capabilities but lacks personnel with international management capabilities. What will you advise the management to do?

4. You are an international management consultant hired by the government of a less developed country wishing to begin industrializing. The country is relatively poor economically and has an abundance of untrained labor. The government needs your advice on establishing policy relating to technology imports. What advice will you give to the government?

5. You are an international management consultant hired by a domestic company that wants to expand its operations into foreign markets via the Internet. What advice would you give your client?

ASSIGNMENT

Scan business periodicals. Select an article describing a company's international strategy. (The Practical Perspectives should help you in this respect.) Provide a brief summary of the major themes contained in the article for class discussion.

CASE 4-1

Levi's International Strategies

As the U.S. denim jeans market continued to shrink, foreign sales were driving Levi's growth. In the nine months ended in August 1990, about 39 percent of the company's total revenues and 60 percent of its pretax profit before interest and corporate expenses came from abroad. . . . Ironically, it hadn't been that long ago that Levi's stumbled around overseas like a clumsy American tourist. Back in 1984 and 1985, its international operations were losing money . . . By the mid-1980s, then Levi's Chief Executive, Robert D. Haas recognized that Levi's was squandering its brand identity in jeans. So, he dumped the fashion businesses and focused anew on blue jeans, at home and abroad.

Then, in 1985, the great-great-grandnephew of company founder Levi Strauss, a Bavarian immigrant who sold canvas pants to California gold seekers, took Levi's private in a leveraged buyout. The restructuring paid off: Operating income hit $589 million in fiscal 1989, up 50 percent since 1986. Sales rose 31 percent, to $3.63 billion. . . . Levi's foreign ads have played up the company's American roots. An Indonesian television commercial showed Levi's-clad teenagers cruising around Dubuque, Iowa, in 1960s convertibles. In Japan James Dean served as the centerpiece in virtually all Levi's advertising. And in most foreign ads for Levi's 501 button fly jeans the dialogue was usually in English. Said John G. Johnson, president of VF International: "The positioning of the 501 really set them apart." In more ways than one. Overseas, Levi's cultivated a top-drawer image that would surprise most Americans, and the company was pricing accordingly. A pair of 501 jeans sold for $30 in the USA but fetched up to $63 in Tokyo and $88 in Paris.

To protect that tony image, Levi's eschewed mass merchants and discounters abroad. Levi's snob appeal has meant lush profit margins. The company's international operation had the highest profit per unit of the company's seven operating divisions. Levi's garnered gross margins of 45 percent on 501s sold outside the USA, compared with less than 30 percent domestically, figured Bernard Duflos, then chairman of the North American unit of London-based Pepe Clothing Inc., a jeans marketer. . . . To provide merchandise for its foreign subsidiaries, Levi's stitched together a global manufacturing network. With a mix of its own 11 sewing plants and contract manufacturers, Levi's could supply foreign customers from nearby factories. And by shortening shipping times, Levi's could react speedily to fads in denim shading. . . . Technology also helped Levi's stay on top of global fashion trends. Through its Levi-Link system, retailers could transfer sales and inventory data from bar-coded clothing direct to Levi's computers. . . .

Levi's innovative approach overseas has allowed it to penetrate one of the world's toughest markets—Japan. The company set up its Japanese subsidiary in 1971. "That was a very important strategic decision—not to go the joint-venture or licensing route," said David E. Schmidt, a Canadian who ran Levi Strauss Japan. . . . In Brazil, Levi's prospered by letting local managers call the shots on distribution. For instance, Levi's penetrated the huge, fragmented Brazilian market by launching a chain of 400 Levi's Only stores, some of them in tiny, rural towns. The stores were pulling in 65 percent of Levi's $100 million-a-year Brazilian women sales. . . . Levi's also was sensitive to local tastes in Brazil, where it developed the Feminina line of jeans exclusively for women there. Brazilian women traditionally favor ultra tight jeans and the curvaceous cut provides a better fit. What Levi's learned in one market could often be translated into another. Take the Dockers line of chino pants and casual wear. The name originated in Levi's Argentinean unit and was applied to a loosely cut pair of pants designed by Levi's Japanese subsidiary. The company's U.S.A operations adopted both in 1986.

Questions

1. Is Levi's seizing opportunities, or combating threats, or both? Explain your answer.

2. Did Levi's "lead from strength"? Explain.

3. Is Levi's strategy ethnocentric, multidomestic, global, or transnational, or a combination? Explain your answer.

4. How effective was Levi's in using IT?

5. This case is dated, so for class discussion, go on the Internet and obtain Levi's global standing today.

SOURCE: Excerpted from M. Shao, R. Neff, and J. Ryser, "For Levi's, a Flattering Fit Overseas," *Business Week* (November 5, 1990), pp. 76–77. Copyright © 1990, McGraw-Hill. All rights reserved. Used with permission.

CASE 4-2

This E-Biz Early Bird Didn't Get the Worm

Lots of companies claim to be pioneers in e-business, but few can match the bona fides of Open Market, Inc. Founded in May 1994—one month before Netscape Communications Corporation—Open Market spotted back in the early days the critical need for software that lets companies offer their wares on the Internet. It attracted an A-list of strategic partners, including AT&T Corporation and Time Warner, Inc. And with the dawn of Internet commerce being widely anticipated, the company's initial public offering in May 1996 was a spectacular hit, placing a market cap of $1.2 billion on a company with only $1.8 million in revenues the previous year.

By 1999, three years later, Open Market's lead all but disappeared. Although the company was still the No. 1 seller of consumer e-commerce software, its market share fell to 22% in 1998, down from 31% the year before, even as competitors such as BroadVision, Inc. and Intershop Communications, Inc. gained ground, according to Dataquest. Four of the company's top managers defected in six months, including Robert Weinberger, its vice president for marketing. Worse yet, all this was happening when the e-commerce software market was finally exploding . . . "The market for commerce software was taking off. Open Market wasn't," according to the analyst Greg P. Vogel at Bank of America Securities.

Easy Errors

What went wrong? The Burlington (Massachusetts) company's executives made a series of fundamental mistakes—which serve as valuable lessons for other e-biz entrepreneurs. For starters, they chose the wrong market initially, investing $50 million in complex software plumbing best suited to large Web sites. The real hot spot was supplying easy-to-build electronic storefronts.

(Continued)

(Continued)

Then, they branched out into the lesser market of electronic catalogs instead. And they stumbled when it came to acquisitions. An ill-conceived merger with Folio Corporation saddled Open Market with a money-losing business that stalled its annual revenue growth at around 12%. That was a disaster in a business where growth rates of 100% were common.

The formidable advantages that Open Market started out with just melted away—in spite of its promising technology and a ready-made market. Its struggles showed just how difficult it is to make smart choices in the chaotic e-business environment, where conventional business logic goes out the window. Normally, seeking out the largest customers, acquiring companies to fill in gaps in a production line, and building up a broad portfolio of proprietary technology are considered wise moves. In Open Market's case, they were blunders . . . CEO Gary B. Eichhorn, who was hired in 1995, promised to deliver a new suite of products . . . that includes less-expensive versions of its software, with simpler tools for setting up electronic storefronts. "They're providing a very robust product," said James R. Preissler, an analyst at PaineWebber, Inc., who believed that the company will eventually recover.

At that time, though, Open Market found itself in a sort of purgatory. In most industries, the rank of various players can change over time. But e-business enforces a harsh discipline: The leading companies tend to get big quickly, and they snap up the lion's share of the market. That leaves precious little room for players who don't execute crisply. "Very few Internet companies occupy the middle, like Open Market," said Shikhar Ghosh, the company's founder and chairman. "The vast majority is either in the high stratosphere of market valuations, or they've died." . . . Ghosh and Eichhorn's first mistake was aiming too high. They focused on developing complex systems to help companies such as AT&T and Time Warner build online shopping malls. The price, including services: $1 million and up. Meanwhile, competitors such as BroadVision were building simple products for individual businesses. They focused on creating a satisfying shopping experience. Open Market paid less attention to shoppers and got left behind.

When Ghosh and Eichhorn finally decided to branch out, they picked the wrong target. Instead of going after the storefront business, they added an electronic product catalog to their lineup. And they acquired a company to do it—Folio in Provo, Utah. Open Market's strategy was to increase sales quickly by introducing its e-commerce software to Folio's customers. But they weren't interested. Worse, integrating Folio's operations proved hugely distracting. "What we lost in focus, we didn't gain back in business," admitted Eichhorn.

Inflexible

At the same time, Open Market was wasting precious cash by investing needlessly in technologies that weren't absolutely vital. When it started, it had to build its own Web application server software—which makes e-commerce Web sites run faster. Later, after Netscape and other companies started specializing in such software, Open Market continued to pour money into the project. Partly, it was misdirected pride. "We considered ours to be better than Netscape's," said Ghosh. When Ghosh finally realized that he was wasting money on something that wasn't strategic, switching over to Netscape's Web server "was very expensive."

Another costly blunder was spreading resources too thin by expanding overseas. After only one year of business, Open Market was offering its software in 25 countries. That played to the strengths of its software, developed from the ground up to have the capacity to handle e-commerce transactions in multiple currencies and different tax regimes. But updating software for all those companies was expensive and didn't pay off. "There is usually one customer in each country who wants this stuff," said Ghosh. "It's very seductive." Open Market was behind—and, what's more, it was having real trouble winning over new customers. In some cases, it was because the company wasn't flexible enough. Kirk Sanders, CEO of Professional Golf Commerce Inc., which sells golfing gear on the Web to 17,000 pro shops, found Interworld Corporation to be more willing to modify its software to his requirements. "Open Market thought they were the only solution," he said. Other times, Open Market was said to be a technology laggard. Cozone.com, CompUSA Inc.'s online computer retail store, chose BroadVision over Open Market . . . Open Market "is on the right track," said R. Stephen Polley, Cozone.com's CEO. "But BroadVision is six to eight months ahead. We wanted someone geared to staying ahead, who can work with us to push the envelope."

Eichhorn was pushing hard to catch up with rivals. He believed that the company would ultimately regain momentum, thanks to the powerful sales-transaction technology that Ghosh started investing in five years earlier. He was betting that it would become vital to thousands of Web sites as they grow and that the competition wouldn't be able to match Open Market's capabilities. "In two years people might look at us and think it was a brilliant strategy," he said.

Open Market had a second chance—rare for startups that make this many mistakes . . . But it had to do much more to deliver on all its early promise.

Questions

1. Discuss this case in the context of "lead from strength."

2. What are Open Market's strengths and weaknesses?

3. How should Open Market have handled its overseas expansion?

4. For discussion, go on the Internet and ascertain Open Market's current standings.

SOURCE: Adapted from Paul C. Judge, "Where Is It Now: Open Market's Fall," *Business Week* (November 1, 1999), pp. EB76, EQ78. Copyright © 1999, McGraw-Hill. All rights reserved. Used with permission.

NOTES

1. Alex Taylor III, "Rough Road Ahead," *Fortune* (March 17, 1997), p. 114.

2. See Dexter Roberts, Michael Arndt, and Pete Engardio, "Why U.S. Companies Love China," *Business Week Online* (September 13, 2005). www.inhome.rediff.com/p/articles/mi_mOBJK/is_1_19/ai

3. Part of this discussion draws from S. Rose, "Why the Multinational Is Ebbing," *Fortune* (August 1977), pp. 111–120. Rose uses the labels "aggressive" and "defensive" reasons.

4. M. Schuman and V. Reitman, "A Worldwide Glut Doesn't Sway Samsung from Auto Business," *The Wall Street Journal* (August 25, 1997), pp. A1, A11.

5. A. Bernstein, S. Jackson, and J. Byrne, "Jack Cracks the Whip Again," *Business Week* (December 15, 1997), pp. 34–35.

6. J. Sapsford and J. T. Areddy, "Why Delphi's Asia Operations Are Booming," *The Wall Street Journal* (October 17, 2005), pp. B1, B4.

7. S. K. Yoder, "U.S. Technology Firms Go Global to Offset Weak Domestic Market," *The Wall Street Journal* (November 14, 1989), p. A1.

8. A. G. Holzinger, "Selling in the New Europe," *Nation's Business* (December 1991), p. 18.

9. I. Teinowitz, "Kobs Looks to Growth Overseas," *Advertising Age* (February 27, 1989), p. 70.

10. J. B. Treece et al., "New Worlds to Conquer," *Business Week* (February 28, 1994), p. 50; see also Larry Greenemeier, "New Worlds to Conquer," *InformationWeek* (September 8, 2002).

11. Khozem Merchant, "The Year of Taking India Seriously," *Financial Times* (October 18, 2005), Corporate Strategy section.

12. V. O'Connell and M. Fong, "Saks to Follow Luxury Brands Into China," *The Wall Street Journal* (April 18, 2006), pp. B1, B2.

13. Janet Morrissey, "GE Real Estate Plans to Launch and Invest in China Markets," *The Wall Street Journal* (March 22, 2006), p. B1.

14. Rik Kirkland, "The Man With the Golden Gut," *Fortune* (October 17, 2005), p. 157.

15. Dexter Roberts, "A Hard Sell for Microsoft," *Business Week* (November 1, 1999), p. 60.

16. The editors of *Fortune* and Joe McGowan, *Fortune Advertiser* (1998), p. 84.

17. For information on how firms grow, see Elizabeth Maitland, Elizabeth Rose, and Stephen Nicholas, "How Firms Grow: Clustering as a Dynamic Model of Internationalization," *Journal of International Business Studies,* 36 (2005), pp. 435–451.

18. S. K. Yoder, "U.S. Technology Firms Go Global," op cit.

19. E. D. Welles, "Being There," *INC* (September 1990), p. 143.

20. J. R. Emshwiller and F. Rose, "Guess's Ambitious Design for Global Expansion Falters," *The Wall Street Journal* (November 26, 1997), p. B4.

21. M. Halkias, "Frito-Lay to Buy Snack Brands Abroad," *Dallas Morning News* (November 18, 1997), pp. D1, D10.

22. D. C. Shanks, "Strategic Planning for Global Competition," *Journal of Business Strategy,* 5, no. 3 (Winter 1985), p. 80.

23. James Brooke, "South Korea Becoming a Big Investor," *The New York Times, International Business* (October 20, 2005), pp. 1, 4.

24. Bernard Condon and Michael Freedman, with Naazneen Karmali, "Globetrotter," *The Forbes Global 2000* (April 18, 2005). www.forbes.com/free forbes/2005/2005/0418/068 3.html

25. S. K. Yoder, "U.S. Technology Firms Go Global," op cit.

26. Ibid.

27. K. H. Hammonds and J. Friedman, "Who's That Knocking on Foreign Doors? U.S. Insurance Salesmen," *Business Week* (March 6, 1984), p. 8.

28. "Spain Puffs On," *Economist,* 5 (December 19, 1987), p. 47.

29. R. A. Melcher, J. Flynn, and R. Neff, "Anheuser-Busch Says Skoal, Salude, Prosit," *Business Week* (September 20, 1993), p. 6.

30. M. Bernstein and M. Weinstein, "Globalshakeout: The Changing Landscape of Financial Services," *Prudential Leader,* no. 2 (February 1998), p. 9.

31. Jeffrey E. Garten, "Troubles Ahead in Emerging Markets," *Harvard Business Review* (May–June 1997), p. 38.

32. Hassan M. Fattah, "Chinese Leader Increases Trade Ties With Saudi Arabia," *The New York Times* (April 23, 2006). www.nytimes.com/chinarises

33. R. Brady, M. Maremont, and P. Galuszka, "Aeroflot Takes Off for Joint-Ventureland," *Business Week* (October 30, 1989), pp. 48–49.

34. SOURCE: http://en.wikipedia.org/wiki/Aeroflot

35. Paul Horn, "Boomers Wealth of Knowledge," *Business Week Online* (October 18, 2005). www.businessweek.com/technology/content/oct2005/te20051018 271109.htm

36. For a recent study on this topic, see K. Bunyaratavej, E. D. Hahn, and J. P. Doh, "International Offshoring of Services: A Parity Study," *Journal of International Management,* 13, no. 1 (March 2007), pp. 7–21.

37. Seth Lubove, "We Have a Big Pond to Play In," *Forbes* (September 13, 1993), p. 216.

38. Frank E. Bair (Ed.), *International Marketing Handbook,* 2nd ed. (Detroit: MI: Gale Research Company, 1985), p. 1582.

39. B. Dumaine, "The Bureaucracy Busters," *Fortune* (June 17, 1991), p. 46.

40. J. Dupuy, "Learning to Manage World-Class Strategy," *Management Review* (October 1991), p. 40.

41. For a study on strategic alliance-based sourcing, see Janet Y. Murray, Masaaki Kotabe, and Joe Nan Zhou, "Strategic Alliance-Based Sourcing and Market Performance; Evidence From Foreign Firms Operating in China," *Journal of International Business Studies,* 36 (2005), pp. 187–208.

42. J. G. Wissema and L. Euser, "Successful Innovation Through Inter-Company Networks," *Long-Range Planning,* 24 (December 1991), pp. 33–39.

43. B. Dumaine, "The Bureaucracy Busters," op cit., p. 46.

44. Andrew C. Inkpen, "Learning and Knowledge Acquisition Through International Strategic Alliances," *Academy of Management Executive,* 12, no. 4 (1998), p. 70.

45. Ibid.

46. See Mark de Rond, *Strategic Alliances as Social Facts: Business, Biotechnology and Intellectual History* (Cambridge, UK: Cambridge University Press, 2003).

47. See R. J. Barnet and J. Cavanagh, *Global Dreams* (New York: Simon & Schuster, 1994); W. J. Holstein, "The Stateless Corporation," *Business Week* (May 14, 1990), pp. 98–106.

48. A. M. Rugman and A. Verbeke, "A Perspective on Regional and Global Strategies of Multinational Enterprises," *Journal of International Business Studies,* 35 (2004), pp. 3–18.

49. Thomas Hout, Michael E. Porter, and Eileen Rudden, "How Global Companies Win Out," *Harvard Business Review* (September–October 1982), p. 103.

50. Fred L. Steingraber, "How to Succeed in the Global Marketplace," *USA Today Magazine* (November 1997), p. 32.

51. Hout et al., "How Global Companies Win Out," op cit.

52. Ibid.

53. George S. Yip, "Global Strategy . . . in a World of Nations?" *Sloan Management Review* (Fall 1989), p. 29.

54. Ibid.

55. Regina Fazio Maruca, "The Right Way to Go Global: An Interview With Whirlpool CEO David Whitwam," *Harvard Business Review* (March–April 1994), p. 136.

56. Yip, "Global Strategy . . . in a World of Nations?" op cit.

57. SOURCE: www.nestle.com (February 8, 1998).

58. M. A. Hitt, B. W. Keats, and S. M. DeMario, "Navigating in the New Competitive Landscape: Building Strategic Flexibility and Competitive Advantage in the 21st Century," *Academy of Management Executive,* 12, no. 4 (November 1998), p. 23.

59. See Whitaker Penteado, "Fast-Food Franschises Fight for Brazilian Aficionados." Used with permission of publisher from *Brandweek* (June 7, 1993), p. 20.

60. Peter Drucker, *The Practice of Management* (New York: Harper & Row, 1954).

61. SOURCE: K. C. Swanson, "We've Got the Solid Grounding, Now for Creative Thinking," *Financial Times* (October 19, 2005), p. 8.

62. J. R. Basch Jr. and M. G. Duerr, *International Transfer of Technology: A Worldwide Survey of Executives* (New York: The Conference Board, 1975), p. 1.

63. S. H. Robock and K. Simmonds, *International Business and Multinational Enterprises* (Homewood, IL: Richard D. Irwin, 1983), p. 461.

64. Basch and Duerr, *International Transfer of Technology,* op cit.

65. Ibid. p. 8.

66. Ibid, pp. 10–11.

67. "China and India: The Challenge, The New World Economy," *Business Week Online* (August 22, 2005). www.businessweek.com/print/magazine/content/0534/b3948401.html? chan=gl

68. John Tagliabue, "Fakes Blot a Nation's Good Names," *The New York Times* (July 3, 1997), pp. D1, D2.

69. SOURCE: http://en.wikipedia.org/wiki/Agreement_on_Trade-Related_Aspects_of_ Intellectual_Prope (February 28, 2007).

70. Masaaki Kotabe, "A Comparative Study of U.S. and Japanese Patent Systems," *Journal of International Business Studies,* 23, no. 1 (First Quarter 1992), p. 148.

71. Ibid. p. 149.

72. See "Limitations and Exceptions to Copyright." http://en.wikipedia.orn/wiki/ Exceptions and limitations to copyright (February 28, 2007).

73. Ford S. Worthy, "Japan's Smart Secret Weapon," *Fortune* (August 12, 1991), p. 72.

74. John R. Engen, "Getting Your Chinese Workforce Up to Speed," *International Business* (August 1994), p. 48.

75. Toshio Nakahara and Yutaka Isono, "Strategic Planning For Canon: The Crisis and the New Vision," *Long Range Planning,* 25 (February 1992), p. 63.

76. This information was obtained from colleagues in Honduras during this author's visit to Honduras in 2003.

77. SOURCE: "International Data Development." http://idc.com/prodserv/maps/bric.jsp (August 22, 2006).

78. Charles K. Kao, *A Choice Fulfilled: The Business of High Technology* (New York: St. Martin's Press, 1991).

79. For a further discussion on this topic, see Thomas L. Friedman, "It's a Flat World, After All," *The New York Times* (April 3, 2005). www.freerepublic.com/focus/f-news/1378440/posts

80. "IDC Says India Will Be the Next 'Potential' Rich Online Gaming Market." http://idc.com/prodserv/maps/bric.jsp (August 22, 2006).

81. Ann Saccomano, "Time for Wine Online," *Traffic World,* 259, no. 8 (August 23, 1999), p. 14.

82. Sunny Baker, "Global E-Commerce, Local Problems," *Journal of Business Strategy,* 20, no. 4 (July–August 1999), pp. 32–38.

83. Ibid.

84. See Arvind Parkhe (Ed.), "International Outsourcing of Services: Introduction to the Special Issue," *Journal of International Management,* 13, no. 1 (March 2007), pp. 3–6.

85. Nabil Adam, Baruch Awerbuch, Jacob Slonim, Peter Wagner, and Yelena Yesha, "Globalizing Business, Education, Culture through the Internet," *Communications of the ACM,* 40, no. 2 (February 1997), pp. 115–121.

5

INTERNATIONALIZATION STRATEGIES

Wal-Mart Stores, Inc. is finding out [1997] that what plays in Peoria isn't necessarily a hit in suburban Sao Paulo. Tanks of live trout are out; sushi is in. American footballs have been replaced by soccer balls. The fixings for feijoadas, a medley of beef and pork in black bean stew, are now displayed on the deli counter. American style jeans priced at $19.99 have been dropped in favor for $9.99 knockoffs. But adapting to local tastes may have been the easy part. Three years after embarking on a blitz to bring "everyday low prices" to the emerging markets of Brazil and Argentina, Wal-Mart is finding the going tougher than expected. Brutal competition, market conditions that don't play to Wal-Mart's ability to achieve efficiency through economies of scale, and some of its own mistakes have produced red ink. Moreover, the company's insistence on doing things "the Wal-Mart way" has apparently alienated local suppliers and employees.[1] In 2006 Wal-Mart is still encountering the same problems in other markets and it is pulling its operations out of Germany.[2]

Learning Objectives of the Chapter

Because of changes taking place around the globe, to remain competitive and to increase their opportunities, domestic enterprises will need to develop strategies for entering the international business arena. Effective internationalization of business operations relies on managers' abilities to develop internationally effective product/service, entry, price, and promotion strategies in light of the enterprise's external environment (discussed in Chapters 3 and 4), as well as in light of the firm's internal situation (discussed in Chapter 4). After studying this chapter, you should be able to do the following:

1. Discuss international product/service strategy

2. Discuss international entry strategy

3. Discuss international pricing strategy

4. Discuss international promotion strategy

5. Discuss the impact of the Internet on internationalization strategies

Product/Service Strategy

In developing product/service strategy, managers are typically concerned with what the product or service should look like and what it should be able to do. In conducting this assessment for foreign markets, managers must overcome the self-reference criterion (SRC). They must determine whether their product or service can be sold in standard form or whether it must be customized to fit differing foreign market needs. Managers must also understand that many products or services do not immediately sell well in foreign markets and must undergo a diffusion process.

The Self-Reference Criterion (SRC)

The SRC is the unconscious reference to one's own cultural values. This unconscious reference is the root of many international business problems.[3] Complex problems can occur when the SRC leads a manager to assume that a product or service that sells well in the home market will sell well in foreign markets in the same form. In many cases it does not because, culturally, people in different societies require the products and services in a different form.

Managers can eliminate the SRC by first defining the problem in terms of the home society's cultural traits, values, habits, and norms and then redefining the problem, without value judgments, in terms of the foreign market's cultural traits, values, habits, and norms. The difference represents the cultural influence on the problem. The manager subsequently restates and solves the problem in the context of both cultures.

For example, Americans like moist, creamy cakes for dessert, purchased ready-baked in grocery stores. However, attempting to market moist, creamy cakes in grocery stores in England may result in failure because the English generally like dry cakes that can be eaten with their fingers with their tea, and when the occasion calls for moist, creamy cakes, they like to bake their own. General Mills ran into this problem when it took Betty Crocker to England many years ago.[4] J. C. Penney made a mistake when it put up a store in the affluent Santiago neighborhood of Las Condes in 1996. It misread Chilean taste, which favors simple clothes, and offered expensive lines in the flashy colors popular in tropical markets such as Miami and Mexico.[5] From the start (1985), IKEA's U.S. foray has run into problems, starting with its failure to tailor its European products to U.S. tastes. IKEA sold European-size sheets and curtains that did not fit U.S. beds and windows,[6] and it sold mattresses in Canada that were too large for the bedsheets sold in Canadian stores. Americans developed a liking for commodious cup holders in their cars, but Mercedes-Benz and BMW, the European car manufacturers, rejected the notion of installing cup holders in their socially prestigious automobiles.

Eventually, they bowed to U.S. drivers' wants; they have installed cup holders.[7] (For another example, read Practical Perspective 5.1, the case of Disney's expansion to France. Note that Disney's management had to repackage some of the original Disney characters.)

PRACTICAL PERSPECTIVE 5-1

Disney Goes to France

A few days after Disney' theme park opened in Tokyo, an amazed Japanese girl asked an American visitor, "Is there really a Disneyland in America?" That should have been music to the mouse ears of Euro Disneyland's management, beleaguered by charges that they were defining the Frenchness of France. Ah, to convince the French that Mickey and Donald belong as much to Marne-la-Vallee as they do to Anaheim, Orlando, and Tokyo. Sensitive to the charge that Euro Disneyland amounted to what the theater director, Ariane Mnouchkine, in a widely quoted assessment, called a "cultural Chernobyl," the company tried for months to persuade Europeans that, in the words of a Disney spokesperson, "It's not America, it's Disney." On opening (April 1992), Disney's chairman Michael Eisner stressed, like a guest too eager to please, that the company had repackaged original European characters: the French Cinderella, the Italian Pinocchio, the German Snow White. More truculently, a Euro Disneyland spokesperson said, "Who are these Frenchmen, anyway? We offered them the dream of a lifetime and lots of jobs. They treated us like invaders."[a]

Disney's entry mode into Japan was via franchising [covered in a subsequent section of this chapter], but in Europe it went at it alone, bringing its U.S. Disney American management style.[b] But after several years of learning through the "school-of-hard-knocks," Disney eventually appointed a French executive to head the park. Euro Disneyland, now Disneyland Paris, opened the Walt Disney Studios Park in March 16, 2002, as part of The Walt Disney Company's $2 billion pledge to try to rescue its operations in Paris, as well as to open a new theme gate at each of their resorts around the world. Disney Resort Parks is currently owned and operated by a French company [like in Tokyo], but the Walt Disney Company does own 39.78 percent of its stock. The restructuring planned for Disney Resorts Parks to receive a major new attraction each year from 2005 to 2009. On January 11, 2005, two new attractions were announced at Disney Park Studios: Space Mountain: Mission 2 (2005) and Buzz Lightyear Laser Blast (2006), and Toon Studio is planned for June 2007 and The Twilight Zone Tower of Terror for late 2007/early 2008.[c]

SOURCES:

a. Abstracted from Todd Gitlin, "World Leaders: Mickey, et al.," *The New York Times,* sec. 2 (May 3, 1992), p. 1. Copyright © 1992 by The New York Times Company. Reprinted by permission.

b. Abstracted from Dr. Tung-Hung, "Euro Disneyland," a case prepared for Carl Rodrigues, *International Management,* 2nd ed. (Cincinnati, OH: South-Western College Publishing, 2001).

c. M. Schuman and J. Ressner, "Disney's Great Leap Into China," *Time,* 166, no. 3 (July 18, 2005); "Walt Disney Studios Park" (March 18, 2007). http://en.wkipedia.org/wiki/Walt_Disney_Studios_Park-55k

It should be noted that the assessment may sometimes reveal that the firm's product or service, because of cultural or other factors, cannot be customized for a foreign market. For example, in the 1970s, Kentucky Fried Chicken (KFC), the popular U.S.-based fast food chain, as pointed out in Chapters 1 and 3, expanded its operations to

Brazil. The expansion was a failure. A Brazilian marketing executive believes that KFC failed because Brazilians do not much care to eat chicken outside their homes.[8] KFC, however, tried again, this time targeting only specific market groups. Campbell's soups also had little success in Brazil, where most housewives felt the need to do more than merely heat up a ready-to-eat soup.[9] But Campbell's soup, as Practical Perspective 5.2 indicates, seems to have learned. Home Depot learned the hard way by failing in Chile and Argentina. But it is currently entering China very carefully.[10]

PRACTICAL PERSPECTIVE 5-2

Campbell's Soup: Expanding an International Presence

By the year 2000, Campbell's hoped to generate half its revenue from outside the USA. Gaining global share was not going to be easy, however, as its major competitors, CPC International and H. J. Heinz, were well-entrenched and generated a significant portion of their sales outside the USA market.

A key component of Campbell's strategy was to develop products suited to local tastes in various foreign markets. In Poland, where soup consumption was three times higher than in the USA, they developed varieties of condensed soup, including chicken noodle and flaki, a peppery tripe soup. For China, Campbell kitchens in the USA and Hong Kong developed an extensive array of exotic soups, including duck gizzards, watercress, and scallop broth, and radish-and-carrot, pork, fig, and date soup. In Mexico, they developed Crema de Chile Poblano, and in the Argentine market, split pea with ham has proven popular.

Developing varieties that suit local tastes is not the only challenge that Campbell faced. In Argentina there was a strong preference for powdered soups and CPC's Korr brand controlled 80 percent of the market. Campbell enjoyed some success by stressing the fresh ingredients in Sopa de Campbell. In Poland, where 98 percent of the soup was homemade, Campbell targeted working mothers while stressing the convenience of its product. Here again, however, they faced competition from CPC, owner of the Polish soup market, Amino. Campbell and others in the food industry have recognized the need to develop new products and brand extensions that are geared to local market tastes.[a] Today [September 5, 2006], Campbell's name stretches to China, Australia, Argentina, and beyond. Its products are available in every country in the world. It continues offering products suited to the local culture, like Watercress and Duck-Gizzard Soup in China and a Cream of Chili Poblano soup in Mexico.[b]

SOURCES:

a. Excerpted from G. S. Graig and S. P. Douglas, "Developing Strategies for Global Markets: An Evolutionary Perspective," *The Columbia Journal of World Business* (Spring 1996), p. 73. Reprinted with permission.

b. Campbell's Soup Company History (September 6, 2006). www.campbellsoupcompany.com/history.asp?cpovisq=

Therefore, international strategists should seek answers to four basic questions:[11]

1. Who in the foreign market uses the product? In what ways are the targeted foreign buyers similar to or different from domestic buyers? How can this product be incorporated into the foreign market's lifestyle?

2. What are the values of the people in the foreign market? Is their value based on timeliness, quality, service, or price? What changes in the products/services need to be made to meet the foreign customers' needs?

3. What are the signals that indicate change in the market? Does the market accept foreign ideas? Are there cross-cultural trends?

4. How can the firm increase market share? Who are the local competitors? Who are the foreign competitors? How much disposable income do consumers have?

Product Strategy

Customization Versus Standardization

Fundamentally, there are three viable alternatives when entering a foreign market: (1) market the same product everywhere (standardization), (2) adapt the product for foreign markets (customization), and (3) develop a totally new product for the foreign market(s). By combining these three alternatives with promotional efforts, five different product strategies can be developed.[12]

1. *Standardize product/standardize message:* Using this strategy, a firm sells the same product and uses the same promotional appeals in all markets. In other words, product and promotional appeals are globally standardized. Coca-Cola, Pepsi Cola, Avon, McDonald's, Sony Walkman, Levi's, and Maidenform are some examples of products that follow this strategy. Military products also follow this strategy. But it should be pointed out that there is no truly global product. For example, Coca-Cola and Pepsi Cola still have to make some minor product customization by changing the taste to fit specific cultures.

2. *Standardize product/customize message:* Enterprises using this approach customize only the promotional message. For example, a bicycle may be sold in the U.S. market for joyriding. In an economically poor country, however, the promotional message may have to be customized to stress economy; that is, the bicycle would be promoted as a means of relatively inexpensive basic transportation.

3. *Customize product/standardize message:* Using this strategy, the company customizes the product to meet the needs of the specific foreign market but promotes the same use as it does in the domestic market. For example, electric sewing machines manufactured for the U.S. market would not sell well in a market where few residents have access to electricity. The manufacturer could, however, customize the machine to sell in that market by producing hand- or foot-cranked sewing machines. The hand- or foot-cranked machine would be promoted in the foreign market in the same way it is in the U.S. market—to sew clothes. Moviemakers at Hollywood in the United States also employ this strategy—they make films, which with customization, such as dubbing in the local language or inserting language translation subtitles, can be distributed globally but are promoted as entertainment worldwide.

4. *Customize product/customize message:* Manufacturers applying this strategy customize the product to meet different use patterns in the foreign market and customize the promotional message attached to it as well. For example, bicycles in the United States are usually lightweight and are generally promoted for use in leisure activities. In many less developed countries, Honduras, for example, however, because of rough roads, the need may be for a stronger bicycle, and the bicycle is often used as a major form of transportation. China is another example of a country where bicycles are heavyweight and are used as a major means of transportation.

5. *Different product:* Using this approach, rather than adapting an existing product, the manufacturer invests in the development of a totally new one to fit the needs of specific foreign markets. For example, Coca-Cola's and Pepsi's diet sodas do not sell well in Asia and Europe because consumers there prefer the creamy sweetness of regular Coke or Pepsi and consider sugar-free sodas as drinks for diabetics and the obese, not for the young and energetic. To deal with this problem, Pepsi designed a new diet cola, called Pepsi Max, specifically for these and other markets. Pepsi Max uses a sweetener that makes it close to the regular colas in taste.[13] Hollywood can make a film specifically for one market. (Refer to Practical Perspective 5.3.) Practical Perspective 5.4 presents Microsoft's strategy to develop a product for the Chinese market. For many years, General Motors was losing billions of dollars in the European market, and to recover in that market, it produced a new car specifically for it—the Astra OPC.[14]

Standardization Is Ideal, but Not Realistic

Of course, manufacturing and selling standardized products worldwide is more efficient because it eliminates the cost of customizing products. For example, it costs moviemakers a lot of money to dub in the local language for different foreign markets. The American professor of marketing Theodore Levitt contended that in an era of global competition, the product strategy of successful firms is evolving from offering

PRACTICAL PERSPECTIVE 5-3

Script Locally

Sony, in 1998, became the first global company to go into foreign-language film production when Columbia TriStar set up shop in Germany at Babelsberg, the long-dormant Potsdam studio where Fritz Lang shot Metropolis. Sony execs figured English-language pictures still commanded nearly 80 percent of the world's box office—but for how long? "When you've got that kind of market share," worried Columbia TriStar film chief Ken Lemberger, "you can only go down."

In television, that was happening already: For two years running, the big news at Mipcom, the global television sales fest at Cannes, had seen American series being pushed out of prime time by the local stuff. Network hits like ER were still big, but the fledgling satellite and cable companies that bought American shows wholesale a few years earlier, outfits like Canal Plus in France, were then billion-dollar enterprises with the resources to fill their evenings with local programming. "As the European marketplace continues to mature, you won't find a lot of American series in prime time," said Andy Kaplan of Columbia TriStar Television.

That was bad news for Hollywood studios, which had been relying on international sales to make up the difference between the $1.5 million or so that it cost to produce an hour-long drama episode and the $1 million a USA network typically paid for it. But in the emerging markets of Asia and Latin America, where the big media conglomerates owned channels instead of just selling to them, they had even more at stake. Sony Entertainment Television in India, Time Warner's HBO Olé and HBO Brasil partnerships in Latin America, News Corporation's Star TV in Asia—these companies sunk billions into pipelines for delivering entertainment, partly to exploit the millions of hours of American movies and television shows they owned. Blockbuster Hollywood movies were still a huge draw worldwide, but most audiences preferred local TV shows—and if that's what they want, that's what they'll get.

SOURCE: Excerpted from Frank Rose, "Think Globally, Script Locally," *Fortune* (November 8, 1999), pp. 157–158.

PRACTICAL PERSPECTIVE 5-4

A Hard Sell for Microsoft

Meet Wu Yanbin, a 21-year-old college student checking out [in 1999] the new computers at the Xidan Department Store in western Beijing. He was a devoted techie who surfed the Internet every day. So asking him what he thought about Microsoft Corporation's key China strategy: promoting set-top boxes with its WinCE software that allows anyone with a TV Set to go on-line. "Microsoft is a giant. I really admire it," he said. But would he buy one of their set-top boxes? No way. Said Wu: "Their functions are too limited for me."

Both blessing and curse—that refrain seemed to run through Microsoft's attempts to do business in China. After months of setbacks, Microsoft said that its new technology, known as the Venus project, would be rolled out at the end of October [1999]. The box, with TV-customized software, lets users read e-mail, surf the Internet, and do simple word processing while sitting in front of the tube with a remote keyboard.

The plan certainly had potential: Then, more than 300 million households in China owned a television. And Chinese so far owned just 2 million PCs. So Microsoft wanted to "stake a claim in the living room," said Sean Zhang, [then] managing director of the Microsoft (China) Research & Development Center and initiator of the project. Analysts said the set-top-box market could be worth several hundred million dollars.

SOURCE: Excerpted from Dexter Roberts, "A Hard Sell for Microsoft," *Business Week* (November 1, 1999), p. 60. Reprinted with permission.

customized products (a multidomestic strategy) to offering globally standardized ones (a global strategy). Such a product strategy requires the development of universal products or products that require no more than a cosmetic change for adaptation to different local needs and use conditions[15] (e.g., Coca-Cola and Pepsi Cola mentioned in Strategy 1 above fit this mode). As was pointed out in Practical Perspective 4.9 (Chapter 4), the Japanese automobile manufacturer Honda has a strategy to build a global car. The strategy entails using a new standardized manufacturing system with flexibility to build cars customized to fit specific market needs. Using this new manufacturing system, the costs of customization are far lower than when using the older systems. In the United States, Ford Motor Company and General Motors have a similar strategy.[16] Strategy 1 discussed above fits this mode, and so does Strategy 2.

As was also discussed in Chapter 4, both the multidomestic and the global strategy approaches have advantages and disadvantages. The global strategy may be appropriate for some products and services and for some nations but not for many other products and services and nations. For example, Japan is a difficult market for many foreign companies—especially U.S. companies—to penetrate because of cultural barriers. To penetrate Japan's market, most products and services require customization. For instance, when KFC entered the Japanese market, it had to make adaptations to cater to the tastes of the local people, including taking the mashed potatoes and gravy off the menu and substituting it with french fries, and halving the sugar in the slaw recipe.[17] Furthermore, some products and services have global appeal only by age groups. For example, teenagers are the most global market of all age groups. Teenagers almost everywhere purchase a common gallery of products: Reebok sports shoes, Procter & Gamble Cover Girl makeup, Sega and Nintendo video games, Nike sports gear, Macintosh computers, and Red Hot Chili Peppers music tapes and CDs.[18] And Gucci, a luxury goods enterprise that targets affluent customers throughout the world, believes that similar demographics and income levels promote similar attitudes and behavioral patterns worldwide. Thus, in 1990, when it relaunched the Gucci name with a print campaign, its "from the hand of Gucci" message was the same in the United States, the United Kingdom, Japan, France, and Italy.[19]

Subhash C. Jain, a professor of international marketing at the University of Connecticut, reviewed published sources to develop a framework for determining the extent of standardization feasible in a particular case. The determining factors in Professor Jain's framework are depicted in Box 5.1.[20]

Box 5.1 Factors That Help Determine Standardization or Customization

- In general, standardization is more practical in markets that are economically alike.
- Standardization strategy is more effective if worldwide customers, not countries, are the basis of identifying the segment(s) to serve.
- The greater the similarity in the markets in terms of customer behavior and lifestyle, the higher the degree of standardization.
- The higher the cultural compatibility of the product across the host countries, the greater the degree of standardization.
- The greater the degree of similarity in a firm's competitive position in different markets, the higher the degree of standardization.
- Competing against the same adversaries, with similar share positions, in different countries leads to greater standardization than competing against purely local companies.
- Industrial and high-technology products are more suitable for standardization than consumer products.
- Standardization is more appropriate when the home market positioning strategy is meaningful in the host market.
- The greater the difference in physical, political, and legal environments between home and host countries, the lower the degree of standardization.
- The more similar the marketing infrastructure in the home and host countries, the higher the degree of standardization.
- Companies in which key managers share a worldview, as well as a common view of the critical tasks flowing from the strategy, are more effective in implementing a standardization strategy.
- The greater the strategic consensus among parent-subsidiary managers on key standardization issues, the more effective the implementation of standardization strategy.
- The greater the centralization of authority for setting policies and allocating resources, the more effective the implementation of standardization strategy.

Service Strategy

As indicated above, a dilemma in global strategy for manufacturing businesses is the need to balance standardization with local customization. In contrast, in service delivery, in many cases, standardization and customization are equally feasible. There are three broad service categories: people-processing, possession-processing, and information-based services.[21]

People-Processing Services. In these services, customers become part of the production process. Such services include passenger transportation, health care, food services, and lodging services. The customer is present during the service. For example, Disney provides entertainment services in theme parks in Paris, Tokyo, and Hong Kong. (Of course, Disney also provides these services for foreign customers in California and Florida.) London hospitals maintain a lucrative business caring for wealthy patients from the Middle East, as do hospitals in Miami, Florida, for patients from Latin America.

Possession-Processing Services. Services of this nature involve tangible actions to tangible objects to enhance their value to customers. The customer need not be present. These services include transporting freight, installing equipment, and maintenance. For example, an American living near the Canadian border can go to Canada to have his or her car serviced because of lower costs resulting from favorable exchange rates. For instance, if it costs $300 in both countries to have a car tuned up and the exchange rate is U.S.$1 equals Canadian $1.50, an American who goes to Canada for the service would save U.S. $100 less the expense of driving across the border. An international corporation might provide, for example, bridge repair services or elevator repair services throughout the world.

Information-Based Services. The provision of these services involves collecting, manipulating, interpreting, and transmitting data to create value. Examples include services such as accounting, banking, consulting, education, insurance, legal services, and news. For instance, CNN provides news in most countries. Prudential provides insurance in many countries. Citigroup provides banking services in many parts of the world. Many U.S. colleges and universities provide education to a multitude of students from foreign countries around the globe, and a number of them (e.g., American University in Cairo, Egypt,) have established satellites in foreign countries to help educate students abroad. Many American students are now pursuing college degrees in Canadian universities because the cost of tuition there is much lower than at home.[22]

Information Technology and Service Strategy

For all three types of services described above, use of current information technology, such as the Internet, may enable businesses to benefit from favorable labor costs or exchange rates by consolidating operations of supplementary services (such as reservations) or certain office functions (such as accounting) in just one or a few countries. Practical Perspective 5.5 describes a company in India that provides software services from home to businesses in other countries. Note that the cost of the software is about two thirds cheaper in India than in the United States.

Barcelona, Spain, in part because of the sun and the fun, is currently a hot spot for outsourcing such functions. Citigroup has 1,200 employees in Barcelona handling customer support and Internet services for Western Europe. General Motors has outsourced its European accounting, financial services, and human resources support to 450 employees of the U.S.-based IT services company ACS; Hewlett-Packard handles internal and some external tech support using 120 staffers from the French IT services outfit Teamlog; and Agilent Technologies runs administration, finance, and customer service for Europe, the Middle East, and South America using 600 staffers.[23] As pointed out in Chapter 4, outsourcing IT services is the current trend.[24]

Of course, employees in the home country do suffer from the loss of service jobs. (Lou Dobbs, a CNN News commentator, as of 2007, has for several years been on a crusade protesting against the outsourcing of U.S. service jobs.)

PRACTICAL PERSPECTIVE 5-5

Programmers From Abroad

The nation had a shortage of techies... But corporate America had already hit on a response. It's global telecommuting, through which this nation's technology companies had [in 1999] created a whole new realm of international trade by exporting their work and hiring programmers overseas to do it.

Having already scooped up any American programmers they could by offering them the chance to ride the Internet to work from their homes in Jackson Hole, Wyoming, or Boulder, Colorado, the corporations were reaching out to places like South Africa and the Philippines.

So increasingly, the world's commerce involved not just tankers filled with Brent crude or container ships laden with VCRs but cables buzzing with computer programming code, product designs, and engineering, diagrams and formulas, not to mention overhauls of American software gone too soft...

Some companies brought the workers to work, searching the world for computer specialists willing to come to the United States. But virtual immigration, where the workers stay put, became far more common, and remains much cheaper. The software unit of a single company, Tata Sons Ltd., of India, had 5,000 developers, a maquiladora of the mind that can immediately deploy 100 techies on a U.S. corporation's mission. India's software exports had grown from $225 million in 1992 to $1.15 billion in 1996, with a year 2000 goal of $3.6 billion. [As mentioned in the chapter, in 2007, this practice continues, and Lou Dobbs, a CNN newscaster, has for years, during the 2000s, been crusading against the ongoing increase in outsourcing these types of U.S. American jobs.]

Technical advances have made this kind of rapid growth possible. Although banks, among other global institutions, have been electronically advantaged for years, the expense has fallen dramatically. Instead of high-capacity leased lines that can cost hundreds or thousands of dollars a month, a plain old phone connection and an Internet service provider will often do.

"It's no longer an international phone call. Now, it's an Internet file exchange," said Ester Dyson, author of *Release 2.0: A Design for Living in the Digital Age*. A cyber diplomat known for striving to make Eastern Europe at least as wired as its Western neighbors, Dyson also served on the board of the PRT Group in Barbados, a software and computer systems design firm, and Softstep, a company doing Year 2000 fixes from Kyrgyzstan in Central Asia.

While some global telecommunicators, like many Americans, work at home, most are clustered in the foreign quarters of U.S. companies or in the offices of foreign contractors like Tata. Projects can receive round-the-clock attention as they are handed from continent to continent. IBM teams in Europe, India, and the West Coast have kept the development of Java software for the Internet going at all hours, with handoffs over the Internet itself. Even as the giants like Tata prosper, the Internet is also allowing pip-squeaks to be heard and seen, offering electronic sales pitches and work samples. Corporations like IBM find themselves hiring tiny foreign firms that could never have found their way through these companies' front doors.

Those specialists who do migrate to the United States have an advantage in spotting talent back home. Under Sanjiv Sidhu, a native of Hyderabad, India, and Sandy Tungare, an executive from Bombay, 12 Technologies of Dallas runs software development centers in Bombay and Bangalore, where the neighbors include Motorola, Intel, and Hewlett-Packard. "Software developers who would earn at least $50,000 in the United States can be had for about a third as much in India," Tungare said.

SOURCE: Excerpted from Allen R. Myerson, "Need Programmers? Surf Abroad," *The New York Times* (January 18, 1998), p. WK4. Copyright © 1998 by The New York Times Company. Reprinted by permission.

Diffusing Innovations

Not all products and services introduced in a foreign market will be immediately accepted by the prospective customers. Many products and services that are new to a market must go through the diffusion process. Basically, diffusion is "the process by which innovation is communicated through certain channels over time among members of a social system."[25] This means that the product or service is adopted by more and more members of society gradually over time. For example, in September 1998, Starbuck's Coffee signed an agreement to open franchise (discussed later in the chapter) outlets in Beijing, China. The challenge Starbuck's faced was to diffuse its brand name and to persuade the (for the most part) tea-drinking Chinese culture to switch to java.[26] Another problem Starbuck's faces in China is that the Chinese typically do not consume cow's milk; instead, they consume soy bean milk. Of course, this problem can be solved by product adaptation. The American mystique Starbuck's carried to China helped in this respect as well as with competing with the Chinese coffee shops already in existence. (As another example, read Practical Perspective 5.6, which discusses how Budweiser diffused its brand name in China.) Many companies introducing a new product or service often incur losses in the beginning years because the company does not yet have the number of buyers required to cover the fixed costs of investment. In later years, however, after the product or service has been diffused, the enterprise should be able to earn enough money to recapture the early years' losses.

PRACTICAL PERSPECTIVE 5-6

Budweiser's China Challenge

"When we arrived in 1995, virtually no one knew the name 'Budweiser,'" says [Jack] Purnell [CEO, Anheuser-Busch International]. "So we focused immediately on simply building awareness. The first year we put most of our efforts into electronic media. We discovered the 'Ants' commercial created for use in the United States played very well in China, so we ran that, as well as specially created sequel showing the ants' party underground. We also developed another spot for China."

PRACTICAL PERSPECTIVE 5-6 (Continued)

Although China is considered a developing country, the vast majority of Chinese households have access to TV sets, which means that the majority of people can be reached through mass electronic media. The TV ads were supplemented with highly visible sponsorships, such as the World Cup, China National Basketball League, and the China Central TV World Sports Report, as well as with point-of-sale items and promotions at accounts. [It was reported in 2004 that about 600 million people in China watched America's NBA's All-Star game on TV because one of the players was from China.]

The all-out effort worked. In Budweiser's first year on the market, awareness rose from zero to nearly 30 percent in the 22 key cities where the brand was sold. Through all of theses challenges, product quality remained top of mind. After all, that is the single greatest competitive advantage that Anheuser-Busch offers. And it was never compromised.

After two years of operations in China, Budweiser's success speaks for itself. The brand will approach the million-barrel mark this year [1997], and the overall operations are on a strong path to begin to show a profit in the year 2000.

Purnell attributes this success to four things: "First, Budweiser has an appealing taste that is refreshingly different and consistent the world over. Second, the brand has an appealing image with American ties. As the best-selling beer in the world, it's an icon brand. That means a lot to Chinese consumers and elevates the brand's status. Third, we have an innovative and effective distribution system that allows us to gain effective placements in key accounts. And finally, we have a very enthusiastic and talented team of Chinese employees who have joined the Anheuser-Busch family. We are very proud of what they have accomplished in such a short period of time."

That winning formula has resulted in a 20 percent backlog on orders, which in turn has prompted Anheuser-Busch to accelerate its brewery expansion schedule. The Wuhan brewery is currently being doubled in size. When completed in 1998, it will have a capacity of 2.1 million barrels, and Anheuser-Busch's investment in China will exceed $150 million.

"Our short-term goal is to double Budweiser sales to 2 million barrels in the next four years," says Purnell. "This will make Budweiser the fastest-growing premium beer and will result over the longer term in Budweiser becoming the No. 1 premium brand in China. We have a leadership position in 9 of the 27 markets we're in, and we're focusing on increasing that ratio. There are 70 more cities with a population of at least 1 million, so we'll expand our distribution area as we grow.[a]

As of September 5, 2006, Anheuser-Busch International operated 15 breweries—14 in China and one in the United Kingdom. Budweiser also is locally brewed through license agreements in eight countries outside the U.S. under the direct supervision of Anheuser-Busch brewmasters. They are: Argentina, Canada, Ireland, Italy, Japan, Russia, South Korea and Spain. In 2005, Anheuser-Busch's International sales volume (excluding equity affiliate brands) grew by 50 percent to 20.8 million barrels. The company's share of its equity affiliates' volume was 36.4 million barrels, giving Anheuser-Busch a combined international volume of 47.2 million barrels for 2005.[b]

SOURCES:

a. Excerpted from "The China Challenge," *Anheuser-Busch Horizons* (Third Quarter 1997), p. 6. Reprinted with permission.

b. Anheuser-Busch International, Inc. (September 6, 2006). www.anheuser-busch.com/overview/international.html

How Quickly Can a New Product/Service Be Diffused in a Culture?

The way people respond to a new product affects how quickly it is diffused. All new products and services can be categorized according to their varied degrees of newness, and the consumer reactions to each category affect the quickness or slowness of diffusion. Generally, the more disruptive the innovation is, the longer the diffusion process will take. Innovations can be categorized as congruent, continuous, dynamically continuous, and discontinuous.[27]

Congruent Innovations. Congruent innovations do not disrupt established consumption patterns. Congruent innovation means introducing variety and quality or functional features, style, or perhaps a duplicate of an existing product. Introducing vegetable oil as a substitute for olive oil is an example of congruent innovation.

Continuous Innovations. Continuous innovation involves altering a product to enhance the satisfaction derived from its use. Menthol cigarettes, new-model automobiles, and fluoride toothpaste are examples of continuous innovations. Continuous innovations have little disruptive influence on the culture's established consumption patterns.

Dynamically Continuous Innovations. Dynamically continuous innovation usually involves creating a new product or substantially altering an existing one to fulfill new needs created by changes in lifestyles or new expectations. Examples are frozen dinners, electric toothbrushes, and electric lawn mowers. These innovations are normally disruptive and therefore are resisted because the old patterns of consumption must be changed. Consumer behavior must be transformed if users are to recognize and accept the value of dynamically continuous innovations.

Discontinuous Innovations. Discontinuous innovation introduces an entirely new idea or behavior pattern. It means establishing fresh and untried consumption patterns. This would be the most disruptive innovation. An example is the introduction of a banking system into a traditional society where people tend to keep their money hidden at home or somewhere else.

Dualistic Technological Structures

Diffusion of new products or services is also affected by the technological structure of the country. A dualistic technological structure exists in the economies of most developing countries.[28] It refers to the simultaneous existence of a modern industrial sector and a traditional sector involved in agricultural and craft production. The modern sector involves large-scale, capital-intensive industries utilizing modern technologies and technically skilled labor to manufacture basic industrial goods such as energy, construction materials, and electrical and mechanical equipment. The traditional sector of many less developed economies is characterized by small-scale, labor-intensive industries using simple technologies with low capital investment and unskilled labor to produce agricultural and consumer products for domestic markets. For example, China modernized its industrial sector at a much faster rate than its agricultural sector. A reason for this might be that if modernization of the industrial sector is not substantially ahead of the modernization of the agricultural sector, the former may not be ready to employ those workers who became unemployed due to the modernization of the latter—thus generating problems stemming from high unemployment.

Managers should thus be aware that a developing nation may need advanced technologies in one sector and older technologies in another. They should also be aware that a developing nation may need both *adaptive technological innovations* and *transformative technological innovations.*[29]

Adaptive technological innovations are important to the modern industrial sector. They aim at modifying and adjusting modern technologies to the needs of domestic markets. An example of an adaptive technological innovation would be the introduction of a more modern tractor into an area where tractors with older technology are in use.

Transformative technological innovations are important to the traditional sector economically, socially, and culturally. An example of a transformative technological innovation would be the introduction of washing machines into a region where laundry is being done manually or the introduction of farming tractors into a region where horses and plows are being used.

Entry Strategy

Managers of business enterprises must determine how their products or services will reach the consumer—the entry strategy. Distribution methods generally require variations from country to country as well as within each country. Generally, the methods are shaped by the size of the market, by the scope and quality of the competition, by the available distribution channels, and by the firm's resources. (For an illustration, read Practical Perspective 5.7, the case of Fusion Systems Corporation.) Distribution methods are also shaped by the laws of the country (the laws of some countries require foreign companies to use local distribution systems) and by the firm's entry strategy.[30]

Basically, manufacturing enterprises can enter a foreign country by

1. manufacturing the product at home and exporting it to the foreign country for distribution in the local market;

2. manufacturing parts at home and exporting them to the foreign country for assembly, for distribution in the local market, and/or for export to other markets (including back to the home market); or

3. manufacturing the product in the foreign country for distribution in the local market and/or for export to other markets (including back to the home market).

With respect to service enterprises,

1. some, such as consulting companies, can provide the services from their home country or they can set up subsidiaries in the foreign country and

2. others, such as insurance and banking companies, generally must establish subsidiaries in the foreign country.

The above suggests that firms enter a foreign market either by exporting its products to that country or by setting up manufacturing facilities in it.[31] Of course, if a firm in a country exports to another country, there has to be an importer in that country— either its own or through an alliance. National cultural differences have an impact on the choice of entry. Adapting to local cultural values that are transmitted through countries' political economy, education, religion, and language are likely to create additional burdens for international businesses operating in different nations.[32] Furthermore, historically, domestic companies internationalizing their enterprises start out by first using an experienced distributor (below termed *the indirect approach*). After they have gotten some knowledge about how to conduct business in foreign cultures, they start their own exporting operations. Subsequently, as they have learned more about cross-cultural business, they move on to direct investment in their foreign markets—via a joint venture, a strategic alliance, or a wholly owned investment.[33]

The point here is that successful international enterprises evolved into international business (refer to Case 5.1) and domestic enterprises that ventured into international business failed miserably or learned through costly blunders (refer again to Practical Perspective 4.4 and to Case 4.2 in Chapter 4). The ensuing sections describe various strategies enterprises use in exporting and manufacturing in foreign markets.

Exporting Strategy

When a firm decides to export, it must choose between indirect and direct exporting. Indirect exporting involves using experienced middlemen to handle export functions, and direct exporting involves assigning the export functions to employees of the company. In general, when a firm lacks personnel with exporting expertise, it usually prefers to start out using the indirect method, and after the enterprise has developed personnel with exporting expertise, and if it is more efficient, it develops its own export division.

PRACTICAL PERSPECTIVE 5-7

Fusion Systems Uses Local Distributor to Enter the Japanese Market

Fusion Systems Corporation, a Rockville, Maryland, company, [in 1990] made sophisticated industrial equipment used to produce numerous goods, including optical fibers, automobile parts, graphic arts printing plates, and semi-conductor chips.... Fusion had been in the Japanese market since 1975, four years after its founding by its president, Donald M. Shapiro, and four colleagues.... Because of its small size when it entered the Japanese market, Fusion lacked the resources to hire its own sales force there. It had to rely on a Japanese distributor. "We knew we couldn't just hire a trade house that would buy and resell our product," said David Harbourne, a [then] Fusion vice president and manager of its core business. "We can always teach a distributor how to sell our product, but if it doesn't have strong service, we can't do much about that. Our philosophy at Fusion is to look for strong service organizations that have a lot of after-sales support."[a]

On October 24, 1996, Fusion Systems signed a cross-license agreement with Asyst Technologies, which has operations in the Far East, relating its Mechanical InterFace technology.[b] Fusion Systems has since been acquired by the Cleveland, Ohio-based Eaton Corporation. Spinoffs of Fusion Systems include Fusion UV Systems and Fusion Lighting Inc.

SOURCES:

a. Excerpted from Edward O. Welles, "Being There" (Inc, September 1990), p. 143. Permission conveyed through Copyright Clearance Center, Inc.

b. "Fusion Systems and Asyst Technologies Sign Technology Cross-Licensing Agreement" (October 24, 1996). www.asyst.com/nevents/1996/pr961024.asp

c. Eastland Scientific Enterprises Corporation (September 6, 2006). www.eastlandscience.com/aboutfounder.html

Indirect Exporting

There are two basic types of middlemen: agent middlemen and merchant middlemen. The agent middlemen represent the principal directly, and the merchant takes title to the goods. Agent middlemen include the export management company, the manufacturer's export agent, the broker, and buyers and selling groups. Merchant middlemen include export merchants and jobbers, export buyers and foreign importers, trading companies, and complementary marketers.

Middlemen may be located at home (domestic middlemen and exporters) or in the foreign country (foreign middlemen or importers). Some firms prefer to deal with middlemen who are located in the foreign market. An advantage of using foreign middlemen is that they provide a channel that is closer to the customer than are domestic middlemen; that is, they provide personnel who are in constant contact with the foreign market. A disadvantage of using these middlemen is that the employing firm does not have the close contact it enjoys when dealing with a middleman located in the domestic market. Another disadvantage of using foreign middlemen is that language or communication barriers between the producer and the middlemen are more likely to develop than with the domestic middlemen. Elements that affect the indirect exporting strategy include the availability of middlemen, the cost of their services, the functions performed, and the extent of control the manufacturer can exert over the middlemen's activities.

Direct Exporting

To obtain greater control over their foreign distribution systems and the volume of sales, firms often develop their own export organization. There are several approaches to establishing direct exporting means, such as setting up an international sales force, a sales branch, a sales subsidiary, or the company's own distribution system, or through the Internet.

International Sales Force. An enterprise may establish an international sales force that travels abroad to sell the product. This may be the least expensive choice since the firm does not have to invest in any facilities abroad. This solution, however, would not give foreign customers immediate access to the firm's representatives, nor would the firm be able to effectively monitor foreign market changes. And the costs of cross-cultural training of sales people are high, and the current costs of cross-national travel and lodging are also very high.

Sales Branch. A firm may choose to establish a sales branch in the foreign country. This approach requires investment in foreign facilities. It enables the firm to be closer to the market, however.

Sales Subsidiary. The manufacturer may also choose to establish a sales subsidiary abroad. A sales subsidiary differs from a sales branch in that it is an entirely separate entity, even though it is under the control of the company.

Setting Up the Company's Own Distribution System. If the foreign country's legal system permits it, a company can elect to set up a chain of wholly owned outlets, which may consist of retail shops. For example, in the 1800s, the British were importing tea from China (until recently, tea was one of China's largest exports), which led to a trade deficit. At that time the British were colonists in the Middle East, where they cultivated opium in abundance. To close the trade deficit with China, the British set up or forced the Chinese government to set up "smoke shops" throughout China to sell the opium.

The Internet. Many firms now sell products and services on the Internet. For example, many newly started businesses think globally from day one. Amazon.com, a bookstore on the Internet, relies on book lovers anywhere on the globe being able to tap into its site to place orders. During its fiscal year ending in 1997, the company sold $16 million worth of books to 180,000 customers in more than 100 countries.[34] Sony's president in 1999, Nobuyuki Idei, indicated that Sony would revamp its distribution system. He didn't see much future for the traditional distribution of music CDs and movies from its Columbia TriStar studio. He was determined to transform the world's leading maker of consumer electronics into a fleet-footed player on the Web. He expected to provide interactive versions of music, movies, and games that can be downloaded onto Sony-made devices. And he expected Internet-related revenues eventually to surpass its then $45 billion-a-year electronics sales.[35]

Since many people around the globe still do not have access to PCs, businesses still must use a traditional distribution approach, thus increasing the costs. However, when using the Internet, a business cuts costs by cutting out the middleman. For example, Dell was able to lower the prices of computers sold in China because it sold them over the Internet. And to lower prices in China, Ford planned to sell its cars over the Internet.[36] It should be pointed out that the individualism-collectivism and uncertainty avoidance cultural dimensions discussed in Chapter 1 affect the use of the Internet as a distribution mode. Collectivist and strong uncertainty avoidance cultures show a lower Internet shopping rate than individualistic and low uncertainty avoidance cultures.[37]

Firms should not adhere to any one approach; they should be flexible and conform to the situation. The choice of approach depends on a number of factors, including the following:

1. The philosophy and aims of the company

2. The traditions of the target market

3. The competition's behavior

4. The existing and potential future size of the market

5. Legal restrictions

6. Usual patterns of distribution of the particular product(s)

7. Financial and staffing problems[38]

8. The firm's CEO's capabilities (discussed in Chapter 12)

Direct or Indirect Exporting?

Both approaches have advantages as well as disadvantages. The advantages of the direct approach include the following:

1. The sales staff are more loyal than the sales staff of an intermediary.

2. The sales staff have greater knowledge of the product line of the firm than does an outside vendor.

3. The sales staff can be trained by the parent company according to its individual sales methods.

4. Salaries of the sales staff can be set in accordance with the long-term goals of the firm instead of on a commission basis.

5. The sales staff can keep personal contact with the end users and retailers.

6. The manufacturer has a channel to receive feedback information on new marketing opportunities and trends that might not be available to a firm using sales intermediaries.

7. The manufacturer has a means of getting information about competitors, evaluating product acceptance, and gathering a multitude of useful information.

8. The sales branch or subsidiary can spend promotional money to advertise a new product, concentrating on building product acceptance in a wide region, which might not be the goal of the sales intermediary.[39]

The disadvantages of using the direct approach include the following:

1. It is usually very expensive to start. (Refer again to Practical Perspective 5.7.)

2. A large inventory is usually needed.

3. The establishment of a complex organization, including a warehousing network, an administrative organization, and a trained staff, is often required.[40]

Manufacturing in a Foreign Country

After they have acquired experience in the international arena, many enterprises find it profitable to produce in foreign countries. Six of the most common approaches to foreign production are licensing, franchising, management contracting, equity-based joint ventures, non-equity-based contractual alliances, and wholly owned subsidiaries. Many companies sometimes use a mix. For example, in 1989, KFC had outlets in 58 countries, and these international outlets generated almost half of KFC's $5 billion per year in sales. But KFC's success was especially notable with its 1,324 outlets in the Pacific Rim. KFC's director of public affairs in 1989, Richard Detwiller, said, "We operate all our outlets on a joint venture or franchise basis, and the licenses are mostly held by local nationals."[41] As of 2007, KFC has restaurants in Canada, Mexico, the United States, Australia, New Zealand, 6 countries in Europe, and 14 in Asia.

The key to transferring operations to a foreign country is that the transferring enterprise must convince the country's government of how the transfer will benefit the nation economically and socially, such as creating jobs and wealth for its residents. Japanese corporations tend to do this very well—for example, Honda and Toyota in the United States. The old ruthless practice of "I came, exploited your resources, and left" is no longer effective. The governments of many countries now insist that a foreign company reinvest its profits or at least a part of its profits for growth in their respective countries; for instance, China has done this through government mandate, *but international businesses would operate far more effectively internationally if they did this on a voluntary basis*, for example, Honda has been reinvesting and creating jobs and generating wealth in the United States for U.S. residents for decades without the U.S. government's mandate, theoretically anyway. (Refer to Chapter 3.)

Licensing/Franchising

Licensing involves granting a foreign enterprise the use of a production process, the use of a trade name, or permission for the distribution of imported goods for a fee. Licenses allow for expansion without a great deal of capital investment or personnel commitment. However, supervising licenses may sometimes be a problem and, because of the partnership, profits may be lower. Nevertheless, overall, licensing can be profitable for many companies, especially those that are no longer producing the product at home and could lose their patent protection for lack of use and those that would incur many expenses by entering a market.

For example, some years ago, Denmark's Carlsberg, an internationally popular brand of beer, which typically exported its product, found the licensing approach to be the most feasible way of entering the Canadian market, which was relatively small and whose local beer producers were highly protected by the Canadian government. The licensing agreement in small print on the bottles' label indicated that the beer was produced by a Canadian beer company under Carlsberg's supervision. But this beer actually tasted nothing like the original Carlsberg beer; it tasted more like Canada's Molson Beer. Thus, people were buying a foreign brand but getting a local beer. Budweiser beer also uses this entry approach in some countries, including Canada. (Refer to Practical Perspective 5.6.)

In franchising, the contractor provides a standard package of products, systems, and management services; grants permission to use a certain product, including a special name or trademark; and often incorporates a special set of procedures for making the product. Under franchising agreements, the parent firm maintains a reasonable degree of control. The Disneyland located in Tokyo, Japan, is a franchise arrangement. Under the agreement, Walt Disney Productions was to receive 10% of every admission fee from the Tokyo Park and 5% of the revenues from restaurants and shops.[42]

Numerous other companies have been entering the complex Japanese market via franchising or licensing arrangements, including 7-Eleven Stores, Stained Glass Overlay, Tiffany & Company, and Barney's of New York.[43] Starbuck's Coffee entered China via a franchising agreement.[44] Whirlpool Corporation entered China via joint ventures to make refrigerators and air conditioners, but in 1997 it began withdrawing from the joint ventures to focus less on manufacturing its own products abroad and more on licensing.[45]

Management Contracts

Using the management contract method, a firm provides managerial know-how in all or some functions to another organization for a stated fee or a percentage share of the profits. For example, BBA Group of Britain possesses general airport-management skills. In the United States, BBA operates the Indianapolis airport under a 10-year management contract and provides retail management at the Air Mall in the Pittsburgh airport.[46] Many of the U.S. ports are currently (in 2007) being managed by foreign-owned managing companies.

An upside of this approach is that the firm is not investing its assets abroad, and when an enterprise licenses production abroad, it can maintain control through a contract. Furthermore, the enterprise can maintain control of an investment abroad in which it is a minority owner. A downside is that these contracts are sometimes executed in hostile environments, thus exposing employees to danger—for instance,

Halliburton (discussed in Chapter 3) has been contracting security for its operations in Iraq, and during the U.S.-Iraq war several contractors were killed. (Assigning employees to foreign sites is discussed in Chapters 7 and 8.)

This approach has also been used when a foreign nation's government nationalized or took over an industry but needed the managerial know-how of the previous foreign owners to manage the enterprise. For a contracted fee, the previous owners managed the enterprise for the government. This occurred numerous times decades ago in South America. Closely related to this matter, in 2005, Venezuela's president, Hugo Chavez, announced that all foreign oil companies with contracts must agree to form joint ventures.[47] On April 10, 2007, Hugo Chavez announced his plan to wrest control oil projects from U.S. and European companies by May 1, 2007.[48]

Joint Ventures/Contractual and Strategic Alliances

Many enterprises' entry strategy is via a joint venture or a contractual alliance. Many companies use a mix to attain the most efficient entry.

Joint Ventures. A joint venture is an arrangement whereby a company joins in a partnership or a merger between one or more other companies.[49] Some governments require that their citizens have majority ownership of foreign-owned firms located in their country. (Refer to Chapter 3.) Advantages of a joint venture include the following:

1. It enables a firm to use the foreign partner's skills.

2. It enables a firm to gain access to the foreign partner's distribution system.

3. It requires less capital investment than if the investment were wholly owned, therefore reducing the size of the risk.

For example, many years ago, when it was popular, Toys "R" Us Inc. had planned to open 100 stores in Japan via joint ventures. Its strategy was to maintain 80% ownership. To compensate for its lack of understanding of Japan's real estate and cultural nuances, Toys "R" Us teamed up with McDonald's Japan, whose management had experience in these matters.[50] Walt Disney Company, when it planned to build a theme park in Hong Kong—its third theme park outside the United States—said it will create the park through a joint venture with Hong Kong International Parks Ltd., 57% to be held by Hong Kong and 43% by Disney.[51] The park opened in 2005, and much of it has been customized to fit Chinese culture.[52] Practical Perspective 5.8 describes a joint venture between Suzuki and General Motors, and Practical Perspective 5.9 describes a joint venture between Telmex and Microsoft.

There are some disadvantages in this approach, however. First, profits must be shared with the partner, and second, because some nations require majority control by local people, the home company might lose managerial control. (A management contract, however, can mitigate this problem.) For example, in 1990, a U.S. household products company entered into a joint venture in China with Shanghai Jahwa Corporation, then China's largest cosmetics manufacturer. The U.S. company intended to capitalize on Jahwa's brand equity and distribution to push its own product line, and it hoped that the Chinese partner would provide the connections required to do business in China. The Chinese partner hoped that the U.S. company would upgrade its technology and increase its competitive capabilities both locally and abroad. The two companies, as it

PRACTICAL PERSPECTIVE 5-8

Frugal Head of Suzuki Drives Markets in Asia

In the U.S., Suzuki had some early success, introducing its small Jeep-like Samurai years before the Toyota RAV4 and Honda CR-V models. But Suzuki's fortunes sank after Consumer Reports magazine in 1988 branded the little truck prone to rolling over, a rating Suzuki still protests. U.S. sales peaked at 81,349 that year and dropped to 29,283 in 1997.

Suzuki [in 1998] has 60 plants in 27 countries from Hungary to Ecuador and Nigeria. "Years ago, the company's products weren't good enough to get into the U.S. and Europe," Mr. Suzuki says. So he decided to enter the developing world.

His strategy is to start small. Mr. Suzuki describes the Vietnam factory as "just a hut" that produces 12,000 "two-wheelers" (motorcycles) and 500 "four-wheelers" a year. In India, Suzuki churns out 350,000 cars a year in a joint venture forged with the government. In China, it builds 260,000 cars and commercial vehicles a year at its five plants.

Suzuki pulled out of a joint venture in Spain about three years ago [1995]. Spanish regulations required paying workers until they were 65, even if they were laid off. So Suzuki sold out and now makes more money selling parts to its former plant than it did when it owned the facility.

Seeking to benefit from Suzuki's developing-world experience, GM has approached Suzuki about forging joint ventures in Asia and Eastern Europe. Combining volumes in the smaller-car market could lead to purchasing economies of scale, says Lou Hughes, GM's executive vice president, but no agreement has been reached. The two companies complement each other in a Canadian assembly joint-venture. Suzuki gets the benefit of GM's huge sales and purchasing network, while GM benefits from Suzuki's engineering skills.

"But Suzuki holds the advantages in the developing world, and the two companies may not be as complementary there," Mr. Suzuki says. Mr. Suzuki makes most decisions himself, enabling his company to move more quickly than GM or other Japanese companies, which are ruled by consensus. A framed calligraphy of the Japanese characters for "being alone" hangs behind his desk.[a]

Suzuki has continued to grow worldwide. Its consolidated sales grew from 1,668 billion Japanese yen in fiscal year 2001 (as of September 6, 2006, equal to approximately US $14.4 billion) to 2,747 billion yen in fiscal year 2005 (approximately US $23.7 billion). Its automobile production jumped from 1,642,000 in fiscal year 2001 to 2,200,000 in fiscal year 2005 and its motorcycle production jumped from 1,625,000 to 3,138,000 during the same period worldwide. Suzuki now sells its products in Europe, North America, Asia, Japan, and other areas as well. It also sells other products, such as fishing boats, outboard boat motors, and motorized wheelchairs. And it has over the years formed numerous alliances with other companies, including General Motors of Argentina, GM Colmotores, the Columbian subsidiary of GM, Nissan Motor Company, Maruti Udyog Limited, India.[b]

SOURCES:

a. Excerpted from Valerie Reitman, "Fresh Head of Suzuki Drives Markets in Asia," *The Wall Street Journal* (February 26, 1998), p. A12. Permission conveyed through Copyright Clearance Center, Inc.

b. SUZUKI Online (September 6, 2006). www.globalsuzuki.com/corp info/2.htm

turned out, had different dreams; their dispute over direction and resources paralyzed operations for three years. In 1993, Jahwa withdrew its top brands from the joint venture and sold its share, leaving the U.S. partner scrambling for another local partner to salvage its investment and save face.[53]

As a result of this experience, currently, many companies seek to enter the Chinese market via a wholly owned investment.[54] (Refer to Case 3.1, "Protecting the Pepsi

PRACTICAL PERSPECTIVE 5-9

Telmex and Microsoft Team Up on a Hispanic Portal

Over the years, Mexican mogul Carlos Slim spent billions assembling a sprawling communications empire. He started out with the acquisition of Teléfonos de México (Telmex), the former telecoms monopoly, in 1990. Investment in computers, media companies, and Internet service providers followed. But investors and analysts kept wondering when Slim would start up a truly multinational operation. On October 18 [1999], they got their answer. Slim announced a $100 million joint venture with Microsoft Corporation to create a Spanish-language Internet portal for the Americas. For Microsoft, this was a chance to expand into foreign-language Internet services with a savvy Latin American partner. Telmex's pockets were nearly as deep as Microsoft's, to boot. For Slim, the venture was the key to his plans to go regional.

It was also part of his strategy to reduce Telmex's dependence on long-distance telephony, with its ever-smaller margins, and move into the fast-growing market for data transmission and Internet-related services . . . "The Internet is in its diaper stage," said Slim. "We want to develop as many associated businesses as possible."

Telmex and Microsoft were going head to head with big players throughout the region. U.S. heavyweights such as American Online Inc. and Yahoo! Inc. and homegrown Internet service providers such as Brazil's Universo Online were already battling for position. Early entrants such as New York–based StarMedia Network, Inc. will not give up market share easily. "We are far ahead not only in product development but audience creation," said StarMedia CEO Fernando J. Espuelas.

SOURCE: Excerpted from Geri Smith, "Mr. Slim, Meet Mr. Gates," *Business Week* (November 8, 1999), p. 5. Reprinted with permission.

Taste," in Chapter 3.) In 1999, however, General Motors entered into a joint venture in China (becoming the largest U.S. joint venture in China). Many critics, including *Fortune*, slammed General Motors for giving away too much technology and getting locked into making Buick sedans that were too expensive for the market. (General Motors acknowledged that the investment entailed a lot of risk but defended the investment on the basis that it sees China as the world's last big growth market[55]— which it is as of 2007.)

Contractual and Strategic Alliances. Many joint ventures are in the form of a contractual alliance. *Contractual alliances* are formed to reduce costs at home. As pointed out in Chapter 4, currently (2007) many U.S. corporations are contracting with companies in India and China to provide some of their IT requirements (for instance, *The New York Times*, the popular New York City–based newspaper is as of May 1, 2007, making plans to transfer much of its IT operations to India).

Strategic alliances are formed to share costs, to share risks, to gain additional market knowledge, to combine technical and market knowledge, to serve an international market, and to develop industry standards together.[56] They are also formed, as discussed in Chapter 4, to allow companies to focus on their strengths; that is, they do what they can do best (to "lead from strength" and contract for other functions). For example, Nissan and Volkswagen have an arrangement whereby Nissan distributes Volkswagens in Japan and Volkswagen sells Nissan's four-wheel-drive cars in Europe.

In describing such an alliance, Professor Thomas G. Cummings of the University of Southern California used the term *transorganizational systems.*[57] He described such systems as a group of two or more enterprises engaged in collective efforts to achieve goals they could not achieve by themselves. Riad Ajami, a former professor at Ohio State University, proposed that such systems are characterized "by a shift from an equity-based investment . . . to that of a service-based organization providing technology know-how and other managerial services . . . ownership rests upon contractual arrangements rather than conventional ownership arrangements."[58] Ajami listed 15 examples of such collaborative ventures, including Toyota/General Motors, General Electric/Salelni (an Italian construction firm), and MW Kellogg Company of Houston/China Petrochemical International Corporation.

Kenichi Ohmae, formerly a management consultant for McKinsey, an international management consulting firm, described this type of arrangement as follows:

- There is no formal contract.
- There is no buying and selling of equity.
- There are few, if any, rigidly binding provisions.
- It is a loose, evolving kind of relationship.
- There are guidelines and expectations. But no one expects a precise, measured return on the initial commitment.
- Both partners bring to the alliance a faith that they will be stronger than either would be separately.
- Both believe that each has unique skills and functional abilities the other lacks.
- Both have to work diligently over time to make the union successful.[59]

Ohmae proposed that a non-equity-based alliance in many instances has advantages over the equity-based joint venture. He contended that when equity enters the picture, one becomes concerned with control and return on investment, and one cannot manage a global company through control—it demoralizes workers and managers. Furthermore, he contends that equity poisons the relationship, which can lead to the prevention of the development of intercompany management skills, which are crucial for success in today's global environment.[60]

There are certain problems in using this approach, however. Premature dissolution of the agreement by one partner can create problems for the other partner(s). There is always the risk that a partner may not really be in it for the long-term, which is required for it to be successful.[61] For example, a British whisky company used a Japanese distributor until it felt it had acquired sufficient experience to begin its own sales operations in Japan, and Japanese copier makers and automobile producers have done the same to their U.S. partners.[62] The effectiveness of the approach depends on a solid relationship between partners. It may be a very lengthy and expensive process to find the right partner(s) and develop the required relationship.

Wholly Owned Subsidiaries

Using the strategy of a wholly owned subsidiary, the firm establishes an entity in a foreign country, paying all the costs incurred. To establish a wholly owned foreign subsidiary, an enterprise may acquire or merge with an existing company in the foreign country or build one from scratch.[63] For example, to maintain its growth, Wal-Mart

Stores, Inc. entered foreign markets. Moving to Europe for the first time, Wal-Mart acquired the German retailer Wertkauf GmbH, giving it a foothold in a large market. The purchase was a key step for Wal-Mart in its continuing effort to expand internationally. The move parallels Wal-Mart's acquisition strategy in other countries, such as Canada, where in 1994 it acquired 120 stores from Woolworth Corporation. In December 1998, Wal-Mart bought another 74 German stores from Spar Handels Company.[64] (As of 2006, Wal-Mart is not doing well in Germany and some other foreign markets, thus it may have done better if it had formed a joint venture with a local partner who understood the local culture and business practices.) Disney also failed miserably when it opened its theme park in Paris, going it alone and not using a local partner, as it had done when entering Japan and China. (As of 2007, Disney has learned from its mistakes in Paris and made the necessary adjustments and is doing quite well there.)

Recognizing that the U.S. market is close to saturation point, Merrill Lynch made overseas acquisitions a central part of its strategy to capture more customers. The firm established objectives to make non-U.S. revenues account for 50% of its business within a five-year period. Within the first three years, Merrill acquired enterprises worldwide. In 1995, the company purchased the London-based broker Smith New Court PLC to improve its penetration into Asian markets. In 1997, Merrill acquired McIntosh Securities, one of Australia's leading brokerage houses. And Merrill's acquisition of Mercury Asset Management, Britain's second largest asset management company, cemented its position in Europe's financial capital.[65]

In early 1998, it was announced that the German carmaker Daimler-Benz and the U.S. carmaker Chrysler Corporation, both international corporations, would merge to become the fourth largest car manufacturer in the world. The reason for the merger was that Daimler-Benz wanted a car company that was not dependent solely on luxury cars, and Chrysler wanted entry into the exclusive luxury car market that Daimler-Benz would provide.[66] (As it turned out, Daimler actually acquired Chrysler, but in 2007, Daimler announced plans to sell Chrysler—see Case 8.2 in Chapter 8.) Acquisition of foreign enterprises can be very risky if the acquiring firm is not very familiar with its target market, as it may be difficult for it to assess the value that it brings to the acquisition.[67]

Advantages of the Wholly Owned Subsidiary

1. The firm maintains total control and authority over the operation.

2. Profits need not be shared with anyone outside the company.

3. Because they do not need to consult a partner, firms have more flexibility to adapt faster to market demands and labor needs.

4. The enterprise is able to protect trade secrets.

Disadvantages of the Wholly Owned Subsidiary

1. It does not generate "goodwill" because profits are not shared with local people. Also, many acquirers, for example, Wal-Mart, try to change the nature of the acquired organization's culture, which is resented by some of the stakeholders, such as the suppliers and the employees.[68]

2. Government officials in many countries tend to view wholly owned foreign investments in their nation unfavorably.

3. The risk is greater since it is totally company borne.

Within the past two decades or so, government officials in many countries have become uncomfortable with the situation in which much of their nation's industrial sector is controlled by foreigners. As a result, many governments have established policies mandating that the majority of control of foreign investments in their country must be in the hands of local citizens—although this trend currently seems to be declining. China, for example, which in the past mandated entry via joint venture, now more readily allows entry via wholly owned investment.

Export or Manufacture Abroad?

Both approaches have advantages and disadvantages. The general advantages of investing in manufacturing facilities abroad, as opposed to exporting, include the following:

1. Capitalizing on low-cost labor

2. Avoiding high import taxes

3. Reducing transportation costs

4. Gaining access to raw materials

5. Developing "goodwill" in the foreign nation because direct investment may help in that nation's economic development

The general disadvantages include the following:

1. Subsidiaries are far removed from the home country and are thus often difficult and expensive to control.

2. The risk of nationalization, confiscation, domestication, and expropriation exists to a greater degree than when using other methods. (For example, Iraq's invasion of Kuwait in the early 1990s was an attempt to integrate Kuwait into Iraq's domain and to nationalize its oil industry. Of course, since U.S. oil companies had heavy investments there, the U.S. military stopped the invasion by sending 500,000 or so U.S. troops there to abort Iraq's efforts.)

Which strategy option, manufacture abroad or export, should a firm select?[69] Naturally, the firm chooses the one that is the most efficient. And it is often most efficient for a company to manufacture in one country and export to another; that is, it is best to use a mix. Furthermore, firms sometimes shift back and forth from one strategy to another, as efficiency dictates. For example, in 1990, McIlhenny Company of Avery Island, Louisiana, was shipping its product to Europe, where distributors get it onto grocery shelves. But McIlhenny did not always export its sauces abroad. The firm used to manufacture in England through a licensing agreement with a British company. Carlos E. Malespin, then vice president in charge of the company's international operations, said, "Although it's now more profitable for us to use distributorship arrangements . . . we can fall back on our former strategy of licensing for manufacture in Europe if import tariffs are raised significantly after 1992."[70] (As of June 23, 1995, McIlhenny Company was still exporting, and it had no plans to manufacture in Europe.) Another example is Guess? Inc.'s shift in strategy in Europe. In 1997, in Europe, a region then targeted for particularly aggressive growth, Guess? had taken on a partner to share expenses. Earlier that year, Guess? had sold part of its Italian unit and granted licensing rights to a joint venture. The move was made, in part, to relieve Guess? of the burden of financing the substantial capital expansion needed to build new Guess? stores in Europe.[71]

Think Global, Act Local[72]

In the 1960s and 1970s, U.S. domestic businesses were encouraged to internationalize their business operation, and the slogan adopted was "Think global, act local," meaning internationalize your business but make the necessary adaptations required by the foreign country's culture and other factors (described in Chapter 3). Many companies in the United States, followed by Europe and Japan have done this. But most of the companies, such as America's KFC, Coca-Cola, McDonald's, Wal-Mart, France's Carrefour, Japan's Honda and Toyota, and many others, promote their home brand name. They do make some adaptations, either by design or through the school of hard knocks, to meet the local culture's needs. Some of these companies, because they have created jobs for the locals, have tried to convince the locals that they are a local company, but in the eyes of the local people, Wal-Mart and McDonald's are American companies and Toyota and Honda are Japanese companies no matter where they are located.

Wal-Mart and Carrefour are competing to become the largest global retailer. They are both using their brand name as a "Think global, act local" strategy to grow. But competing against Wal-Mart for the No. 1 spot is the Taiwanese company President Enterprise Corporation (PEC), founded on July 1, 1967. In 1996, its president, Kao Chin Yen, developed a strategy to become the world's No. 1 food producer by 2017. But PECs "Think global, act local" strategy is different. Whereas Wal-Mart mainly acquires foreign companies and attaches its brand name to most of them, PEC mainly acquires many companies the world over and keeps their original local brand name—it does not have a Taiwanese global brand name anywhere. For example, it owns a great number of 7-Eleven convenience stores in Taiwan.[73]

U.S. brand names do often have a competitive advantage over local brands. However, a global brand name, especially a U.S. brand, can sometimes backfire, for example, the French burning down a McDonald's restaurant because of the American stigma, and they have given rise to the notion of American imperialism. Certainly, Japanese brand names were not taken too kindly in the United States in the 1980s, when the Japanese were being criticized by many Americans for their "buying America" foreign investment activities.

Furthermore, localizing means more than just translating the words on a label. For example, Henry Estate, a winery in Umpqua, Oregon, had for the past 10 years been exporting its wine to Canada, the United Kingdom, and Japan. In the fall of 2004, the company had some marketing materials translated into Mandarin, attached some Chinese-language labels to the bottles, and found a distributor, and soon 700 cases of red wine were en route to China, and the company was set to handle a demand of 500 cases per month. Four months later, most of that wine was still on the shelves in Chinese stores. But no one in China, including the local distributors, the retailers, and the consumers, seemed to know the first thing about red wine. The wine, which retails for $62 a bottle, was being sold in convenience stores, and the bottles were being delivered by motorcycle, after being exposed to the sun for hours.[74]

Price Strategy

Operating in foreign markets brings new price strategy challenges as there are new market variables to consider. For example, local culture plays an important role in pricing. In many countries, as has been pointed out in previous chapters, people will pay more for American products and services simply because of the American mystique. For example, in 2000, in Taipei, Taiwan, Tony Roma's Ribs sold its ribs for a much higher price than it did in the U.S. market—even though the per capita income in Taiwan was much lower than the U.S. per capita income. And the restaurant was always filled to capacity with a long waiting line. Furthermore, in Tegucigalpa, Honduras, where the per capita income is very low, in 2003, Tony Roma's Ribs restaurant was charging the same price as it did in the United States.

Also, the attitudes of foreign governments are important, and serious pricing problems that differ from one country to another need to be considered. Sometimes, foreign governments act as price arbiters. Therefore, effective price setting consists of much more than mechanically adding a standard markup to cost. Thus, international pricing strategy is much more complex than domestic pricing strategy.

International Pricing Strategy

International pricing strategy is made complex by monetary exchange factors as well as by firms often being required to countertrade—that is, to trade by barter or a similar system (which is discussed more thoroughly later in the chapter). Pricing policy is also affected by the commercial practices of the country in which the firm is doing business, by the type of product being merchandised, and by existing competitive conditions.

In establishing pricing policy, some firms are influenced by the view that pricing is an active tool by which to accomplish their marketing objectives, and some are influenced by the belief that price is a static element in business decisions. Furthermore, some firms emphasize control over final prices and some control over the net price received by the enterprise.

Pricing as an Active Tool

Using the view that pricing is an active tool, the firm uses pricing to accomplish its objective relative to a target return from its overseas operations or to accomplish a target volume of market share. (For an illustration of pricing as an active tool strategy, read Practical Perspective 5.10, the case of Dell Computer Corp. in Japan. Dell used pricing as an active tool in the early 1990s, and as indicated earlier, it is currently using the Internet to lower its prices.)

Pricing as a Static Element

If a firm follows the view that pricing is a static element, it will most likely be content to sell what it can overseas and consider it to be a bonus value.

Pricing as an active tool is more closely allied with firms that make direct investment in the foreign country, whereas pricing as a static element is more closely allied with firms that export.

Control Over Final Prices

To achieve a desired level of foreign market penetration, a firm must have the ability to control the end price. Enterprises with the desire to attain a high level of market penetration therefore attempt to obtain all possible control over the final price. These firms are more likely to view pricing as an active tool than as a static element.

PRACTICAL PERSPECTIVE 5-10

Dell Computer Corporation Wages Price War in Japan

Dell Computer Corporation escalated a personal computer price war in Japan by unveiling plans [in 1993] to sell six types of high-end PCs in Japan at prices 25 to 60 percent lower than those of its rivals. At a news conference in Dell's Tokyo offices, Chief Executive Officer Michael Dell outlined the company's plans to target corporate customers through "direct sales," the company's preferred euphemism for mail order, its main avenue for PC sales in the U.S. According to Mr. Dell, the company's "more efficient mode" will allow Dell to undercut its competitors' prices because the company can avoid paying the added costs of distribution. Dell's kickoff of its full-scale Japanese operations, foreshadowed for weeks by press leaks and speculation about the company's sales strategy, marks the latest move in aggressive U.S. marketing tactics into the once-placid world of Japanese PC sales.

Dell joined Compaq Computer Corporation and International Business Machines Corporation, both of which announced low-priced PCs for sale in Japan . . . The U.S. companies had set their eyes on the world's second largest market for personal computers, once ruled by NEC Corporation. With an iron grip on its network of retail distributors and huge library of software, NEC had for years enjoyed a market share of more than 50 percent and the luxury of selling its computers at high prices. . . . Dell, [in 1992] the world's fifth largest PC maker, seemed intent on pushing such competition even further. Officials at the news conference presented a price comparison of three Dell computers and machines from Compaq, IBM, and NEC with identical speed and memory and comparable hard-disk storage capacities. NEC's prices were as much as 60 percent higher than Dell's. Compaq's prices were generally closest to Dell's, at one point coming within 25 percent.[a]

Dell has continued to grow. It reported revenue of $14.1 billion for the second quarter of fiscal year 2007 (an industry leading global share of 19.3 percent), an increase of 5 percent year-over-year.[b]

SOURCES:

a. Excerpted from David P. Hamilton, "Dell Computer Escalates Price War in Japan by Introducing Low-Cost PCs," *The Wall Street Journal* (January 22, 1993), p. 5. Permission conveyed through Copyright Clearance Center, Inc.

b. "About Dell." www.dell.com/content/topics/global.aspx/corp/en/home?c=us&1=en&s=corp (November 16, 2007).

Net Price Received

Firms using this approach do not attempt to control the price at which the product is finally sold. The enterprise's main concern is with the net price it receives. This type of firm most likely shares the view of pricing as a static element more than as an active tool.

Foreign National Pricing and International Pricing

Pricing for foreign markets is further complicated by managers' having to be concerned with two types of pricing: foreign national pricing and international pricing. Basically, the former is pricing for selling in another country, and the latter is pricing in another country for export.

Foreign National Pricing

A firm's foreign national pricing is influenced by its international pricing strategy, discussed above, as well as by foreign governments. A government can influence its nation's prices by taking various actions. It can institute national price controls. These controls may encompass all products sold within the nation's borders or impose them on only specific products. Some governments influence prices on foreign imports by levying higher import duties or subsidizing local industries. Governments can also affect prices by applying legislation relative to labor costs. For example, the government of Thailand, besides imposing steep taxes on cars, unofficially controls their prices. Of course, the steep taxes raise prices dramatically. For instance, in 1997, in Thailand, a Honda Accord, nearly identical to the one sold in the United States, sold for $35,520, about a 50% premium.[75] Higher labor costs mean higher prices, and vice versa.

As another example, in 1995, the Chinese government levied high tariffs on products such as Japanese motorcycles and air conditioners—products it did not deem essential to its economic growth endeavors. For example, the price of a Japanese imported motorcycle had been doubled by a U.S. $1,000-equivalent tariff. But the Chinese government waived the tariff on one transaction for visiting foreigners who purchased the product. So young Chinese men were offering foreign tourists U.S. $500 if they would take their passport and go with them to the retail outlet to purchase the motorcycle for them—the buyer would save $500, and the tourist would get $500.

A recent trend, however, among many nations is to open up their markets to price competition laws. Prices are likely to be lower in competitive environments. Because of globalization, competition is currently intensifying throughout the world. Therefore, many international corporations' strategies are now influenced by price. For example, the European retailer Carrefour acquired Promodès Group, becoming Europe's No. 1 retailer. The merger aimed to create a much tougher playing filed for Wal-Mart Stores, Inc. in its drive to expand internationally. Carrefour is the No. 1 retailer in Argentina, Brazil, and Taiwan, as well as in Belgium, France, Greece, Portugal, and Spain. To counter Wal-Mart, Carrefour seeks ways to slash prices—of course, Wal-Mart is doing the same.[76]

Currently (2006), Wal-Mart is having problems in the price war because in some foreign markets it has not been able to muscle suppliers into lowering their prices (which is how Wal-Mart became the largest retailer). Practical Perspective 5.11 describes IKEA's international pricing strategy. The product life cycle in a specific

PRACTICAL PERSPECTIVE 5-11

IKEA: Furnishing a Big World

"IKEA [a Swedish corporation] recognized that the value added in making furniture wasn't necessarily in manufacturing," explained Robert Atkins, [in 1997] a vice president of Mercer Management Consulting in Boston. "They designed kits that put the consumer in the middle of the value chain, giving them lots of things to do that were traditionally done by the manufacturer. This took incredible amounts of cost out of their system."

IKEA further reduced its costs by becoming production oriented. The company strived to carry out product development on the shop floor. It sent its 10 in-house designers into its suppliers' factories to learn the capabilities and limitations of their machinery so that product designs can be adapted to the machines, instead of the other way around. "Most designers look at the form and the function, but ours must also look at the price," explained [Jan] Kjellman [president of IKEA North America]. "We don't want to make limited-edition products. We want to mass produce them."

Sometimes keeping costs down means that an IKEA design will be made of a lesser quality material. For example, the company does not hesitate to make a painted tabletop out of a lower grade of wood, or substitute a simpler material for a base that isn't seen. And furniture that would be too expensive to make in birch is made out of pine. While the company aimed to provide a good quality product, price was still the main reason people shop IKEA. "The easiest way to enter a market is with a low price," said Atkins.

SOURCE: Excerpted from Sharen Kindely, "IKEA: Furnishing A Big World," *Hemispheres* (February 1997), p. 32. Reprinted with permission.

market also influences the price. If it is a new product and there is a demand for it, a higher price can often be charged. On the other hand, to achieve market penetration where the product is in a late life cycle stage, a firm may have to charge a lower price. Of course, as discussed in Chapter 3, businesses must avoid committing the illegal act of "dumping."

International Pricing

International pricing basically relates to the managerial decision of what to charge for goods produced in one nation and sold in another. A common practice of global corporations has been to establish a strong position in global markets by intracorporate sales. In applying this practice, a global corporation attempts to rationalize production by requiring foreign subsidiaries to specialize in the manufacture of some items while importing others. The subsidiaries' imports may consist of components assembled into the end product, or they may be finished products imported to complement their product mix.

This import-export practice among subsidiaries located in different countries enables the global corporation to control and transfer prices and to control the profits and losses of its subsidiaries. These corporations will realize no profits in a country where, for reasons discussed below, it is not beneficial to do so and will realize them in a country where it is beneficial to do so.

Avoiding a Country's High Tax Rate. Both foreign and domestic governments are interested in profits and the role of transfer prices in their attainment. This is because of the consequences profits have on the amount of taxes paid. Because of the differences in tax structures among nations, global corporations can often obtain significant profits by instructing a subsidiary in a country that has a high corporate tax rate to sell the product at cost to another subsidiary in a country where taxes are lower. The profit is thereby earned in the country where taxes are lower.

Avoiding a Country's Currency Restrictions. Transfer pricing may also be used to get around currency restrictions. For example, a nation suffering from a lack of foreign hard currencies may impose controls that limit the amount of profit (hard currency) that can be repatriated—that is, profits that can be transferred back to the corporation's home base. For instance, suppose Country X imposes controls on the amount of profits that can be repatriated and there is trade with Country Y, which does not have such controls. The corporation at home could instruct the subsidiary in Country X to sell its product to a subsidiary in Country Y at cost. This would transfer X's profit to Y, from where the global corporation can repatriate profits (hard currency).

Avoiding Currency Devaluations, Having to Reduce Prices, and Having to Increase Wages. The international pricing approach could also be employed by global corporations when a foreign nation's currency is devaluated, when there is government pressure in the foreign country to reduce prices because of excessive profits, and when labor in the foreign country demands higher wages because of high profits earned.

Arms-Length Pricing. Because of these manipulative practices, many governments insist on arms-length pricing—that is, the price charged to company affiliates must be the same as that paid by unrelated customers. For example, under Section 482 of the U.S. Internal Revenue Code, U.S. tax authorities are empowered to reconstruct an intracorporate transfer price. When they suspect that low prices were set to avoid taxes, they may alter the tax structure.[77] It should be noted that many U.S. executives prefer the arms-length approach because it enables them to properly monitor and evaluate foreign managements' performance.[78] They also tend to prefer it because profit transfers to another subsidiary can demoralize the management of the foreign subsidiaries that do not show positive results.

Fluctuating Exchange Rates and Costs

Fluctuating exchange rates force periodic adjustments in price. For example, Zenith Electronics Corporation incorrectly estimated the fluctuating direction of the U.S. dollar when it hedged in forward exchange contracts, resulting in a $13 million loss in its 1989 second quarter, even though its sales grew.[79] In 1996, Whirlpool lost $13 million in Europe, blaming it on the rising Italian lira (now the euro).[80] To deal with the problems fluctuating currency exchange rates create for international businesses, the European Union has introduced a single currency—the euro dollar. There is currently a move to introduce a single currency in Asia as well.[81] The same principle applies to fluctuating costs, including costs of raw materials and supplies, inflation, and interest rates. When a firm enters into a long-term contract at a fixed rate, shifts can prove disastrous if the firm cannot adjust its prices in some way. The bottom line is that in international pricing, a firm must develop strong international money management skills. (Refer again to the case of Laker Airways, the British firm discussed in Chapter 3, which went into bankruptcy because it did not manage well in this respect.)

Currently, many international companies use international price indices (IPCs) as critical tools for conducting international business. IPCs help international managers in predicting exchange rates, as well as in calculating escalator clauses in long-term contracts (termed *hedging* in Chapter 3), in conducting strategic market analyses, and in assessing international competition.[82]

Countertrade

The swapping of goods is a practice that has been around for thousands of years. A well-known swap occurred in 1626, when European settlers in America traded with America's Aborigines $24 worth of cloth and trinkets for Manhattan Island (New York City).[83] Today (2007), oil-producing countries are trading oil for food, and technology-producing countries are trading technology know-how for oil.

Pricing strategies are further complicated by the fact that not all foreign transactions can be in cash. For example, sales to communist countries and to less developed countries with "soft currency"—currency that is not readily accepted in international transactions—often take place in the form of countertrade, which fundamentally means that the buyer of a product pays the seller with another product that has an equivalent monetary value. The pricing problem derives from the difficulty of assessing the value of the product received in exchange. A miscalculation could lead to financial disaster, but it could also lead to "windfall profits." There are four basic types of countertrade transactions: barter, compensation, switch, and counterpurchase.[84]

Barter. Barter is an arrangement in which the exporter sells goods to a foreign importer without the exchange of cash. That is, specified goods are sold to the importer for other specified goods.

Compensation. Using the compensation procedure, the exporter sells technology and equipment to an importer in the foreign market. The importer pays the exporter with goods produced with the imported technology or equipment.

Switch. In the switch procedure, the exporter transfers the commitment to a third party who may be an end user of the product received by the exporter or to a trading house employed to dispose of the product. An advantage here is that the third party can be highly effective in selling the product. A disadvantage is that the third party often seeks to obtain the product at a bargain price, therefore lessening profit and complicating negotiations.

Counterpurchase. Under a counterpurchase agreement, two parties agree to sell each other products or services with some balancing of values. The exporter sells goods, technology, or services to the foreign importer for hard currency, but agrees to purchase goods with the hard currency equivalent from the importing country within a specified period—the goods are selected from a list that usually excludes those items produced by the technology being imported. An advantage of this approach is that the exporter has use of the hard currency for the specified period.

Exporters entering into countertrade agreements must often use a trading firm to market the goods they purchase. However, the goods purchased can often be distributed or used by a subsidiary of the exporter. For example, as mentioned in Chapter 3, during the U.S.S.R. regime, PepsiCo was selling to Russia the concentrate for the drink to be bottled and sold in Russia, and in return, PepsiCo was paid with vodka, which it distributed through a U.S. subsidiary. Also, often, exporters receive raw materials or parts that can be used in their production process as payment.

In general, the major problem in countertrade is determining the value and the potential demand of the goods offered by the other firm, and it is time-consuming. Firms, however, are motivated to participate in countertrade for various reasons, including making sales in nonmarket nations and in many less developed countries and adjusting their accounting records to enable them to pay lower taxes and tariffs. This occurs when both parties underestimate the value of the goods.

The Brazilian government conducts training programs for companies, which help them seize business opportunities in untapped markets in less developed countries. Hence, Brazilian companies are much better at conducting business transactions through countertrading than U.S. companies, which tend to prefer cash business transactions.

Promotion Strategy

In general, problems related to international promotion strategy include the legal aspects of the country, tax considerations, language complexities, cultural diversity, media limitations, credibility of advertising, and degree of illiteracy. Some governments regulate advertising more closely than others. Laws in some nations restrict the amount of money that may be spent on advertising, the utilization of media, the types of products advertised, the methods used in advertising, and the ways in which the prices are advertised. Some nations levy special taxes on advertisements. Language translation, which is discussed in Chapter 9, presents many barriers. For example, translating semantic and idiomatic meanings across languages is difficult, thus presenting a huge impediment to communication.

Why International Promotional Strategies Fail

International promotional strategies fail because of numerous reasons, including insufficient research, poor follow-up, narrow vision, overstandardization, and rigid implementation.[85]

Insufficient Research

Insufficient research prior to making international strategic decisions generally leads to failure. For example, Lego A/S, the Danish toy company, had improved its penetration in the American market by offering "bonus" packs and gift promotion. Encouraged by its success in the United States, Lego decided to apply the same approaches, unaltered, to other markets, including Japan, where penetration had been lagging. These tactics, however, failed to impress the Japanese customers. A later investigation revealed that Japanese consumers viewed the promotions as wasteful, expensive, and not too appealing. The results were similar in other countries as well.

Overstandardization

Some commodities, such as Coca-Cola, have a global appeal. In this situation, the message to be communicated can be much the same throughout the world. Many products, however, do not have a universal appeal.[86] The message to be communicated must therefore be tied to individual motivation; the promotional campaign, instead of being overstandardized, must reflect local tastes. The foreign environment thus has a significant effect on promotional strategy. Failure to adapt promotional strategy to the foreign environment inevitably creates difficulties. Managers therefore need to determine whether or not a promotional message is appropriate for the foreign culture, and if not, what adaptations must be made. (Refer again to the earlier discussion on SRC.)

For example, the Marlboro cigarette advertisements, which showed a man projecting a strong Western masculine image, were unsuccessful in Hong Kong. Philip Morris subsequently changed its ad to reflect a Hong Kong–style man, still a virile cowboy, but younger, better dressed, and depicted as owning the truck and the land he stood on.[87]

Another example is a laundry detergent company's promotional campaign in the Middle East. The advertisement on the box showed a picture of soiled clothes on the left, a picture of the soiled clothes being washed with the detergent in the middle, and a picture of sparkling clean clothes on the right. This works in Western cultures, where people read from left to right (as you are doing right now). But in some languages, people read from right to left, therefore some individuals interpreted the message to mean that you put clean clothes in the washer, you use the detergent to wash them, and then you get soiled clothes.[88] In the 1970s, Polaroid began selling its pathbreaking SX-70 camera in Europe. It used the same advertising strategy—TV commercials and print ads—that was successful to launch the product in the U.S. market. Although the product itself had global appeal, the TV commercials featuring personalities well-known in the United States did not. Testimonials by well-known personalities did not stimulate European consumers' interest. Polaroid subsequently researched and adhered to European promotional practices that were known to work. (For further illustration, refer to Practical Perspective 5.12.)

PRACTICAL PERSPECTIVE 5-12

Advertising in Saudi Arabia Must Adhere to Local Customs

Saudi Arabia plays a key role in the Gulf Co-operation Council (GCC)....An understanding of advertising regulation in this gateway country thus becomes essential for marketers interested in the region....As do many other developing countries, Saudi Arabia strongly adheres to local customs. Age-old traditions continue to be observed in dress, salutations, hospitality, and so forth. Although no laws specifically regulate the culture contents of ads, insensitivity may destroy credibility. A major tea company alienated Saudi customers after it aired a commercial that showed a Saudi host serving tea with his left hand to one of his guests, moreover, the guest was shown wearing shoes while seated, which is considered disrespectful by traditional Saudis [which, as discussed in Chapter 10, is a don't do].

SOURCE: Excerpted from M. Luqmani, Z. Quraeshi, and U. Yavas, "Advertising in Saudi Arabia: Content and Regulation," *The International Executive* (November–December 1989), pp. 35–38. Reprinted with permission.

Poor Follow-Up

Failure to monitor the promotional campaign for problems and solve them as they arise will contribute to failure. For instance, a U.S.-based computer company implemented a software house cooperation program in Europe to help penetrate the small- and medium-sized accounts market segment, where it was weak. The program needed a large change in sales force operation. The sales force, no longer in control of the hardware and software package, had to determine its content together with a software house that had access to the smaller accounts. The success of the new program depended on how effectively the sales force carried out its new assignments as well as on central coordination and attention, which it never got. Lacking central coordination and follow-up, there was no communication channel for sharing and building on the experiences of subsidiaries.

Narrow Vision

An enterprise may either centralize promotional strategic decision making or decentralize it to its local managers. Both approaches have pros and cons. The centralized approach can be effective by providing an overall global perspective, but it can be ineffective because decision making is not close to the market. The decentralized approach may be effective since decision making is close to the market; however, it may be ineffective because it does not provide a global perspective. (For an illustration, refer to Practical Perspective 5.13.)

PRACTICAL PERSPECTIVE 5-13

Nestlé's Decentralization of Promotion Proves Less Than Satisfactory

Nestlé's experiences with laissez-faire in sales promotion are typical of the problems faced by many multinationals. In the early 1980s, management delegated to the local organizations many decisions that had traditionally been made or strongly influenced by the headquarters. Of all the marketing decisions, only branding and packaging were kept at the center. The rest, including consumer and trade promotions, became the domain of the company's country operations around the world. Although decentralization has helped enhance Nestlé's performance internationally, it has been less than satisfactory in sales promotion.

The problem had to do with two developments over time: a worldwide shift in emphasis and budget allocation in favor of sales promotion and away from media advertising and increasing reliance on price promotion to boost short-term local sales results, particularly in countries with a powerful trade and/or limited electronic media advertising. The outcome: reduced brand profitability, contradictory brand communication, and a serious potential for dilution of brand franchises with consumers. [In 1990] Nestlé was trying to put some central direction back into its worldwide communication practices, including sales promotion. Management was painfully aware of the damage "brand management by calculators" and "commodity promotion" can do to its international brands and their long-term profitability. Laissez-faire in sales promotion was no longer considered a virtue at Nestlé.

SOURCE: Excerpted from K. Kashani and J. A. Quelch, "Can Sales Promotions Go Global?" *Business Horizons* (May–June 1990), pp. 37–43. Reprinted with permission.

Firms that apply just one of the two approaches possess a narrow vision. For example, in the 1970s, the Anglo-Dutch company Unilever targeted its household cleaner, Domestos, for international expansion. Management assigned the development of a global "reference mix" to Britain, where the brand had been established. After several years and numerous market entries, Unilever's top management was still waiting to repeat the success it had attained in the British market. The failure was attributed to the lead market's insistence that their strategy be followed in other markets (centralization), while the success was attributed to deviation from the lead market's strategy (decentralization). However, in the markets where there was deviation, the global theme also deviated. For instance, the theme for Domestos in West Germany (now Germany) was as an "all-purpose sanitary cleaner," and in Australia, it was as a "bathroom plaque remover." To attain a balance between centralization and decentralization, Unilever's detergent unit subsequently established a multisubsidiary structure, the European Brand Group, to coordinate brands in Europe. The group consisted of executives from the central headquarters and from numerous large subsidiaries.

Rigid Implementation

High-level managers sometimes ignore local managers' reservations about rigidly implementing a standardized promotional program and force compliance, which usually leads to failure. This is because local managers' reservations are often based on a solid understanding of local conditions. For example, Nestlé launched an innovative cake-like chocolate bar in Europe. The British unit, however, refused to accept the product because of its knowledge that a soft bar would not appeal to British tastes. Forced adoption of the product would therefore have resulted in failure.

Top management may also become inflexible to changing market conditions. For instance, Lego pioneered standardized marketing in its field and became a genuine global corporation by marketing its educational toys in the same way in more than 100 countries. However, Lego eventually encountered competition from look-alike and lower-priced rival products from Japan, the United States, and other countries. Tyco, a leading competitor in the United States, began packaging its toys in plastic buckets that could be used for storage after play. Lego, however, used elegant see-through cartons standardized worldwide. American parents preferred the functional toys-in-a-bucket idea over the cartons. Lego's U.S. managers sought permission from the central managers in Denmark to package Lego's toys in buckets. The central managers refused because they believed that packaging toys in buckets could lower Lego's reputation for high quality and change it from innovator to follower, and that it deviated from the company's policy of standardization.[89] Massive losses eventually led Lego to change its stand and develop its own innovative buckets.

Developing an Effective International Promotional Strategy

To develop an effective international promotional strategy, strategists must determine (a) the promotional mix—the blend of advertising, personal selling, and sales promotions—needed for each market; (b) the extent of worldwide promotional standardization; (c) the most effective message; (d) the most effective medium; and (e) the necessary controls to aid in assessing whether or not the potential objectives are being met.[90] Practical Perspective 5.14 reports how Procter & Gamble penetrated the Japanese market with its Joy dishwashing soap. For another illustration, refer to Practical Perspective 5.6, which describes Budweiser's development campaign in China.

PRACTICAL PERSPECTIVE 5-14

P&G's Joy Makes an Unlikely Splash in Japan

Just two years ago [in 1995], two powerful consumer-products concerns, Kao and Lion Corporation, each controlled nearly 40 percent of the kitchen-soap market with several brands and had essentially declared a truce. The rest of the market was cornered by private brands at chain stores. Meanwhile, the Japanese were cooking less at home and thus buying less dish soap every year. P&G actually washed out of the Japanese kitchen-detergent market during an earlier attempt. It withdrew in the late 1970s after failing to make a dent with Orange Joy, a product that it transplanted from the U.S. But by 1992, it had succeeded in marketing other products, such as Pampers, in Japan. The home office told its Japanese unit to find new markets for products in which P&G was strong elsewhere in the world.

So that year P&G sent out researchers to study Japanese dishwashing rituals. They discovered one odd habit: Japanese homemakers, one after another, squirted out more detergent than needed. It was "a clear sign of frustration" with existing Japanese products, said Robert A. McDonald, [then] head of P&G's Japanese operations. He saw the research as a sign that an "unarticulated consumer need" was more powerful soap. "We knew we had something to go after," he said.

"Some P&G executives were concerned about entering such a mature market," said McDonald. But P&G's lab in Kobe went to work to create a highly concentrated soap formula, based on a new technology developed by the company scientists in Europe, specifically for Japan.

The first hint that Joy was a hit came in March 1995 in the region around Hiroshima, 400 miles west of Tokyo, where P&G started test-marketing it. Four weeks into the test, Joy had become the most popular dish soap in the region with a 30 percent market share. P&G marketing pitch was deceptively simple: A little bit of Joy cleans better, yet is easier on the hands. "The message hit a chord," said Ayumi Osaki, a 31-year-old homemaker who rushed off to buy Joy after seeing pilot commercials. "Grease on Tupperware, that's the toughest thing to wash off," said Osaki, a mother of three in Hiroshima. "I had to try it."

SOURCE: Excerpted from Norihiko Shirouzu, "P&G's Joy Makes an Unlikely Splash in Japan," *The Wall Street Journal* (December 10, 1997), p. B1. Permission conveyed.

Want to Go International?

Factors to Consider

Chapters 3 to 5 discussed the international planning process. This section presents some questions that the strategist should answer, or factors that should be considered, to be successful doing business abroad.

- Does your firm have a mission statement? That is, do you know why the company exists and what it plans to do? If you don't, you won't have a sense of direction.
- Why do you want to go international? Is it for opportunity or threat reasons or both? Or is it because it is currently fashionable to internationalize? If it is the latter, you might not apply the intensity required to be successful abroad.
- Are you ready to go abroad? Will going abroad really solve your problems? How long has the company been in business? Is it stable enough (financially and psychologically) to endure the initial hardship of internationalization? Does it have

a national reputation? Will being successful at home help mitigate the hardship of internationalization?

- Have you done your homework? That is, have you ascertained where there may be a demand for your product/service? Are you totally familiar with domestic and international environments? Have you thoroughly familiarized yourself with the potential market's cultural, economic, legal, political, competitive, trade and monetary barriers, and labor relations factors? That is, are your thoroughly familiar with the challenge you will be facing in internationalizing?

- Are you thoroughly familiar with your strengths and weaknesses? That is, do you have a thorough understanding of your international management capabilities? Do you have a clear understanding of the nature of your product/service? Do you know how to capitalize on your product's/service's strengths, how to minimize its weaknesses, how to correct its shortcomings, and how to customize it to fit the needs of the foreign market? How strong or weak is your firm with respect to e-commerce?

- Have you developed viable product/service, place/entry, pricing, and promotion strategies that are based on the answers to the questions posed above as well as to the issues to be presented in Chapters 6 to 13?

In essence, the above means that to be successful in internationalizing a business, the strategist must do his or her homework. As the many practical anecdotal cases presented throughout this book illustrate, those who do their homework have a far greater chance of succeeding abroad than those who do not.

Summary

This chapter has proposed that when managers develop an international product/service strategy, they must consider the SRC, which often leads one to assume that what sells at home will sell abroad in the same form—which usually is not true. Some products and services can be sold globally in standardized form, but most products and services must be customized to fit the varying needs of different societies. Managers must also consider that many products/services introduced into a society will not sell well right away; they must be diffused into the society over time.

The method of getting the product or service to foreign customers will vary from nation to nation. The fundamental approaches are exporting the products to a country or manufacturing it there. Six approaches to manufacturing abroad have been discussed: licensing, franchising, management contracts, joint ventures, contractual alliances, and wholly owned subsidiaries. The chapter also described how various factors influence international pricing strategy, such as the foreign government, monetary exchange, and the requirement for barter trade. Some international firms use pricing strategy to develop foreign markets; others are content to simply get some revenues from the foreign market. Some international firms use a transfer of pricing approach to get around a country's high tax rate, currency restrictions, currency devaluations, and mandate to reduce prices and increase wages. Four types of barter trade were discussed: barter, compensation, switch, and counterpurchase.

Relative to promotion strategy, it was proposed that various factors influence international promotions, including the legal aspects of the country, language differences, and cultural diversity. Several reasons for the failure of international promotional strategies were discussed: insufficient research, overstandardization, poor follow-up, narrow vision, and rigid implementation.

KEY TERMS AND CONCEPTS

1. Product/service, place/entry, pricing, and promotion strategies

2. Self-reference criterion

3. Standardization versus customization

4. Cultural barriers

5. People-processing, possession-processing, and information-based services

6. The diffusion process

7. Quickness or slowness of diffusion

8. Dualistic technological structure

9. Adaptive transformative and transformative technological innovations

10. Exporting to or manufacturing abroad

11. Indirect and direct exporting

12. Agent and merchant middlemen

13. Domestic and foreign middlemen

14. International sales force

15. Foreign sales branch, foreign sales subsidiary, and company's own foreign distribution system

16. Internet sales

17. Firms should not adhere to any one approach

18. Licensing, franchising, management, contractual alliances, and wholly owned subsidiaries

19. "Goodwill"

20. A mix of strategies

21. Think global, act local

22. International pricing strategy

23. Pricing as an active tool and as a static element

24. Control over final prices and net price received

25. Foreign national and international pricing

26. National price controls

27. Getting around a country's high tax, currency restrictions, currency devaluations, and requirements to reduce prices and increase wages

28. Arms-length pricing

29. Barter, compensation, switch, and counterpurchase

30. Insufficient research, overstandardization of promotion, poor follow-up on promotion program, narrow vision, and rigid implementation of promotion program

DISCUSSION QUESTIONS

1. Why is it important that managers of international firms remain informed about their enterprises' external environment and internal situation?

2. Briefly discuss the five different product strategies.

3. Some writers on international strategy contend that the effectiveness of international businesses relies more and more on the offering of standardized products (a global strategy). Do you agree or disagree? Why?

4. Discuss the ways information technology enhances the provision of information-based services and products.

5. Discuss the dualistic technological structure.

6. Differentiate between an international sales force, sales branch, sales subsidiary, and firm's own distribution system. Discuss some of the factors that affect the various approaches taken.

7. Discuss some advantages and disadvantages of direct exporting over indirect exporting.

8. Discuss the six strategic options for manufacturing abroad.

9. Discuss the advantages and disadvantages of the wholly owned strategy.

10. Discuss the advantages and disadvantages of manufacturing abroad over exporting.

11. Discuss the two approaches to "Think global, act local."

12. Operating in foreign markets brings new pricing challenges. Discuss some of them.

13. Discuss the following pricing strategies: pricing as an active tool, pricing as a static element, control over final prices, and net price received.

14. Differentiate between foreign national pricing and international pricing.

15. Why do international managers currently prefer arms-length pricing?

16. How do fluctuating exchange rates and costs affect pricing strategy?

17. Discuss the four approaches to countertrade. What is the major problem with countertrade?

18. Discuss the general problems related to an international promotion strategy.

19. Discuss the factors with which a strategist should be familiar when developing an internationalization strategy.

EXERCISES

1. You are the strategic planner for a domestic firm that produces soft drinks. Your firm's sales at home are stagnant. As a solution, you have decided to sell your product in Europe and Asia. What should your next step be?

2. You are an international management consultant hired by a domestic company that invented a unique product for its home market. The firm's management is now considering expansion into foreign markets and is currently considering the financial aspects of the transfer. With respect to revenues, what would you advise your client?

3. A domestic firm, whose managerial personnel lack international business experience, is considering entering a foreign market. What would be its logical entry strategy? Why?

4. A domestic firm, whose managerial personnel have had considerable prior experience in international business in a similar industry, is considering entering a foreign market. What would be its logical entry strategy? Why?

5. An international business has been exporting to a foreign market. The firm's product is well diffused in the market. Because of high local labor costs, rises in transportation costs, and increases in tariff costs, the firm has been incurring financial losses. The firm's management has decided that it is time to manufacture abroad. The management of the cash-strapped firm likes to be in control of total operations. Which of the six options to manufacture abroad do you believe would be best suited for this firm? Why?

6. You are an international promotion consultant hired by a firm getting ready to develop a massive international promotion program. What advice would you give your client?

7. Chapter 2 discusses ethics and social responsibility. In this context, refer to the International Pricing section. Do you think these practices are ethical or unethical? Why? Do you think they are socially responsible? Why or why not?

ASSIGNMENT

Interview an international executive of an international business firm. Ask him or her to describe the enterprise's general international strategies. How did the firm enter the foreign arena? What were some of the factors that affected the strategy? Has the firm changed strategies? If not, does it plan to do so? Prepare a short report for class discussion.

CASE 5-1

Keep On Trekking

Surrounded by Wisconsin's gently rolling hills, the town of Waterloo (population 2,888) is the last place you would associate with high-flying international business. License plates on the pickup trucks that dominate the roads here read America's Dairyland, football fans at Green Bay Packers games wear giant foam cheese wedges on their heads, and the conversations on Main Street are conducted in slow, flat Midwestern cadence, not the impatient shorthand of international trade—NAFTA, ASEAN, Mercosur, WTO. But here, in the heartland of America, a remarkable tale of globalization is unfolding. In the past ten years, international exports from Wisconsin have nearly quadrupled, reaching $10.6 billion in 1996, projections of $13 billion by 2000. Much of this growth has been generated by small and midsize firms that found themselves doing business around the world before they even thought much about it—companies like Trek Bicycle.

Trek made its first road bicycle in 1976 in a tiny workshop in a rented barn outside Waterloo, less than an hour from Milwaukee, the state's commercial center, and Madison, the state capital. The company still builds its high-tech, Y-suspension bicycle frames in that red barn, but in the intervening two decades, it has become the world's biggest specialty bicycle maker, ringing up nearly $400 million in sales in 1996, of which 38 percent comes from its international business. Mountain biking may have originated in the United States, but today it's a global obsession, and Treks are exported to more than seventy countries through seven wholly owned subsidiaries in Europe and Japan and 65 independent distributors on six continents. Last year, Wisconsin governor Tommy G. Thompson named Trek one of the state's top exporters. How a tiny company that had just $18 million in sales in 1986, smack in the middle of Wisconsin farm country, managed to pull off this feat is a lesson in serendipity propelled by tenacity.

Joyce Keehn, Trek's worldwide sales director, still smiles in amazement when she recounts the events that catapulted international sales from zero in 1985 to well over $100 million in little more than a decade. It all began when a handful of letters came across her desk requesting information about exporting Trek bicycles to Canada. She was the telemarketing sales manager at the time, and Trek had no international sales division, so she took the letters to the national sales manager, John Burke. Those were the tight years of Reaganomics, of astronomical interest rates, bankruptcies, and the Third World debt crisis. Wisconsin was at the heart of the Midwest's rust belt, the depressed swath of the states where factories closed their doors when they were unable to ride out years of recession. Residents by the tens of thousands were moving south to try their luck in the booming Sun Belt.

Exporting was the last thing on anyone's mind. When she proposed that Trek find out how to export to Canada, Keehn recalls, "Burke just looked at me for a while. Then he said, 'Okay. Do it.' I said, 'Me?' 'Yeah you.'" Keehn had absolutely no experience with the laws or the practice of international trade, but she rolled up her sleeves and set about learning how to export with the same diligence that had gotten her out of bed before dawn to milk the cows on her family's dairy farm.

It is not uncommon for small- and medium-size companies to be introduced to international trade in just this way. Initially, most are content simply to fill overseas orders that arrive unsolicited. When results aren't immediately impressive or problems with tariffs and customs and distributors begin to crop up, many would-be exporters give up. But that didn't happen at Trek. Because Burke gave the telemarketing sales manager the leeway to develop the business and Keehn was determined to learn what it takes to be an exporter, the company was able to come up with the staff and budget to actually develop a global market rather than just fill orders for bikes. Following through made the difference.

Of course, it didn't hurt that Wisconsin had at that moment hit on the idea of international trade as a way out of its economic doldrums. Governor Thompson was setting up programs to teach local businesses about foreign markets, pushing through tax cuts for Wisconsin exporters, and leading trade missions all over the world. Because of the tone he set, when Keehn turned to the state export authority (a commercial office most states maintain), she found a staff that was enthusiastic and well-informed. They gave her advice on legal and logistical challenges and suggested she attend a state-sponsored trade seminar that brought together potential local exporters and international buyers. Keehn decided that Trek should sell directly to bicycle shops in Canada. The alternative, going through a distributor, would push the retail price too high.

With that strategy in mind, Keehn flew to Canada, flipped through phone directories to find likely bicycle shops then set out to visit each one. "You can tell which shops are at the high end, which ones are discounters, which you think you can work with," she says. "It's a lot of gut work." Back in Waterloo, with orders to fill, she handled all that paperwork needed to get each bicycle shipment through customs. And she made a trip to the warehouse before each shipment to make sure the papers were in order; even the tiniest slip could cause costly delays.

A year later, a Swiss dealer called, asking for bicycles to sell, and the whole process started again. By now, Keehn was an old hand. Within months, the Swiss orders multiplied from fifty bikes at a time to a hundred to a container of more than three hundred. Suddenly Keehn's boss realized he had good reason to pay attention to exporting. "It really didn't take a genius to figure out there were opportunities for us in Europe," says Burke, who is now Trek's president. The numbers told the story: Europeans buy fifteen million bikes a year, while Americans and Canadians together buy ten million. Because of the size of the European markets, Trek ponies up the money in the late '80s to establish its own wholly owned subsidiaries in six countries, including the U.K., Germany, and Austria, to distribute bicycles directly to retail outlets. The offices handle sales, inventory, warranties, and customer service. Although owning these operations was more expensive than using local distributors, it gave the company more control over how it sold its products, not to mention higher profits. That was the heart of the lesson Keehn was learning: Strive for as much control as possible, run your own operations on the ground, and build solid relationships worldwide.

As Trek set up European subsidiaries, Keehn began building a complementary network of independent distributors in countries where it made sense to do so. With greater distance and cultural and language barriers, Keehn had to rely on the expertise of local distributors rather than approach retailers on her own. To find partners, she attended trade shows and enlisted the help of private and state groups and the U.S. Department of Commerce. When she found likely prospects, she solicited proposals, then visited their offices and warehouses and asked questions. How would they advertise? How big was the market potential? Were there English speakers on staff? What were their marketing plans? How would they price the bikes? Did they sell competitors' bicycles? If so, the deal was usually off; Trek generally makes exclusive distributor agreements, renewable annually.

Often prospective partners came to the company. "Mountain biking was hot, and Trek was a hot brand. There was a lot of interest," Keehn says. At one trade conference, she offered a cough drop to a man sitting next to her with a terrible cold. When he thanked her, she noticed a Brazilian flag in his lapel pin and handed him a card; she was looking for a distributor in Brazil. His face lit up when he found out she was from Trek. He was looking for new products to add to his sports equipment business.

(Continued)

(Continued)

There were times, of course when her luck wasn't so good. In Brazil, Argentina, China, and Australia, Trek had to fight to protect its trademark. In South America and Indonesia, customs inspection delays sometimes held up shipments for so long that the letters of credit needed to ensure payment for the bicycles nearly expired. In Mexico, cargo was often pilfered while waiting to clear customs, making insurance hard to get. France and Denmark imposed all sorts of special requirements for the bikes, such as lights, bells, or engraved serial numbers, that made business difficult and costly.

And there was the constant risk of inadvertently offending customers through some cultural misunderstanding. Like the time Trek sent out catalogs decorated with pictures of Betty Boop, only to get a frantic fax the German subsidiary explaining that the character had adorned Allied bombers during World War II. A buyer from Singapore shied away from green helmets: in his country, he explained, if a man wears green on his head, it means his wife is having an affair. Often, however, international demands made the product better. Germany's strict environmental requirements led Trek to redesign its packaging, helping to bolster the company's environmentally conscious image.

The Internet, by making it much easier for companies to advertise around the world, posed another problem. About a third of the visits to Trek's Web site (www.trekbikes.com) come from abroad. But international sellers must charge more than their U.S. counterparts to make up for costs like shipping, customs duties, and currency exchange. If customers around the world could buy bicycles from the Web site, foreign distributors would be forced to compete with U.S. dealers. And price is no small matter: Trek's products are top of the line. Its famous Y-frame model, constructed of extremely light, strong carbon fiber, looks like something Batman might ride. The U.S. Secret Service uses it to patrol the White House grounds. Most of the mountain bikes the company exports are in the $300 to $1,500 range, with top models fetching more than $4,000. To protect its international sellers, Trek does not post prices on its Web site. It also forbids U.S. dealers to sell to international customers. Both policies demonstrate to Trek's overseas affiliates that it will stand behind them.

That is especially important for foreign partners, who have to grapple with red tape, wild swings in the value of their national currencies, and arbitrary import regulations. Last summer, for example, Brazil barred importers from borrowing for periods of less than 360 days, an extraordinarily long and expensive proposition for U.S. exporters, which normally don't extend credit for more than 90 days. And in 1996, the South African rand tumbled 30 percent on rumors (later proved false) that President Nelson Mandela had suffered a heart attack. American bicycles, therefore, were 30 percent more expensive for South Africans.

The last thing foreign distributors need is to sell against the more stable prices of the U.S. dealers. "Our local importer can absorb only so much of the price increase before it has to be passed on to the consumer," says Steve Bowman, a bike-racing champion whose Cape Town bike shop, Hopkins Cycle Inn, is Trek's top South African dealer. "From one month to the next, bike prices could go up 200 or 300 rand [about $40 to $60]." Trek brings dealers like Bowman to Wisconsin for regular visits to its factory and Madison store, where they've given sales and product training on Trek brands, including Fisher, LeMond, Klein, and Bontrager. In exchange, the company has high expectations of profits from Trek's team abroad. In five years, Trek projects exports to grow to 50 percent of its total sales.

What's next? Trek is considering building an assembly plant in Europe, a move that could cut delivery time by thirty days and eliminate 15.8 percent import duty it currently pays European

Union member countries. Meanwhile, the company is active in seminars, mentoring programs, and state-level policy initiatives to help other firms get their global business going. Not that these efforts are completely altruistic: building a wider base of small-to-medium-size companies interested in export policies is good for business. A bunch of small companies can exert a lot of influence when it comes to trade policy. John Burke no longer greets international topics with blank stares but rather with impassioned arguments in favor of breaking down trade barriers. He's particularly incensed about China, which levies a hefty import tax on bicycles of at least 50 percent and pays only 11 percent on the three million bikes it ships to the United States every year. "They pay their workers a dollar a day and no benefits, they are subject to no environmental standards, and still they charge those kinds of tariffs," he says. "It's totally unbelievable to me that the U.S. government won't say to the Chinese. 'As of this date, we will permit no bikes to enter the United States until you open up your markets.'"

It's the kind of debate heard more often these days in small towns like Waterloo and in once-small companies like Trek Bicycle. But it shouldn't be surprising. The American economy is being fueled by two forces: small business and exports. The National Association of Manufacturers and the Institute for International Economics have found that exporters create 20 percent more jobs— and are 9 percent less likely to go under—than purely domestic firms. Exporters like Trek helped the Wisconsin job market grow 13 percent in the last five years, outrunning the 9 percent rate in the rest of the economy.

The latest bright idea to come out of Wisconsin is a kind of statewide export-import bank to finance new exporters. On a crisp fall day in Madison, in a brand new building covered with Wet Paint signs, Governor Thompson and three dozen of Wisconsin's international business pioneers mulled the matter over at a regular quarterly strategy session. "Every time you sell one billion dollars of goods and services, you create 22,000 good jobs here in the state of Wisconsin," the governor said in an interview after the meeting. Today that translates into 220,000 jobs in Wisconsin that are all directly related to exports, he said, "and we're not even scratching the surface."

Questions

1. Discuss Trek's internationalization strategies within the context of the 4 Ps. How effective was Trek?

2. How might the Internet enhance its international operations?

3. Compare and contrast this case with Case 4.2 and Practical Perspective 4.4 (both in Chapter 4).

4. The article was written in 1999. For class discussion, check Trek's current status on the Internet.

SOURCE: Michele Wucker, "Keep On Trekking," *Working Woman* (December–January 1998), pp. 32–36. Reprinted with permission of MacDonald Communications Corporation. Copyright © 1999 by MacDonald Communications Corporation. www.workingwoman.com

NOTES

1. J. Friedland and L. Lee, "The Wal-Mart Way Sometimes Gets Lost in Translation Overseas," *The Wall Street Journal* (October 8, 1997), pp. A1, A12.

2. See M. Lander and M. Barbaro, "Wal-Mart Finds That Its Formula Doesn't Fit Every Culture," *The New York Times* (August 2, 2006), pp. C1, C4.

3. James E. Lee, "Cultural Analysis in Overseas Operations," *Harvard Business Review* (March–April 1966), pp. 106–114.

4. Len Lewis, "Growing Global," *Progressive Grocer,* 78, no. 9 (September 1999), pp. 22–28.

5. Clifford Krauss, "Despite Uncertain World Markets, a Big U.S. Retailer Bulls into Latin America," *The New York Times* (September 6, 1998). www.latinamericanstudies.org/economy/home-depot.htm

6. J. Flynn and L. Bongiorno, "IKEA's New Game Plan," *Business Week* (October 6, 1997). www.businessweek.com/1997/40/971006.htm-26K

7. Martha T. Moore, "Meeting the Cupholder Challenge," *USA Today* (May 2, 1994), p. 1B.

8. Whitaker Penteado, "Fast-Food Franchises Fight for Brazilian Aficionados." Used with permission of publisher from *Brandweek* (June 7, 1993), p. 20.

9. H. Riesenbeck and A. Freeling, "How Global are Global Brands?" *The McKinsey Quarterly* (November 4, 1991), p. 353.

10. F. Balfour and B. Grow, "Home Depot: One Foot in China," *BuinessWeekonline* (May 1, 2006). www.businessweek.com/print/magazine/content/06 18/b3982066.htm?chan=gl.

11. Adapted from Allison Lucas, "Market Researchers Study Abroad," *Sales and Marketing Management* (February 1996), p. 13.

12. Warren J. Keegan, "Multinational Product Planning: Strategic Alternatives," *Journal of Marketing* (January 1969), pp. 58–62.

13. Laurie M. Grossman, "PepsiCo Plans Big Overseas Expansion in Diet Cola Wars With Its Pepsi Max," *The Wall Street Journal* (April 4, 1994), p. B6.

14. David Welch, "GM Starts Getting Traction in Europe," *Business Week* (September 25, 2005), p. 60.

15. Theodore Levitt, "The Globalization of Markets," *Harvard Business Review,* 61 (May–June 1983), pp. 92–102.

16. K. Naughton, E. Thorton, K. Kerwin, and H. Dawley, "Can Honda Build a World Car?" *Business Week* (September 8, 1997), pp. 101–102.

17. Global Strategies, "The Colonel Comes to Japan," *The International Executive* (July–August 1989), pp. 28–29.

18. Shawn Tully, "Teens: The Most Global Market of All," *Fortune* (May 16, 1994), p. 90.

19. H. Riesenbeck and A. Freeling, "How Global are Global Brands?" op cit., p. 349.

20. Subhash C. Jain, "Standardization of International Marketing Strategy: Some Research Hypotheses," *Journal of Marketing,* 53 (January 1989), pp. 70–79.

21. This discussion draws from C. H. Lovelock and G. S. Yip, "Developing Global Strategies for Service Businesses," *California Management Review,* 38, no. 2 (Winter 1996), pp. 64–86.

22. William M. Bulkeley, "Having High-Tuition Blues? Look North," *The Wall Street Journal* (November 26, 1997), pp. C1, C19.

23. A. Reinhardt and C. Vitzthum, "Cafes, Beaches, and Call Centers," *Business Week* (September 5, 2005), p. 51.

24. See Arvind Parkhe, "International Outsourcing of Services: Introduction to the Special Issue," *Journal of International Management,* 13, no. 1 (March 2007), pp. 3–6.

25. Everett M. Rogers, *Diffusion of Innovations,* 3rd ed. (New York: The Free Press, 1983), p. 10.

26. Joanne Lee-Young, "Starbucks' Expansion in China Is Slated," *The Wall Street Journal* (October 5, 1998), p. A27.

27. The discussion of these categories draws from P. R. Cateora and J. M. Hess, *International Marketing* (Homewood, IL: Richard D. Irwin, 1979), p. 377.

28. This discussion draws from Paul Shrivastava, "Technological Innovation in Developing Countries," *Columbia Journal of World Business,* 19, no. 4 (Winter 1984), pp. 23–39.

29. Ibid., p. 26.

30. For a current study on entry strategies, see P. J. Buckley and P. N. Ghauri, "Globalization, Economic Geography and the Multinational Enterprises," *Journal of International Business' Studies,* 35 (2004), pp. 81–98.

31. For information regarding the evolution of foreign entry in the form of joint ventures and wholly owned enterprises, see Mauro F. Guillen, "Experience, Imitation, and the Sequence of Foreign Entry: Wholly Owned and Joint-Venture Manufacturing by South Korean Firms and Business Groups in China, 1987–1995," *Journal of International Business Studies,* 34 (2003), pp. 185–198.

32. See L. Tihanyi, D. A. Griffith, and C. J. Russell, "The Effect of Cultural Distance on Entry Mode Choice, International Diversification, and MNE Performance: A Meta-Analysis," *Journal of International Business Studies,* 36 (2005), pp. 270–283.

33. See A. Delios and W. J. Heinisz, "Policy Uncertainty and the Sequence of Entry by Japanese Firms, 1980–1998," *Journal of International Business Studies,* 34 (2003), pp. 227–241.

34. Kevin Maney, "Technology is 'Demolishing' Time, Distance," *USA Today Tech Report* (September 2, 1997). www.linkinghub.elsevier.com/retrieve/pii/50360835298000527

35. Irene M. Kunii, "Here Come the Sony Netman," *Business Week* (November 1, 1999), p. EB47.

36. Brian Palmer, "The View from China," *Fortune* (November 8, 1999), p. 214.

37. See K. H. Lim, K. Leung, C. L. Sia, and M. K. O. Lee, "Is eCommerce Boundary-Less? Effects of Individualism-Collectivism and Uncertainty Avoidance on Internet Shopping," *Journal of International Business Studies,* 35 (2004), pp. 545–559.

38. *Distribution in Asia/Pacific's Developing Markets* (Hong Kong: Business International Asia/Pacific Ltd., March 1978), pp. 1–3.

39. Ibid.

40. Ibid., pp. 3–4.

41. Global Strategies, "The Colonel Comes to Japan," op cit.

42. John Marcom Jr., "Japan to Host World's 3rd Disneyland but Park May Run Short of Funds, Fans," *The Wall Street Journal* (November 17, 1982), p. 36.

43. Ted Holden, "Who Says You Can't Break into Japan?" *Business Week* (October 16, 1989), p. 9.

44. Lee-Young, op cit. p. A27.

45. Carl Quintanilla, "Despite Setbacks, Whirlpool Pursues Overseas Markets," *The Wall Street Journal* (December 9, 1997), p. B4.

46. "BBA Takes Majority Stake in Naples," *Airports International* (March 1997), p. 3.

47. The Associated Press, "Chavez: Oil Co's. Must Form Joint Ventures," *abcNews* (2005), abcnews .go.com/search?searchtext=Chavez%3A%200ie%20Co%27s%20Must%20Form%Joint%20Ventures&type=

48. See S. Romero and C. Krause, "Deadline Nears in Chavez Fight Against Big Oil," *The New York Times* (April 10, 2007), sec. A, p. 1.

49. For further information on international equity joint ventures, see Y. Luo and S. H. Park, "Multiparty Cooperation and Performance in International Equity Joint Ventures," *Journal of International Business Studies,* 35 (2004), pp. 142–160.

50. Ted Holden, "Who Says You Can't Break into Japan?" op cit.

51. Dirk Beveridge, "Disney to Build in Hong Kong" (November 1, 1999). http://dailynews.yahoo.com/h/ap/19991101/bs/hong_kong__disney_13. html

52. M. Schuman and J. Ressner, "Disney's Great Leap Into China," *Time* (July 11, 2005). www.time.com/time/magazine/article/0,9171,108137...-38K

53. Wilfried Vanhonacker, "Entering China: An Unconventional Approach," *Harvard Business Review* (March–April 1997), p. 131.

54. Ibid.

55. Hu Mao Yuan, "China's Car Guy," *Fortune* (October 11, 1999), p. 240.

56. J. G. Wissema and L. Euser, "Successful Innovation Through Inter-Company Networks," *Long Range Planning,* 24 (December 1991), p. 35.

57. Thomas G. Cummings, "Transorganizational Development," in B. Staw and L. L. Cummings (Eds.), *Research in Organizational Behavior,* Vol. 6 (Greenwich, CT: JAI Press, 1984), pp. 367–422.

58. R. Ajami, "Designing Multinational Networks," in R. H. Kilmann and I. Kilmann (Eds.), *Making Organizations Competitive* (San Francisco: Jossey-Bass, 1991), pp. 309–326.

59. Kenichi Ohmae, "The Global Logic of Strategic Alliances," *Harvard Business Review* (March–April 1989), p. 151.

60. Ibid., pp. 147–149.

61. Helen Becket, "Bridging the Cultural Divide," *ComputerWeekly.Com* (January 23, 2006). www.computerweekly.com/Articles/2006/01/23/213761/Bridgin

62. Ibid., p. 152.

63. For information on developing acquired foreign subsidiaries, see Klaus Uhlenbruck, "Developing Acquired Foreign Subsidiaries: The Experience of MNEs in Transition Economies," *Journal of International Business Studies,* 35 (2004), pp. 109–123.

64. L. Lee and C. Rohwedder, "Wal-Mart to Acquire German Retailer, Moving to Europe for the First Time," *The Wall Street Journal* (December 19, 1997), p. A2; "Wal-Mart Goes Shopping in Europe," *Fortune* (June 7, 1999), p. 105.

65. M. Bernstein and M. Weinstein, "Globalshakeout: The Changing Landscape of Financial Services," *Prudential Leader,* 3, no. 2 (February 1998), pp. 9, 17.

66. Frank Gibney Jr., "Worldwide Fender Blender," *Time* (May 24, 1999), pp. 58–62.

67. See J. J. Reuer, O. Shenkar, and R. Ragozzino, "Mitigating Risk in International Mergers and Acquisitions: The Role of Contingent Payouts," *Journal of International Business Studies,* 35 (2004), pp. 19–32.

68. See Klaus E. Meyer, "Perspectives on Multinational Enterprises in Emerging Economies," *Journal of International Business Studies,* 35 (2004), p. 265.

69. For further information on this issue, see H. Zhao, Y. Luo, and T. Suh, "Transaction Cost Determinants and Ownership-Based Entry Mode Choice: A Meta-Analytical Review," *Journal of International Business Studies,* 35 (2004), pp. 524–544.

70. Seth J. Margolis, "Middle Market Companies Prepare for '92," *The International Executive* (January–February 1990), p. 41.

71. John R. Emshwiller and F. Rose, "Guess?'s Ambitious Design for Global Expansion Falters," *The Wall Street Journal* (November 26, 1997), p. B4.

72. For additional discussion on this topic, see Gianfranco Zaccai, "Global or Local? Make It Both," *BusinessWeekonline* (August 22, 2005). wwwbusinessweek.com/print/innovate/content/aug2005/id20050822_950630.htm

73. SOURCE: Adapted from a case study prepared and contributed to the second edition of this book by Long W. Lam and Louis P. White, "Internationalization of the President Enterprise Company," University of Houston, Clear Lake, TX (February 2000).

74. Allen P. Roberts Jr., "Localizing the Brand," *Inc. Magazine* (October 2005). www.inc.com/magazine/20051001/global-entrpreneur.html

75. Alex Taylor III, "Rough Road Ahead," *Fortune* (March 17, 1999), p. 116.

76. C. Matlack, I. Resch, and W. Zellner, "En Garde, Wal-Mart," *Business Week* (September 13, 1999), p. 55.

77. See L. Eden, L. F. J. Valdez, and D. Li, "Talk Softly But Carry a Big Stick: Transfer Pricing Penalties and the Market Valuation of Japanese Multinationals in the United States," *Journal of International Business Studies,* 36 (2005), pp. 398–414.

78. J. Greene and M. Duerr, *International Transactions in the Multinational Firm* (New York: The Conference Board, 1970), p. 8.

79. Stephen Kreider Yoder, "U.S. Technology Firms Go Global to Offset Weak Domestic Market," *The Wall Street Journal* (November 14, 1989), p. A1.

80. G. Steinmetz and C. Quintanilla, "Whirlpool Expected Easy Going in Europe, and It Got a Big Shock," *The Wall Street Journal* (April 10, 1998), p. A6.

81. Barry Eichengreen, "Is There a Monetary Union in Asia's Future?" *The Brookings Review* (Spring 1997), pp. 33–35.

82. For a deeper discussion on this topic, see L. Eden and P. Rodriguez, "How Weak Are the Signals? International Price Indices and Multinational Enterprises," *Journal of International Business Studies,* 35 (2004), pp. 61–74.

83. Arley A. Howard and John A. Yeakel, "Who Wins in International Countertrade," *Financial Executive* (January–February 1990), p. 49.

84. This discussion draws from P. Maher, "The Countertrade Boom," *Business Marketing* (January 1984), pp. 50–52; "Countertrade Without Cash?" *Finance and Development* (December 1983), p. 14.

85. The following discussion is adapted from Kamran Kashiani, "Beware the Pitfalls of Global Marketing," *Harvard Business Review* (September–October 1989), pp. 91–98.

86. "Global Messages for the Global Village Are Here," *Business World* (Autumn 1983), p. 51.

87. David A. Ricks, *Big Business Blunders: Mistakes in Multinational Marketing* (Homewood, IL: Dow Jones/Irwin, 1983), p. 52.

88. Ibid., p. 55.

89. For a current discussion on international marketing strategies, see L. K. S. Lim, F. Acito, and A. Rusetski, "Development of Archetypes of International Marketing Strategy," *Journal of International Business Studies,* 37 (2006), pp. 499–524.

90. Adapted from Cateora and Hess, *International Marketing,* op cit., p. 417.

Part III

ORGANIZING INTERNATIONAL ENTERPRISES

Two key questions managers must answer when they decide to market their firms' products or services in the international arena are how they will handle their foreign business and how they will structure their organization to conduct that business in the most efficient and effective manner. The success of an international enterprise depends on many crucial factors. One is its organizational structure. The structure is the organization's "skeleton"; it provides support and ties together disparate functions. Therefore, it is imperative that managers totally understand the structuring factors to be considered and the structuring problems to be overcome when attempting to expand into foreign markets. Chapter 6 discusses various basic organizational structures in an international context.

6

INTERNATIONAL DIMENSIONS OF ORGANIZATIONAL STRUCTURES

To support Gillette's increasingly global focus, the company went through a restructuring in 1988, creating three principal divisions. The North Atlantic Group manufactured and marketed the company's traditional shaving and personal care products in North America and Western Europe. The Diversified Group comprised the Stationery division's North Atlantic arm as well as the Braun, Oral-B, and Jafra companies, each organized on a worldwide product line basis. The International Group produced and sold the company's shaving, personal care, and stationery products in all markets except North America and Western Europe. The International Group was divided into three regions: Latin America; Africa, Middle East, and Eastern Europe (AMEE); and Asia-Pacific.[1]

Learning Objectives of the Chapter

Organizational structures generally establish the internal authority relationships, responsibility for work performance, and paths of communication and control required for a company to achieve its objectives. These structures are typically set up to blend the specialized expertise needed to facilitate decision making on a variety of short- and long-range problems. The development of structures should generally be planned and managed. The type of structure managers select should take into consideration the social and psychological aspects of the environment and personnel and should be designed to achieve operational efficiency and control without inhibiting individual creativity and initiative. This task becomes much more complex when a domestic enterprise desires to internationalize its operations. This is because organizations' managers need to establish lines of authority and responsibility from top headquarters management to managers in a variety of foreign environments and at the same time keep open the necessary lines of communication required to manage effectively and efficiently in all the diverse environments.[2] After studying this chapter, you should be able to do the following:

1. Describe the basic traditional international organizational structures

2. Present the advantages and disadvantages of each structure

3. Discuss contemporary thinking on the structuring of international organizations

4. Discuss the impact of the Internet on international organizational structures

Traditional and Contemporary International Structures

The three basic dimensions of an international business enterprise are technical or product needs, functional needs, and regional or environmental needs. Technical or product needs are specialized factors such as construction, operation, manufacturing, research and development, special knowledge, and experience. Functional needs refer to special knowledge of functions such as personnel, planning, purchasing, and finance. Regional or environmental needs involve special knowledge of areas such as the foreign country's culture, government, politics, trends, and economy. To attain maximum overall benefit and to ensure effective communication and develop the means to make effective decisions, the international organizational structure managers must effectively integrate these three basic dimensions throughout the organization.[3]

An organization's international structure is usually based on one of seven traditional or contemporary models. The traditional models include the functional structure, international division, foreign subsidiary, product division, and regional structure. The contemporary models include the matrix organization, the non-equity-based contractual/strategic alliance, and the mixed (hybrid) structure. These are discussed in the ensuing sections. Large international corporations tend to use similar basic structures the world over, but one will find many variations, as managers create a structure that best suits their organizational needs.

The Functional Structure

Under the functional structure, major functions are the focus. Product knowledge is centered in manufacturing, engineering, and marketing, and management of each of these departments is responsible for both domestic and international activities. Large international companies rarely use this structure at the corporate level; it is sometimes used in regions, divisions, and/or subsidiaries. The functional structure is traditionally European. It is typically used by smaller firms, or by larger firms with one major product and stable demand. Domestic firms whose internationalization strategy (discussed in Chapter 5) entails indirect exporting often use this structure.

A firm's low dependence on foreign sales and its staff's lack of international business experience often lead it to adopt this structure, as opposed to the international division structure (discussed next). A typical functional structure is illustrated in Figure 6.1. Note that the organizational chart in Figure 6.1 shows a manager of domestic operations and a manager of foreign operations for each function. However, these two roles are often carried out by one individual. Two people might be used when there is a large volume of international sales, but even then, the domestic manager may appoint an assistant manager to oversee international sales for him or her.

Advantages of the Functional Structure[4]

1. *Emphasis on functional expertise:* The key business tasks define work, and functional expertise is brought to bear on all aspects of the operation.

2. *Tight control:* This centralized functional approach permits a small staff to control the firm's operations. Top management has authority and operational responsibility.

3. *Prevents "we" versus "them" conflicts:* The absence of secondary profit centers (there is no international division) prevents internal conflicts—the "we" versus the international division problem (discussed in the next section) is prevented.

Disadvantages of the Functional Structure

1. *Weak regional coordination:* Disputes between functional managers must often be resolved at the corporate level. The CEO is often asked to solve problems in areas in which he or she lacks expertise, such as international business.

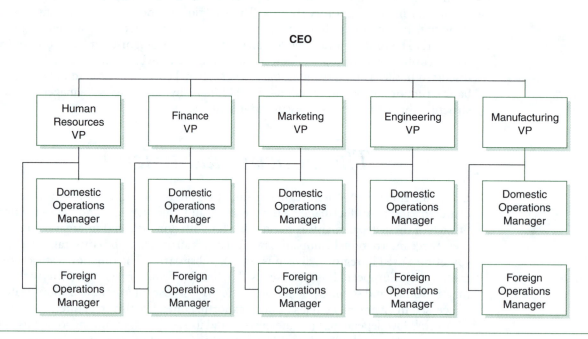

Figure 6.1 An Illustration of a Functional Structure

2. In firms with multiple product lines, the functional structure can lead to top heaviness. In multiproduct firms, functional managers need expertise in each product, or a functional manager is needed for each product. The latter, which is often the case, would lead to an expensive, top-heavy structure. For example, if the volume of international business is high, a domestic functional manager and a foreign functional manager may be needed (as shown in Figure 6.1).

3. Much greater emphasis is often placed on domestic sales than on foreign sales. For example, in a study of 185 medium and large successful Australian exporters, it was found that those firms that make a commitment to support exports through the formation of a separate export unit within their organizations outperform firms that treat exports as just a part of their domestic business.[5]

The International Division

After they have acquired some international business experience through indirect exporting and their reliance on international business has increased somewhat, many companies internationalize their operations further by creating an export department. Typically, the aim of the export department is simply to handle the shipment of existing domestic products to foreign markets. But when firms' foreign transactions subsequently increase, the export department is generally developed into an international division. The international division usually supervises exports, distribution agreements, foreign sales forces, foreign sales branches, and foreign sales subsidiaries. Staff members in the international division are selected on the basis of their general familiarity with corporate products, technology, and culture, combined with their ability to be "hands-on" managers who are culturally sensitive and adaptable to the constraints imposed by the foreign environmental factors (as discussed in Chapters 1 and 3).

In the international division structure, functional staffs such as marketing, finance, and research and development are typically established, and an executive responsible for international operations is appointed. International businesses adopt this structure when they desire to have an expert responsible for managing each specialized function. Managing these functions across countries requires skills beyond those required for managing them in the home country. One of the earliest users of this type of structure was International Harvester.[6] Canon Corporation, before it became a multiproduct enterprise, also used this structure. To expand into markets abroad, Wal-Mart was using this structure, as was Bally's Total Fitness.

The international division is generally given total authority and responsibility for the enterprise's foreign operations and activities. Historically, some smaller enterprises for whom an international division was not really necessary (an export department would have sufficed) have nevertheless adopted such a structure because they saw it being used by larger, successful enterprises.[7] A typical international division structure is illustrated in Figure 6.2.

Advantages of the International Division[8]

1. *Focused international responsibility and authority:* Foreign operations are generally more complex than domestic operations and distant from the home base.

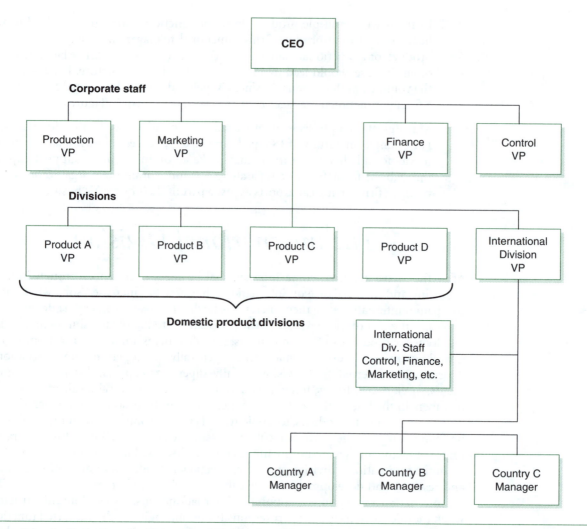

Figure 6.2 An Illustration of an International Division Structure

An experienced executive whose sole responsibility and authority is the international division is therefore freer to react to the needs of such areas than would be an executive whose responsibility and authority are for both domestic and international operations.

2. *International executive development:* Managers and employees in such a division are forced to develop expertise in international business and will subsequently be able to participate in, or direct, operations in foreign sites.

3. Managers of the international operations have a single, strong voice in the company's strategy/policy-setting process. Since heads of international divisions are usually totally responsible for the profits and losses of the foreign operations, they will be forceful in acquiring the share of resources necessary to accomplish the firm's international goals. On the other hand, an executive in charge of both

domestic and foreign operations may focus more on obtaining resources for domestic activities than for foreign operations.

4. *Company-wide view of international operations:* Managers in the international division are usually concerned with the success of all the firm's products in foreign markets. These managers are therefore impartial in determining the best overall corporate strategy for international profits. On the other hand, managers of individual product lines made responsible for both domestic and foreign operations may be partial to their own international operations as opposed to the firm's overall international strategy.

5. *Top management is cognizant of consequences:* Because of the complexity of international business, many domestic executives focus mainly on their home-country operations and lose themselves in domestic issues, thereby ignoring global operations. By having an international division, top management is made cognizant of the consequences of focused decisions on global operations.

Disadvantages of the International Division

1. *Bottleneck:* Managers of international divisions sometimes lack adequate product or technical expertise, and the physical separation between domestic and foreign operations often precludes enterprises from providing adequate technical support to international divisions. This causes bottlenecks.

2. *Exports slowdown:* Production divisions may not always adequately supply what the foreign division needs because they favor the domestic operations. Consequently, foreign orders may go unfilled even if the profit potential is higher than for domestic orders. On the other hand, the heads of product divisions who are responsible for both domestic and foreign business may pay more attention to foreign operations when they see a higher profit potential than in the domestic market.

3. *Conflict between employees in the domestic division and the employees in the international division:* Organizational struggles between domestic and foreign operations often occur. Because the international division cuts across all product areas, a "we-they" situation can occur.

4. *International versus other divisions:* In the ideal corporate organization, operating divisions should be equal in size and profit. In reality, however, the international division often becomes more profitable than the product divisions. When this occurs, the product divisions sometimes "gang up" to reduce the international division's powers.

5. *International managers spread too thin:* Managers of international divisions are often made responsible for several disparate markets, such as South America, Europe, and Asia. This makes developing expertise difficult.

The Foreign Subsidiary Structure

Environmental changes, such as increased demand in foreign markets, a foreign government's mandate, or changing conditions in the home market, often force international corporations to cease exporting and begin establishing manufacturing facilities in the foreign markets—they establish subsidiaries in foreign countries. These firms thus restructure their organization; they change from an international division structure to a foreign subsidiary structure. Each foreign subsidiary is treated as an entity. Each reports directly to top management at headquarters. Coordination between product and service departments is carried out at the headquarters office. These firms therefore apply the multidomestic strategy (discussed in Chapter 4). Applying a multidomestic strategy, the headquarters' managers generally allow the subsidiaries to function as a loose federation with local managers possessing substantial autonomy, allowing them to respond quickly to local situations.[9] (Refer to Practical Perspective 6.1.) A typical foreign subsidiary structure is illustrated in Figure 6.3.

Advantages of the Foreign Subsidiary Structure[10]

1. *Autonomy of affiliates:* The affiliate subsidiaries operate free of layers of management between them and top management. These independent affiliate companies are generally allowed to operate with little control from above and can thus develop their own local identity.

2. *Direct top management involvement:* Problems beyond the affiliate's talents go to top management for response and resolution. This enables top management to reflect long-range corporate goals rather than parochial interests. Also, it forces top management to develop a stake in international business and acquire knowledge in that area.

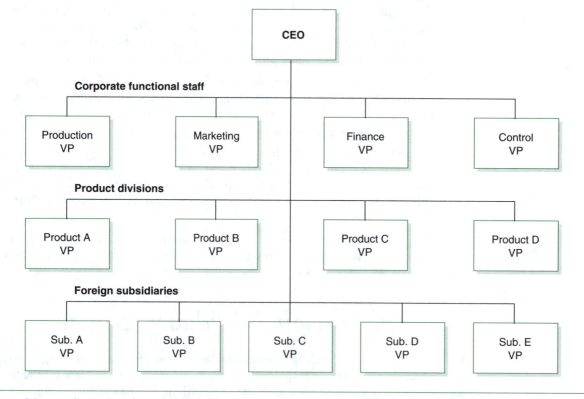

Figure 6.3 An Illustration of a Foreign Subsidiary Structure

PRACTICAL PERSPECTIVE 6-1

Wal-Mart Spoken Here

Wal-Mart has had to cope with political and economic instability. In Mexico, for example, it first bought 80 percent of its goods locally to get the best prices. But customers, many of whom had shopped at Wal-Mart in the USA, were disappointed at the lack of American products, so the retailer changed course. Then came the peso devaluation in December 1994, and Wal-Mart flip-flopped again. Now, only 10 percent of the goods sold in the Mexican stores are imported. What emerged from those early lessons is an overseas blueprint calling for a slightly different kind of Wal-Mart in each country. Though USA managers have been a big presence so far, the company hopes to create nearly autonomous units run by native managers who will handle their own buying, training, accounting, and other functions in two to three years. Managers will tweak the Wal-Mart formula to serve their local markets better. "We're building companies out there," says Martin. "That's like starting Wal-Mart all over again in South America or Indonesia or China."

But not everything will be decentralized. In the longer term, stores in different markets will coordinate purchasing to gain leverage with suppliers. Developing new technology—a key Wal-Mart strength—and plotting overall strategy will be done from Bentonville. And in Mexico, Wal-Mart plans to merge its stores with CIFRA's successful chains, once it completes the takeover of its Mexican partner. That will let the chains streamline costs.

SOURCE: W. Zellner, I. Katz, and D. Lindorff, "Wal-Mart Spoken Here," *Business Week* (June 23, 1997), pp. 141. Reprinted with permission.

Disadvantages of the Foreign Subsidiary Structure

1. *Diffuseness of international responsibility:* There is no center for international operations responsibility. With so many groups reporting directly to the board, clarity and focus can be lost—although the board can delegate the responsibility to certain expert members.

2. *Potential unwieldiness:* Many items that could be resolved without board action, such as by experts, are often pushed to the board level—again, the board could delegate many responsibilities to expert members.

The Product Division Structure

Many corporations are diversified (multiproduct) and use the product division structure. Under the product division structure, each of the enterprise's product divisions has responsibility for the sale and profits of its product. Therefore, each division has its own functional, environmental, sales, and manufacturing responsibilities. When a product division decides to internationalize its operations, it might first begin by using the indirect export strategy. Then, after becoming more experienced in international business, it might use the export division strategy. Subsequently, it might be necessary for it to adopt the foreign subsidiaries strategy. This means that if sales in foreign markets by firms with numerous product divisions become substantial, these enterprises could end up operating numerous subsidiary companies in a single foreign territory. Ford Motors began restructuring itself along the product line in the early 1990s.[11] Canon Corporation used the product division structure when it became a multiproduct enterprise in 1962. Practical Perspective 6.2 presents Procter & Gamble's (P&G's) plan to restructure from a regional to a product structure by 2005. As of March 9, 2007, P&G is operating under this structure. It has regional Web sites in the Balkans, Central Asia, and Western Europe, as well as local Web sites in all the countries in which it operates. A typical product division structure is shown in Figure 6.4.

Advantages of the Product Division Structure[12]

1. *Product and technology emphasis:* Since both domestic and international units report to the product division and, compared with the whole, product divisions tend to be small, closer ties could result. Therefore, because of the common product benefit and the closer ties, products and technology can be easily transferred between the domestic and international units.

2. *Worldwide product planning:* Foreign and domestic plans can be more easily integrated in a product division than in an international division. A worldwide division perspective could therefore evolve.

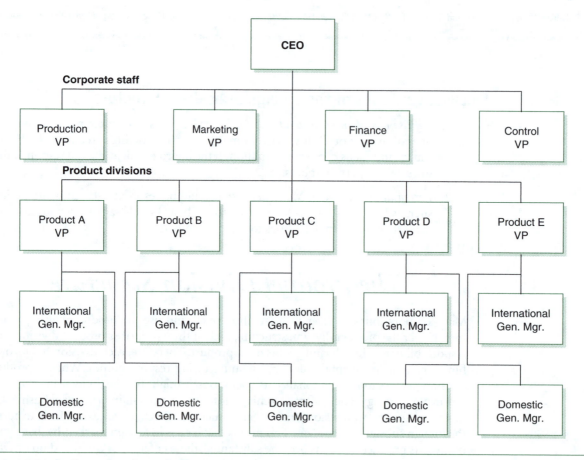

Figure 6.4   An Illustration of a Product Division Structure

PRACTICAL PERSPECTIVE 6-2

From Country to Product

Procter & Gamble's [in 1998] Chief Executive John E. Pepper will step down about two years early to make way for President and Chief Operating Officer Durk I. Jager, who will drive the changes. It's a shift away from internal themes of recent years in which Procter focused heavily on such tasks as cost-cutting and shedding underperforming brands. But even as the giant revs its engines to push for faster sales growth, critics wonder if it can overcome both economic turmoil around the world and what will surely be cultural turmoil within its own ranks. "This is a very big deal, for Procter and for all the companies that watch Procter's moves," said Watts Wacker, chairman of consulting firm FirstMatter in Westport, Connecticut. "But great plans often come with great obstacles."

In preparation for the task, Pepper and other top execs have been traversing the country, visiting the CEOs of a dozen major companies, including Kellogg Company and 3M, in search of advice. Pepper went to Jack Welch at General Electric Company to learn how the company streamlined global marketing. He persuaded Hewlett-Packard Company CEO Lewis E. Platt to share enough secrets about new-product development to make a 30-minute instructional video for P&G staffers. The message from all was clear, said Pepper: "What thousands of people have been telling us is that we need to be simpler and move faster."

The result of this unprecedented road trip is Organization 2005, a shuffling of the P&G hierarchy and a new product-development process designed to speed innovative offerings to the global market. The old bureaucracy, based on geography, will be reshaped into seven global business units organized by category, such as baby care, beauty care, and fabric-and-home care. The global business units will develop and sell products on a worldwide basis, erasing the old system that let Procter's country managers rule as colonial governors, setting prices and handling products as they saw fit. [As of 2007, P&G is using the foreign subsidiary structure.]

SOURCE: Excerpted from P. Galuszka, E. Neuborne, and W. Zellner, "P&G's Hottest New Product: P&G," *Business Week* (October 5, 1998), pp. 92, 96. Reprinted with permission.

3. *Conflict minimized:* The problem of substantiating the difference between international and domestic needs may be less difficult than when the international function is in the international division. Having both functions in the same division may lead to similar loyalties, and the "we-they" conflict often caused by placing the international function in an international division may be mitigated.

Disadvantages of the Product Division Structure

1. *Weakness in worldwide know-how:* Managers of individual product divisions may become knowledgeable in operating in certain markets, but worldwide knowledge is often impossible. For example, in the past, many managers of U.S. domestic enterprises that internationalized their operations have developed strong skills in the Canadian and European markets but weaker skills in other parts of the world. This may result in weak performance in certain markets.

2. *Inherent weakness of multiproduct systems:* Managers of the overall corporate system may encounter conflicting international demands from the different product divisions. Since managers are part of the overall corporate system, they may not possess adequate abilities to handle such conflicting demands.

3. *Division managers often lack international skills:* International product managers are often selected on the basis of domestic performance and may therefore lack the required international skills. (This problem is addressed in Chapter 8.)

4. *Foreign coordination problems:* Managers of different product divisions operating in the same foreign country may not coordinate efforts to attain overall corporate efficiency because they are too busy looking out for their own interests. For example, to cut costs, perhaps some support functions typically carried out in all product divisions, such as personnel and payroll, could be carried out by a single unit.

Canon Corporation dealt with these disadvantages by developing a divisional structure at the corporate level as well. It established a system consisting of 8 product groups at the corporate level and 21 product divisions.

The Regional Structure

Under the regional structure, regional heads are made responsible for specific territories, usually consisting of areas such as Europe, Asia, South America, North America, and so on, and report directly to their CEO or his or her designated executives at the headquarters. In general, firms with low technology and a high marketing orientation tend to use this structure. Firms whose foreign subsidiary or foreign product structure has become too large and too complex to manage from a single headquarters often restructure themselves using this form. This type of structure enables regional heads to keep abreast of, and provide for, the needs of their respective regional markets. Managers at regional headquarters are typically responsible for a range of activities, such as production for and marketing in their respective regions. Pharmaceutical, food, and oil companies tend to use this structure. Whirlpool Corporation is organized regionally in North America, Europe, Latin America, and Asia (whirlpoolcorp.com). A typical regional structure is illustrated in Figure 6.5.

Advantages of the Regional Structure[13]

1. *Decentralization:* Authority and responsibility, and therefore performance accountability, are delegated directly to the regional office. The management tasks of planning and strategy are less complex than if the central headquarters were to hold this responsibility. Also, management response time to environmental changes is shorter because a regional manager's knowledge of local conditions is greater than that of headquarters manager.

2. *Adaptation:* Regional managers are better able to adapt to local needs than headquarters managers because they are in closer touch with local changes and requirements.

3. *Single management units possess regional knowledge:* Regional managers develop local expertise because they are responsible for regional strategies and daily operations. Regional differences exist throughout the world. Inputs from knowledgeable regional managers can enable central headquarters managers to use these differences effectively in developing and attaining overall corporate objectives.

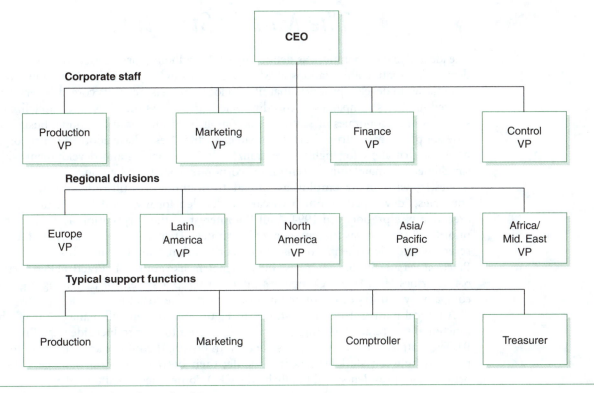

Figure 6.5   An Illustration of a Regional Structure

Disadvantages of the Regional Structure

1. *Weak worldwide product emphasis and technical knowledge:* Because technical knowledge is spread out, a global perspective on products is sometimes difficult to attain. And because the emphasis is usually on regional concerns, the formulation of worldwide strategy formulation can be difficult.

2. *Technology transfer barriers:* Employee loyalty is often focused on the region rather than on the overall organization, and each regional manager tends to claim that things are different in his or her region. Therefore, when headquarters managers attempt to implement new technology on an overall corporate basis, it may not be readily accepted by the regionals.

3. *Policy barriers:* Inconsistent overall corporate management practices may evolve. This is especially so when central management tries to, or is persuaded to, satisfy specific regional needs.

4. *Costly application:* The typical support functions shown in Figure 6.5 exist in each regional division, resulting in costly duplication of effort. Efficiency could be achieved if these support functions were combined, but in this structure, the number of functional product staff specialists tends to increase through the years.

5. *Weak communication:* Necessary information may not reach top management because of the regional managers' focus on regional performance. Overall corporate performance may therefore be weakened.

The Matrix Structure

The ideal global corporation, as defined by Carl Lindholm, former executive vice president of international operations at Motorola, is strongly decentralized. It allows local subsidiaries to develop products that fit into local markets. Yet at its core, it is very centralized; it allows companies to coordinate activities across the globe and capitalize on synergies and economies of scale.[14] To accomplish this, many international businesses have adopted matrix structures.[15] Companies such as Nestlé have adopted matrix organizations that allow for highly decentralized decision making and development while simultaneously maintaining a centralized corporate strategy and vision.

Nestlé, with many employees spread throughout a multitude of sites in 60 countries, "developed as much as can be decided locally," said Peter Brabeck, its executive vice president in 1994. "But the interest of the corporation as a whole has priority."[16] Many firms that apply a global strategy (firms that rely heavily on foreign revenues and view themselves as global corporations) tend to use this structure.[17] Practical Perspective 6.3 describes Gillette's matrix-like approach. Practical Perspective 6.4 describes H. J. Heinz Company's intent to scrap a system of managing a global company by country or region in favor of a matrix-like structure.

A typical matrix structure is shown in Figure 6.6. In general, managers from the functional side (e.g., Marketing, Africa) assign a staff to the product side (e.g., Product B). The staff leader is then responsible to both bosses. If conflicts arise, they are to be resolved between staff leaders if possible; then between general managers; then between vice presidents; and finally by the CEO, sometimes called the fulcrum.

Advantages of the Matrix Structure[18]

1. Coordination and cooperation across subunits enable the firm to use its overall resources efficiently and therefore to respond well to global competition in any market.

2. Overall corporate global performance is highlighted.

3. Many internal conflicts are resolved at the lowest possible level, and those that cannot be resolved are pushed up.

Disadvantages of the Matrix Structure

1. Worldwide responsibility may be given to product managers with weak international experience. (This problem is addressed in Chapter 8.)

2. The organization tends to create a mountain of paperwork.

3. The dual-boss, cross-communication system is expensive and complex.

4. Decisions sometimes must be made quickly. Quick decisions can be made by one person. In the matrix group decision-making process, decisions are usually made slowly.

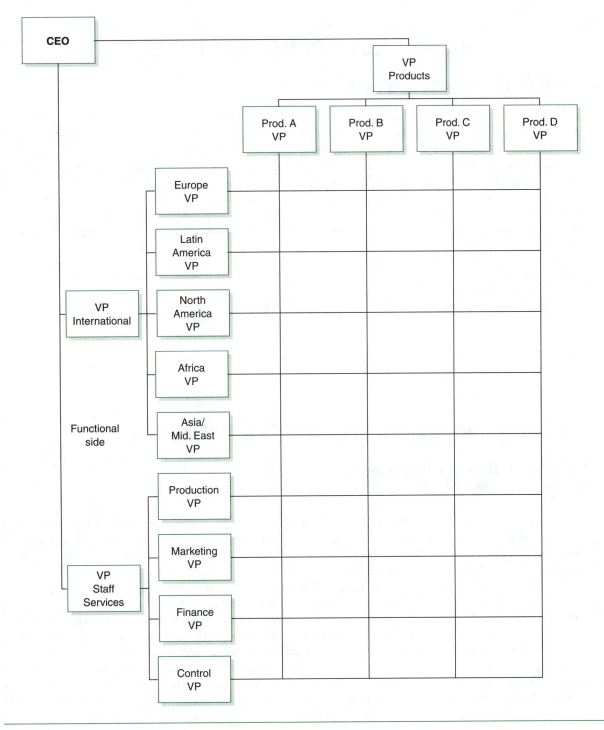

Figure 6.6 An Illustration of a Matrix Structure

PRACTICAL PERSPECTIVE 6-3

Gillette's International Organization

Gillette's global strategy [in 1998] includes a clear understanding of local differences—that each market presents unique challenges, requirements, and opportunities. In the rapid-growth Asia-Pacific region for example, Gillette has used merger integration as a vehicle for developing a wholly integrated approach to individual markets. In Singapore, the acquisition of Parker Pen in 1993 triggered the establishment of a new organizational structure that has allowed Gillette to show one face to the customer and act as a single, integrated entity to suppliers in the region. While the integration reflects a global strategy, the ability to pull it off required a local sensitivity and orientation. Indeed, the story of Gillette Singapore's merger with Parker Pen illuminates the link between global strategy and local mastery. It demonstrates how managing local integration is the key to unleashing the power of global brands.

SOURCE: Excerpted from R. M. Kanter and T. D. Dretler, "'Global Strategy' and Its Impact on Local Operations: Lessons from Gillette Singapore," *Academy of Management Executive,* 12, no. 4 (1998), p. 62.

PRACTICAL PERSPECTIVE 6-4

Heinz's Johnson to Divest Operations, Scrap Management of Firm by Regions

H.J. Heinz Company's newly [in 1997] appointed chief executive said he plans to centralize management, divest unrelated operations, and add another strategic business to the big food company. William R. Johnson, unveiling his plans in an interview and a speech at a meeting of food brokers here Saturday, made it clear that, in his opinion, Heinz could perform better. "We haven't been adept at internationalizing our business," he said.

The appearance came only days after Heinz, owner of Star-Kist Tuna and Weight Watchers in addition to the Heinz brand, announced that Johnson, its president and chief operating officer, would succeed Anthony O'Reilly as chief executive in April. The 48-year-old Johnson said he will scrap a system of managing the global company by country or region. Instead, he will run the business by categories so that tuna managers in Europe will work with tuna managers in Asia, Latin America, and other regions, allowing the best brand manager to advise all the countries.

Johnson will also accelerate the expansion of successful products in one country or region into others. At the moment, he said, the company is test marketing in the USA products that have worked in Europe, such as frozen tuna filets and flavored tuna. At the same time, Johnson said he intends to increase the role of Heinz's headquarters in monitoring sales performance and serving as a think tank for international growth.

SOURCE: Excerpted from Rekha Balu, "Heinz's Johnson to Divest Operations, Scrap Management of Firm by Regions," *The Wall Street Journal* (December 8, 1997), p. B12. Permission conveyed through Copyright Clearance Center, Inc.

Some international business enterprises have had an unhappy experience with the matrix structure. For example, in 1994, Digital Equipment announced that it was getting rid of its matrix system in a global restructuring that would cost $1 billion and 20,000 jobs. Dow Chemical went back to its conventional structure with clear lines of responsibility given to geographic managers.[19]

In 1999, the giant corporation General Electric established plans to restructure, to replace its matrix structure with a functional organization—marketing, sales, manufacturing, and so on[20] (although perhaps not in the same way as the functional structure described earlier).

Contractual Alliance Structure

As discussed in Chapters 4 and 5, many enterprises enter foreign markets via non-equity-based joint ventures, often referred to as contractual alliances and strategic alliances.[21] For example, one firm's strength may be production and another firm's, distribution. Instead of these two firms forming an equity-based joint venture to capitalize on each other's strengths, they form a non-equity-based contractual alliance. Thus, when the two firms no longer need each other, in theory, they simply break up the partnership. The advantage of this partnership arrangement is that when there is a breakup, there is no long drawn out fight for the division of assets, as often is the case when equity-based partnerships break up.

There are disadvantages to this approach, however. For instance, when one partner acquires the other partner's skills, and the reverse is not the case, the former may leave the latter in a dubious situation or may easily take over the latter. Of course, this type of arrangement can work only when neither partner possesses an ulterior motive—for example, "I'm really going into this arrangement to acquire the partner's skills, and once I have done so, I will break up the partnership." Furthermore, these arrangements are extremely difficult to manage on a global scale. At one time, AT&T formed an alliance with Philips in Europe to swap technology for access to local markets. The alliance did not meet expectations, mostly because the companies failed to understand each other's strategic objectives.[22]

Developing an organizational structure to manage and control alliances can thus be extremely difficult, especially in the areas of quality control and human rights control (such as employee health and child labor abuses), which international corporations are typically responsible for, otherwise media exposure of corporations that fail to act on such events can lead to boycott.

Network Agreements

Somewhat similar to the contractual alliance arrangement is networking. Applying this approach, a corporation subcontracts its manufacturing function to other companies. For example, Nike, the American shoe manufacturer, subcontracts the manufacture of its athletic shoes and clothing to 40 separate locations, mostly in Asia.[23]

When an organization enters into such contractual alliances or network agreements, it must create a unit whose responsibility is to monitor the arrangement.

For instance, IBM has created an alliance council of key executives who meet monthly to keep track of more than 40 partnerships throughout the globe.[24] But contemporary thinking is that these independent organizations must in some way be interconnected (see, e.g., Practical Perspective 6.5).

PRACTICAL PERSPECTIVE 6-5

Asia's New Competitive Game

As the millennium approaches, business based on family ties is giving birth to a new type of organization. Instead of building either a centralized bureaucracy or a set of independent, far-flung subsidiaries to manage increasing complexity and geographic spread, Asia's new competitors [in 1997] are building extended networked organizations that rely on continual sharing of information among all their business units. In such organizations, information flows in many directions between nodes, each of which may act as an information supplier at one moment and as a receiver at the next. The process of information sharing is similar to the process by which data flow in a network of computers as opposed to in a centralized mainframe computer system. This style of sharing is especially important for Asian companies, for which key technologies and market intelligence are relatively hard to come by.

One of the companies that typify this new style of organization is Acer, which is driven by the vision of its chairman and CEO, Stan Shih. The structure of Acer's client-server organization is familiar: strategic business units (SBUs), each responsible for a group of products, and regional business units (RBUs), each responsible for a geographic area.

At Acer, each SBU and RBU has independent capabilities. RBUs, for example, are not simply distributors. They have the capability to assemble a product that has been locally customized to meet local needs, augmenting standard technologies and components in what Acer calls the fast-food model of the computer supply chain. Shih believes that as they develop, RBUs should move from being wholly owned subsidiaries of Acer to becoming minority-owned affiliates of the network, thereby ensuring that they develop as truly local competitors. In addition to acting as clients for the SBUs' products, the RBUs act as servers, providing local market intelligence and informing the SBUs and RBUs of local best practices.

Maintaining excellent multilateral communication among different groups within a company becomes more difficult when the groups are linked to the parent company only by minority shareholdings. But according to Shih, the advantage in such situations is that each group must continually prove the worth of its role in the network, an effort that reduces the risk of complacency. If the benefits of the linkages do not justify the costs, the subsidiary organization will be spun off.

SOURCE: Excerpted from Peter J. Williamson, "Asia's New Competitive Game," *Harvard Business Review* (September–October 1997), pp. 61–62.

The well-known Harvard Business School professor Michael E. Porter describes a similar arrangement as a "cluster." According to him, clusters are "geographic concentrations of interconnected companies and institutions in a particular field." They encompass "an array of linked industries and other entities important to competition." And they include, according to Porter, "suppliers of specialized inputs such as components, machinery, and services, and providers of specialized infrastructure."[25] Japan's *keiretsu* is a world-known form of interorganization networking.[26] Practical Perspective 6.6 describes FedEx's and DHL's networking operations. And as discussed in Chapters 4 and 5, many corporations, such as banks and other financial institutions, are currently (2007) outsourcing certain functions, such as the IT functions, to foreign lands.

PRACTICAL PERSPECTIVE 6-6

Warehouses That Fly

DHL [in 1999] has assembled an extensive network of express logistic and strategic-parts centers across Europe. For instance, in its Brussels logistics center, DHL does upgrading, repair, and final configuration of Stratus and Fujitsu computers, InFocus projectors, and Johnson & Johnson medical equipment. Adam Ludwig, operations manager at the center, says DHL is currently negotiating similar logistics contracts, each worth $15 million and more, with about 60 companies. The supply of spare parts and products replacements within Europe is another fast-expanding business. For instance, DHL stores and supplies parts for EMC and Hewlett-Packard and replaces Nokia and Philip mobile phones. "If something breaks down on a Tuesday at four o'clock, that warehouse knows at five past four, and the part is on a DHL plane at seven or eight that evening," trumpets [Robert] Kuijpers [CEO, DHL International]....

Dell Computer's build-to-order, time-compression model hinges on fast and reliable air express service. FedEx consolidates parts for Dell at Subic, flies them to Dell's big plant in Penang, Malaysia, then, the next day, whisks the machines to Japan, where FedEx handles final configuration for the Japanese market.

DHL's arrangement with Lucent shows how a manufacturer's life can be simplified. DHL moves integrated circuits from Lucent plants directly to customers anywhere in the world within 48 hours. Cranfield's Peter says that the contract with DHL replaced contracts with 51 freight-forwarders and transporters. Likewise, before Toshiba Medical turned over its warehouses in Miami, Brussels, and Singapore, the Japanese firm stockpiled its medical systems and parts in 50 locations around the world.

SOURCE: Excerpted from Andrew Tanzer, "Warehouses That Fly," *Forbes* (October 18, 1999), p. 125. Reprinted by permission of *Forbes Magazine* © 1999.

The Mixed (Hybrid) Structure

The traditional and contemporary alternative structures described above are not independent entities that cannot coexist within the same company. By mixing the structural types, the weaknesses of each type can be minimized. For example, companies with a worldwide product division structure can appoint regional coordinators who supply the concentrated environmental expertise that is usually absent in the product division structure. Similarly, companies with regional structures (either worldwide or within an international division) can set up positions for product coordinators. While such coordinator positions are not particularly new, giving them some real influence short of classical line authority is a relatively recent development.[27] Furthermore, international organizations can centralize some functions, such as an accounting division that provides services for all worldwide subsidiaries, while other functions, such as marketing, remain decentralized.

A General Framework for Decision Making

The preceding discussion described several traditional and contemporary international organizational structures and presented the general advantages and disadvantages of each. The word *general* is used because what is advantageous and disadvantageous does not apply to all situations. For example, one of the disadvantages of the international division structure is conflict; the structure often creates organizational struggles between employees in the domestic divisions ("we") and employees in the international division ("they"). In most cases it may be true that conflict causes harmful organizational disruptions, especially in organizations that rely on "team spirit" for effectiveness. But in some organizational situations, conflict can actually be advantageous, especially when it leads the groups to try to outperform each other. Thus, if the international division outperforms the domestic division, the latter may be stimulated to try to outperform the former, and so on. Therefore, the stated advantages and disadvantages are intended to serve as a general framework for decision making, not as a prescription. All situations must be examined separately because different situations sometimes require different prescriptions. For instance, the knowledge a firm transfers to a foreign country will determine the structural mode the firm uses in the foreign market.[28]

Flat Structures

Regardless of which structure is used, it should be as flat as possible. That is, it should have fewer managerial layers than traditional hierarchical organizations. A flat structure is needed because a 12-layer company cannot compete with a 3-layer company. For example, a decade or so ago, General Motors, the U.S.-based car manufacturer, had an organizational structure consisting of more than 15 managerial levels. General Motors had a problem competing with Toyota, the Japanese car manufacturer, at least partly because Toyota's organizational structure contained only 4 managerial levels. (This is in part because Japanese employees are not as motivated by the opportunity to climb up the hierarchy as are U.S. employees.) One reason why companies with tall structures are less competitive than firms with flat structures is that they have to pay more managers at more levels, thus increasing their costs.

Another reason is that an organization can create an atmosphere of maximum creativity only if it reduces hierarchical elements to a minimum and creates a corporate culture in which its vision, company philosophy, and strategies can be implemented by employees who think independently and take initiatives.[29] Furthermore, as Henry Mintzberg, a well-known professor at McGill University in Canada, once proposed in his explanation of adhocracy, having many levels of administration restricts the organization's ability to adapt.[30]

The Internet's Impact on the Tallness of Organizational Structures

A flatter structure means that managers have to communicate with more employees than do managers in tall structures. The ability to communicate with more subordinates has been made possible by the enormous advancements in communication technologies, which, as the American management authority Peter F. Drucker noted, enables managers to communicate with a far wider span of individuals than was possible in the past.[31] Spans of control thus give way to spans of communication. For example, at Cypress Semiconductor, CEO T. J. Rodgers established a computer system that enabled him to keep abreast of every employee (1,500) and team in his rapidly moving, decentralized, constantly changing organization.[32] The Asea Brown Boveri Group's structure is relatively flat. DuPont, the U.S.-based manufacturing and processing company had a goal to develop a flat organization that operates by network rather than by hierarchy. DuPont sought to establish an organization with the flexibility to be able to quickly form and dissolve the local, regional, and global networks needed to solve business problems and meet customers' needs.[33]

Organic Versus Mechanistic Structures

Another problem confronting international managers is determining how organic or how mechanistic the organizational structure should be. Basically, managers in organic structures give their employees considerable discretion in defining their roles and the organization's objectives.[34] In mechanistic organizations, roles and objectives are clearly and rigidly outlined for employees—managers and subordinates are allowed little or no discretion.[35] Historically, large organizations have tended to adopt the mechanistic form, and small organizations adopt the organic form. Mass-producing organizations have tended to adopt the mechanistic form, and firms producing specialized products have tended to adopt the organic form. Thus, the form an organization adopts is determined by varying situational factors.

In determining which approach is appropriate for an organization functioning across nations, managers also need to consider national cultural factors. For example, organizational structures tend to be more mechanistic in strong uncertainty avoidance cultures (discussed in Chapter 1), such as France and Germany, than in weak uncertainty avoidance cultures, such as Sweden, and organic structures tend to be more prevalent in weak uncertainty avoidance cultures than in strong uncertainty avoidance cultures. See, for example, Jane Pickard's article "German Way Holds Sway in Britain."[36] This concept of national cultural factors, as well as the situational approach discussed in the paragraph above, will be discussed more thoroughly in Chapters 11 and 13. As will be shown, national cultural factors provide international managers a starting point for decision analysis; but ultimately they must consider specific situations carefully. If one adheres to the national cultural factors model, subsidiaries in some nations will be more structured than subsidiaries in other nations; but if one adheres to the situational factors model, the same structure is applied in the same situation in all cultures. As will be demonstrated in Chapters 11 and 13, reconciling the national cultural factors model and situational factors model as determinants of the appropriate structure is a monumental task confronting all managers of international organizations.

Adaptable Management

Similar to the above discussion, the international organizational structure adopted by a firm's management is influenced by many factors, including the firm's economic situation; the type of product or technology; managerial preference (organizational culture); the foreign country's cultural, economic, technological, and political conditions; the wide separation of operations; and the different foreign market characteristics, including the nature of competition. Therefore, organizational structures that work well for domestic operations are often not suitable for multinational operations. For example, matrix organizations are very scarce in Latin America. This is in part because Latin America's patron system does not lend itself to the power sharing that characterizes matrices.[37] The structure is also influenced by the firm's level of experience in international business and its dependence on revenues from foreign markets. Table 6.1 presents the international organizational structures that might be appropriate for various levels of a firm's dependence on revenues generated from foreign sales.

Historically, when firms first ventured into foreign markets, and when both foreign sales and the diversity of products sold in the foreign country were limited, global companies generally managed their international operations through indirect exporting, and subsequently through an international division. Companies that subsequently expanded their sales in foreign markets without significantly increasing foreign product diversity generally adopted the regional structure. Those enterprises that subsequently increased foreign product diversity tended to adopt the product division structure. Firms that increased both foreign sales and foreign product diversity tended to adopt the matrix structure.[38]

International business executives must be thoroughly familiar with the strengths and weaknesses of each organizational structure and be ready to switch from one form to another as a means of adapting to changing environments, including moving an important business unit's headquarters to foreign soil. (For an illustration, read Practical Perspective 6.7.) The right structure must be matched to the right environment as both internal and external situations change. And the fit must attain a balance between organizational complexity and simplicity. Adopting an organizational structure too complex for its environmental demands can be as ineffective as adopting a structure too simplistic to operate in a turbulent environment.[39] Not adopting the right structure can be very costly—not only in the sense that it will be ineffective but also because reorganizing is very expensive. For example, AT&T indicated that global reorganization accounted for most of the $347 million it paid in fees to consultants in 1993.[40]

TABLE 6.1	Dependence on Foreign Revenues and Organizational Structures	
Organization's International Level of Dependence on Foreign Sales	Unit Responsible for Foreign Business	Potential Organizational Structure
Very little	Middle person (indirect exporting)	The functional structure; contractual alliance/network
Somewhat	Export department	The functional structure; the international division; contractual alliance/network
Substantial	International division	The international structure; contractual alliance/network
Considerable	Foreign subsidiary	The subsidiary structure; the product structure
Very much	Foreign subsidiary/regional headquarters	The regional structure; contractual alliance/network
Extensive	Foreign subsidiary/central headquarters	The mixed (hybrid) structure; matrix

PRACTICAL PERSPECTIVE 6-7

Moving Headquarters of Business Units Abroad

Increasingly, going global means "move 'em out"—by transferring world headquarters of important business units abroad. In the process, many companies put a non-American in charge of the unit. And USA operations that once reported to Wilmington, Delaware, or Parsippany, New Jersey, now report to Tokyo—or the French Riviera. Multinational corporations are making these shifts, risking a loss of control, because they want to operate near key customers and tough rivals in fast-changing markets far from home. More big businesses "recognize that they can't rule the world from one single location" any longer, says Ingo Theuerkauf, an international management specialist [in 1992] for consultants McKinsey & Company. In ten years, Theuerkauf predicts, "we will see maybe 50 percent of Fortune 500 companies making [such] moves."

This fall [1992], American Telephone & Telegraph Company moved the headquarters of its traditional corded-telephone business to France from Parsippany, N.J. It marked the first overseas move by a unit of AT&T, whose ranks of non-USA workers have jumped to 50,000 from 50 in 1984. The corded-telephone business had scant international sales until two years ago. Its approximately 2,000 employees around the globe now report to a Frenchman in Sophia Antipolis, a high-technology center near Nice on the Riviera. Other examples abound. In August, E.I. DuPont de Nemours and Company announced the shift of its world-wide electronics operation from the USA to Tokyo, nearer its big base of Asian customers. DuPont already manages its global agricultural-products operation and parts of two other large businesses from Geneva.

Going the other direction, Hyundai Electronics Industries Company in April moved its personal computer division to San Jose, California, from Seoul, South Korea, so it could better compete in that industry's biggest market. International Business Machines Corporation, Hewlett-Packard Company, and Germany's Siemens AG have taken similar steps since 1989 by moving units' global headquarters out of their home countries. "The name of the game is to get close to the customer and to understand the customer," says Jack Malloy, a DuPont senior vice president. With the chemical giant growing fastest in non-USA markets, he says, "it wouldn't be surprising to see a couple more" units move their headquarters overseas.

Robert Bontempo, [in 1992] an assistant professor of international business at Columbia University, sees "a strategic competitive advantage" in uprooting operations from a parent's home country and basing them abroad. Relocated units often gain marketing power by acquiring the image of "a global firm with a global reach," he suggests. The strategy also helps to break down parochialism and to groom global managers, management experts say.

SOURCE: Excerpted from Joann S. Lublin, "Firms Ship Unit Headquarters Abroad," *The Wall Street Journal* (December 9, 1992), p. B1. Permission conveyed through Copyright Clearance Center, Inc. As an example, on February 9, 2007, Honda Aircraft Company announced that it will establish its world headquarters in Greensboro, NC.

An Example of a Modern Manufacturing Corporation in China[41]

As pointed out earlier, different businesses worldwide adopt differing structures. This author visited communist China in the summer of 1995, when China was in the early stages of transition to a modern economy. Under the old economy, the communist government fully owned and operated its enterprises, called state-owned enterprises (SOEs). At that time, China's government was also attempting to make the SOEs more competitive and starting to partially privatize them, but at the same time it was implementing modern competitive market enterprises. While there, this author visited a modern manufacturing corporation, which was manufacturing weaving machines for the textile industry, an industry in which China was about to assume world leadership. Figure 6.7 presents the organization's structure.

The corporation's financial structure consisted of three types of stock: Stock A, Stock B, and Stock C. The communist government, as was the case in all of China's new modern enterprises, owned 52% of the three types of stock. Stock A was purchased by the company's employees, Stock B was sold in China's stock exchange, and Stock C was sold in foreign stock exchanges. Thus, technically, China's government had majority control of all of China's enterprises. However it was beginning to decentralize management of many of its SOEs and fully decentralized management of the modern enterprises. As Figure 6.7 depicts, the enterprise this author visited was governed by the board of directors, consisting of China's government representatives, employee representatives, and representatives from the stock exchange owners, through three CEOs. The CEO on the center of the organizational chart was the entrepreneur, and he in reality controlled the enterprise. He used the CEO on the left to motivate the company's workers and the CEO on the right to obtain the resources he needed from the government.

The entrepreneurial CEO, whom this author interviewed, had spent a few years visiting corporations in Europe and North America. He used the external organizational ideas he had learned in his travels and adapted them to establish an organizational structure that fitted to China's needs.

Anyway, the point of all this is that the Western structures discussed in this chapter are fairly similar in MNCs throughout the globe, but not in all situations.

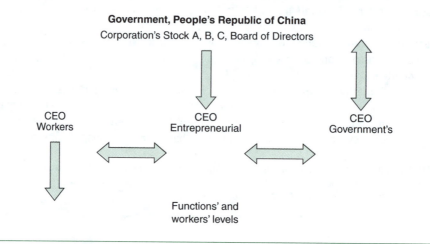

Figure 6.7   Organizational Structure of a Modern Chinese Corporation

Information Technology and Organizational Structure[42]

The advent of new information technologies such as the Internet, videoconferencing, teleconferencing, and portable telephones now allows organizations to implement inter- and intra-organizational structures that were impossible or economically unfeasible not too long ago. And the introduction of Blackberry in 2007 enables one to send and receive e-mail from anywhere on the planet. These technologies enable small, medium, and large organizations to access information from most parts of the world. This suggests that companies, usually smaller ones, organized under the functional structure, can now have access to the same information as large companies. Therefore, smaller companies, by selling their products/services through electronic commerce, can compete more effectively with larger corporations.

Companies such as Wal-Mart that are organized under the international division structure, with subsidiaries located in many parts of the world, can now manage more effectively from a single location and may often avoid the cost of establishing physical regional offices when they have grown. And many companies with regional offices throughout the globe can now revert to a single location or at least reduce the number of locations. For example, Eastman Kodak Company consolidated 17 data centers (on four continents) into 7.[43]

Perhaps some of the larger companies can even restructure themselves using the functional structure. As mentioned earlier, General Electric, one of the largest corporations in the world, had plans to restructure itself from the matrix to the functional structure. Many of the functions carried out at several points in the matrix structure can now be performed more easily than in the past, when they were centralized. Therefore, the mixed structure is easier to manage, and information technology makes global strategic alliances and networks easier to manage.

Organization Communication Flow

Identifying the ideal international organizational structure is a huge challenge for the managers of any organization; there may not even be an ideal structure. Nevertheless, regardless of which organizational structure a firm adopts, a neat chart with neat boxes is useless unless information and communications flow freely to develop proper business decisions. The relationship of domestic, international, and senior corporate organization can be described by three general guidelines.[44]

1. The organization must be formulated in such a way that planning and decision making on every aspect of the firm's operations can be done by people with the breadth of functional, geographic, and/or product knowledge and responsibility necessary to develop the potential for a unified strategy.

2. The channels for the flow of important or recurring decisions and information should be as direct and as short as possible.

3. Individuals with expert international knowledge and competence in overcoming the obstacles to international communication should be readily available within the organization and be used wherever their capacities are needed.

This means that top management in all organizations must incorporate the following dimensions into their systems:[45]

1. The structure must allow for the development and communication of a clear corporate vision.

2. It must allow for the effective management of human resource tools to broaden individuals' perspectives and develop identification with corporate goals.

3. It must allow for the integration of individual thinking and activities into a broad corporate agenda.

Information Technology and Organizational Communication

The advent of the new information technology previously discussed also allows organizations to implement inter- and intra-organizational communication flows that were impossible or economically unfeasible not very long ago. These new technologies enable companies to vastly increase information flow across world operations. Companies can create a globally integrated information infrastructure that electronically links their entire supply chains (refer again to Practical Perspective 6.6)—their sales, production, and delivery processes—into one seamless flow of information across national borders and time zones with both real-time and store-and-forward access to information from any location. The following are some examples:[46]

- Nike, Inc. implemented a global electronic supply chain to share information with its partners around the world and facilitate better decision making.
- The Body Shop created an intranet to link the head offices in each of the 47 countries in which it operated (1999). Its headquarters is in the United Kingdom.
- Tricon Global Restaurants, Inc., which operates 30,000 fast food restaurants worldwide (Pizza Hut, Taco Bell, and KFC), standardized its back office operations at all stores. Tricon's new proprietary global information system will allow all stores to order supplies through one global clearinghouse.

Of course, cross-country language and cultural barriers present a challenge for the implementers of such systems. (These problems are discussed in Chapters 9 and 10.) However, the problem is mitigated because English is rapidly becoming the international language for conducting commerce. For example, Cap Gemini Sogeti, a French company with operating units in the United States and Europe, recently (in 1999) made a $40 million investment to become more transnational. The firm chose English as the common language for all correspondence and business documentation.[47] But it should be pointed out that as of 2007, international corporations' Web sites by country are still widely presented in the local language.

Summary

This chapter has discussed numerous international organizational structures, such as the international division and the matrix structure, adopted by international corporations, by multinational corporations, and by global corporations, and the advantages and disadvantages of each structure. Managers must be flexible regarding which structure to adopt for their organizations because different structures fit different environments and environments change often. Regardless of which structure is adopted, it must allow information and communications to flow freely.

KEY TERMS AND CONCEPTS

1. International organizational structures
2. Functional structure
3. International division structure
4. Foreign subsidiary structure
5. Local managers
6. Product division structure
7. Regional structure
8. Matrix structure
9. Contractual alliances
10. Networks, clusters
11. Mixed (hybrid) structure
12. Flat structures
13. Organic vs. mechanistic organizations
14. Adaptable management
15. Information technology and structure
16. Information and communications must flow freely
17. Information technology and communication flow

DISCUSSION QUESTIONS

1. In the functional structure, who is usually responsible for the firm's international business activities?

2. When an international corporation establishes a single subunit to manage all its international business activities, which international organizational structure is the firm using?

3. Briefly discuss some advantages and disadvantages of the structure you gave as an answer to Question 2.

4. "Autonomy of affiliates" and "direct top management involvement" are advantages of which international organizational structure?

5. Which international structure is prone to "foreign coordination problems"?

6. A global corporation establishes a headquarters to manage its business activities in Africa and a headquarters to manage its activities in Asia. Which international organizational structure is the firm using?

7. Which international organizational structure allows local subsidiaries to use discretion in developing products or services to fit local markets and at the same time allows headquarters to coordinate activities around the globe to capitalize on synergies and economies of scale?

8. Discuss strategic alliances, networks, and clusters.

9. Which structure enables organizations to minimize the weaknesses of the other structures?

10. Managers must be flexible to the extent that they can adopt different structures in different environments. Discuss the environments that are conducive to the use of the international division, the regional structure, the product division, and matrix structures.

11. Read Practical Perspective 6.7. Discuss some of the pitfalls of such reorganization.

12. Discuss the impact of modern technology on structuring of organizations.

13. Discuss the impact of modern technology on organizations' communication flow.

EXERCISES

1. You are the consultant advisor to a small company that wishes to internationalize its business operations. Its management has no international business experience at all. Which organizational structure would you advise your client to adopt? Why?

2. You are the consultant for a firm whose management has acquired some international business experience and wants to establish its own international division. Your client wants to know the problems that might be encountered. What would you tell your client?

3. An international company operating with an international division structure wants to adopt the foreign subsidiary structure. Discuss some of the problems the company might encounter in adopting the new structure.

4. You are the consultant to an international company currently using the subsidiary organizational structure. Over the years, the company has established many subsidiaries throughout the globe, and its management is encountering coordination problems. What would you advise the management to do? Why?

5. You are the consultant to an international corporation that has recently set up subsidiaries in Denmark. The corporate culture is strong control through a rigid organizational structure. The company's management is encountering many problems in managing its Danish subsidiaries. What would you recommend as a solution to the problem? Why? (You may need to refer to Chapter 1.)

ASSIGNMENT

Obtain the most current annual report of a multinational corporation. Prepare a short report describing the corporation's structure for class presentation.

CASE 6-1

Toys "Я" Us

Charles Lazarus founded Toys "Я" Us on the premise that "when Mama went back to work, department stores were dead." He argued that "working women wanted a store where they could shop for their children quickly, easily, and cheaply." Toys "Я" Us offered a warehouse full of play items. Said Lazarus, "We don't want to decide which toys you should buy. We have everything." When focusing on domestic markets, Toys "Я" Us selected store locations where the rent was low, mainly along major highways as opposed to expensive shopping malls. The company's strategy of warehouse-size stores built away from shopping malls enabled it to slash prices on merchandise. Toys "Я" Us, in essence, invented the toy supermarket. By being big, Toys "Я" Us could buy merchandise at large volume discounts. Toys "Я" Us [in the early 1990s] stocked about 8,000 items, and it expects to raise that level to 15,000 over time.

Toys "Я" Us went international in 1984. The company began operating first in Canada, then it subsequently opened stores in Europe, Hong Kong, and Singapore. Japan was always tempting, but the country's Large-Store Law, aimed at protecting Japan's small shopkeepers, was too great a barrier to overcome . . . until December 1991. Japan has the second largest toy market in the world. The Japanese spent $4.7 billion on toys in 1991. It was for this reason that Toys "Я" Us launched its Japanese effort. The first Japanese store was opened on December 20, 1991, in Ami, north of Tokyo.

Toys "Я" Us' international growth is as follows. During 1984, 5 stores were opened. By 1985, 13 had been opened. By 1986, 24 had been opened, and by 1987, 37 had been opened. By 1988, 52 international stores were in operation, 74 had been opened by 1989, and in 1990, 97 international stores were open for business. As of January 1992, Toys "Я" Us was operating 497 stores in the United States and 126 outlets overseas (including the two already opened in Japan), plus 189 Kids "Я" Us stores. Combined, these stores generated approximately $6 billion in sales in 1991.

Everyday low pricing has been a success in Europe, since it is virtually nonexistent there. Toys "Я" Us plans to continue its aggressive pricing policy to obtain a greater market share. It had planned to open 10 foreign stores per year from 1993 through the end of the decade. According to Lazarus, at least 100 stores might be opened in Japan alone within the next 10 years, depending on the absence of red tape and the ability to find real estate there. The goal of Toys "Я" Us for the future is to open 3,001 European stores.[a] The following is a list of Toys "Я" Us stores in the United States and abroad in 1999:[b]

Store Locations

Stores Across the United States (1999)

	Toys	Kids	Babies
Alabama	8	1	2
Alaska	1	—	—
Arizona	11	—	2
Arkansas	4	—	—

(Continued)

(Continued)

	Toys	Kids	Babies
California	87	23	8
Colorado	11	—	2
Connecticut	11	6	—
Delaware	2	1	1
Florida	47	10	10
Georgia	18	4	6
Hawaii	1	—	—
Idaho	2	—	—
Illinois	34	19	5
Indiana	13	7	2
Iowa	8	1	—
Kansas	5	1	1
Kentucky	8	—	1
Louisiana	11	—	1
Maine	2	1	1
Maryland	19	9	3
Massachusetts	19	6	1
Michigan	25	13	5
Minnesota	12	2	1
Mississippi	5	—	—
Missouri	13	5	3
Montana	1	—	—
Nebraska	3	1	—
Nevada	4	—	2
New Hampshire	5	2	—
New Jersey	26	18	7
New Mexico	4	—	—
New York	46	23	3
North Carolina	16	1	5
North Dakota	1	—	—
Ohio	33	18	6
Oklahoma	5	—	1
Oregon	8	—	1

	Toys	Kids	Babies
Pennsylvania	33	15	3
Puerto Rico	4	—	—
Rhode Island	1	1	1
South Carolina	9	—	3
South Dakota	2	—	—
Tennessee	14	2	4
Texas	54	9	13
Utah	6	3	1
Vermont	1	—	—
Virginia	22	7	7
Washington	14	—	1
West Virginia	5	—	—
Wisconsin	10	3	—
Total	704	212	113

Toys "Я" US International—452 (1999)

Australia	24	Netherlands	9
Austria	8	Portugal	6
Belgium	3	Saudi Arabia	3
Canada	64	Singapore	4
Denmark	10	South Africa	8
France	44	Spain	29
Germany	59	Sweden	5
Hong Kong	5	Switzerland	5
Indonesia	3	Taiwan	6
Israel	5	Turkey	5
Japan	76	United Arab Emirates	4
Luxembourg	1	U.K.	61
Malaysia	5		

In July 2005, Toys "Я" Us was acquired by an investment group consisting of affiliates of Bain Capital Partners LLC, Kohlberg Kravis Roberts & Company, and Vornado Realty Trust for $6.6 billion. The acquisition encompassed all worldwide operations of Toys "Я" Us, Inc., including the Toys "Я" Us and Babies "Я" Us businesses, and each of the investors owns an equal stake in Toys "Я" Us,

(Continued)

(Continued)

Inc. As of September 11, 2006, Toys "R" Us is one of the leading retailers of toys and baby products, with more than 1,400 freestanding destination toy and baby specialty stores worldwide. The company sells merchandise through 587 toy stores in the United States and nearly 650 international toy stores, including licensed and franchise stores, as well as through the Internet. Babies "R" Us is the largest baby product specialty store chain in the world and a leader in the juvenile industry; it sells merchandise through 232 stores in the United States as well as the Internet. Toys "R" Us, Inc. currently operates the following divisions:

- Toys "R" Us, US
- Toys "R" Us, International
- Babies "R" Us
- Toyrus.com

Toys "R" Us International has stores in Asia, Africa, Australia, Europe, and North America.[c]

Questions

1. Design the appropriate international organization structure for Toys "R" Us.

2. Why did you select that structure?

3. If the company continues growing, will the structure be different in 10 years? Why or why not?

SOURCES:

a. Adapted from Stuart Gannes, "America's Fastest Growing Companies," *Fortune* (May 23, 1988); Holt Hackney, "How Do You Say Toys Я Us in Germany?" *Financial World* (September 5, 1989); Anthony Ramirez, "Can Anyone Compete with Toys Я Us?" *Fortune* (October 28, 1985); Robert Neff, "Guess Who's Selling Barbies in Japan Now?" *Business Week* (December 9, 1991); "Toys "R" Us Seeks Bigger World Market," *Discount Merchandiser* (July 1989); Isadore Barmash, "Toys Я Us: 1990 Outlook," *Stores* (December 1989); Patrick Oster, "Toys "R" Us: Making Europe Its Playpen," *Business Week* (January 20, 1992).

b. *1998 Annual Report,* www.toysrus.com (October 16, 1999). Reprinted with permission.

c. www9.toysrus.com/guest/sitemap.cfm (2007).

NOTES

1. Excerpted from R. M. Kanter and T. D. Dretler, "'Global Strategy' and Its Impact on Local Operations: Lessons from Gillette Singapore," *Academy of Management Executive,* 12, no. 4 (1998), p. 62.

2. William A. Dymsza, *Multinational Business Strategy* (New York: McGraw-Hill, 1972), p. 17.

3. *Designing the International Corporate Organization* (New York: Business International Corporation, 1976), p. 17. For additional information about organizational structures, refer to Michael Z. Brooke, *International Management: A Review of Strategies and Operations* (London: Hutchinson, 1986); W. H. Davidson and P. Haspeslagh, "Shaping a Global Product Organization," *Harvard Business Review,* 60 (1982), pp. 125–132; C. A. Bartlett and S. Ghoshal, "Tap Your Subsidiaries for Global Reach," *Harvard Business Review,* 64

(November–December 1986), pp. 87–94; Daniel Robey, *Designing Organizations: A Macro Perspective* (Homewood, IL: Richard D. Irwin, 1982); Thomas H. Naylor, "International Strategy Matrix," *Columbia Journal of World Business,* 20 (Summer 1985), pp. 11–19.

4. Adapted from *Designing the International Corporate Organization,* op cit., pp. 32–33.

5. P. W. Beamish, L. G. Karavis, and C. A. Lane, "The Relationship Between Organizational Structure and Export Performance," *Management International Review,* 39, no. 1 (1999), pp. 37–54.

6. W. A. Dymsza, *Multinational Business Strategy,* op cit., p. 23.

7. John M. Livingstone, *The International Enterprise* (New York: John Wiley & Sons, 1975), p. 95.

8. Adapted from *Designing the International Corporate Organization,* op cit. pp. 19–25.

9. C. A. Bartlett and S. Ghoshal, *Managing Across Borders: The Transnational Solution* (Boston: Harvard Business School Press, 1989).

10. Adapted from *Designing the International Corporate Organization,* op cit., pp. 33–36.

11. "The Discreet Charm of the Multicultural Multinational," *The Economist* (July 30, 1994), p. 58.

12. Adapted from *Designing the International Corporate Organization,* op cit., pp. 25–29.

13. Ibid., pp. 29–31.

14. Joshua Greenbaum, "View From the Top: Survival Tactics for the Global Business," *Management Review* (October 1992), pp. 50–51.

15. "The Discreet Charm of the Multicultural Multinational," op cit., p. 58.

16. Ibid.

17. Bartlett and Ghoshal, *Managing Across Borders,* op cit.

18. Stefan H. Robock and Kenneth Simmonds, *International Business and Multinational Enterprises* (Homewood, IL: Dow Jones-Irwin, 1983), pp. 387–388.

19. "The Discreet Charm of the Multicultural Multinational," op cit., p. 58.

20. Thomas A. Stewart, "See Jack, See Jack Run Europe," *Fortune* (September 27, 1999), pp. 124–127.

21. See K. Ohmae, "The Global Logic of Strategic Alliances," *Harvard Business Review,* 67 (March–April 1989), pp. 143–154.

22. "The Discreet Charm of the Multicultural Multinational," op cit., p. 57.

23. Ibid.

24. Jeremy Main, "Making Global Alliances Work," *Fortune* (December 17, 1990), p. 121.

25. Michael E. Porter, "Clusters and the New Economics of Competition," *Harvard Business Review* (November–December 1998), p. 77.

26. See J. McGuire and S. Dow, "The Persistence and Implications of Japanese Keiretsu Organization," *Journal of International Business Studies,* 34 (2003), pp. 374–388.

27. Designing the International Corporate Corporation, op cit., p. 36.

28. See S. Tallman, "The Significance of Bruce Kogut's and Udo Zander's Article, 'Knowledge of the Firm and the Evolutionary Theory of the Multinational Corporation,'" *Journal of International Business Studies,* 34 (2003), pp. 495–497; see also J. W. Spencer, "Global Gatekeeping, Representation, and Network Structure: A Longitudinal Analysis of Regional and Global Knowledge-Diffusion Networks," *Journal International Business Studies,* 34 (2003), pp. 428–442.

29. H. H. Hinterhuber and W. Popp, "Are You a Strategist or Just a Manager?" *Harvard Business Review,* 70 (January–February 1992), pp. 105–113.

30. Henry Mintzberg, *Structures in Fives: Designing Effective Organizations* (Englewood Cliffs, NJ: Prentice Hall, 1983).

31. Jeremy Main, "The Winning Organization," *Fortune* (September 26, 1988), p. 60.

32. B. Dumaine, "The Bureaucracy Busters," *Fortune* (June 17, 1991), p. 46.

33. Sunny Baker, "Global E-Commerce, Local Problems," *Journal of Business Strategy,* 20, no. 4 (July–August 1999), pp. 32–38.

34. See John Miner, *The Management Process: Theory, Research and Practice* (New York: Macmillan, 1973), p. 270.

35. See Max Weber, *The Theory of Social and Economic Organization,* A. M. Henderson and T. Parsons, Trans. (New York: Oxford University Press, 1947).

36. Jane Pickard, "German Way Holds Sway in Britain," *People Management* 5, no. 17 (September 2, 1999), p. 15.

37. J. S. Osland, S. DeFranco, and A. Osland, "Organizational Implications of Latin American Culture: Lessons for the Expatriate Manager," *Journal of Management Inquiry,* 8, no. 2 (June 1999), pp. 219–234.

38. J. Stopford and L. T. Wells Jr., *Managing the Multinational Enterprise* (New York: Basic Books, 1972).

39. S. Ghoshal and N. Nohria, "Horses for Courses: Organizational Forms for Multinational Corporations," *Sloan Management Review* (Winter 1993), p. 24.

40. "The Discreet Charm of the Multicultural Multinational," op cit., p. 57.

41. This information draws from the author's memory; the notes he had taken during his 1995 visit are lost, but for more information on the topic, see M. W. Meyer and X. Lu, "Managing Infinite Boundaries: The Strategy and Structure of a Chinese Business Firm," *Management and Organization Review,* 1, no. 1 (March 2005), pp. 57–86.

42. David O. Stephens, "The Globalization of Information Technology in Multinational Companies," *Information Management Journal,* 33, no. 3 (July 1999), pp. 67–71.

43. Ibid.

44. Adapted from John Fayerweather, *International Business Management: A Conceptual Framework* (New York: McGraw-Hill, 1969), p. 185.

45. Adapted from C. A. Bartlett and S. Ghoshal, "Matrix Management: Not a Structure, a Frame of Mind," *Harvard Business Review,* 68 (July–August 1990), pp. 138–145.

46. Stephens, "The Globalization of Information Technology," op cit.

47. Ibid.

Part IV

INTERNATIONAL STAFFING

Basically, staffing involves finding and hiring the right people to fit positions and functions. Accomplishing this is a complex task organizations face in their domestic (home) country, but finding and hiring the right people to fit positions and functions in organizations' foreign country's operations is far more complex. Chapter 7 describes three types of managerial staff used by international companies to staff their foreign operations. Chapter 8 describes the effective international human resource management (HRM) function.

7

INTERNATIONAL MANAGERIAL STAFFING

Dear Mom . . . For Americans sent to work in China, the word "adjustment" takes on new meaning, as is evident by these excerpts taken from a letter sent home by an American Anheuser-Busch employee shortly after his arrival in Wuhan: "I have relocated to sunny (and hot!) Wuhan. Spring lasted about four days and now it is summer. We have recently started bringing restaurant menus to work to have them translated. The last one has such delicacies as 'fish stomach over rice' and 'beef tail.' You have to hand it to the people over here: they know how to get their money's worth out of an animal. Absolutely no waste. . . . Well, I am in my new house. Everything has its own set of challenges. I taught myself how to use the alarm system. This may not seem like much, but you have to understand that while the instruction booklet is in English, the control panel is written in French. . . . I did get my driver's license. Driving is certainly an adventure. This week I am learning how to ignore the stripes on the road, and next week I will work on ignoring red lights. Everything in its own time."[1]

Learning Objectives of the Chapter

Regardless of whether the nature of their business is in commerce, science and technology, education, entertainment, tourism, transportation, religion, or communications, many domestic enterprises that want to remain competitive, as indicated in the previous chapters, must develop strategies in response to the intense global competition they face or in response to declining markets at home. When a domestic corporation develops a strategy to conduct business in a foreign country, it faces a complex set of managerial problems that differ substantially from those it faces at home. One of the complex problems is selecting the most effective managers to staff the firm's foreign operations.

International business enterprises typically use three types of executives to staff their foreign subsidiaries: home-country nationals (expatriates), host-country nationals (locals), and third-country nationals (by definition, also expatriates). Use of host-country nationals by companies to manage their foreign subsidiaries has become more and more popular in recent years. But there is no doubt that the home country and third countries will continue to be important sources of expatriate executives used by international businesses. This is especially true as more and more multinational corporations (MNCs) transform themselves into global corporations and establish a global strategy. These expatriate executives can move readily from country to country and perform effectively no matter where they are. Using expatriates can be very costly, especially when the expatriate wants to return home prematurely from the foreign assignment or when the wrong person was selected for the foreign assignment. After studying this chapter, you should be able to do the following:

1. Discuss home-country national expatriates and their advantages and disadvantages

2. Discuss host-country national expatriates and their advantages and disadvantages

3. Discuss third-country national expatriates and their advantages and disadvantages
   - The factors that influence the choice
   - Why expatriates fail
   - How technology aids expatriation

Three Approaches to Staffing Foreign Subsidiaries

A key problem confronting international corporations is deciding whether to employ an expatriate, a host-country national, or a third-country national to manage their foreign operations. An expatriate is a home-country national, usually an employee of the firm, who is assigned abroad to manage the enterprise's foreign subsidiary(s); a host-country national is a resident of the country where the firm's subsidiary is located, or is to be located, employed to manage the operations; and a third-country national is a resident of a country other than the home country and the host country employed to manage the operations. International organizations must determine which approach is best suited to the needs of each situation.

Advantages and Disadvantages of Using Expatriates

When managers of international businesses are deciding whether to use an expatriate to manage a foreign subsidiary, they must consider both the advantages and the disadvantages of the approach.[2]

Advantages

Knowledge of the Corporation's Culture. Using expatriates is a relatively easy way to obtain personnel with detailed knowledge of company policies, procedures, and corporate culture.[3]

Knowledge of the Company's Management Techniques. Expatriates, because they have worked for the company in the home country, are familiar with the company's management techniques and methods, as well as with the related technology and product and/or service development.

Loyalty. The expatriate approach enables international business corporations to select people with proven loyalty to the company. This helps provide credibility at headquarters when the expatriate conveys information, especially information concerning the adaptations the company must make to succeed in the foreign market.[4]

Influence at Headquarters. Using expatriates places individuals in the foreign subsidiary who are influential at the home headquarters and thus possess the ability to obtain the resources from the home office needed in the foreign subsidiary.[5]

Easier to Assess. Because the expatriate has been employed with the firm for some time, it is not difficult to assess his or her qualifications for the foreign assignment.

Foreign Image. Using expatriates enables companies to maintain a "foreign image" in the host country, which can be an important marketing strategy (many people, e.g., the Chinese, like to purchase goods with foreign labels).[6]

Disadvantages

Expensive Orientation Programs Needed. Expensive programs (which are often unsuccessful) to orient the expatriate to the foreign country's culture and systems are required. This is not as much of a problem for large international business enterprises as it is for small and medium-size companies that compete in the global arena. Smaller companies often do not have the financial means to establish such programs. Smaller companies can send their expatriate candidates to a private training institution, but this is also costly. Yet without such training, small firms' expatriates are likely to make costly blunders in conducting business abroad, thus putting them at a disadvantage. Small businesses can sometimes overcome this difficulty by entering into a partnership with a capable firm in the foreign market—which, as pointed out in Chapters 4 and 5, is what many Western companies do when entering Asia and other parts as well. Nevertheless, while using the expatriate approach is very expensive, it is still a valuable approach to establishing operations abroad and in managing them.[7]

Unfamiliar With the Foreign Environment. Initially, even after going through the orientation program, the expatriate is not familiar with the local culture, laws, political process, legal process, and other subtleties. People can be taught the formal systems, but the informal systems have to be learned through field experience. Lack of information often impairs performance (e.g., refer to Practical Perspective 7.1). But this can sometimes be a problem if the expatriate tries to push its corporate culture in the foreign subsidiary—for instance, in Germany where its operations have

PRACTICAL PERSPECTIVE 7-1

Getting the Job Done

Although most expatriates will have prepared for working with Arab, Italian, Japanese, or other colleagues, there will be cultural and language obstacles for expats to overcome in the workplace. You can master the language, take cross-cultural diversity courses, and read the native literature and never be entirely prepared for all that idiosyncrasies of life in a foreign country.

Just ask Erin Crossland.

The last thing Crossland had to worry about while selling consulting services for Arthur D. Little in Belarus was cordiality. She quickly learned that many Belarussians live up to their reputations for enjoying a vodka or two. Her challenge: not to let their good nature get in the way of doing important business.

Crossland and her colleagues from the Arthur D. Little consulting group spent almost two years in Belarus working on a strategy with the local government to clean up an environmental-hazard site. It was cagey work that required both high-level planning and muscle-wielding manpower. Unfortunately, Crossland says, the work ethic of the Belarussians did not always jibe with that of her American counterparts. She recalls being offered vodka at 10 A.M. breakfast meetings and having to fire a couple of Belarussians for being drunk on the job. But the most wrenching experience took place one night at a banquet Crossland oversaw for several international officials, including some from the U.S. Defense Department and the Environmental Protection Agency. The owner of the restaurant where the dinner was held offered to provide, at no expense, a cultural program as a thank-you for bringing him business. Crossland said sure, and gave it little thought. The oversight has since haunted her. That night, after dinner was served, several scantily clad women appeared in the banquet room to perform a racy dance for the guests. It left Crossland—and the executives—a bit red-faced. "I should have gotten a better explanation of what was meant by a cultural program," she now admits.

SOURCE: Excerpted from Charles Butler, "A World of Trouble," *Sales & Marketing Management*, 151, no. 9 (September 1999), p. 2. Permission conveyed through Copyright Clearance Center, Inc. Reprinted by permission.

failed, Wal-Mart initially installed American executives who had little feel for what German consumers wanted. Wal-Mart has learned to use local managers.[8]

Communication Problems. The expatriate may encounter communication problems in the foreign country, especially if he or she does not have a good command of the local verbal and nonverbal language. This problem impairs the expatriate's performance.

May Not Adapt to Foreign Culture. The expatriate and/or his or her family may not adapt to the local culture and have to be repatriated (brought back to the home country) early. This is an expensive proposition—not only because it is expensive both to send the expatriate abroad and to prepare someone else for the assignment but also because the expatriate may not have been very effective in the assignment. It was estimated that in 1990, moving an expatriate and his or her family members from the United States to Europe cost about $50,000 and twice that figure to send them to Japan.[9] In 1999, it was estimated to cost as much as $300,000.[10] It was found that between 10% and 20% of all U.S. managers sent abroad returned early because of job dissatisfaction or difficulties in adjusting to a foreign country. Of those who stayed for the duration, nearly one third did not perform up to the expectations of their superiors, and one fourth of those who completed the assignment left their company within one year of repatriation.[11]

The best-qualified people sometimes do not want the assignment. It may be difficult to find highly qualified people who want to work at the foreign subsidiary.[12] Many employees are motivated to elevate themselves in the corporate hierarchy, and they fear that by working in the foreign country, they may not rise as quickly as they would if they remained in the mainstream at home. For example, Ted Patlovich, then vice chairman of Loctite Corp., indicated that "generally, people are not champing at the bit to go [on a foreign assignment]." "It is a major plus to have international experience these days, but you may get lost there," said Chuck Campbell, then senior vice president of Federal Signal Corporation. "You aren't as visible as the guy who is working away in front of the CEO's eyes."[13] And in a survey of personnel managers at 56 MNCs, 56% of the respondents believed a foreign assignment to be immaterial or detrimental to their careers.[14]

When, prior to the 1970s, U.S. international corporations faced low competition, they tended to assign their weakest managers to their international divisions or abroad. However, currently, it is generally acknowledged that executives cannot elevate themselves in the organization without substantial foreign experience. According to Michael Angus, former chairman of Unilever PLC, "Most people who rise toward the top of our business will have worked in at least two countries, probably three."[15] It may thus now be less difficult to find highly qualified people for foreign assignments than in the past.

Highly qualified executives may also refuse a foreign assignment because of a dual-career family situation, an increasing phenomenon in the United States. This means that to get highly qualified executives in such a partnership, international business enterprises may have to take on the costly burden of having to find a job in the foreign country for the spouse or pay for some other arrangement, such as commuter marriage support. The strategies that some companies are applying to this problem include intercompany networking, job-hunting/fact-finding trips, and intracompany employment.[16]

Very Expensive Incentives Required. To get these highly qualified people to accept a foreign assignment, very expensive incentives, such as much higher salaries and benefits, are often required. The average cost of an international assignment in 1998 was estimated at $1 million.[17] In 1999, a fully loaded expatriate package, including benefits and cost-of-living adjustments, cost anywhere from $300,000 to $1 million annually.[18] Because of such high costs, some companies in Asia terminated expatriate assignment during the recent (1998) economic downturn (see Practical Perspective 7.2). Given today's (2007) international state-of-nature, for example, the world's war on terrorism, the costs are likely to be much higher.

Low Productivity in Early Part of Assignment. The expatriate may not be very productive in the earlier part of the assignment because he or she needs time to adapt to the new environment.

No "Goodwill." Employing foreigners could fail to generate "goodwill" because local people may prefer to see residents of their country managing the foreign subsidiary.

Expensive Repatriation Programs Needed. Expensive programs to reorient the expatriate when he or she returns (repatriation) are required. (This is discussed more thoroughly in Chapter 8.)

PRACTICAL PERSPECTIVE 7-2

Down and Out

Twenty-seven-year-old Ravi Menon arrived in Indonesia from India four years ago [1994]. Then, Indonesia was an "expatriate heaven," a land of high salaries, big houses, company cars, great holidays, and full medical insurance. But this [1998] January, his employer, the giant Bakrie group, told Menon and its other expatriate staff that their U.S. dollar salaries would in the future be paid entirely in rupiah. What's more, the conversion would be at 3,500 rupiah to the dollar, less than half the market rate. "It was a good trip while it lasted," Menon says wryly.

Menon isn't the only one lamenting the end of the good times. Expatriates have been among the first to feel the heat of Southeast Asia's meltdown—dramatically so in Indonesia but also in Thailand, Malaysia, and Singapore.

Before the crisis, replacing expensive foreigners with cheaper locals was a long-term goal for most employers of expatriates. Suddenly it has become a matter of immediate necessity.

Pummeled by currency devaluations, local companies can no longer afford U.S. dollar salaries. They and, to a lesser extent, multinationals are now trying to make their expatriates cheaper and more effective or getting rid of them altogether.

SOURCE: Excerpted from Joanna Slater, with S. Jayasankaran, "Down and Out," *Far Eastern Economic Review* (April 2, 1998), p. 1.

Expatriate may have an ulterior motive for accepting the assignment. If an expatriate is resentful of his or her country's political system and/or governmental policies, his or her motivation for wanting the foreign assignment may be "escaping" from the country. At the foreign site, the expatriate's energies may be used to attain his or her objectives instead of the company's. In past decades, some expatriates from communist countries on assignment in democratic countries have spent much of their time finding ways to obtain political asylum.

Japanese Expatriates in the United States as an Illustration of the Disadvantages

An influential Japanese organization once employed Matthew D. Levy, principal of WSY Consulting Group, and Soji Teramura, president of the consulting firm Teramura International, to analyze the experiences of 50 foreign-owned enterprises in the United States. The following are some of their findings:[19]

- A large majority of Japanese executives and about half the American executives find miscommunication (language barriers) to be a significant obstacle to successful operations.
- More than half the American executives, and nearly as many Japanese executives, find cultural differences in the U.S. workplace to be a problem.
- Smaller Japanese companies, which tend to be less experienced in international management, have the most difficulty managing cultural differences.
- Family adjustment and lack of preparation for life in the United States were cited as problems by about half the Japanese executives.

- Japanese families have problems readjusting when they return to Japan.
- Some Japanese executives have problems dealing with American-style unions.
- Some Japanese executives, coming from a homogeneous society, encounter difficulties in dealing with America's culturally diverse workforce.
- Some Japanese executives have difficulty dealing with the negative feelings some American workers have toward Japanese management.
- Many Japanese executives have problems dealing with U.S. federal, state, and local government regulations.
- Some Japanese executives cannot effectively handle community relations.

Advantages and Disadvantages of Using Host-Country Locals

As indicated above, when managers of international enterprises are determining whether to use an expatriate to manage a foreign subsidiary, they must consider both the advantages and the disadvantages. If the disadvantages of using an expatriate outweigh the advantages, they may have to consider the option of using a host-country national.[20]

Advantages

Familiar With Local Environment. Host-country nationals are already familiar with the local language, culture, and customs. They do not require expensive training in language proficiency or acculturation. Ted Patlovich, then vice chairman of Loctite Corporation, saw great advantages in having a local manager running things overseas. "We would rather have nationals be country managers than foreigners," Patlovich said. "The national knows his [or her] way around. He [or she] knows the lawyers, the financial people, and the bankers. He [or she] knows everybody."[21] As indicated above, Wal-Mart learned this the hard and costly way.

Can Sometimes Be Productive Right Away. Unlike expatriates, nationals do not need time to adapt to the local environment and can sometimes be productive from the beginning of the assignment.

Knows Local Business Subtleties. Nationals grasp the subtleties of the local business situation, information that may be vital to the establishment of a good relationship with customers, clients, government agencies, employees, and the general public.

"Goodwill." Having local nationals in management positions, especially at higher levels, may enhance the company's image (it develops "goodwill"), especially in very nationalistic countries. It may also enhance host-country employees' morale because these employees may appreciate working for a boss of the same nationality rather than for a foreigner and/or they may appreciate the opportunity for growth in the organization.

Usually Less Expensive to Employ. Employing host-country nationals is often less expensive than employing home-country or third-country nationals, especially in lower-wage nations. Salaries and other benefit packages are often lower than the expatriate's and the third-country national's, and no expensive repatriation programs are needed.

Disadvantages

Loyalty May Be to the Country, Not to the Company. In a conflict between national policy and the company's interests, host-country managers may favor national policy over the company's interests.[22]

Often Difficult to Find Qualified People. It is often difficult, especially in the less developed countries, to find people at the local level with the right skills for the assignment.

More Difficult to Assess Abilities. It is usually more difficult to assess nationals' skills and abilities than to assess someone who is working for the corporation.

Does Not Understand the Corporation's Culture. The national probably does not have sufficient knowledge of the firm's policies and culture, including the informal decision-making network in the home office.

Problems in Communicating With Home Office. The national may have difficulty communicating with the home-office manager and other employees.

May Not Be Mobile. Host-country managers, once appointed, may be difficult to move; they may want to remain on the job until retirement. For example, the Japanese have tended to prefer lifetime employment in the same company.

May Have Ulterior Motives. Local managers may become bored with the job itself and concentrate on building a name and reputation in the community for themselves, thus ignoring the managerial function.

May Be Weak in Dealing With Local Government Officials. A host country manager may be weak in dealing with the local authorities.[23]

Expensive Training and Development Programs Needed. To deal with the problems outlined above, expensive programs, such as assigning the national to the corporate headquarters for a lengthy period of time to acquaint him or her with the corporation's formal and informal methods of operation may be required. (These programs are addressed in Chapter 8.) This would eliminate the advantage of the local manager's being productive right away. And the host-country local himself or herself becomes an expatriate when sent back to his or her country, thus inheriting the problems for the expatriate previously discussed. Nevertheless, as Morislav Lansky, former human resource (HR) and corporate programs manager at IBM Czech Republic, indicated, "It's better to train locals in corporate culture than to train expatriates in local culture."[24]

Advantages and Disadvantages of Using Third-Country Personnel

If the disadvantages of using an expatriate or a host-country national outweigh the advantages, managers can consider another option: using a third-country national to manage the foreign subsidiary—in essence, an expatriate from another country. This approach, too, has advantages and disadvantages.

Advantages

Additional Source of Personnel. Third-country nationals are a source of personnel when there is a shortage of qualified host-country and home-country nationals who are able or willing to take foreign assignments.

Usually Costs Less Than the Home-Country Expatriate. The costs of maintaining third-country nationals are often less than the costs of maintaining home-country expatriates, especially if the home-country expatriates are from high-income nations, such as the United States and Japan.

Greater Adaptability Than the Expatriate. Third-country nationals from a country in the same region as the foreign assignment are likely to possess greater cultural adaptability and greater flexibility and ease of adjustment in the host country than home-country personnel. For instance, a Brazilian national probably would adapt more readily in Chile than a Danish national. There will be even greater adaptability if the third country and the host country share a common language and a similar cultural background. A Portuguese national may be able to work in Brazil more easily than a British national because Portuguese is spoken in both Brazil and Portugal. And it would be easier for a Taiwanese to work in the People's Republic of China than it would for a French individual because Taiwan and the People's Republic of China, to a great extent, share a common culture and language (Mandarin). Over the years, U.S. companies have hired English or Scottish executives for top management positions in their subsidiaries located in countries that were former British colonies, such as Jamaica, India, and Kenya.

Advantageous When the Home Country Does Not Maintain a Good Relationship with the Host Country. Hiring a third-country national is especially advantageous when the home-country government does not maintain a positive relationship with the government of the nation in which the subsidiary is located. For instance, an Iranian enterprise with a subsidiary in the United States may be better-off employing a Canadian citizen to manage the subsidiary because the Iranian government's relationship with Canada is better than its relationship with the United States.

Disadvantages

The employee's country does not maintain a good relationship with the host country. Problems arise with this staffing strategy if the qualified employee is from a country that does not maintain a good relationship with the country where the assignment is to take place. In certain parts of the world, animosities of national character exist between neighboring countries: India and Pakistan, Greece and Turkey, Ireland and Northern Ireland (the United Kingdom), Denmark and Sweden, to name just a few. Transfers of third-country nationals must take such factors into account very seriously, keeping in mind that local workers may dislike working for the third-country manager simply because he or she is from that third country.

Locals may prefer their own citizens in managerial positions. Another problem, similar to the use of the home-country expatriate option, is the desire of the host-country's government to elevate its own people to responsible managerial positions. Even if the third-country national is better qualified, the government may prefer that a local citizen be appointed.

Appointee may have an ulterior motive. Yet another problem, also similar to the home-country expatriate approach, may occur if the candidate is dissatisfied with his or her country's political system and/or governmental policies. His or her motive for wanting the assignment may be to "escape," and he or she may work toward this end while ignoring the company's objectives.

Factors Influencing the Choice

Many factors influence the choice of whether to use an expatriate, a host-country national, or a third-country national. The factors include top management's staffing outlook and perceived needs, the corporation's characteristics, the characteristics of the personnel available at home, and the host country's characteristics.[25]

Top Management's Staffing Outlook

The varying staffing views of international business corporations influence the decision. A company's view can be ethnocentric, polycentric, regiocentric, or geocentric.[26]

Ethnocentric

The ethnocentric view holds that key positions in the foreign subsidiary should be staffed by citizens from the parent company's home country. An enterprise develops such an outlook because its top management perceives a deficiency in the qualifications, experience, and competence of host-country nationals to fill management positions in the foreign subsidiary. These firms use expatriates to manage their foreign operations. Japanese international businesses are reputed to adhere strongly to this view. For example, Japanese international business corporations have been found to employ considerably more parent-country nationals at the senior- and middle-management levels in their foreign operations than do U.S. and European international business enterprises, and they do not use third-country nationals at any level of management in their foreign operations, except in Africa.[27] Procter & Gamble endured a series of painful product failures because of its policy (now abandoned) of imposing managers from headquarters on overseas subsidiaries.[28]

Polycentric

The polycentric view holds that key positions in the foreign subsidiary should be staffed by locals (host-country nationals). A corporation's top management holding this view will employ host-country locals to ensure that the foreign subsidiary's operation follows overall company policy. However, polycentric enterprises do usually send expatriates to start the foreign subsidiary and to train and develop locals to assume the managerial responsibility. For example, in its international expansion efforts, Wal-Mart tried to have two American managers in each store for the first year or two, but in Mexico it employed more than two.[29] In addition, although Japanese international businesses have tended to apply the ethnocentric approach, some of them are starting to think polycentric—for example, Sony now aims to give the top job in each of its subsidiaries to a manager from the host country.[30] Isao Tsuruta, formerly senior vice president for JUSCO, a retail giant based in Tokyo with operations in many parts of the globe, including the United States and the United Kingdom, indicated that in their international expansion, as local people matured in the company, they gradually assumed key managerial positions. In Talbot's, their U.S. affiliate, according to Tsuruta, there is not a single JUSCO employee among its managers, and of the eight members of Talbots' board of directors, only four were JUSCO people.[31]

A company may be polycentric in one country and, at the same time, ethnocentric in another. Polycentric firms send expatriates to the foreign subsidiary not only to train and develop the locals but also to develop or enhance their managerial skills and to develop an informal communication network in the foreign market.[32] For example, Becton Dickinson promotes cross-posting of managers. The firm accomplishes this by sending managers to different foreign subsidiaries for a period of time and having them take on general management responsibilities. This gives members of the strategy teams a broad international profile, enabling them to be more effective when making organizational decisions.[33] Historically, hierarchical opportunities for host-country locals in these enterprises have generally been limited to top management of the local subsidiary.[34]

Regiocentric

The regiocentric view holds that key positions at the regional headquarters should be staffed by individuals from one of the region's countries (the regional organizational structure is discussed in Chapter 6). These firms will use expatriates to develop a regional organization and, as in the case of the polycentric approach, to enhance their skills and develop an informal communication network.[35] Hierarchical opportunity for host-country locals presented by these businesses (especially U.S. and European international business corporations) tends to be top management at the regional headquarters.[36] This opportunity evolved, in part, because polycentric companies realized that a way to keep effective local managers was to open regional top-level positions to them.

Arthur Pappas, an American who (in 1991) headed Glaxo's regional operations in Asia, "had sent home ten Western managers since 1989, replacing them with locals or one of the growing number of Asians who work in the region but outside their home country. Among his tasks was to train or recruit an Asian to take his place."[37]

These international business enterprises typically do not provide locals the opportunity for top-level positions in the central, home-office headquarters. The lack of this opportunity demoralizes some local and regional managers.

Geocentric

The geocentric view holds that nationality should not influence the assignment of key positions anywhere (local subsidiary, regional headquarters, or central headquarters) and that competence should be the prime criterion for selecting managerial staff. Even though this view (referred to as that of the global corporation in Chapter 1), at least in theory, seems to be catching on, few international business enterprises practice it fully. In 1994, David dePury, the cochairman of Asea Brown Boveri, the Swedish-Swiss electrical engineering giant, informed a recent (1994) international management symposium at St. Gallen in Switzerland that few multinationals produce more than

20% of their goods and services outside their immediate or wider home market, that most boards come predominantly from one culture, and that few multinationals are ready to let their shareholder base become as global as their business.[38]

Coca-Cola Company, however, appears to accept the geocentric view. In 1994, it owned and operated businesses of all sizes in more than 195 nations. Two thirds of its 31,000 employees worked outside the United States. Third-country nationals made up the majority of the international service employees, and individuals of other nationalities were in charge of more of Coca-Cola's division offices than were North Americans.[39] In 1998, two of Gillette's four executive vice presidents, the traditional stepping-stone to the top, were Europeans. In some countries, the Gillette management is beginning to resemble the United Nations. Its business in the former Soviet Union, for instance, is headed by a Frenchman, backed up by an Egyptian controller, an English sales director, and officers from Pakistan and Ireland.[40] These corporations, too, use expatriates for development purposes. Ford Motor Company has recently embarked on a colossal plan to turn itself into a borderless firm.[41] And Japan's Sony recently named Howard Stringer, the Wales-born American, as its first non-Japanese CEO, and Nancy McKinsey was the first American to be named CEO of Wolters Kluwer, the Dutch publisher.[42]

Top Management's Perceived Needs

Some top managers may perceive that an expatriate would work better for them than a local, and vice versa. Louis Jouanny, the manager of international marketing for Grid Systems Corporation (a portable computer maker in California) in 1990, stated, "The experience we had is that you need Europeans to sell in Europe and Asians to sell in Asia. You need local people to sell locally."[43] On the other hand, Jerry Johanneson, the chief operating officer for Haworth Inc. (an office furniture maker from Michigan) in 1990, said, "Because the pricing and design of furniture systems can get complicated, and because we wanted to be certain Haworth's service would be excellent from the outset, we elected to station a U.S. national in the London office."[44]

Company's Characteristics

Companies' characteristics that influence the choice of staffing strategy include the following.[45]

Ownership of Foreign Subsidiaries. The type of staffing strategy an international business company adopts depends on whether the investment is for a short or a long term. If it is for a short term, the firm may use the expatriate approach because there is no time to train locals; if it is for a long term, it may use a development-of-locals approach.

Industry Group. Staffing strategy is likely to vary between the manufacturing and service industries. Service industries such as banking, insurance, and law often hire locals because these people know the practices required to operate the foreign subsidiary effectively. On the other hand, manufacturing enterprises often send expatriates because they have the technical knowledge required to develop and operate the foreign subsidiary effectively.

Technology. The level of technological sophistication and the amount of research needed to sustain it affects staffing strategy. If the level is high, an expatriate may be required. Furthermore, if the enterprise is protective of its technology, it is likely to use expatriates to avoid sharing private information.

Market Influences. Staffing strategies vary according to whether the market for the product is local or international. If the foreign subsidiary is producing for local distribution, employing managers with a local perspective may suffice. If, however, the production is for global distribution, managers with a broader perspective, which expatriates or third-country nationals are more likely to possess than locals, would be required.

Stage of Foreign Subsidiary Development. Traditionally, international business corporations have staffed foreign subsidiaries with expatriates in the early stages of establishing operations in a foreign country. To some extent, this is also true in the developed stages when higher-level positions are involved.[46] In the later stages of subsidiary development, at least at the lower levels, host-country nationals are employed. Research has revealed that in their first stage of internationalization, companies in the United States and Europe export their products to foreign markets. However, as the local market becomes large enough to support local manufacture of the product, home-country managers are sent to the host country to start the operations and manage them during the first few years. Subsequently, the companies replace the expatriates with host-country nationals.[47] The case of Motorola, which has been doing business internationally for many years, is an example:

> Motorola has . . . US managers serving on assignments in Europe, the Mid-East, Asia, Canada, Mexico, and Latin America. In virtually all our operations we use an American manager in the start-up process. We do this because it's very difficult for someone in a foreign country to acculturate to the company's management style and objectives while starting up a facility. It's an awful lot to learn. There are exceptions to that, mainly when we have a longer-than-normal lead time to get the facility going. But a lot of our expansion has happened fairly rapidly with only 9 to 12 months to get a plant up and running.[48]

The cases of Wal-Mart and JUSCO discussed earlier serve as other examples. U.S. international businesses have a tendency to use host-country nationals at all levels of foreign subsidiary management to a much greater extent in the more advanced regions of the world than in the less advanced regions.[49] This suggests that U.S. international business corporations use the ethnocentric approach in less developed countries and the polycentric approach in developed countries. Japanese international corporations have tended to stay with the expatriate staffing approach in key decision-making positions—although, as mentioned earlier, they are currently (2007) starting to employ other staffing approaches.[50]

Organizational Structure. A company's organizational structure also affects its choice of staff. International business enterprises with multidomestic strategies (discussed in

Chapter 4) may use locals more than enterprises with global strategies, which require an expatriate's or a third-country national's global perspective. (Of course, locals can also possess a global perspective.)

Dependence on International Business. Top management in firms with high dependence on international business may feel more secure with an expatriate managing its foreign operations. Firms with low dependence may use locals because they cost less than expatriates. Japan has historically depended much more on international business than has the United States, thus Japanese international companies, as previously indicated, have tended to be far more ethnocentric than U.S. international companies.

Cost-Benefit Factors. The staffing approach with the most favorable cost-benefit ratio is chosen. There is, however, no standard formula for accurately determining the ratio. Decision makers must therefore rely on their intuition.

Style of Management. International business companies apply a staffing strategy that suits their organizational character (or corporate culture) and their style of management. For example, as indicated before, Japanese international businesses tend to staff their foreign subsidiaries' important decision-making positions with Japanese expatriates.

Characteristics of Personnel Available at Home. The choice of staffing strategy is also influenced by the characteristics of the personnel available at home. Are there individuals with

- adequate qualifications and experience,
- a proven record of previous success,
- a commitment to international business, including aspirations for international assignments,
- the ability to adapt to cultural environments different from their own and the sensitivity to adapt to new situations, and
- family commitments that would not hinder the foreign assignment?

If the answer to most of the above questions is no, the firm may have to (1) look for staff in third countries and/or in the host country, (2) implement extensive training and development programs (to be discussed in Chapter 8), or (3) do both (1) and (2).

As an example, refer to the anecdotal example of jewelry manufacturing used to illustrate cheaper labor in Chapter 4. Note that the creative design personnel are to be found in the very expensive New York City, where creative people tend to want to live, and thus are not so readily available in many parts of the world. The manufacturing design is done in Providence, Rhode Island, where the cost of living is substantially lower than in New York City and there are ample personnel living, including people with skills that are not so readily available in many parts of the world. The manufacturing of the product takes place in China, where labor is cheaper, and because so many Chinese have, in recent decades, studied business in U.S. universities, there are ample managerial personnel available there, as well as engineering personnel. As a matter of fact, the head designer in the New York City company was recently (March 2007) offered a lucrative job to become the head designer for a Chinese company based in Hong Kong. Refer to the IPLC (international product life cycle) theory discussed in Chapter 3. This offer is an indicator that a Chinese company will soon take over these three companies, as it now has the manufacturing technology and an ample pool of engineers educated in the United States but needs to import the creative people. Hong Kong is a very exciting city to live in, and the cost of living there is much cheaper than in New York City. Furthermore, since Hong Kong is a former U.K. colony, it has a lot of Western culture. Whereas in Japan, a very homogeneous society as pointed out in Chapter 4, in the 1980s, MNCs possessed strong manufacturing and engineering know-how but relied heavily on creative R&D centers in the West. But numerous U.S. companies did establish creative centers in Japan to bring them closer to their engineering and manufacturing centers. The creative designers in the New York City jewelry company, discussed above, often travel to China, flying business class and staying in five-star hotels.

Host-Country Characteristics

The choice of staffing strategy is also influenced by factors associated with the host country. These factors include the following.

Level of Economic and Technological Development. If the country's level of economic and technological development is low, it may sometimes be difficult for the company's top management to find qualified personnel locally.

Political Stability. If political stability in the country is low and nationalist sentiments are high, and there is great potential for the government to nationalize or expropriate foreign-owned companies, an enterprise's top management may feel more secure sending an expatriate. (Of course, as suggested in Chapter 3, many companies will not establish operations in such a high-risk country.)

Control of Foreign Investments and Immigration Policies. Nations may have a policy mandating that foreign-owned subsidiaries place locals in managerial positions. As pointed out in Chapter 3, when Russia started to attract foreign investment in the late 1980s, its policy was that top management in foreign-owned subsidiaries had to be Russians. Since the policy failed, Russia eliminated it, allowing foreigners to assume top management positions in foreign-owned subsidiaries.[51]

Availability of Capable Managerial Personnel. If managers with the appropriate abilities and experience are not available in the host country, the corporation may have to look for them in third countries or at home and then implement programs aimed at training and developing locals for managerial positions. For example, many MNCs once had difficulty finding capable managers in China because these managers were used to working for China's state-owned enterprises (SOEs) and didn't really know how to manage in a competitive environment[52] (bear in mind that China had a 100% employment policy). While China has made much progress in transforming itself into a market-like economy, Russia is still having the same problems in moving from a centrally controlled economy to a market-like economy—many of its managers manage the old way. China is far ahead of Russia in transforming itself into a market-like economy, in part because Russia's communist regime killed the entrepreneurial spirit while China's entrepreneurial spirit remained alive during its communist regime through "underground" market-like activities. Of course, as discussed in Chapter 1, cultural differences between the two countries have much to do with the differences in the transition progress. Also, as previously mentioned, many Chinese have, for the past few decades, studied business in the West.

Sociocultural Setting. Will it be too difficult for an expatriate to adjust to the country's cultural, racial, language, religious, and political boundaries? If so, the firm may have to look for locals or for third-country nationals. "The country you plan to expand into makes a big difference," said Steven Graubart, manager with the accounting and consulting firm Ernst & Young in 1990. "In Malaysia, Indonesia, Thailand, and the Middle East, for example, [to] hire a local executive to run the operation might be more necessary than it would be in Canada, the United Kingdom, or Hong Kong because differences in language, social customs, and government regulations are far more pronounced."[53]

Geographical Location. If the location is very isolated, adaptation may be very difficult for the expatriate. For example, it may be difficult to find an employee of a company in Hong Kong to accept an assignment in an isolated area of an African or a South American country. The corporation would then have to consider a local national or a third-country national. On the other hand, many expatriates now readily accept assignments in Spain, especially in Barcelona,[54] the sun and fun place.

The three sets of factors—company, home-country individuals, and host-country characteristics—may interact to affect the choice of one particular staffing strategy rather than another. These factors suggest that there may be situations in which international businesses will have to adapt their selection criteria to specific situations; in fact, they may sometimes have to lower their standards. For instance, a position at home may require an employee with a college degree, but in a foreign nation where college graduates are scarce and other factors dictate employing a local, the MNC may have to settle for a high school graduate. Thus, ultimately, the situation will determine the approach an enterprise uses.[55]

Why Expatriates Fail

Reasons for the failure of many expatriates in their foreign assignments include the foreign country's physical and social environments, different level of technical sophistication in the host country, the home country's conflicting objectives and policies, overcentralization, gender, inadequate repatriation programs, and pitfalls in the HR planning function.

The Physical and Social Environments

When expatriates cross national boundaries, they often encounter adaptation problems caused by both the physical and the sociocultural environments—they encounter a culture shock. This is especially true when these environments are at odds with the expatriate's own value system and living habits. For example, geographical distance conflicts with an individual's need to feel secure in the community, and it may result in "separation anxiety" for expatriates and their family members.[56] Such reactions may impair the expatriate's on-the-job effectiveness and lower family morale. The problem is aggravated when the expatriate is not capable of communicating with the local people in their verbal and nonverbal language.[57] These problems will affect expatriates' ability to deal with individuals and business groups outside the subsidiary, including local partners, trade unions, bankers, and important customers.[58] And the current 2007 state-of-nature, the so-called global war on terrorism going on, is making expatriates' lives much more difficult and stressful. Companies are thus taking this issue more seriously than in the past and are investing a large amount of time and money to enable staff to have a better understanding of how to bridge cultural differences.[59] Practical Perspective 7.3 describes Renault-Nissan's training program. Hatachi UK and Hatachi America also implemented similar programs.[60]

PRACTICAL PERSPECTIVE 7-3

Renault-Nissan—Training Staff to Deal With the Diversity of Cultures

When the French car maker Renault bought a controlling stake in Nissan in 1999 and set up the Renault-Nissan Alliance, it decided to learn from past mistakes. Previous experiences of cross-border partnerships, even within Europe, had taught Renault the necessity of understanding the mindset of its Japanese partners. Everyone involved in the new relationship attended half-day courses on Japanese culture and norms. Many of them went on to a two-day "Working with Your Japanese Partners" course to explore Japanese business culture in more depth . . . Some were encouraged to continue their studies, learn Japanese, or improve their English on company time; some attended follow-up days, where they could seek advice from colleagues and consultants on how to tackle day-to-day problems; some of the more senior managers had coaching sessions.

Employees in both companies went on exchange programmes for six months to five years, working in their partner company's offices and plants in France and Japan. Three years later, Nissan started the same process in Japan, running two-day courses on "Working With Your French Partners" and coaching sessions for expatriates.

SOURCE: Adapted from Richard Pool, "Bridging the Cultural Divide," *Computing Business* (April 20, 2006). www.whatpc.com.uk/computing-business/features/2153953/bridgi

Varying Technical Sophistication

Expatriates often encounter differences in technical sophistication in the foreign country, a problem that conflicts with their expectations. The problem becomes critical when an expatriate views the technical differences as insurmountable.[61] Yet another problem for expatriates occurs when they attempt to apply successful home-country managerial and organizational principles in the foreign country. The expatriate may experience considerable frustration because differences in the local culture usually prevent effective implementation.[62]

MNC Country's Conflicting Objectives and Policies

Expatriates also encounter difficulties because they are links between corporate head-quarters and the foreign subsidiary and because they are responsible for implementing the objectives and policies formulated by the home office. Problems often occur when the objectives and policies conflict with the managerial situation viewed by the expatriate manager and with the managerial mandates imposed on him or her by the local government based on immediate national needs, such as job opportunities, and use of local resources, such as land, water, power, and minerals, whereas the MNC expects the local government to provide an open market and reduce bureaucracy and red tape to easily take advantage of cheap resources.[63] That is, the expatriate manager must often conduct the subsidiary's operations within the constraints imposed by the immediate situation and the local government.[64]

Overcentralization

Expatriates face another problem when the home office overcentralizes decision making. The transactions between the employees and the manager are effected when the employees are aware that the power in not embedded in the local manager.[65] If the expatriate manager's authority is visibly constrained, his or her opportunity to establish and maintain an effective relationship with local associates is diminished. This is especially true in host environments where individuals place a high value on authority. If the expatriate manager lacks authority, he or she loses credibility in the eyes of the locals.[66] (Refer to Practical Perspective 7.4.)

PRACTICAL PERSPECTIVE 7-4

Successful MNCs Have Flexible Practices, People, and HR Functions

"If you want to be around 20 years from now, your people must be flexible and willing to make change—or the organization will be gone." This sentiment, expressed by André Rudé, an HR executive at the Hewlett Packard Corporation, summarizes well the opinions shared by the managers at the successful MNCs in our 1998 study. According to Rude, "Flexibility is IN" at Hewlett Packard. In the case of MNCs, flexibility is critical with respect to the policies and practices typically developed at headquarters and then implemented worldwide. Policies and practices are considered flexible if they allow for variation across nations, thereby taking national cultures into account. Yet, all too often, the goal is to maintain consistency across nations, and rigid and inflexible policies and practices are the result.

To illustrate this, some of the executives mentioned the conflict around diversity programs. This conflict arose between those advocating the need for consistency or centralization and those administering policy at the local level. In an extreme case of centralization, corporate headquarters may ask all the managers of the organization's foreign subsidiaries to implement the same very structured program. International managers are likely to become frustrated with the home office for being so culturally insensitive and naïve as to believe that people worldwide hold the same value concerning, for example, individualism and equal opportunity as a fundamental right.

SOURCE: Excerpted from L. K. Stroh and P. M. Caligiuri, "Increasing Global Competitiveness Through Effective People Management," *Journal of World Business,* 33, no. 1 (Spring 1998), pp. 2–3. Reprinted with permission.

Gender

Still another problem is cultural resistance to expatriate women managers. Cultural biases against women in some host countries may deter the acceptance of women as managers. Subordinates in such host-country subsidiaries may interpret the assignment of a woman executive to mean that the central headquarters has low regard for its business with that subsidiary. They may also worry that a woman will have less influence over decisions at headquarters; that is, they may think that she will have less autonomy in local negotiations and will thus be less able to represent the subsidiary in local transactions.[67]

However, using a female expatriate is becoming less and less of a problem—especially when she is viewed by locals as having the authority to make decisions. In Japan, for example, it is well-known that historically, Japanese males felt uncomfortable working for a Japanese female boss, but they feel quite comfortable working with a foreign female expatriate, provided she demonstrates the appropriate skills, of course, and Japanese men actually feel a lot more comfortable working with a female expatriate than they do with a male expatriate.

Repatriation

Repatriation (reassigning the expatriate back home) is a special problem—after having worked and lived abroad for several years, returning home causes a reverse culture shock. A survey revealed that employees found reentry into their home country and home company more difficult than the initial move to the foreign culture. This was, in part, because the managerial skills that they had enhanced abroad generally were neither recognized nor used by the home-country organization. The returnees saw themselves as being most effective when they integrated their foreign with their home-country experiences and actively used these new skills. But their colleagues evaluated them most highly when they did not have characteristics of "foreigners" and did not use their cross-cultural learning in their domestic jobs.[68] In fact, the experience expatriates acquired in the foreign assignment often made them more marketable outside the home corporation.[69]

The problem is magnified when the technological advances made at home make the expatriate's functional abilities obsolete.[70] It is also magnified when the returnee finds that he or she has missed opportunities in the organization. An investigation showed that returning managers encountered problems because important career and professional opportunities had passed them by.[71] Many expatriates have returned home only to find that their peers had been promoted ahead of them to higher-level positions.[72] Other problems include returnees' complaints that the length of their foreign assignment adversely affected their lifestyles, their ability to plan for their future professional careers, and their children's education.

Some returnees complained about losing social and professional prestige. For example, being in a country where the cost of living is relatively low, coupled with the higher salary expatriates normally draw, the executive may have had a very large house with servants, may have had his or her children sent to an expensive private school, and may have been in top management at the subsidiary. Back at home, where the cost of living is relatively high, the employee may have to settle for a smaller house; no domestic help; and a less expensive, lower-quality school for the children. The returnee may no longer be in a focal position at work—even if the executive was promoted on return, in many cases he or she felt professionally "demoted," as the new position usually did not allow the same freedom and stimulation that the foreign position did.[73]

Also, as previously pointed out, the repatriate and his or her family may experience "reverse culture shock" on return, as the environment is no longer as familiar as it was when they left.[74] Or the assignment may have been in a European cultural center, and the returnee is assigned to a remote rural town. (Refer to Practical Perspective 7.5.)

PRACTICAL PERSPECTIVE 7-5

Coming Home

In 1993 Thorpe McConville was sent to Shanghai to open Diebold, Inc.'s China subsidiary. As the general manager and CEO of the operation, McConville had considerable responsibilities. He would be preparing Diebold to tap a market with immense potential for his company's product, ATM machines. Over the course of the next five years, McConville accomplished a great deal: He had a manufacturing plant designed and built, recruited local sales and marketing executives, set up a distribution system, and negotiated tariff agreements with the government. Every day, he said, brought a challenge.

In 1999 he was back at Diebold's headquarters in Canton, Ohio. His job? Head of internal auditing. Not exactly a sexy title befitting a cosmopolitan executive.

The entire time he was in China, McConville knew he would one day return to work in the Canton headquarters. He expected there would be a job—doing what was in the back of his mind. "One of the things about foreign assignments is, it's very difficult to find a job back in the U.S. that fits you," McConville said, "After five years I knew I wanted to come home because companies tend to forget you by then. So about year four, we came to an agreement that that was long enough. But I had mixed emotions about leaving." McConville was like many expats. After all the nagging issues of being sent abroad are overcome—finding housing, making new friends, developing a network within the organization—these workers finally get comfortable. It lasts for about a week. Then a creepy feeling envelops many. It's the fear that the home office will no longer need them when it's time to return. A merger might have eliminated jobs, or a mentor may have retired, or a host of other scenarios. The bottom line: The promise made earlier of a job, maybe even a promotion, has faded with the years. The reality is, there may be no position to promote an expat to once he or she returns. Even the most senior executives get anxious.

SOURCE: Excerpted from Charles Butler, "A World of Trouble," *Sales & Marketing Management*, 151, no. 9 (September 1999), p. 3. Reprinted with permission. Permission conveyed through Copyright Clearance Center, Inc.

These potential repatriation problems may hinder the expatriate's performance abroad, or, as pointed out earlier, the better-qualified executives may not even accept the foreign assignment, forcing companies to assign less qualified people.

Pitfalls in the Human Resource Planning Function

The above reasons for expatriate failures stem, in part, from poor HR planning. A study revealed that many pitfalls in the HR planning function of U.S. multinationals helped cause expatriate failures.[75] The HR planning function in many U.S. international business enterprises tended to suffer because of several major limitations.

Lesser Role Assigned to HR Planning.[76] HR managers generally played a less active role in companies' overall planning processes than did managers of other functions.[77] Based on a content analysis of interviews conducted to identify aspects of people management that were critical to MNCs' success in the global arena, it was concluded that the more successful companies had more effective initiatives to address the issue of including the HR function as a strategic partner in global business than the less successful companies.[78] Today (2007), senior management of MNCs is recognizing the significance of the HR department to their financial success.[79]

Evidence suggested that business failures in foreign countries were often linked to poor management of human resources.[80]

Inadequate Selection Criteria for Foreign Assignments. A study of international business enterprises' practices in selecting personnel for foreign assignments showed that international corporations with lower failure rates tended to use criteria specifically appropriate for selecting expatriate personnel.[81] Another study showed that most U.S. international businesses used technical competence as the primary criterion for selecting expatriate personnel. This practice derived from two primary reasons: (1) the difficulty in identifying and measuring attitudes appropriate for cross-cultural interaction and (2) the self-interest of the selectors—since technical competence usually prevented immediate failure on the job, particularly in high-pressure situations, the selectors played it safe by placing a heavy emphasis on technical qualifications.[82]

An abundance of research shows that while technical competence is the most important factor in the overall determination of success, relational abilities appear to increase the probability of successful performance considerably, and lack of relational skills is frequently the principal cause for expatriate failure.[83]

Failure to Consider the Family Situation Factor. Another important reason for expatriate failure is the family factor.[84] This refers to the inability of the expatriate's family to adapt to living and working in the foreign country. This creates stress for the expatriate's family members, who then create stress for the expatriate, often resulting in on-the-job failure.[85] The majority of the respondents in a survey of personnel administrators indicated that they recognized the importance of this factor to successful performance in a foreign assignment.[86] Of 80 U.S. multinationals surveyed, 52% interviewed spouses as part of the selection procedure for managerial positions, and only 40% interviewed spouses for technically oriented positions.[87] The same study revealed that those U.S. multinationals that conducted interviews with the candidate and his or her spouse to determine his or her suitability for the foreign assignment experienced significantly lower incidents of expatriate failure than those that did not.

Lack of Adequate Training for Foreign Assignments. Ineffective international training and management development have considerable adverse impact on MNCs.[88] The use of more rigorous training programs could significantly improve the expatriate's performance in an overseas environment, thus minimizing the incidence of failure.[89] (Refer again to Practical Perspective 7.3.)

However, changing the behavior of experienced managers can be an insurmountable task for a company's training system (the "you-can't-teach-an-old-dog new tricks" syndrome, so to speak). First, prospective expatriates without a background in the behavioral sciences generally do not consider the training function to be an effective agent. Second, many prospective expatriates are inclined to believe that they are more familiar with the organizational environment and problems, both at the headquarters and at the foreign subsidiary, than the training department, and thus believe that they do not need its help. Third, a prospective expatriate whose past behavior has proven to be highly successful finds it hard to accept that similar behavior may be dysfunctional in the foreign assignment. Fourth, prospective expatriates may consider such training efforts as criticism of their past behavior; they may also interpret it to mean that top management has doubts about their ability to adapt their behavior on their own. Fifth, their workload in the midst of preparation for their transfer may not leave sufficient time for an intensive training program. Finally, top managers tend to underrate the need for such training.[90]

Duration of Assignment and Performance Evaluation. [91]Foreign assignments with a short duration are not conducive to effective performance because the expatriate is not allowed sufficient time to become acquainted with, and adapt to, the new environment. Many international businesses, especially U.S. companies whose management tends to be short-range oriented, tend to expect immediate results from their expatriates. These MNCs evaluate expatriates who do not produce positive results right away as low on performance. This evaluation is not reasonable because expatriates need time to adapt. To mitigate the acculturation problem and to avoid costly mistakes, expatriates should be exempted from active management activities during the first six months after arrival in the foreign market.[92] The amount of time expatriates require for adaptation has been estimated at six months, broken down into four phases: the initial phase, disillusionment phase, culture shock phase, and positive adjustment phase.[93] These are depicted in Table 7.1. The model presented in Table 7.1 is general, and some exceptions may occur. As will be discussed later, Japanese corporations have tended to give their expatriates a year or two to adapt.

Underutilization of Women as Sources of Expatriates. The option of using women expatriates has been underutilized by international businesses—as pointed out earlier, female expatriates can be more effective in some cultures than male expatriates. A 1983

TABLE 7.1	The Expatriate Adaptation Process
The initial phase	When the expatriate transfers to the foreign assignment, the newness of the culture creates a great deal of excitement for him or her.
The disillusionment phase	After about 2 months, the novelty of the new culture wears off, and day-to-day inconveniences caused, for example, by different practices in the local culture and by not being able to communicate effectively create disillusionment for the expatriate.
The culture shock phase	After about 2 months of the day-to-day confusions, the expatriate faces cultural shock. By now, the expatriate is ready to go back to his or her old, familiar environment.
The positive adjustment phase	If the expatriate remains, at about Month 4 of the assignment, he or she begins to adapt, and by Month 6, he or she feels more positive about the foreign environment; he or she does not regain the "high" of the first 2 months but does not repeat the "low" of the next two months.

SOURCE: Based on data from K. Oberg, "Culture Shock: Adjustment to New Cultural Environments," *Practical Anthropology* (July–August 1960), pp. 170–182.

study of 686 U.S. and Canadian firms revealed that only 3% of expatriate managers were women.[94] The October 21, 1994, edition of the *Wall Street Journal* (p. A1) reported this figure to be 5%. Today, the figure is likely to be only slightly higher. This underutilization of women in foreign assignments may derive in part from the presumption that, as pointed out earlier, for cultural reasons many male managers in foreign countries do not accept women as business partners and equals. (Refer to Practical Perspective 7.6.)

PRACTICAL PERSPECTIVE 7-6

Work vs. Life vs. The World

Each country has different work/life issues to balance. It all depends on your perspective. In the USA the biggest work/life anxiety for an employee with flexible work arrangements might be arranging his or her schedule to finish a work assignment and still see his or her son's music recital and daughter's basketball game in the same day.

Elsewhere in the world, work/life concerns can be quite different—and much more basic. Indeed, the biggest work/life issue that Mhpo E. Letlape, in 1999 human-resource director for IBM–South Africa, faced was simply the anxiety that sets in, she said, while "waiting for the gates to open at my home when I had to leave work after dark"—even though her home was only six kilometers from her office.

"Crime and violence are becoming a greater problem because the same work/life imbalances—workload problems, skills shortage, and business pressures—that exist around the world are surfacing in South Africa for the first time, creating [social] problems," said Letlape, one of the speakers at a seminar on international work/life issues cosponsored by the Conference Board and the Families & Work Institute. Indeed, she worried about her teenage children going to shopping malls where she said "drugs and rape are rampant."

By contrast, the most important work/life issues in Japan have been gender issues because there is little equity for women in the workplace. But even that equity issue has temporarily been pushed into the background by the economy. Now the key work/life issue in Japan—because of the unprecedented layoffs in firms that once boasted lifetime employment—is "simply survival as opposed to the perks and benefits" people in the USA often believe they are entitled to have, says Susan Seitel, president of Work & Family Connection, Inc. of Minneapolis, Minnesota.

Venezuela had similar gender issues. Women needed a mentor—and their husbands' approval—to get a job, and it was taboo for women to be invited out for drinks, even for after-work business get-togethers, said Patricia Marquez Otero, associate professor of organizational behavior at the Institute of Higher Studies in Administration in Caracas, Venezuela. "How can we talk about work/life [issues], when we are not even willing to talk about gender differences?"

Unlike other countries, Venezuela had no difficulty balancing work and life issues because in that culture, work is secondary to or part of social, personal, and family lives of people. "We work as part of our social life, not as a competitive thing," said Otero.

In Chile the quality-of-life issues were similar to those in Venezuela. "Women have conquered new places of work," said Aníbal Oyarzún-Lobo of Serviceo Médico Cámara, Chilena de la Construcción, Chile, "but there is still discrimination in [the kinds of jobs they can hold] and in compensation. And because government policies mandate 18 weeks of full pay for maternity leave, free medical care for newborns, and paid time off to take care of the sick children under age one, companies don't like to hire married women," he said.

SOURCE: Excerpted from Michael A. Verespej, "Work vs. Life vs. the World," *Industry Week* (April 4, 1999). www.industryweek.com/ReadArticle.aspx?ArticleID=349. Reprinted with permission.

While such barriers do exist, male managers in many countries do make a distinction between foreign women professionals and local women; as was also pointed out, many male managers may not accept local females in managerial roles but will accept foreign females. In a survey of female expatriates, many of the respondents indicated that they were viewed by locals as foreigners who happened to be women; they also said that the added visibility of being the first female manager in the region gave them greater access to clients because of the curiosity factor.[95] (For an illustration, refer to Practical Perspective 7.7.)

PRACTICAL PERSPECTIVE 7-7

An American Businesswoman's Guide to Japan

"Japanese men aren't used to dealing with woman as equals in a business setting," said Diana Rowland, 1999 author of the book Japanese Business Etiquette, and owner of a San Diego-based cross-cultural consulting firm. "They are uncomfortable simply due to a lack of experience." That lack of experience can severely handicap an American woman executive working in Japan—but it can also be an asset. "I've been asked at meetings if I'm married and when I say no then I've been asked why I don't want to be," Rowland said. "You just have to gracefully deal with these questions and move on."

As intrusive as they may appear, personal questions help a Japanese businessman determine how serious a woman might be about the project at hand. After all, lingering in his mind is the idea that a woman would rather be home, not on the job. Why an American woman would choose to work rather than raise a family is almost incomprehensible to the Japanese. It doesn't jibe with their cultural experience of what a woman ought to do.

In Japan, where gender roles are rigidly defined, most Japanese women choose to root their identities in motherhood and marriage.... Some Japanese businessmen—especially those accustomed to dealing with Americans—sidestep the "female issue" altogether, preferring to somewhat desexualize their image of American women. "There are three kinds of people in Japan: men, women, and foreigners," said Nancy Noyes, who ran Salomon Brothers' hedge desk in Tokyo for six months in 1988. "In the Japanese male's mind, I was not a woman, but a foreigner."

Many American businesswomen say the sheer uniqueness of being a woman is an advantage in Japan. "Once I asked my Japanese associates how they felt about working with me," said a 32-year-old stockbroker for a large U.S. brokerage firm. "They said it was so easy to remember me because they'd always get Bob confused with Jim, Jim confused with John and John mixed up with Bob." ... More and more Japanese men are discovering that they actually like working with American women. "As a group, we're probably more diplomatic and less threatening than American men," Rowland said. "Japanese men don't perceive us as trying to dominate them, nor do they feel the need to be overly competitive with us."

SOURCE: Excerpted from Deidre Sullivan, "An American Businesswoman's Guide to Japan," *Overseas Business* (Winter 1990), pp. 50–55. Reprinted with permission.

This suggests that MNCs need to explore the possibilities of using female expatriates more than in the past. As noted earlier, many expatriates fail because of a shortage of relational skills. These skills are abilities generally ascribed to female managers. Women managers, compared with their male counterparts, experience significantly lower levels of boundary-spanning stress; that is, women cope better with the pressures and strains resulting from the foreign environment.[96] (Also, refer again to the Trek case in Case 5.1, Chapter 5, and note the success of a female international manager.)

The author's own experience in developing and managing an administrative division at a Native American Indian reservation also provides support for the contention that women are more adaptable than men in a culture very different from their own. Many years ago, the author was employed by a Native American Indian tribe to aid it in developing a division in the tribal organization. Non-Native American males and females were hired, but by the conclusion of the development period (four years later), the division employed the author (a male) and 15 females. The males who were hired quickly became frustrated with the cultural differences and left, but many of the females who replaced the males were much more tolerant and stayed.

The above means that managers of international businesses will need to establish programs that help them place the right expatriate in the right position, programs that help them manage its foreign personnel effectively. Many large corporations establish international human resource management (HRM) programs to help them do this, but many smaller businesses often rely on external sources, usually international management consultants. The effective international HRM function is discussed in Chapter 8.

Technology and Expatriation

Technology can play a role in easing some of the staffing problems discussed in this chapter. The Internet, e-mail, teleconferencing, videoconferencing, and computer networks now enable many companies in some situations to work globally in ways they could not before. For example, a group of computer programmers at Tsinghua University in Beijing, China, wrote software using Java technology. They worked for IBM. At the conclusion of each workday, they sent their work over the Internet to an IBM facility in Seattle, Washington. In Seattle, programmers built on it and used the Internet to send it to the Institute of Computer Science in Belarus and Software House Group in Latvia. From there, the advanced work was sent to India's Tata Group, which passed the software back to Tsinghua by morning, back to Seattle, and so on until the project was completed. Caterpillar was working on ways to let engineers in different countries collaborate on tractor designs by simultaneously working on a 3-D model over a computer network. And ParaGraph International, a software company started by Russian Stepan Pacikov, developed products in Moscow and Campbell, California, linking the two via Internet and e-mail.[97]

Furthermore, technologies such as videoconferencing, teleconferencing, e-mail, cell phones, and frequent-flier miles now enable some expatriates to manage abroad but live at home (see Practical Perspective 7.8). Of course, even though global teams do not have to come together face-to-face and international managers can often carry out many of their managerial duties from the home office, they still must learn the others' cultures (discussed in Chapter 8).

PRACTICAL PERSPECTIVE 7-8

"Virtual" Expatriates Work Abroad but Live at Home

London—Michael D. Bekins spent three years on a "virtual" assignment.

As head of Asia-Pacific operations for executive-recruiting firm Korn/Ferry International, of Los Angeles, Bekins was officially based in Singapore. But he didn't rent an apartment there because he wasn't spending enough time in the country to justify the expense. Instead, with his firm's approval, he lived in a hotel when he was in Singapore or elsewhere in Asia and kept his Los Angeles house as his home base.

With more employees refusing to uproot themselves and their families for foreign postings, "virtual" expatriates like Bekins are on the rise, according to a survey by PriceWaterhouseCoopers.

Virtual expatriation arises when someone takes an assignment to manage an operation or area abroad without being located permanently in that country. By accumulating frequent-flier miles and using videoconferencing and communications technology to stay in touch with far-flung troops, the virtual expat is a new breed of manager that is multiplying.

For one thing, they are often less expensive than the traditional expatriate, whose allowances and other perks can end up costing employers three times as much as local hire.

More importantly, more executives are balking at an offer to pick up and move overseas for three or four years, particularly when working spouses and school-age children are involved. It is these reluctant employees who are forcing employers to come up with short-term and virtual international postings instead.

Virtual Postings Increase

According to the PriceWaterhouseCoopers survey of 270 organizations in 24 European countries employing 65,000 expatriates, there has been an increase in shorter-term, commuter, and virtual assignment during the past two years. Since the last survey in 1997, 44 percent more employers report increases in virtual assignments, and 54 percent report a boost in short-term postings. Overall, about two thirds of the companies surveyed employ virtual expats, up from 43 percent two years ago.

"Virtual assignments are a sign of how companies are being forced to become more flexible," says PriceWaterhouseCoopers's Mari Simpson, who edited the study. "They have to, if they don't, more and more employees will refuse to go on assignment." The survey included responses from such companies as Italy's Flat SpA, Hoechst AG of Germany, and Norsk Hydro ASA of Norway.

More than 80 percent of companies surveyed reported employees had turned down assignments because of dual-career problems or family issues. Other reasons for balking at overseas postings were the career risk of being far away from headquarters and less attractive overseas packages being offered by companies scrutinizing their expat costs.

Staying Close to Headquarters

Ian Hunter, for one, thinks it makes more business sense for him to be close to where budgeting decisions are made. Although he is in charge of the Middle East and Pakistan for SmithKline Beecham PLC, the Scottish-born Hunter isn't based in Istanbul, Turkey or Dubai, United Arab Emirates, but rather at the drug maker's London headquarters. "My role is to get resources for my team, and being based at headquarters helps me lobby for them," he says.

(Continued)

PRACTICAL PERSPECTIVE 7-8 (Continued)

Hunter, who is 57 years old, notes that being a "virtual" expat is less expensive for the company, even counting the cost of 16 to 17 weeks a year he travels. Yet he still sees a role for traditional expats, particularly as a way of quickly broadening the experience of promising young managers. Indeed, in the office next to his sits a young Arab assigned to London as an expatriate manager, and on the other side is a young Pakistani expatriate, who is his unit's newly appointed finance director.

To be sure, the survey found the traditional expat, with more than 50 percent of companies reporting growth in the number of assignments overall, is still out there. About 70 percent of companies also said they had focused on cutting expatriate costs during the past two years, with the main focus on reducing pay packages rather than cutting benefits such as housing and cost-of-living allowances.

It also found some companies were rejiggering compensation packages to reward expats who stuck it out through their entire foreign stint. One method: paying bonuses, allowances, or other forms of compensation near the back end of an employee's assignment rather than spreading it out on a monthly basis, which is commonly done now.

Korn/Ferry's Bekins asked his employer for location flexibility. "My job required me to be out of the office most of the time, so it really didn't matter where I was based," says Bekins, who accepted a new assignment [in early 1999] as head of the executive-search firm's European operations based in London. In his new role, Bekins says he sees more employers offering virtual postings to help lure top executives to their companies.

Theoretically, the virtual posting allows an executive to take an assignment without subjecting his or her family to the culture shock of an overseas move. These arrangements also expose the employee to global management issues, while permitting closer touch with the home office.

Improved Technology Is Key

Technology has made that much easier. Gerald Lukomski, 63, a Detroit native now based in Slough, England, as Motorola Inc.'s corporate vice president and director of Central Eastern Europe, the Middle East, and Africa, estimates he spends about 75 percent of his working time traveling. He never leaves home without a laptop and cell phone. And as an empty nester, he sometimes travels with his wife. "Our kids refer to us as 'runaway parents' because we are seldom in one place for very long," Lukomski says.

Of course, there are drawbacks to virtual assignments. Parachuting into a country for a few weeks every quarter may not be the most effective way of leading or building a local team. "Nothing can replace face-to-face communication," says Christine Communal, a senior researcher at England's Cranfield University's Center for Research into the Management of Expatriation. "If you do hit problems, the risk is that you haven't had time to properly build up a relationship with your local employees to help you work them out."

SOURCE: Excerpted from Julia Flynn, "E-mail, Cell Phones and Frequent-Flier Miles Let 'Virtual' Expats Work Abroad But Live At Home," *The Wall Street Journal* (October 25, 1999), p. A26. Permission conveyed through Copyright Clearance Center, Inc.

Summary

This chapter has described three options for international business enterprises to use in selecting management staff for their foreign operations: send someone from the home country, hire someone in the host country, or hire someone from a third country. It has also discussed the advantages and disadvantages of each option and presented the factors HRMs must consider when deciding whether to use a home-country national, a host-country national, or a third-country national. Also discussed are the various reasons why some expatriates fail in their foreign assignments.

KEY TERMS AND CONCEPTS

1. International human resource management function
2. Global mindset
3. International relocation and orientation
4. Risk exposure
5. Expatriate
6. Home-country, host-country, and third-country nationals
7. Familiarity with internal aspects of the firm
8. Not familiar with local culture, laws, political process, legal process, and other subtleties
9. Family may not adapt to local environment
10. Repatriate
11. Adaptation
12. "Goodwill"
13. The ethnocentric, polycentric, regiocentric, and geocentric staffing views
14. Characteristics that influence the choice of strategy
15. Stage of subsidiary development
16. Organizational structure
17. Style of management
18. Characteristics of personnel available at home
19. Host-country characteristics
20. Technology and expatriation

DISCUSSION QUESTIONS

1. Fundamentally, the international HRM functions consist of interplay among three dimensions. What are the three dimensions?

2. How does the international HRM function differ from the domestic HRM function?

3. Briefly describe the three approaches to international managerial staffing.

4. Discuss some of the advantages and disadvantages of each approach.

5. What are some of the problems Japanese expatriates encounter in the U.S. environment?

6. What is the appropriate staffing strategy for the following company characteristics?
   a. Has established foreign operations for a short period of time
   b. Has established a banking subsidiary in a foreign country
   c. Is transferring advanced, sophisticated technology to the foreign country
   d. Has an established foreign subsidiary in the foreign country to produce for local consumption
   e. Is to establish a new subsidiary in the foreign country
   f. Has developed a multidomestic strategy
   g. Has total revenues that rely only slightly on foreign sales

7. Discuss the host-country characteristics that influence the staffing method.

8. Discuss the way current technology aids HR managers in dealing with the international staffing problems discussed in the chapter.

EXERCISES

1. You are the manager of the international HRM function for a firm that needs to assign an executive to manage a subsidiary in a foreign country. You have approached a top-notch executive who refused the assignment because he or she wishes to remain in the home office because of upward movement aspirations. How would you convince the executive to accept the assignment? What would you say to him or her?

2. You are the manager of the international HRM function for a firm located in the United States that needs to assign an executive to Iran to establish operations there. The top management of the firm is inclined to send one of its own executives. What advice would you give to the top management?

3. You are the manager of the international HRM function for a firm whose staffing view is ethnocentric. You noticed that the firm has been spending far too much money assigning expatriates to manage its foreign operations and that the host-country nationals working for foreign subsidiaries are disgruntled because their managers are foreigners. What would you advise the firm's management to do?

4. You are the manager of the international HRM function for a firm located in Japan that needs to assign an executive to the United States to establish operations there. The top management of the firm is inclined to send one of its own executives. What advice would you give to the top management?

5. You are the manager of the international HRM function for a firm located in France that needs to assign an executive to the United States to establish operations there. The top management of the firm is inclined to send one of its own executives. What advice would you give to the top management?

ASSIGNMENT

Contact the manager of an international business corporation's international HRM function. Ask him or her to describe the company's international managerial staffing approaches. Prepare a short report for class presentation.

CASE 7-1

Deep in the Republic of Chevron

The Delta region of Southern Nigeria, where the mighty Niger River drains into the Atlantic Ocean, includes some of the most inhospitable territory on earth. It's the world's largest mangrove swamp, 14,000 square miles of thickets, channels, and lagoons all but impenetrable to any but the most practiced eye. It's also oil country, dotted with wells and flow stations, where about two million barrels of crude are collected each day and piped to central stations for transport abroad.

Helicopter is the preferred mode of transport, for the lucky few who can afford it. One of those is Leonard Hutto, the superintendent of Chevron operations in the eastern Niger Delta, and on this day, it was his chopper that hovered tentatively above one of Chevron's 30-odd oil stations in the area. The landing pad, a few hundred feet below, was thronged with hundreds of angry young Nigerians peering up at the midmorning sky, clearly shouting and shaking their fists. Seeing that they did not have guns, Hutto finally told the pilot to land.

At the same moment, down on the flow station, standing atop a table inside a tiny office, surrounded by dozens of young men brandishing machetes, Hutto's Nigerian assistant, Tony Okoaye, was relieved to hear the helicopter's engine drown out the shouts of his captors. To hear Okoaye tell it, a predawn phone call had jerked him out of bed: 400 villagers had invaded the site, carrying with them a long list of demands. By 7 A.M. Okoaye had driven to the station, only to be taken hostage. Okoaye, an American-educated engineer, normally prone to fits of delirious laughter, was not laughing. The young men, many drunk or high on marijuana, made him stand on the table for hours, slapping his pudgy frame and jabbing forefingers into the soft belly above his Tommy Hilfiger jeans. "Ah, hah!" they taunted, "You're a big man!"

They ordered him to shut down the oil wells. Okoaye did so, reluctantly. "You don't want to lose one barrel." Then they demanded to see his boss, Hutto. "We want to see the white man," they told him. "The American."

And so after a half-hour helicopter ride from Chevron's eastern headquarters in the city of Port Harcourt, the American oilman from south Texas had arrived. "What a pain," Hutto remembers thinking, as his chopper descended from the sky and the Nigerians scattered.

What came next on this particular morning would nonplus the most seasoned executive at a *Fortune 500* company, but to the Chevron oilman it was Kabuki. After the youths agreed to let him call a police escort, Hutto got into a Toyota pickup and drove a few miles to the village.

There, in the shade of a huge tree, he sat on a folding chair through the afternoon, listening to the community's grievances and demands: more scholarships for its youngsters and more regular meetings with Chevron, which the locals would get, and other demands, which they would not, including 25 jobs on the spot, about $27,000 in cash and an unspecified amount for wages they had lost while busy invading the oil station. Hutto instead, slipped $50 to the town chiefs for drinks, $20 to the youths, and another $20 to a group of young men who had let the air out of the tires of the Toyota—to reinflate them.

His assistant was released, the valves were opened at the oil wells and crude began coursing through the pipelines to the flow station. A few thousand barrels had been lost.

"Not a big deal," Hutto says.

Routine, in fact, in the Niger Delta, where men usually focused on finding and extracting hydrocarbons are forced to act as politicians, diplomats, and mediators. These are roles that

(Continued)

(Continued)

Western oilmen are increasingly playing as they seek crude in war-ravaged and lawless places like Angola and Congo, nations in name alone. Hutto spent 12 years in Congo, the former Zaire, where frequent crises forced him to sleep on an offshore oil platform, a fortress in the Atlantic Ocean several miles from a land of chaos. . . .

After work, Hutto drives home in his white Toyota Landcruiser through Port Harcourt's "go slows," or traffic jams. Boys hawking everything from toilet paper to power tools dart to his side with cries of "Master!" But they turn away quickly: a Nigerian policeman, gripping a tear-gas rifle in his hands, rides shotgun.

More policemen guard Hutto's villa, a two-story white house. Never married, Hutto lives alone, not counting the houseboy in the backyard bungalow. In the kitchen, Hutto shows me a large refrigerator and freezer. He keeps inside the 50 New York sirloin and T-bone steaks that he brought back from his last visit to the United States and has been cooking, at the rate of one a week, on a grill that he keeps in his living room.

He drops off his briefcase and gets ready for a visit to an expat bar called Cheers. As Hutto pulls out of his driveway, a skinny African dog watches indifferently. When he moved in, Hutto explains, the houseboy told him that the previous tenant had left the dog behind.

"Now it's yours," Hutto told the houseboy.

Hutto, 43, grew up in the small town of Taft in south Texas, watching his father and grandfather supplement their farmers' incomes by working in oil fields. Hutto got a degree in petroleum engineering at Texas A & M, then joined Chevron and worked in west Texas and the company's headquarters in San Francisco. But it was the Congo that hardened him for battle. Like many expatriate oilmen in Africa, he worked nonstop for 28 days, then went home for 28 days, in his case to a ranch-style house in Las Vegas. . . .

A year ago, Hutto accepted the assignment in Port Harcourt, a position Chevron considers difficult to fill because there is no rotation schedule, no other Americans, and constant interaction with Chevron's delta neighbors. In Lagos, the Americans live inside Chevron's headquarters, a sprawling campus surrounded by high walls, a surreal replica of America with wide streets and suburban houses straight out of Westchester County. Hutto is alone.

Questions

1. Discuss the appropriateness of Chevron's staffing approach, including Hutto and Okoaye in your discussion.

2. No doubt, this staffing approach is very expensive. Are there other viable staffing approaches available to Chevron? Why or why not?

3. Do you believe Chevron has a strong expatriate risk briefing program? Why or why not?

4. Is Chevron's staffing outlook in this case ethnocentric, polycentric, or geocentric? What in the case led you to that conclusion?

SOURCE: Excerpted from Norimitsu Onishi, "Deep in the Republic of Chevron," *The New York Times Magazine* (July 4, 1999), pp. 26–27. Copyright © 1999 by The New York Times Company. Reprinted by permission.

NOTES

1. Excerpted from "The China Challenge," *Anheuser-Busch Horizons* (Third Quarter 1997), p. 3.

2. For an account of the problems expatriates face, see R. L. Thornton and M. K. Thornton, "Personnel Problems in 'Carry the Flag' Missions in Foreign Assignments," *Business Horizons* (January–February 1995), pp. 59–65. For a discussion on the advantages and disadvantages of using expatriates see "Expatriates," *China-Britain Business Council* (2004). www.cbbc.org/market_ intelligence/hr/expats.html

3. The source of this discussion is S. B. Prasad and Y. K. Shetty, *An Introduction to Multinational Management* (Englewood Cliffs, NJ: Prentice-Hall, 1976), p. 152.

4. C. K. Prahalad and K. Lieberthal, "The End of Corporate Imperialism," *Harvard Business Review* (July–August 1998), p. 75.

5. For further discussion on this issue, see Y. Ling, S. W. Floyd, and D. C. Baldridge, "Toward a Model of Issue-Selling by Subsidiary Managers in Multinational Organizations," *Journal of International Business Studies,* 36 (2005), pp. 637–654. See also Y. Gong, Y. Luo, and M. K. Nyaw, "Human Resources and International Joint Venture Performance: A System Perspective," *Journal of International Business Studies,* 36 (2005), pp. 505–518.

6. E. L. Miller and J. L. Cheng, "A Closer Look at the Decision to Accept an Overseas Position," *Management International Review,* 18, no. 1 (1978), pp. 25–27.

7. See Denise E. Welch, "Globalization of Staff Movements: Beyond Cultural Adjustment," *Management International Review,* 43, no. 2 (2003), p.149.

8. M. Landler and M. Barbaro, "No, Not Always: Wal-Mart Discovers That Its Formula Doesn't Fit Every Culture," *The New York Times* (August 2, 2006), p. C4.

9. Charles Siler, "Recruiting Overseas Executives," *Overseas Business* (Winter 1990), p. 31.

10. Charles Butler, "A World of Trouble," *Sales Marketing Management,* 151, no. 9 (September 1999), p. 45.

11. Charles Butler, "A World of Trouble," *Sales Marketing Management,* 151, no. 9 (September 1999), p. 45.

12. Simcha Ronen, *Comparative and Multinational Management* (New York: John Wiley & Sons, 1986), pp. 505–554.

13. Siler, "Recruiting Overseas Executives," op cit., p. 77.

14. Cecil G. Howard, "Profile of the 21st-Century Expatriate Manager," *HR Magazine* (June 1992), pp. 93–100.

15. Ibid., p. 97.

16. C. Reynolds and R. Bennett, "The Career Couple Challenge," *Personnel Journal* (March 1991), p. 48.

17. Ken Coles, "Prudential Prepares People for Life Overseas," *Prudential Leader* (February 1998), p. 24.

18. J. S. Black and H. B. Gregersen, "The Right Way to Manage Expatriates," *Harvard Business Review* (March–April 1999), 53.

19. Matthew D. Levy and Soji Teramura, "Foreign Ownership: Japanese in U.S. Overcome Barriers," *Management Review* (December 1992), pp. 10–15.

20. For an in-depth discussion on the challenges foreign firms' managers face in managing personnel in China, see David Ahlstrom, "HRM of Firms in China: The Challenge of Managing Host Country Personnel," *Business Horizons* (May 2006). www.findarticles.com./tn-bus?pqt=HRM+of+firms+in+China&3A+The+challenge+of+managing+host+country+personnel%X=16%=9

21. Siler, "Recruiting Overseas Executives," op cit., p. 77.

22. Prasad and Shetty, *Introduction to Multinational Management,* op cit., p. 153.

23. F. Adams Jr., "Developing an International Workforce," *Columbia Journal of World Business,* 20 (20th Anniversary Issue 1985), pp. 23–25.

24. Byron Sebastian, "Integrating Local and Corporate Culture," *HR Magazine,* 41, no. 9 (1996), p. 114.

25. For a discussion on whether to use expatriates or locals in China, see "Expatriates," *China-Britain Business Council,* op cit.

26. H. V. Perlmutter and D. A. Heenan, "How Multinational Should Your Top Managers Be?" *Harvard Business Review,* 52 (November–December 1974), pp. 121–132. See also S. H. Robock and K. Simmonds, *International Business and Multinational Enterprises* (Homewood, IL: Irwin, 1989); J. L. Calof and P. W. Beamish, "The Right Attitude for International Success," *Business Quarterly* (Autumn 1994), pp. 105–110.

27. Rosalie L. Tung, "Selection and Training Procedures of U.S., European, and Japanese Multinationals," *California Management Review*, 25, no. 1 (1982), p. 61.

28. "The Discreet Charm of the Multicultural Multinational," *The Economist* (July 30, 1994), p. 58.

29. W. Zellner, L. Shepard, and D. Lindorff, "Wal-Mart Spoken Here," *Business Week* (June 23, 1997), p. 141.

30. "The Discreet Charm of the Multicultural Multinational," op cit., p. 8.

31. Deloitte and Touche Representatives, "One Company's Approach to Global Expansion," *Stores* (January 1998), p. S14.

32. A. Pazy and Y. Zeira, "Training Parent-Country Professionals in Host Organizations," *The Academy of Management Review*, 8, no. 2 (1983), pp. 262–272. See also Y. Zeira and A. Pazy, "Crossing National Borders to Get Trained," *Training and Development Journal*, 39 (October 1985), pp. 53–57.

33. Denis McCauley, "How Becton Dickinson Uses Cross-Border Teams to Make 'Transnationalism' Work," *Business International* (February 26, 1990), pp. 63–68.

34. Daniel Ondrack, "International Transfer of Managers in North American and European MNEs," *Journal of International Business Studies* (Fall 1985), pp. 1–19.

35. Ibid.

36. Ibid.

37. Ford S. Worthy, "You Can't Grow If You Can't Manage," *Fortune* (June 3, 1991), p. 88.

38. "The Discreet Charm of the Multicultural Multinational," op cit., p. 57.

39. "Corporate Coaches Support Global Network," *Personnel Journal* (January 1994), p. 58.

40. William C. Symonds, "The Next CEO's Key Asset: A Worn Passport," *Business Week* (January 19, 1998), pp. 76–77.

41. "The Discreet Charm of the Multicultural Multinational," op cit., p. 57.

42. Carol Hymowitz, "More American Chiefs Are Taking Top Posts at Overseas Concerns," *The Wall Street Journal Online* (October 20, 2005).

43. Siler, "Recruiting Overseas Executives," op cit., p. 76.

44. Ibid.

45. Prasad and Shetty, *Introduction to Multinational Management*, op cit., p. 154.

46. M. Z. Brooke and H. L. Remmers, *International Management and Business Policy* (Boston: Houghton Mifflin, 1978).

47. Lawrence G. Franko, "Who Manages Multinational Enterprises," *Columbia Journal of World Business*, 2, no. 8 (1973), pp. 30–42.

48. David Pulatie, "How Do You Ensure Success of Managers Going Abroad?" *Training and Development Journal* (December 1985), pp. 22.

49. Tung, "Selection and Training Procedures," op cit., p. 61.

50. For further information on this issue, see R. A. Belderbos and M. G. Heijltjes, "The Determinants of Expatriate Staffing by Japanese Multinationals in Asia: Control, Learning and Vertical Business Groups," *Journal of International Business Studies*, 36 (2005), pp. 341–354.

51. R. Brady and R. Boyle, "Combustion Engineering's Dislocated Joint Venture," *Business Week* (October 22, 1990), pp. 49–50.

52. See David Ahlstrom, "HRM of Foreign Firms in China," op cit.

53. Siler, "Recruiting Overseas Executives," op cit., p. 77.

54. See A. Reihart and C. Vitzhum, "Spain: Cafes, Beaches, and Call Centers," *BusinessWeek* (September 5, 2005), p. 51.

55. See D. Rouzies, M. Segalla, and B. A. Weitz, "Cultural Impact on European Staffing Decisions in Sales Management," *International Journal of Research in Marketing*, 20, no. 1 (2003), pp. 67–85.

56. D. A. Heenan, "The Corporate Expatriate: Assignment to Ambiguity," *Columbia Journal of World Business* (May–June 1970), pp. 49–54.

57. A. J. Almaney, "Intercultural Communication and the MNC Executive," *Columbia Journal of World Business*, 9, no. 4 (1974), pp. 23–28.

58. A. Rahim, "A Model for Developing Key Expatriate Executives," *Personnel Journal* (April 1983), pp. 312–317.

59. Richard Pooley, "Bridging the Cultural Divide," *Computing Business* (April 20, 2006). www.whatpc.com.uk/computing-business/features/2153953/bridgi

60. See Helen Becket, "IT Management: Supplier Relationship Management" (April 23, 2006). www
.ComputerWeekly.com/Articles/2006/01/23/213761/Bridgin

61. Heenan, "The Corporate Expatriate," op cit.

62. F. E. Cotton, "Some Interdisciplinary Problems in Transferring Technology and Management," *Management International Review,* 13, no. 1 (1973), pp. 71–77.

63. Rahim, "A Model for Developing Key Expatriate Executives," op cit.

64. See Joseph Gamble, "Introducing Western-Style HRM Practices to China: Shopfloor Perceptions in a British Multinational," *Journal of World Business,* 41 (2006), pp. 328–343.

65. See Joseph Gamble, "The Rhetoric of the Customer Control in China," *Work, Employment & Society,* 21, no. 1 (2007), pp. 7–25.

66. Heenan, "The Corporate Expatriate," op cit.

67. D. N. Israeli, M. Banai, and Y. Zeira, "Women Executives in MNC Subsidiaries," *California Management Review,* 23, no. 1 (1980), pp. 53–63.

68. Nancy J. Adler, "Re-entry: Managing Cross-Cultural Transitions." Paper presented at the annual meeting of the Academy of International Business New Orleans, LA (October 1980).

69. L. Clague and N. B. Krupp, "International Personnel: The Repatriation Problem," *The Personnel Administrator* (April 1978), p. 32.

70. See Rosalie L. Tung, "Career Issues in International Assignments," *The Academy of Management Executive,* 2, no. 3 (1988), pp. 241–244.

71. Cecil G. Howard, "The Expatriate Manager and the Role of the MNC," *Personnel Journal,* 10, no. 10 (October 1980), pp. 830–844.

72. Michael G. Harvey, "The Other Side of Foreign Assignments: Dealing with the Repatriation Dilemma," *Columbia Journal of World Business,* 17, no. 1 (Spring 1982), p. 53.

73. D. W. Kendall, "Repatriation: An Ending and a Beginning," *Business Horizons* (November–December 1981), p. 23.

74. Harvey, "The Other Side of Foreign Assignments," op cit.

75. Rosalie L. Tung, "Strategic Management of Human Resources in the Multinational Enterprise," *Human Resource Management,* 23, no. 2 (1984), pp. 129–143.

76. For further discussion on this issue, refer to T. Buck, I. Filatochev, N. Demia, and M. Wright, "Insider Ownership, Human Resources Strategies and Performance in a Transition Economy," *Journal of International Business Studies,* 34 (2003), pp. 530–549.

77. P. Lorange and D. C. Murphy, "Strategy and Human Resources: Concepts and Practices," *Human Resource Management,* 22, no. 1–2 (1983), pp. 111–113.

78. L. K. Stroh and P. M. Caligiuri, "Increasing Global Competitiveness Through Effective People Management," *Journal of World Business,* 1, no. 1 (Spring 1998), p. 2.

79. SOURCE: U.S. Department of Labor, Bureau of Labor Statistics (March 2007). www.stats.bls.gov

80. R. L. Desatnick and M. L. Bennett, *Human Resource Management in the Multinational Company* (New York: Nichols, 1978).

81. Rosalie L. Tung, "Selection and Training of Personnel for Overseas Assignments," *Columbia Journal of World Business,* 16, no. 1 (1981), pp. 68–78.

82. Edwin L. Miller, "The Selection Decision for an International Assignment: A Study of Decision-Makers' Behavior," *Journal of International Business Studies,* 3, no. 2 (1972), pp. 49–65.

83. Tung, "Selection and Training of Personnel," op cit.

84. Charles Butler, "A World of Trouble," *Sales and Marketing Management,* 151, no. 9 (September 1999), p. 5.

85. G. M. Harvey, "The Executive Family: An Overlooked Variable in International Assignments," *Columbia Journal of World Business* (Spring 1985), pp. 84–91.

86. Tung, "Selection and Training Procedures of U.S., European, and Japanese Multinationals," op cit., pp. 57–71.

87. Tung, "Selection and Training of Personnel," op cit.

88. See Jie Shen, "International Training and Development: Theory and Reality," *Journal of Management Development,* 24, no. 7 (2005), pp. 656–666.

89. Tung, "Selection and Training Procedures," op cit.

90. E. Harari and Y. Zeira, "Training Expatriates for Assignments in Japan," *California Management Review*, 20, no. 4 (1977), pp. 56–61.

91. For extensive coverage of this topic, refer to Charlene Marmer Solomon, "How Does Your Global Talent Measure Up? (International Personnel Performance Measures)," *Personnel Journal*, 73, no. 10 (October 1994), pp. 96–108.

92. Harari and Zeira, "Training Expatriates," op cit.

93. J. T. Gullahorn and J. E. Gullahorn, "An Extension of the U-Curve Hypothesis," *Journal of Social Sciences*, 19, no. 3 (1963), pp. 33–47.

94. Nancy J. Adler, "Cross-Cultural Management Research: The Ostrich and the Trend," *The Academy of Management Review*, 8, no. 3 (1983), pp. 226–232.

95. Ibid.

96. Tung, "Selection and Training of Personnel," op cit.

97. This discussion draws from Kevin Maney, "Technology Is 'Demolishing' Time, Distance," *USA Today Tech Report* (April 24, 1997). linkinghub.elssevier.com/retrieve/pii/50360835298000527

8

EFFECTIVE INTERNATIONAL HUMAN
RESOURCE MANAGEMENT

Michael Bonsignore, in 1997 chairman and CEO of $7 billion instrument-controls maker Honeywell, was the quintessential global executive. Having traveled extensively as the son of an Army doctor, during his own stint as an officer in the Navy and for Honeywell, Bonsignore has lived around the world—in Venezuela, Peru, Mexico, Germany, and Belgium. He spoke four languages: English, Spanish, French, and Italian. Since becoming head of the company in 1993, he had made sure that other executives at the Minneapolis-based company mirrored his own broad exposure to various cultures. In several key instances, he's picked foreign-born managers for his most senior posts and ensured that other executives routinely were given short- and long-term assignment around the globe. By 1997, 40 percent of Honeywell's sales and one-third of its employees were outside the United States.[1] In 2002, David M. Cote was appointed chairman and CEO. As of March 2007, Honeywell International employs more than 100,000 people in 95 countries (www.honeywell.com).

Learning Objectives of the Chapter

As indicated in Chapter 7, international business enterprises use three types of executives to staff their foreign subsidiaries: home-country nationals (expatriates), host-country nationals (locals), and third-country nationals (by definition, also expatriates). Use of host-country nationals by companies to manage their foreign subsidiaries has become more and more popular in recent years. But there is no doubt that the home country and third countries will continue to be important sources of expatriate executives used by international businesses. This is especially true as more and more multinational corporations (MNCs) transform themselves into global corporations and establish a global strategy. These expatriate executives can move readily from country to country and perform effectively no matter where they are. As pointed out in

Chapter 7, using expatriates can be very costly, especially when the expatriate wants to return home prematurely from the foreign assignment or when the wrong person was selected for the foreign assignment. This suggests that international business enterprises need to develop and implement effective international human resource management (HRM) programs. After studying this chapter, you should be able to do the following:

1. Discuss the additional functions of the international HRM

2. Propose how to reduce expatriate failures

3. Point out how to select the right expatriate

4. Discuss how to find and develop global expatriates

5. Show how to administer expatriate programs

6. Discuss expatriate compensation policy

7. Discuss international labor laws

8. Discuss organizational culture and development of multicultural teams

9. Show how current technologies help the HRM function

The International HRM Function

International HRM consists of an interplay among three dimensions:[2]

1. The broad function: procurement, allocation, and utilization.

2. Country categories: the home country, or where the headquarters is located; the host country, or where the subsidiary is located; and third countries, or other countries that may be a source of labor.

3. Types of employees: home-country employees, host-country employees, and third-country employees.

The factors that differentiate international from domestic HRM are additional functions and activities, a broader perspective, more involvement in employees' personal lives, changes in emphasis as the workforce mix varies, risk exposure, more external influences, and aiding management in staffing foreign operations (discussed in Chapter 4).[3]

Additional Functions and Activities

Operating in an international environment, an MNC's HRM department performs numerous activities that would not be required in the domestic environment. The department must deal with developing a global mindset, international taxation, exchange rates, international relocation and orientation, administrative services for expatriates (employees sent from the home country to manage firms' foreign subsidiaries), host government relations, language and cultural training, and establishing training programs for local workers in the foreign market.

Developing a Global Mindset in the Organization. A key issue HRM is confronted with is how to transform the organization internally to become globally oriented. In today's environment, even for employees who may not go abroad, it is necessary to constantly sensitize everyone to the notion that the company is in a global business and that different cultures require unique managerial styles.[4] In this respect, most colleges and universities have implemented some sort of program to develop an international mindset in their students. (For example, that is what this book aims to do.)

International Taxation. Expatriates normally have both home- and host-country tax liabilities. HRM must ensure that there is neither a tax incentive nor a tax disincentive attached to any particular assignment.[5]

Exchange Rates. Fluctuating exchange rates with regard to payroll for employees working abroad must be monitored at all times, and as in the case of tax incentives or disincentives, HRM must make sure that the employee is not financially harmed by negative fluctuating exchange rates. For instance, U.S. major league baseball players who sign contracts to play with a team in Canada or Canadian major league baseball players who sign contracts to play with a team in the United States at a set amount of money could lose or gain by fluctuating exchange rates—depending on the direction of the fluctuation. If in Canada they were paid in Canadian dollars while the U.S. dollar became more expensive, they would be taking a pay cut—the Canadian dollars would buy fewer U.S. dollars. Of course, in this case a Canadian who came to play for a team in the United States would have great benefits due to the weakening of the U.S. dollar against the Canadian dollar—the U.S. dollars would buy more Canadian dollars. As another example, on January 1, 2002, the European Union (EU) adopted a single currency, the euro. On that day, 1 euro cost U.S.$0.98; today, March 9, 2007, 1 euro costs U.S$1.30. Thus, the effects would be the same as in the Canadian example.

International Relocation and Orientation. International relocation and orientation entails making arrangements for predeparture training; providing immigration and travel details; providing housing, shopping, medical care, recreation, and schooling information; and finalizing compensation details such as the issuance of salary in the foreign country, determination of various overseas allowances, and taxation treatment.

Providing International Administrative Services. Providing administrative services is a time-consuming and complicated activity, in part because policies and procedures are not always clear-cut and sometimes conflict with local conditions. For example, the practice of testing employees for alcohol and drugs may be legally required in a foreign country but may not be legally required in the home country, or vice versa. As another example, the Chinese government once passed a mandate requiring that expatriates had to take an AIDS test on returning to China after being away for a certain length of time—although the mandate was not enforced. Had the Chinese government enforced this mandate, how would a Chinese company have reconciled this with the prospective expatriate who may refuse the assignment because of such conditions?

Foreign Government Relations. It is usually much less difficult for HRM managers to obtain work permits and other important documents required by the expatriate if the international business enterprise maintains a good relationship with the host-country's government. Of course, in many countries, obtaining work permits and other important documents requires payment of "whitemail" bribes to the issuing officials, as discussed in Chapter 2.

Providing Foreign Language and Cultural Training. Providing verbal and nonverbal language and cultural training is another important activity of the international HRM. Expatriates require at least some basic knowledge of the language of the country in which they will be conducting business, as well as a lot of its cultural ways; otherwise, how will they communicate?

Establishing Programs Aimed at Developing Local Workers' Skills. The international HRM department must create and implement programs aimed at training local workers—that is, at developing local workers' skills to fit the needs of the organization, especially in transitional economies such as China,[6] and the techniques used to train workers usually must be modified to fit the specific culture.[7] For example, as pointed out in Chapter 4, Panasonic implemented a military-like boot camp for workers at its Beijing television tube plant. Xian-Jenssen Pharmaceutical Ltd., a Chinese-U.S. joint venture, spent several thousand dollars to train each local employee; it offered in-house courses in sales, accounting, English, and computer usage.[8]

Broader Perspective

International HRM managers are confronted with the problem of designing and administering programs for more than one national group of employees. As a result, they need to take a more global view; for example, they must make sure that employees are treated fairly, regardless of nationality.

More Involvement in Employees' Lives

Because the international HRM department must be involved in the selection and training of expatriates, and because it must ensure that expatriates understand housing arrangements, health care, cost-of-living allowances, taxes, and so on, it becomes much more involved in their personal lives than in the personal lives of domestic employees. For example, Jeanne Dennison, former director of HR of International Telecommunications Group at Bell Atlantic, said that expatriate employees will often look to HR to learn all about things that affect their families, and you can get involved with them at a level unheard of with domestic employees.[9]

Changes in HRM Emphasis as the Workforce Mix Varies

As the corporation's foreign operations mature, the HRM department may have to change its international functions. If the enterprise employs mostly host-country nationals, the department would no longer place as much emphasis on expatriate training, relocation, and tax programs. The emphasis would probably shift to other programs, such as bringing host-country nationals to the home office for development.

Risk Exposure

There is a risk of possible terrorist attacks in the foreign country, especially in countries where some groups hold hostile feelings toward a country or where there is a strong possibility of the expatriate being kidnapped for ransom or for political reasons, such as the current (2008) terrorists' war against Western values, especially U.S. values. The September 11, 2001, attack on the United States is of great concern to U.S. international business corporations and their expatriates. In the Middle East, expatriates live in gated communities.[10] Mexico and Colombia, for example, are very high-risk nations with respect to kidnapping for ransom, and the Middle East is a very dangerous place with respect to kidnappings and killings for political reasons.

In 1996, a Japanese Sanyo executive was taken hostage and released only after a $2 million ransom was paid. According to American International Group, an insurer, U.S. companies pay fat premiums as kidnapping insurance for their executives in Mexico. And many top American businessmen live as virtual prisoners of their own security.[11] Of course, kidnapping for ransom is not the only problem expatriates face—they are often attacked for robbery as well (see Practical Perspective 8.1). And some U.S. and other Western expatriates working in Iraq during the war have been kidnapped and killed. The training programs administered by the HRM department must therefore include briefing the expatriate about such risk exposure.[12] Box 8.1 describes four steps for helping the expatriates abroad.

Furthermore, preparing an employee to work abroad is very costly. This preparation investment is high-risk in the sense that many employees want to return home soon after they land in the foreign country. The international HRM department must make great efforts to lower the incidence of expatriates returning early from foreign assignments.

PRACTICAL PERSPECTIVE 8-1

Very Risky Business

The last phone call Peter Zarate, an ex-Navy SEAL from California, made was to his wife. A commercial real-estate broker working in Mexico City, Zarate stayed late at the office one night in mid-December to close several big deals. Around 8 o'clock, he picked up his cell phone, called his wife and told her that he would be home soon. Ten minutes later, carrying a briefcase and dressed in a dark blue pin-stripe suit, he walked out of the three-story building on Galileo Street where his employer, the American company Cushman & Wakefield, has its offices.

Apparently Zarate had trouble getting a cab, because around 8:20 he called his wife again and said that he was going to walk to a taxi stand down the street. These would be "sitio" cabs—meaning they had license plates and were registered with the government—and so would be more or less safe. Unlicensed gypsy cabs have become infamous in Mexico City for elaborate mugging and kidnapping schemes, and in fact, a few days earlier an American had been savagely beaten in the back of one. The United States Embassy has issued strong warnings against taking them.

PRACTICAL PERSPECTIVE 8-1 (Continued)

According to the account of a friend who was later involved in the police investigation, Zarate never made it to the taxi stand. He may have been shoved into a gypsy cab or he may have just gotten into one. At any rate, he found himself held at gunpoint by at least two men and tailed by several more in another gypsy cab. First they beat him—beat him so badly that the friend, who identified the body, thought Zarate had been shot in the head. And then they did what robbers in most gypsy cab holdups do: they drove him around from one automatic teller to another, taking out cash. The problem was that Zarate's bank account limited the amount of cash he could withdraw to around $200, and he wasn't even wearing any expensive jewelry. But the robbers looked in his briefcase and there they struck gold. They found papers that told them where he lived.

SOURCE: Excerpted from Sebastian Junger, "Very Risky Business," *The New York Times Magazine* (March 8, 1998), p. 52. Used with permission of the author.

Box 8.1   Protecting Businesspeople Abroad

[Chris] Marquet [senior managing director (1998) of Kroll International, a New York–based security firm] describes four steps for helping protect businesspeople abroad.

Step 1: *Information and intelligence.* Companies should assess the risks in the countries where they send employees. Such information is available through the U.S. State Department, the British Foreign Office, and private firms. The information should include travel advisories, such as what parts of certain cities to avoid, and there should be a mechanism for getting that information to anyone who needs it via the Internet, company intranet, or fax.

Step 2: *Planning and preparation.* Have a crisis plan and test it frequently. The plan should describe specific solutions for hypothetical crises, such as kidnapping or extortion.

Step 3: *Prevention.* A preventive program involves special training on how to ward off incidents. For example, awareness training can teach people how to avoid being followed. Prevention also involves policies and procedures such as making sure all travelers are met at the foreign airport, sometimes with an escort or armored vehicle. It's also necessary to protect an expatriate's home as well as his or her office.

Step 4: *Response mechanism.* Companies should have plans in place to respond quickly and effectively to crises. In some countries, an evacuation plan may be necessary.

SOURCE: Helen Frank Bensimon, "Is It Safe to Work Abroad?" *Training & Development,* 52, no. 8 (August 1998), p. 20. Reprinted with permission.

In 2006, there were numerous conflicts in the Middle East that required several thousands of expatriates to be repatriated (brought back home or to a safe place), presenting multinational enterprises' HRM with an enormous challenge. As this was being written (September 19, 2006), CNN News reported a military coup that had just occurred in Bangkok, Thailand, where there are several thousands of expatriates. Martial law was eventually imposed in Thailand. HRMs in many enterprises in that country were faced with the challenge of carefully monitoring the situation and making plans for taking the expatriates out or determining ways to protect them if the coup presented any danger to them. (Martial law was lifted on January 26, 2007, in 41 of Thailand's 76 provinces but remained in place in the other 35 provinces.)

More External Influences

The type of government, the state of the country's economy, and the generally accepted business practices in the host countries are factors that affect international HRM. These factors vary from one host country to another. The cost of labor and the extent to which labor is organized also vary from country to country. Unions in Japan are far less hostile toward management than unions in Detroit, Michigan.

To find the right managers for foreign operations, managers of international HRM must study the complex situations that exist in each country. In other words, to be effective in their role, international HRM managers must do their homework.

Aiding Managers in Staffing Foreign Operations

As discussed in Chapter 4, a challenge that management faces is placing the right managers in their foreign operations. International HRM managers can help management in this respect by helping them reduce expatriate failures. Understanding Japanese and European expatriation practices can be helpful to HRM managers in this respect.

Japanese MNCs' Expatriation Practices

A comparative study of the expatriate selection and training procedures of U.S. and Japanese MNCs found that Japanese MNCs experienced a significantly lower incidence of expatriate failure than U.S. MNCs. Eighty-six percent of the Japanese companies reported a recall rate of less than 5% (in the United States, 24% reported a recall rate of less than 10%), 10% reported a recall rate between 6% and 10%, and 14% reported a recall rate of between 11% and 19%.[13] The study's results provided numerous insights into the strengths of Japanese MNCs relative to their strategies in the HRM function.

Importance of the HR Function. The HR function is centralized, and the head of the personnel division reports directly to the CEO.[14] The HR division wields considerable authority in the overall aspects of the corporation's operation, such as recruitment, career development, evaluation, promotion, and compensation for all employees.

Long Duration of Foreign Assignments. The average duration of foreign assignments in Japanese corporations is 4.67 years.[15] (Foreign assignments in U.S. companies are usually for 3 years or less.) During the first year of his or her foreign assignment, the Japanese expatriate would focus mainly on adaptation. In the second year, the expatriate would become more active in managerial activities, but this year is still considered a period of adjustment. In the third year, the expatriate begins to function at full capacity.

Support System at Corporate Headquarters. Japanese firms provide a comprehensive support network established for the purpose of setting the expatriate's mind at ease once he or she arrives at the foreign market. The support network includes a division whose sole purpose is to look after expatriates' needs, including the provision of mental and financial support; a mentor system, which implies certain obligations and responsibilities on the part of the corporation toward the expatriate; the showing of greater concern for the total person, including the company's trying to find reasons for expatriates who have gone to the foreign country alone to periodically visit the headquarters or some other operation in Japan, enabling them to visit their families at the same time; and the practice of having expatriates who have been around for a long time provide assistance to new expatriates.[16]

Criteria for Selecting Expatriates. Because the prospective expatriate usually has been with the enterprise for many years, managers of Japanese international firms normally have access to the information required to assess the candidate's suitability for the foreign assignment. The strong group orientation and the after-hours socializing practices of Japanese corporations enable managers to become familiar with employees' family background. And most Japanese companies keep a detailed personnel inventory on all their permanent staff.[17]

Training for Foreign Assignments. The system of lifetime employment and the long-range perspective of many Japanese firms results in their investing large sums of money to train and develop employees for future foreign assignments. The results of one study indicated that 57% of the Japanese MNCs surveyed sponsor formal training programs for their expatriates. The programs, in general, consist of the following components: language training, general training, field training, graduate programs in a foreign country, in-house training programs, and use of external agents.[18] The study also revealed that American MNCs tend to be reluctant to invest as much as Japanese firms do in such programs because employment in American MNCs tends to be short term—if they invest in an employee's development and he or she leaves, the company will not retrieve the costs.[19]

The above suggests that Japanese firms place much greater emphasis on preparing expatriates than do U.S. firms. This may be because Japan's large population, in a small country with relatively few natural resources, forces Japan to rely on international business much more than does the United States, which is a large country with an abundance of resources. Japanese firms must therefore invest more in preparing expatriates than do U.S. firms, although the changes that have taken place around the globe during the past couple of decades are making U.S. firms more and more dependent on international business. In effective preparation of expatriates, Japanese firms have an advantage over U.S. firms in part because of the programs the Japanese have implemented and in part because they hold a wider global business perspective. But it should be pointed out that the number of employees in Japan working under the lifetime employment system is gradually lessening as Japanese MNCs, like U.S. MNCs, gradually transfer operations to foreign countries—for example, Honda and Toyota moved some of their assembly plants to the United States.

However Japanese expatriation practices are not devoid of problems. Japan's culture is very homogeneous, unlike U.S. culture, which is very heterogeneous. Thus, lengthy foreign assignments often create problems in children's education, and if the family adopts new cultural traits in the foreign country, they may be ostracized by the community for "foreign" behavior when they return to Japan. Furthermore, reluctance among the younger generation in Japan to undertake a foreign assignment is increasing.[20]

European MNCs' Expatriation Practices

A study revealed that like Japanese MNCs, European MNCs have had a much lower expatriate recall rate than U.S. MNCs.[21] The executives interviewed in the study believed that the strong global orientation of their organization is a primary reason for the low expatriate failure rate. This orientation derived in part from the "spirit of internationalism" among the Europeans. This spirit is attributed to several factors.[22]

Smallness of European Markets. Domestic markets in European nations tend to be small, and firms have had to export in order to expand market size. On the other hand, the vastness of the United States has for most of its existence been able to sustain most firms' growth objectives. Historically, U.S. firms did not needed to transact business in foreign markets to the extent they do today. As a result, European firms have over time developed a much greater global perspective than have U.S. firms.

Europeans like to travel abroad. Europeans tend to travel extensively. Because of the size and proximity of neighboring nations, Europeans are naturally exposed to numerous foreign people and cultures, and they learn multiple languages, unlike Americans, who tend to learn only their own culture and language. Europeans have therefore developed an international perspective to a much greater extent than have Americans—most Europeans can easily identify any country on a global map.

A Tradition of Interaction in Foreign Lands. European traditions and economic conditions have for many centuries encouraged interaction in foreign markets and even emigration to foreign lands. The United States has not developed such a tradition to the extent that Europe has.

A History of Colonization. In Europe, there is a legacy of "the empire," the colonization of nations around the globe. Portugal, Spain, England, and France once colonized much of the world. Therefore, European commercial enterprises have a long history of establishing operations in foreign nations and have accumulated much experience in dealing with people in other nations. Many European expatriates are therefore assigned to well-established foreign markets.

This spirit of internationalism provides European international businesses a large pool of individuals who can easily be developed for cross-national assignments. This spirit also makes European spouses more adaptable to foreign cultures than American spouses. In addition, as in the case of Japanese MNCs, European MNCs have had a long-range orientation and a low rate of turnover among managerial personnel. As a result, they are also willing to invest heavily in training and development programs, and they have designed comprehensive expatriate support programs.[23] Therefore, European corporations, like their Japanese counterparts, have had a greater pool of adaptable employees to transfer to foreign nations than have U.S. businesses. Nevertheless, many European companies now face new expatriation problems, such as the need to assign expatriates from dual-career families.

Implications of U.S., Japanese, and European MNCs' Expatriation Practices

Based on the analysis of the problems in HR planning in many U.S. international business enterprises and of the comparative strengths of their Japanese and European counterparts, the following expatriate staffing implications may be drawn:[24]

1. Top management in international firms must pay a great deal more attention to the international HRM function. This function should have adequate representation in the overall corporate strategic planning.

2. Since inadequate relational skills contribute heavily to expatriate failures, managers selecting expatriates need to pay more attention to this criterion.

3. Top management in international businesses must sponsor rigorous training programs aimed to prepare expatriates for foreign assignments. This means choosing the right program for the right person and for the right nation. Since the expatriate's lack of sensitivity to the foreign country's culture is a primary reason for his or her failure, the programs must include cross-cultural sensitivity development. The programs should also address potential repatriation problems.

4. Top management may have to be flexible regarding the length of the foreign assignment. In some situations, a short-term assignment may be appropriate—for example, when an expatriate is sent abroad to repair some aspect of the manufacturing facilities. In other situations, however, such as sending an expatriate to develop a new foreign market, a longer-term assignment may be appropriate.

5. International business enterprises must also develop programs to attend to the needs and aspirations of expatriates and eliminate the information gap so that expatriates do not feel too alienated from their old environment. In this respect, the following ideas have been proposed:[25]

   - A mentor program should be established to keep abreast of the expatriate's career progression throughout his or her international and domestic experience.
   - The international business enterprise should establish a unit in its HRM function for career planning, meeting regularly with expatriates and repatriates.
   - The firm's home office should maintain contact with expatriates by sending them newspapers, company newsletters, and mail.

   And these days, the advent of new information technology, such as the Internet, e-mail, voice mail, videoconferencing, teleconferencing online newsletters, and shared databases, provides ways for global employees to easily remain linked to their home country and colleagues.[26]

6. Since the family is a prime reason for expatriate failures, managers making the selection must assess the expatriate's spouse and children to ascertain their adaptability to the foreign country.

7. International enterprises need to use women in their foreign operations to a much greater extent then they do now. In the United States, this can perhaps be facilitated by the fact that in U.S. colleges there are now more female M.B.A. students than male M.B.A. students enrolled.

Incorporating the above framework into the international business enterprise's overall HRM strategies will have positive consequences. It is likely to reduce the incidence of ineffective or poor expatriate performance. MNCs can no longer rely solely on technology to gain a competitive edge in international markets; they must also rely on international HRM planning because the organization and technology are managed and operated by people.

Selecting and Training the Right Person

In essence, expatriate failures can be reduced by selecting the right person and implementing programs for assessing a prospective expatriate's effectiveness potential, finding and developing global executives, preparing expatriates, and providing effective compensation.

Selecting the Right Expatriate

As suggested above, expatriate failures can be reduced by selecting the right person for the assignment. "When an expatriate manager fails in a foreign assignment, it is usually not due to technical incompetence; it is due to improper selection."[27] To select the right expatriate for the assignment, David Pulatie, the former vice president and director of employee relations at Motorola, Inc., recommended the following steps:[28]

1. Do an extremely sophisticated job of selecting the people you send to the foreign country—not only the expatriate, but his or her family as well. This requires private, extensive interviews to evaluate each candidate's family situation, lifestyle, and financial picture. For example, if the expatriate has family problems or schooling, medical, or financial responsibilities, adjustment overseas will be difficult. The expatriate will not be able to devote his or her full attention to the assignment.

2. Find out why the candidate wants the foreign assignment; what he or she expects to get out of it, and if the expectations are realistic; what his or her attitude is about living in a foreign country; and what his or her tolerance is.

3. Select only top-notch, proven people. This will help in both the expatriation and the repatriation processes (discussed later).

4. Familiarize the expatriate and the accompanying family members with the country they are going to (discussed later).

5. Set up an administrative branch whose sole function is supporting your international staff (as previously discussed).

Rosalie L. Tung, a professor of international business at Simon Fraser University in Canada, has developed a framework of the expatriate selection process.[29] Her framework contains several notable features.[30] First, by requiring information about whether the position could be filled by a host-country national, the framework brings up the issue of employee nationality. Second, the framework follows a low-risk strategy in selecting expatriates. Third, the framework takes a contingency approach to selecting and training expatriates in that it recognizes that varying assignments require different degrees of interaction.

Assessing Expatriates' Effectiveness Potential. It is apparent from the preceding sections that individuals being considered for foreign assignments require certain characteristics that would not be required for local assignments. (For an illustration, refer again to Case 7.1 in Chapter 7.) As executive search consultants agree, to be effective, expatriate managers must listen well, be patient, and have respect—perhaps even enthusiasm—for other cultures.[31] Kai Lindholst, formerly a managing partner for Egon Zehnder International Inc., a leading executive search firm, puts it this way:

> You are looking for an open-minded person who is quite flexible and tolerant of other ways of doing things. If the person can only eat at McDonald's every day of the week, why go abroad? If the expatriate manager has a family also making the move, they must share in the enthusiasm in order for the relocation to work. Uprooting a family can be traumatic. . . . Most overseas managers seem to know of at least one divorce resulting from an overseas assignment.[32]

Based on published research, Professors Mark Mendenhall and Gary Oddou developed a framework outlining the special characteristics required by expatriates.[33] Their framework, which can be used to assess expatriates' effectiveness potential, consists of four dimensions as components of the expatriate adjustment process. The four dimensions and subfactors are outlined in Box 8.2. If a prospective expatriate demonstrates weakness on those dimensions, he or she may not be adaptable in a foreign culture. Mendenhall and Oddou also identified some techniques currently available to test the strengths and weaknesses in the dimensions and subfactors outlined in Box 8.2.[34]

Box 8.2   Dimensions of the Effective Expatriate

The Self-Oriented Dimension

- The effective expatriate has the ability to replace pleasurable activities at home with similar, yet different, activities in the foreign culture—for example, replacing baseball in the United States with soccer in Brazil.
- He or she is able to deal with the stress that the foreign culture generally produces for expatriates. He or she has "stability zones"—for example, meditation, writing in diaries, engaging in favorite pastimes, and religious worship—to which he or she can retreat when conditions in the host culture become overly stressful.
- He or she possesses the necessary technical competence.

The Others-Oriented Dimension

- The effective expatriate is able to develop long-lasting friendships with locals. The close relationship aids local mentors in guiding the expatriate through the intricacies and complexity of the new culture; for example, the local mentor provides feedback that helps the expatriate understand local worker expectations and attitudes and helps the expatriate in his or her efforts to train and develop local replacements.
- The expatriate is able to communicate with locals (he or she has a good command of the local language). This enables the expatriate to become more familiar and intimate with locals and to create and foster interpersonal relationships.

The Perceptual Dimension

- The effective expatriate has the ability to understand why locals behave the way they do and to make correct attributions about the causes of locals' behavior. This helps the expatriate predict how the locals will behave toward him or her in the future.
- The expatriate is nonjudgmental and nonevaluative when interpreting the behavior of locals. He or she seeks to update his or her perceptions and beliefs as new information arises.

The Cultural-Toughness Dimension

- The effective expatriate is able to adapt to the toughness of the specific culture (for example, it may be more difficult for a Canadian expatriate to adapt in Nigeria than in England).

SOURCE: Adapted from M. Mendenhall and G. Oddou, "The Dimensions of Expatriate Acculturation: A Review," *The Academy of Management Review,* 10, no. 1 (1985), pp. 39–47. Used by permission of the Academy of Management.

Relative to *the self-oriented dimension*, assessors already possess the means of evaluating technical expertise. They have access to various psychological tests and evaluation techniques, as well as to numerous instruments for measuring stress levels and stress-reducing programs. To assess *the others-oriented dimension*, assessors can solicit in-depth evaluations from a prospective expatriate's superiors, subordinates, friends, and acquaintances. Regarding *the perceptual dimension,* there are numerous psychological tests available to measure the rigidity and flexibility of an individual's perceptual and evaluative tendencies. These tests include the Cognitive Rigidity Test, the F-test, the Guilford-Zimmerman Temperament Survey, and the Alport-Vernon Study of Values. The prospective expatriate's cultural-toughness dimension can be assessed on the basis of the toughness of the specific country in concert with the above needs. That is, the assessor should feel confident that the applicant's scores on the battery of evaluation tests are high enough to handle the specific country.[35]

Professor S. Ronen also identified a group of attributes for expatriate success, including the following:

- Tolerance for ambiguity
- Behavioral flexibility
- Nonjudgmental
- Cultural empathy and low ethnocentrism
- Interpersonal skills
- Belief in the mission
- Interest in foreign experience
- Willingness to acquire new patterns of behavior and attitudes
- An adaptive and supportive spouse
- A stable marriage
- Nonverbal communication skills[36]

A supportive spouse and a stable marriage are important because in the foreign country, work may be filled with frustrations, and the spouse may be the only one available with whom the expatriate can talk about them. The above framework also applies to the evaluation and selection of third-country nationals, who, because they are being assigned to a foreign country, are also expatriates, and even to the evaluation of host-country locals who are being expatriated to the home office for development.

However, psychological testing is not without its critics. Considerable debate goes on among scholars and practitioners about the reliability and accuracy of tests in predicting cross-cultural adjustments.[37] Furthermore, since these tests were developed in the United States, they may be "culture bound" and may be even less reliable and accurate when applied to non-Americans.[38] Also, in some countries (e.g., Australia), use of psychological tests is controversial.[39] Use of tests is limited by law in some countries (e.g., Italy). And somewhat different conclusions regarding test use have been found, with a greater use of personality measures by French compared with British organizations.[40]

Determining the effectiveness potential of expatriates is further inhibited by a nation's legal system. In some countries, a candidate may not be asked about his or her religion, smoking habits, drug and alcohol consumption, and other such behaviors about which an assessor needs to know in order to make a determination about the candidate's adaptability. For instance, an individual who smokes and consumes alcohol may not adapt well in Saudi Arabia, where consumption of alcohol is unacceptable.

Finding and Developing Global Expatriates

Many international business enterprises, especially global corporations, require a group of executives who are ready to perform effectively in foreign assignments when and where needed. Many successful organizations, including Coca-Cola, have created the position of chief learning officer (CLO). Somewhat like a chief financial officer, who is dedicated to building the organization's financial strength, the CLO is responsible for developing—on a worldwide scale—the organization's human talent and for utilizing the human knowledge present in the organization.[41] Where do global corporations get such expatriate managers? Professor Cecil G. Howard identified a general recruitment and developmental process consisting of four sources: domestic operations; managers currently on a foreign assignment; external sources, including worldwide competitors; and educational institutions.[42]

Domestic Operations. A source available to international firms for recruiting and developing global expatriates is their home operations. The following are the steps an MNC can use when developing expatriate managers from its domestic operations.

Identify potential expatriate managers within the parent company at early stages of their careers. In other words, find out which young managers might do well in international assignments.

Prepare an individual development plan for each prospective expatriate manager. This entails conducting a training and developmental needs analysis, including discussions with the potential expatriate's supervisor and peers. (Development should include the characteristics identified in Tables 8.1 and 8.2.) It should be noted that standardized training programs may not always be effective because different individuals have different learning/training style preferences.

Table 8.1 presents 10 typical learning/training styles and the preference rating by students with different cultural dimensions. Note that "lectures by instructors" is the highest rated style, followed by "classroom discussions" and "reading textbooks." By far the lowest rated is "classroom presentations by students." "Computerized learning assignments" received the highest rating from students from Confucian cultures, followed by the large power distance and the strong uncertainty avoidance students, and it received the lowest rating by the small power distance and the weak uncertainty avoidance students (both mostly American students). It has been found that language and culture present problems in administering training programs.[43]

Table 8.2 presents the percentage of students—by level of education (bachelor's/M.B.A.), gender, and nationality (U.S./foreign)—who rated the 10 learning/teaching styles listed in Table 8.1 "very important." Some of the key findings are that the U.S. students rated "classroom discussions" much higher than the foreign students, but the foreign students rated "computerized learning assignments" much higher than the U.S. students, which may help explain why many U.S. firms are outsourcing these types of jobs to India and China. The undergraduate students also rated "computerized learning assignments" far higher than the M.B.A. students, who tend to be much older and are already in the corporate world, which may mean that in the future U.S. firms will have a better HR source for these jobs at home. (Of course, labor costs will remain a factor in the recruitment process.)

TABLE 8.1

Importance Level of 10 Learning/Teaching Styles: A Comparison of Students' Ratings by Culture

Learning Styles	Overall Ratings[b] (rank)	Cultural Dimensions[a]				
		LPD (n = 121)	SPD (n = 189)	SUA (n = 89)	WUA (n = 280)	Confucianism (n = 57)
Case studies	2.55 (4)	2.69	2.47	2.66	2.51	2.39
Individual research projects	2.39 (5)	2.58	2.27	2.53	2.32	2.44
Group projects	2.23 (6)	2.43	2.12	2.35	2.21	2.39
Classroom discussions	2.99 (2)	2.90	3.09	2.83	3.08	2.63
Lectures by instructor	3.27 (1)	3.33	3.23	3.33	3.25	3.16
Reading textbooks	2.59 (3)	2.74	2.49	2.67	2.55	2.40
Guest speakers	2.19 (7)	2.21	2.18	2.24	2.13	2.02
Videos shown in class	2.20 (8)	2.24	2.17	2.25	2.18	1.93
Classroom presentations by students	1.87 (10)	2.15	1.69	2.13	1.77	2.02
Computerized learning assignments	2.14 (9)	2.43	1.95	2.38	2.05	2.58

SOURCE: Carl A. Rodrigues, "Culture as a Determinant of the Importance Level Business Students Place on Ten Teaching/Learning Techniques: A Survey of University Students," *Journal of Management Development*, 24, no. 7 (2005), p. 615.

a. LPD = large power distance; SPD = small power distance; SUA = strong uncertainty avoidance; and WUA = weak uncertainty avoidance.
b. Ratings are computed on the average of not important = 0; a little important = 1; somewhat important = 2; important = 3; and very important = 4.

TABLE 8.2

Percentage of Students Who Rated the Learning/Teaching Styles "Very Important" by Degree Level, Male/Female, and U.S./Foreign Students

Learning Styles	Overall (n = 310)	Bachelor's (n = 246)	M.B.A. (n = 64)	Male (n = 148)	Female (n = 162)	U.S. (n = 181)	Foreign (n = 129)
Case studies	54.0	50.4	68.7	56.8	51.9	50.8	58.9
Individual research projects	48.6	47.7	51.6	51.4	46.0	44.7	53.9
Group projects	44.9	44.9	45.3	51.4	39.2	43.3	47.3
Classroom discussions	76.4	77.9	70.3	75.5	77.0	82.1	68.3
Lectures by instructor	87.1	88.6	79.7	84.3	88.9	86.2	87.3
Reading textbooks	59.6	62.4	48.5	55.5	63.2	56.2	64.1
Guest speakers	39.8	38.6	44.5	41.1	38.7	41.6	40.2
Videos shown in class	39.0	39.9	35.5	40.4	37.6	37.3	41.2
Classroom presentations by students	31.3	31.3	31.3	37.0	25.9	25.3	38.7
Computerized learning assignments	39.8	43.2	25.4	39.3	40.3	31.5	51.6

SOURCE: C. A. Rodrigues and E. Kaplan, "The Importance Level of Typically Used Training/Teaching Styles as Rated by Undergraduate, MBA, Male, Female, and Foreign Business Students," Paper presented at the 6th Conference on Business and Economics, Cambridge, MA (October 15–17, 2006).

Give those selected as prospective expatriate managers training and skills development related to potential foreign assignments. The training and development should include practical on-the-job experience in a foreign site. (Practical Perspective 8.2 describes the development programs implemented by some international business enterprises.)

The domestic operations approach has at least three advantages: (1) the MNC has a captive pool to tap, (2) those selected are expected to be in tune with the corporate culture and its managerial philosophy, and (3) the process of assigning those selected to foreign projects helps eliminate those not really qualified for global managerial assignments. There are disadvantages, however. The process is quite costly and time-consuming, and there is a strong possibility that some of the trained executives will sell their newly acquired skills to another international business firm.

PRACTICAL PERSPECTIVE 8-2

Younger Managers Learn Global Skills

A growing number of global-minded U.S. companies have been giving fast-track managers a global orientation much sooner in their careers. "It's a pretty significant trend," said David Weeks, in 1992 a researcher who was completing a Conference Board study of 130 large multinational companies in the U.S., Europe, and Japan. The study found "a certain sense of urgency" among American companies about "trying to build an internationally experienced cadre of executives," Weeks said.

A number of European and Japanese corporate giants had already installed elaborate training and career-tracking mechanisms to develop such executives. Unless U.S. companies equip their best managers with global skills at younger ages, "they are going to come up short" in global competition, warned Michael Longua, then Johnson & Johnson's director of international recruiting.

American Express Company's Travel Related Services unit gave American business-school students summer jobs in which they worked outside the U.S. for up to ten weeks. [It] also transferred junior managers with at least two years experience to other countries. Colgate-Palmolive Company trained about 15 recent college graduates each year for 15 to 24 months prior to multiple overseas job stints. General Electric Company's aircraft-engine unit exposed selected midlevel engineers and managers to foreign language and cross-cultural training even though not all would live abroad.

American Honda Motor Company, Inc. [as of 1992] had sent more than 40 U.S. supervisors and managers to the parent company in Tokyo for up to three years, after preparing them with six months of Japanese language lessons, cultural training, and lifestyle orientation during work hours. PepsiCo, Inc.'s international beverage division brought about 25 young foreign managers a year to the U.S. for one-year assignments in bottling plants. Raychem Corporation assigned relatively inexperienced Asian employees (from clerks through middle managers) to the U.S. for six months to two years.

SOURCE: Excerpted from Joann S. Lublin, "Younger Managers Learn Global Skills," *The Wall Street Journal* (March 31, 1992), p. A1. Permission conveyed through Copyright Clearance Center, Inc.

Managers Currently on a Foreign Assignment. Another source for recruiting and developing global expatriates is the people working in a corporation's foreign subsidiaries. Using this approach involves the following steps:

1. Survey eligible expatriate managers worldwide. It should be noted that the managers in the foreign subsidiaries do not necessarily have to be expatriates; they can be locals who have been developed or are being developed for local managerial assignments. Many international business enterprises, especially those with a multidomestic and global strategy, have training and development programs aimed at developing local managers. For example, Procter & Gamble once asked the Chinese University of Hong Kong to develop a training program for young managers in its plant in Guangzhou, China. Japan's Matsushita's Human Development Center in Singapore trained more than 500 employees in 1990–1991.[44] And current general thinking is that the development of global leadership skills should not stop with home-country employees; it should involve host-country nationals as well. Prudential, for example, uses both.[45]

2. Identify the need for further training and development for those who wish to fit into a new and more demanding managerial role in the future.

3. Prepare independent development plans for those willing to fit into the new managerial role.

4. Provide the skills and knowledge identified on the independent development plans.

5. Place expatriate managers in worldwide subsidiaries.

This approach, because the candidates are already working abroad, can be somewhat less expensive and less time-consuming than developing domestic talent, and besides, they (other than the host-country nationals) have proven adaptability in a foreign culture. However, finding these individuals and administering and coordinating the development process can be a problem if the corporation's subsidiaries are geographically dispersed.

External Sources. Using this approach involves recruiting and developing people with foreign experience from outside sources. The steps in this recruitment and development process are as follows:

1. Recruit qualified individuals from competing and noncompeting companies, both at home and in foreign countries. For example, Chinese companies are energetically wooing executives away from multinationals.[46] Executive-search firms may be helpful in this respect. It should be pointed out that the cultural classifications outlined in Table 1.8 in Chapter 1 (and Table 8.3) may be helpful in determining if the individual is OK or not OK for the position. Individuals in some cultures may believe that they are OK, but they're not—if this is the case, the candidate may not be right for the assignment; he or she will not support the firm's objectives. Table 8.2 presents a cultural framework that can be helpful as a starting point in the assessment.

2. Identify the training and development candidates' need to fit into the new corporate culture.

3. Prepare an individual development program.

4. Provide the required skills and knowledge.

5. Place them in strategic foreign management positions.

The advantages of this approach include the fact that the new employee brings seasoned foreign management experience and personal maturity, reducing training and development costs and time. However, the search can be very expensive—the executive-search companies, also known as "headhunters," charge a high finder's fee. Also, the recruiting can take a long time, especially when local talent is scarce (refer to Practical Perspective 8.3). And the new hire may take a long time to fit into the new corporate culture, or he or she may not fit at all. These factors add to the cost of this approach.

TABLE 8.3 Cultural Classifications and Whether the Culture is "Really OK" or "Really Not OK"

Cultural Classifications	Really OK	Really Not OK
Master of destiny	X	
Fatalism		X
Quest for improvement	X	
Maintaining status quo		X
Enterprise is important	X	
Relationships are important		X
Selection based on merit	X	
Selection based on relationship		X
Accumulation of wealth	X	
"Just enough"		X
Sharing in decision making	X	
Few people make decisions	X	
Decisions based on data	X	
Decisions based on emotions		X
High-context cultures	X	
Low-context cultures	X	
Large power distance	X	
Small power distance	X	
Collectivism	X	
Individualism		X
Strong uncertainty avoidance	X	
Weak uncertainty avoidance	X	
Masculinity		X
Femininity		X
Confucianism	X	

SOURCE: Carl Rodrigues, "Developing Expatriates' Cross-Cultural Sensitivity: Cultures Where 'Your Culture's OK' Is Really Not," *Journal of Management Development,* 16 (1997), p. 692.

PRACTICAL PERSPECTIVE 8-3

Consider the Quality and Availability of the Local Labor Force

The greatest challenge in entering a new market is often the workforce, specifically senior management. "After you determine that you have a marketplace that's going to utilize what you're producing, you need to see if there is the capability and talent in the local workforce to support the endeavor," said Richard Bahner, in 1998 human resources head at New York City–based Citicorp [now Citigroup]. "You really need to do a total, balanced evaluation. Some of these places offer less expensive labor, but if they don't have the capabilities you're looking for, it may not be a savings because you'll have to supplement it with a large amount of computer support, training, or expatriates."

The extent of the staffing challenges depends on your industry. "If you're distributing Pepsi™, you can manufacture it locally and teach people how to sell it easily enough, but if you're in global banking, you've got a lot more restrictions," Bahner explained.

Citibank had experienced this in the Asia-Pacific region. With relationships in China and Hong Kong for almost a century, it had an advantage when it looked to expand into Indonesia and Thailand. But it was hampered by the need for an educated workforce. Citibank developed the market in Indonesia and taught the people about electronic banking—eventually generating millions of Citibank Visa cardholders. But the HR issues were daunting.

"The biggest problem is the dearth of qualified locals," said Bill Fontana, formerly of Citibank in Indonesia and in 1998 vice president of international HR for the National Foreign Trade Council. It's a big, big problem. There were so few qualified people who could take senior positions (among 200 million Indonesians), that other U.S. companies would bid for this unique individual. "It jacks up the cost of your senior local person, and then you begin to pirate people away from other companies because they speak English, they've worked at another multinational organization, and therefore, you would pay almost anything to get them onto your payroll. It leads to spiraling inflation in the workforce."

As an example, Fontana was recruiting for a treasury head at Citibank in Indonesia. The position was staffed with an expat, and he wanted to fill it with a local. It took more than one year to identify a qualified person. [In 1998] Citibank offered the man $150,000 and a guaranteed base of $100,000. "He turned me down," said Fontana. "He told me that the Bank of Bali was offering him more money! And the expatriate was only making about $115,000."

SOURCE: Excerpted form Charlene Marmer Solomon, "Don't Get Burned by Hot New Markets," *Global Workforce* (January 1998), pp. 12–13. Reprinted with permission.

Educational Institutions. College and universities are another source for recruiting and developing global expatriates. Many of these institutions, especially in the United States, have implemented or are currently implementing programs aimed at internationalizing their students, including offering degrees in international business and programs encouraging study abroad. (Refer to Practical Perspective 8.4.) Gillette International implemented a program to groom executives to fill global management positions. Initially, Gillette worked with the New York City–based AIESEC (an international student exchange program) in identifying students for the program. In 1993, Gillette's personnel director and general manager for each of the company's worldwide operations were responsible for identifying the top business students in prestigious universities worldwide.[47] Emerson Electric's biggest hurdle in entering China was finding the right managers. To jump that hurdle, Emerson sought graduates of top local universities, offering them a generous pay, and brought them to the United States for intensive training.[48]

PRACTICAL PERSPECTIVE 8-4

The Call for Training

Business schools in Europe and the United States are beginning to understand the requirements for these new managerial marvels and modify their programs. The educational infrastructure is coming, but not soon enough ... We should look to three familiar sources for this training, but each source will have to reorder its priorities, change its curriculum, and deliver in wholly new ways. The first source, business schools, are rushing to change their curriculum to include global management issues. But that's not enough. Every course should be designed from a global perspective, with cases on cross-border alliances, cross-cultural issues, and global markets and competition. Today's student in the United States must understand how Japanese and Indian managers think, not just to compete against them but also to partner with them.

Many companies also are already investing in internal development programs and sending managers to executive courses offered by graduate business schools to help develop the level of understanding needed in alliances. But most are not taking the necessary actions. Motorola University has multiple course offerings on cultural awareness and alliances training ... Hewlett-Packard has an intense alliance development program. Internally, its best practices program in alliance management consist of training sessions, case histories, tool kits, and checklists. Externally, HP obtains assessments form its partners and benchmarks the best practices of other successful companies.

The third source is the individual. Anyone who wishes to be a business leader in the twenty-first century should read as much as possible about managing in an intercultural environment and participative management. Accept an assignment to live outside your home country, be part of a team managing a strategic alliance, put yourself in the line of fire.

SOURCE: Excerpted from Cyrus F. Faidheim Jr., "The Battle of the Alliances," *Management Review*, 88, no. 8 (September 1999), pp. 46–51.

The college recruiter is encouraged to become familiar with the college's international program because an effective program will equip its students with professional skills, including cross-cultural sensitivity and linguistic capability. However, the programs in some colleges develop only a narrow functional specialization and a parochial perspective to managing in a foreign culture.

Expatriate Preparation Programs

A selectee being sent to a foreign site needs extensive preparation. This means that international businesses require an expatriate preparation program and a program administrator who can effectively administer such a program. The preparation program should consist of four phases: understanding the corporate international environment, pre-expatriation, expatriation, and repatriation.[49]

The Corporation's International Environment

Before the program administrator can properly administer an expatriation program, he or she must become totally familiar with the following:

1. The enterprise's foreign involvements, including operations, investments, business goals, and strategies

2. The staffing needs of overseas operations, including qualifications, duties, the expected duration of the assignment, and the goals and objectives of the position (e.g., whether the expatriate is needed only to run the day-to-day operations, to develop new operations and/or train locals for managerial positions, or to simultaneously run the operations and develop locals—each job may require different skills)

3. The environmental aspects of the nation where the assignment is to take place, such as geographic isolation, level of urbanization, economic development, culture, and political and legal systems

The above knowledge enables the program administrator to (a) better understand the organization's international commitments; (b) determine the skills, objectives, and relative hardships of foreign assignments; (c) make better selections for foreign positions; and (d) better judge the level of adjustment and readjustment necessary in each case.[50]

Pre-Expatriation

In the pre-expatriation phase, the selectee becomes involved in the preparation process.[51] The objective of this phase is to make sure of the following:[52]

1. The individual has a complete understanding of the foreign assignment, including its purpose, goals, objectives, duties, and relationship to his or her career objectives.

2. He or she is aware of the realities of expatriation, including the professional and personal problems foreign assignments may often create. This should include making the expatriate and his or her family aware (but not "scared to death") of the potential psychological and emotional strains created by being separated from friends and other family members. In other words, the expatriate and his or her family should be made aware of all the advantages and disadvantages of the foreign assignment.

3. The expatriate and his or her family are educated and oriented about their temporary foreign home before leaving. The orientation should include the elements discussed in the following paragraphs.

Cultural Briefing

This should include the country's cultural traditions, history, government, economy, living conditions (including foods, education, medical facilities, and entertainment), climate, and clothing requirements. Books, maps, brochures, films, and slides would help in this respect. It should be noted that the cultural training program must be extensive, otherwise it won't be very effective.[53]

Assignment Briefing

This briefing includes details about the length of the assignment, vacation policy, holidays, allowances, tax consequences, and repatriation policy, as well as the expatriate's tentative work plan, the basis of his or her evaluation, and his or her authority and degree of autonomy in the foreign operations.

Relocation Requirements

Shipping, packaging, storage, and home disposal and acquisition should be addressed and settled.

Language Training

Introducing the selectee to the country's language is essential. Not only does it help the communication process, but it also helps him or her better understand the country's culture. The language training methods commonly used include instruction at a language school and do-it-yourself kits such as records, cassette and CD recordings, and books.

Expatriation

The expatriation phase takes place while the expatriate is working in the foreign operations. It involves communication and information delivery. It is imperative that the following steps are taken by the home office:

1. Keep the expatriate well-informed about domestic operations and plans; different time zones and the location of the assignment being out of the organizational mainstream make it easy for the home office to ignore the expatriate and make him or her feel professionally and personally isolated, thus increasing anxiety. As mentioned earlier, the new technologies available, such as e-mail, help in this respect. Periodically bringing the expatriate to the home office for a meeting would help in this respect as well. (Refer to Practical Perspective 8.5.)

2. Review and discuss the expatriate's performance and career path, emphasizing the assignment's purpose and what the expatriate can expect to gain on returning home. In other words, provide feedback and motivation.

PRACTICAL PERSPECTIVE 8-5

Out of Sight, Out of Mind

Paris-based Stephen Gates, [in 1997] a senior research associate at the Conference Board, asked 152 HR managers with international work experience to identify the pitfalls of an overseas assignment. The survey's results appeared in a report titled "Managing Expatriates' Return." Here are the key findings:

Repatriation

After a lengthy assignment in a foreign country, the repatriate and the repatriate's family will encounter a high level of pressure and anxiety. The longer the assignment, the greater the pressure and anxiety, and on the expatriate's arrival home, the following must be done:[54]

1. Provide intensive organizational retraining for the repatriate. The retraining should provide information on policy and procedural changes, shifts in corporate strategy, and new and promoted personnel, with a detailed description of his or her new position. (If the expatriate phase has been carried out effectively, this should not be too difficult.) He or she should not be pushed into a new position and be expected to produce immediately but should be given ample time to adjust. Andy Knox of Korn/Ferry says that it generally takes a returning expatriate up to 18 months to readjust to working in the States.[55] Also, the new position should, as much as possible, be challenging and should use the skills acquired in the foreign assignment.

2. Provide some form of financial counseling for the family, especially when there is a reduction of income.

3. Provide housing assistance. If the repatriate did not sell his or her house and instead rented it, help him arrange to have the house vacated and prepared for the family to move into it. If he or she has sold the house, help him or her obtain a new one, including a low-interest loan, a lump-sum bonus, or compensation for increased housing prices.

4. Assist the repatriate financially so that his or her children can continue receiving the quality education that the foreign country provided.

5. Help pay for psychological consultation if some repatriates and repatriate families experience personal and psychological problems readjusting.

Expatriate Compensation

Ineffective expatriate compensation can also lead to expatriate failures. Thus, international firms need to establish policies for effective management of expatriate compensation, and to do so requires knowledge of the foreign country's laws, customs, environment, and employment practices, as well as understanding of the effects of currency exchange fluctuations and inflation on compensation. And, within the context of changing political, economic, and social conditions, establishing policy also requires an understanding of why certain allowances are necessary. Ron Ashkenas described the relocation problems that merit additional compensation:

As more territories open up to global business, some will be remote, inconvenient, and disturbingly different. Organizations must develop programs to maintain fairness when hardship or disruption of families is an issue. While the manager may personally accept and even want the foreign assignment, he or she may have legitimate concerns about the schooling for the children, employment opportunities for the spouse, or the effects of cultural differences and language barriers. New incentives and supports must be offered to help compensate for the feelings of loss that these situations trigger.[56]

An assignment in a hostile or undesirable environment would require greater compensation than an assignment to a friendly, desirable environment. For instance, Frans Ryckebosch, who was the overseas assignment general manager for Xerox in Shanghai, China, negotiated with Xerox for a 25% hardship allowance on top of the standard Xerox package before taking the assignment.[57] Box 8.3 (with data from 1998) presents the top 10 hardship locations. Of course, since the global war on terrorism started in 2001, this list is likely to have changed. For example, this author spent six months in Taipei, Taiwan (No. 6 on the list) in 2000, and he found it quite safe, fun, and interesting living there. This author also lived for eight months in Honduras during 2002 and 2003, and the danger elements there were very high.

Box 8.3   Top 10 Hardship Locations According to ECA Windham's Location-Ranking System

Based on such criteria as security, sociopolitical tension, housing, and climate, here are the 10 countries or regions that ranked highest in hardship:

1. Kinshasa, Zaire

2. Almaty, Kazakhstan

3. Moscow, Russia

4. Beijing and Shanghai, China

5. New Delhi and Mumbai, India

6. Taipei, Taiwan

7. Lima, Peru

8. Sofia, Bulgaria

9. Warsaw, Poland

10. Jakarta, Indonesia

SOURCE: Helen Frank Bensimon, "Is it Safe to Work Abroad?" *Training & Development*, 52, no. 8 (August 1998), p. 24. Reprinted with permission.

Expatriate compensation policies seek to satisfy numerous objectives:[58]

- The policy should be consistent and fair in its treatment of all categories of expatriate employees.
- The policy must work to attract and retain expatriates in the areas where the corporation has the greatest need.
- The policy should facilitate the transfer of expatriates in the most cost-effective manner.
- The policy should be consistent with the overall strategy and structure of the organization.
- The compensation should serve to motivate employees.

A decision must be made about whether to establish an overall policy for all employees or to distinguish between home-country, third-country, and host-country nationals. It is common for international businesses to distinguish between them; they even distinguish between the types of expatriates. For example, different policies may be set on the basis of length of assignment or on the type of function to be carried out.[59] In all cases, the policy should be based on the idea that the expatriate must not suffer a loss because of his or her transfer. Furthermore, the approach selected should not demoralize the foreign subsidiary's staff; for example, visible pay inequity between the expatriates and their local peers can create bad feelings, thus undermining morale.[60] Table 8.4 presents the home-based balance sheet calculation of expatriate pay.

Expatriate Base Salary

MNCs have tended to use the expatriate's home-country base salary as the primary component for determining his or her package of compensation for undertaking the foreign assignment. They tended to use third- and home-country nationals' home salary base to determine their compensation when they are selected for the assignment.

The conditions that force compensation policies to differ from those used for home-country expatriates include inflation and cost of living, housing, security, school costs, and taxation.[61] Furthermore, home-country and third-country expatriates often require a salary premium as an inducement to accept the foreign assignment or to endure the hardships of the foreign transfer. In the United States, when an international business enterprise has determined the type of hardship, it can refer to the U.S. Department of State's Hardship Post Differentials Guidelines to ascertain the appropriate level of premium compensation.

The practice of international businesses paying a higher salary to home-country than to third-country expatriate managers and to host-country managers can "demotivate" managers in the latter two categories, especially when they have an equal level of authority and responsibility. A problem currently confronting MNCs is how to deal effectively with such inequities. Some managers think that MNCs should have a global standard policy relating to compensation; that is, regardless of the varying costs of living existing in

---

TABLE 8.4   Calculation of Expatriate Pay

A pure home-based balance sheet calculation of expatriate pay works something like this:

1. Start with home-based gross income, including bonuses.

2. Deduct home tax, social security, and pension contributions (either a hypothetical tax or a real tax).

3. Add or subtract a cost-of-living allowance. Usually, companies don't subtract. Instead, they allow the expatriate to benefit from the negative differential.

4. Add a housing allowance, with or without a housing norm deduction.

5. Add incentive premiums, including general mobility premiums and possibly hardship premiums.

6. Add or subtract to equalize taxes. In other words, gross the net salary to protect against the double tax obligations in the home and host countries.

Of course, that can't be all there is to it. There are also many modified versions of the balance sheet approach and other unrelated compensation systems, including the host-based system. The balance sheet and host-based systems are at opposite ends of a continuum, with many hybrids in between.

SOURCE: Valerie Frazee, "Is the Balance Sheet Right for Your Expats?" *Workforce,* 77 no. 9 (September 1998), p. 19. Reprinted with permission.

countries, all the corporation's managers in all countries should be compensated on the basis of a standard global salary range based on the level of authority and responsibility. This policy, of course, is arguable and difficult to implement.

Taxation

For the expatriate, a foreign assignment can mean being double-taxed—by the home country and the foreign country governments. This problem, however, is mitigated in the United States by Section 911 of the Internal Revenue Service Code, which has an exclusion provision permitting only a specific deduction. It is also mitigated by the United States having an obligation agreement with some countries whereby an expatriate would pay taxes only in the United States and not in the host country, but in most cases double taxation applies.[62] International firms are subject to varying tax rates around the globe.

The rates are different from country to country, and they change within countries from time to time. For example, the maximum marginal rate in Belgium was 72% in 1985 and 70.8% in 1988; in the United States it was 50% in 1985 and 33% in 1988.[63] (Current rates may be different.) A corporation's compensation packages must consider how specific practices can be adjusted in each nation to provide, within the context of the corporation's overall policy, the most tax-effective, appropriate rewards for home-country, host-country, and third-country managers.

Benefits

Benefits such as pension and medical plans and social security are difficult to transfer across national borders. When considering expatriate benefits, international enterprises need to consider numerous issues, including the following:[64]

- Whether or not to maintain expatriates in home-country programs, particularly if the company does not receive a tax deduction for it
- Whether companies have the option of enrolling expatriates in host-country benefit programs and/or making up the difference in coverage
- Whether host-country legislation regarding termination affects benefit entitlements
- Whether expatriates should receive home-country or host-country social security benefits (refer to Practical Perspective 8.6)
- Whether benefits should be maintained on a home-country, third-country, or host-country basis, which is to be responsible for the cost; whether other benefits should be used to offset any shortfall in coverage; and whether home-country benefit programs should be exported to local nationals in foreign countries

U.S. firms' home-country expatriates generally remain under their home-company's benefit program.[65]

Social Security. There is an agreement between the United States Canada, and several European countries that eliminates dual social security coverage of citizens from one country working in another on a temporary basis. In some nations, however, expatriates must participate in local social security programs. In these cases, the international companies normally incur the additional costs.[66]

PRACTICAL PERSPECTIVE 8-6

International Social Security

Around the globe, social security isn't just a tax to be avoided; it is a social policy that provides benefits including medical care, retirement, and disability pensions. Policies vary widely across countries.

For the expatriate, social taxation can become a complex issue that requires careful planning to make sure that accumulated entitlements are protected in the home country, that benefits continue to accrue while on foreign assignment, and that the employee isn't taxed by both the home and host countries.

Within the European Union, and between the EU and the European Economic Area of Iceland and Norway, legislation specifies that normally an expatriate will enroll in the host-country program for the duration of the assignment and continue to accrue benefits. Similar agreements exist between the United States and most industrialized nations.

Reciprocal agreements between countries usually mean the employee can remain in the home-country system for a few years before being required to switch to the host-country scheme.

If expatriates eventually enroll in the host-country program, they will earn some benefits there. This situation can prove financially difficult if:

- The pension earned in the host assignment country is significantly less than home social security benefits;
- Pensions earned abroad are payable in the host country currency and exchange rates are expected to worsen prior to retirement; and
- Payment from the host country may be difficult to claim and collect, especially if many years pass between the expat assignment and retirement.

Because of these concerns, many expats choose to remain in their home social security plan, even if this requires paying into both home and host country programs.

Assignments to countries without reciprocal agreements require protecting both existing and future social security benefits. "If the expatriate can be retained in his home country scheme, probably through voluntary contributions by employee and/or home employer, the problem is to a great extent solved," said Gunter Becher, [in 1996] director of international consulting in Europe for Watson Wyatt. "Certainly this is so in regard to continuing entitlement to long-term benefits. In these cases, short-term benefits such as medical care must often be arranged through private insurance.

"International social security matters require considerable knowledge and research," emphasized Becher, "more particularly because systems are changing all the time."

To be safe, expats should remain in their home-country social security system whenever possible and for as long as possible. "In fact, this can frequently be achieved," said Becher, "and is the one solution that is readily acceptable to—and understood by—almost every expatriate."

SOURCE: Excerpted from Leigh and Collinns Allard, "Managing Globe-Trotting Expats," *Management Review* (May 1996), p. 39. © 1996 American Management Association International. Reprinted by permission of American Management Association International, New York. All rights reserved. www.amanet.org.

Payroll and Payment Currency. Expatriate employees are often kept on the home-country payroll to retain home-country employment status. From a company perspective, to commit expatriate salary and allowance payments in home-country currency, the currency of payment ought to be clearly established at the beginning. The issue is one of currency conversion risk. The most company-favorable currency commitment by the company is to home-country currency payment, and the employee bears the conversion risk. The most employee-favorable commitment by the company is to local currency payment, and the company bears the conversion risk.[67]

Allowances

International businesses generally pay expatriates certain allowances. These include cost-of-living, housing, education, and relocation allowances. Cost-of-living allowances pay the expatriate for differences in expenses between the home and the foreign country. Housing allowances help the expatriate maintain his or her home-country living standards. Education allowances ensure that the expatriate's children will receive at least as good an education as they would receive in the home country. Relocation allowances usually pay for the expatriate's moving, shipping, and storage expenses; temporary living expenses; and other related expenses.[68]

The preceding discussions suggest that international business enterprises tend to apply an ethnocentric compensation policy—the home-country expatriate, as previously indicated, receives compensation and benefits that are different from those received by third-country and host-country managers. However, as companies become more globally oriented, they will rely more on third-country managers to manage global operations. Some of these firms may be able to apply a more geocentric compensation policy—that is, a more globally uniform compensation and benefits package.

However, when polled, 80% of international management listed discrepancies between their compensation packages as their biggest personal HR problem, and more than 50% felt that compensation discrepancies among their different pools of international management employees were a significant HR problem, and these discrepancies exist at managerial levels as well as across home country, third country, and host country. But a consistent compensation package was viewed as not being feasible. Thus, one will find a host-country expatriate manager in Colombia receiving a hardship allowance, but his or her French counterpart in Peru does not. And it was found that 85% of host-country expatriate managers and supervisors received tax equalization and only 30% of third-country managers and executives got the same and no third-country supervisor received the same benefits. The discrepancies most cited as being the biggest HR problem were, in order, as follows:[69]

- Base salary
- Overseas premiums
- Housing allowances
- Education allowances
- Cost of living allowances
- Tax equalization
- Repatriation allowances
- Performance-based incentives

Countries' Labor Laws and International HRM

As pointed out in Chapter 3, a country's labor laws have a great impact on international HRM. The following are some illustrations.[70]

The Netherlands. Under employment laws in the Netherlands, for an indefinite period of employment agreement, the probationary period is at most two months, and specifying a longer period will result in there being no probationary period at all. If an employer seeks termination of an employee by judicial order, the court may order reinstatement and that the parties make an attempt in good faith to make the employment successful, and an employer found not to make such an effort may incur substantial financial penalties.

Thailand. Under Thailand labor laws, employees have the right to take sterilization leave and be paid full wages by the employer during the leave period. Also, under Thailand labor laws, material relocation of the place of work by an employer gives employees the right to refuse assignment and claim 50% of the customary severance pay for not-for-cause dismissal. Employment termination with cause is governed by the provisions of Section 583 of the Civil Commercial Code and Section 119 of the Labor Protection Act, and includes gross negligence, willful disobedience, dishonesty, or a criminal act. When there is employment termination without cause, it is mandatory for the employer to make severance payment to the employee based on the length of unbroken time employed:

From 120 days but less than 1 year, the amount is 30 days' pay.

From 1 year but less than 3 years, the amount is 90 days' pay.

From 3 years but less than 6 years, the amount is 180 days' pay.

From 6 years but less than 10 years, the amount is 240 days' pay.

From 10 years and more, the amount is 300 days' pay.

Furthermore, under Thailand labor laws, all employers are required to provide employees at least 13 official public holidays per year; employees are entitled to 30 working days of annual sick leave with full pay; and a pregnant woman is entitled to 90 days of maternity leave (inclusive of holidays), including 45 workdays with full pay.

China. In the People's Republic of China (PRC), businesses may grant stock options to their employees, but national currency may not be transferred abroad for their exercise. Also, by PRC statute, the time employees spend in social activities at the workplace, such as political study, promoting, family planning, and so on, must be compensated by the employer. Furthermore, most foreign companies elect not to directly employ local Chinese employees. Under PRC employment law, a foreign enterprise can enter into an employment contract with local PRC staff, while a representative office must employ local staff through an authorized foreign enterprise service corporation such as FESCO (Foreign Enterprise Service Company). Under PRC employment laws, a foreign enterprise can enter into individual labor contracts with each individual PRC employee and is required to submit the labor contracts for certification by the local labor bureau. The local staff working in a representative office is technically not employed by the representative office, but they are employees of FESCO seconded to the representative office. This peculiar feature doesn't carry much practical significance in terms of the actual performance in terms of work by employees.

Brazil. The employment relationship in Brazil is governed by Law Decree No. 5452 of May 1, 1943, Consolidacao das Leis do Trabalho (CLT). At least two thirds of the employees of any employer, whether a resident company or other business, must be Brazilian nationals. Brazilian employees must be employed by an employer registered to do business in Brazil.

France. Direct employment of a French national in France by a foreign company is not permitted, with the limited exception of one sales employee, engaged in direct sales, working from the employee's home. French employment agreements are advised. The termination of an employment contract by an employer must be carefully done.

Posted Worker Directive in the EU. A posted worker is an employee who for a limited time carries out his or her duties in the territory of an EU member state other than the state in which he or she normally works. On December 16, 1999, the EU implemented the Posted Worker Directive, which requires that where a member state has certain minimum terms and conditions of employment, these must also apply to workers posted temporarily for their employer to work in that state. The terms of EU Directive 96/71 include maximum work periods and minimum rest periods; minimum paid annual holidays; minimum rates of pay, including overtime rates; conditions of hiring workers, in particular the supply of workers by temporary employment undertakings; health, safety, and hygiene at work; protective measures in the terms and conditions of employment of pregnant women or those who have recently given birth, of children, and of young people; equal treatment for men and women; and other provisions on nondiscrimination.

Application of the EU Posted Worker Directive in Italy. When implementing EU Directive 96/71 by means of Legislative Decree 72/2000, Italian legislation extended the scope of application of the EU Posted Worker Directive so that the relevant provisions apply not only to employers located in EU member states but also to employers located in non-EU countries. The main labor area that is relevant in the case at issue, as a consequence of the above provisions, is vacation (expatriates shall benefit from the same number of days of vacation or holidays established in the applicable collective agreement), the others being minimum salary, daily and weekly days off, safety at work, maternity, and parity between men and women.

The EU Posted Worker Directive and U.S. expatriates in Italy. A U.S. expatriate manager assigned to Italy, under the Italian application of the EU Posted Worker Directive, is considered equivalent to Italian national employees covered under the collective bargaining agreement for *dirigenti* in the commercial and tertiary sector (CCNL). Such *dirigenti* employees contractually must receive no less than 30 days of vacation per year. Italian application of the EU Posted Worker Directive thus means that the assigned employee must receive 30 days of vacation, even though the terms of the U.S. policy may provide for only two weeks of vacation.

The above paragraphs presented some of the challenges international HR managers face in internationalizing and managing their organizations in a few countries and one region. There are more than 200 countries on the planet, each with unique HR management distinctions.

Organizational Culture and Developing Multicultural Teamwork

As cross-national/cross-cultural acquisitions, mergers, and formations of partnerships take place among organizations with differing cultures, such organizations must be innovative. Innovation is often best generated through teams whose members have diverse views—that is, members who come from varied cultures. But people typically have difficulty accepting views that are different from their own and seek to eliminate diversity. Therefore, implementing multicultural teamwork is a challenge organizations face. Thus, HR managers will need to develop and implement programs that bring the team members together for the following purposes:[71]

- Providing team members with an awareness of cultural difference and its impact on organizational structure and systems, management style, decision making, and interpersonal behavior
- Helping team members become aware of their different roles, preferences, and strengths and how these complement each other
- Helping team members develop methods of communication swiftly and effectively with each other
- Helping team members develop a set of shared ground rules for maintaining team effectiveness when working together and working apart
- Beginning the process of developing a shared vision for the team and an implementation strategy

Hence, to be effective, team members need to establish the behaviors outlined in Box 8.4. This requires that HR managers possess the strong global perspective and high level of understanding needed in alliances, mergers, acquisitions, and partnerships.[72]

Box 8.4 Characteristics of an Effective Team

1. *Members trust and respect each other:* Trust is the antidote to a proliferation of rules and regulations. It simplifies life. Without trust, the team would not be able to effectively deal with external threats.

2. *Members protect and support each other:* Members of the team must share the conviction that they can rely on each other. As such, each member's self-esteem must be maintained.

3. *Members engage in open dialogue and communication:* Subordination to an authority figure is minimal, and all members must participate—every member can expect it, every member can demand it, and every member is supposed to participate.

(Continued)

(Continued)

4. *Members share a strong common goal:* Certain mutually agreed on qualitative and quantitative goals need to be established by the team. This helps them determine the degree of their success in pursuing their tasks.

5. *Members have strong shared values and beliefs:* Shared values and beliefs define the team's attitudes and the norms that guide their behavior, and they play the role of a social control mechanism.

6. *Members subordinate their own objectives to those of the team:* Team members operate within the boundaries of team rules, they understand personal and team roles, and they do not let their own needs take precedence over the team's needs.

7. *Members subscribe to "distributed" leadership:* Team members are not intimidated by rank, seniority, or status. All members of the team are empowered to make decisions. Team leadership is based on knowledge and expertise.

SOURCE: Abstracted from Manfred F. R. Kets De Vries, "High-Performance Teams: Lessons From the Pygmies," *Organizational Dynamics,* 27, no. 3 (Winter 1999), pp. 66–77.

It should be pointed out that in the late 1990s, Nissan was a company in distress, looking for a partner to help solve the short-term issues, and Renault was a successful European carmaker looking to expand its business internationally. Nissan's partnership with Renault began in March 1999. Renault's $9.5 billion infusion and top management resources provided the necessary catalyst that led to the start of Nissan's revival. From the start, the decision to form an alliance was not so much a financial decision as a strategic decision about the future of each company. To avert the clash of corporate cultures, Renault and Nissan are partners linked by a cross-shareholding. Renault holds 44.4% stake in Nissan, and Nissan owns 15% of Renault shares. Both companies have a direct interest in the results of its partner, but each company is responsible for its own performance. Renault and Nissan retain their own distinct brand identities. Product planning is separate. Corporate identities are separate as well. Each company implements its own strategy and manages its operations under its respective executive committee. Each is accountable for specific results to its own board of directors, and ultimately to its own shareholders. Nissan and Renault consult each month about potential synergies through the alliance board, which steers the alliance's medium-term and long-term strategy and coordinates joint activities on a worldwide scale. But decision making is clearly divided between Nissan's headquarters in Tokyo and the Renault headquarters in Paris. Corporate cultures are intact.[73]

Technology and Cross-National HRM

The advent of the new technologies described earlier, such as e-mail, cellular phones, teleconferencing, and videoconferencing, enable international organizations to develop a system to keep track of people and people's skills worldwide. For example, Cypress Semiconductor, a maker of specialty computer chips in San Jose, California, has developed a computer system that keeps track of its 1,500 employees as they criss-cross between different functions, teams, and projects. Apple has developed a computer network called Spider—a system that combines a network of personal computers with a videoconferencing system and a database of employee records. A manager assembling a team can, using this system, call up profiles of employees who are stationed anywhere in the world. A color photo of the person can be seen on the screen, where he or she works, who reports to him or her, to whom he or she reports, and his or her skills. If the manager wants to interview a candidate in, for instance, Frankfurt, he or she can call him or her over the Spider network and talk with him or her in living color on the computer screen.[74]

Furthermore, the Internet and intranets, including e-mail, are the most democratic form of overseas deployment, enabling communication among employees regardless of organizational level. Videoconferencing has a similar advantage; however, such facilities are scarce compared with e-mail in most organizations. In the future, as costs of such systems are lowered, more organizations will be able to use videoconferencing. Dow and Merck have videoconferencing systems, and their managers said that their videoconferencing rooms are in constant use.[75]

Summary

This chapter has discussed the functions of effective international HRM, the foreign country's physical and social environments, differences in technical sophistication, gender bias, inadequate repatriation programs, and the pitfalls in the HR planning function. Based on Japanese, European, and U.S. MNCs' expatriation practices, a framework for reducing expatriate failure was presented. Other ways to reduce expatriate failure were also introduced, including a framework for selecting the right person for the foreign assignment. Also presented were frameworks for finding and developing effective expatriates, administrating expatriate programs, administrating expatriate compensation, and developing multicultural teamwork. The chapter also discussed the ways in which current technologies aid the HRM function.

KEY TERMS AND CONCEPTS

1. Expatriates
2. Adaptation problems
3. Differences in technical sophistication
4. Company-country conflicting objectives and policies
5. Visibly constrained authority of expatriate managers
6. Cultural bias against women
7. Repatriation
8. Repatriation programs
9. Skills acquired in foreign country not used at home
10. Missed opportunities
11. Reverse culture shock
12. Human resource managers play a less active role in companies' overall planning process
13. Inadequate selection criteria for foreign assignments
14. Inability of expatriate's family to adapt to foreign environment

15. Lack of adequate training for foreign assignments

16. Expatriates need time to adapt

17. The initial, disillusionment, culture shock, and positive-adjustment phrases

18. Underutilization of women as expatriates

19. Lower incidence of expatriate failure experienced by Japanese MNCs than by U.S. MNCs

20. The "spirit of internationalism"

21. New information technology

22. Reducing expatriate failure

23. Selecting the right expatriate

24. Assessing expatriates' effectiveness potential

25. Cultural-toughness dimension

26. Finding and developing global managers

27. Chief learning officer

28. Expatriation programs and program administrators

29. Pre-expatriation, expatriation, and repatriation phases

30. Expatriate compensation policy

31. Visible pay inequity

32. Double taxation

33. Home-country's benefit package

34. Cost-of-living allowances

35. Internet and intranets

36. Information technologies

DISCUSSION QUESTIONS

1. State and explain the fundamental reasons why expatriates fail and what MNCs can do to reduce failure.

2. What are the international staffing implications that can be drawn from the Japanese, European, and U.S. MNCs' expatriate practices?

3. Refer to Exercise 2 below. What questions would you ask the top management to make sure that the right expatriate has been selected?

4. To be effective, consultants agree, expatriates require certain characteristics. What are those characteristics?

5. Discuss the significance of the self-oriented, others-oriented, perceptual, and cultural-toughness dimensions in the selection of expatriates.

6. Discuss the four sources for recruiting and developing a pool of global expatriates.

7. Discuss the pre-expatriation, expatriation, and repatriation administration programs.

8. What type of knowledge is required for the effective administration of expatriate compensation?

9. What is meant by "a global standard policy" relating to compensation?

10. How do information technologies assist in managing global human resources?

EXERCISES

1. You are the manager of the international HRM function for a firm whose top management is assigning an executive from the home office to head one of the firm's foreign subsidiaries. Relative to the cultural adaptation phases, what would you advise the top management?

2. A European MNC is looking to fill an important position in one of its subsidiaries in Japan. It has narrowed down its candidate pool to two women: One is Japanese and the other is American. Which one would you advise management to select? Why?

3. An MNC is having problems managing its foreign subsidiaries. With respect to HRM, what would you advise its management to do to solve the problem?

4. An MNC has been spending a lot of money sending its employees on foreign assignments, but soon after they get there, they want to return home. What should management do to solve this problem?

5. An MNC is looking to fill some key managerial positions in some of its foreign subsidiaries. Where should management look for candidates?

ASSIGNMENT

Contact the manager of the HRM function for an MNC. Ask him or her to describe the company's policy relating to expatriate development. Prepare a short report for your class.

CASE 8-1

Trouble Abroad

The line went dead. Steve Prestwick slowly hung up the telephone, wondering what he could possibly say to the executive committee monitoring the Singapore R&D center project. Shortly after being assigned to help staff the facility, he had attended a committee meeting that left him excited about tapping into the potential of the company's large global workforce. "Get the best people from everywhere," said one executive. "Don't just rely on information from headquarters. Try to find out what the people in Europe or Japan might know," chimed in another. And from the CEO, "Let's use this as an opportunity to develop a global mindset in some of our more promising people." The vision sounded great, and Steve's role seemed simple: Put together a team with all the experts needed to get the new facility up and running smoothly in its first two years.

Right away Steve began having trouble finding out who had the right skills, and even where the choices seemed obvious, he wasn't getting anywhere. The engineer who refused the assignment over the telephone was the best the company had in her field. She told him that spending two years in Singapore wouldn't really help her career. Plus, it would be hard on her children and impossible for her husband, a veterinarian with a growing practice. Not only did he need a top engineering manager, but Steve also had to find a highly competent corps of technical researchers who knew about the company and its approach to R&D. He also needed technicians who could set up the facility. He thought he would bring in people from the USA to select and set up equipment, then lead a research team of local engineers that the USA engineers would train in company practices and technologies. To his chagrin, most of the USA technical people he had talked to weren't interested in such an assignment. A European perspective might be useful, but he didn't even have records on possible candidates from the other overseas offices. Steve was on his own and he had less than a week to come up with a plan.

Questions

1. How could this problem have been avoided?

2. What can Steve do?

SOURCE: Excerpted from K. Roberts, E. E. Kossek, and C. Ozeki, "Managing the Global Workforce: Challenges and Strategies," *Academy of Management Executive*, 12, no. 4 (November 1998), p. 92. Copyright by Oxford University Press. Reprinted with permission.

CASE 8-2

DaimlerChrysler: Steering Around Culture Clashes

It's 9 a.m. and the early shift at the Mercedes-Benz assembly plant was headed for its vesper, the first of the workday's ritual beer breaks. Once back on the floor of the cavernous workshops, the newly refreshed employees, in their uniform blue coveralls and safety glasses, lit up their cigarettes at the control panels and machining stations. Robots did all the heavy lifting in this high-tech automotive heartland these days, but the workforce here remained overwhelmingly male.

Issues such as the risk of alcohol-related accidents, nonsmokers' rights, sexual harassment, and diversity in the workplace were sources of bemusement for those who turned out the cars whose name had become synonymous with perfection.

And one had only to glance at the official portrait of the new board of directors—18 members, all middle-aged, all white, all male—to be reassured that nothing had changed in Germany's hidebound automaking culture just because of the November [1998] merger of Daimler-Benz and Chrysler Corporation.

"We're not trying to bring two worlds together to create a new one. The ideal merged company will still have noticeable differences, like a choir that needs different voices to achieve the perfect sound," said Dirk V. Simmons, a corporate strategist from Daimler-Benz serving on the Daimler-Chrysler integration team. Those guiding history's biggest industrial marriage through its first daunting stages insisted that the objective of uniting the two auto giants was to preserve each working environment's unique qualities.

But cultural frictions were identified as the primary pitfalls in unsuccessful cross-border joint ventures, of which there had been many. More than 70 percent of such mergers were given up as failures within three years, according to Daimler's own extensive pre-merger research. As a hedge against those discouraging statistics, DaimlerChrysler managers put together PMI (Post-Merger Integration), a 100-member team that had combed through the sorry details of 50 failed cross-border partnerships to identify the frictions before they could begin grating on this merger.

With trademark German efficiency, the integration specialists had produced lists of *do's* and *don'ts* for industrial partnerships, isolating 98 miserable marriage traps and consigning them to 12 hit lists to be tackled by a bicultural team. The themes targeted for scrutiny ran from the broadly divergent packages of compensation and benefits accorded auto workers on opposite sides of the ocean to sensitivity training to help each side's executives understand the complexities of the other's industrial culture.

Late-night brainstorming sessions and videoconferences between the headquarters in nearby Stuttgart, Germany, and in Auburn Hills, Michigan, had themselves produced more issues for the strategists to ponder. "We noticed right away that the American executives were more casually dressed," said corporate communications director Roland Klein, one of the younger German executives to whom the notion of casual Fridays had some appeal. "You would never see anyone here without a tie on, even if they came in on a Saturday."

The *lingua franca* of all management meetings was English, which spared German executives the need to converse with each other using the informal *du* manner, as agreed by the PMI team. But Klein noted that the encouraged familiarity had not caught on: "As soon as two Germans are on their own again, they immediately revert to using *Sie*," he said, referring to the formal German

(Continued)

(Continued)

word for "you." German executives on the PMI team, which was supposed to finish its work and dissolve within two years, insisted that the new cross-cultural partnership had the ideal qualities for a corporate marriage because Daimler-Benz had been evolving toward a more American style of corporate management since Juergen Schrempp took over as chairman in May 1995. His introduction of performance-related bonuses and streamlining of the industrial conglomerate to focus on its core products transformed Daimler-Benz into a profitable company that should adjust more easily to the U.S. strategies for doing business.

Under Schrempp's guidance, Daimler-Benz became one of the first German companies to switch to U.S. accounting methods. Initiatives launched in February 1997 to create a more globally competitive company included the German automaking world's first labor agreement allowing management to change production schedules to fulfill orders more efficiently. In exchange, Daimler-Benz workers were promised there would be no layoffs through the end of 2000.

Fear of job losses was the main theme of resistance to the $33 billion merger before it was approved by both companies and their unions last year, and employees recognized that the merger meant eventual setbacks on the job market.

"People are worried, but that's not surprising in the current circumstances," said Gerhard Maier, a product manager whose extended family was dependent on the DaimlerChrysler empire for its livelihood. "The generation of my father expected to work for Mercedes-Benz until the end of their working lives, but those of us today can't be so sure."

Most workers shrugged off the effects of the merger as imperceptible at the production level. "I come through here 16 times a day, and I can't find one thing that is different now," said Herbert Spies, who conducted tours through the assembly facilities for visiting executives and new hires. Finding a delicate balance between preserving a familiar working atmosphere and getting across to employees that their company has a new identity was one of the most challenging tasks for the integration team, said Simmons, the corporate strategist.

Although cultural differences were said to be the downfall of most failed cross-border ventures, the merger's promoters cited production issues in arguing that their corporate marriage will be a success. The most important factor in DaimlerChrysler's favor, Klein said, is that there is virtually no overlap in the combined product line spanning Plymouth subcompacts up to the Mercedes-Benz luxury S-Class. Even the few models that appeared to compete for similar markets, such as the Jeep Grand Cherokee and Mercedes M-Class sport-utility vehicles, appealed to different types of consumers, he said. . . .

The joined manufacturers expected to achieve $1.4 billion in cost-saving "synergies" in the first year alone by combining purchasing operations and some technology products, for example. The company said bigger economies may become possible later if the automakers produce future models together. And Daimler may not yet be done shopping for partners and new opportunities for growth; the company was among the rumored suitors for all or part of the troubled Nissan Motor Company of Japan. But industry analysts were less sanguine about the very qualities that DaimlerChrysler strategists were promoting as keys to success.

"There is hardly any overlap in the product range of DaimlerChrysler, which means the potential for cost-savings in pretty limited," said Lothar Lubinetzki, automotive analyst for Enskilda Securities in London. "The real benefits of a merger come only with the implementation of a platform strategy, and there is no indication DaimlerChrysler is going to do this." That strategy aimed to cut costs by using common platforms—or the same basic underpinnings—for vehicles in more than one product line. Such a move required redesign and departure from the new company's vehement insistence on preserving the individuality of each partner's output.

If DaimlerChrysler were to engage in joint manufacturing, it would be confronted by the cultural clashes of the American and German workforces and the intense pride autoworkers on both sides of the Atlantic take in their products, Lubinetzki said.

"The Mercedes guys think they're brilliant because their product is respected for its quality," the analyst said. "But Chrysler people feel the same way about their reputation for efficiency. You put the two together, and you are going to have clashes. The biggest challenge in a merger like this is on the production floor. The chairmen and boards of directors can be all for it, but it eventually comes down to the workforces."

One major difference between German and U.S. auto production is the relationship between management and labor. At DaimlerChrysler, as at all German automakers, representatives of the powerful IG Metall labor union sat on the board of directors. The common German industrial practice of *mitbestimmung*, or co-determination, seeks to head off labor disputes by involving union leadership in decisions about production. The newly constituted supervisory board of DaimlerChrysler included a representative of the United Auto Workers.

Mixing management and labor in the boardroom may help avert trouble on the production floor, but fluctuations between the wages and benefits of the two workforces could introduce new disputes at the executive level. U.S. assembly line workers earned more per hour than their German counterparts, but their benefits and insurance packages often pale against those of the Europeans, who enjoyed a minimum of six weeks vacation each year, fully paid health care and education, and the right to a soul-soothing spa break every three years. When it came to the boardroom, though, U.S. executives were usually far better compensated than their German equivalents. . . .

Although a fatal collision was unlikely for the two automakers, the fact remains that most of those who have gone before them have crashed and burned.[a]

As of March 19, 2007, DaimlerChrysler was attempting to sell Chrysler to a private-equity buyer, Cerberus Capital Management LLC.[b] On May 14, 2007, Daimler announced that it is selling Chrysler for $7.5 billion. Major reasons include Chrysler's huge healthcare and pension benefits and Chrysler's poor consumer ratings of its output.

Questions

1. The merger actually turned out to be an acquisition of Chrysler by Daimler. Discuss the major issues that confronted Daimler Chrysler from the beginning from the HRM perspective developed in this chapter. What are the major HRM issues in this case?

2. How might have Daimler and Chrysler averted the clash of corporate cultures?

3. Do you believe that Daimler's top management adequately used its HR executives in the decision-making process to merge with Chrysler?

SOURCES:

a. Carol J. Williams, "Steering Around Culture Clashes," *Los Angeles Times* (January 17, 1999), Pt C, p. 1. Copyright © 1999 Times Mirror Company.

b. Brilliant, "Unions Vowing to Fight Chrysler Sale" (March 19, 2007). http://freerepublic.com/tag/UAW/index?tab=articles

NOTES

1. Excerpted from "Today's Issue: What It Means to Be a Global Corporation," *USA Today* (December 8, 1997), p. 15B.

2. P. V. Morgan, "International Human Resource Management: Fact or Fiction," *Personnel Administrator*, 31, no. 9 (1986), pp. 43–47.

3. P. J. Dowling, R. S. Schuler, and D. E. Welsh, *The International Dimensions of Human Resource Management* (Belmont, CA: Wadsworth Publishing, 1994), pp. 2–10.

4. K. Robert, E. E. Kossek, and C. Ozeki, "Managing the Global Workforce: Challenges and Strategies," *Academy of Management Executive*, 12, no. 4 (1998), p. 95.

5. See D. L. Pinney, "Structuring an Expatriate Tax Reimbursement Program," *Personnel Administrator*, 27, no. 7 (1982), pp. 19–25.

6. See Joseph Gamble, "Multinational Retailers in China 'McJobs' or Developing Skills?" *Journal of Management Studies*, 43, no. 7 (2006), pp. 1463–1490.

7. See David Ahlstrom, "HRM of Firms in China: The Challenge of Managing Host Country Personnel," *Business Horizons* (May 2006). www.findarticles.com./tn-bus?pqt=HRM+of+firms+in+China&3A+The+challenge+of+managing+host+country+personnel%X=16%=9

8. John R. Engen, "Getting Your Chinese Workforce Up to Speed," *International Business* (August 1994), p. 48.

9. Carla Joinson, "Why HR Managers Need to Think Globally," *HR Magazine* (April 1998), p. 2.

10. See Eric Washington, "There's No Place Like Home," *BusinessWeekonline* (October 9, 2001). www.businessweek.com/careers/content/oct2001/ca2001108 3942.htm

11. Sebastian Junger, "Very Risky Business," *The New York Times Magazine* (March 8, 1998), p. 53.

12. See J. Kapstein "How U.S. Executives Dodge Terrorism Abroad," *Business Week* (May 12, 1986), p. 41.

13. Rosalie L. Tung, "Selection and Training Procedures for U.S., European, and Japanese Multinationals," *California Management Review*, 25, no. 1 (1982), pp. 57–71.

14. J. C. Baker, K. Ryans, and G. Howard, *International Business Classics* (Lexington, MA: D. C. Heath & Co., 1988), pp. 283–295.

15. Ibid.

16. Ibid.

17. Ibid.

18. Tung, "Selection and Training Procedures," op cit.

19. Ibid.

20. Rosalie L. Tung, "Strategic Management of Human Resources in the Multinational Enterprise." *Human Resource Management*, 23, no. 2 (1984), pp. 129–143.

21. Rosalie L. Tung, *The New Expatriate* (Cambridge, MA: Ballinger, 1988), pp. 161–172.

22. Ibid.

23. Ibid.

24. Adapted from Rosalie L. Tung, "Human Resource Planning in Japanese Multinationals: A Model for U.S. Firms," *Journal of International Business Studies*, 15, no. 2 (Fall 1984), pp. 139–150.

25. Tung, *The New Expatriate*, op cit.

26. Brian Croft, "Use Technology to Manage Your Expatriates," *Personnel Journal* (December 1995), p. 115.

27. Paul E. Illman, *Developing Overseas Managers and Managers Overseas* (New York: Ama Com, 1980), p. 15.

28. David Pulatie, "How Do You Ensure Success of Managers Going Abroad?" *Training and Development Journal* (December 1985), pp. 22–23.

29. Rosalie L. Tung, "Selection and Training of Personnel for Overseas Assignments," *Columbia Journal of World Business*, 16, no. 1 (1981), pp. 68–78.

30. Dowling and Schuler, *The International Dimensions of Human Resource Management*, op cit., p. 53.

31. Charles Siler, "Recruiting Overseas Executives," *Overseas Business* (Winter 1990), p. 31.

32. Ibid.

33. M. Mendenhall and G. Oddou, "The Dimensions of Expatriate Acculturation: A Review," *The Academy of Management Review*, 10, no. 1 (1985), pp. 39–47.

34. For another framework on assessing expatriate candidates, refer to Charlene Marmer Solomon, "Staff Selection Impacts Global Success," *Personnel Journal* (January 1994), pp. 88–101.

35. Mendenhall and Oddou, "The Dimensions of Expatriate Acculturation," op cit.

36. S. Ronen, "Training the International Assignee," in I. Goldstein (Ed.), *Training and Career Development* (San Francisco: Jossey-Bass, 1989), p. 438.

37. I. Torbioro, *Living Abroad: Personnel Adjustment and Personnel Policy in the Overseas Setting* (New York: John Wiley, 1982).

38. H. L. Willis, "Selection for Employment in Developing Countries," *Personnel Administrator,* 29, no. 7 (1984), p. 55.

39. P. J. Dowling, "Psychological Testing in Australia: An Overview and an Assessment," in G. Palmer (Ed.), *Australia Personnel Management: A Reader* (Sydney, Australia: Macmillan, 1988), pp. 123–135.

40. A. M. Ryan, L. McFarland, H. Baron, and R. Page, "An International Look at Selection Practices: Nation and Culture as Explanations for Variability in Practice," *Personnel Psychology,* 52, no. 2 (Summer 1999), p. 359.

41. L. K. Stroh and P. M. Caligiuri, "Increasing Global Competitiveness Through Effective People Management," *Journal of World Business,* 33, no. 1 (1998), pp. 1–16.

42. Cecil G. Howard, "Profile of the 21st Century Manager," *HR Magazine* (June 1992), pp. 97–100.

43. See Robert W. Hornaday, "Using a Computer Simulation in Multicultural Management Development: An Indonesian Example, *Journal of Management Development,* 12, no. 3 (1993), pp. 12–20.

44. Ford S. Worthy, "You Can't Grow If You Can't Manage," *Fortune* (June 3, 1991), p. 86.

45. L. K. Stroh and P. M. Caligiuri, "Increasing Global Competitiveness Through Effective People Management," op cit., p. 10.

46. F. Balfour and D. Roberts, "China: Stealing Managers From the Big Boys," *Business Week* (September 25, 2005), pp. 54–55.

47. Jennifer J. Laabs, "How Gillette Grooms Global Talent," *Personnel Journal* (August 3, 1993), pp. 64–76.

48. Ronald Henkoff, "Growing Your Company: Five Ways to Do It Right," *Fortune Advisor 1998* (New York: Fortune Books, 1998), p. 84.

49. N. Sleveking, K. Anchor, and R. C. Marston, "Selecting and Preparing Expatriate Employees," *Personnel Journal* (March 1981), pp. 197–200. See also Solomon, "Staff Selection Impacts Global Success," op cit.; J. L. Calof and Paul W. Beamish, "The Right Attitude for International Success," *Business Quarterly* (Autumn 1994), pp. 105–110. See also Robert Kramer, "Developing Global Leaders: Enhancing Competencies and Accelerating the Expatriate Experience," Report # 1373–05-WG (New York: The Conference Board, 2005).

50. M. Harvey, "The Other Side of Foreign Assignments: Dealing with the Repatriation Dilemma," *Columbia Journal of World Business,* 17 (1982), pp. 53–59.

51. For further discussion on this issue, see J. M. Mezias and T. A. Scandura, "A Needs Approach to Executive Adjustment and Career Development: A Multiple Mentoring Perspective," *Journal of International Business Studies,* 36 (2005), pp. 519–538.

52. R. L. Thornton and M. K. Thornton, "Personnel Problems in 'Carry the Flag' Missions in Foreign Assignments," *Business Horizons* (January–February 1995), pp. 59–65; Harvey, "The Other Side of Foreign Assignments," op cit., p. 56; Cecil G. Howard, "How Relocation Abroad Affects Expatriates' Family Life," *Personnel Administrator* (November 1980), p. 71; Michael A. Conway, "Reducing Expatriate Failure Rates," *Personnel Administrator* (July 1984), pp. 31–34; David M. Noer, *Multinational People Management* (Washington, DC: Bureau of National Affairs, 1975).

53. See Richard Pooley, "Bridging the Cultural Divide," *Computing Business* (April 20, 2006). www.whatpc.com.uk/computing-business/features/2153953/bridgi

54. SOURCES: Harvey, "The Other Side of Foreign Assignments," op cit., p. 58; Clague and Krupp, "International Personnel: The Repatriation Problem," *Personnel Administration,* 23 (1978), pp. 29–33.

55. Charles Butler, "A World of Trouble," *Sales and Marketing Management,* 151, no. 9 (September 1999), p. 5.

56. Excerpted from Ron Ashkenas, "Breaking Through the Global Boundaries," *Executive Excellence,* 16, no. 7 (July 1999), p. 8.

57. Eric Matson, "How to Globalize Yourself," *Fast Company* (April–May 1997), p. 134.

58. Dowling and Schuler, *The International Dimensions of Human Resource Management,* op cit., p. 117.

59. Ibid.

60. Valarie Frazee, "Is the Balance Sheet Right for Your Expats?" *Workforce,* 77, no. 9 (September 1998), p. 19.

61. Dowling and Schuler, *International Dimensions of Human Resource Management,* op cit., pp. 120–121.

62. Carolina Esquenazi-Shaio, "Just Rewards: Compensating Managers Abroad is Tough," *International Business* (April 1996), p. 33.

63. Dowling and Schuler, *International Dimensions of Human Resource Management,* op cit., p. 124.

64. Ibid., p. 125.

65. Ibid.

66. Ibid., p. 126.

67. SOURCE: www.worldwideconsulting.com/expatriate.htm (March 12, 2007).

68. Ibid., p. 129.

69. SOURCE: "Discrepancies in International Compensation" (March 12, 2007). www.worldwideconsulting.com/compdiscr.htm

70. This discussion is adapted from Worldwide Consulting Corporation's Web site, www.worldwideconsulting.com (March 13, 2007).

71. This concept draws from R. Neale and R. Mindel, "Rigging Up Multicultural Teamwork," *Personnel Management* (January 1992), p. 37.

72. For an example, see Debee Doke, "Perfect Strangers: Cultural and Linguistic Differences Between U.S. and U.K. Workers Necessitate Training for Expatriates," *HR Magazine* (December 2004). www.findarticles.com/p/articles/mi_m3495

73. SOURCE: Carlos Ghosen, "Creating Value Across Cultures," *Global Agenda Magazine* (2004).

74. B. Dumaine, "The Bureaucracy Busters," *Fortune* (June 17, 1991), p. 41.

75. K. Roberts, E. E. Kossek, and C. Ozeki, "Managing the Global Workforce: Challenges and Strategies," op cit., p. 99.

Part V

CROSS-CULTURAL COMMUNICATION, BUSINESS PRACTICES, AND NEGOTIATIONS

Communication is the process of transmitting information, ideas, and attitudes (a message) from one person (the sender) to another (the receiver). In practice, this is an extremely difficult process to apply effectively because receivers often do not interpret messages as intended by the sender; messages are often not understood or are misinterpreted. This occurs when senders encode messages using words, symbols, and concepts/ideas that are unfamiliar to the receiver or receivers. Unfamiliarity results especially when senders' and receivers' frames of reference and means of communication have been developed in different cultures. Cultures typically develop unique ways of communicating; they develop formal languages, idioms, slang, jargon, and nonverbal means of communication (body language) as well as norms and values that are unique to their own society. And they develop unique ways of conducting and negotiating business. This uniqueness makes communicating, and conducting and negotiating business across nations/cultures challenging tasks for international managers. International managers who possess strong skills in this area are likely to be far more successful in international management than those who possess weak skills. Chapter 9 discusses cross-cultural communication and Chapter 10, cross-cultural business practices and negotiations.

9

CROSS-CULTURAL COMMUNICATION

Stiff and ill at ease at first [at a training program], the Japanese said little, and some of what they said was hard to understand. The Americans talked too much and wondered when the Japanese would make a contribution. . . . [Professor Hirotaka Takeuchi from Hitotsubashi University, Japan] explained to the others why the Japanese spoke so little. . . . Unlike Americans, who like to jump in and grab control of a meeting, said Takeuchi, the Japanese prefer to wait and listen; the higher their rank, the more they listen. This group of Japanese was the elite, he explained, and therefore listened a lot. He added that the Japanese have a not-so-subtle saying: "He who speaks first at a meeting is a dumb ass."[1]

Learning Objectives of the Chapter

Effective communication across nations/cultures can take place only when the sender encodes the message using language, idioms, norms and values, and so on that are familiar to the receiver or when the receiver (or receivers) is familiar with the language, idioms, and so on used by the sender. Attaining familiarity with language, slang, norms and values, and so on across nations/cultures is by no means an easy task because words and concepts are often not easily translatable (and sometimes not translatable at all) from one culture to another. For example, the concept of "self-fulfillment" is well understood in American culture, but such a concept is not translatable to many cultures throughout the world, which understand better the concept of "group fulfillment." Furthermore, words often have different meanings when translated into another language. For instance, the U.S. manufacturer General Motors Corporation advertised on many of the automobiles it produced that the body was made by Fisher ("Body by Fisher"). The Flemish in Belgium interpreted it to mean "Corpse by Fisher."

In the United States, the slang *knocked-up* means a female has been impregnated, but in England the slang *knock-up* means to pick up someone at his or her home at a preestablished time. In Portugal, the title of the American book *Knocked Up* was translated into Portuguese as "Damn It, What Bad Luck."

The above suggests that communication is bound to create many problems for people conducting international/cross-cultural business. And international managers cannot generally be effective if they do not possess strong cross-cultural communication skills. After studying this chapter, you should be able to do the following:

1. Discuss the communication process (ideation, encoding, transmission, and decoding) in an international/cross-cultural context

2. Discuss the cultural and language barriers and the ways of dealing with them, including the use of translators

3. Discuss the ways to develop the ability to communicate effectively across cultures

The Cross-Cultural Communication Process

Figure 9.1 presents the communication process. Communication is the process of conveying a message (a concept or idea) from one party to another or others. The message can be transmitted orally (spoken words), visually (written words), or nonverbally (body/facial expressions). Concepts have different meanings and different levels of importance in different cultures throughout the globe, and many societies have adopted a unique language or multiple unique languages (e.g., China has one written language but more than 50 distinct spoken languages, such as Mandarin, Cantonese, Shanghainese). Mandarin has been made China's national language, but (in 2006) only about half of China's 1.3 billion people speak Mandarin; there is only one written language that is common to all dialects.

Since meanings and languages vary so much from one culture to another, people conducting business across cultures and languages will often encounter communication difficulties that they would not encounter in their own culture and language. Therefore, to communicate effectively across cultures and languages, international businesspeople must develop the ability to adapt to the differences. Lacking this ability, they will often find themselves in embarrassing situations.[2]

Relative to differing verbal languages, English appears to be emerging as the language of choice in conducting business across countries. Nevertheless, cross-cultural, cross-national communication problems remain because different cultures have developed different social values. Thus, a concept perceived in a certain way in one culture, is perceived differently in another. Also, different cultures have developed different nonverbal languages. Therefore, differing gestures and facial expressions still present cross-cultural communication problems. Furthermore, "it is blind provincialism to believe that English will continue to be used everywhere for all occasions."[3]

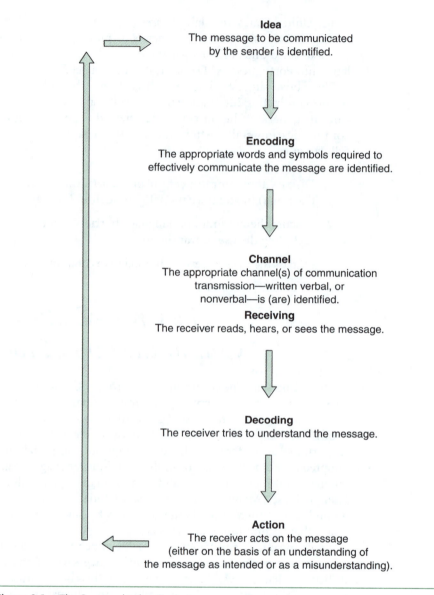

Idea
The message to be communicated
by the sender is identified.

Encoding
The appropriate words and symbols required to
effectively communicate the message are identified.

Channel
The appropriate channel(s) of communication
transmission—written verbal, or
nonverbal—is (are) identified.

Receiving
The receiver reads, hears, or sees the message.

Decoding
The receiver tries to understand the message.

Action
The receiver acts on the message
(either on the basis of an understanding of
the message as intended or as a misunderstanding).

Figure 9.1   The Communication Process

This means that quite often, international business is conducted between parties who speak different languages (either verbal or nonverbal, or both). When senders of messages and receivers speak different languages, communication barriers arise. To help eliminate the verbal and nonverbal barriers, the parties involved in the communication process must often employ a language translator. The ensuing sections describe the ideation, encoding, transmission, and decoding stages of the communication process in an international/cross-cultural context; discuss effective translation skills; propose a framework for communicating across countries using the English language; and propose ways to develop cross-cultural communication skills.

The Ideation Stage

At the ideation stage, senders (communicators) must identify clearly and specifically what it is that they want the receivers (the listeners) to do as a result of the communication—that is, they must determine what their objective is.[4] Is it to get the receiver(s) to buy a product or service? Or to perform a certain task? Or to sign a contract? Or to find a solution to a problem? Or to approve a solution to a problem? Or to provide certain information? Or to approve a certain recommendation?

When individuals are communicating in cultures different from their own (and realistically, differences do not occur only across nations; they can often be found within nations, as well as within nations' regions; between cities/towns; and in cities such as New York, within blocks and even apartments in the same building), they should ask themselves two basic questions: In light of the culture, is the objective realistic? In light of the culture, is the time frame realistic?

Realistic Objective

A society's culture determines to what extent an objective is realistic. For example, an objective requiring that the receiver carry out the sender's directives may not be realistic in small power distance cultures such as Sweden, Norway, and Israel, where individuals culturally expect to participate in decision making. It may, however, be realistic in large power distance cultures such as France, where individuals culturally expect to be directed. (See Practical Perspective 9.1.) Objectives to sell beef in India or pork in Israel would not be realistic. An objective to sell toothpaste that makes teeth sparkling white may not be realistic in many parts of Southeast Asia where betel nut chewing is an elite pastime and stained teeth are a symbol of high esteem. An objective to mass-sell Western-style, sitting-height toilet bowls in China, where ground-level bowls were (prior to modernization) widely used (to use, one squats over them), would not have been realistic before China's economic transformation. An objective to obtain a signature on a lengthy contract may be realistic in America, where it is an accepted practice, but not in Japan, where verbal contracts ("a gentleman's agreement/a handshake") or written contracts consisting of only a few pages are the accepted practice.

PRACTICAL PERSPECTIVE 9-1

An Illustration of Cross-Cultural Communication Ineffectiveness

Behavior	Attribution
American: "How long will it take you to finish this report?"	American: I have asked him to participate.
	Greek: His behavior makes no sense. He is the boss. Why doesn't he tell me?
Greek: "I don't know. How long should it take?"	Greek: I asked him for an order

PRACTICAL PERSPECTIVE 9-1 (Continued)

American: "You are in the best position to analyze time requirements."

American: I press him to take responsibility for his actions

Greek: What nonsense! I'd better give him an answer

Greek: "Ten days."

American: He lacks the ability to estimate time; this time estimate is totally inadequate.

American: "Take fifteen days. Is it agreed? You will do it in fifteen days?

American: I offer a contract.
Greek: These are my orders: fifteen days.

In fact, the report needed 30 days of regular work. So the Greek worked day and night, but at the end of the fifteenth day, he still needed to do one more day's work.

Behavior	Attribution
American: "Where is the report?"	American: I am making sure he fulfills his contract.
	Greek: He is asking for the report
Greek: "It will be ready tomorrow."	Both attribute that it is not ready.
American: "But we had agreed it would be ready today"	American: I must teach him to fulfill a contract.
	Greek: The stupid, incompetent boss! Not only does he give me the wrong orders, but he doesn't even appreciate that I did a 30-day job in sixteen days

The Greek hands in his resignation. The American is surprised. Greek: I won't work for such a man.

SOURCE: From H.C. Triandis, *Interpersonal Behavior*, 1st ed. (Monteray, CA: Brooks/Cole Publishing, 1977). Copyright © 1977. Reprinted with permission of Wadsworth, a division of Thomson Learning. Fax: 800–730–2215.

An objective to obtain a firm employee commitment to a project in Islamic cultures—which exist anywhere from North Africa to the Middle East to Indonesia—may not be as realistic as it is in Western cultures. Islamic cultures tend to be guided by a fatalistic view that events are controlled by external forces ("God wills it") and they therefore have no power to make things happen, whereas the latter cultures tend to be guided by a master-of-destiny view that events are controlled by people themselves. An objective to discuss business during a lunch or dinner meeting in many parts of Asia, Europe, and South America, where such meetings are used mainly for the development of social relations, may not be a realistic objective, but it may be realistic in North America, where such meetings are typically held for the purpose of discussing business.

Realistic Time Frame

Culture also determines the definition of a realistic time frame. Different cultures hold different concepts of time. In some cultures, for example, Germany and Switzerland, timetables are exact and precise, and people tend to meet deadlines. In some cultures, including some Latin American and African cultures, individuals possess a relatively more relaxed attitude toward time; unlike in the United States, time is not a commodity, and the completion of tasks moves relatively slowly. Deadlines given to employees in these cultures often will not be met and often will demotivate them. The objective to build a bridge in, for instance, a 24-month span of time is therefore more realistic in the former cultures than in the latter.

The Encoding Stage

After the message to be communicated has been ascertained, the next step is to determine and organize the words, expressions, and nonverbal signals needed to communicate the message effectively. Language and cultural differences exist among nations. Vast language differences occur even within a single nation. For example, Canada has two official languages; Switzerland has four; and China, as previously indicated, has more than 50 different languages. These differences create difficulties in identifying the words, expressions, and nonverbal signals required to communicate effectively across nations and cultures. Therefore, the encoding process for cross-cultural communication must take into consideration the many language and cultural differences existing around the globe. Some of the differences are discussed below.

Language

Unique idioms, slang, similes, metaphors, and jargon are components of languages that people use without being aware that they are doing so, and many are not easily translatable from one language to another. For example, the promotional term *come alive with Pepsi* in the United States means to become invigorated or energetic, whereas when translated into German, it communicates the thought of "coming alive from the grave with Pepsi." Even though the Latin word *nova* actually means "new," the label on Chevrolet's Nova automobile was interpreted by many Spanish-speaking individuals to mean "doesn't go" (*no va*)—who would buy a car that does not go? America's Colgate-Palmolive Company introduced its Cue brand of toothpaste in French-speaking countries. The word "cue" in French translates into a pornographic word that offends many French-speaking people. How does a non-English-speaking person using a language translation dictionary readily translate the English phrase "as easy as duck soup" or "a ballpark figure" or "a monkey on my back" or "a pain in the neck" into his or her language? How does an English-to-Russian translator interpret terms such as *consumer market* or *market-driven* economy to a Russian?

Furthermore, U.S.-made movies, which are popular exports, use swear words a lot. But in many cultures, swearing is unacceptable. Therefore, the swear words are given an acceptable translated meaning. The translation in many American movies is made via written subtitles, and countries that do not accept swearing will use different, acceptable words; for example, in some Spanish-speaking countries swear words are posted in the subtitle in parentheses as *mal decion*, which means "bad word."

Even within a language, many words have different meanings to different people. For example, Parker, the well-known maker of ballpoint pens, had to change its advertising in Latin America after learning that *bola*, the Spanish translation of "ball," does not mean *ball* in all Spanish-speaking countries; in some, it actually means "revolution" or "lie." In the United States, *tabling something* means "postponing it"; in

England, it means "discussing it now." In Canada, a *pothole* is where one goes swimming; in New York City, it is where one smashes an automobile's wheels and shock absorbers. Imagine the embarrassment of an American named Randy, who when visiting in England, approached a lady at a social gathering and introduced himself: "Hi, I'm Randy." In England, *to be randy* means to be sexually aroused. In the United States, *to be pissed* means to be mad, while in England it means to be drunk. In Portugal, the word *rapariga* simply means "girl," but in Brazil calling a girl *rapariga* will get you into trouble, as there the word is used to describe a street walker or a prostitute. And when United Airlines entered the Pacific market, one of United's in-flight magazine covers showed the Australian actor Paul Hogan wandering through the outback. The caption read, "Paul Hogan Camps It Up." Hogan's lawyer called United Airlines to let them know that *camps it up* is Australian slang for "flaunts his homosexuality."[5]

Also, some languages are read from left to right (just like you are reading now), thus *A, B, C* would be read as "A, B, C"; but some languages read from right to left, and *A, B, C* would thus be read as "C, B, A." This could cause many business presentation problems when issues are displayed from left to right to a culture that reading the displays from right to left. For instance, a box of detergent used to wash clothes in a washing machine may display on the box from left to right dirty clothes first, then the clothes being washed with the detergent, and shining clean clothes last. The right-to-left cultures might read the displays as "You have clean clothes, wash them in the detergent, and you get dirty clothes." They may not want to buy the detergent. Furthermore, the September 11, 2001, attack on the United States is often referred to by Americans as the 9/11 incident. People in many countries would read it as the November 11 incident because in their country, the day is placed first, the month second, and the year last. Therefore, in those countries, the attack on the United States took place on 11 November 2001. Also, measures and weights used in the United States are different from those used in other parts of the world. For example, the United States uses miles, while many countries use kilometers.

Letters and Characters

Letters and characters also differ across cultures. Japanese characters and English letters, for example, are very different. The Japanese written language consists of thousands of picture characters. The Japanese language, however, uses a combination of two syllabifies, *kana* and *kanji.* Kana are the phonetic sounds of the 113 possible syllables, and kanji are characters that stand for sound plus meaning. To read a Japanese newspaper, the reader must know 2,000 kanji characters, and the reader who knows 4,000 characters is considered well educated. (This may help explain why the Japanese culturally prefer oral over written communication and short, as opposed to long, written communication.) Such differences also make language interpretations difficult. The Chinese language also uses many thousands of picture characters.

For example, when America's Coca-Cola Company initially introduced its beverage in China, only its Coca-Cola label appeared on the can. Since Coca-Cola is not translatable into Mandarin (the official language of China), to write the label, local vendors used Mandarin characters to phonetically spell the sound of Coca-Cola. The characters the vendors selected actually meant "bite the wax tadpole." To deal with this problem, Coca-Cola's translators eventually selected a group of characters that are interpreted by the Chinese to mean "may the mouth rejoice" and now place those characters on the cans along with the English letters.[6]

Effective translation of languages is therefore vital in cross-national business negotiations—in promotion and labeling as well as in writing of contracts and reports, in written and/or oral communications between domestic and foreign employees, and in the general management of foreign subsidiaries.

Expressions and Nonverbal Communication

Expressions and nonverbal communication play an important role in cross-cultural encoding. For example, U.S. moviemaking firms export movies and television programs made for American audiences. Usually, these must be modified by dubbing in the local language or translating it by using subtitles. Accurate language translation is therefore essential. But what is also important is the nonverbal communication contained in the films or TV programs. For example, the ways of depicting affection in American-made movies and television programs are viewed by some cultures as being offensive. Gestures are widely used as a means of communication in films and television programs, and the same sign has different meanings across different cultures. Some gestures may offend many foreign viewers and must therefore be edited out or somehow isolated before the film is distributed in the foreign culture. For example, in the United States, Americans form a circle with their index finger and thumb to communicate that something is "OK." Imagine the embarrassment of a former U.S. president who visited Brazil, stepped out of the airplane, and made that gesture to a waiting crowd of Brazilians. The same sign in Brazil means that one is interested in having sex. The same OK sign means "zero" in France and is a symbol for money in Japan.

In many cultures, including those of the United States and China, pointing one's thumb up is a gesture meaning "good" or "great," but in Australia it is a crude gesture. The showing of affection in public is offensive in some cultures. For instance, in April 2007, the famous U.S. movie actor, Richard Gere, who contributes to socially oriented programs in India, while visiting there, passionately hugged a famous, very attractive, female Indian movie star on stage, seemingly in jest. She had just finished making a new movie. That display led to public riots, with the demand that Richard Gere and the actress be incarcerated because they have offended the Indian people—such public display is a no-no in Indian culture. Geer and the actress were accused of promoting immoral behavior in Indian culture, of being culturally insensitive. That kind of controversial behavior used to promote movies in the United States works well for moviemakers in the United States. Will it work in India?

The Role of Formality and Informality in Communication

Cultures vary in their requirements for formality and informality, and these variations also affect cross-cultural communication encoding. Some cultures, especially American and Australian, value informality in communication, but most cultures throughout the world value formality.[7] Individuals in cultures that value informality place low importance on the use of rank, status, and position in communication and often use first names when communicating with each other, even in business settings. On the other hand, individuals in cultures that value formality place high importance on the use of last names, titles, and other indications of rank and status in communication.

For example, in Italy, many people are addressed as Dottore or Dottoressa, whether or not they hold a Ph.D. degree, and an individual can hold such a title by simply holding a college degree. In many Latin American cultures, the title is more important than the name. Therefore, the title *Ingeniero* (Engineer) is used before the person's last name (e.g., Ingeniero Vargas). The French demonstrate status, rank, and privilege by the type of language used in correspondence. They often use flowery, effusive, complex syntax when communicating with higher-ranking individuals. The French do not use the term *Dear* to begin a formal letter; the letter would simply start with the person's name—for instance, "P. Rousseau." In France, individuals can work together in the same place for many years and still greet each other with a formal handshake and by the formal name— for example, "Bonjour, M. Rousseau." In Germany, a doctor is addressed as "Herr Doctor," not "Doctor Schilling," and one does not use first names until invited to do so.

In many cultures, rank and status are shown by seating arrangements, by the way individuals enter a room, and by who speaks first. In Japan, for instance, the oldest male is normally the most senior, and he must not be the first to enter a room; he is preceded by his assistants and followed by other assistants, and he sits in the middle. Correspondence to people of higher status must be written individually, and mass mails are often disliked because they emphasize efficiency over the honoring of individuals' rank and position. People in cultures that value informality, such as Americans, often become frustrated when forced to pay deference to someone simply because of his or her status (family ties, schooling, age, and so on) and not because of the person's accomplishments.

How Much Information Is Needed?

Individuals in some cultures, such as Japan, France, and Germany, can be generally categorized as conservative or risk-avoidant. These individuals make decisions slowly, avoid risks, and dislike ambiguity. (Conditions of uncertainty and ambiguity make them feel uncomfortable.) They, therefore, have a strong need for much detail and information. On the other hand, people in some cultures, such as Singapore, the United States, and Australia, feel relatively more comfortable with risk and ambiguity, make decisions more quickly, and require less detail and information.[8]

Language Translation

The above suggests that cross-cultural, cross-national communicators, to communicate effectively, must make certain that the language used, including the words, symbols, context,[9] slang, formal and informal behaviors, as well as nonverbal behaviors, is the one that will be understood by the receiver(s). In conducting global business, businesspeople often do not possess the command of the language necessary to communicate effectively with foreign associates. These senders therefore have to find a way to convert the language they understand into the language understood by the foreign associates (the receivers).

Translating one language into another is a huge problem confronting cross-cultural, cross-national communicators. To overcome translation problems in written communications, international businesspeople often use the dual-translation approach. This involves having a translator in the home country interpret and convert the message into the foreign language, and before the message is communicated, having another translator in the foreign country interpret and convert the message back into the home country's language. For example, a communicator transmitting a message from the United States to Angola, where Portuguese is spoken, first has a translator of English to Portuguese in the United States translate the message from English to Portuguese; the translated message is then sent to a translator of Portuguese to English in Angola to be translated back to English. The sender will transmit the message after he or she has been assured that the translated message will be understood by the receiver(s) as intended.

The Translator's Role

A translator acts as an interpreter for two or more people who wish to communicate with each other but speak different languages. The interpretation may involve written messages, oral messages, nonverbal messages, or a combination of the three types. The translator's job is complex, as he or she must effectively decode the sender's message and encode it into the receiver's language, and then decode the receiver's (now the sender's) reply and encode it into the sender's (now the receiver's) language. (See Figure 9.2.)

Oral Translators. There are two types of oral translators: those who are engaged in simultaneous interpretations and those involved in sequential interpretations.[10]

Simultaneous oral interpreters are usually used by speakers in formal presentation situations, such as conferences, where the audience (the receivers) and the speaker (the sender) communicate using different languages. In this situation, the translator interprets the sender's formal presentation and passes it on to the audience. (This type is used in United Nations' meetings.) Usually, the speaker communicates a small group of words, pauses to allow the interpreter to translate them and pass them on to the audience, and so on.

For example, a few years ago, this author spent three weeks lecturing in English at a university in Shanghai, China. The lecture topic was "Current Western Management Theory and Research." The audience consisted of the university's management professors, some high-level executives from Chinese business enterprises, and several of the university's management graduate students. Most of the participants did not understand English or their understanding was weak. The presentations therefore required use of a translator. Two Mandarin-speaking graduate students at the university who also spoke English fairly fluently were assigned to the author to act as translators. Both students were management majors who had studied Western management theory. They acted as translators in shifts. The lectures were held daily from 9 a.m. to 4:30 p.m., with an hour and a half for lunch. It is virtually impossible for one person to be effective in a translator's role for such a long period of time. The author made formal presentations, with many pauses to allow the translator to interpret the message and pass it on to the audience. But the author was not sure his intended message was really translated as intended because some contexts are not translatable as there is no equivalent in the culture and he was not sure the translators could come up with a near-equivalent context. For example, one of the participants asked the author to explain America's concept of freedom of the press. He did, but he could tell from the nonverbal feedback that the participants were not really grasping the concept.

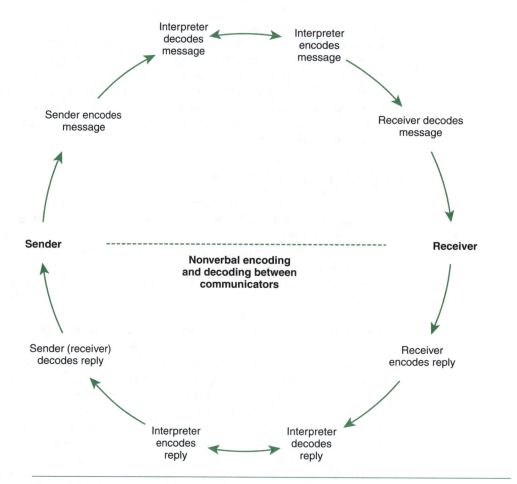

Figure 9.2 Cross-Language Interpretation

SOURCE: Adapted from Lyle Sussman and Denise M. Johnson, "The Interpreted Executive: Theory, Models, and Implications," *Journal of Business Communications*, 30, no. 4 (1993), p. 421. Reprinted with permission.

Sequential oral interpreters are typically used by clients involved in cross-language business negotiations and social functions. Unlike the simultaneous interpreter, the sequential interpreter normally requires negotiation and diplomatic skills, the ability to transmit personality and style, as well as knowledge of the language and culture.

The Effective Translator

It is obvious that the lack of an effective translator will lead to problems. Several factors help define the effective translator.[11]

Characteristics of the Message Itself. The translator is aware of the underlying substantive content of the message—both implicit and explicit—that the sender wishes to convey to the receiver(s). This suggests that a translator with a business background is likely to be more effective in business transactions than a translator with a liberal arts background. The former is likely to be more familiar with business jargon, idioms, and so on than the latter. For instance, the former is more likely to know what the business term *bull market* means than the latter. On the other hand, the translator with the liberal arts background may be more effective at social gatherings, where a broad range of topics are typically discussed, than the translator with the business background.

Characteristics of the Language Involved. The translator is familiar with the sociolinguistic properties of the languages, including formality (discussed above) and the role of gender, status, verb, tense, and standard syntax in the language. For example, the effective translator knows that it is not inappropriate to use first names in small power distance societies, but it is in large power distance societies, where use of titles is customary. As previously indicated, in the United States, bosses and subordinates often communicate with each other on a first-name basis, but not so in France, where titles are used.

Interpreter's Relationship With the Client. The translator has a personal involvement and familiarity with the client and the topic to be communicated. For example, when the author was lecturing in China using two translators, both were familiar with the topic. A problem that arose, however, was that the author did not meet with the interpreters before beginning the lectures to orient them specifically on the matters to be covered. Interpreters not given advance notice of the specific contents of the message can make translation errors and interrupt the flow of communication.

Context.[12] The time, place, and purpose of the meeting affect a translator's ability. High-stakes negotiations that take place in a hostile environment and that must be accomplished in a short period of time create stress for the translator and for the communicator, reducing their effectiveness. Negotiations should therefore be arranged to cause minimum stress for the translator and the communicator.

Interpreter's Skills. The effective translator has command of the languages being interpreted, active listening skills, sensitivity to explicit and implicit meanings, and the ability to bridge cultural gaps. These skills must be optimum. Many language specialists believe that to master a language, especially its idiomatic meanings and slang, it is necessary to live in the foreign country for a few years. As a matter of fact, many expatriate professional translators periodically return to their native countries so that they can update their translation skills. They believe that prolonged absences reduce translation ability because idioms, slang, jargon, and cultural behaviors change rapidly.

For instance, in the United States, the meaning of the word *gay* not too long ago, was generally taken to mean "happy"; today, many people use the word to describe a homosexual male. The word *bad* has historically meant just that; today, in describing an individual's behavior in some situations, such as in sports, the word is actually used to mean "good." For example, a basketball player is "bad" if he or she possesses "good" playing skills. His or her being so good makes it "bad" for the opposing team, therefore he or she "is bad." And within the past few decades, the slang word used to describe unconventional individuals in the United States changed from "bohemian" to "beatnik" to "hippie." Not too long ago, in the United States *hunk* was slang for a good-looking guy, but today the same slang means "a cool guy." Earlier, it was posited that slang should be avoided in cross-cultural communication; but the author once inadvertently described himself as a "hunk" to a female friend in Honduras. Not knowing what it meant, his female friend looked it up in the dictionary, which told her it meant "a big piece of meat." Later, the author explained that *hunk* means a good-looking guy and asked if there was a Spanish equivalent in Honduras. She said that *mangito*, the fruit mango, was the equivalent; but he stopped right there because *fruit* also used to be slang for "a male homosexual" in the United States.

At a recent social gathering in New York, the author met an expatriate from Portugal whose profession is translating English to Portuguese and Portuguese to English for businesses. She writes business contracts, is involved in oral translations, and so on. She said that to maintain her translating skills, she goes back to Portugal every year and a half or so and lives there for about six months, spending that time updating her Portuguese language skills. She believed that if a professional translator is away from the foreign language for much longer than a year and a half, his or her effective translation skills will diminish.

Characteristics of the Parties. The effective translator is familiar with the personal styles, idiosyncrasies, and communication strengths, including encoding and decoding abilities, of the parties for whom he or she is interpreting.

Cultural Norms and Values. The effective translator is familiar with the cultural norms and values of both cultures. For example, as discussed in Chapter 1, some cultures are high context and some are low context. When conducting business, people in high-context cultures (1) establish social trust first, (2) value personal relations and goodwill, (3) make agreements on the basis of general trust, and (4) like to conduct slow and ritualistic negotiations.[13] People in these cultures prefer that messages not be structured directly, that they do not get right to the point and state conclusions or bottom lines first. Instead, they prefer that a message be indirect, building up to the point and stating conclusions or bottom lines last.[14] On the other hand, individuals in low-context cultures (1) get down to business first, (2) value expertise and performance, (3) like agreement by specific, legalistic contract, and (4) like to conduct negotiations as efficiently as possible.[15] Individuals in these cultures prefer that messages be structured directly, that they get immediately to the point and state conclusions or bottom lines first.[16]

The translator can guide the communication flow accordingly, and when the parties for whom he or she is acting as intermediary are opposites (one is high context and the other low context), the translator educates his or her clients accordingly and applies the most viable communication customs. For instance, if a Japanese businessperson is competing with other companies to obtain a contract from a German company, the German customs are likely to be the most applicable. If, however, a German businessperson is competing with other companies to obtain a contract from a Japanese company, the Japanese customs are likely to be the most applicable. (Practical Perspective 9.2 describes an American expatriate in Japan who became a cultural translator.)

PRACTICAL PERSPECTIVE 9-2

The Tale of a Cultural Translator

Joint ventures in Japan between Western and Japanese companies usually run into a series of small conflicts that escalate over the years. They easily become big emotional battles, mainly due to cultural differences. Both parties exclaim: "Here they go again. Can't they understand that . . . "

A company I [Gunnar Beeth] worked for, as director of international operations, avoided this entire problem thanks to an employee, George Schreiber. I will describe him because he became what I call a "cultural translator" between the American headquarters and its Japanese joint venture.

Schreiber was an installation engineer, in charge of starting up our equipment. The company needed to send a person to train the new Japanese employees in the unique technology. Schreiber accepted a two-year contract for temporary transfer to Japan. He was first sent to an intensive course in Japanese.

Schreiber did not belong to the management group in the American company but had a solid understanding of the technical products, their installation, and use. So he was highly qualified for training the Japanese engineers.

Schreiber became well accepted by all of the Japanese employees. The Japanese managers felt that the nonassertive Schreiber was no threat to their management careers, despite representing the U.S. owner. So they did not hesitate to ask his advice on a great many matters, some outside his expertise but within his good common sense. The engineers throughout the company appreciated Schreiber's frequent help with a multitude of problems they ran into in the beginning. It became their habit to ask him when they had a problem, any problem. The secretaries in the office were eager to help this nice gaijin bachelor with his wretched Japanese.

Before expected, the joint venture was profitable, thriving, and growing. Schreiber's first two-year contract came to an end. By then, he had learned Japanese habits. His spoken Japanese became good. He drank green tea at all hours, ate rice at all meals, and liked to sleep on Japanese tatami mats instead of a bed. He had become "tatamized."

Schreiber was offered a second two-year Japanese contract, which he accepted at once. Other contracts followed. The joint venture soon had more than 100 Japanese employees, and the Japanese engineers soon surpassed Schreiber in the intricacies of the new equipment, which changed rapidly, so he had nothing left to teach them in technical matters.

What could he do in that mature joint venture? Schreiber became a "cultural translator."

When a message arrived from the American headquarters and the capable Japanese joint-venture president felt offended, he stormed into Schreiber's small office and threw the message in front of him, fuming. George read it and explained in his calm manner that the Americans had not really meant it in the way such a message would be understood in Japan.

For communication from Japan to the United States, the written English of one of the Japanese secretaries was quite adequate. But, at times, something far more important than good English was needed, such as when the Japanese accountant explained to the American auditor why they had spent $46,534 on 847 December holiday presents or when the Japanese personnel manager explained why they continued to keep a chemist on the payroll whose specialty had become obsolete a year earlier.

In these instances, they all went to Schreiber with their drafted messages. Somehow or other, he made them sound at least halfway sane in the American environment. It wasn't easy.

At times, when not even Schreiber could get it to sound sane in the American culture, he would write over his own signature, "This will sound crazy in the United States, but you should go along with it anyway for the following reasons . . ."

When the western managers came traveling to Japan (myself included), Schreiber accompanied us to ensure that we didn't do or say anything too stupid, from the Japanese viewpoint. Whenever we did that anyway, he corrected us at

Identify the Right Audience

To encode their messages effectively, senders must ascertain the correct receivers and see that the message appeals to them.[17] In many cultures, those persons involved in the decision or action phase are not readily obvious. Tailoring a message to the obvious receivers and appealing to them can often create communication problems. A culture's views on authority, rank, and group definition often force a sender to include additional or different primary audience members—those who will be receiving the message directly. They may also force a sender to include a secondary audience—those who will hear about the message, participate in decision making, or be affected by the message.

The sender must also identify the key decision makers in the audience. These could include superiors and subordinates, influential officials, opinion leaders, power brokers, contacts, tribe or sect members, or family members. How are the power brokers identified? In Western cultures, an individual's power is demonstrated by how much "proactivity" he or she brings to a situation. In Asia, the powerful do not reveal their inner feelings and thoughts, and they display their authority by the silence and stillness they maintain in response to situations. In Latin America, those in power are often also poets and musicians, and they are trusted because they are able to reveal their inner feelings and thoughts eloquently. The message must be tailored to these audiences and appeal to their motivations.

Appeal to Receivers' Motivations

Motivations are affected by the economic and political conditions confronting the audience. Obviously, an American sending a message to a group of locals in Rwanda about his or her mansion in California or his or her recent vacation in Hong Kong probably will not be heard; the Rwandans probably would hear a message about how to solve their hunger and other problems. That message also probably would not be heard by a group of individuals who are politically repressed; a message explaining how to attain more freedom would probably be heard by these people.

Individuals' motivations are also influenced by culture. For example, people in high-masculinity cultures, such as the United States, Austria, and Switzerland, may be motivated by material wealth and accumulation, while people in low-masculinity cultures, such as Denmark and Norway, may value a clean environment and altruism more than material wealth. Thus, a message promising material wealth may be heard more by listeners from a high-masculinity culture than by listeners from a low-masculinity culture. People in weak uncertainty avoidance cultures, such as Israel, the United States, and Denmark, may be motivated by task enhancement, career advancement, achievement, and challenge, while people in strong uncertainty avoidance cultures, such as France, Portugal, and Greece, may be motivated by job security and a safe work environment. Therefore, listeners from weak uncertainty avoidance cultures may be more interested in a message promising challenging tasks than listeners from strong uncertainty avoidance cultures. People in low-individualism cultures, such as Japan, may be more motivated by group relationships than by career advancement, while people in high-individualism cultures, such as Australia and the United States, may be motivated more by challenging work than by group relationships. A message promising individual rewards would probably be more appealing to listeners from high-individualism cultures than to listeners from low-individualism cultures.

Furthermore, individuals from some cultures, have a negative attitude toward work activities and a positive attitude toward leisure, community, religious, and family activities. The message must therefore appeal to these attitudes, otherwise it may be difficult to get such people to listen. (Practical Perspective 9.3 presents an insight on making presentations across cultures.)

PRACTICAL PERSPECTIVE 9-3

A Time to Talk, a Time to Dance

Picking up a little local color in advance, and using it appropriately, can endear you to an audience, says Richard Marker, a veteran of presentations in more than 20 countries, from Italy to Argentina.

"In Buenos Aires, I was invited to speak to a group of students at 10 p.m. on Saturday evening." He recalls. "We were convinced that we would arrive to an empty room, but found it was standing room only. In Buenos Aires, on the weekends, most people don't eat dinner until midnight, so this was the pre-dinner-and-dancing entertainment. The group was alive! And when I mentioned the local hot disco, El Cielo, I became a hero."

That, he added, was a nice happenstance, considering that the conference organizer had inspired local derision by scheduling dinner for 6 p.m. and the evening sessions for an 8 p.m. start. "In Buenos Aires, even on weekdays, dinner isn't served until 9 or 10 p.m.," Marker points out, "The organizer had violated one of the basic principles of international business: Learn a little about the local scene."

Yogi Berra once noted that you can observe a lot just by watching. In planning your itinerary, reserve a little time after arrival to gain some familiarity with local conditions and culture.

"When you arrive you need to observe what the local people are doing," Bosrock says. "Ask whenever communication or expected behavior seems unclear. Listen actively and assertively to what people say."

Remember that the more you can acclimate to local customs and habits, the better your chance of presentation success. You need to be willing to try to greet people properly, taste the local food, and learn others' behaviors," Bosrock says. "People can tell when you're trying, and they appreciate it."

But in your quest to be culturally sensitive, don't obsess on tiny nuances of meaning. "We don't communicate perfectly even within our own culture, so we certainly shouldn't expect to do so in someone else's." notes Bosrock. "But when you try, people all over the world understand that you are taking a risk and making an effort to reach out to them."

PRACTICAL PERSPECTIVE 9-3 *(Continued)*

Adjust to the Situation

Some cautions are so basic as to seem almost condescending—but as many veteran presenters can attest: The Basics are basic for a reason. "Speak more slowly and with less slang than to a U.S. audience," Marker says, repeating perhaps the most common caveat. Even articulate audiences will miss references to American cultural icons and misunderstand popular expressions.

Working with translators can present some unaccustomed challenges. In situations that require a translator, Marker advises modifying your pacing to speak in one- or two-sentence bursts. The goal is not to slow down so much that the audience becomes restless, but to give the translator time to keep up with you—and to keep the audience involved. When hearing a lengthy paragraph in someone else's language, "people tune in and out," he points out.

For women presenters, there remain some special concerns. "In many countries, a woman may still need a male spokesperson with her, at least in the beginning," says Dana May Casperson, president of the Professional Resource Institute in Santa Rosa, California. "She needs to dress conservatively—dark neutrals are best—and in the highest-quality clothing and jewelry."

The extra scrutiny women often receive in other countries extends to both what they say and how they say it. Here again, advance preparation is crucial. Before you go, you need to identify issues or presentation styles that might affect your credibility, offstage as well as on. That might include, in some cultures, being less open about family and personal matters, Casperson says.

Those, however, are the kind of subtleties that have to be dealt with on a country-by-country basis; broad rules simply don't apply. The support of credible local contacts can be invaluable in such instances not only for the advance heads-up they can provide but also for the role they can play as host, facilitators, and sponsors.

SOURCE: Excerpted from Dick Schaaf, "How to Prepare When You Are Presenting There," *Presentations*, 13, no. 6 (June 1999), pp. A1–A3. Permission conveyed through Copyright Clearance Center, Inc.

English as the Language of Communication in Global Business[18]

As indicated above, English appears to be emerging as the universal language for conducting international business. English, now, has special status in more than 100 countries, far more than any other language. In addition, English is the most widely taught as a foreign language—in more than 100 countries worldwide. More than a quarter of the world's population is already fluent or competent in English—and the number is growing rapidly, and no other language even comes close to this level of growth.[19] To deal with this evolution, many countries' governments now require that English be taught in their education systems, and in countries whose governments do not mandate the study of English, many students study English for competitive advantages in the job market, as many foreign businesses now require command of the English language as a basis for employment.[20] As a result, English is often the second or third language for many businesspeople around the globe. This, however, does not mean that these people are proficient in the use of the English language. Many of these individuals have learned English by reading and listening and therefore possess a weak ability to communicate in English. In addition, many people learn primarily just the English that relates to their specific industry; for example, large hotels often employ teachers to teach their staff English so that they can accommodate English-speaking customers. These hotels will invest just enough money to train employees in the language commonly used in the business—for example, "The restaurant is on the second floor" or "May I help you with your luggage?" Many understand only dictionary (literal) meanings. Therefore, quite often, a correspondence in English from foreign business associates is the consequence of considerable time and effort on their part. Given a choice, most receivers with English as a second or third language would probably prefer to communicate in their native language and would appreciate your acknowledgment of their first-language skills.

This suggests that senders from English-speaking countries should, when possible, attempt to communicate using the foreign receivers' language.[21] They should learn the foreign language or at least have the communication translated. At the very least, senders should communicate some phrases using the foreign language. This shows respect for the culture, acknowledges that there are differences, and informs the receivers that they are not viewed as a branch of the English-speaking nation.[22] Furthermore, perhaps the most compelling reason for learning the language of one's international affiliate is that it provides considerable insights into that culture.[23] It provides the means of entering into the "worldview" of another culture—it reveals the important values found in the culture, gives insights into how directly or indirectly people in the culture communicate with one another, and reflects social realities such as status differences within the culture.[24]

Although it is important that senders from English-speaking countries make some use of other languages, they should also be sensitive to the struggle that receivers with English as their second or third language encounter with the English language and should attempt to maximize their use of English (practice makes perfect). Box 9.1 provides some ground rules for communicating in English with receivers whose knowledge of English is secondary to their native language.

Box 9.1   A Framework for Dealing With Language Differences

- Keep your communications simple, short, and to the point. Do not use complicated English words. Monosyllables are fine, if they say what you mean.
- Try to eliminate all words that have more than one meaning (e.g., does "right" mean "correct," "the opposite of left," or to "re-do"?).
- Don't make nouns into verbs.
- Don't use industry-specific jargon, acronyms, or abbreviations. Avoid all "professionalese." There simply are no equal translations.
- Use action words and verbs to describe exactly what you mean (e.g., don't say "take the bus"; instead, say "ride the bus"), and avoid word pictures unless they are exactly what you mean (e.g., don't say, "walk me through this again" or "run that by me again").
- Always start out and stay formal unless and until your correspondent informs you to do otherwise; use titles, last names, and so forth.
- Avoid humor: It doesn't translate well. What is hysterically funny in one culture can be meaningless in another.

(Continued)

(Continued)

- Eliminate all slang, idioms, and sports-related terms from your English. Business English is loaded with them, and terms like "give me a ballpark figure," "hit a home run," "pinch hit for me in the morning," "that idea is out of left field," "he really threw me a curve ball," and "I'll touch base with you tomorrow" all have absolutely no meaning in cultures where they don't play baseball.
- On the telephone and in person, speak slowly, simply, and deliberately. Show respect and empathy. Never shout to be understood.
- On long-distance communications, the rule should be only one communication per item or question. A comprehensive fax of 15 major points and sub-points requiring a response, in English, to a group-oriented culture will either engender no response at all (they will be overwhelmed at the task) or can cause a delay of anywhere between several months to a decade or two.
- Be realistic: They don't speak English, they have to translate the document, they have to consider it as a group and then find someone available who speaks English to retranslate their final answer back to you.

SOURCE: Dean Foster, "Business Across Borders: International Etiquette for the Effective Global Secretary," *The Secretary* (October 1992), p. 24. Copyright © 1992 International Association of Administrative Professionals. All rights reserved. Used with permission.

Identifying the Right Transmission Channel Stage

A message is typically transmitted in writing, orally, and nonverbally (body/facial expressions). Ongoing advancements in communications technologies present new means of transmitting messages. Written messages can now be transmitted via mail, computer, fax, and e-mail. Oral messages can be transmitted via meetings, telephone, cell phone, and videoconferencing. Nonverbal messages can be sent via videoconferencing. Some of these communication channels are not available in many countries, especially in the less developed countries.

Written or Spoken Message?

Regardless of the channels available, the sender must decide whether to transmit the message orally or in writing. Cultural norms affect the decision. Some cultures prefer written messages, and others prefer spoken messages. Individuals in high-context cultures, which value trust, tend to prefer spoken communication and agreements; confirming an idea in writing may be taken as an indication that you think their word is no good. On the other hand, people in low-context cultures, which value efficiency, tend to prefer written communication and agreements.[25] Also, as indicated earlier, many people who know English as a second or third language learned it by reading and listening and have not developed a strong command of the language. These receivers may, therefore, feel more comfortable with written communication than with oral communication because written communication gives them more time to understand the message. The literacy level of the audience also affects the decision. If the illiteracy rate is high, oral messages would be more effective than written messages.

Format of Messages

There is no universal written message format. For example, standard paper sizes differ among many countries. The standard letter-size paper in the United States is 8.5 inches by 11 inches; in Europe, the page is longer, but in many countries it is narrower and shorter. This can create filing, printing, duplicating, and other problems. The physical format of the message must be adapted to different cultures. Similarly, presentation formats, including presentation length and timing, the number of visual aids, flamboyance, and the nature of interaction with the audience, also vary among cultures.[26] For example, when the author was lecturing in China, he sometimes wrote on the blackboard in front of the participants, which is a "don't" in China; it should have been written before the audience's arrival or printed on a poster or on an overhead transparency ahead of time. (PowerPoint presentation technology was not yet available there.)

Body Language

Body language, including eye contact, physical distance and touching, hand movements, pointing, and facial expressions, which vary across cultures,[27] also affects the transmission of a message.

Eye Contact. Eye contact between superiors and subordinates is avoided in many Southeast Asian cultures because it is a sign of disrespect. On the other hand, in Western cultures, avoiding eye contact is a sign of disrespect. Therefore, an American and a Malaysian subordinate may very well view each other as being disrespectful when the American attempts to make eye contact and the Malaysian avoids it.

Physical Distance and Touching. In Asia, once a relationship is established between individuals, physical distance is placed between them, and touching or display of emotions are substantially reduced. On the other hand, in Latin America, once a relationship is established between individuals, physical distance between them is reduced, and touching and display of emotions are increased.

Hand Movements. Some cultures make greater use of hand movements when communicating than others. For example, Italians tend to use their hands extensively, while Americans make limited use of hand movements—they believe that too much hand movement while communicating orally distracts the receiver(s).

Pointing. Pointing with the index finger is rude in some cultures, including those of Sudan, Venezuela, and Sri Lanka. Pointing your index finger toward yourself is insulting in Germany, the Netherlands, and Switzerland.

Facial Expressions. Russians do not use facial expressions very much, and Scandinavians do not use many gestures. This does not mean that they are not enthusiastic.[28]

Transmission of Messages Through Mediators

Messages (written, spoken, and nonverbal) are typically sent directly to the receiver(s). In some situations, in some cultures, it is not wise to send messages directly to the receiver(s); it is wise to use a mediator—the encoder sends the message to a mediator (a third party), who in turn conveys it to the receiver(s). For example, sincere Americans are often factually blunt and frank, even if it upsets the listeners.[29] The Japanese, however, culturally neither practice nor accept overt criticism and bluntness well; in Japan, to be sincere means having concern for the emotional, not the factual. In fact, to avoid being offensive (a concern for the emotional), a Japanese receiver may not even say "no" to a request from a sender with which he or she does not want to comply; instead, he or she would respond, "Maybe" (which really means "no" in Japan); in fact, the Japanese do not use the word *no* at all. Therefore, when a message being transmitted to a Japanese receiver must contain critical and blunt facts, it is better to submit it through a mediator. The bluntness is mitigated because the message was only indirectly passed from the sender to the receiver.

In Japan, when use of a mediator or a message is too impractical, the Japanese use informal get-togethers to discuss formal matters. At the informal meeting's setting (often after work hours in bars, nightclubs, and restaurants), serious matters can be obscured as entertainment. Discussions in such settings can be semiserious and hint of disagreements (the message can be blunt, but not too blunt) that would be unwelcome in formal settings.

Communication Principles

There is no doubt that the ability to communicate across cultures and languages is one of the most important skills required in global managers and businesspeople. Professors Ronald E. Dulek, John S. Fielden, and John S. Hill, all with the University of Alabama, devised a three-set series of cross-cultural communication do's and don'ts.[30] These are outlined in Box 9.2. The three sets of principles are conversational principles, those that senders must remember in all aspects of cross-cultural communication; presentation principles, those applicable when making oral presentations to a foreign audience; and written principles, those that must be remembered when transmitting written messages across cultures.[31]

Box 9.2 Do's and Don'ts of Cross-Cultural Communication

Conversational Principles

1. High-context cultures need to know as much as possible about the sender, such as what makes him or her "tick" and the company he or she represents. Conversations about the sender's family, company, and current events are used to "warm up" relationships. And these people like to know about senders even before they meet them.

2. Foreigners often learn only formal English. Thus, the sender should speak slowly, clearly, and simply, and he or she should avoid use of jargon, slang, clichés, and idioms.

3. It is polite and diplomatic to learn and speak a few phrases using your host's language.

4. Pay close attention to your body language and tone of voice. Communicating disinterest or impatience will embarrass or insult many people. Loud oral communication is socially unacceptable in many parts of Asia and the Middle East, but it is acceptable in many parts of Europe and Central America.

Presentation Principles

1. Americans tend to like spontaneous, unrehearsed presentations. In most other nations, however, such presentations convey the impression that the speaker has not bothered to prepare sufficiently, thus demonstrating disrespect for the audience. Disrespect is further shown when a speaker writes on the blackboard or on transparencies during the presentation. Customized presentations are therefore appreciated in most cultures.

2. Be sensitive to the fact that different audiences in different cultures behave differently during presentations. In Japan, for example, during presentations, businesspeople generally sit quietly and nod their heads to indicate that they understand—not that they agree. When they talk frenziedly among themselves, it is an indication that the speaker has said something offensive. Also, be sensitive that in many cultures the audience's not looking at you while you speak does not mean that they are disinterested—in the United States, the audience's not looking at the speaker is a sign of disinterest.

3. Design your presentation's length, completeness, and interruptability to the culture and language capabilities. For example, Americans, Swiss, and Germans like fast-paced, efficient presentations. Most cultures, however, prefer slower, more deliberate presentations. Slower-speaking paces are definitely mandatory when a translator is needed or when the audience does not have a good command of the language that the speaker is using. Also, never show any sign of impatience when a member of the audience who does not have command of your language is struggling or is clumsy in encoding a question. In high-context cultures, presentations should be short, separate segments, with questions and answers in between. In low-context cultures, such as the United States, questions are usually reserved for the end of the presentation.

4. Match age and rank of presenter to the audience's cultural expectations. For example, in high-context cultures age and seniority are a major indicator of status and wisdom, so a young speaker in these cultures may not be appreciated. For instance, if an American firm sends a young executive to negotiate a business deal, the other culture may interpret this as a lack of real interest in negotiations.

Writing Principles

1. In low-context cultures, where efficiency is highly valued, written communication should be organized so that the central point is immediately and directly stated. In high-context cultures, where efficiency is valued less, the communication should be less focused on getting the job done and more personally revealing. For example, people in high-context cultures will not read a detailed contract; they think that no one will be so ill-bred as to camouflage anything in fine print.

2. The style should be adapted to cultural preferences. Individuals in high-context cultures place great emphasis on respect and politeness, and writing etiquette requires that subordinates are asked to "consider" performing a task or "if it is possible at all" to complete a task. Arab and Latin American cultures tend to be poetic in their writing styles, and communications are filled with exaggerations, colorful adjectives, and metaphors. People in many cultures think that Americans tend to demonstrate egocentricism by overusing *I* and *my*.

3. If the message is important, enclose a translation in the receiver's native language whenever possible. Translations are both helpful and diplomatic.

SOURCE: Adapted from Ronald E. Dulek, John S. Fielden, and John S. Hill, "International Communication: An Executive Primer," *Business Horizons* (January–February 1991), pp. 21–24. Copyright © 1991 JAI Press Inc. Used with permission from JAI Press Inc. All rights reserved.

The Receiving-Decoding Stage

In cross-cultural communication, decoding by the receiver of signals is subject to social values and cultural variables not necessarily present in the sender. Therefore, the most effective way to understand cross-cultural communication is to focus on the decoding process and the role of perception in communication. Communication itself is best understood from the perspective of the receiver, not the sender, the channel, or the encoded message itself.[32] This means that transmission of a message is, by itself, not communication; a conscious perception of signals at the receiver's end is necessary for communication to have occurred.

This suggests that an effective sender of a message understands the receiver's perceptions, which in essence means that he or she is both an encoder and a decoder. For effective communication to take place when the sender does not understand the receiver's perceptions, the receiver must understand the sender's perceptions; he or she is both an encoder and a decoder. Either the sender or the receiver (or both) must have knowledge of the other's environmental, cultural, sociocultural, and psychocultural contexts; thus, when the amount of such knowledge is small on both sides, communication ineffectiveness results.

For example, in American culture, it is quite acceptable to pass food at a dinner table using one's left hand, but in some Middle East cultures, it is quite unacceptable. If an American transacting business in the Middle East is aware of this custom, when out to dinner or lunch with local clients, he or she will pass food only with his or her right hand. Doing so will permit communication between the American and the locals to proceed smoothly. If, however, the American is not aware of the custom and passes food with his or her left hand, it will offend the locals and the communication flow is impaired. On the other hand, if the local is aware that Americans instinctively pass food with either hand, depending on which is more convenient (efficient), and the local is "understanding," the communication flow may proceed smoothly.

In reality, it may be difficult to find "understanding" locals, as most will expect you to come to their territory prepared. If you are an American conducting business in China and go out to dinner with local business clients, it may be difficult to find one whose respect you will not lose if you ask for a fork, as opposed to eating with chopsticks. Also, it may be amusing if at first you are clumsy using chopsticks; however, in a long-term relationship, the clumsiness will cease to be amusing, and it may actually become a handicap. Of course, in the United States, the Chinese clients would have to be understanding, and they might have to use forks as well. But even in this situation, much may depend on who needs whom the most. It might be wise for the American to show courtesy by occasionally taking the Chinese visitors to a local Chinese restaurant where they can use chopsticks, and the Chinese hosts might occasionally take visiting Western clients to a local Western restaurant, where they can use forks. This would symbolize a show of mutual understanding and respect for both cultures. And it certainly would be intellectually self-enhancing if one learned to do it either way. The late CEO of Sony, Akio Morita, as shown in Practical Perspective 9.4, seemed to possess strong encoding-decoding ability.

The Nature of Received Signals

Receivers take signals transmitted by senders, decode them, and try to understand them. The receiver-decoded signal is a "sign" constructed of two parts: the signifier and

PRACTICAL PERSPECTIVE 9.4

Mr. Sony's Struggle

In the 1970s and 1980s [Akio] Morita [the late CEO of Sony] built his presence in the global business establishment to a level not previously attained by any Japanese businessman. The phenomenon was so remarkable that it gave rise to perhaps the most important question above him; how did he do it?

What accounted for Akio Morita's unique ability as a businessman to establish and sustain beneficial relationships with the most important Western business and political leaders? There is striking agreement among those who knew him over time that he was special because he was someone who seemed to understand them and, as important, whom they could understand. Longtime acquaintance Peter Peterson, an investment banker and Sony board member, put it as well as anyone: "When it came time for Akio to do business in the U.S., whether it was joint ventures or licensing or whatever, he could pick up the phone and talk to almost any businessman in America. And instead of its being 'Who is this again?' and interpreters and all that sort of thing, Akio knew these people at the human level, at the personal level. And let's be honest: To many American businessmen, the Japanese business culture is foreign: they don't feel comfortable with Japanese businessmen, and they don't know them to a large extent as human beings. But they did know Akio in that way, and therefore when he called, people listened."

Henry Kissinger was more theoretical: "First of all, the Japanese in my experience are not great communicators. They tend to operate within their consensus, and when they get dropped out of the consensus and get into dialogue with other cultures, it's tough because they don't feel they have the authority to make independent decisions. So even for many of us who have Japanese friends whom we value, the problem of communication is very difficult. Morita could conduct a dialogue, and while he was a very patriotic Japanese and a firm defender of the Japanese point of view, he could communicate it in a way that was meaningful to non-Japanese . . . He was probably the single most effective Japanese spokesman I ever met." . . .

Morita was raised in a traditional Japanese family in which all things were understood implicitly, where communication, when it occurred, was oblique and equivocal. With this background, how can the aggressive outspokenness and confrontation at the heart of American business behavior have come naturally to him? How, indeed, can he have been naturally at ease with American social style in general? Was Akio Morita, the strict Japanese traditionalist, as effortlessly at home in the West as he appeared to be, or was he simulating Western behavior?

The following excerpt is from a televised dialogue with a well-known Japanese commentator, Saburo Shiroyama, about the differences in Japanese and American management style:

Morita: Grammar and pronunciation aren't as important as expressing yourself in a way that matches the way Westerners think, which is very different from our thought process. You have to switch off your Japanese way of seeing things, or they will never understand what you are saying. First of all, they want to hear the conclusion right away; in English sentence structure, the conclusion comes first.

Shiroyama: I've heard that one of our Prime Ministers was on his way to the United States for the first time and asked you for advice, and you suggested the critical thing was to start right out with a "yes" or "no" followed by a brief explanation.

Morita: When they ask questions or express an opinion, they want to know right away whether the other party agrees or opposes them. So the English, "yes" or "no" comes first. We Japanese prefer to save the "yes" or "no" for last. Particularly when the answer is "no," we put off saying that as long as possible, and they find that exasperating.

PRACTICAL PERSPECTIVE 9-4 *(Continued)*

Shiroyama: But in Japan, as you explained, we don't come out with "yes" or "no" but prefer expressions like, "I'll take this under consideration." Our feeling is that vagueness in these cases in less offensive. So when you're in America, you must be clear, and when you return to Japan you must be vague. Is it hard to switch back and forth?

Morita: It's more difficult than you can imagine.

Despite Westerners' impression that he was one of them, this small critique reveals Morita's appraisal from the opposite side of a cultural divide, as he worked hard to decipher the puzzle that stood between him and successful communication.

the signified.[33] A sign is a signal that is recognized, structured into a category, and assigned meaning. The signifier is the sound or shape of the signal, which is sensorally perceived without meaning attached to it; the signified is the meaning attached to the signifier. "The linkage of new, unattributed signifiers to already-existing signifieds is a large part of the process of decoding communication messages."[34] "Cross-cultural communication is ineffective when signs are not recognized because they differ from the signs in the culture-driven repository."[35] (See Figure 9.3.)

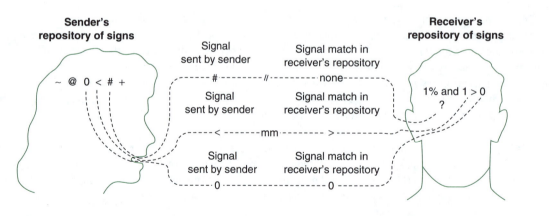

Figure 9.3   Attaching Meaning to Signals

NOTES: The # signal sent does not match a corresponding sign in the receiver's repository (?), so communication has not taken place (//). The sign # may signify "large" in the sender's repository, but "large" is signified by "&" in the receiver's repository. Therefore, for effective communication to take place, either the sender must add "&" to his or her repository or the receiver must add "#" to his or her repository.

The < signal sent is matched by the receiver with the seemingly corresponding sign > in his or her repository. Both believe that the signs are the same, and communication has taken place. But ineffective communication (mm) has actually taken place because while the signs appear the same, they actually point in different directions. The signs < and > may signify "He's old." To the sender, "He's old," in a certain context, may mean "He's not qualified for the job"; but to the receiver, in the same context, it may mean "He has wisdom and experience and is qualified for the job." For effective communication to take place, either the sender or the receiver must understand the contextual differences and encode or decode the meaning accordingly.

The "O" signal matches the signal in the receiver's repository precisely. Effective communication has taken place.

Receivers of cross-cultural messages continually adjust and adapt incoming signifiers to the existing repository of signs, and adapt and adjust the repository of signifieds to create new signs. Thus, a competent cross-cultural receiver constantly challenges his or her repository of existing signs and expands it to participate in the matching of signs with the sender.[36] (Learning to use both a fork and chopsticks enhances cross-cultural competence.)

To communicate effectively across cultures, the transmission of signs to a receiver must take into account the cultural factors—values, attitudes, beliefs, and behaviors—that shape the structuring categories of the receiver's repository. Cognitively learned knowledge of the cultures involved may be the basis for developing effective cross-cultural competence. Barriers to cross-cultural communication can be reduced by knowledge and understanding of varying cultural factors, along with a genuine desire to communicate effectively. All this means that "intercultural communication competence is the encoding and decoding of attributed signifieds to signifiers in matches that correspond to signs held in the other communicator's repository."[37]

To communicate effectively across cultures also requires good listening skills. One must be able to listen to spoken as well as to nonverbal (such as facial expressions) messages. An impatient American who constantly looks at his or her watch is not likely to communicate effectively across cultures.

Developing Cross-Cultural Communication Competence

Professor Linda Beamer of California State University, Los Angeles, has developed a model for the purpose of describing the process of developing cross-cultural communication competence.[38] The model proposes five levels of learning: (1) acknowledgment of diversity, (2) organizing information according to stereotypes, (3) posing questions to challenge the stereotypes, (4) analyzing communication episodes, and (5) generating "other culture" messages. The intent of the learning process, according to Beamer, "is to develop the ability to decode effectively signs that come from members of other cultures, within a business context, and to encode messages using signs that carry the encoder's intended meaning to members of other cultures."[39] The five levels do not cease to exist once attained; they are continually revisited in the process of learning. This means that newer differences in a culture are constantly being discovered. The ensuing sections describe Beamer's model.

Acknowledging Diversity

At this level of learning, the learner becomes aware of cultural differences. He or she addresses the initial issue of perception—the recognition that formerly unknown and unrecognized signs are being sent. Individuals in homogeneous, high-context cultures, who possess limited experience of cultural diversity, need to start by acknowledging the diversity of signifiers for signifieds already understood. At this level, definitions of basic concepts for discussing diversity are important, such as bias, ethnocentricity, stereotype, value, and culture. Especially when discussing signifiers, language is the most apparent cultural difference, but becoming proficient in the target language does not always generate cultural fluency.

Organizing Information According to Stereotypes

At this level, stereotypes that distinguish a particular culture and its members are identified. Stereotypes are normally simple or brief: "Americans are efficiency-oriented"; "Latin Americans place the well-being of family members and friends ahead of organizational efficiency"; "the French are rude to non-French-speaking visitors." Stereotypes provide some familiarity with a culture, and they may be helpful and even accurate to some extent, but they are myopic insights that reveal only part of the entire culture. Therefore, knowledge of a culture's stereotypes does not constitute understanding of a culture, and it may actually be an obstacle to the development of cross-cultural communication competence. Stereotypes fail to challenge the signs within their own repository of meanings—they fail to ask if some other signified can be associated with the signifier. One must progress beyond this level of cross-cultural communication.

Posing Questions to Challenge the Stereotypes

At this level, stereotypes are challenged. The learner asks questions about how members of a business enterprise describe that organization, their relationships to one another and to their material environment, and their position in relation to the universe. Asking questions is apt to disclose attitudes that are crucial for understanding business activities, such as individuals' attitudes toward time, status, and role; obligations in relationships; responsibility and the decision-making processes; the role of law; and the role of technology. Questions challenge stereotypes, and can be patterned to probe what members of a culture "value, how they behave in certain circumstances because of their values, [and] what their attitudes are toward institutions in their society and toward events beyond their control."[40] Primary and/or secondary research will help provide answers to the questions.

Beamer developed a framework outlining several questions that must be answered. The questions relate to the cultural differences in behavior and attitude that affect business communication.[41] The framework develops five areas of value orientations: thinking and knowing, doing and achieving, the self, social organization, and the universe.[42]

Thinking and Knowing

This value orientation relates to how people in a culture obtain, organize, and communicate information about the culture. A group of questions about the culture must be answered:

1. *Ways to know:* In some cultures, an individual only knows something when it is conceptualized and abstracted; in others, what a person knows is contingent on firsthand experience.

2. *Activity that results in knowledge:* In some cultures, knowing is attained by probing, questioning, and atomizing; in others, it is attained by mastering a received body of knowledge to the point where it may be reproduced.

3. *Extent of knowledge:* In some cultures, everything is knowable; in others, the indescribable nature of some things precludes their being known totally.

4. *Patterns of thinking in the culture:* Some cultures use mainly cause-and-effect patterns; they value planning, and their conceptualizations, language, and institutions divulge linear thinking patterns. Other cultures stress "context in patterns of

thinking: the interconnections and relationships between things are important and a lattice or net pattern emerges."[43]

Doing and Achieving

This orientation relates to activity and achievement. Some cultures identify goals, work to achieve them, and are result oriented; other cultures emphasize the present, commemorate simply being, and are relationship oriented. Furthermore, some cultures apply a sequential approach to the completion of tasks (e.g., they can serve only one customer at a time), while others apply a simultaneous approach (they can serve several customers at a time). Some cultures have more tolerance for uncertainty and ambiguity than others. And some cultures view luck as a significant influence on outcomes; other cultures assign little or no importance to luck.

The Self

The self value refers to the relative importance of individualism versus interdependence. In cultures where individual efforts are rewarded, personal competitiveness is high; in interdependent cultures, where people are not interested in individual achievement and groups are rewarded, competitiveness may be detestable. In some cultures, age is more important than training and experience, but not in other cultures. In hiring practices, some cultures prefer one sex over the other.

The Organization of Society

Cultures' value orientations relate to social structure contrast. The contrasts include (a) a tendency toward temporary versus permanent group membership, (b) a preference for private ownership of material goods versus community ownership, (c) a tendency to distrust form versus a preference for form, (d) an egalitarian versus a hierarchical structure, and (e) a general practice of approaching authority directly versus using a mediated link to authority. These orientations affect the format, organization, and tone of business communication documents as well as interpersonal communication.

The Universe

Cultural contrasts in this respect include humans dominating nature versus nature dominating humans, time being linear versus time being cyclical, human activity at the center of the universe versus divine beings at the center of all activities, change as good versus change as bad, and death as the end of life versus death as merely a part of life.[44]

Analyzing Communication Episodes

The understanding obtained by challenging cultural stereotypes can be used to analyze events in actual situations. Situations may reveal effective communication, ineffective communication, or both. As the situation is analyzed, new meanings for communication behavior can be ascribed. At this point of developing cross-cultural communication abilities, "learning focuses on depth of understanding, and application of the abstractions in level three [posing questions to challenge the stereotypes] during the plotting of a culture's value orientations."[45] The pool of questions about a culture's values is cultivated and enlarged with the addition of new insights from particular communication cases. This increases competence in both encoding and decoding cross-cultural messages.

Generating "Other-Culture" Messages

At this level, the communicator becomes cross-culturally competent "when messages may be encoded and directed as if from within the new culture and when messages from the new culture may be decoded and responded to successfully."[46] He or she has developed the ability to "become the other." At this level of cross-cultural competence, communicators continually evaluate "other-culture" messages against the repository of signs they have stored in their mental databases. They can modify the database or match incoming signs and messages to those already known. They are "able to manipulate information received as well as information stored and to make linkages between levels of understanding."[47]

Information Technology and Global E-Communication

Online information technology, such as the Internet, e-mail, the Web, and video-conferencing, now enables organizations to more readily communicate with networks located around the globe. It also enables an organization's employees to more readily communicate with each other from sites located around the globe. This type of globalization, however, mandates the management of multilingual and multicultural implementation of applications and data, thus generating a new challenge for organizations. For example, consider the challenge of obtaining a consistent definition of data elements within only one business group. Anyone who has gone through the data definition process knows that it requires skill and patience to bring a group to consensus. Now consider the complexity of the problem when those same definitions must be shared worldwide among groups with different linguistic[48] and cultural practices.[49]

Many of the problems and solutions discussed in this chapter have application in electronic communication; for example, simplifying the language and omitting idioms, slang, and so on, as outlined in Figure 9.3, helps mitigate the problem in global e-communication. Information technology itself is helping in this respect as well. It is interconnecting the world, which in turn helps advance learning about other cultures, thus facilitating effective cross-language and cultural communication.[50]

A few examples illustrate the point. Brazilian TV soap operas are very popular in Portugal. As a result, the Portuguese are learning about Brazilian culture as well as the Brazilian Portuguese verbal and nonverbal language. Also, American TV programs are quite popular in other countries, as are American movies. This helps advance an understanding of American culture. (Of course, "Americanization" is upsetting many Tribal leaders or protectors of local culture throughout the globe.[51]) To enhance their learning, many students of English watch TV programs and movies in which the local language has not been dubbed; so students simultaneously learn the language and culture of the English-speaking characters. Many people now have access to the Internet and, therefore, to information from all parts of the world. (Previously, governments could control the information available to their citizens more easily than they can today.) This also helps develop cross-cultural awareness and understanding, which helps improve cross-cultural and language communication effectiveness.

Furthermore, because of new technology, such as the Web, more and more domestic enterprises are able to internationalize their business activities. But companies that want to take on the global marketplace successfully via the Web will have to deal with four major issues.[52]

First, and most obvious, is the wide array of languages and localized settings that must be supported. For example, in international e-commerce, Web customers are three times more likely to purchase at sites that are presented in their native language. Again, the problems and solutions discussed in this chapter help in this respect. Second, some languages are not well suited to non-PC-device rendering. For instance, Japanese characters and Thai accent marks do not display well in devices such as cellular phones. Global organizations will need to address such issues and implement technology solutions. The third and fourth issues concern multiple locales and content management. Many Web applications will require content that is created at different locations to support the local culture and customs of multiple countries simultaneously.

To help in this respect, there is Global Sight's Ambassador (www.globalsight.com), a product that provides Web-based work flow and tools that support distributed team creation of multilingual Web sites. The Ambassador is adept at language translation. It can translate any source or target language as long as Web browsers support it— currently (1999), Web browsers support more than 50 languages. It also integrates easily with existing management products and Web servers that may be running. Once a translation is completed, it is available for subsequent reuse. For example, one can perform translation task on an entire Web site initially and then reuse the memory capabilities to shorten subsequent translation activities during site maintenance.

The new information technology is revolutionizing the ways in which organizations around the globe interact and communicate with each other. E-mail enables employees to communicate effectively with each other across 24 time zones, and it helps break down the communication hierarchy. (An employee at a lower level can readily communicate with an employee at a higher level.) But it also presents new challenges in the need to reengineer organizations' communications systems and corporate cultures (including traditional nations' governmental culture).

Summary

This chapter has presented the communication process in an international/cross-cultural context. How cross-cultural communicators (senders) construct ideas to be communicated is influenced by the receivers' culture. The same concepts will be perceived differently across cultures. Thus, what works in one culture will not necessarily work in another, and adaptations must be made. The words, gestures, symbols, idioms, jargon, and slang a sender uses to communicate an idea are also affected by the particular receivers' culture. Different societies use different languages and social behaviors to communicate. Therefore, for effective communication to take place, the appropriate adaptations must be made.

The means—written, oral, or nonverbal— of transmitting the message is also affected by the receivers' culture. Culturally, some people prefer oral communication, and others prefer written communication. Some cultures prefer flamboyant, flashy presentations; other cultures are offended by such presentations. The cross-cultural communicator must use the means most fitted to the receivers' culture. In essence, the sender of the message must know and use the words, concepts, and behaviors that the receivers will understand, which means that to be effective, a cross-cultural communicator must learn to be both a sender and a receiver.

KEY TERMS AND CONCEPTS

1. Cross-cultural communication
2. Unique written, oral, and nonverbal languages
3. English as the language of communication in global business
4. Unique social customs and behaviors
5. Language translator
6. Realistic objectives
7. Realistic time frame
8. Same word, different meanings
9. Requirements for formality and informality
10. Dual-translation
11. Simultaneous and sequential oral translators
12. Effective translator
13. Updating translator skills
14. High-context and low-context cultures
15. Primary and secondary audiences
16. The audience's motivations
17. English as a second or third language
18. Dictionary translation
19. Body language
20. Eye contact, physical distance, and touching
21. Hand movements, pointing, and facial expressions
22. Mediators
23. Informal get-togethers
24. Conversational, presentation, and written principles
25. Environmental, cultural, sociocultural, and psychocultural contexts
26. Signal, sign, signifier, and signified
27. Cross-cultural message adjustment
28. Developing cross-cultural communication competence
29. Cultural fluency
30. Stereotyping
31. Challenging cultural stereotypes
32. "Other-culture" messages
33. Repository of signs
34. Global e-communication

DISCUSSION QUESTIONS

1. What are the major causes of cross-cultural communication ineffectiveness?
2. Discuss some of the factors that affect the development of an idea to be communicated across cultures.
3. Discuss some of the major factors that must be considered when encoding a message to be sent across cultures.
4. Discuss some of the ways expressions and nonverbal communication affect the cross-cultural encoding process.
5. How do "formality" and "informality" affect the cross-cultural encoding process?
6. Discuss the dual-translation process.
7. Discuss the two types of translators.
8. Discuss the factors that describe an effective translator.

9. Discuss the role audience-motivation plays in encoding messages.

10. English appears to be emerging as the language of global business. You are from England, and you are going to speak to an audience for whom English is a second or third language. Discuss the "do's" and "don'ts" of delivering the message.

11. Discuss the ways culture affects the selection of the right transmission channel.

12. How are mediators useful in cross-cultural transmission of messages?

13. What are the fundamentals of the three communication principles?

14. "The most effective way to understand cross-cultural communication is to focus on the decoding process and the role of perception in communication." Explain this statement.

15. Differentiate between "a sign," "the signifier," and "the signified."

16. Discuss how cross-cultural communication competence is developed.

EXERCISES

1. A U.S. executive's firm has just completed negotiating a business deal with a company in Japan. You have been employed to help him or her write the contract. What would you advise your client to do?

2. A U.S. executive who is preparing to communicate with a French audience enlists your services to help him or her write the substance of the message. With respect to the amount of information a culture requires, what would you advise your client to do?

3. You are an executive from a low-context culture preparing a message to be delivered orally to an audience from a high-context culture. How would you structure the message?

4. A German executive's firm has just completed negotiating a business deal with a company in the United States. You have been employed to help him or her write the contract. What would you advise your client to do?

5. You are a cross-cultural communication consultant employed by a domestic company that wants to internationalize its operations because of the current e-commerce revolution. What would be your advice to the firm's management?

ASSIGNMENT

Select a short story written in English and write a dictionary translation of the story into a foreign language that you do not understand. Then have someone who speaks both English and the foreign language fluently interpret it back to English. How does the new translation compare with yours? Share the experience with your classmates.

CASE 9-1

The Efficient Cross-Cultural Communicator

I [Dean Foster] was speaking recently with an American manager quite down in the dumps and befuddled over the fact that cooperation from the Mexicans, with whom his office did a great deal of work, was becoming increasingly difficult. He just could not figure out why. I asked him to outline all major changes he could think of that occurred around the time that cooperation began to change and he admitted that he had replaced his assistant around the same time. "Was this assistant responsible for communications between your office and the Mexicans?" I inquired, and got a positive response. "Is your new assistant similarly responsible?" Yes, he said.

By the look of things, the new assistant was certainly doing her job. There was no doubt about the efficiency of the letters, e-mails, faxes, and the like that went out like clockwork to the Mexico office. In fact, the new assistant had streamlined the communications system within the office significantly. Now there was a specific form to be used for different types of letters, more precise, straight to the point, and usable for mailing lists. Different criteria were now used for sending out different types of correspondence, time periods had been established that would automatically signal certain types of correspondence to be released to certain individuals, and so forth. Then I looked at the previous assistant's correspondence. It certainly was more cumbersome: Each letter was individually written, following no predetermined form, and was quite customized, depending on to whom it was written and the circumstances. In fact, each correspondence usually acknowledged the individual to whom it was being written in quite personal ways. All correspondence seemed to be about 30 percent greetings, with much inquiry into the health and happiness of the reader's business and family. The significant issues—the reason for the letter in the first place—usually were embedded somewhere in the middle of all this, and constituted only about half of the total letter. A final 20% percent was spent at the end, once again, on all sorts of non-business-related issues, from hoping to see you next month in Guadalajara, to the recounting of a memorable meal that was shared the last time they were together.

Comparing these two very different styles of correspondence, my American manager friend agreed that he regretted replacing his former assistant, but that the company simply couldn't grow spending so much time and resources on old-fashioned, inefficient patterns and systems of communication. I asked him if Mexico constituted an important market for him. He answered that more than 80 percent of his business was with Mexico.

Questions

1. Discuss how the concept of low-context and high-context cultures led to this problem.

2. Assume that you are a consultant hired by this manager to solve the problem. What would you advise the manager to do?

CASE 9-2

The Elusive System

GBAH, the General Bureau of Animal Husbandry, is a division of the huge Chinese Ministry of Agriculture. It received its first grant from the UNDP—the United Nations Development Program—shortly after China joined the UN. It was a grant to study the feasibility of irrigation in the Mongolian grasslands, but one condition of the grant required the GBAH to demonstrate that it had adequate systems for safeguarding and accounting for the funds. So the GBAH reluctantly allocated some of the precious funds to employ a Western consulting firm to show them the systems they should have. That's what I [Roderick MacLeod] was in China for, in part—to snag opportunities like that for my firm—so I was delighted. Since we looked upon it as an entry to the "China market," which we believed to be potentially huge and profitable, we scoured our worldwide resources for a UNDP expert and for Chinese-speaking staff.

Even though the fee would adequately compensate only for one, we sent a team of four people, a UNDP and cattle-farming expert, two Chinese-speaking consultants, and me, for the purpose of doing a bang-up job that we could use as a future reference.

We arrived as scheduled and went to the Beijing Hotel as directed. We weren't expected. It took a couple of hours to get somebody from the GBAH, accompanied by a person from the ministry's Foreign Affairs Department, down to the hotel to work on the problem, and it took another twelve hours to get the four of us into rooms in the Yanjing Hotel, a couple of miles away and several steps down on Beijing's prestige scale. Sitting for fourteen hours in the barroom of the Beijing Hotel, anxious and helpless, unwashed and unloved, is not the best way to start coping with combined jet lag and culture shock.

The next day, the GBAH officials came to the hotel, and the day was spent going over the contract, discussing arrangements, and having a congratulatory banquet. The day after that, twenty Mongolian accountants arrived to be trained in the UNDP accounting requirements. They looked like country people and farm people: weather-beaten faces, callused hands, worn Mao jackets, and the bemused expressions country people have all over the world on their first visit to the city. Each was the accountant for his "Banner" (Mongolian communes are called Banners, evoking images of troops of wild horsemen, although they are really political and economic units of up to several hundred thousand people) and thus was a responsible and experienced official.

We got to work, proud of the charts and tables we had laboriously drawn by hand and labeled in Chinese, and of the overhead projector we had brought along for displaying them. The two Chinese-speaking consultants had been told what to say by the expert, they had spent a week or more at the difficult task of translating it from English to Chinese, and they were ready to give all-day lectures in Chinese. The expert and I sat in ready to answer questions or help out as we could. The Mongolians listened quietly, diligently taking notes, for two days.

The third day, the GBAH officials were back and a long discussion with the two Chinese-speaking consultants delayed the opening of the session. It appeared that what the Chinese were being told wasn't what they had contracted to find out. The Mongolians sat idly in the meeting room for another several hours while we tried to find out what the GBAH wanted and tried to convince them that they knew all there was to know and should be satisfied. The GBAH wasn't satisfied.

(Continued)

(Continued)

We stayed up all night, literally. The expert and I redid the lectures and charts, and the other two did their best to put them into Chinese. Ordinarily, it takes at least three times as long to put a lecture into Chinese as it does for the expert to write it in English. They didn't have that much time; they did it between eleven at night and seven in the morning.

The next day was a tiring one, and at the end of it the expert, who didn't like Chinese food, went off to call on his country's ambassador. (He happened to be Irish, but that's incidental; it seemed to me that all citizens of small countries treated their embassies in Beijing as homes-away-from-home.) The rest of us worked away at the charts and transparencies and lectures, and fell into bed exhausted.

Next day the GBAH officials were back. It still wasn't right. Since it was Saturday (the Chinese work a six-day week), we gave the Mongolians a long weekend and spent Saturday and Sunday trying to get it right. Except for the expert: He worked Saturday and then went to the embassy for Saturday night and Sunday.

Monday morning, there was a conference to see if we were getting it. The expert said there were only so many ways you could slice up one piece of cake, and he thought they'd tried them all. The GBAH still wasn't satisfied. The Mongolian accountants had typically impassive faces, but not so much so that their irritation and frustration weren't showing through.

It went on and on like that. The GBAH had spent their money and wanted what they had paid for. The Mongolians wanted to be sure that they could measure up in the frightening new world of international agencies. We had our professional pride in our work, and also visions of future assignments driving us, and we were determined to get it right: Except for the expert, who spent more and more time at the embassy.

Finally, everybody was exhausted and the allotted time was up. The GBAH officials put a good face on it, saying the Chinese equivalent of "it had been a learning experience." Everybody went home, hurt and sad.

Questions

1. Based on what you learned in this chapter, what do you believe went wrong in this case? In answering the question, you should relate to the communication process.

2. How could the problem have been avoided?

SOURCE: Roderick MacLeod, *China, Inc.: How to Do Business With the Chinese* (Toronto, Ontario, Canada: Bantam Books, 1988), pp. 33–35. Copyright © 1988 by Roderick MacLeod. Used by permission of Bantam Books, a division of Bantam Doubleday Dell Publishing Group, Inc.

NOTES

1. Excerpted from Jeremy Main, "How 21 Men Got Global in 35 Days," *Fortune* (November 6, 1989), p. 71.

2. See, for example, David Ricks, *Big Business Blunders: Mistakes in Multinational Marketing* (Homewood, IL: Dow Jones-Irwin, 1983).

3. R. E. Dulek, J. S. Fielden, and J. S. Hill, "International Communication: An Executive Primer," *Business Horizons*, 34, no. 1 (1991), p. 20.

4. This discussion draws from Mary Munter, "Cross-Cultural Communication for Managers," *Business Horizons*, 36 (May–June 1993), p. 69.

5. J. R. Zeeman, "Service—the Cutting Edge of Global Competition: What United Airlines Is Learning in the Pacific," Remarks before the Academy of International Business Annual Meeting, Chicago (November 14, 1987).

6. *Going International, Part 1: Bridging the Culture Gap* [Video] (San Francisco: Copeland Griggs Productions).

7. This discussion draws from Dean Foster, "Business Across Borders: International Etiquette for the Effective Global Secretary," *The Secretary* (October 1992), pp. 20–24.

8. Ibid., p. 24.

9. On the topic of context, see D. L. Shapiro, M. A. Van Glow, and Z. Xiao, "Toward Polycontextually Sensitive Research Methods," *Management and Organization Review*, 3, no. 1 (2007), pp. 129–152.

10. This discussion draws from Lyle Sussman and Denise M. Johnson, "The Interpreted Executive: Theory, Models, and Implications," *The Journal of Business Communication*, 30, no. 4 (1993), pp. 415–434.

11. Ibid., pp. 419–420.

12. See Shapiro, Van Glow, and Xiao, "Toward Polycontextually Sensitive Research Methods," op cit., pp. 129–152.

13. Edward T. Hall, "How Cultures Collide," *Psychology Today* (July 1976), pp. 67–74.

14. Munter, "Cross-Cultural Communication for Managers," op cit., p. 74.

15. Hall, "How Cultures Collide," op cit., pp. 67–74.

16. Ibid., p. 74.

17. This discussion draws on Munter, "Cross-Cultural Communication for Managers," op cit., p. 73.

18. A guide to writing correspondence, reports, and technical pages for a global audience is provided by Edmund H. Weiss, *The Elements of International English Style* (Armonk, NY: M. E. Sharp, 2005); A framework for analyzing the multinational corporation (MNC) as a multilingual community in which a parent functional language and subunit functional languages are spoken is presented in Y. Luo and O. Shenkar, "The Multinational Corporation as a Multilingual Community: Language and Organization in a Global Context," *Journal of International Business Studies*, 37 (2006), pp. 321–339.

19. Cynthia L. Kemper, "Sacre Blue! English as a Global Lingua Franca?" *Communication World*, 16 (June–July 1999), p. 42.

20. Alan Weiss, "Global Doesn't Mean Foreign Anymore," *Training* (July 1998), p. 51.

21. See Daren Fonda, "Selling Tongues," *Time Magazine* (November 26, 2001). www.time.com/time/global/november'cover.html

22. This discussion draws from Foster, "Business Across Borders," op cit., p. 24.

23. See Steven E. Grump, "Bridging the Culture Gap: A Practical Guide to International Business Communication/Culture Intelligence: A Guide to Working With People From Other Cultures," *The Journal of Language for International Business*, 17, no. 1 (2006), p. 134.

24. Gary P. Ferraro, "The Need for Linguistic Proficiency in Global Business," *Business Horizons* (May–June 1996), p. 40.

25. Munter, "Cross-Cultural Communication for Managers," op cit., p. 74.

26. Ibid., p. 75.

27. Ibid.

28. Ibid., p. 76.

29. This discussion draws from Jon P. Alston, "Wa, Guanxi, and Inhwa: Managerial Principles in Japan, China, and Korea," *Business Horizons*, 32, no. 2 (March–April 1989), pp. 27–28.

30. Dulek, Fielden, and Hill, "International Communication," op cit., pp. 21–24.

31. Ibid., p. 21.

32. This discussion draws from Linda Beamer, "Learning Intercultural Communication Competence," *The Journal of Business Communication*, 29, no. 3 (1992), pp. 285–303.

33. L. A. Saussure, *Course in General Linguistics*, R. Harris, Trans. (cited in Beamer, op cit., p. 247).

34. Beamer, op cit., p. 387.

35. Ibid.

36. Ibid., p. 289.

37. Ibid.

38. Ibid., pp. 291–301.

39. Ibid., p. 291.

40. Ibid., p. 294.

41. See also Anna Brown, "Bridging the Gap Between Cultures," *Conference and Incentive Travel,* (February 2006), p. 19.

42. Ibid, pp. 296–300.

43. Ibid., p. 296.

44. Ibid., p. 300.

45. Ibid.

46. Ibid., p. 301.

47. Ibid.

48. See Pete Engardio, "Making Bangalore Sound Like Boston," *BusinessWeek* (April 30, 2003), p. 48.

49. This discussion is adapted from Sunny Baker, "Global E-Commerce, Local Problems," *Journal of Business Strategy,* 20, no. 4 (July–August 1999), pp. 32–38.

50. Dick Schaaf, "Speaking Abroad," *Presentations,* 13, no. 6 (June 1999), pp. A1–A15.

51. See Janet Guyon, "The American Way," *Fortune* (November 26, 2001), pp. 114–120.

52. This discussion draws from Maggie Biggs, "Globalization Issues Forced to the Front Lines by Changing Online Demographics," *InfoWorld,* 21, no. 36 (September 6, 1999), p. 52.

10

CROSS-CULTURAL BUSINESS PRACTICES AND NEGOTIATIONS

Companies that have a strong track record with expats place a candidate's openness to new cultures on an equal footing with the person's technical know-how. After all, successfully navigating within your own business environment and culture does not guarantee that you can maneuver successfully in another. We know, for instance, of a senior manager at a U.S. carmaker who was an expert at negotiating contracts with his company's steel suppliers. When transferred to South Korea to conduct similar deals, the man's confrontational style did nothing but offend the consensus-minded South Koreans—to the point where suppliers would not even speak to him directly. What was worse, the man was unwilling to change his way of doing business. He was soon called back to the company's home office, and his replacement spent a year undoing the damage he left in his wake.[1]

Learning Objectives of the Chapter

In this era of globalization of business activities, managers from one country will often be conducting business and/or sitting at negotiating tables with managers from other nations and cultures. Conducting business and negotiating in one's own culture are complex tasks; they are, however, far more complex when they are conducted across cultures. Each side tends to have perceivable differences in ways of conducting business, language, dress, preferences, and legal and ethical considerations. Understanding and minding the cultural variables of the country where business transactions are taking place is one of the most important aspects of being successful in any international business endeavor. A lack of understanding and/or a disregard for the variables will most likely lead to failure. Practical Perspective 10.1 presents an illustration of how an internationalizing firm's not heeding local culture led to problems. (Disney's managers insisted on doing things the way they did them at home.) After studying this chapter, you should be able to do the following:

1. Discuss the ways business practices vary across cultures

2. Discuss the ways negotiating tactics vary across cultures

3. Discuss the ways negotiating styles vary across cultures

4. Discuss the negotiating styles in numerous countries

PRACTICAL PERSPECTIVE 10-1

Blundering Mouse

Europe got its first taste of the management style of Walt Disney Company when Joe Shapiro started kicking in a door at the luxury Hotel Bristol here [Paris]. It was 1986, and Disney was negotiating with the French government on plans to build a big resort and theme park on the outskirts of Paris. To the exasperation of the Disney team headed by Shapiro, then the company's general counsel, the talks were taking far longer than expected. Jean-René Bernard, the chief French negotiator, says he was astonished when Shapiro, his patience ebbing, ran to the door of the room and began kicking it repeatedly, shouting, "Get something cheap to break!" Shapiro doesn't remember the incident, though he adds with a laugh, "there were a lot of histrionics at the time." But Disney's kick-down-the-door attitude in the planning, building, and financing of Euro Disney accounts for many of the huge problems that plague the resort.

The irony is that even though some early French critics called the park an American cultural abomination, public acceptance hasn't been the problem. European visitors seem to love the place ... Euro Disney's troubles, instead, derive from a different type of culture clash. Europe may have embraced Mickey Mouse, but it hasn't taken to the brash, frequently insensitive, and often overbearing style of Mickey's American corporate parent. ... Disney's contentious attitude exacerbated the difficulties it encountered by alienating people it needed to work with, say many people familiar with the situation. Its answer to doubts or suggestions invariably was: Do as we say, because we know best. "They were always sure it would work because they were Disney," says Beatrice Descoffre, a French construction industry official who dealt with the U.S. company. "Disney," adds a colleague, "came here like the Marines going to Kuwait."

SOURCE: Peter Gumbel and Richard Turner, "Fans Like Euro Disney But Its Parent's Goofs Weigh the Park Down," *The Wall Street Journal* (March 10, 1994), pp. A1, A12. Permission conveyed through Copyright Clearance Center, Inc.

Cross-Cultural Business Practices

As corporations become increasingly international and competition for global markets increases, business managers who are not attentive to cultural differences will not be able to function in foreign markets effectively—they will make their companies less competitive. Effective international managers have learned how varying cultural practices across societies affect business and management practices and how to adapt to the differences. Learning something about the culture of a country before transacting business there shows respect for that culture, and those who understand the culture are more likely to develop successful, long-term business relationships than those who do not.[2] The ensuing section discusses business practices in a cross-cultural context.

The Impact of Culture on Business Practices

Approaches to conducting business vary from culture to culture, making the practice of business at the international level much more complex than in the home market. Some factors that affect cross-cultural business include time, thought patterns, personal space, material possessions, family roles and relationships, competitiveness and individuality, and social behavior,[3] as well as whether a culture is high context or low context (discussed in Chapter 9).[4]

Time

"Time Equals Money" Versus Relationships. Some cultures, the United States, for example, perceive time as a commodity and an asset, and it is greatly valued—"time equals money." The conservation of time is therefore an efficient process in these cultures. Punctuality is expected behavior; tardiness is unacceptable. People in other cultures, however, do not place as much of a premium on time and punctuality; to them, time does not equal money, and tardiness is quite acceptable; and in some cultures, punctuality is viewed as unreasonable behavior. For example, when an Italian is late for a meeting, he or she is not being rude; he or she is simply acting out his or her philosophy that time is a guide rather than a rule.[5] Individuals in these cultures place a much greater premium on relationships and a more relaxed lifestyle than on time and punctuality.

Businesspeople in these cultures generally would be offended by individuals applying time-oriented behavior in business transactions; they prefer that an amicable relationship be established before business is conducted. Charles Ford, who used to be a commercial attaché in Guatemala, has said,

> *The inexperienced American visitor in Guatemala often tries to force a business relationship. The abrupt "always watching the clock" style is often ineffective in Guatemala. A more informed businessperson would engage in small talk about Guatemala, show an interest in the families of his or her associates, join them for lunch or dinner, and generally allow time for a personal relationship to develop. This holds true for Latin America in general.[6]*

Schedules. Schedules are important to individuals in some cultures, but relatively unimportant to people in other cultures. In other words, individuals in some cultures possess an "it must be done by tomorrow" mentality, but people in other cultures possess a "when it gets done is when it is done" mentality. Furthermore, in some cultures which task gets done first depends on the importance of the task (need-based), but in other cultures it depends on factors such as relationship. For instance,

> *in the Arab East, time does not generally include schedules as Americans know and use them. The time required to get something accomplished depends on the relationship. More important people get fast service from less important people, and close relatives take absolute priority; nonrelatives are kept waiting.[7]*

Therefore, telling someone in the Middle East that something must be done now or by the end of the day or by tomorrow may prove to be a mistake. The recipient of the direction may stop work because he or she is placed under pressure and/or because he or she may view the person issuing the directive as being rude or "too pushy."

Time and Decision Making. Some cultures take a long time to make important decisions; other cultures make important decisions quickly. Consequently, low-level managers in cultures that take a long time to make important decisions often try to enhance their work status by lingering over routine decisions. And foreign managers who try to make important decisions quickly in these cultures are likely to downgrade their importance in the eyes of the local people's:

> *For example, in Ethiopia, the time required for a decision is directly proportional to its importance. This is so much the case that low-level bureaucrats there have a way of trying to elevate the prestige of their work by taking a long time to make up their minds. (Americans in that part of the world are innocently prone to downgrading their work in the local people's eyes by trying to speed things up.)*[8]

Thought Patterns

Some cultures' thought patterns are circular. Circular cultures believe that since individuals can see what has happened in the past, their past is ahead of them, and since they cannot see into the future, their future is behind them. Many people in these cultures view change as being bad, so they do not see the business opportunities that lie ahead. In contrast, some cultures' thought patterns are linear. Linear cultures such as the United States view the past as being behind them and the future in front of them. Individuals in these cultures tend to view change as good and attempt to take advantage of the business opportunities they foresee. Circular-oriented people are likely to view a future-oriented person's behavior as forward and aggressive. People in linear cultures are far more open to new ideas and the setting of objectives than are people in circular cultures.

Personal Space

Cultures generally develop informal rules on the distance individuals maintain from one another during face-to-face interactions. People in the United States, for example, prefer a wide distance from those with whom they are involved in face-to-face communication, and they usually feel uncomfortable when the distance is narrowed. In contrast, people in Arab cultures, for instance, prefer a very short distance between themselves and those with whom they are communicating, and they feel offended or rejected by those individuals who maintain a wide distance or keep backing away.

Americans tend to feel comfortable in the following zones of space: 0 to 18 inches for comforting or greeting; 18 inches to 4 feet for conversing with friends; 4 to 12 feet for conversing with strangers; and more than 12 feet in public spaces (lobbies or reception areas). Venezuelans generally prefer much closer space and may view it as rude if someone backs away. On the other hand, the British tend to prefer more space and may view it as rude if one moves too close to them.[9] And the Japanese tend to prefer an even wider space than the British.

Material Possessions

How individuals value material wealth varies from culture to culture. Individuals in high-masculinity cultures tend to value material possessions more than do people in low-masculinity cultures, where they tend to place greater value on things such as a clean environment and a sense of equity/fairness. Individuals in some cultures, the United States, for example, equate success with material wealth—expensive clothes, automobiles, houses, large offices, expensive furnishings, and so forth. Individuals in many cultures, including the English, however, place relatively little importance on material possessions and view the flaunting of wealth as disrespectful:

> *Middle East businessmen look for something else—family, connections, friendship. They do not use the furnishings of their office as part of their status system, nor do they expect to impress a client by these means or to fool a banker into lending more money than he [or she] should. They like good things, too, but feel that they, as persons, should be known and not judged solely by what the public sees.*[10]

The American notion that "money talks" is far from true in many cultures. Furthermore, some cultures use material possessions differently from the way they are used in the United States. For example, the Japanese take pride in relatively "inexpensive but tasteful arrangements that are used to produce the proper emotional setting."[11] Europeans are embarrassed when guests compliment them on their personal possessions; they are not likely to value an object because of its monetary worth—they appreciate an object for its age, beauty, and form, for example, items that have been in the family for a long time.[12] Therefore, in most cultures, when one comments about the value of someone's material possessions, the comment should reflect the aesthetic value, as opposed to the monetary value, of the possession. For example, in American accounting, debits (assets, what you own) are placed on the left side of the balance sheet, thus one sees your wealth first and one is judged on the wealth, and the credits (your liabilities, what you owe) are placed on the right side. But in English accounting, credits are placed on the left side of the balance sheet and debits on the right side, thus one is judged on what he or she owes.

Family and Friendship Roles

In many cultures, family roles are highly traditional and personal. Members of the family have predictable, designated roles and a responsibility for maintaining the status quo. In these cultures, family responsibilities have a greater influence on members' behavior than do work situations and business interactions; family-related matters are more important than work-related matters. On the other hand, in some cultures, especially in the United States, work matters often take precedence over family matters. Americans tend to make friends quickly and become disassociated from them just as fast. In other countries, however, friendships form more slowly, and once made, they are deeper, last longer, and involve real obligations. Friends, as well as family, tend to provide some sort of social insurance:

> *It is important to stress that in the Middle East and Latin America, your "friends" will not let you down. The fact that they personally are feeling the*

pinch is never an excuse for failing their friends. They are supposed to look out for your interests.[13]

Competitiveness and Individuality

Competitiveness and individuality are valued by Americans. A statement made by the late Vince Lombardi, a famous, highly successful American football coach, characterizes the typically American view of competition: "Winning isn't everything, it's the only thing." Many cultures, including European cultures, reject this attitude. Instead, they emphasize team and consensus values; they value modesty, team spirit, and patience. Individuals in these cultures are likely to be offended by those who apply haste and aggressive behavior in the pursuit of business transactions; they prefer business relationships that have a more relaxed atmosphere.

Social Behaviors

Many social habits, such as eating, the types of foods eaten, gift giving, and greetings vary from culture to culture.

Eating. Behaviors such as noisy eating and belching are quite acceptable in some cultures but are totally unacceptable in others. Eating noisily and belching mean that the meal is being enjoyed, and failure to do either may actually be offensive to the hosts because their absence indicates that the meal is not good. In some cultures, such as the Chinese, spitting residuals, such as chicken bones and shrimp shells, on the table is appropriate behavior at home or in a restaurant. Removing the residuals with your fingers and placing them on the table is actually crude behavior to people in these cultures. The French, who think Americans are repulsive because they switch forks from one hand to the other while eating, may find these types of behavior quite gross. Furthermore, flatulence at the dinner table is quite crude and offensive in many cultures, but not so in some cultures, such as the French.

Foods. Types of food vary from culture to culture, and what foreigners are expected to eat when dining with local hosts can be a traumatic culture shock to many. For example, in China ceremonial lunches and dinners often consist of as many as 15 courses, and sometimes more. Chinese hosts typically expect guests to try at least a bit of each course—not doing so would be offensive. China, with a land base smaller than Canada's, has a population of about 1.3 billion people (about 25% of the world's population). How, one might wonder, is such a population fed? One way is by being efficient, by not wasting food and maximizing use of the foods that "Mother Nature" provides. People in China generally eat a greater variety of foods than do people in most Western cultures. Therefore, a foreign guest should not be too surprised when he or she finds fish heads, chicken heads, chicken feet, and "night duck" soup (bat soup) included in the 15 or so courses.

An American might not enjoy snails, a popular local dish in France, and might not enjoy blood pudding sausages, which are popular in Portugal; he or she may not understand the appeal of "fragrant meat" (dog meat) eaten in Taiwan or horse meat, which used to be eaten in some parts of Italy and in some parts of Canada. Global travelers who have participated in such lunches or dinners may suggest that in such situations it is best to just eat and not ask what it is. However, this author's own experience has been that it is polite and diplomatic to ask what food is being served, but in a polite, curious, inquisitive way (the hosts appreciate that you have taken an interest in their culture). Never ask in a "What is that?" tone of voice, which may sound as if you find it strange that they would eat such a thing.

Gift Giving. In some cultures, gifts are expected, and failure to present them is considered an insult, whereas in other cultures, offering a gift is considered offensive. For example, gifts are rarely exchanged in Germany and are usually considered inappropriate, although small gifts may be appropriate. In some cultures, the gift is given during the initial visit, while in others it is given afterward. In some cultures, the gift is given in private, whereas in other cultures it can be given in public. In Japan, where gift giving is an important part of doing business (it helps symbolize the depth and strength of a business relationship), the exchanging of gifts usually takes place at the first meeting. The gift given to a Japanese associate should consist of multiple contents that can be shared with the group. And gifts to the Japanese should not be too elaborate or too expensive. Such gifts may create awkwardness.[14] Some countries, such as Paraguay, tend to view gifts as bribes.

Countries in which a gift is expected:

Europe	Czech Republic, Poland, Russia, Ukraine
Latin America	Bolivia, Colombia, Costa Rica
Pacific Rim	China, Hong Kong, Indonesia, Japan, (South) Korea, Taiwan, Malaysia, Philippines, and Thailand.

Countries in which a gift is not expected on the first visit but would be expected on a subsequent visit:

Europe	Portugal, Spain
Latin American	Brazil, Chile, Guatemala, Nicaragua, Panama, Peru, Venezuela

Countries in which a gift is not expected or gifts are less frequently exchanged:

Africa	
Europe	England, France, Hungary, Italy
Latin America	Uruguay
Scandinavia	Denmark
Middle East	Pakistan, Saudi Arabia
United States[15]	

The type of gift given also varies from one culture to another. For example, white flowers are typically not given in Asia, where white is symbolic of death. In China, giving a clock shakes the superstitious. The phrase "to give a clock" when uttered in Chinese sounds like an expression that means "to care for a dying patient."[16] In Belgium, gift giving is not a normal custom—flowers may be given as a gift when invited to someone's home, but do not take chrysanthemums, as they are used mainly for funerals.

Greetings. Knowledge of a culture's way of greeting is important because first impressions are vital to the development of relationships. Many cultures greet with a handshake, some give a hug, some a combination of a handshake and a hug, but some cultures do not greet by touching. For example, Australians and Americans use a strong handshake, but the French and the Asians use a light, gentle, single handshake. Many Latin European cultures greet with an *abrazo*—a combination of handshake, hug, and shoulder pats. The Japanese greet by a bow, and the Laotians greet by bringing palms together in prayer-like form and bowing.[17]

High-Context Versus Low-Context Cultures

Some cultures are high context, and some are low context. The degree affects the business tempo in the society. As discussed in Chapters 1 and 9, in the transaction of business, people in high-context cultures establish social trust first, value personal relations and goodwill, make agreements on the basis of general trust, and like to conduct slow and ritualistic negotiations.[18] On the other hand, individuals in low-context cultures get down to business first, value expertise and performance, reach agreement by specific, legalistic contract, and like to conduct negotiations as efficiently as possible.[19] The following is the advice that an American Embassy attaché gave to an executive from the United States (a low-context culture) seeking to do business in a South American, Spanish-speaking country (a high-context culture):[20]

1. You don't do business here the way you do in the States; it is necessary to spend much more time. You have to get to know your man and vice versa.

2. You must meet with him several times before you talk business. . . .

3. Take your price list and put it in your pocket. . . . Down here price is only one of the many things taken into account before closing the deal. In the United States, your past experience will prompt you to act according to a certain set of principles, but many of these principles will not work here. Every time you feel the urge to act . . . suppress the urge. . . .

4. Down here people like to do business with men who are somebody. In order to be somebody, it is well to have written a book, to have lectured at a university, or to have developed your intellect in some way. The man you are going to see is a poet. He has published several volumes of poetry. Like many Latin Americans, he praises poetry highly. You will find that he will spend a good deal of business time quoting his poetry to you, and he will take great pleasure in this.

5. You will also note that the people here are very proud of their past and of their Spanish blood, but they are also exceedingly proud of their liberation from Spain and their independence. The fact that they are a democracy, that they are free, and also that they are no longer a colony is very, very important to them. They are warm and friendly and enthusiastic if they like you. If they don't, they are cold and withdrawn.

6. And another thing, time down here means something different. It works in a different way. You know how it is back in the States when a certain type blurts out whatever is on his mind without waiting to see if the situation is right. He is

considered an impatient bore and somewhat egocentric. Well, down here, you have to wait much, much longer, and I really mean much, much longer, before you can begin to talk about the reason for your visit.

7. There is another point I want to caution you about. At home, the man who sells takes the initiative. Here, they tell you when they are ready to do business. But, most of all, don't discuss price until you are asked and don't rush things.

Business Customs in China, Japan, and South Korea

People transacting business across cultures must be sensitive to the above dynamics, as well as to varying business customs. Culture affects business behavior and customs. For example, writing in red is seen as rude in China, and so is giving clocks or umbrellas as gifts. Furthermore, the Chinese do not appreciate a discussion about Taiwan or Tibet, and the number 4 should be avoided because the pronunciation of *four* sounds similar to the pronunciation of the word *death* (in Chinese) and it's considered an unlucky number in Asia (like the number 13 in America), while the number 8 is considered lucky.[21] This means that meetings scheduled for the fourth of the month might best be avoided.

This section describes how *guanxi* affects business culture and customs in China, how *wa* affects business culture and customs in Japan, and how *inhwa* affects business culture and customs in South Korea. Some other interesting business customs from around the world that differ from country to country are presented in Table 10.1. Note that the descriptions in Table 10.1 are generalizations. Not all residents of a country necessarily adhere to those customs—especially the immigrants in a country. For example, many people in Australia are from other countries, such as China and Italy. These people may adhere to the customs of their country of birth.

Guanxi

The Chinese are excessively polite, but are tough bargainers; they like to entertain and expect reciprocal dinner parties; and they avoid all unnecessary physical contact. In China, contracts are binding only if the conditions present at the time the contract is signed are also present when the contract is executed.[22]

A major dynamic of Chinese society is *guanxi,* which refers to the special relationships between two people.[23] The two individuals who share this relationship assume that each is fully committed to the other, that they have agreed to exchange favors, even when official commands mandate that they act neutrally. The *guanxi* relationship, even though it is preferred, does not have to be between friends. In the relationship, an individual who refuses to return a favor loses face and becomes known as untrustworthy. Foreigners planning to do business in China who have not established a *guanxi* relationship may very well have to deal with uninterested officials. When the relationship is between two people of unequal rank, the relationship favors the weaker person. The weaker person can claim inadequacy and ask for special favors that he or she does not have to reciprocate equally. The unequal exchange gives respect and honor to the stronger party, who voluntarily gives more than he or she receives.

Thus, to do business in China effectively, good personal connections must be established first. Note that the decision-making process in China is slow even when bureaucracy is circumvented by *guanxi.* This is because decisions in China are made hierarchically, and superiors in each *guanxi* link must agree.[24] The financial crisis and

TABLE 10.1	Business Customs Around the World
Australia	Business is almost always conducted over drinks, and it is considered rude to buy out of turn. Australians like to be addressed by their titles.
Austria	Austrians prefer to be addressed by their titles and consider it rude if a business associate tries to pick up the tab for a lunch or dinner they have initiated. They enjoy discussing art and music as well as skiing.
Belgium	Belgians like to get down to business immediately and are very conservative and efficient in their approach to business meetings. One must address French-speaking Belgians as "monsieur" or "madame," while Dutch-speaking Belgians must be addressed as "Mr." or "Mrs."
Egypt	Egypt is dominated by the Moslem faith, and their business customs reflect this. Business is slow paced, and the red tape is limitless. Egyptians take offense at refusals and at the use of direct negatives.
France	Conducting business in France in August is difficult because most people are on vacation. The French use titles until use of first names is proposed. In negotiations, they like to debate issues; they like to show their intellect and to challenge your intellect. To successfully sell the French requires convincing them of the merits of the product/service through intellectual debate, not through flashy, high-powered presentations. They have sophisticated table manners.
Germany	One should expect much handshaking, but in order of the person's importance in the enterprise. Germans insist on using titles, seldom use first names, use the surname preceded by the title, dislike small talk, and are very punctual. Germans are competitive negotiators who get straight to the point and leave little room for debate. German executives tend to have an engineering and science background, and one must therefore appeal to their technical tastes—glitzy presentations are likely to fail. They do not strongly emphasize the development of personal relationships with business associates—they value their privacy and keep business and private matters separate.
Greece	The Greeks are famous for their extensive bargaining and for never discussing business without a cup of coffee. Building a personal rapport with Greeks is important. Business entertaining normally takes place in the evening at a local tavern, and spouses are often included. It is important that a business relationship be built on trust. The government plays an important role in business, which means that one must work through the bureaucracy. Business is highly personalized—family connections, political connections, and business connections. How one connects is often more important than the quality of the product/service. In Greece, negotiations are not finished even after the contract has been awarded—a contract is viewed as an evolving document of agreement.
Guatemala	A luncheon set for a specific time means that some guests may arrive 10 minutes early, while others may be 45 minutes late.
India	Business is conducted at an extremely leisurely pace; therefore, Indians are very patient, unlike their American counterparts. When invited to dinner, one should accept and pass the food with the right hand only and expect to be asked many personal questions—which Indians see as a sign of politeness. Indians avoid discussing political issues with their business contacts.
Ireland	Do not confuse it with Northern Ireland or the United Kingdom—it is politically and culturally distinct from both.
Republic of Italy	Italians use a handshake for greetings and goodbyes. Unlike in the United States, men do not stand when a woman enters or leaves a room, and they do not kiss a woman's hand—this is reserved for royalty. Appearance and style are very important to Italian businesspeople. The appeal and polish of a presentation reflect the quality of the product/service or the firm itself. Italian businesspeople are confident, shrewd, and competent negotiators, and they tend to rely mainly on their instincts and not as much on the advice of specialists.
Malaysia	Most Malaysians are Muslims, so they do not eat pork, drink alcohol, or party on Friday night, the eve of the Muslim Sabbath. They are very status and role conscious and therefore do not readily mingle at social gatherings, particularly if men and women are together at the same gathering.

TABLE 10.1 (Continued)

Mexico	Local contacts (connections) are required prior to arrival in Mexico. It is impolite to make extended eye contact with Mexicans. Timeliness is not important—it is OK for your host to keep you waiting. Don't say "America" to mean the United States because Mexicans are Americans too, and don't say "the United States" to mean the country because Mexico is a "United States" too—the United States of Mexico. Don't get down to business right away. First, get to know your prospective Mexican clients and their families by socializing.
Netherlands	The Dutch are competitive negotiators who get straight to the point and normally have little conflict or debate.
Nigeria	Business is slow paced and never conducted over the telephone.
Pakistan	The Islamic faith is a dominant factor in Pakistani life and in business as well. It is a male-dominated country where women are largely confined to the domestic sphere; hence, Pakistani men are uncomfortable or may even refuse to transact business with a woman. They refuse alcohol, cigarettes, and pork. One should never try to take a picture of a Pakistani without his or her permission.
Portugal	One must take the time to establish a rapport with Portuguese business associates.
Saudi Arabia	Business is informal, slow paced, and male dominated. The Saudies are insulted if forced to deal with a representative rather than with the main person. When invited to a Saudi home, never bring flowers or gifts for the lady of the house, never eat or drink with the left hand, and never praise the house furnishings unless you would like to receive them as a gift the following day.
South Africa	Businesspeople like to discuss politics with their peers, and they are generally ultraconservative.
Spain	The Spanish work long days and break appointments often. The business lunch is an important part of conducting business in Spain, and there is great ceremony in lunch meetings. Lunches stretch from 2:30 p.m. to 5:00 p.m.; then work goes on until 8:30 p.m. or 9:00 p.m. These lunches are used to develop the relationship required before business can be conducted.
Thailand	Thailand's traditional greeting is the *wai*, which is made by the placement of both hands together in a prayer-like position at the chin and bowing slightly. The gesture means "thank you" and "I am sorry," as well as "hello." The higher the hands, the more respect is symbolized. The fingertips, however, should never be raised above the eye level. Failure to return a *wai* is equivalent to refusing to shake hands in the West. In Thailand, it is considered offensive to place one's arm over the back of the chair in which another person is sitting, and men and women should not show affection in public. First names are used, and last names are reserved for very formal occasions or in writing.
United Kingdom	In the United Kingdom, never sit with the ankle resting on the knee; one should instead cross one's legs with one knee on top of the other. Avoid backslapping and putting an arm around a new acquaintance. Use titles until use of first names is suggested. Gift-giving is not a normal custom in the United Kingdom. The British are very civil and reserved; they do not admire overt ambition and aggressiveness and are offended by hard-sell tactics. They do not brag about their finances or positions. And they are good negotiators but do not have a high regard for bargaining in general.
United States	Americans often feel that the European practice of meticulously cultivating personal relationships with business associates slows the expedient conduct of business; they agree that time is money and that Europeans waste time. Business comes first, and friendship or pleasure comes later, if at all.

SOURCE: Adapted from David Altany, "It Takes Cultural Savvy," *Industry Week* (October 2, 1989); M. Katherine Glover, "Do's and Taboos: Cultural Aspects of International Business," *Business America* (August 13, 1990), p. 3; Dean Foster, "Business Across Borders: International Etiquette for the Effective Secretary," *The Secretary* (October 1992), p. 23; Valerie Frazee, "Getting Started in Mexico," *Workforce*, 2, no. 1 (January 1997), pp. 16, 17.

corruption in Asia in the 1990s was attributed to this Asian value. (Some academics use the word *cronyism* to describe this type of behavior.)[25] Many Asian banks sanctioned loans not on the basis of merit (as defined in the Western financial systems) but on the basis of these types of connections.[26] The International Monetary Fund (discussed in Chapter 2) has started and implemented programs aimed at encouraging Asian financial institutions to apply America's prudent investment system.

Wa

The Japanese entertain exhaustively but in a very businesslike manner. To them, business is family, and therefore they are usually selfless—unlike the cutthroat business styles of many Americans. The Japanese, like the Chinese, avoid physical contact as much as possible, and they require even more space than Americans. No matter how poorly negotiations may be proceeding, the Japanese see direct negative statements as rude and offensive. Asians are not very open to criticism and may consider it insulting, even if it's constructive criticism.

Arriving late for a business meeting is considered rude, while it is quite acceptable to be late for a social occasion. The Japanese bow is a well-known form of greeting; it symbolizes respect and humility. When receiving a business card, take it with both hands, observe it carefully, acknowledge it with a nod that you have taken in the information, and make a relevant comment or ask a polite question about it. In other words, treat the card as you would treat its owner—with respect. When presenting the card, use both hands and position the card so that the recipient can read it. The information should be printed in Japanese on the reverse side of the card. (The above process of presenting business cards applies in China, Taiwan, as well as in many East Asian countries.)

The Japanese concept of *wa* necessitates that members of a group, be it a work team, a company, or a nation, cooperate with and trust each other. Consequently, the Japanese usually prefer, or even demand, that business dealings occur among friends, and they do not like to deal with strangers. Therefore, proper introductions are crucial when business relationships are launched. Before business transactions can begin, the Japanese must first place the foreigner within some group context (a *wa* relationship must be established).[27] Furthermore, in Japan telling the truth, or, as it is called in the United States, "laying one's cards on the table," does not work well because it may upset someone and threaten the group's *wa*. The Japanese, thus prefer ensuring harmony and goodwill over the truth, as well as long-term over short-term relations.[28]

Inhwa

South Korean business behavior is heavily influenced by *inhwa*, which stresses harmony; linking of people who are unequal in rank, prestige, and power; loyalty to hierarchical rankings; and superiors being concerned for the well-being of subordinates.[29] Corporations are viewed as a "family" or a "clan." As a consequence, South Korean businesspeople prefer to establish personal ties with strangers before they transact business deals with them. Unlike the Japanese, but like the Chinese, the binding of Koreans' relationships is between individuals, and there is no strong loyalty to the organization—they will readily change companies when it suits them. *Inhwa* relationships are long-term and require a long time and much patience to cultivate. Once relationships have been established, they must be continually maintained and strengthened. Business contracts are interpreted through the personal relationships of those who agree. Therefore, an agreement is only as good as the personal relations that made it possible; lawyers should not take over from the original signatories.

Furthermore, in South Korea contracts are not simply documents indicating mutual obligations and rights; they are declarations of intentions supported by the integrity of the signatories. As a result, renegotiation of contracts is expected behavior in South Korea. South Koreans do not consider a contract binding if conditions change. Since the emotional aspects are more valuable than the contents of a contract, foreigners must cultivate a strong relationship with their South Korean associates before signing a contract. The original signatories should be prepared to continually maintain that relationship and interest in the project after the contract has been signed because any change of those in power could lead to problems.

Government officials direct much of South Korea's economy; therefore, most major ventures require the approval of one or more government officials. Foreign businesspeople must establish relationships with government circles as well. Senior South Korean officials deal only with other senior officials, not junior officials. If the South Korean company is using its president as the negotiator, then the foreign corporation should also make sure that its negotiator is its president. Also, South Koreans do not like bad news, and when it must be delivered, it should be done toward the end of the workday, and suddenly.[30]

Cross-Cultural Generalizations: A Caveat

The international businessperson should be aware that while the culture influences the mode of conducting business in a country, the introduction of new technology changes the practical aspects of culture. Historically, cultural borrowing between countries has been a common practice. Strategists should thus be cautious about using outdated information about a nation's culture. They should also be aware that generalized information about nations, though often true, serves mainly to describe stereotypes, and stereotypes are useful mainly as starting points for analysis.[31] Ultimately, specific situations must be analyzed and considered to make the final decision. For example, it may be true that many Americans do regard time as money, but not all of them do.

Cross-Cultural Adaptation: A Caveat

Those who offer advice on international negotiations advocate adaptation—an attempt to obtain approval from members of a foreign culture by becoming behaviorally similar to them. ("When in Rome, do as the Romans do.") This advice is based on research findings that when individuals were perceived as similar in areas of beliefs, attitudes, dialect style, and socioeconomic class, they were viewed more favorably. These advocates do not specify a degree of adaptation, however. Other research findings suggest that the positive correlations between similarity and attraction may be true only at moderate levels of similarity and that substantial levels of adaptation actually result in negative relationships.[32] In other words, if one does not adapt to the local culture, a negative relationship will occur, as it will if one attempts to adapt too much. It is therefore moderate adaptation that leads to a positive relationship. A possible explanation for this is that substantial adaptation efforts may be perceived as presumptuous, while moderate adaptation efforts may reflect respect and sensitivity to the local culture.[33]

For example, a male Japanese executive conducting business in Texas may actually be offensive if at a business meeting with his traditionally dressed Texan associates he dresses in traditional Texas clothes (big hat, big boots, etc.). In the same context, an American conducting business in Malaysia may offend some Malaysians if he or she dresses in traditional Malaysian clothes. Simply acknowledging and respecting that traditional dress style differs in many countries would suffice. Not violating local rituals, such as hurrying the conducting of business in a culture where business activities typically are not hurried, will result in a better relationship. Furthermore, a male Texan conducting business in India may actually command respect if he dresses in traditional Texas clothes—it would be interesting to the locals.

Cross-Cultural Negotiations

Negotiating across cultures is far more complex than negotiating within a culture because foreign negotiators have to deal with differing negotiating styles and cultural variables simultaneously. In other words, the negotiating styles that work at home generally do not work in other cultures. As a result, cross-cultural business negotiators have one of the most complex business roles to play in organizations. They are often thrust into a foreign society consisting of what appears to be "hostile" strangers. They are placed in the precarious position of negotiating profitable business relationships with these people or suffering the negative consequences of failure. And quite often they find themselves at a loss as to why their best efforts and intentions have failed them. (Practical Perspective 10.2 presents an insight in this respect.)

PRACTICAL PERSPECTIVE 10-2

Be Aware of Cultural Differences When Selling Abroad

When Shannon Small began her marketing presentation, she had no idea it was about to backfire on her.

A vice president for Bethesda, Maryland-based Iconix Group and a seasoned pro at corporate image-building and technology branding, Small started her pitch to a French firm recently with a tactic that had proven effective for Iconix when presenting to domestic companies. She showed the firm a side-by-side comparison of its Web site and those of its competitors. She evaluated the strengths and weakness of each, including where the prospective client's Web site fell short. The reaction was swift.

"They said, 'If you send us anything like this again, we will never work with you,'" Small recalls of the response. Far from viewing the comparison as constructive and insightful criticism, the clients perceived it as "confrontational, rude, typical ugly American," Small says.

For a young technology company doing business overseas, the episode was a telling lesson in negotiating Old World cultural subtleties.

"Basically what they told us was, 'You can tell us those things, but we don't want to know anyone is doing it better,'" Small says. With a little finesse, she ultimately salvaged the account. What Small took away from that unexpected encounter was that the American penchant for the cards-on-the-table, straight talk approach in business meetings must give way to coaxing egos and using polite gestures in France.

This type of scenario may be ancient history for large American corporations that have been working in overseas markets for decades now. But as technology companies run by headstrong entrepreneurs are going international at earlier and earlier stages in their life cycles, they are facing such subtleties for the first time.

No longer the exclusive province of Fortune 500 companies, international markets are opening up to small firms riding the Internet's conquest of the globe. As digital connectivity eliminates the cost of doing business over long distances and as language barriers become a thing of the past, young tech executives are rushing into foreign markets hungry for American Internet and software expertise. But the roadblock time and time again for this aggressive generation is its lack of Miss Manners properness in dealing with other cultures. For all the talk of the Internet breaking down barriers and making the world a cozy global village, the reality is that age-old cultural differences still persist.

These cultural differences in the tech world include misunderstandings of behavior and speech, and societal differences in the proper ways of relationship building and deal signing. And gender issues, though not included in this list, still affect many international business ventures—after all, professional American women still encounter sexism and unequal treatment when doing business in certain countries of South America, the Middle East, and the East Asia.

Large tech companies, like IBM, Hewlett Packard, and General Electric, learned their overseas cultural lessons 30 or more years ago. But the next generation is up against the same curve.

"The smaller companies have so much learning to do," says Neil Goodman, who heads Global Dynamics, an international business protocol consulting firm in Randolph, New Jersey. "They stumble a lot more in international settings, and it's very hard to recoup from that bad first impression."

SOURCE: Excerpted from Dan Egbert, "The New Generation Learns an Age-Old Lesson Overseas," *Tech Capital*, 3, no. 4 (July 1999), p. 78. Reprinted with permission.

How to Avoid Failure in International Negotiations

Negotiators in a foreign country often fail because the local counterparts have taken more time to learn how to overcome the obstacles normally associated with international/cross-cultural negotiations. Failure may occur because of time and/or cost constraints. For example, a negotiator may be given too short a period of time to obtain better contract terms than were originally agreed to in a country where negotiations typically take a long time. A negotiator may think that "what works in the home country is good enough for the rest of the world," which is far from the truth. In fact, strategies that fail to take into account cultural factors are usually naive or misconceived. Typically, the obstacles to overcome include the following:

- Learning the local language, or at least being able to select and use an effective language translator
- Learning the local culture, including how the culture handles conflict, its business practices, and its business ethics, or at least being able to select and use an effective cultural translator
- Becoming well prepared for the negotiations (i.e., along with the above, the negotiator must have a thorough knowledge of the subject matter being negotiated)

Effective cross-cultural negotiators understand the cultural differences existing between all parties involved; and they know that failure to understand the differences serves only to destroy potential business success.[34]

How Much Must One Know About the Foreign Culture?

Realistically, it is nearly impossible to learn everything about the culture of another country, although it may be possible if one lives in that country for several years. The reason for this is that each culture has developed, over time, multifaceted structures that are much too complex for any foreigner to understand fully. Therefore, foreign negotiators need not be fully aware of the foreign culture; they do not need to know as much about the foreign culture as the locals, whose frames of reference were shaped by that culture. However, they will need to know enough about the culture and about the locals' negotiating styles to avoid being uncomfortable during (and after) negotiations.[35] Besides knowing enough not to fail, they also need to know enough to win. For example, in negotiations between Japanese and American businesspeople, Japanese negotiators have sometimes used their knowledge that Americans have a low tolerance for silence to their advantage.

In other words, for negotiations to take place, the foreigner must at least recognize those ideas and behaviors that the locals intentionally put forward as part of the negotiation process—and the locals must do the same for the foreigners. Both sides must be capable of interpreting these behaviors sufficiently to distinguish common from conflicting positions, to spot movement from positions, and to respond in ways that sustain communication.[36] Practical Perspective 10.3 describes negotiating in Mexico. Boxes 10.1 and 10.2 present the recommended behavior for negotiating with the Japanese, Table 10.1 for negotiating with the French, and Table 10.2 for negotiating in China. Appendix 10.1 presents the negotiating styles of various European nations, and Appendix 10.2 presents the negotiating style in Asia. It cannot, however, be overemphasized that these are stereotypes or generalizations and, while they are often accurate, should serve only as starting points in understanding a culture. Not all individuals in a culture adhere to these practices. Ultimately, cross-cultural negotiators must determine their counterparts' personal motivations and agendas and adapt the negotiation style to them.

The purpose of the ensuing sections is to develop a cross-cultural negotiations process. The process includes both strategy and tactics. Strategy refers to a long-term plan, and tactics refers to the actual means used to implement the strategy.[37]

PRACTICAL PERSPECTIVE 10-3

Negotiating Successfully In Mexico

Negotiating in Mexico is non-confrontational; it may seem more like a polite conversation than the give-and-take process many Americans are accustomed to. Agreements are developed in a more casual environment, but the deal is expected to be honored. Mexicans keep their word and expect us to do the same.

Although our counterparts will likely speak English, bring someone who speaks Spanish, preferably someone from Mexico. This encourages familiarity, which will be conductive to negotiations.

Warming Up

Mexicans have a warm-up period that greatly influences how negotiations will proceed and their outcome. U.S. political and military interventions in Mexico are still alive in Mexican education, so Mexicans are wary of being taken advantage of by "gringos." Wariness needs to be overcome, and trust must be built. Demonstrate that you are willing to negotiate on a level playing field.

Mexicans need to feel their counterparts are *simpático* (being warm and likable) to feel comfortable negotiating and enjoy doing business with them. This comes from a cultural emphasis on the importance of relationship. U.S. businesspeople are sometimes perceived as *antipático* (impersonal or aloof). Mexicans use the warm-up period to determine whether their counterparts are simpático or antipático. Decisions are based not only on the decision maker's assessment of the negotiations but also on feelings about the U.S. company and the individuals representing it.

In the United States, decisions tend to be reached by committee or group consensus. This is not the case in Mexico. The decision maker is one person, which comes from a historical and cultural emphasis on *personalisimo* (personalism). This value has developed strong political leaders and predominates in Mexican businesses. Americans should use the warm-up period to determine who the decision maker is.

Mexicans are very hierarchical, and by interacting with your counterparts socially, you may discover that the person you are dealing with defers to someone else. Also, many Mexican companies are family businesses. By doing research, you will know what family names are associated with the owners of the company. If you are not dealing with the decision maker, you are going through an extra step in the negotiations.

It's How You Say It

Mexican society is high-context, meaning much of the information transferred between people, especially in negotiations, is in the context rather than the content. A great deal of information is transmitted nonverbally. Less emphasis is placed on words, numbers, and written documents, and much more on inflection, tone of voice, setting, past history of your relationship, how they feel about you, trust, and so on.

Because it is a high-context culture, Mexicans use body language. Less eye contact would indicate reluctance to commit. Less distance, more touching, and warm *abrazos* (hugs) are signs of acceptance.

Lengthy proposals written in legalese will intimidate your Mexican counterparts and can scare them away from the deal.

Negotiations may not proceed in an orderly fashion by U.S. standards. Discussions are not necessarily sequential or logical. Mexicans are quite comfortable with this as it allows them to be creative and demonstrate their personal flair. If you present a checklist-style negotiation schedule and stick to it rigidly, the Mexicans may feel confined and pressured.

The Mexican culture is far more concerned with status than ours is. Therefore, it is important that your negotiators' status matches theirs. If the U.S. company sends mid-level managers, the Mexicans may be offended. If the opposite is true, you will be wasting your time because the decision will come from higher ranks. The larger company and the buyer will have more status.

Dealing With Difficulties

Your Mexican counterparts have less control over things than we might have in this country. Rather than pretend difficulties will not arise (for example, delivery dates might not be met), it is much more useful for both companies to recognize these potential problems and build into the contract a way to deal with them. This foresight will also show your counterparts that you understand their business environment.

If negotiations are not working out, it is important not to end abruptly. If you have an attitude that indicates, "This is our bottom line. We cannot go any farther, and the negotiations are over," you may hinder future business opportunities. They need to feel they can come back to you later and still have a *simpático* relationship.

Reaching an Agreement

We like to end negotiations on a clear, definitive note. Mexicans need a more flexible ending. This "open-endedness" allows Mexicans to deal with unforeseen eventualities—changes in price, political climate, etc. Mexican businesspeople deal with much more change and uncertainty than we do and would be uncomfortable with an iron-clad document at the end of negotiations. This does not mean they are trying to find an escape clause. The real substance of the agreement is in the quality of the relationship that has been established.

SOURCE: *International Business* (February 1997), p. 15. Reprinted with permission.

Box 10.1 Recommended Behavior for Negotiating With the Japanese

Employ

- Use an "introducer" for initial contacts (e.g., a general trading company).
- Employ an agent the counterpart knows and respects.
- Ensure that the agent/advisor speaks fluent Japanese.

Induce

- Be open to social interaction and communicate directly.
- Make an extreme initial proposal, expecting to make concessions later.
- Work efficiently to get the job done.

Adapt

- Follow some Japanese protocol (reserved behavior, name cards, gifts).
- Provide a lot of information (by American standards) up-front to influence the counterpart in making a decision early.
- Slow down your usual timetable.
- Make informed interpretations (e.g., "It is difficult" means "No").
- Present positions later in the process more firmly and more consistently.

Embrace

- Proceed according to the information-gathering, *nemawashi* (not exchange) model.
- "Know your stuff" cold.
- Assemble a team (group) for formal negotiations.
- Speak in Japanese.
- Develop personal relationships, and respond to obligations within them.

Improvise

- Do your homework on the individual counterpart(s) and circumstances.
- Be attentive and nimble (improvising entails different behaviors for different Japanese).
- Invite the counterpart to participate in mutually enjoyed activities or interests (e.g., golf).

These are examples, not a complete listing, of attitudes and behaviors implied by a negotiator's use of each strategy.

SOURCE: Stephen E. Weiss, "Negotiating With 'Romans'—Part 1," *Sloan Management Review* (Winter 1994), p. 58. Copyright © 1994, Sloan Management Review Association, Massachusetts Institute of Technology, Sloan School of Management. Used with permission. All rights reserved.

Box 10.2   How to Behave During Negotiating Sessions in Japan

- Don't get too involved with the details of the contract too early in the session. The Japanese may feel that the details can be worked out as the relationship continues to grow.
- Try not to use an aggressive approach in selling your idea. Japanese believe that your idea or product should speak for itself. A low-key approach is better.
- Don't interrupt when someone is speaking. This is considered rude by most Japanese.
- Try to be formal. Do not ask if it would be OK to call them by their first names or if everyone can take off their coats to relax. This type of atmosphere or approach tends to give the Japanese a feeling of ack of sincerity.
- Always bring as much information as possible about your plans and your firm. Published articles are of great advantage.
- It is better to not approach the Japanese alone. Send a group (two or three) to conduct negotiations. This is a sign of earnestness to the Japanese. Make certain you send the appropriate individuals who can make the decisions.
- Do not demand an immediate decision on the points covered in the meetings. As most decisions are made in groups, the Japanese team needs time to compare notes and discuss matters.
- Do not be offended if the Japanese enquire about your religious or political beliefs. These are common questions used in Japan because they are interested in knowing as much about you and your company as possible. It is a confidence builder.
- If you get stuck on a point, don't continue to beat away on it. Move on to other points and come back when the other team has had time to think about it.
- Keep reviewing those points that were agreed on during the meeting, trying to move forward in a constructive manner.
- Maintain good communication with your interpreter. The interpreter may be able to inform you on the progress of the contract or perhaps of possible conflicts that may be avoided.
- Speak slowly and with patience. Do not rattle off numbers to indicate your knowledge of the project. Numbers can be studied in detail by the Japanese at a later date.
- Be prepared for misunderstandings and clarify the points with sincerity and a willingness to assist.
- Don't cover difficult points first on the agenda. Work toward a common ground, but be flexible enough to realize that ground may totally change before the contract is signed.

SOURCE: Robert T. Moran, *Getting Your Yen's Worth: How to Negotiate With Japan, Inc.* (Houston, TX: Gulf Publishing, 1985), pp. 123–124. Copyright © Gulf Publishing Company, Houston, TX, 800–231–6275. All rights reserved.

Strategic Planning for International Negotiations

Strategic planning for international negotiations involves several stages: preparation for face-to-face negotiations, determining the settlement range, selecting the form of

TABLE 10.2 Culturally Based Guidelines for Negotiating Business Conflict Resolutions in China

1. Expand Your Cultural Comfort Zone

"Learn something from 5,000 years of Chinese history."—Jiang Zemin

Implications for American Managers Who Are Negotiating Conflict Resolutions in China:
a. Embrace the unusual as normal.
b. Get rid of any misplaced sense of (American) cultural arrogance.
c. Seek all forms of knowledge about China's history and culture.
d. As a result of this cultural immersion, seek to absorb strategic thinking unconsciously. Then strive to accept the mental "thrust-and-parry" associated with strategic thinking as a natural part of human interaction in China.

2. Last Things First

"Reng Qing, the belief that the human should never be removed from business affairs."—Confucius

Implications for American Managers Who Are Negotiating Conflict Resolutions in China:
a. Learn that in the face of Chinese conflict not having goals may be worse than not being able to achieve them.
b. Welcome conflicts as an opportunity for creative expression within the context of the business relationship.
c. Learn how to create obligations (in one's Chinese counterparts) through gestures or actions that cost little. Also, learn when and how to subtly call the debt due. In short, learn the essence of Reng Qing.

3. Anticipate Conflict

"He who excels at resolving difficulties does so before they arise. He also excels in conquering his enemies triumphs before threats materialize."—Sun Tzu

Implications for American Managers Who Are Negotiating Conflict Resolutions in China:
a. Learn that active measures should be taken in anticipation of conflict rather than dispassionately waiting for disagreements to arise.
b. Learn that the opportunity to act in China turns on the ability to make small adjustments or corrections in advance of significant disagreements.
c. Learn to separate essential (hard-boundary) issues or concepts from nonessential ones and do not allow hard-boundary issues to be violated by Chinese partners.
d. Learn to specify hard-boundary issues or concerns to Chinese counterparts very early in the relationship; otherwise, doubts may arise.

4. Do Not Resist Resistance

"Travel where there is no enemy"—Bing Fa
"Understand your adversary thoroughly and lead him to where he is without fault."
—Chuang Tzu
"Become your opponent."
—Bing Fa

Implication for American Managers Who Are Negotiating Conflict Resolutions in China:
a. Accept Chinese resistance to Western business practices.
b. Learn to maintain organizational flexibility (except with respect to hard-boundary issues) in the face of conflict; then strive to blend with and redirect attacks.
c. Put yourself in your opponent's place, consider his goals, and develop empathy toward him.
d. Work toward a solution that allows each party to achieve what it desires.

5. Retreat Gracefully

"Retreat is another form of advance. Good men do fight a losing battle."—Bing Fa
"If I can fight and win, I will I fight. If I cannot fight, I will escape."—Ancient Chinese schoolchild adage

Implications for American Managers Who Are Negotiating Conflict Resolutions in China:
a. Develop alternatives for every negotiating response expected from the Chinese and create exit strategies for each business.
b. When original positions are knocked down, compensate as gracefully as possible and retreat slowly toward hard-boundary issues.
c. Accept that U.S. firms in China will sometimes find it necessary to accept temporary defeat and attempt to preserve strength for other days (and future conflicts).

TABLE 10.2   (Continued)

6. Understand the Role of Deception	
"Offer the enemy a bait to lure him; then feign disorder and strike him." "Pretend inferiority and encourage his arrogance" Do not gobble proffered baits."—Bing Fa	Implications for American Managers Who Are Negotiating Conflict Resolution in China: a. Do not idealize Western traditions of openness and fair play while in China. b. Be aware of the likelihood that deception will be used in China. These illusions are likely to assume the form of "hiding the truth," "showing false strength," or "bait-and-switch" tactics. c. Reserve a place for illusion in one's own business practices in China, but use the tactic sparingly, selectively, and properly.
7. Give Your Opponent Face	
"Gentleman call attention to the good points in others; they do call attention to their defects."—Confucius	Implications for American Managers Who Are Negotiating Conflict Resolutions in China: a. Acknowledge opponents' potential for future excellence. b. Remember that taking away an opponents' face is perhaps the worst tactical error that can be made in China. c. Always acknowledge the value, dignity, and position of one's adversaries. Whenever possible, feed their self-worth. d. Remember that if your firm is the selling partner in a Chinese business alliance, it operates under a culturally induced obligation to defer to the buying partner.
8. In Death Ground, Fight	
"In death ground, fight." —Sun Tzu	Implications for American Mangers Who Are Negotiating Conflict Resolution in China: a. When encountering a worst-case scenario, recognize the danger. b. Quickly and accurately analyze the direct threat to your firm's survival in China. c. Integrate all available resources and energies into a single, focused ("zero-doubt") strike at the heart of your adversary. d. Use this sort of "zero-doubt" negotiating style only when absolutely necessary.

SOURCE: David Strutton and Lou Pelton, "Scaling the Great Wall: The Yin and Yang of Resolving Business Conflicts in China," *Business Horizons* (September–October 1997), pp. 26–27. Reprinted with permission.

negotiations, determining where the negotiations should take place, deciding whether to use an individual or a group in the negotiations, and learning about the country's views on agreements/contracts.

Preparation for Face-to-Face Negotiations

Generally, at the preparation stage, the issues to be identified are common interests, desired outcomes, possible conflicts (and tactics for handling them), participants' abilities and limitations, business markets, financial status, participants' reputation, and similar products/services.[38]

Typically, the negotiating strategy that is effective in the home market will have to be modified for negotiating with foreign businesses; as indicated above, cultural factors, business customs, and ethical standards of the foreign country must be considered.[39] For instance, in negotiating with the Chinese, Americans want to agree on specific terms first, while the Chinese want to determine general principles (the "spirit of the contract") and then discuss specifics. In other words, Americans tend to be concerned with short-term goals, such as profits, while the Chinese are more concerned with long-term interests, such as the procurement of American technology and business techniques.[40]

Determining a Settlement Range

At this phase, a negotiation or settlement range (all possible settlements a negotiator would be willing to make) must be established. The "least acceptable result" (LAR) and the "maximum supportable position" (MSP) must be identified. In this respect, the Japanese have a saying, "*Banana no tataki uri*," which means "ask outrageous prices and lower them when faced with buyer objections."[41] Establishing a range provides negotiators the ability to make concessions and, therefore, more flexibility in the negotiations. Some cultures, Russia, for example, view concessions as a sign of weakness, not gestures of goodwill or flexibility. To be able to establish a reasonable negotiating range, an accurate analysis of the nature of all relevant markets must be conducted.[42] If there are other options, that is, if either the seller or the buyer has other forms of leverage or enticement, he or she may not need to make as many concessions or may not need to make any concessions at all.

Technological Forms of Negotiation

International negotiations can take place via telephone, telex, e-mail, fax, face-to-face videoconferencing, face-to-face meetings, and use of third parties.[43] Using a telephone, telex, e-mail, or fax is relatively inexpensive, but because the personal presence is missing, it is usually not a viable approach in important negotiations.

Global videoconferencing can be an effective negotiating form. There is face-to-face communication, yet unlike in face-to-face meetings, negotiators do not have to travel to unfamiliar places, and the costs of airfare and lodging are saved. However, the development of global videoconferencing technologies is still at an early stage. It is not yet widely used by negotiators, but as technological advancements are made, its use may become more widespread. Note that videoconferencing will not be a viable form for all face-to-face negotiations. In many cultures, China, for example, carrying out certain rituals and ceremonies are an important part of negotiations, and in many negotiating situations the person's presence is needed. (Refer to Table 10.2 for guidelines for negotiating business in China.) In important negotiations, the face-to-face meeting is the most widely used, and this is likely to continue. Using a third party in face-to-face meetings sometimes works best, especially when one or both of the parties involved are not knowledgeable about cross-cultural negotiations and when there is political and/or social hostility between the two countries involved in the negotiations.

Where Should Negotiations Take Place?

Negotiations can take place in the home country, in the counterpart's country, or in a neutral venue. Most negotiators would prefer that negotiations take place on their home turf. Familiar surroundings and easy access to information provide more leverage; the fatigue and stress associated with foreign travel are not experienced; and, of course, travel costs are reduced.[44] On the other hand, negotiating in the foreign country does have its advantages, such as sometimes receiving certain concessions because you have endured the burden of traveling. And quite often it is a good idea because one gets firsthand information about the site, and hence decisions can be based on one's own observations—for example, you get to see the plant where your product is going to be manufactured. A neutral venue that is equally advantageous to both parties is also often ideal. For example, an American executive from Park Avenue in New York City may not adapt well in a Brazilian village in the Amazon, and an executive from this village may not adapt well in New York City. A negotiating venue that falls between the two extremes may be the most viable.

Individual or Team Negotiations?

An organization can assign one individual or a group of individuals to conduct the negotiations. The obvious advantages of using one person are that it is cheaper and a decision can be made quickly. An obvious disadvantage is that one person may not have sufficient ability to deal with the other side, which typically consists of a group of experts and negotiating specialists—an advantage of the group approach. Furthermore, in Japan, for instance, not using a group may be interpreted to mean that you are not very serious about the negotiation or the business deal. Also, the individual negotiator often finds himself or herself pressed to make a decision when it is not the right time to do so. In a group, the members can always take a break to confer, therefore "buying time" to assess the situation and develop new strategies and tactics. (The Japanese typically use this method because their decisions usually require group consensus.) Thus, in negotiating situations where the cost and speed of a decision are more important than the other factors, use one negotiator; otherwise, use a group of experts and negotiating specialists.

To speed up decision making a bit and still have access to expert input, a team of negotiators can be used, but one member is given full negotiating authority (Americans generally use this approach). Of course, the other side may know this. And in the negotiations game, for tactical reasons, both parties try to learn who the decision maker is. In this respect, American decision makers usually reveal themselves quickly because they tend to be very active in the negotiations. On the other hand, Japanese decision makers are usually not very active in the negotiations—they simply remain silent and listen. It should also be noted that the Japanese tend to include several young executives in the negotiation team simply for exposure and on-site development purposes.[45]

What Are the Country's Views on Agreements/Contracts?

Countries existing on a high commercial level have generally developed a working base on which agreements can rest. The base may be on one or a combination of three types:[46]

1. Rules that are spelled out technically as laws or regulations

2. Moral practices mutually agreed on and taught to the young as a set of principles

3. Informal customs to which everyone conforms without being able to state the exact rules.

Some cultures favor one type and some, another. Americans, for example, rely heavily on written contracts, and signing the contract marks the end of the negotiations. Many societies, however, do not place much importance on written contracts; they rely more on the development of a social relationship. And in many countries, Greece, for instance, a signed contract is simply a starting point for negotiations, which end only when the project is completed—the clauses in the contract are subject to renegotiation. Thus, the international negotiator must understand the nature of the other country's views and practices relating to agreements and contracts.

Tactical Planning for International Negotiations

Tactical planning for international negotiations involves determining how to obtain leverage, use delay, and deal with emotions.

Leverage

In negotiations, it is generally accepted that the more options you have, the more leverage you get and the more concessions your opponents may be willing to make. For example, if you are negotiating with the Argentinean government to establish a manufacturing subsidiary in Argentina, and the Argentinean negotiators know that their site is the only viable one you have, they will not make any concessions and are likely to ask you for some concessions. But if the Argentinean negotiators believe that you can just as easily set up the subsidiary in Peru or Brazil, and they need the technology—as most less developed nations do, they are likely to be willing to make concessions.

Less developed countries appear to have leverage over multinational corporations because they control access to their own territory, including markets, local labor supplies, investment opportunities, sources of raw materials, and other resources that multinational corporations need or desire. China, for instance, has been developing economically rather quickly these days. Its more than 1 billion prospective customers, along with its relatively inexpensive cost of labor, make China an attractive place for many foreign companies to establish operations. This, it seems, gives Chinese negotiators considerable leverage, and concessions would often have to be made by the foreign negotiators. This may be true in some cases, but in many instances, multinational corporations have negotiating advantages because they possess the capital, technology, managerial skills, access to global markets, and other resources that governments in less developed countries need for economic development.[47]

Delay

Applying delay tactics is another form of leverage. If you walk away from the negotiations and your opponents become overly anxious, they may be willing to make some concessions. On the other hand, if you become anxious before your opponent does, you may have to make some concessions. Furthermore, the pause in the negotiations enables you to rest and recuperate, assess progress, obtain other information, and reformulate strategy.[48] In this context, patience is generally recognized as being a key personal attribute in negotiators. Americans tend to be low on patience, while the Japanese tend to be high. For an illustration, refer to Practical Perspective 10.4.

PRACTICAL PERSPECTIVE 10-4

Don't Just Sit There—Do Something!

A close friend and executive in a large Japanese company spoke very frankly to me one day. He said, "You Americans are fond of the expression 'Don't just sit there—do something.' Once in a while, you should reverse that advice. We Japanese would prefer to say 'Don't just do something—sit there.' Contemplation may be more productive than action."

It is true that U.S. businesspeople have always been action-oriented. Only when rushing to an endless series of appointments and conferences do they really feel productive. For many, perpetual motion seems to be their ultimate goal. It was Santayana who once observed that Americans are possessed by an obscure compulsion that will not let them rest, that drives them on faster and faster—not unlike a fanatic who redoubles his effort when he has lost sight of his goal. The greatest compliment that can be paid a U.S. executive is to call him dynamic. . . .

Furthermore, foreign visitors are startled by Americans' typically low tolerance of silence. Most Asians, in contrast, can endure long periods during which nobody says anything. They feel that these opportunities for organizing and evaluating one's thoughts may be the most productive in any conference or negotiation.

Their relative inability to tolerate long periods of silence has gotten many American negotiators into serious trouble when the other side feels no comparable frustration and tension. As one foreign consultant cautions, "This is a bad trait indeed when the negotiation game is being played in a boardroom in Rio or in a Ginza nightclub, and when the other side is playing by Brazilian or Japanese rules."

The international vice president of a large U.S. corporation confessed to his own experience with the consequences of failing to understand foreign negotiating patterns. He said, "In one of my company's deals overseas, our buyer was sitting across the table from the Japanese manufacturer's representative for the purpose of bidding on an item in which we were interested. Following the usual niceties, our man offered $150,000 per batch. On hearing the bid, the Japanese sat back and relaxed in his chair to meditate. Our buyer, interpreting this silence to be disapproval, instantly pushed his offer higher. It was only after the session was over that he realized he had paid too much."

It is true that Americans are considered an outspoken lot. Masaaki Imai contrasts this with the behavior of his own compatriots in saying, "Sitting mute is clearly a minus at the Western conference, while silence is still silver, if not golden, in the Japanese mind-set. Many Japanese sit silently throughout the conference. Nobody thinks the worse of them for that. They are like oxygen; their views may not be visible, but they are making a positive contribution nonetheless."

Unless and until American business leaders can learn to live more comfortably with silence and to value thinking and listening as highly as mere physical activity, foreign executives will enjoy an easy advantage. It has been suggested that top U.S. executives keep a tiny replica of the giant Buddha of Kamakura, Japan, on their desks at all times. Its typical posture of quiet and peaceful meditation should serve as a constant reminder that great leaders are remembered for their thoughts as well as their deeds.

SOURCE: Excerpted from Arthur M. Whitehill, "American Executives Through Foreign Eyes," *Business Horizons* (May–June 1989), p. 44. Copyright © 1989, JAI Press Inc. Used with permission from JAI Press Inc. All rights reserved.

Emotions

Even though behavior in negotiations is mainly intuitive, it should never be judgmental. To be able to listen to other negotiators, you should exclude your subjective opinions, preconceptions, and emotional filters. By becoming aware of your emotions, you can learn to change your reactions and avoid being manipulated by others or by the emotions themselves—you prevent emotion from controlling a negotiation. On the other hand, if you negotiate solely on the basis of logic, you will miss emotional signals sent out by the other negotiator. Thus, the key to negotiations is to be perceptive of feelings (yours and theirs) without being reactive.[49] For an illustration, refer again to Practical Perspective 10.4.

Ethical Constraints

Business ethics and corporate social responsibility (discussed in Chapter 2) place constraints on negotiators. For example, a negotiator's ethical concerns for honesty and fair dealings, regardless of the power status of negotiating parties, will affect the outcome. As was pointed out in Chapter 2, there is no global standard or view of what is ethical or unethical behavior in business transactions—what is viewed as unethical behavior in one culture may be viewed as ethical in another culture, and vice versa. For instance, if a negotiator on one side "pays off" an influential decision maker on the other side to obtain a favorable decision, it would be an unethical business practice in some cultures (and illegal in the United States), but it would be quite acceptable in other cultures.

Conflict Resolution

Cross-cultural business negotiations often generate considerable conflict. The conflict stems mainly from cultural differences and/or misunderstandings.[50] This chapter (as well as the entire textbook) has focused on bringing countries' cultural differences and approaches to management, including confrontation, to the forefront. Conflict resolution therefore requires that both sides possess an understanding of the other's culture. To put it better, conflict can be avoided if both sides possess an understanding of the other's culture and learn to deal with it in a compromising or nonconfrontational way. For example, the Chinese are more for conflict avoidance than Americans. This is because the Chinese expect that direct confrontation will hurt the relationship with the other party.[51] To do this requires that both sides use savvy cross-cultural interpreters (as discussed in Chapter 9).

Summary

This chapter has discussed how differing cultural views on time, material possessions, family roles, relationships, and so forth affect the ways one transacts business across societies. For example, in the United States, "time is money," but in many parts of the world, people value relationships more than time. Thus, the "hurry up" business approach used by Americans would not be effective in, for instance, Spain, where establishing a relationship is more important than "time equals money." The business practices in a number of countries have been briefly discussed. How negotiating styles vary from culture to culture has also been discussed. If a cross-cultural negotiator does not become familiar with, and adapt to, the style of the society where he or she is negotiating for business contracts, the consequence is likely to be failure. Issues related to strategic and tactical planning for international negotiations were addressed. The negotiation styles of numerous nations were examined.

KEY TERMS AND CONCEPTS

1. Cross-cultural business practices
2. "Time is money"
3. Circular- and linear-oriented cultures
4. Material possessions
5. Haste and aggressive behavior
6. *Guanxi, wa,* and *inhwa* relationships
7. "When in Rome, do as the Romans do"
8. Cross-cultural negotiations
9. Learning the local language and culture
10. Strategic and tactical planning for international negotiations
11. Settlement range
12. Face-to-face in-person negotiations
13. Use of a third party in negotiations
14. Individual versus team negotiations
15. Countries' views on agreements/contracts
16. Leverage
17. Delay tactics
18. Emotions
19. Ethical considerations

DISCUSSION QUESTIONS

1. Discuss how a culture's views on "time is money," relationships, and material possessions affect cross-cultural business transactions.

2. Discuss the effect of a culture's thought patterns—linear or circular—on cross-cultural business activities.

3. "Winning isn't everything, it's the only thing." Discuss this statement in a cross-cultural context.

4. Discuss some of the ways social customs differ across cultures.

5. Describe the business tempo for the following cultures: Greece, Spain, Italy, England, and Germany.

6. Discuss the major business dynamics of China, Japan, and South Korea.

7. How does one avoid failing in cross-cultural negotiations?

8. You are the negotiator for a firm that wishes to negotiate a contract in a foreign country. What must you do before you depart?

9. What are the forms of international negotiations?

EXERCISES

1. You are the vice president of marketing for Company Y. You need to send an executive to Brazil to negotiate a contract. Your firm's personnel files indicate that one of your marketing executives has a college degree with a major in Brazilian culture. Would you feel comfortable sending this executive to Brazil to negotiate the contract? Why?

2. You are a cross-cultural consultant specializing in negotiating in Japan and China. Two clients come to you for guidance—one on Japan and the other on China. In broad terms, what would you tell your clients to do?

3. As a classroom exercise, your professor will appoint two groups of at least five students each. One group will act the part of a team of negotiators sent to China by a U.S. automaker to negotiate a contract with Chinese government officials and businesspeople. The company has decided to establish a subsidiary in the People's Government of Yue Cheng District Shaoxing (about 200 miles southwest of Shanghai) to manufacture automobile parts to be sold back to the parent company in the United States. The group has decision-making authority. If available, students who are U.S. citizens will be preferred for this role.

The second group is to represent the Chinese side. This group is represented by the district head and vice-head, who are concerned with the long-range economic development of their district, and by three top-level local factory executives who are seeking to import the manufacturing technology they need to update their current unproductive operations. This group also has decision-making authority. If available, students who are either Asians or who are not from the United Sates are preferred for this role.

The demands are as follows:

- The Chinese side wants Chinese managers in charge of the subsidiary; the American side believes that the Chinese do not yet have managers capable of managing this type of advanced technology and wants Americans in charge.
- The Chinese side does not want the parent company to repatriate any profits for 10 years. (They want profits to be reinvested in China.) The Americans, who have short-range pressures to increase employee salaries and issue dividends to stockholders, want to be able to repatriate profits after 2 years.
- The Chinese want the American side to pay for all the expenses of building a new plant or refurbishing an old one; the Americans believe that since they are contributing the technology, which is very important to China's economic development, the Chinese side should pay for the entire investment.

In 45 minutes or less, the two groups should negotiate an agreement in class. The groups should draw on this chapter, including Appendix 10.2 and Table 10.5, as well as on previous chapters, especially those on international human resource management. After the agreement is negotiated, hold a class discussion about the negotiating difficulties and possible compromises.

ASSIGNMENT

Select a country that was not extensively discussed in this chapter. Research the country and prepare a short report on how to transact business there—the do's and don'ts. Present your findings (in three to five minutes) to your class.

CASE 10-1

The Impatient American Sales Manager

A Latin American republic had decided to modernize one of its communication networks to the tune of several million dollars. Because of its reputation for quality and price, the inside track was quickly taken by American company "Y." The company, having been sounded out informally, considered the size of the order and decided to bypass its regular Latin American representative and instead send its sales manager. The following describes what took place. The sales manager arrived and checked in at the leading hotel. He immediately had some difficulty pinning down just whom he had to see about his business. After several days without results, he called at the American Embassy, where he found that the commercial attaché had the up-to-the-minute information he needed. The commercial attaché listened to his story. Realizing that the sales manager had already made a number of mistakes, but figuring the Latins were used to American blundering, the attaché reasoned that all was not lost. He informed the sales manager that the Minister of Communications was the key man and that whoever got the nod from him would get the contract. He also briefed the sales manager on methods of conducting business in Latin America and offered some pointers about dealing with the minister.

The next day, the commercial attaché introduced the sales manager to the Minister of Communications. First, there was a long wait in the outer office while people kept coming in and out. The sales manager looked at his watch, fidgeted, and finally asked whether the minister was really expecting him. The reply he received was scarcely reassuring: "Oh yes, he is expecting you, but several things have come up that require his attention. Besides, one gets used to waiting down here." The sales manager irritably replied, "But doesn't he know I flew all the way down here from the United States to see him, and I have spent over a week already of my valuable time trying to find him?" "Yes, I know," was the answer, "but things just move much more slowly here."

At the end of about 30 minutes, the minister emerged from the office, greeted the commercial attaché with a *doble abrazo*, throwing his arms around him and patting him on the back as though they were long-lost brothers. Now, turning and smiling, the minister extended his hand to the sales manager, who, by this time, was feeling rather miffed because he had been kept in the outer office so long. After what seemed to be an all-too-short chat, the minister rose, suggesting a well-known café where they might meet for dinner the next evening. The sales manager expected, of course, that, considering the nature of their business and the size of the order, he might be taken to the minister's home, not realizing that the Latin home is reserved for family and very close friends.

Until now, nothing at all had been said about the reason for the sales manager's visit, a fact that bothered him somewhat. The whole setup seemed wrong; neither did he like the idea of wasting another day in town. He had told the home office before he left that he would be gone for a week or 10 days at most and made a mental note that he would clean this order up in 3 days and enjoy a few days in Acapulco or Mexico City. Now, the week had already gone, and he would be lucky if he made it home in 10 days. Voicing his misgivings to the commercial attaché, he wanted to know if the minister really meant business, and, if he did, why could they not get together and talk about it?

The commercial attaché by now was beginning to show the strain of constantly having to reassure the sales manager. Nevertheless, he tried again: "What you don't realize is that part of the time we were waiting, the minister was rearranging a very tight schedule so that he could spend tomorrow night with you. You see, down here they don't delegate responsibility the way we do in the States. They exercise much tighter control than we do. As a consequence, this man spends up to 15 hours a day at this desk. It may not look like it to you, but I assure you he really means business. He wants to give your company the order; if you play your cards right, you will get it."

(Continued)

(Continued)

The next evening provided more of the same. Much conversation about food and music, about many people the sales manager had never heard of. They went to a night club, where the sales manager brightened up and began to think that perhaps he and the minister might have something in common after all. It bothered him, however, that the principal reason for his visit was not even alluded to tangentially. But every time he started to talk about electronics, the commercial attaché would nudge him and proceed to change the subject.

The next meeting was for morning coffee at a café. By now, the sales manager was having difficulty hiding his impatience. To make matters worse, the minister had a mannerism he did not like. When they talked, he was likely to put his hand on him; he would take hold of his arm and get so close that he almost "spat" in his face. As a consequence, the sales manager was kept busy trying to dodge and back off.

Following coffee, there was a walk in a nearby park. The minister expounded on the shrubs, the birds, and the beauties of nature, and at one spot, he stopped to point at a statue and said, "There is a statue of the world's greatest hero, the liberator of mankind!" At this point, the worst happened, for the sales manager asked who the statue represented and, being given the name of a famous Latin American patriot, said, "I never heard of him," and walked on. . . . The sales manager did not get the order.

Questions

1. It appears that the sales manager did not follow the commercial attaché's instructions. What do you believe were the attaché's instructions?

2. The sales manager was sent to a foreign country to negotiate a business contract. Discuss what should have been done before he or she was sent.

CASE 10-2

A Failed Cross-Cultural Negotiations Attempt

An Italian director of a construction company went to Germany to negotiate for a project. He began the discussion with a presentation of his company that vaunted its long history and its achievements. The German managers first looked startled, then bored, and then they excused themselves and walked out the door, without even listening to the Italian manager's offer.

Question

1. Discuss what you believe went wrong.

CASE 10-3

The Long Printed Contract

There is a popular story making the rounds of Japanese business circles. So legalistic was the representative of an American candy company that he ruined his chances to establish a potentially profitable joint venture with a Japanese corporation. The product was a top-quality, prestige chocolate with a fine reputation already established in the United States. The goal was to establish a plush retail outlet on Tokyo's glittering Ginza. Many days were spent by the U.S. company's legal department in drawing up a lengthy, complete contract before their representative packed his bags for a trip to Tokyo. He was proud of the leather-bound, printed contract with almost 50 pages of fine print. No detail had been omitted. All that was lacking were the two signatures needed to launch the new enterprise.

With no knowledge of the Japanese language or culture, the U.S. representative faced a half dozen Japanese negotiators. He had a copy of the contract for each member of the Japanese team. But he was crushed when not one of them even opened the impressive legal document before them. Instead, a pleasant and inconclusive discussion of general business conditions in the two countries took up the whole afternoon. No decision on the proposed joint venture was made then—nor was the possibility ever discussed again.

Question

1. Discuss what you believe went wrong.

SOURCE: Arthur M. Whitehill, "American Executives Through Foreign Eyes," *Business Horizons* (May–June 1989), p. 46. Reprinted with permission.

CASE 10-4

Profitable Genuineness

Years ago, when I [Gunnar Beeth] was starting the European operations of an American company, I was considering appointing a popular general distributor for France. This family-held company was a leader in the industry and was located in the small town of Amboise in the Loire valley. My repeated letters and calls to them, though, did not produce a sufficiently large initial order.

So I went to see them. A long, heavy day's work in their offices with all their specialists, discussing packaging, branding, designs, advantages, prices, delivery, and competitors, did not produce the order. Despite my efforts, all I got was an invitation to dinner with the owner, le patron.

Even during dinner, my attempts to turn the conversation from wine, food, theater, literature, and our families to business were waived away by le patron. I admit that with each bottle of wine my attempts grew feebler, while the conversation grew livelier and more interesting.

Question

1. What must Beeth do to secure the order?

SOURCE: Excerpted from Gunnar Beeth, "Multicultural Managers Wanted," *Management Review* (May 1997), p. 21. Copyright © 1997 American Management Association International. Reprinted by permission of American Management Association International, New York. All rights reserved. www.amanet.org.

APPENDIX 10-1: NEGOTIATING IN EUROPE

The following are generalizations, based on expert opinion, about the negotiating style found in Europe's major markets:

Germany

In the preliminary stages of negotiations, German managers are often tough, cold, and impassive. They grill their prospective partners on all the technical aspects of their businesses, and it's bad luck for them if they don't have all the answers. "A mistake at this stage means that you're lost," comments the cross-cultural negotiating consultant Prabhu Guptara, the chairman of ADVANCE: Management Training Ltd. in London. Once the Germans are satisfied about technical matters, they begin to think they can trust the other negotiators. The difficulty at this point is to make German managers change their position. "At times they can stick to one point and refuse to budge," says [Ann] Bengtsson [a management consultant based in Stockholm]. Still, consultants agree that German managers are, in general, quite practical at this stage. Finalizing a negotiation is not difficult with German managers. However, it is important to know if the person you are dealing with has the authority to close the deal. "Germans believe in 'consensus management,'" comments [Vincent] Guy [a consultant specializing in international business communication with Canning International Management Development in London]. Patience may be required to get the final word.

Italy

Human relationships are most important here. Italian managers need to believe that they can get along as well with their foreign partners as they would with managers from Italian companies. Initial negotiations with Italians can include a lot of idle talk and some chess playing. These preliminaries will last until they feel secure and comfortable. When they do, the negotiation process actually starts. But here the foreign businessperson may be baffled by circumlocutions: "Italian managers may take ages to get to the point," Guptara points out. But be sure not to interrupt. As far as Italians are concerned, they are simply giving you the benefit of a complete understanding of their position. Concluding a negotiation with Italian managers can go quite quickly. But a surprise may be in store for the foreign manager because of the fluid nature of Italian corporate hierarchy. Titles mean relatively little in Italian companies, and very often the person who would normally have decision-making authority turns out to need approval. "Watch for someone sitting on the sidelines who's said nothing so far," warns Bengtsson. That person may leap into the fray at the end, make some changes, and then conclude the negotiation.

France

The French have their own way of doing most things, and negotiation is no exception. As a result, the French do not quite fit into the North-South dichotomy. The art of diplomatic negotiations was invented in France in the 14th century, and the French embrace that long tradition. Yet because French education stresses mathematics and logic, doing business is a highly intellectual process for French managers. "They see the negotiating process as a means to solve a logical problem," points out Robert Moran, Professor of Cross-Cultural Communication and International Studies at the American Graduate School of International Management in Glendale, Arizona.

French managers will have carefully prepared for the negotiations, but they will generally begin with some light, logical sparring. "The French love discussion and often handle negotiating as though it were a debate," Moran adds. In general, French managers don't like to work on one point at a time. "They like to outline the entire structure of a potential agreement abstractly," explains Guptara. "Then they look at the details briefly, moving quickly from one to another." Throughout the preliminary and middle stages of negotiating, the French manager will judge the partners carefully on their intellectual skills, their ability to reply quickly and with authority. As one French businessman puts it, "Sometimes I am more impressed by a brilliant sally than by a well-reasoned argument." But generally one has to be able to do both. Because the details come last in French negotiations, the finalizing stage can be very tricky. "French managers tend to slip in little extras when finalizing, like executive bonuses," comments Bengtsson. It's important to insist on what one wants at this stage and be prepared to refuse, even if days have been spent getting to this point.

Scandinavia

While it is always difficult to generalize about four separate nations like Norway, Sweden, Finland, and Denmark, consultants agree that the business culture is quite similar in these countries. Scandinavian managers tend to be frank, open, and relatively sincere. They like to get right down to work and expect their partners to do the same. This makes the preliminary stages relatively brief, but the foreign manager should not confuse Scandinavian frankness with the easy establishment of a relationship of trust. "If the foreign manager becomes too friendly too quickly, the Scandinavian partner will construe this as weakness," comments Bengtsson. In fact, time must be taken to develop a real relationship. In the middle stages of negotiations, foreigners may be surprised to find a Scandinavian manager become inflexible, sticking to a technical point. "These are often not negotiable in Scandinavia," Guptara says. "It is best to research technical questions carefully beforehand to be prepared for the Scandinavian's reaction." After this stage, finalizing is usually relatively quick and simple.

Spain

Preliminaries to negotiations in Spain may take several days. The foreign businessperson may be asked to spend a day touring the city, having long meals, with business barely being mentioned. Here, the establishment of a good, friendly relationship with a partner precedes all else. "It is very important not to appear impatient, not to seem in a hurry to get it over with," says Thorne. The foreigner should show interest in Spain and its culture without being unctuous. When finally the Spanish managers get down to business, the negotiation process can be elaborate and theatrical. "Sometimes a Spanish manager will just storm out of the room, right in the middle of negotiations," Bengtsson says.

One has to be prepared for long and complex discussions in the middle stages. It is important at this time to earn the respect of the Spanish manager with intelligent and straightforward replies. Finalizing can be difficult in Spain because of the strict hierarchy in Spanish companies. Approval may take a long time.

Britain

British managers tend to be curious negotiators. They are usually open in the preliminary stages of negotiations, and they like to get down to work fairly quickly. They are very practical and well prepared. Yet in the middle stages of negotiations, British managers may become "a bit vague," Bengtsson points out. Sometimes they can become cagey about details, refusing to provide information. Here, the foreign manager must be patient. Finalizing can be complex in Britain because it may take time and more negotiating to get approval from the right people. Patience and tact are required to reach a conclusion.

The Netherlands

Dutch managers are generally among the most cosmopolitan of Europe's businesspeople, consultants agree. With a long history of trade, the Dutch are experienced in adapting to foreign cultures. They are likely to be familiar with the customs in a foreigner's country and to change their negotiating style accordingly. It is possible to offend your Dutch partners, though. Beating around the bush and too much dallying will eventually make the Dutch manager annoyed and ultimately distrustful. The Dutch appreciate efficiency above all.

Eastern Europe

"The countries of Eastern Europe are rapidly learning modern negotiation techniques, but it is too early to analyze cultural differences," Moran points out. These countries need to attract business from all the industrialized nations, and that makes the negotiating process somewhat special. The same general rules apply in Eastern Europe as they do in all international negotiations. Be polite, earn the trust and respect of the partner, and you will succeed. All the consultants agree that this approach applies everywhere in the world.

SOURCE: Adapted from Alex Blackwell, "Negotiating in Europe," *Hemispheres* (United Airlines, July 1994), pp. 43–48. Reprinted with permission from *Hemispheres*, the inflight magazine of United Airlines, Pace Communications Inc., Greensboro, NC.

APPENDIX 10-2: ASIAN BARGAINING TACTICS

Westerners can enhance their negotiating power in Asia by recognizing a set of strategic archetypes used by Asian negotiators. Most Asian negotiators imitate military tactics developed in China thousands of years ago and passed down through mentor-apprentice relationships. Eight strategic archetypes are commonly encountered in Asia.

Strategy 1. Playing the Orphan

> Use humility to make them haughty.
>
> —*Sun Tzu*

Throughout Asia, one encounters business situations in which the Asian company claims to be weaker and more vulnerable than it really is. The Asian side claims it is a small or backward company in order to elicit sympathy in the form of concessions. This seems odd to North American executives who typically try to convince a negotiating partner that their company is large and powerful. Sun Tzu taught: "Even though you are competent, appear to be incompetent." Sun Tzu's commentator, Mei Yaochen, elaborated: "Give the appearance of inferiority and weakness, to make [your enemy] proud."

Asians may open a negotiation by dwelling on their company's vulnerabilities, small size, and other feigned weaknesses to swell Westerners' confidence and induce them to ask for less in return for the concessions that the Westerners are prepared to request. Some Westerners might think the orphan strategy is an expression of Asian humility. Instead, it often conceals a hidden agenda. For example, a claim of weakness is soon followed by a request that the foreign side ease its credit terms to lighten the financial burden on the Asian side. Or, the Asians demand conciliatory "favors" outside the contract.

Strategy 2. Team-Driven Intelligence Gathering

Comparisons give rise to victories.

—*Sun Tzu*

"By the comparisons of measurements, you know where victory and defeat lie," Cao advises in *The Art of War*. What Asian counterparts can find out about a Western company will be used against the company during negotiations—how large or small the company is, what sort of technological know-how it possesses, and the tone of its financial muscle. A concerted effort may be underway to transfer to the Asian side as much of the company's know-how as possible, free of charge.

Westerners who have negotiated in Asia report that Asians value detail in formulating their business decisions; they consider information gathering to be the heart of a negotiation. However, what they call a "know-how exchange" often becomes "information rape," with the Asian side planning to reverse-engineer a Western product from the outset of collaboration with the firm. The effort will be a concerted team objective. If Western negotiators are not on guard against it, their firm is likely to find itself the victim of information rape.

The Asians' objective of sharing in a company's know-how without paying for it may be partially cultural in origin. In Asia, no notion of proprietary know-how took root; new technology was shared by all. Knowledge was kept public, and to imitate or adopt someone else's methodology was considered virtuous, and a great compliment to the person who created it. Borrowing another person's expertise was considered neither thievery nor unethical. The Japanese have long conducted a policy of "selective borrowing" from foreigners. Industrial Japan borrowed extensively from the West and adapted Western production and quality control techniques to its own needs.

All of this is not to suggest that Asia hasn't developed technologies on its own; its well-known inventions through the centuries have had dramatic effects on all of civilization. Today, technological innovations travel back and forth across the Pacific with amazing frequency. The flow of innovation, however, is moving faster toward the East than toward the West. Japanese companies, for example, purchased over half of American high-technology firms that were sold during a 30-month period from 1989 to 1991, according to a study by the Economic Strategy Institute, a Washington think tank. Increasingly, North American corporations have found it necessary to forge "strategic alliances" with Asian companies (mostly Japanese) in order to acquire know-how from Asia, rather than vice versa. Facilitating the flow of technical information and human know-how has proven easier said than done.

Strategy 3. The Haughty Buyer

The customer is God. Sellers of products and services in the West defer to their buyers to some degree, but sellers and buyers ultimately deal with one another as social equals. Not so in Asia: buyers and sellers differ fundamentally in social status.

In North America, buyers and sellers maintain a somewhat adversarial relationship; in order to get a lower price, buyers ask vendors to bid against each other, and sellers seek out those buyers who will pay a premium price. When monetary advantage can be found elsewhere, buyers have few qualms about terminating their relationship with a seller. Business is business.

In much of Asia, however, buyers and sellers forge long-term bonds of trust and partnership. Sellers tend to respond to every wish and whim of their buyers. In Japan, and increasingly in Korea, as well as in other parts of Asia, the customer is not only king, but God. Asian buyers look after their suppliers in ways their North American counterparts do not.

Asian sellers tend to overserve their buyers because they can trust them to stay loyal if times get tough. A buyer might pay an above-market price, find a seller new customers, and even help [protect] the seller's business from foreign competitors. In Japan, the relationship between buyer and seller is based on *amae* (a paternalistic, dependent relationship). Paternalistic buyer-seller bonds are hard to break, especially for a newcomer in the market.

Westerners' typical unwillingness to accept the lower-status position of suppliers in Asia and to enter into paternalistic relationships with buyers is a primary reason, though not the sole one, that American executives often hear their potential Asian customers say, "We'll contact you when we are prepared to buy," which means, "Thanks anyway." Asian buyers are not exactly "haughty" as part of a strategy; they are demanding, and possibly condescending, because of conditioning.

To sell, Westerners may have to enter *amae* relationships and accept the lower status. They have to satisfy what they may consider unreasonable demands such as fast delivery, costly product modifications, and strictly enforced quality specifications. Some companies have not survived the rigorous requirements of being sellers in Asia. Still, there are ways to reach arrangements that will satisfy both sides.

Strategy 4. Outlasting the Enemy

> It is easy to take over from those who have not thought ahead.
>
> —*Li Quan in The Art of War*

Asian negotiations can, as the Chinese saying goes, be like "grinding a rod down to a needle." When the Taoist concept of wu wei (nonassertion) is applied to business negotiation, the strategy is to seek long-term success through minimal short-term effort: state a position and wait, hoping that opponents will yield on concessions in order to close the deal. Time is not money for Asian negotiators; it's a weapon.

Asian negotiators often open a negotiation, extend an invitation to visit their country, supply some technical information, and dedicate time and resources to forging an agreement. Unfortunately, the final contract remains elusive. Some Japanese investors, according to a number of American real estate developers I know, will sit down with them and sign on for a mutually beneficial deal, but problems set in at the last minute, when they balk and push for concessions. Then they initiate delay tactics, all the while pushing for more and more concessions in the gray areas of the contract. The foreign side often gives in because a costly delay may jeopardize firm financial commitments.

When Asian negotiators use delay tactics that push foreigners to the brink of anger, they may be seeking more than concessions. They may be testing the Westerners' commitment to a deal or their accountability. They may want to clarify the unequal status between buyer and seller. By delaying, they send a message that their interest may be waning; the Westerners may weaken in their resolve to hold out for a stated price.

I've seen this strategy used on youthful foreigners (myself included) as a way of testing their will and trying to intimidate them—to put them in their youthful place. Another possible reason for delay is that an Asian wants to kill a deal without losing face and hopes that the Westerner will take a hint and walk away as a friend, not a frustrated foe.

Strategy 5. Hidden Identities

> The inscrutable win, the obvious lose.
>
> —*Du Mu in The Art of War*

In the city of Hefei, in China's Anhui Province, I came across two Canadian representatives of a water purification equipment company. They were to have an important meeting with local import officials the following morning in the conference room at our hotel.

I met them the next day as they emerged confidently from their meeting. I also recognized a past acquaintance, the leading official from the Ministry of Foreign Economic Relations and Trade. After he left the hotel, I complimented the Canadians on obtaining a meeting with such a prominent official and suggested that this official's presence indicated significant interest in the water purification system on the part of the Chinese.

"Who, him?" one of the Canadians blurted. "He said he was just our interpreter for the meeting!"

This high official had concealed his true identity in order to eavesdrop on the Canadians in the guise of an interpreter. They had been burned by the hidden identity strategy.

Although a meeting in Asia usually begins with an exchange of business cards and handshakes, the true identities of the real decision makers on the Asian negotiating team may remain unknown—sometimes indefinitely. Ascertaining precisely who the key players are and how much influence they wield is difficult because some persons may vanish and later reappear at a banquet or sightseeing excursion.

The hidden identity strategy may also involve sudden changes among the Asian side's negotiating personnel. The number of Asian negotiators may swell over time, while the foreign side generally depends on the same team throughout. Being forced to defend a proposal before a new team can be maddening or can lead to making extra concessions or giving up some that have already been won. More innocently, the Asian negotiator whom the company hosted in the West for a factory visit and a side trip to Disneyland may have suddenly moved to another division of the Asian company. All the concessions won with him are now gone, and the process must start all over again with a new negotiator. In China, this problem has been exacerbated by the massive reorganization that has taken place since the Tiananmen Square massacre.

It would be unfair to Asians, however, not to mention that the same problem occurs in North America for different reasons. With the constant merging of North American companies and the high turnover of their executives, whether through departure, relocation, or promotion, the appearance of new negotiators can be difficult and disconcerting for Asians who desire to forge long-term, ongoing relationships with Western companies.

Strategy 6. The Trust Game

> Honey in mouth but dagger in heart.
>
> —*Chinese saying*

A well-known American cable television company recently signed a deal with a comparable cable network in Taiwan. The agreement was based on a royalty to be paid by the Taiwanese company to the U.S. company for each television show aired. To guarantee its 10 percent share, the American company requested that the contract enable it to periodically view the Taiwanese company's accounting books.

The president of the Taiwanese company took the request as a grave insult. He was livid and nixed the entire deal, which had taken months to put together. "The American company is implying that we are liars," he railed. "If the Americans can't trust us, then we won't trust them!"

The irony is that most Taiwanese companies (this one included) keep two, or even three, sets of books, and a demand to have the accounting records made public in a deal of this size would be reasonable anywhere else in the world.

As part of what I call the trust game, the Asian doesn't want to trust the Westerner but reacts negatively to any suggestion that the mistrust is mutual. Asians may even purposefully personalize negotiations in order to give Westerners a feeling that trust has been generated, and thus lure them into a deal; Westerners may find they are being called "old friend" at the second meeting. The Asian side's personalization of the negotiation may be a good thing for the long-term relationship between the two companies. However, it may be merely a tactic to obtain proprietary information about the firm—its size and past endeavors, the price and marketability of its products, its experience in Asia, and so on. Trust has to work both ways.

The trust game in Asia can be especially brutal on "middlemen" and firms that share their technology. "When the hares have been killed, the hounds are cooked," as the Chinese say. That is, the middlemen are discarded once they have fulfilled their purpose. I recommend that middlemen sign a bomb-proof contract with the manufacturer they represent, guaranteeing them total exclusivity to represent the product in Asia. They should conclude the contract before they disseminate information or quote prices of equipment among potential Asian customers.

Often Asian customers will contact the manufacturer directly and attempt to cut the middlemen out. The motive may not be to avoid paying an added commission, but simply to forge a relationship directly with the manufacturer and get closer to its technology.

In another trust game, the Asian side signs a "symbolic agreement." The Asians win over the Western firm by signing a well-drafted contract but then fail to implement what they have agreed to do. Some Asians may sign a "symbolic contract" knowing full well that governing bodies with oversight of the venture will not accept the conditions of the deal. Requests for major revisions in the contract arrive soon after.

A recent case in Korea involved the purchase of agricultural goods from the United States. The goods were refused by Korean Customs. The Korean customer had guaranteed that the government would enact a regulation allowing the import of the goods long before the contract was signed. Unfortunately, the Korean government was unwilling to enact the law. The deal died, along with a shipment of perishable product.

Strategy 7. Sacrifice Something Small for Something Big

Cast a brick to attract a piece of jade.

—*Chinese saying*

In this strategy, Asian counterparts attempt to trick Westerners into trading something significant for something insignificant. An Indonesian or Chinese joint venture partner might assure a Western company of access to a large untapped market or offer unlimited numbers of inexpensive workers in exchange for cash, technology, and worker training.

Many gullible Westerners have fallen victim to this strategy, believing the numbers that appear in feasibility studies presented by the Asians. The market may be both smaller than the numbers claim and quite inaccessible despite promises of access. The building space and land offered may appear to be a real break but could cost a fortune to upgrade.

Some Asian managers wish to connect with a foreign firm to gain the benefits that accrue to an Asian factory that forges a joint venture with a foreign company. In China, for example, these benefits can include the right to hire and fire workers, the unilateral right to buy imports without government approval, and the right to pay more to workers than regular Chinese enterprises can, thus allowing the manager to attract more workers with higher skills.

Some foreign companies have been asked by Chinese enterprises to form a joint venture but to station only one foreign manager in China—an easy way for the Chinese enterprise to enjoy the benefits of being a "foreign-invested enterprise." They sign a contract to manufacture and sell a foreign product, but the interests of the foreign partner become secondary to their own the moment the contract is signed.

A weak Asian company can obtain a new lease on life by merging with an unsuspecting, richer foreign partner. Even a near-bankrupt Asian company gains leverage over its Asian competitors by becoming a partner of a large foreign company. "If you forge alliances with strong partners, your enemies won't dare plot against you," Cheng Shi comments in *The Art of War*. For the foreign company, having an Asian partner with this objective usually leads to disaster.

Strategy 8. The Shotgun Approach

Foreign business negotiators most often experience the "shotgun approach offer" when dealing with individual overseas Chinese entrepreneurs (briefcase companies); their locale is just about all of Asia except Japan and Korea. The Westerners begin by presenting a product for sale to the Asian side, and within minutes they find themselves talking about transferring technology, transferring a management model, and setting up a manufacturing joint venture in Asia. They have been lured off course by the "shotgun strategy."

We don't need to dwell long on this tactic; most of us have dealt with it in some form on our home turf. Chinese Malay business people might negotiate like the proverbial used car salesmen of the West; they want a deal, any deal, now. Owners of Asian "trading companies" tend to work alone and to negotiate as individual (one-person) companies.

They start by saying, "I can get you anything in Asia that you want. Bamboo furniture, tropical fish, orchids, anything. My brother has an orchid farm near Kuala Lumpur, you know." "Okay, okay," you say, "let's concentrate on orchids. Can you get 8,000 stems by February?"

"Well, I don't know, 8,000 is a lot of orchids. Let me call my brother. Maybe we start slow with about 200 per week."

Your expected sigh only triggers another onslaught.

"We should grow orchids here! Set up a greenhouse. Start small. Big profit. You make a mint. Why didn't you guys think of it? It'll be like having the right to print money!"

You sigh again and balk at the whole idea of collaborating at all.

These dealmakers try to make Westerners feel guilty about not trusting them. In fact, the obstacle in the negotiation is that they can't perform what they originally claimed they could do. Wise Westerners stay polite and collected, and they keep communication lines open. Getting irate is the only sin that Westerners can commit in dealing with these "pushy" overseas Chinese: It robs Westerners of face and gets their name around as a company to avoid.

SOURCE: Excerpted from Christopher Engholm, "Asian Bargaining Tactics: Counter Strategies for Survival," *East Asian Executive Reports* (July 1992), pp. 9, 22–25 and (August 1992), pp. 10–13. Copyright © 1992, International Executive Reports, Ltd. and Christopher Engholm. Reprinted with permission. All rights reserved.

● ●

NOTES

1. Excerpted from J. S. Black and H. B. Gregersen, "The Right Way to Manage Expats," *Harvard Business Review* (March–April 1999), p. 58.

2. M. Katherine Glover, "Do's and Taboos: Cultural Aspects of International Business," *Business America* (August 13, 1990), p. 3.

3. Adapted from R. Knotts, "Cross-Cultural Management: Transformations and Adaptations," *Business Horizons* (January–February 1989), pp. 29–33.

4. This idea draws from Edward T. Hall, "How Cultures Collide," *Psychology Today* (July 1976), pp. 67–74.

5. Anna Bowden, "Bridging the Gap Between Cultures," *Conference and Incentive Travel* (London: February 2006), p. 19.

6. Glover, "Do's and Taboos," op cit., p. 3.

7. Edward T. Hall, "The Silent Language in Overseas Business," *Harvard Business Review* (May–June 1960), p. 87.

8. Ibid.

9. Mary Munter, "Cross-Cultural Communication for Managers," *Business Horizons* (May–June 1993), p. 77.

10. Hall, "The Silent Language," op cit., p. 90.

11. Ibid.

12. John Hill and Ronald Dulek, "A Miss Manners Guide to Doing Business in Europe," *Business Horizons* (July–August 1993), p. 50.

13. Hall, "The Silent Language," op cit., p. 90.

14. Amanda Mayer Stinchecum, "Everyone Gives at the Office," *World Traveler* (June 1997), p. 20.

15. Kimberly Roberts, "International Success Tips: Business Meeting Gifts—Part 1," *International Business Center* (2003–2004). www.international-business-center.com/international business gifts meetings.html

16. Frederick H. Katayama, "How to Act Once You Get There," *Fortune* (Pacific Rim, 1989), p. 88.

17. Munter, "Cross-Cultural Communication for Managers," op cit., p. 77.

18. E. T. Hall, *Beyond Culture* (Garden City, NY: Doubleday, 1976).

19. Ibid.

20. Hall, "The Silent Language," op cit., p. 96.

21. Anthony Clark, "Facing the Dragon: To Do Business in China, An Understanding of the Cultural Differences Is Important," *LookSmart* (March 2, 2006).www.findarticles.com/p/articles/mi_ mOKZC/is_ 2006_ March 2/ai_ n1611212165/print

22. Cindy P. Lindsay and Bobby L. Dempsey, "Ten Painfully Learned Lessons About Working in China: The Insights of Two American Behavioral Scientists," *Journal of Applied Behavioral Science,* 19, no. 3 (1983), pp. 265–276.

23. This discussion draws from Jon P. Alston, "Wa, Guanxi, and Inhwa: Managerial Principles in Japan, China, and Korea," *Business Horizons,* 32, no. 2 (March–April 1989), pp. 28–29.

24. Ibid., p. 29.

25. See N. Khatri, E. W. K. Tsang, and T. M. Begley, "Cronyism: A Cross-Cultural Analysis," *Journal of International Business Studies,* 37 (2006), pp. 61–75.

26. Paul Krugman, "Saving Asia: It's Time to Get Radical," *Fortune* (September 7, 1998).

27. Alston, "Wa, Guanxi, and Inhwa," op cit., p. 27.

28. Ibid.

29. Ibid., pp. 29–30.

30. Ibid.

31. See A. Bird, J. S. Ogland, M. Mendenhall, and S. C. Schneider, "Adapting and Adjusting to Other Cultures: What We Know But Don't Always Tell," *Journal of Management Inquiry,* 8, no. 2 (June 1999), pp. 152–165.

32. Cited in June N. P. Francis, "When in Rome? The Effect of Cultural Adaptation on Intercultural Business Negotiations," *Journal of International Business Studies* (Third Quarter, 1991), pp. 403–428.

33. Ibid.

34. Dean Allan Foster, *Bargaining Across Borders* (New York: McGraw-Hill, 1992), p. 5.

35. Ibid.

36. Stephen E. Weiss, "Negotiating With 'Romans'—Part 1," *Sloan Management Review* (Winter 1994), p. 52.

37. Hokey Min and William Galle, "International Negotiation Strategies of U.S. Purchasing Professionals," *International Journal of Purchasing and Materials Management* (Summer 1993), p. 43.

38. Trenholme J. Griffin and W. Russell Daggatt, *The Global Negotiator* (New York: Harper Business Publishers, 1990), p. 74.

39. Min and Galle, "International Negotiation Strategies," op cit., p. 42.

40. Robert O. Joy, "Cultural and Procedural Differences That Influence Business Strategies and Operations in the People's Republic of China," *SAM Advanced Management Journal* (Summer 1989), p. 31.

41. Griffin and Daggatt, *The Global Negotiator,* op cit., p. 77.

42. Min and Galle, "International Negotiation Strategies," op cit., p. 43.

43. Ibid., pp. 43–44.

44. Ibid.

45. Ibid., p. 44.

46. Hall, "The Silent Language," p. 93.

47. Shah M. Tarzi, "Third World Governments and Multinational Corporations: Dynamics of Host's Bargaining Power," in Jeffrey A. Frieden and David A. Lake (Eds.), *International Political Economy: Perspectives on Global Power and Wealth* (New York: Bendford/St. Martin's, 1991), p. 237.

48. Griffin and Daggatt, *The Global Negotiator,* p. 120.

49. Ibid., p. 106.

50. See E. U. Weber, D. R. Ames, and A.-R. Blais, "'How Do I Choose Thee? Let Me Count the Ways': A Textual Analysis of Similarities and Differences in Modes of Decision-Making in China and the United States," *Management and Organization Review,* 1, no. 1 (2005), pp. 87–118.

51. R. Friedman, S.-C. Chi, and L. A. Liu, "An Expectancy Model of Chinese-American Differences in Conflict-Avoidance, *Journal of International Business Studies,* 37 (2006), p. 78.

Part VI CROSS-CULTURAL COORDINATION

Some managers make decisions participatively; they involve those subordinates who will be affected by the decision in the decision-making process. Others make decisions authoritatively; instead of involving subordinates who will be affected by the decision, they make the decision by themselves. One theory posits that a manager's approach is influenced by national culture. Another theory is that the approach is influenced by specific situations in all cultures. These theories are discussed in Chapter 11. American-based theories posit that participative leadership behavior produces better results than authoritative behavior. However, in many cultures, authoritative behavior produces better results. Culture also has an effect on employee motivation. In some cultures, employees are motivated by the opportunity to obtain challenging work, but in other cultures, they are motivated by the opportunity to socialize. Cross-cultural leadership and motivation are discussed in Chapter 12.

11

CROSS-CULTURAL DECISION MAKING

Bosses in France tend to be Napoleonic. They are, as a rule, graduates of one of the elite Grands Ecoles and are expected to be brilliant technical planners, equally adept at industry, finance, and government. They can be vulnerable to surprise when the troops below fail to respond to orders from on high. Stiff hierarchies in big firms discourage informal relations and reinforce a sense of "them" and "us." Managers in Italy tend to be more flexible. Firms' rules and regulations (where they exist) are often ignored. Informal networks of friends and family contacts matter instead. Decision making tends to be more secretive than elsewhere, and what goes on in a meeting is often less important than what happens before and after.[1]

Learning Objectives of the Chapter

In essence, every aspect of management (planning, organizing, staffing, coordinating, and controlling), in one form or another, involves decision making. Decision making is thus the manager's most difficult task, and when managers cross national borders and cultures, the task becomes even more difficult because people in different cultures view problems differently and apply unique decision-making processes. (For illustrations, read Practical Perspectives 11.1 and 11.2.) A decision or a decision-making process that works in one culture is often ineffective in another culture. Furthermore, different situations also require different decision-making styles. After studying this chapter, you should be able to discuss the following:

1. The decision-making process in a cross-cultural context

2. The differing cultural factors that affect managers' decision-making style, authoritative/consultative or participative

3. The varying environmental factors/situations that affect the decision-making style

PRACTICAL PERSPECTIVE 11-1

Choosing a Local Manager in Russia

In choosing a general manager (in Russia), Western companies are often misled by the false conventional wisdom that insists there never was such a thing as effective Soviet management. Considering the enormous handicaps imposed on them by perennial shortages and centralized command and control, the general managers of many Soviet enterprises accomplished wonders. These managers still have no training in Western management theory and practice, of course, but their own Russian management style, deeply rooted in the resilient culture of the Russian *mir*, or collective, has its own considerable strengths. For example, Russian executives are often strong personal leaders who practice hands-on, walk-around, face-to-face management. They develop direct bonds of loyalty with employees at all levels. They also practice a unique form of decision making that combines consultation and command by alternating periods of open, widespread discussion of options with moments of strong, top-down authority in making final decisions.

SOURCE: P. Lawrence and C. Vlachoutsicos, "Joint Ventures in Russia: Put Locals in Charge," *Harvard Business Review* (January–February 1993), p. 45.

PRACTICAL PERSPECTIVE 11-2

The Quiet Indonesian

Machmud was promoted to a position of authority and was asked to represent his company and Indonesia's needs at the head office in Butte, Montana. Relationships with fellow workers seemed cordial but rather formal from his perspective. He was invited to attend many policy and planning sessions with other company officials where he often sat, rather quietly, as others generated ideas and engaged in conversation. The time finally came when the direction the company was to take in Indonesia was to be discussed. A meeting was called to which Machmud was invited to attend. As the meeting was drawing to a close after almost two hours of discussion, Machmud, almost apologetically, offered a suggestion—his first contribution to any meeting. Almost immediately, John Stewart, a local vice president, said, "Why did you wait so long to contribute? We needed your comments all along." Machmud felt that Stewart's reply was harsh. In Indonesia, the group often comes before any action of the individual. Machmud was acting as one would in a meeting in his home country. Rather than standing out as an idea-person seeking attention, suggestions are often quickly presented toward the close of a meeting, with hope that little attention will be paid to the originator of the idea.

SOURCE: Excerpted from R. W. Brislin, K. Cushner, C. Cherrie, and M. Yong, *Intercultural Interactions: A Practical Guide*, Vol. 9 (Newbury Park, CA: Sage Publications, 1986), pp. 169, 185. Copyright © 1986, Sage Publications, Inc. Reprinted with permission. All rights reserved.

The Decision-Making Process: A Cross-Cultural Perspective

When making decisions, managers in organizations apply either a programmed or a nonprogrammed decision-making process. Both processes are affected by the culture of the society in which the decision is being made. For example, managers in countries with relatively low tolerance for ambiguity, such as Japan and Germany, avoid nonprogrammed decisions as much as possible by using standard operating procedures (programmed decision making). Operating manuals in organizations in these cultures tend to be relatively thick. In contrast, managers in countries with relatively high tolerance for ambiguity, such as the United States and Norway, seek responsibility for nonprogrammed decision making.[2]

The Programmed Decision-Making Process

The programmed decision-making process, which is by far the most commonly used in organizations, entails making decisions based on precedent, custom, policies and procedures, and training and development. An advantage of this approach is that the basis for a decision can be pretested for efficiency, which reduces risk and stress for decision makers ("I followed the procedures manual," "I did it the way it is supposed to be done," or "I did it the way it has always been done"). A disadvantage of this approach is that when the organization's environment changes, the programmed bases for decision making often become obsolete and ineffective, which can lead to decision-making ineffectiveness. Of course, some of the advantages and disadvantages are culturally determined. For example, people in some cultures—strong uncertainty avoidance cultures, for example—do not like too much challenge; they prefer a structured environment that provides certainty and become frustrated in ambiguous, challenging situations. People in other cultures prefer challenge and become bored in an environment that provides too much structure. (This is discussed in more detail later in this chapter.)

The Nonprogrammed Decision-Making Process

The nonprogrammed decision-making process entails analyzing current data and information, obtained through a systematic investigation of the current environment, for the purpose of identifying and solving a problem.

The Rational Decision-Making Process

In Western culture, the steps in the rational decision-making process are as follows: (1) through investigation, define the problem; (2) identify a set of minimum criteria on which to base the decision; (3) identify multiple viable choices; (4) quantitatively evaluate each viable choice on the basis of each criterion; (5) select the optimum choice, the one with the highest quantitative value; and (6) implement the choice. In Western cultures, the "ideal" decision model thus presumes an optimum choice among viable alternatives.

The Impact of Culture on Nonprogrammed Decision Making

The validity of the nonprogrammed decision-making process as a prescription for decision-making behavior (DMB) is affected by culture. Culture has been defined as "the interactive aggregate of common characteristics that influence a group's response to its environment."[3] Since the characteristics vary from group to group, people in different cultures are likely to have different preferences for a certain state of affairs, for specific social processes, and for "general rules for selective attention, interpretation of environmental cues, and responses."[4] As such, people in different cultures view and react to problems differently. What is rational in one culture may be irrational in another, and vice versa. In a broad context, we do not know whose views are right.[5] Presented below are some examples of how contrasting views affect the decision-making process.

Problem Recognition

The master-of-destiny and fatalistic cultural concepts described in Chapter 1 affect problem definitions. Managers in master-of-destiny cultures tend to perceive most situations as problems to be solved, and they seek improvement through change. On the other hand, managers in fatalistic societies tend to accept situations as they are, and they do not seek improvement or change; they believe that fate or God's will intervenes in decision making. U.S. society is an example of the master-of-destiny culture, and Indonesia is an example of a fatalistic society.[6] American decision makers would thus act more quickly on a problem than would Indonesian decision makers.

Criteria

Some cultures possess a "collective" orientation (discussed in Chapter 1 and to be discussed later on in this chapter as "low individualism") and some, an "individualistic" orientation (also discussed in Chapter 1 and to be discussed later on in this chapter as "high individualism"). The collectivist orientation implies that individuals in the culture possess a group orientation; they emphasize group objectives in arriving at decisions, the rights of both current and future generations, and group harmony and discipline. In contrast, the individualistic orientation implies emphasizing the functional definition of relationships, utilitarianism in problem solving, a shorter time perspective, and the freedom to choose and compete.[7] Decision makers in the two cultures are thus likely to use different criteria to make a decision. For example, collectivist decision makers may use maintaining group harmony as the major criterion on which to base the decision; in contrast, individualistic decision makers may use cost-benefit as the major criterion (evident in the United States, an individualistic society).

Information Gathering

As pointed out in Chapter 1, decision makers in some cultures rely on "hard facts" and data as bases for a decision. The nonprogrammed approach to decision making would therefore be applied in these cultures. In many cultures, however, decision makers do not place a high premium on factual information and data; instead, they rely more on their instincts as a basis for decision making. Since decision makers in these cultures rely on their intuition, they would not be highly receptive to the application of the nonprogrammed decision-making process.

Choice and Implementation

In some cultures, such as the United Kingdom and Canada, the choice and implementation tactics are determined either by the highest-ranking member of the decision-making team or by a majority vote. But in collectivist cultures, such as Japan and Africa, to maintain harmony and unity, decisions are made by consensus. When group consensus is required, decisions normally take a long time to make. The process of obtaining consensus is often more important than the choice itself. In contrast, choice and implementation decisions in individualistic societies are normally made quickly because decision makers tend to be autocratic and make decisions by themselves. (The ensuing sections will discuss this more thoroughly.) Furthermore, decision makers in individualistic cultures are likely to select the most economically efficient choice. On the other hand, decision makers in collectivist societies are likely to select a choice that does not offend members of the group. Thus, in troubled times, an American corporation might lay off employees as a way of dealing with the problem, whereas a Japanese corporation would not—it would seek to maintain group harmony and therefore seek other solutions.

In some cultures, decision makers are very methodical, and they carefully evaluate numerous alternative choices before making a selection; in other cultures, decision makers use an incremental approach—they discuss alternatives in a preplanned sequence, making decisions as they go along. Furthermore, as is also discussed in the ensuing sections, individuals in some cultures take greater risks than individuals in other cultures. For instance, in deciding on a foreign market entry strategy, decision makers in the lower-risk-taking cultures may select the safer exporting approach; decision makers in the higher-risk-taking cultures may select a riskier approach, such as producing abroad.

Decision-Making Behavior: Authoritative or Participative?

Decision makers use two basic types of DMB: authoritative and participative. Decision makers using authoritative behavior decide alone what is to be done and/or how it is to be done and inform their subordinates; however, they may consult their subordinates about decisions before they finalize them. Using participative behavior, decision makers ask their subordinates what should be done and/or how it should be done, and together they reach an agreement and/or a consensus. Both approaches have advantages and disadvantages.

An advantage of the authoritative approach is that decisions can be made quickly. A disadvantage, however, is that not involving the subordinates in the decision-making process can lead to their demoralization, which often leads to decision sabotage and slow implementation. An advantage of the participative approach is that it can lead to greater subordinate satisfaction and performance, especially when participation makes work more challenging for them, and the multiple inputs from subordinates can result in higher-quality decisions than those made authoritatively by one person. A disadvantage is that the decision-making process can take too long, although this disadvantage can be offset by the decision making not being sabotaged and therefore being implemented more quickly.

The management theorist Rensis Likert has hypothesized that authoritative decision making leads to "mediocre" organizational performance, consultative to "good" organizational performance, and participative to "high levels of productivity."[8] It should be noted, however, that the concept of authoritative or participative DMB is explained from a Western cultural perspective. Some cultures may not even possess such a perspective. In other words, many concepts are not readily transferable across cultures. For example, many people in some cultures, such as Swedish, perceive the authoritarian decision maker in a negative way: "Who made him/her king/queen?" But in some cultures, the same DMB is perceived favorably: "By dictating to me, he or she is communicating God's will to me, so I feel good."

Thus, people in some cultures perceive participative DMB positively. But in many cultures it is perceived negatively: "He or she is asking me what I think. . . . Doesn't he or she know how to do his or her job? It's not my responsibility to make decisions." In these cultures, the participative decision maker loses credibility in the eyes of subordinates and may even frustrate and demoralize them. For example, in their study of Mexican workers in a Mexican plant and of American workers in a U.S. plant, cross-cultural management researchers T. Morris and C. M. Pavett concluded that U.S. management systems do not have to be applied in the Mexican plant to extract the same level of production as in the U.S. plant. They found that the management systems used in the two plants reflect some of the salient cultural differences between the United States and Mexico. Americans have been characterized as less accepting of authority, autocratic decision making, and unequal power distributions (to be discussed in the ensuing sections) than are people of Mexico. Mexican workers are characterized as expecting an authority figure to make decisions and assume responsibility.[9]

It should be noted that in applying participative decision making, some managers apply the management by objectives (MBO) approach, while others apply the *ringi* approach. The use of these approaches is also dictated by culture. The major features of a typical MBO program are as follows:[10]

1. Manager and subordinate meet and together set objectives for the subordinate.

2. Manager and subordinate attempt to establish realistic, challenging, clear, and comprehensive objectives related to organizational and personal needs.

3. Criteria for measuring and evaluating the objectives are agreed on by both the manager and the subordinate.

4. The manager and the subordinate establish review dates when objectives will be reexamined.

5. The manager plays less the role of a judge and jury and more of a coach, counselor, and supporter.

6. The overall process depends on results accomplished and counseling subordinates and not on activities, errors, and organizational requirements.

7. After establishing goals and objectives and identifying the activities necessary to accomplish them, subordinates are allowed to pursue their goals and objectives essentially in their own manner. However, as indicated above, there are periodic reviews by the manager. The subordinate also reviews his or her own progress.

Many decision makers, especially in Japanese organizations, use a group-oriented consensus building process known as *ringi* to establish objectives. The *ringi* participative approach is as follows:[11]

1. All subordinates who are to be involved in the execution of the decision must have the opportunity to voice their views.

2. The manager meets with the group responsible for carrying out the decision.

3. During the meetings, all issues are considered and all members of the group contribute to the discussion of options, facts, and the philosophy underlying the decision. Therefore, when a decision is reached, everyone involved knows what he or she must do. And because everyone has agreed to the decision, its execution can proceed quickly.

The MBO process is likely to work best in "individualistic" cultures such as the United States, where individuals tend to prefer to work on their own, and the *ringi* process is likely to work best in group-oriented, "collectivist" cultures such as Japan, where people tend to like to work in groups.

Subordinates' views on how they should be used in the decision-making process vary from culture to culture, as do managers' views. For example, French executives tend to assume that the authority to make decisions is a given right of office and a privilege of rank, and therefore they make decisions authoritatively. On the other hand, executives in the Netherlands, Scandinavia, and the United Kingdom expect their decisions to "be challenged, discussed or, more probably, made on a consultative, group basis in the first place."[12]

Which approach works best? It is, as suggested above, contingent on many factors. The aim of the ensuing sections is to explain the concept of contingency DMB. Different situations and cultures require dissimilar behavior, and decision makers therefore have to be flexible in their decision-making style when confronted with varying situations and when crossing national boundaries and cultures. Failure to apply the right DMB will result in ineffective decisions, which in turn will make the enterprise less competitive in the global economy.

Decision-Making Behavior: Two Contingency Frameworks

Decision makers who are not bound to just one approach or style are often confronted with the problem of determining which DMB, authoritative/consultative or participative, is applicable in a given situation. Using several existing theories, concepts, and research findings, the ensuing sections develop two contingency DMB frameworks that can assist cross-cultural managers in determining the appropriate DMB for specific situations and cultures.[13] The first framework, called *the country-related cultural factors framework*, identifies certain national cultural dimensions and their impact on DMB. This framework is "culture specific"; it assumes that different societies possess distinct and relatively stable cultures that serve as determinants of the DMB.[14] The second contingency framework, termed the *universal factors model*, identifies various situations and their impact on DMB. This model is "culture free"; it assumes that certain situational factors have an impact on DMB in all cultures.[15]

The Country-Related Cultural Factors Framework

A key study used in developing the *country-related cultural factors framework* was conducted by Professor Geert Hofstede, who developed a typology consisting of four national cultural dimensions by which a society can be classified: power distance, uncertainty avoidance, individualism, and masculinity.[16] (These are discussed in Chapter 1.) As pointed out in Chapter 1, Hofstede and his colleague Michael Bond subsequently identified a fifth dimension, called the *Confucian dynamism dimension*. The ensuing sections describe these five cultural dimensions and discuss whether DMB tends to lean toward authoritative/consultative or participative (see Table 11.1).

DMB as a Factor of the Country's Power Distance

As indicated in Chapter 1, Hofstede found that some of the countries included in his study are classified by a moderate to large power distance cultural dimension. Individuals dominated by this dimension, according to him, tend to accept centralized power and depend heavily on superiors for structure and direction. Hofstede also noted that different laws and rules for superiors and subordinates are accepted.

TABLE 11.1 The Country-Related Cultural Factors Model

Factors	DMB
Large power distance	A
Small power distance	P
Low individualism	A
High individualism:	
Employees show low concern for organization's well-being	A
Employees show high concern for organization's well-being	P
Strong uncertainty avoidance	A
Weak uncertainty avoidance	P
Confucianism	A
High masculinity	A
Low masculinity	P

NOTE: A = authoritative; P = participative; DMB = decision-making behavior leaning toward.

Therefore, authoritative DMB probably would be preferred by subordinates dominated by this cultural dimension. On the other hand, Hofstede found that some nations are classified by a moderate to small power distance cultural dimension. Individuals dominated by this dimension do not tolerate highly centralized power and expect to be consulted in decision making. Furthermore, Hofstede remarked that status differences (large power distance) in these countries are suspect. Thus, subordinates in these cultures probably would favor participative, or at least consultative, DMB. For example, subordinates in the United States, a moderate power distance society, tend to favor consultative DMB.

The cross-cultural researcher O. J. Stevens conducted a research project including M.B.A. students from Germany, Great Britain (both small power distance societies), and France (a large power distance society). This study provides some support for the above propositions about a country's power distance measure influencing DMB. He asked the students to write their diagnosis of and solution to a case problem. The majority of the French referred the problem to the next higher authority—they sought direction. The British handled the problem. The Germans attributed it to a lack of formal policy and proposed establishing one.[18] Studies by researchers S. Kakar and by L. Williams, W. Whyte, and C. Green also lend support to these conclusions.[19] Kakar reported that the paternal type of superior-subordinate relationships, especially in the form of assertive behavior, dominates the authority relations in organizations in India, a large power distance society. He attributed this pattern to sociocultural factors, as well as to the hierarchical development of modern work organizations in India.[20] Williams and his colleagues concluded that in societies where there are small power differences, such as Sweden, Austria, and Israel, subordinates and managers are highly interdependent in the completion of tasks, and status differences are downplayed. In cultures where there are large power differences, such as the Philippines, Mexico, and Venezuela, a more autocratic management style is not only more common but also expected by subordinates.[21]

DMB as a Factor of the Country's Individualism Measure

Hofstede found that many societies are classified by a moderate- to low-individualism (collectivist) cultural dimension. Low-individualism societies are tightly integrated, and individuals belong to "in-groups" from which they cannot detach themselves. People think in "we," as opposed to "me," terms and obtain satisfaction from a job well done by the group. Since most of the societies that measured low individualism also measured large power distance (as shown in Table 1.6, Chapter 1), the DMB applied by decision makers in organizations in these countries probably leans toward the authoritative.

On the other hand, Hofstede concluded that some nations are classified by a moderate- to high-individualism cultural dimension. Individuals in these societies look primarily after their own interests. Since employees in these cultures often consider their own objectives to be more important than the organization's, decision makers are likely to apply DMB leaning toward the authoritative, as evidenced by the authoritative/consultative DMB usually applied by decision makers in U.S. organizations, a country with a high individualism measure. As Practical Perspective 11.3 indicates, the management of Japanese MNCs tend to behave authoritatively with American executives working for their subsidiaries in the United States. In these societies, the subordinates themselves probably would prefer that participative or at

PRACTICAL PERSPECTIVE 11-3

The Authoritative Japanese Management

The Japanese need American executives' expertise to sell their products in the United States and are willing to pay top salaries to get them. But in company after company, the Americans complain about a system of subtle and debilitating discrimination in which they are treated as necessary but inferior outsiders—lacking both the authority to get things done and upward mobility. . . . This is hardly surprising, given the chasm that separates the American and Japanese corporate cultures. The qualities admired in American managers—ambition, risk taking, independence—are handicaps in Japanese companies, where group cooperation and a strict decision-making hierarchy prevail. Japanese managers generally choose a company for life and they move up the corporate ladder very slowly and according to seniority rather than ability. . . .

Japanese companies have been described as Machiavellian bureaucracies where absolute loyalty is demanded. . . . As a result, the Japanese have a hard time dealing with the mobility of American executives, whose tendency to move from company to company to take advantage of better opportunities breeds distrust and makes their loyalty automatically suspect. . . . A study on the organization of Japanese subsidiaries in the United States by the Boston Consulting Group shows that while the formal corporate chain of command includes American executives at the second and third level, the actual decision-making system cuts out the Americans altogether. "You have a situation in which business is conducted at night on the telephone in Japanese between Japanese," says Kazuo Nomura, who is consul for the Boston Consulting Group and helped put the study together. "They come back in the morning and tell the Americans what has been decided, and sometimes they even make it seem like the Americans made the decision."

SOURCE: Excerpted from Leah Nathans, "A Matter of Control," *Business Month* (September 1988), pp. 46, 50. Reprinted with permission.

least consultative DMB be applied. This contention is based on Hofstede's conclusion that for these individuals, a high quality of life means individual success and achievement, which is perhaps best attained in organizations whose decision makers apply participative DMB. Therefore, in societies with a high individualism measure, decision makers in organizations whose employees are strongly concerned with the enterprise's well-being probably apply DMB leaning toward the participative.

The above contentions are partially supported by the researchers E. F. Jackofsky and J. W. Slocum Jr. They argue that in low-individualism cultures, employees attach more importance to structure than to freedom in their jobs and are more emotionally and morally involved with their organizations than are employees in cultures that stress high individualism.[22]

DMB as a Factor of the Country's Uncertainty Avoidance Measure

Many societies, Hofstede found, are classified by a moderate to strong uncertainty avoidance cultural dimension. Individuals in these cultures feel uneasy in situations of uncertainty and ambiguity and prefer structure and direction. Therefore, authoritative DMB, because the uncertainty involved in decision making is assumed by someone else, probably would be preferable to these subordinates. Hofstede has proposed that improving the quality of life for employees in these societies implies offering more security and perhaps more task structure on the job. On the other hand, Hofstede found that numerous countries are classified by a moderate to weak uncertainty avoidance cultural dimension. People in these cultures tend to be relatively tolerant of uncertainty and ambiguity and require considerable autonomy and low structure. Since it allows for some degree of autonomy, participative DMB probably would be preferred by subordinates dominated by this dimension.

This conclusion is supported by the cross-cultural researchers R. N. Kannungo and R. Wright, who discovered that many managers in Britain, a weak uncertainty avoidance culture, placed greater importance on individual achievement and autonomy than managers in France, a strong uncertainty avoidance society. The French valued competent supervision, sound company policies, fringe benefits, security, and comfortable working conditions.[23] This suggests that British subordinates prefer participative DMB, and the French prefer authoritative DMB.

DMB as a Factor of the Country's Masculinity Measure

Many countries, Hofstede found, are classified by a moderate- to strong-masculinity cultural dimension. Societies classified by this dimension stress material success and assertiveness and assign different roles to males and females. Males are expected to carry out the assertive, ambitious, and competitive roles in the society; females are expected to care for the nonmaterial quality of life, for children, and for the weak—to perform society's caring roles. In such societies, a male might be the manager of finance, and a female might be his secretary; a role reversal would be an exception to the rule. In strong-masculinity countries, where such behavior is perceived as inequitable, mandating authoritative DMB emphasizing reduction of such social inequities would probably be applied in many organizations. One finds evidence of this in recent programs in the United States, a society with a moderate- to strong-masculinity dimension, which enacted programs such as the Equal Pay Act of 1963, Title VII of the Civil Rights Act of 1964, and affirmative action and equal employment opportunity; in Japan, with its very strong-masculinity culture, which enacted the Employment Opportunity Law of 1986; and in Great Britain, another high masculinity culture, which enacted strong equal opportunity laws in 1976. Furthermore, the assertive behavior of male managers is likely to lead them to making decisions authoritatively. It has been proposed that in Latin American cultures, which tend to rank high on masculinity, women's leadership style may be more participative than autocratic (but this proposition may be difficult to test, since there are few female leaders in Latin American organizations).[24]

Hofstede also concluded that numerous nations are classified by a moderate- to weak-masculinity cultural dimension. Societies classified by this dimension stress interpersonal relationships, a concern for others, and the overall quality of life, and they define relatively overlapping social roles for males and females. In these cultures, neither males nor females need be ambitious or competitive; both may aspire to a life that does not assign great value to material success and that respects others—both may perform society's caring roles. Male secretaries, female truck drivers, and male nurses would be far more acceptable in such societies than they would in societies classified by a strong-masculinity cultural dimension. According to Hofstede, improved quality of work life for individuals in these societies means offering opportunities for developing social relationships on the job, which is perhaps best accomplished through participative/consultative DMB. Sweden, a weak-masculinity society, which generally exhibits participative DMB, is a good example. Findings by the cross-cultural researchers B. M. Bass and L. Eldridge support Hofstede's contention. They discovered that successful managers in Denmark (a low-masculinity society) emphasized societal concerns in decision making, whereas successful U.S., British, and German (all high-masculinity societies) managers strongly valued a profit motive.[25]

DMB as a Factor of Confucianism

As pointed out earlier and in Chapter 1, research by Hofstede and Bond revealed a fifth cultural dimension, termed *Confucian dynamism*, a dimension by which many societies can be classified. This dimension applies mainly to East Asian cultures based on Confucian philosophy (the People's Republic of China, South Korea, Japan, and Singapore).[26] As indicated in Chapter 1, Confucianism is not a religion but a system of practical ethics; it is based on a set of pragmatic rules for daily life derived from experience. The key tenet of Confucian teachings is that unequal relationships between people create stability in society.

In essence, individuals in Confucian-based organizations are forced to adhere to rigid, informal group norms and values, which include the subservient relationships aspects of Confucianism described in Chapter 1. Since individuals are so strictly bound to group norms, decision makers in organizations based on the Confucian cultural dimension, in reality, apply authoritative DMB. Support for this contention is provided by the cross-cultural studies conducted by K. H. Chung and by W. S. Nam, who found that South Korean managers demonstrate the Confucian virtues of loyalty and obedience to authorities, and by G. W. England and R. Lee and by J. Harbron, whose studies revealed that South Korean managers tend not to adopt systems of shared management and power equalization within organizations. It is also supported by research conducted by L. W. Pye and by R. H. Solomon, who described Chinese subordinates as passive and as preferring that others make decisions for them.[27] And it is generally known that Japanese culture teaches its children submissiveness to elders and authority.[28]

As discussed earlier, Japanese managers use a participative approach called *ringi*. Many Japanese managers, however, prior to the group's meeting, "discuss" the issue or decision one-on-one with individual members. They use a technique called *nemawashi*—a term borrowed from gardening, which refers to the process of gradually snipping the roots of a tree or bush that is to be transplanted to reduce the shock to the plant. In business terms, *nemawashi* means many private or semiprivate meetings in which true opinions are shared before a major decision-making meeting takes place.[29] In essence, the *ringi* method appears to be a formal and informal authoritative decision-making approach—not only does the manager enforce rigid group norms and values, but so do the group's members. It has been proposed that the Japanese prefer to work in groups and put the group's interests above their own, but once out of the group's institutional controls, they become egoistic.[30] The real objective of participative decision making is to generate and allow the introduction of varying views and alternative choices. The group-oriented cultures, however, tend not to allow the introduction of views that differ from the group's norms and values—which, in a Westerner's view, translates into repressive, authoritative behavior. In fact, a trend currently catching on in Japan is Japanese executives seeking employment in foreign companies, where they can be more autonomous.[31]

Other Support for the Country-Related Cultural Framework

Numerous theorists accept the country-related cultural factors model.[32] They conclude that managerial attitudes, values, and beliefs are functions of a society's culture, and many studies support these theorists' contention. The cross-cultural researchers A. Sorge and M. Warner, for example, found substantial differences between West German (now Germany) and British factories with respect to the shape of organizations, functional differentiation and integration mechanistics, the basic features of industrial systems, and the process of education; they attributed these differences to distinct national technical cultures.[33] The researchers M. Maurice, A. Sorge, and M. Warner studied similar factories in France, West Germany, and Great Britain and proposed that organizational processes of differentiation and integration interact with the processes of educating, training, recruiting, and promoting manpower; that these processes develop within an institutional logic that is distinct to a society; and that nationally different shapes of organization result.[34]

The cross-cultural researcher D. Gallie studied the work attitudes of employees in four oil refineries owned by a multinational corporation. The refineries, two situated in Great Britain and two in France, were matched for technology and size. Gallie found considerable contrast in the attitudes of workers and their relations with management; he attributed the differences to national culture.[35] Professor A. Laurent researched employees of a multinational enterprise in different nations and found that the employees retained their culturally specific work behaviors despite the existence of common management policies and procedures.[36]

The researcher P. Blunt studied an organization employing about 160 people in Brunei to determine whether or not the employees' values compared with Brunei's national values of large power distance, strong uncertainty avoidance, and low individualism. Brunei was not included in Hofstede's study, but Blunt equated Brunei with similar countries in the region that Hofstede had categorized as such. Blunt found that commonalities did exist between the values of the firm's employees and Brunei's national values. For example, employees showed a considerable unwillingness to make a decision without referring it to the most senior manager in the organization—an indication that the employees were exhibiting large power distance and strong uncertainty avoidance.[37]

Jackofsky and Slocum examined published sources to ascertain whether or not the behaviors of two French CEOs, three German CEOs, two Swedish CEOs, one Taiwanese CEO, and three Japanese CEOs compared with their respective country's culture as identified in Hofstede's study. Although they detected a few deviations, for the most part, they found commonalities in the CEOs' behavior and their country's value system.[38] The above-cited cross-cultural studies thus provide strong support for the "culture-specific" theory.

Questions About the Country Factors Framework

Despite support for the country-related cultural factors framework, many unanswered questions remain. For example, how does the framework apply to multicultural centers, such as the United States and Canada? For instance, British Americans can be individualistic and Japanese Americans collectivistic; German Americans can have strong uncertainty avoidance and Swedish Americans weak uncertainty avoidance. From a global perspective, can we even conceptually define the meaning of the labels used, such as uncertainty avoidance? Are not the more educated members of societies generally better equipped to deal with conditions of high uncertainty than the less educated members?

Furthermore, how does this framework apply to the archetypes described by the researchers W. D. Guth and R. Tagiuri—Economic Man, Theoretical Man, Political Man, Religious Man, Aesthetic Man, and Social Man, labels that reflect the personal values of decision makers existing in societies?[39] For instance, the Theoretical Man, who relies on tangible evidence in seeking the truth, would probably have low tolerance for power from above and high tolerance for uncertainty. The Religious Man, who relies on mysticism (faith) and the intangible, would probably have higher tolerance for power from above and lower tolerance for uncertainty. The Economic Man is practical and concerned with what is immediately useful, the Social Man is driven by benevolence, the Political Man is driven by challenge, and the Aesthetic Man is driven by savoring the moment's beauty—would not these individuals also have different tolerances for different decision-making styles, and would not they themselves apply different DMBs? For instance, would not the more liberal values of the Aesthetic Man generate more participative DMB than would the more power-oriented values of the Political Man? These questions thus lead us to the universal factors framework.

The Universal Factors Model

Many theorists argue that irrespective of a society's culture, individuals are forced to adopt attitudes and behaviors that comply with the imperatives of industrialization.[40] (For an illustration read Practical Perspective 11.4.) These theorists believe that other transnational factors affect DMB in all countries. For example, the management theorists V. Vroom and P. Yetton contend that participation is not an ideological or cultural phenomenon but an "instrumental" phenomenon. They propose that U.S. managers use participation to enhance both quality and acceptance.[41] Therefore, many cross-cultural theorists adhere to a universal factors framework, which posits that DMB is influenced not as much by broad cultural factors as by varying situational factors, such as subordinates' work environment, motivation, maturity level, and managerial level and functions. These situations and the DMB associated with each are discussed below. (See Table 11.2.) It should be noted that numerous management textbooks, especially those addressing leadership, list many other situations that affect DMB. These few were selected to illustrate the framework.

PRACTICAL PERSPECTIVE 11-4

Participative Management Comes to the Far East

Taiwan and South Korea, the two heavyweights among the newly industrialized economies, face not so much a quantitative shortage as a qualitative one: The skills its managers have are simply no longer appropriate for the changing competition they face. As wages have risen, the region's traditionally low-tech companies have had to move into higher-value-added products dependent upon expertise—overseas marketing sophistication, for instance—that their old-line managers often do not have. As authoritarian governments in both countries loosened up, workers began to challenge their bosses for the first time, creating a whole new set of managerial problems. Says Lee Hak-chong, a dean at

PRACTICAL PERSPECTIVE 11-4 (Continued)

Yosei University in Seoul: "Democratization has produced a tough and loud labor force." The search for more of the right kind of managers is challenging some of the region's most basic values....

A new wave of thinking is bringing forward a fresh generation of managers, men like Ng Pock Too and Nelson An-ping Chang. After getting an MBA degree from New York University, Nelson Chang went back to Taiwan. He heads an innovative computer services firm and a large cement manufacturing company that his father founded in 1954.... Chang, 38, could easily fill the part of the omnipotent dictatorial boss, the role favored by his father's generation. He has instead renounced that style because he thinks it stifles productive ideas. Says he, proudly: "I am a participative manager." The participation can get rough. To make certain that his senior executives take issue with him, Chang sometimes deliberately sets overambitious goals that they must argue against—or suffer penalties if the objectives are not met.

Belatedly, the region's universities are trying to respond.... Business schools are broadening curriculums in response to criticism that they have been turning out narrow specialists. In 1991, they began requiring the National University of Singapore business majors to take courses in such areas as psychology and Japanese culture. Chow Kit Boey, director of the school's Centre for Business Research and Development, says professors are now challenging students to become more "participative" and "free-thinking."

SOURCE: Excerpted from Ford S. Worthy, "You Can't Grow If You Can't Manage," *Fortune* (June 3, 1991), pp. 83–88. Copyright © Times, Inc., New York. Reprinted with permission. All rights reserved.

TABLE 11.2 The Universal Factors Model

Factors	DMB
Subordinates' work environment	
Crisis conditions	A
Ambiguous conditions	A
Competent individuals	Pe
Individuals' motivation	
Need for affiliation individuals	Ac
Need for achievement individuals	Pe
Need for power individuals	Pe
Individuals' maturity level	
Low-maturity individuals	A
Low- to moderate-maturity individuals	Ac
Moderate- to high-maturity individuals	P
High-maturity individuals	Pe
Managerial level and functions	
Upper-level managers	Pe
Lower-level managers	A
Structured functions	A
Unstructured functions	P

NOTE: DMB = decision-making behavior leaning toward; A = authoritative; Ac = authoritative/consultative; P = participative; Pe = participative/extensive.

Subordinates' Work Environment

Regardless of national culture, in crisis situations and in conditions where a group of individuals are under extreme pressure to perform a difficult task or survive in a hostile atmosphere, they generally prefer that the decision maker behave in a directive manner.[42] A decision maker who authoritatively makes and communicates decisions to correct the undesirable conditions is likely to be welcomed. Individuals confronted with ambiguous or unclear assignments also generally prefer a manager who provides much structure, clearly defining roles and expectations.[43] On the other hand, in situations where individuals feel competent, an effective decision maker is likely to be one who asks them to participate extensively in the decision-making process. This is because competent people, those with a higher degree of perceived ability relative to the task demands, usually have low tolerance for authoritative behavior.[44]

Individuals' Motivation

In many societies, some individuals are motivated by the need for affiliation, others by the need for achievement, and still others by the need for power.[45] Individuals whose primary motivator is the need for affiliation are interested in warm, friendly relationships, social interaction, communication, and collaboration. Such people generally dislike making unpopular decisions, even when it is necessary for organizational effectiveness. These individuals may not like the responsibilities that come with participative DMB, and they may prefer authoritative DMB with consultation. People motivated by the need for achievement are interested in attaining specific objectives, will work hard to achieve them, and tend to be more interested in personal success. It is likely that these individuals will want to be very involved in making decisions. People motivated by the need for power are interested in controlling and influencing situations; they like to get things done through people, and they like to teach and inspire other individuals. Since such people want to have an impact on the organization, they probably would prefer to participate extensively in the decision-making process—although they themselves may prefer to apply authoritative DMB with their subordinates.

Individuals' Maturity Level

According to theorists Paul Hersey and Kenneth Blanchard, individuals function at four maturity levels: (1) low maturity, (2) low-to-moderate maturity, (3) moderate-to-high maturity, and (4) high maturity.[46] Individuals at a low maturity level have a negative attitude; they are unwilling and unable to assume responsibility. With such people, the effective manager applies directive (authoritative) DMB. Some individuals attain a low-to-moderate maturity level. These people are willing to assume responsibility, are confident, and have a positive attitude but lack the skills to make decisions. A combination of directive (authoritative) and supportive (consultative) DMB would work best with them. The manager, engaging in both kinds of DMB and using two-way communication, tries to improve the subordinates' decision-making abilities.

Other individuals develop to a moderate-to-high maturity level. Through coaching, training, and development, they have acquired the ability to make decisions but are unwilling to do so because of a lack of confidence. Participative DMB, which provides strong emotional support and encouragement and helps build confidence, would work well with these individuals. People with a high maturity level are able and willing and possess the confidence to make decisions. Because they are at a maturity level where they need little direction and little emotional support, these individuals are likely to prefer a participative approach that allows them a great deal of responsibility in the final decision. Hersey and Blanchard's theory thus suggests that DMB is not a factor of national culture but a factor of individuals' differing maturity level in their culture.

Decision-Making Level and Functions

Regardless of national culture, lower-level decision makers generally provide more direction than do upper-level decision makers; upper-level decision makers normally delegate more than those at a lower-level.[47] This means that upper-level decision makers apply participative DMB more than lower-level decision makers, and lower-level decision makers apply authoritative DMB more than upper-level decision makers. Decision makers for functions such as production, especially when the tasks are structured, tend to be directive and apply authoritative behavior. Decision makers for functions such as sales, where much of the employees' work is self-initiated, usually apply participative DMB.[48]

Some Problems With This Framework

The above discussion has presented some ideas that may aid decision makers in determining the appropriate DMB for certain situations in all national cultures. One problem in applying the above framework is reconciling the conflicting demands of a situation. For example, when a crisis confronts a group of achievers, which behavior would be most appropriate? Another problem is how to identify individuals' motivation at all levels—not all upper-level managers are willing to delegate authority to the lower levels, nor do all lower-level managers want to behave autocratically. Furthermore, some organizational behavioralists have questioned the utility of complicated situational theories as a means of improving managerial effectiveness.[49] They believe that these theories can only be applied when the manager has time to analyze the situation and select the style that works best. But managers, according to those behavioralists, are so busy making decisions and responding to crises in a hectic and fragmented fashion that they do not have adequate time to evaluate the situation. The complexity of managing in the international environment is likely to increase, which means that managers will have even less time to analyze and apply a situational approach in the international environment than they do in the domestic one.

Which Framework Is Correct?

Since the two frameworks are well supported by existing literature, can they both be correct? An analysis of the study by Jackofsky and Slocum, cited earlier, can be used to lend support to both models. They found that, in some instances, the behavior of one of the French CEOs was influenced more by his own personal characteristics than by his country's cultural characteristics. This CEO acted boldly in acquiring two competing firms—behavior that stands in marked contrast to France's culture of strong uncertainty avoidance (conservative behavior). He also decentralized management in the acquisitions—conduct that is also opposed to France's large power distance culture. Jackofsky and Slocum surmised that this CEO's behavior of not conforming to national culture eventually led to his demise—which supports the country-related cultural factors framework. However, this CEO's behavior also violated the universal factors framework. This contention is based on the idea that often acquisitions are made when the firm being acquired is encountering difficulties (crisis) and that ambiguous conditions often arise in newly acquired firms. In such situations, the universal framework proposes application of directive DMB,[50] yet the CEO decentralized decision making. This CEO's unorthodox behavior, which led to his failure within the company, thus can also be interpreted to support the universal framework.

The other CEO, also eventually released from his position, generally conformed to France's national culture. He made conservative decisions (high uncertainty avoidance behavior), even when his firm was confronted with crisis conditions. However, his behavior contradicts the universal framework, which proposes that individuals confronted with a crisis generally prefer an authoritative manager who makes decisions that communicate potential for correcting the situation. This CEO made a somewhat bold decision in trying to cut 9,000 jobs to save money. But this action seems to go against both models. It violates the universal framework in the sense that the solution does not develop hope for subordinates confronted with crisis conditions, and it violates the country-related framework in the sense that the French display strong uncertainty avoidance and search for security; eliminating 9,000 jobs certainly does not make one feel secure.

The cases of these French CEOs, therefore, lend validity to both frameworks—as does Professor Herbert Simon's famous, older work. He discusses the "zone of acceptance" concept, which is the extent to which a subordinate accepts another's decisions as governing his or her behavior. Individuals with a wide zone accept more; individuals with a narrow zone accept less. Simon proposes that the zone is socially determined and varies with the social situation, which in some ways equates with the country-related framework. On the other hand, he notes that "there are wide differences, too, among different types of employees in their expectation of authority relations in their positions. Professional men and skilled workmen are apt to have relatively narrow zones of acceptance."[51] This provides support for the universal framework.

In their research findings, Eylon and Au concluded that subjects of both high power distance and low power distance cultures were more satisfied with their jobs when empowered (to make decisions) than when not empowered.[52] C. Robert et al. examined the effects of empowerment on job satisfaction in four nations: India, Mexico, Poland, and the United States. They found that in India, a high power distance culture, empowerment was negatively associated with job satisfaction (which provides support for the country-related cultural factors model), but they found no significant association between empowerment and job satisfaction in Mexico and Poland, both strong power distance cultures, and in the United States, a small power distance culture[53] (which provides support for neither model). A more recent and more extensive study by M. K. Hui et al. revealed that empowerment has a stronger effect on job satisfaction in small power distance cultures than in high power distance cultures[54] (providing support for the country-related cultural factors model).

Even though we know that both frameworks can be used to help predict DMB in organizations, we do not know yet which one is the best predictor. That is, we do not know when the determinants in one framework have a greater impact on DMB than the determinants in the other. Are there any situations (e.g., crisis) that make the determinants in one framework more dominant than the determinants in the other? For example, would the two French CEOs discussed above have been more effective if their behavior emphasized the universal model's determinants when they seemed the most relevant and the country-related determinants when they seemed the most appropriate? How is such a determination made? It seems that to make such a determination, managers require a great deal of managerial savvy, including global, cross-cultural savvy. Not understanding the other's cultural traits would be a crucial mistake.[55]

Implications of the Two Frameworks for Cross-Cultural Decision Making

The two frameworks developed in this chapter are still being refined, but they do have some implications for cross-cultural decision making. The country-related cultural factors framework can serve as a general starting point for analysis. For example, it may be accurate to state that culturally, the British tend to be highly individualistic and the Portuguese tend to be less individualistic. But it would be risky to make a blanket decision based on this belief, as not all British rank high on individualism, nor do all Portuguese rank low on individualism. Thus, ultimately, each specific situation must be studied. For instance, when the Japanese Honda Motor Company penetrated the European market, it discovered that it was not sufficient to have abstract knowledge about a foreign country—a deeper understanding had to be developed. Honda learned the importance of adopting a locally oriented approach and building up a new way of doing work in the host country. As its success indicates, Honda learned how to blend its corporate culture with the cultural background of the host nation.[56]

The two frameworks also imply that cross-cultural decision makers need to determine to what extent individuals in different situations and cultures tolerate or expect different DMB. They also imply that effective cross-cultural decision makers are flexible in their approach to making decisions in different situations and across cultures; they understand that the behavior that works in one situation or culture will not necessarily work in another.[57] Historically, managers doing business across foreign borders have made many costly blunders, in part because they did not adopt managerial styles appropriate to specific situations and cultures.[58] For example, David Pulatie, the vice president and director of employee relations at Motorola, Inc., stated that there has been a tendency on the part of American managers to simply go into nation X, Y, or Z and try to introduce the American mentality and decision-making process without considering the reactions of the host country's citizens.[59] For example, there was a situation in which an Asian employee working in an American firm was threatened with termination. The reason given was that he asked too many questions. The Asian was deeply bewildered by this criticism; he could not imagine how to act differently. The manager, being a good American, expected employees to act independently after receiving initial instructions. The manager was annoyed by the Asian's constant questions and decided that he was too ignorant for the job. Actually, however, the Asian was asking questions as a way of strengthening his dependent relationship with his supervisor and to be sure that he was proceeding properly.[60] In view of the huge costs managerial blunders can generate in the global economy, it is imperative that international decision makers learn and apply theDMB appropriate to the situation and culture.[61]

Before a corporation sends someone abroad, it must identify the effective management style for that place and, as indicated in Chapters 7 and 8, select and train the right person for the assignment. For example, Reynolds International's training director, Thomas Kruse, explained that to determine the right management style for a country, they rely on managers who have worked there before, and they talk to Peace Corps volunteers who have worked in the country. They also obtain information from the American Management Association in New York, which offers country profiles and arranges seminars in which natives of a specific nation provide information on management styles that work in their country.[62] In the long run, the investment of time and effort put into assessing the situation, culture, and appropriate managerial behavior will be regained by avoiding costly blunders.

Group Decision Making and Information Technology

More and more international organizations (and domestic ones as well) are now making important decisions by using input from groups consisting of employees and sometimes outsiders. In face-to-face group decision making, it is well-known that, in both small and large power distance societies, a certain member or certain members of the group (often those with status) usually influence the other members' decisions. Questions one might ask include the following: Can the use of newer technologies—for example, using e-mail instead of face-to-face communication, in offering input for group decision making—reduce the powerful group member's influence on the group's decision-making process? Can the more impersonal means of group decision making allowed by the Internet induce group members holding a large power distance cultural orientation to participate more in the organization's decision-making process? Some initial research in this respect involving computer-mediated communication (CMC) conducted using United States (small power distance) and Singapore (large power distance) decision-making groups suggests that the answer to the above questions might be yes—the groups supported by CMC were less influenced by member status than the groups that were not supported by CMC.[63] This suggests that in the future, the Internet might have a positive effect on the democratization of societies throughout the world.[64]

Summary

This chapter has discussed the programmed and nonprogrammed decision-making processes in a cross-cultural context, including a discussion on how a society's culture affects the rational decision-making process. The MBO and *ringi* participative decision-making approaches were also described in a cultural context. Two frameworks, each presenting several factors that influence DMB—authoritative or participative—were discussed. The country-related cultural factors framework proposes that certain cultural dimensions affect DMB. The universal factors framework posits that certain specific situational factors affect DMB in all cultures. Questions about how to apply both frameworks were posed. The implications of both frameworks were put forth—mainly that cross-cultural decision makers, to apply the appropriate DMB, must understand each situation and culture thoroughly.

KEY TERMS AND CONCEPTS

1. An effective decision-making process in one culture may be ineffective in another
2. Programmed and nonprogrammed decision making
3. "Master of destiny" and "fatalistic" cultures
4. Consensus; group harmony
5. Authoritative and participative decision making
6. Participative DMB is perceived negatively in many cultures
7. MBO and *ringi*
8. Contingency decision making
9. The country-related cultural factors framework
10. The universal factors framework
11. The "culture-specific" and "culture-free" theories
12. Power distance
13. Individualism
14. Uncertainty avoidance
15. Masculinity
16. Confucianism
17. Nemawashi
18. Cross-cultural research
19. Multicultural centers
20. Subordinates' work environment
21. Individuals' motivation
22. Individuals' maturity level
23. Decision-making level and function
24. Group decision making and information technology

DISCUSSION QUESTIONS

1. Discuss the ways culture affects programmed and nonprogrammed decision making.

2. Discuss the fundamentals of the country-related cultural factors and the universal factors frameworks.

3. What type of DMB, authoritative or participative, would you apply in the following cultures?
   a. Large power distance
   b. Low individualism
   c. Strong uncertainty avoidance
   d. Low masculinity
   e. High Confucianism

4. What type of DMB, authoritative or participative, would you apply in the following situations?
   a. Crisis conditions
   b. Subordinates are motivated by the need for affiliation
   c. Subordinates function at a high level of maturity
   d. Subordinates carry out the sales function

5. Discuss the problems with the country-related cultural factors and the universal factors frameworks.

6. Fundamentally, what do the two frameworks tell the global manager?

7. Discuss how technology affects cross-cultural group decision making.

EXERCISES

1. Analyze Table 1.6 in Chapter 1, and based on the country-related cultural factors framework, determine the appropriate DMB—authoritative or participative—for each of the 50 countries.

ASSIGNMENT

Interview an executive involved in international business. Ask the executive to describe his or her experiences in making decisions across cultures. Did he or she apply the country-related factors framework or the universal factors framework? Prepare a short report for class discussion.

CASE 11-1

A Dutchman Abroad

A young Dutchman, called Sytze, had recently been transferred from the head office in Rotterdam to his employer's Polish subsidiary. He was in Warsaw on a four-month secondment to help set up a new database. The head of the subsidiary, to whom he reported directly, was also a Dutch and had been in Poland a year. Sytze's boss had overseen the move from the old office in the suburbs to a brand new one in the center of the city. When his boss had seen the architect's plans for the new office, he had insisted that the wooden doors and paneling of each manager's office be replaced with glass. Sytze's new Polish colleagues hated working in these "akwariums." But not one of them expressed their dissatisfaction to Sytze's boss. Sytze realized they hoped he would tell him [the boss] on their behalf. He did. His boss was amazed.

Questions

1. Why had the employees not told him [Sytze's boss] to his face?

2. What kind of problems did the glass doors and paneling present?

SOURCE: Richard Pooley, "Bridging the Cultural Divide," *Computing Business* (April 20, 2006). www.whatpc.co .uk/computing-business/features/2153953/bridgi

CASE 11-2

Cultural Traditions

If you are involved in business with Third World countries, you need to understand three widespread traditions that affect business transactions: the inner circle, future favors, and gift exchange.

Inner Circle

Communal societies divide people into two groups: those with whom they have relationships and those with whom they have none—the goal being group prosperity and protection. There are the "in" people and the "out" people. The "ins" are family and the "outs" are strangers. In East and West Africa, inner circles can be true relatives, comrades, or persons of similar age or region. In China, they may be those who share the same dialect, in India, members of the same caste. These are not unlike the "old boy networks" in the United States. The effect in many of these countries is to restrict social and business dealings to those with whom the business person has safe, trusting relationships.

Future Favors

The system of future favors operates within the inner circles. In Japan, it is known as "inner duty," in Kenya, "inner relationship," and in the Philippines, "inner debt." In these traditions, the person is obligated to another to repay the favor sometime in the future. Some form of favor or service will repay the earlier debt; this repayment then places the grantor of the original favor under future obligation. Lifelong shifting obligations create relationships of trust and are the basis for doing business.

Gift Exchange

In many non-Western circles, the gift exchange tradition has evolved into a business tool: Gifts begin a process of future favors. They are an immediate sign of gratitude or hospitality, but on acceptance, they generate an obligation that the recipient must someday repay.

Questions

1. Discuss some of the ways the above cultural traditions affect the rational decision-making process described in this chapter.

2. Compare the inner circle with the "low-individualism" cultural dimension. What type of decision-making approach, participative or authoritative, is likely to be preferred in the inner circle cultures? Why?

SOURCE: Ken Hodgson, "Adapting Ethical Decisions to a Global Marketplace," *Management Review* (May 1992), p. 55.

CASE 11-3

From Napa Valley, California, to Paris, France

John Terwilick, an executive for Shonteur, Inc., a wine wholesaler based in Massachusetts, was appointed to head Shonteur France, Inc., a subsidiary in Paris, France. The subsidiary had been established to procure wines in Europe for distribution in the U.S. market. The subsidiary employs 179 people. The employees are mostly locals (French), but numerous employees are from Germany, Spain, and Portugal—which are sources of European wines. The company selected Terwilick for the assignment because of his successful experience managing another wine-sourcing subsidiary in Napa Valley, California.

Over the years, Terwilick has attended many management development seminars, where he was taught that participative management, involving employees in the decision-making process, would produce wonders. It did work well for him at the Napa Valley subsidiary, and it helped establish his reputation at the Massachusetts headquarters as an effective manager. These days, however, to

(Continued)

(Continued)

climb to the top of a corporation's headquarters, managers require extensive cross-cultural experience—that is, experience managing diverse cultures. In view of this current managerial trend, Terwilick, with the goal of a high-level appointment at corporate headquarters, happily accepted the appointment in France.

Terwilick was determined to be at least as successful in France as he had been in Napa Valley. On assuming his managerial post as the head of the French subsidiary, Terwilick began applying basically the same managerial style he had applied in Napa Valley. For example, he began delegating some of his decision-making duties to the French supervisors, and in making major decisions, he often solicited their input—he involved them in the decision-making process. Terwilick had been taught in management development programs and had learned through experience at Napa Valley that this would improve employee morale and, thus, productivity. To his surprise, however, he noted that the French supervisors nonverbally expressed anxiety, dissatisfaction, and low morale. Terwilick thought to himself, "What is wrong here? What is the problem?"

Questions

1. What did the company do wrong in sending Terwilick overseas?

2. Can you help Terwilick solve the problem with which he is confronted?

SOURCE: This case was created by the author.

NOTES

1. "The Business of Europe," *The Economist* (December 7, 1991), p. 64.

2. J. S. Black and L. W. Porter, *Management: Meeting the New Challenges* (Upper Saddle River, NJ: Prentice Hall: 2000), p. 54.

3. Geert Hofstede, *Culture's Consequences: International Differences in Work-Related Values* (Beverly Hills, CA: Sage Publications, 1980), p. 19.

4. D. K. Tse, K. Lee, I. Vertinsky, and D. A. Wehrung, "Does Culture Matter? A Cross-Cultural Study of Executives' Choice, Decisiveness, and Risk Adjustment in International Marketing," *Journal of Marketing,* 52 (October 1988), p. 82.

5. See R. Theobald, "Management of Complex Systems: A Growing Societal Challenge," in F. Feather (Ed.), *Through the 1980s: Thinking Globally, Acting Locally* (Washington, DC: World Future Society, 1980), pp. 42–51.

6. Nancy J. Adler, *International Dimensions of Organizational Behavior*, 2nd ed. (Boston: PWS-Kent Publishing, 1991), p. 162.

7. Tse et al., "Does Culture Matter?" op cit., p. 82.

8. Rensis Likert, *The Human Organization: Its Management and Values* (New York: McGraw-Hill, 1967).

9. T. Morris and C. M. Pavett, "Managing Style and Productivity," *Journal of International Business Studies* (First Quarter 1992), p. 177.

10. Anthony P. Raia, "A Second Look at Management Goals and Controls," *California Management Review* (Summer 1966), pp. 49–58; Peter F. Drucker, *The Practice of Management* (New York: Harper & Row, 1954).

11. J. Johnston, "Ringi: Decision Making Japanese Style," *Management Review,* 70 (May 1981), pp.15–21.

12. R. Neale and R. Mindel, "Rigging Up Multicultural Teamworking," *Personnel Management* (January 1992), p. 37.

13. For another discussion on these two frameworks, see E. U. Weber, D. R. Ames, and A-R Blais, "'How Do I Choose Thee? Let Me Count the Ways': A Textual Analysis of Similarities and Differences in Modes of

Decision-Making in China and the United States," *Management and Organization Review,* 1, no. 1 (2005), pp. 87–118.

14. See J. Child and A. Kieser, "Organizations and Managerial Roles in British and West German Companies: An Examination of the Culture-Free Thesis," in C. Lammers and D. Hickson (Eds.), *Organizations Alike and Unlike* (London: Routledge and Kegan Paul, 1979), pp. 251–271.

15. See Child and Kieser, "Organizations and Managerial Roles in British and West German Companies," op cit.; W. Heydebrand, *Comparative Organization: The Results of Empirical Research* (Englewood Cliffs, NJ: Prentice-Hall, 1973); D. J. Hickson, C. J. Hinings, and J. P. Schwitter, "The Culture-Free Context of Organization Structure: A Tri-National Comparison," *Sociology,* 8 (1974), pp. 59–80; M. Haire, E. E. Ghiselli, and L. W. Porter, *Managerial Thinking: An International Study* (New York: John Wiley, 1966).

16. Hofstede, "Culture's Consequences," op cit.; Geert Hofstede, "The Cultural Relativity of the Quality of Life Concept," *Academy of Management Review,* 9, no. 3 (1984), pp. 389–398.

17. G. Hofstede and M. Bond, "The Confucius Connection: From Cultural Roots to Economic Growth," *Organizational Dynamics* (Spring 1988), pp. 5–21.

18. Cited in Geert Hofstede, "Motivation, Leadership, and Organization: Do American Theories Apply Abroad?" *Organizational Dynamics* (Summer 1980), pp. 42–62.

19. S. Kakar, "Authority Patterns and Subordinate Behavior in Indian Organizations," *Administrative Science Quarterly,* 16 (1971), pp. 93–101; L. Williams, W. Whyte, and C. Green, "Do Cultural Differences Affect Workers' Attitudes?" *Industrial Relations,* 5 (1966), pp. 105–117.

20. See also Z. Aayan, R. B. Kanungo, and J. B. P. Sinha, "Organizational Culture and Human Resource Management Practices," *Journal of Cross-Cultural Psychology,* 30, no. 4 (July 1999), pp. 501–526.

21. J. K. Harrison and R. Hubbard, "Antecedents to Organizational Commitment Among Mexican Employees of a U.S. Firm in Mexico," *The Journal of Social Psychology,* 138, no. 5 (1998), pp. 609–623; J. S. Osland, S. Franco, and A. Osland, "Organizational Implications of Latin American Culture: Lessons for the Expatriate Manager," *Journal of Management Inquiry,* 8, no. 2 (June 1999), pp. 219– 234.

22. E. F. Jackofsky and J. W. Slocum Jr., "CEO Roles Across Cultures," in D. C. Hambrick (Ed.), *The Executive Effect: Concepts and Methods for Studying Top Managers* (Greenwich, CT: JAI Press, 1988).

23. R. N. Kannungo and R. Wright, "A Cross-Cultural Comparative Study of Managerial Job Attitudes," *Journal of International Business Studies,* 14, no. 2 (1983), pp. 115–129.

24. H. J. Mullen and M. Rowell, "Mexican Women Managers: An Emerging Profile," *Human Resource Management,* 36, no. 4 (1997), pp. 423–435; J. S. Osland, L. Hunter, and M. M. Snow, "A Comparative Study of Managerial Styles in Nicaraguan and Costa Rican Female Executives," *International Studies of Management and Organization,* 28, no. 2 (1998), pp. 54–73.

25. B. M. Bass and L. Eldridge, "Accelerated Managers' Objectives in Twelve Countries," *Industrial Relations,* 12 (1979), pp. 158–171.

26. Hofstede and Bond, "The Confucius Connection," op cit.

27. K. H. Chung, "A Comparative Study of Managerial Characteristics of Domestic, International, and Governmental Institutions in Korea." Paper presented at the Midwest Conference of Asian Affairs, Minneapolis, MN (1978); W. S. Nam, "The Traditional Pattern of Korean Industrial Management, ILCORK," Working paper No. 14, Social Science Research Institute, University of Hawaii, HI (1971); G. W. England and R. Lee, "Organizational Goals and Expected Behavior Among American, Japanese, and Korean Managers: A Comparative Study," *Academy of Management Journal,* 14 (1971), pp. 425–438; J. Harbron, "Korea's Executives Are Not Quite the New Japanese," *The Business Quarterly,* 44 (1979), pp. 16–19; L. W. Pye, *The Spirit of Chinese Politics* (Cambridge: MIT Press, 1968); R. H. Solomon, *Mao's Revolution and Chinese Political Culture* (Berkeley: University of California Press, 1971).

28. Brock Strout, "Interviewing in Japan," *HR Magazine* (June 1998), p. 72.

29. Black and Porter, *Management: Meeting the New Challenge,* op cit., p. 254.

30. T. Yamagishi, "Cross-Societal Experimentation on Trust: A Comparison of the United States and Japan," in E. Ostrom and J. Walker (Eds.), *Trust and Reciprocity* (New York: Russell Sage Foundation, 2003), pp. 352–370.

31. "Changing Jobs Catching On in Japan," *Focus Japan* (March 1993), p. 6.

32. See M. Crozier, *The Bureaucratic Phenomenon* (London: Tavistock Publications, 1964); S. M. Davis, *Comparative Management: Cultural and Organizational Perspectives* (Englewood Cliffs, NJ: Prentice Hall, 1971); R. Nath, "A Methodological Review of Cross-Cultural Research," *International Social Science Journal,* 20, no. 1

(1968), pp. 35–62; W. Glasier, "Cross-National Comparisons of the Factory," *Journal of Comparative Administration* (May 1971), pp. 67–83; Hofstede, "Culture's Consequences," op cit.; Haire, Ghiselli, and Porter, *Managerial Thinking,* op cit.

33. A. Sorge and M. Warner, "Culture, Management and Manufacturing Organizations: A Study of British and German Firms," *Management International Review,* 21 (1981), pp. 35–48.

34. M. Maurice, A. Sorge, and M. Warner, "Societal Differences in Organizing Manufacturing Units: A Comparison of France, West Germany, and Great Britain," *Organization Studies,* 1 (1980), pp. 59–86.

35. D. Gallie, *In Search of the Working Class* (London: Cambridge University Press, 1978).

36. A. Laurent, "The Cultural Diversity of Management Conceptions," *International Studies of Management and Organization* (Spring 1983), pp. 75–96.

37. P. Blunt, "Cultural Consequences of Organization Change in a Southeast Asian State: Brunei," *The Academy of Management Executive,* 2, no. 3 (1988), pp. 235–240.

38. Jackofsky and Slocum, "CEO Roles Across Cultures," op cit.

39. See W. D. Guth and R. Tagiuri, "Personal Values and Corporate Strategy," *Harvard Business Review* (September–October 1965), p. 126.

40. See R. E. Caves, "Industrial Organization, Corporate Strategy and Structure," *Journal of Economic Literature,* 18 (1980), pp. 317–334; Hickson, Hinings, and Schwitter, "The Culture-Free Context of Organization Structure," op cit.; W. Heydebrand, *Comparative Organization: The Results of Empirical Research,* op cit.

41. V. Vroom and P. Yetton, *Leadership and Decision-Making* (Pittsburgh, PA: University of Pittsburgh Press, 1973); F. Heller and B. Wilpert, *Competence and Power in Managerial Decision-Making* (New York: John Wiley & Sons, 1981).

42. See A. W. Halpin, "The Leadership Behavior and Combat Performance of Airplane Commanders," *Journal of Abnormal and Social Psychology,* 49 (1954), pp. 19–22; E. P. Torrence, "The Behavior of Small Groups Under Stress Conditions of Survival," *American Sociological Review,* 19 (1954), pp. 751–755; M. Mulder and A. Stemering, "Threat, Attraction to Group, and Need for Strong Leadership," *Human Relations,* 16 (1963), pp. 317–334.

43. E. Burack, *Organizational Analysis: Theory and Applications* (Hinsdale, IL: Dryden Press, 1975), pp. 315–318.

44. See A. S. Ashour and G. England, "Subordinates' Assigned Level of Discretion as a Function of Leader's Personality and Situational Variables," *Journal of Applied Psychology,* 56 (1972), pp. 120–123; A. C. Filley, R. House, and S. Kerr, *Managerial Process and Organizational Behavior,* 2nd ed. (Glenview, IL: Scott, Foresman & Co., 1976), p. 215; F. Heller, *Managerial Decision Making: A Study of Leadership Style and Power Sharing Among Senior Managers* (London: Tavistock Publications, 1971).

45. See D. C. McClelland, "Business Drive and National Achievement," *Harvard Business Review,* 40 (July–August 1962), pp. 35–42; D. C. McClelland, *The Inner Experience* (New York: Irvington, 1975).

46. P. Hersey and K. Blanchard, *Management of Organizational Behavior,* 4th ed. (Englewood Cliffs, NJ: Prentice Hall, 1982).

47. See F. Heller and G. A. Yukl, "Participation, Managerial Decision Making, and Situational Variables," *Organization Behavior and Human Performance,* 4 (1969), pp. 227–241; W. W. Tornow and R. R. Pinto, "The Development of a Managerial Job Taxonomy: A System for Describing, Classifying, and Evaluating Executive Positions," *Journal of Applied Psychology,* 61 (1976), pp. 410–418; R. A. Webber, *Time and Management* (New York: Van Nostrand-Reinhold, 1972).

48. See J. K. Hemphill, "Job Descriptions for Executives," *Harvard Business Review,* 37 (September–October 1959), pp. 55–67; R. Stewart, *Contrast in Management* (Maidenhead, Berkshire, England: McGraw-Hill U.K., 1976); B. M. Bass, "A System Survey Research Feedback for Management and Organizational Behavior," *Journal of Applied Behavioral Science,* 12 (1976), pp. 151–171; Heller and Yukl, "Participation, Managerial Decision Making, and Situational Variables," op cit.; Webber, *Time and Management,* op cit.

49. See M. W. McCall Jr., "Leaders and Leadership: Of Substance and Shadow," in J. Hackman, E. E. Lawler Jr., and L. W. Porter (Eds.), *Perspectives on Behavior in Organizations* (New York: McGraw-Hill, 1979).

50. E. P. Torrence, "Behavior of Small Groups," op cit.

51. See Herbert A. Simon, *Administrative Behavior* (New York: The Free Press, 1976).

52. D. Eylon and K. Y. Au, "Exploring Empowerment Cross-Cultural Differences Along the Power Distance Dimension," *International Journal of Intercultural Relations,* 23 (1999), pp. 373–385.

53. C. Robert, T. M. Probst, J. J. Martocchio, F. Drasgow, and J. J. Lawler, "Empowerment and Continuous Improvement in the United States, Mexico, Poland, and India: Predicting Fit on the Basis of the Dimensions of Power Distance and Individualism," *Journal of Applied Psychology*, 85 (2000), pp. 643–648.

54. M. K. Hui, K. Au, and H. Fock, "Empowerment Effects Across Cultures," *Journal of International Business Studies*, 35 (2004), p. 58.

55. Richard Pooley, "Bridging the Cultural Divide," *Computing Business* (April 20, 2006). www.whatpc .co.uk/computing-business/features/2153953/bridgi

56. H. Sigiura, "How Honda Localizes Its Global Strategy," *Sloan Management Review*, 31, no. 1 (Fall 1990), pp. 77–82.

57. "Cultural Differences Affect Decision-Making," *IIE Solutions*, 31, no. 6, p. 8.

58. See D. Ricks, *Big Business Blunders: Mistakes in Multinational Marketing* (Homewood, IL: Dow Jones-Irwin, 1983).

59. D. Pulatie, a section of "How Do You Ensure Success of Managers Going Abroad?" *Training and Development Journal* (December 1985), pp. 22–23.

60. Cornelius Grove, "Easing Overseas Workers Into the U.S. Business Environment," *HR Focus*, 76, no. 10 (October 1999), p. 9.

61. See Weber, Ames, and Blais, "'How Do I Choose Thee? Let Me Count the Ways': A Textual Analysis of Similarities and Differences in Modes of Decision-Making in China and the United States," op cit., p. 115.

62. T. Kruse, a section of "How Do You Ensure Success of Managers Going Abroad?" *Training and Development Journal* (December 1985), p. 23.

63. N. Adam, B. Awaerbuch, J. Slonin, P. Wegner, and Y. Yesha, "Globalizing Business, Education, Culture Through the Internet," *Communications of the ACM*, 40, no. 2 (February 1997), pp. 115–121.

64. B. C. Y. Tan, K. K. Wei, R. T. Watson, and R. M. Walczuch, "Reducing Status Effects With Computer-Mediated Communication: Evidence From Two Distinct National Cultures," *Journal of Management Information Systems*, 15, no. 1 (Summer 1998), pp. 119–141.

12

CROSS-CULTURAL LEADERSHIP
AND MOTIVATION

Not clearly understanding the way people work and the attitudes they have towards work can cause real difficulties, as explained by [Michael] Howlin [a barrister with Dickson Minto in Edinburgh]: "For example, in a highly unionized country such as Italy, even when a company is acting fairly, the workforce may be suspicious because there is a tradition of conflict." However, "there are no real differences in work aspirations between nationalities, more differences in the way such aspirations are expressed," explained Rosemary Neale, managing consultant with Warwick Weston. . . . " For instance, British and American workers felt that to do well, they had to work longer hours and stay late to show commitment, whereas Scandinavians believed that working beyond your allotted hours just demonstrated that you were not doing your job right."[1]

Learning Objectives of the Chapter

Leadership is the act of one person guiding another or others toward the attainment of an objective, and motivation is the act of the leader providing the incentives necessary to induce the follower or followers to attain the objective. Leadership and motivation are therefore interrelated and interdependent. However, the leadership style and the types of inducements to which individuals respond vary from one culture to another. Thus, the managerial behavior that works well in one culture will not necessarily work well in another. For example, culturally, the French and the Swedish tend not to respond to the same leadership style. Americans and Japanese tend to be driven by somewhat different motivations. Therefore, managers of multinational corporations are likely to be ineffective if they attempt to rashly transfer the leadership style and inducements that work in their home country to the management of subsidiaries in other countries. This means that along with having to adapt their business, negotiation, and communication approaches to different cultures, cross-cultural managers must adapt their leadership style and motivation inducements to different cultures as well. After studying this chapter, you should be able to do the following:

1. Discuss how culture affects leadership style

2. Point out that American-based leadership theories do not have a global application

3. Describe the traits, abilities, and behaviors leaders require in varying international strategic situations

4. Discuss how culture affects motivation

5. Point out that American-based motivation theories do not have a global application

6. Discuss how work goals vary across cultures

Cross-Cultural Leadership

There are some universal leadership similarities. For example, managers throughout the globe tend to want to be more proactive and to get work done by applying less authority, and those with greater rates of career advancement view themselves as possessing greater effective intelligence.[2] However, in most cases, national boundaries make a substantial difference in managers' goals, inclination for taking risks, pragmatism, interpersonal skills, and leadership style.[3] This is because, overall, the environments that affect leader-subordinate relations vary across countries and cultures.[4] What is valued in one society in terms of leadership behavior may not be valued as much in another society. For example, the ambitious behavior of American managers is valued less by the British than it is by the Americans.[5] And in the United States, it is quite common for a leader/manager with good technical abilities to be younger than his or her subordinates, but in Africa this would not work well. There, a person younger than his or her subordinates would feel highly uncomfortable supervising them—even if he or she possessed superior technical abilities.[6]

Therefore, to be effective, cross-cultural managers are often required to assume different leadership styles, depending on the culture with which they are interacting. (For illustration purposes, read the case of Glaxo in Practical Perspective 12.1.) It should be noted, however, that, as pointed out in Chapter 11, cross-cultural managers may sometimes find themselves confronted with situations in which other factors are more important determinants of the appropriate leadership style than cultural factors. For example, a manager confronted with the need to make a decision very quickly may not have the time to involve employees who culturally, such as in Denmark, want to be involved in the decision-making process.

American-Based Management Theories

Popular American-based leadership theories include Douglas McGregor's Theory X versus Theory Y manager and Rensis Likert's System 4 management.[7] Fundamentally, these theories advance the notion that participative leadership behavior is more

PRACTICAL PERSPECTIVE 12-1

Leaders Require Cultural Sensitivity

Global corporations are those that consider all nations as sources of managerial, leadership, and technical resources. Glaxo, a pharmaceutical corporation headquartered in London, has intentionally spread its operations throughout the globe in pursuit of cultural diversity and human resource talent. It has research centers in the United States, Italy, Japan, and France. Cross-country partnership means that open-minded leaders must coordinate activities in Glaxo plants. An authoritarian style or a "best-way" technique is not suited to Glaxo's approach to cultural diversity. Glaxo's workforce, managers, and orientation are built on the premise that cultural values must be respected and can be used to the advantage of the enterprise.

SOURCE: Adapted from Paul Girolami, "Why Glaxo Seeks Cultural Diversity," *World Link* (September–October 1990), pp. 108–109.

effective than authoritarian leadership behavior. As pointed out in Chapter 11, this may be true more in small power distance cultures, such as Israel and Denmark, than in large power distance cultures, such as France, Mexico, Spain, and Turkey, where employees tend to expect authoritative leadership.

Relationship-Oriented and Task-Oriented Leadership

In leader-subordinate relationships, some leaders are, by nature, relationship oriented and some, task oriented. *Relationship-oriented leaders* place much more emphasis on maintaining a good relationship with their subordinates than they do on the performance of tasks. *Task-oriented leaders* place more importance on the performance of tasks than they do on maintaining a good relationship with their subordinates.[8] Robert R. Blake and Jane S. Mouton surveyed 2,500 managers from the United States, South Africa, Canada, Australia, the Middle East, and South America, who were participating in Managerial Grid seminars. Most agreed that the ideal leadership style was an integration of the relationship and task orientations, but when these managers described their actual behavior on the job, the practice was more task oriented than relationship oriented.[9]

However, culture has an impact in this respect as well.[10] For instance, Indian leaders have been found to emphasize task orientation.[11] A strong task orientation is also generally found in leaders in North America and in most Western European countries, and a strong relationship orientation is generally found in leaders in African, Arab, and Latin American countries.[12] Using the Least Preferred Coworker (LPC) questionnaire, it was found that high-performing managers in the Philippines had a low score (task oriented), while their counterparts in Hong Kong had a high score (relationship oriented).[13] In a study of American, Indian, and Japanese managers, the Japanese managers indicated that they received more social support from their superiors than did the American and Indian managers, and for Americans and Indians, relatives were more important providers of social support.[14] The Chinese, as Practical Perspective 12.2 indicates, also prefer relationship-oriented leadership. And in Africa, employees prefer a manager who is highly visible, approachable, and genuinely concerned with their welfare.[15]

PRACTICAL PERSPECTIVE 12-2

Managers in the People's Republic of China

Ignoring me (James A. Wall Jr., University of Missouri) as well as her customers, the young salesclerk slowly leafed through her paperback. This I had heard was the best-run clothing store in Nanjing, and I was waiting to talk with its manager. "He's not here," said the translator. "He's on a buying trip, so we'll have to come back later." As we left, I asked the salesclerk, "Would you be reading that book if your manager were here?" "Of course," she snapped. "He's not a cold machine. He's progressive and lets me enjoy my work. He has a reformed management style." I had just been given my first lesson in contemporary Chinese management. . . .

"Dictatorship of the proletariat" dovetails quite easily with ancient Chinese values. In the feudal system, the rulers, landowners, and businessmen treated their subordinates as a large family. The superiors expected obedience, loyalty, and labor from the subordinates. In return, the superiors provided food, care, and protection. Chinese society still views firms from this feudal perspective. The firm is expected to provide for the families of the workers, and managers are expected to attend to the workers' personal problems. Reared under these traditional values and 40 years of socialism, Chinese managers willingly accept their paternal roles. . . .

Chinese managers, it seems, are squeezed into power positions and at the same time instructed by their government to use scientific management, in which pay is tied to productivity. The problem, however, is that the discretionary pay (bonus) of about $5 a month (in 1990) was not large enough to serve as an incentive. As they recognized that they had no effective pay system, the Chinese managers, like their counterparts in the United States, built and relied on other forms of power. And they did so quite pragmatically.

A seemingly preferred method for building power is to loosen the rules; in street jargon, managers "cut workers some slack." Specifically, managers allow cooperative workers to be tardy, take days off, sleep on the job, play cards, or earn extra income using plant tools. . . . In return for their laxness, managers expect to glean workers "on" (obligation), so that they will perform when production is necessary and give moderate attention to quality. In Western terminology, we can say that the Chinese managers develop idiosyncrasy credits with each worker and then call these in as they need loyalty, hard work, and high performance. Managers labor diligently to establish and maintain a strong, warm relationship (i.e., referent power) with each worker. Since the leader traditionally is viewed as a patriarchal figure, this relationship is highly valued by the subordinates. . . . The importance of the leader-subordinate relationship cannot be overly emphasized. It enables leaders to gain worker conformity, and it proves to be an important source of worker satisfaction. . . .

Reform, even though it breaks sharply from tradition, is heartily embraced by managers. Every manager emphasizes that he or she practices a "reformed" leadership style. In practice, though, most pick and choose from the reform package. . . . Many managers, workers complain, lead as they wish and then label their approaches "reformed" management. My interviews with managers in the Nanjing and Shanghai areas strongly validated this assertion. Many were autocratic, expecting subordinates to work hard without complaining. Some held that workers should work for and appreciate their "elementary" pay because it provided them with rice (i.e., life). And others admitted eschewing risk—"No achievement but no failure"—and following the rules. In all these cases, the managers referred to their styles as "reformed."

Bonuses, while used and praised by most managers, were administered effectively by a small percentage. One set of managers pretended to reward productive employees with differential bonuses. Actually, they spread the bonuses around arbitrarily and parroted the reform propaganda. Some only preached bonuses because they did not care to devote the time and resources to monitoring individual production levels. And others eschewed bonuses because they did not want the reform system to work.

SOURCE: Adapted from James A. Wall Jr., "Managers in the People's Republic of China," *Academy of Management Executive*, 4, no. 2 (1990), pp. 19–32. Used with permission from the Academy of Management. All rights reserved. Permission conveyed through Copyright Clearance Center, Inc.

Initiating Structure and Consideration

Leadership behavior, similar to the task and relationship orientations, consists of *initiating structure*, which refers to the leader's efforts in organizing and getting things done, and *consideration*, which relates to the extent of trust, friendship, respect, and warmth that a leader extends to subordinates.[16] It was once believed in the United States that leaders applying consideration behavior were more effective than those applying structure. However, this leadership behavior, too, is affected by culture. For example, it has been found that consideration behavior applied by leaders in a mixed cultural setting in New Zealand did not contribute to managers' effectiveness.[17] A 12-nation study revealed that leaders tend to see the need for consideration behavior more at the lower levels than at the upper levels of management—except for the French and Latin Americans, who regarded being considerate as relatively unimportant at all levels of management. Germans and Austrians viewed consideration as important at all levels. Consideration was highlighted by fast-rising but not by slow-rising managers in Italy, Spain, Portugal, and the United States, and it was deemphasized by managers with accelerated careers in Belgium, Scandinavia, France, Latin America, and India.[18] And in line with consideration, *respect-oriented leadership behavior*, which is characterized by avoiding confrontation, displaying patience, listening to others, and avoiding losing face, is prevalent in China, Japan, Korea, Singapore, and Turkey.[19]

Japanese PM Theory of Leadership

American managers' authoritative leadership approach is poorly suited to Japan's group-controlled style. Building on the American idea of task and relationship leadership, during the past few decades, the Japanese have developed their own theory, called the PM theory of leadership. P stands for performance and M for maintenance. Fundamentally, in the Japanese PM leadership theory, the P refers to leadership oriented toward forming and attaining group goals, and the M refers to leadership oriented toward preserving group social stability.[20] Therefore, as in the case of the American task and relationship leadership style, PM is concerned with both output and people.

However, a fundamental difference between Japan's PM leadership theory and the American task and relationship leadership theory is that the Japanese emphasize groups and Americans emphasize individuals. Another fundamental difference is that, in practice, Americans tend to emphasize the task more than the relationship aspects of leadership, while the Japanese emphasize P and M equally. (Table 12.1 shows a comparison between some American and Japanese management styles.)

Cross-Cultural Leadership Traits, Abilities, and Behavior

Table 1.10 in Chapter 1 and Table 8.1 in Chapter 8 present the characteristics of effective cross-cultural, cross-national managers. Along with those characteristics, cross-cultural leaders also require certain other traits, abilities, and behaviors, as well as the ability to apply different traits, abilities, and behaviors to different leadership situations.[21]

Innovator, Implementer, and Pacifier Leadership

Different situations require a manager with particular leadership characteristics. Three types of leaders, the innovator, the implementer, and the pacifier, require different

TABLE 12.1	A Comparison of American and Japanese Managers	
The American Manager	**The Japanese Manager**	
Is a decision maker	Is a social facilitator	
Heads a group	Is a member of a group	
Is directive	Is paternalistic	
Often has conflicting values	Has harmonious values	
His or her individualism sometimes obstructs cooperation	Facilitates cooperation	
Is confrontational	Avoids confrontation	
Top-down communication	Top-down, bottom-up communication	
His or her authority and responsibility are specified and limited	His or her authority and responsibility limits are not specified	
Is held responsible for performance	Groups are held responsible for performance	
Is held responsible for subordinates' poor decisions	Accepts symbolic responsibility when things go wrong	
Top managers initiate problem statements and propose solutions	Top managers initiate problem statements, and those affected are involved in identifying solutions	
Makes the final decision	Codifies the final decision	
Needs to show immediate results because he or she is reviewed on a short-term basis	The longer-term review period enables him or her to concentrate on long-term plans	

SOURCE: Adapted from Sang M. Lee and George Schwendiman, *Japanese Management: Cultural and Environmental Considerations* (New York: Praeger Publishers, 1982); Sang M. Lee and George Schwendiman, *Management by Japanese System* (New York: Praeger Publishers, 1982).

characteristics (described in Table 12.2). Each type works best in specific situations. Figure 12.1 depicts three problem phases (situations) organizations normally encounter and the appropriate type of leader for each.[22]

As Figure 12.1 indicates, an organization needing an infusion of new ideas (often an organization undergoing a crisis) requires a leader with the characteristics of the innovator. This is because under crisis conditions, subordinates generally prefer a forceful leader who can solve the problem—leadership behavior characteristic of the innovator. The innovator identifies new ideas and visions and "sells" them to the institution. Some aspects of the leadership behavior of Jack Welch, General Electric's former CEO, provide a good illustration of an innovator leader. He recognized the problems created by global competition and redirected GE into broadcasting, investment banking, high-tech manufacturing, and other high-risk ventures. Lee Iacocca's behavior at Chrysler is another example of innovator leadership. Hired by Chrysler when it was confronted with an extreme financial crisis, he came up with the radical idea of getting the U.S. Congress and the United Auto Workers to aid him in saving the company. He persuaded the U.S. government to guarantee bank loans, put the president of the union on Chrysler's board, and received major concessions from the union.

TABLE 12.2	The Traits, Abilities, and Behavior of Three Types of Leaders
The innovator	Likes to compete and win
	Keeps on trying to succeed
	Assumes responsibility for success and failures
	Takes moderate as opposed to high risk (is bold)
	Likes to commit unit to a major course of action
	Is actively searching for new ideas to improve unit
	Seeks organizational growth
	Is motivated by the need to achieve, to be creative
	Centralizes decision making (is in control)
	Wants to stand out from the rest of the group (dares to behave differently)
	Believes the environment can be controlled and manipulated (can "sell" his or her ideas)
	Is long-range oriented (foresees positive results in the distant future)
The implementer	Desires to exercise power, to control and influence situations
	Is actively assertive
	Is able to get things done through others
	Has the ability to assume responsibility for decision making
	Is systematic in analysis and in problem solving
	Is able to integrate decisions and analysis
	Is both long-range and short-range oriented (attends to distant needs as well as to today's)
The pacifier	Has a positive attitude toward authority figures
	Is willing to carry out administrative functions (willing to do the "paperwork")
	Is interested in friendly relationships
	Likes to communicate and collaborate with employees (is socially oriented)
	Likes to improve the social atmosphere in the unit
	Makes decisions that keep everyone moderately happy
	Makes decisions based on feedback from what others have decided
	Allows employees to make many of the unit's decisions (delegates decision making)
	Accepts that decisions in the unit are not in harmony (individuals make conflicting decisions)
	Seeks to satisfy influential individuals
	Believes the environment cannot be controlled and manipulated (cannot "sell" ideas)
	Makes short-range decisions (deals only with day-to-day problems)

SOURCE: Carl A. Rodrigues, "Identifying the Right Leader for the Right Situation," *Personnel* (September 1988), p. 46.

The new ideas introduced by the innovator often create an ambiguous atmosphere in the organization. When individuals cannot tolerate ambiguous or unclear assignments, they generally prefer to have a leader who provides systematic structure to create a stable working environment within the organization. Thus, after the new vision has been initiated, the institution needs a leader who can systematically put into

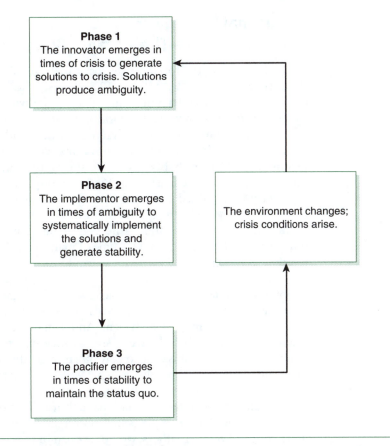

Figure 12.1 Contingency Leadership Cycle

SOURCE: Carl A. Rodrigues, "Identifying the Right Leader for the Right Situation," *Personnel* (September 1988), p. 44.

operation the desired changes, someone whose personality is similar to the implementer's. Some aspects of the behavior of Alfred Sloan Jr. serve as an example of implementer leadership. He generated structure in General Motors after William C. Durant conceived the company. Sloan was a talented operations executive who also possessed competency in financial and organizational matters. He studied the situation at GM and prepared the "Organizational Study," a program proposing a new organizational and business philosophy for GM.[23]

When the organization has attained a certain degree of stability and daily operations are running smoothly, members usually feel more competent and believe that they can perform the task at hand. The higher the degree of perceived ability related to task demands, the less willing subordinates will be to accept strong direction and oversight. In this situation, an organization needs a pacifier-oriented leader. In some respects, the leadership of Reginald H. Jones, Jack Welch's predecessor at General Electric, illustrates pacifier behavior. Prior to the placement of Welch in the top position, Jones emphasized the role of corporate statesman.[24] Figure 12.1 shows that when a crisis arises again, the leadership cycle is repeated.

Managerial Strategy and Application of the Three Leader Types

Table 12.3 depicts the foreign subsidiary managerial strategy and application of the three types of leaders. As Table 12.3 shows, when a company needs to send an expatriate abroad to start a new subsidiary, an individual with the innovator's creative characteristics probably would work best. But once the innovator has conceived the idea for establishing the subsidiary, an individual with the implementer's capabilities to systematically implement the innovator's ideas and to train locals for managerial positions would probably work best. (Many innovators do not possess the implementer's characteristics.) Once the implementer has fully developed the subsidiary and trained the local managers, a pacifier-oriented leader is needed to transfer managerial duties to the locals. Subsequently, a manager with the characteristics of the pacifier is needed at the firm's headquarters to monitor the foreign subsidiary's activities. This type of manager is needed because he or she will not interfere as much in local activities as would the innovator and the implementer, who are hands-on managers.

Some individuals possess the characteristics of both the innovator and the implementer. Thus, instead of sending two individuals, one who has been properly trained to act both ways would be the most cost-efficient. And some individuals actually possess the traits, abilities, and behaviors of all three types—as three-dimensional leaders, they know when it is time to create, when it is time to rally others to get the creation implemented, and when to stay out of the way. Three-dimensional leaders would therefore be ideal. They, however, are hard to find—but can be developed.[25]

It should also be noted that national culture also has an impact on the appropriate leadership style. For example, small power distance individuals, because they want more control over their affairs, would be open to the relatively "hands-off" managerial approach of the pacifier type. On the other hand, large power distance individuals are likely to appreciate the strong "hands-on" managerial approach of the implementer type. And in comparison with weak uncertainty avoidance people, strong uncertainty avoidance people, since they have relatively low tolerance for ambiguity, probably would prefer the structure the implementer provides and probably would be closed to the innovator's creative thinking.[26] In a broader sense, the United States appears to develop more managers with entrepreneurial skills than does Japan—which Japan, in light of its (1990s) financial crisis, views as a problem. (Refer to Practical Perspective 12.3.) Practical Perspective 12.4 attempts to explain this phenomenon.

Cross-Cultural Motivation

In discussing the topic of motivation, some individuals may argue that there are no major differences in what motivates people across countries, that people everywhere, in general, are the same and respond to the same stimuli. This may be true in some respects but not in all. Certainly, just about all individuals are driven by such basic needs as food, water, air, and shelter. However, people are also driven by psychological needs, such as self-esteem and social status. Psychological drives tend to be culture-specific; the stimuli to which an individual responds differ across cultures. For example, people in individualistic cultures, such as the United States, may work toward

TABLE 12.3 Managerial Strategy and Application of the Three Leader Types

Managerial Strategy	Type of Leader Needed		
	Innovator	Implementer	Pacifier
Expatriate to create a new subsidiary abroad	X		
Expatriate to operationalize the new subsidiary		X	
Expatriate to train locals for managerial positions		X	
Expatriate to transfer autonomy to local managers			X
Home-office manager to monitor subsidiary activities			X
Expatriate/local manager to solve crisis in subsidiary	X		
Expatriate/local manager to operationalize solution		X	
Local manager to carry out activities under conditions of stability			X

PRACTICAL PERSPECTIVE 12-3

Learning to Go Against Japan's Corporate Grain

A Japanese executive was describing his company's efforts to spin off a smaller unit when he suddenly leaned forward and asked that his name not be used.

In a low voice, he said with a touch of embarrassment, "If this happens, we will have an image as an innovator." Horrors!

This desire to innovate while not being openly seen as doing so may explain why the Japanese have not quite embraced a concept that has built the United States and contributed to its vitality: entrepreneurship.

They don't even have a good word for it. They have a few expressions, like *kigyo ka* (one who starts a business), but somehow the terms don't quite have the same ringing spirit in a nation not known for a go-it-alone attitude.

So the Japanese have just imported the word *an-torepurenah* whole, along with launching rounds of discussions about its spirit.

As the Asian economic crisis continued, it has became painfully obvious there that traditional Japanese values were interfering with the country's attempt to build the kind of entrepreneurial spirit that could lead it out of its seven-year slump.

Japan feared that it would fall behind the United States and Europe, and perhaps even Asian countries like South Korea, unless it could change the dynamics of its economy.

A Fear of Losing Ground

Although Japan may have the second biggest economy in the world, its companies are vast, bureaucratic conglomerates at a time when entrepreneurial, information-age companies are dominant.

In short, they are too much like Mitsui and not enough like Microsoft. Government officials and business executives feared that their country was losing ground in an emerging global economy that would increasingly reward creativity, flexibility, and entrepreneurship, which was a rarity there. While entrepreneurship was not looked down on, it didn't merit much prestige either.

PRACTICAL PERSPECTIVE 12-3 *(Continued)*

"It's not receiving the appropriate attention or respect," said Yoshihiko Miyauchi, a creative iconoclast and the president of Orix Corporation, a leasing company. "People do not aim to become like Bill Gates."

Japan was grappling with ways to inspire entrepreneurship and innovation in a society that looked askance at those who ventured out alone. The new campaign to create individuals in the most communitarian of societies—and nurture risk takers in a nation exceedingly risk averse—faced huge obstacles. . . .

Upstarts

. . . The need was for software engineers, and Japan lagged behind.

Besides creativity, entrepreneurship also needed a system of venture capital to finance companies so that they could expand.

Japan had almost no true venture capital funds or a system of venture capital. Banks were loath to lend to upstarts, high taxes discouraged success, and stock market listings were extremely difficult to secure.

The government had made a start, particularly in setting up programs to encourage new business with special loans.

On a broader level, Japan was trying to reeducate its people, starting with kindergartners in the hope of cultivating greater creativity and independent thinking . . . entrepreneurship had become a *buzzword* among board directors, the salaried class, government officials, and young students.

Lectures, seminars, and books abounded, all offering step-by-step guidance on how to become an entrepreneur.

The stature of the handful of new entrepreneurs, like Masayoshi Son, who began distributing software and then bought high-technology companies in Japan and in the United States, had been rising within the business community.

But, ultimately, some scholars said, a fundamental shift was needed since Japan's capitalism differs from that of the United States and tends to be less friendly to small start-ups.

"For entrepreneurship to work, you have to have a free market, one where the strong win and the weak lose," said Daizaburo Hashizume, a sociologist at Tokyo Institute of Technology.

"With this kind of market, old companies disappear and new companies rise. But there is no such free market in Japan."

SOURCE: Adapted from Sheryl WuDunn, "Learning to go Against Japan's Corporate Grain," *The New York Times* (Sunday, March 8, 1998) p. wk 3. Copyright © 1998 by The New York Times Company. Reprinted by permission.

PRACTICAL PERSPECTIVE 12-4

In Japan, Nice Guys (and Girls) Finish Together

My intention, honest, was not to scar these Japanese kids for life. I just wanted to give them a fun game to play.

It was the fifth birthday party last year for my son Gregory, and he had invited all his Japanese friends over from the Tokyo kindergarten that he attended. My wife and I explained the rules of musical chairs, and we started the music.

It was not so awful for the Japanese boys. They managed to fight for seats, albeit a bit lamely. But the girls were at sea.

The first time I stopped the music, Gregory's five-year-old girlfriend, Chitose-chan, was next to him, right in front of a chair. But she stood politely and waited for him to be seated first.

So Gregory scrambled into her seat, and Chitose-chan beamed proudly at her own good manners. Then I walked over and told her that she had just lost the game and would have to sit out. She gazed up at me, luminous eyes full of shocked disbelief, looking like Bambi might after a discussion of venison burgers.

"You mean I lose because I'm polite?"

Chitose-chan's eyes asked, "You mean the point of the game is to be rude?"

Well, now that I think of it, I guess that is the point. American kids are taught to be winners, to seize their opportunities and maybe the next kid's as well. Japanese children are taught to be good citizens, to be team players, to obey rules, to be content to be a mosaic tile in some larger design.

One can have an intelligent debate about which approach is better. The Japanese emphasis on consideration and teamwork perhaps explains why Japan has few armed robbers but also so few entrepreneurs. The American emphasis on winning may help explain why the United States consistently racks up Olympic gold medals but also why its hockey players trashed their rooms in Nagano.

The civility that still lingers in Japan is the most charming and delightful aspect of life here today. Taxi drivers wear white gloves, take pride in the cleanliness of their vehicles, and sometimes give a discount if they mistakenly take a long route. When they are sick, Japanese wear surgical face masks so they will not infect others. The Japanese language has almost no curses, and high school baseball teams bow to each other at the beginning of each game.

One can go years here without hearing a voice raised in anger, for when Japanese are furious they sometimes show it by becoming incredibly formal and polite. Compared with New York, it's rather quaint.

The conundrum is that Japan is perhaps too civilized for the 1990s. To revive its economy, mired in a seven-year slump, the country now needs an infusion of economic ruthlessness, a dose of the law of the jungle. Japan desperately needs to restructure itself, which is to say that it needs to create losers—companies need to lay off excess workers, Mom-and-Pop rice shops need to be replaced by more efficient supermarkets, and failing banks need to go bankrupt.

But Japan is deeply uncomfortable with the idea of failures or losers. The social and economic basis of modern Japan is egalitarianism, and that does not leave much room for either winners or losers. In Japan, winning isn't everything and it isn't the only thing; in elementary schools it isn't even a thing at all. . . .

Of course, competition is inevitable in any society, and in Japan, it is introduced in junior high schools, when children must compete intensely to pass high school and college entrance examinations. But the emphasis remains on *wa* or harmony, on being one with the group.

Ask a traditional Japanese housewife what she wants for her child, and you will sometimes hear an answer like "I just want my kid to grow up so as not to be a nuisance to other people." Hmmm. Not a dream often heard in America. . . .

The emphasis on *wa* perhaps arises because 125 million Japanese, almost half the U.S. population, are squeezed into an area the size of California. How else could they survive but with a passion for protocol and a web of picayune rules dictating consideration for others? If 125 million Americans were jammed into such a small space, we might have torn each other to shreds by now.

Building teamwork in Japan starts from birth. When our child, Caroline, was born in Tokyo last fall, the hospital explained that the mothers were to nurse their babies all together in the same room at particular meal times. So on her first day of life, Caroline was effectively told to discipline her appetites to adjust to a larger scheme with others. . . .

So now, Japan is trying to become nastier. Workers are being pushed out of their jobs, occasionally even laid off. Employees are no longer being automatically promoted by seniority. Pay differentials are widening. Companies are becoming more concerned with efficiency and share prices, less concerned with employee welfare.

SOURCE: Adapted from Nicholas D. Kristof, "In Japan Nice Guys (and Girls) Finish Together," *The New York Times* (April 12, 1998) p. 7. Copyright © 1998 by The New York Times Company. Reprinted by permission.

self-actualization as an end, while people in collectivistic cultures, such as China, may work toward self-actualization as a means to a higher end—to better serve society/the group.

Many of the popular motivation theories were developed by Western scholars using Western subjects and concepts. The ensuing sections discuss some of these theories in a cross-cultural context.

A Comparison of Western and Southeast Asian Motivation Theories

More than three decades ago, Douglas McGregor proposed that managers adhere to one of two opposing theories about people: Theory X and Theory Y.[27]

Theory X and Theory Y

Theory X posits that the average human being has an inherent dislike of work and will avoid it if he or she can. Because of this human characteristic of dislike of work, people must be coerced, controlled, directed, or threatened with punishment to get them to put forth adequate effort toward the achievement of organizational objectives. The average human being prefers to be directed, wishes to avoid responsibility, has relatively little ambition, and wants security above all.

Theory Y puts forth that the expenditure of physical and mental effort in work is as natural as play or rest. External control and the threat of punishment are not the only means of bringing about effort toward organizational objectives. People will exercise self-direction and self-control in the service of objectives to which they are committed. Commitment to objectives is a function of the rewards associated with their achievement. The average human being learns, under proper conditions, not only to accept but also to seek responsibility. The capacity to exercise a relatively high degree of imagination, ingenuity, and creativity in the solution of organizational problems is widely, not narrowly, distributed in the population; under the conditions of modern industrial life, however, the intellectual potential of average human beings is only partially utilized.

Several years ago, Geert Hofstede, the European researcher, analyzed these two theories in the context of Southeast Asian culture. He believed that McGregor's assumptions, which are common to both theories, stem from the United States, an individualistic and masculine society. Hofstede outlined the assumptions on which McGregor's theories rest as follows:[28]

- Work is good for people. It is God's will that people should work.
- People's potentialities should be maximally used. It is God's will that you and I should maximally use our potentialities.
- There are "organizational objectives" that exist separately from people.
- People in organizations behave as unattached individuals.

Theory T and Theory T+

Hofstede proposed that American assumptions do not apply in the collectivist (low individualism), large power distance Southeast Asian cultures. He replaced them with Southeast Asian assumptions.[29]

Southeast Asian assumptions are as follows:

- Work is a necessity but not a goal in itself.
- People should find their rightful place, in peace and harmony with their environment.
- Absolute objectives exist only with God. In the world, persons in positions of authority represent God, so their objectives should be followed.
- People behave as members of a family and/or group. Those who do not are rejected by society.

Hofstede proposed that since these assumptions are culturally determined, McGregor's *Theory X* and *Theory Y* distinction becomes irrelevant in Southeast Asia. He developed a Southeast Asian distinction (although he qualifies his distinction in that he is a European and may thus have made cultural mistakes). Theory X and Theory Y are mutually exclusive opposites. Unlike the American distinction, the Southeast Asia distinction that Hofstede proposed, which he named *Theory T* and *Theory T+* (T standing for traditional), is a complementary one—Theory T and Theory T+ fitting harmoniously together. According to Hofstede, Southeast Asian management could be as outlined in Table 12.4.[30] Theory X posits that people dislike work and will avoid it if they can, and Theory T contends that people dislike change and will avoid it if they can. This suggests that both Theory X and Theory T propose that all people would attempt to avoid challenging work. A difference, however, is that Theory T espouses development of people, while Theory X advocates control. Theory T+ indicates that in spite of the wisdom of tradition, the experience of change in life is natural and, similar to Theory X, it is the function of the leader to coerce those who resist change.

People in cultures throughout the world thus behave in dissimilar ways because of the differences in how they view their environment. Their thinking is partly conditioned by national cultural factors, which are passed on from one generation to the next. It would therefore be a critical mistake for an international manager to attempt to apply a set of motivational techniques on a worldwide basis—to reiterate, what works in one culture does not necessarily work in another. Of course, people's thinking does not remain static from generation to generation. As proposed in Chapter 1, the practice aspects of culture do change gradually over time as new technologies are introduced into society. For example, the new economic systems introduced into the former communist nations are changing the ways managers lead and what motivates employees. (For illustration purposes, refer again to Practical Perspective 12.2 and review the case of China presented in Practical Perspective 12.5, as well as the case of Russia in Practical Perspective 12.6.)

Chinese Social Motivation Versus Western Individual Motivation

The Hierarchy of Needs theory developed by Abraham H. Maslow proposes that certain individual needs serve as motivators.[31] Maslow contended that people are first motivated by activities that aim to satisfy their basic needs. Once these needs are reasonably satisfied, they cease to be motivators; and people are then motivated by activities that can satisfy their next level of needs, their safety needs, and when these

TABLE 12.4	Southeast Asian Management
Theory T:	There is an order of inequality in this world in which everyone has his or her rightful place. High and low are protected by this order, which is willed by God.
	Children have to learn to fulfill their duties at the place where they belong by birth. They can improve their place by studying with a good teacher, working with a good patron, and/or marrying a good partner.
	Tradition is a source of wisdom. Therefore, the average human being has an inherent dislike of change and will rightly avoid it if he or she can.
Theory T+:	In spite of the wisdom in traditions, the experience of change in life is natural, as natural as work, play, or rest.
	Commitment to change is a function of the quality of the leaders who lead the change, the rewards associated with the change, and the negative consequences of not changing.
	The capacity to lead people to a new situation is widely, not narrowly, distributed among leaders in the population.
	The learning capacities of the average family are more than sufficient for modernization.

SOURCE: Geert Hofstede, "The Application of McGregor's Theories in Southeast Asia," *Journal of Management Development*, 6, no. 3 (1987), p. 16. Copyright © 1987 MCB University Press. Used with permission. All rights reserved.

PRACTICAL PERSPECTIVE 12-5

Money Works Wonders in China

Attracting workers can be a lot easier than holding on to them. Money is king in contemporary China . . . Stories abound of women from the inner provinces arriving to work long, backbreaking days for a few years and then returning home flush with cash to start businesses or to start up a local gentry. To provide some stability to their workforces, companies are moving to individual contracts. "We want total commitment from our workers," said Mr. Yen of Xian-Janssen (Pharmaceutical Ltd., a Chinese-U.S. joint venture). "They have to sign a pledge. Signing something is very significant here. So once they sign, they are committed."

"Have them sign it before training takes place so you can protect your investment," advised Ralph McIntyre, area director for Asia of Mine Safety Appliances Company in Pittsburgh. Incentives also help restrain potential wanderers and boost performance. "Simple performance-related incentives work best," said Andrew Mok (vice president) of Philips Inc., the Hong Kong subsidiary of a Dutch multinational. "If a unit exceeds its target, the members get extra money. Some of our partners refuse to use incentives, and you can see a marked difference in output." The disinclination to take individual action or responsibility is another trait that can be tackled via incentives. "Anyone who takes a risk is immediately rewarded," says Xian-Janssen's Jerry Norkskog. "I don't care how wrong the risk is."

Of course, even money takes time to move attitudinal mountains. Rich Brecher of the U.S.-China Business Council cites an American company that took over a state-run enterprise. The plant now has one expatriate officer on the floor with hundreds of Chinese workers. The transformation from communism to capitalism is proving slow. "That guy can't do everything," observed Brecher. "The workers have to understand that all decisions don't have be made by the president. But that takes years to teach." All the time and effort will be worth it, however, if China continues shedding communism as an economic philosophy. Companies with well-trained management teams and workforces in place stand to enjoy a great advantage over those who are delaying (entering China) until they can see exactly how the (now deceased) Premier Deng Xiaoping's long march to capitalism pans out.

SOURCE: Excerpted and adapted from John R. Engen, "Getting Your Chinese Workforce Up to Speed," *International Business* (August 1994), p. 44. Reprinted with permission.

PRACTICAL PERSPECTIVE 12-6

Human Resource Management (HRM) in Russia

HRM in Russia in the Communist Era

To understand how to design efficient human resource management systems (HRM) for Russia today, it is important to understand traditional HRM practices in Russia prior to the end of communism. Traditionally, Russian firms have viewed employees as a cost rather than as a resource. In addition, while Russia has had a well-developed and demanding educational system that Russians went through prior to beginning work, relatively little attention was paid to skill development once a Russian was employed in a firm.

The Russian labor market has also historically been inefficient. Artificial constraints (e.g., poor labor mobility due to needing a permit to live in each town) have limited career progression and thereby decreased incentives for people to work hard. Furthermore, salary differentials were very small in Russia during communist times. Even if you could obtain extra money, it had limited value since there were few goods available to purchase. In Russia, it was products and contacts, not money that had the greatest value. All adults were expected to have a job in Russia, and many jobs were created to ensure full employment. Since there was limited focus on the enterprise making money, less attention was given to finding ways to motivate employees to work hard than was the case in the West.

It is also important to note that employment security has been a hallmark of Russian labor policy.

HRM in Russia Today (1999)

When the government was privatizing a firm, a key consideration was often finding a foreign firm that would agree to guarantee job security for at least some of the original employees. Many foreign firms in this situation encountered a problem with the acquired employees not understanding new market conditions. The change in mentality that must occur to facilitate the customer focus needed for success in today's Russia has been difficult to achieve for many firms. HRM is critical for assisting in phasing out the old culture and replacing it with a new one. For many Russians, the concept of HRM is new. One HR manager we interviewed commented that "people are surprised to find out that so much attention is given to personnel management in Western firms.

Many successful foreign companies in Russia today are growing at very rapid rates. This growth increases the HRM difficulties because there is little time to explore different HRM policies. As Dennis M. Krianin, human resource manager at Coca-Cola, explained, "Business in Russia right now is very intensive. Such companies as ours are covering in one year the history that our colleagues in Europe have covered over five years. We are developing incredibly fast."

The high rate of change in Russia is also problematic for firms. As Vera Panova, personnel manager at GPT, explained, "In Russia . . . daily work conditions could be compared to a jungle where you really don't know what is going to fall on your head in the next minute." For firms to survive in this jungle, competent employees are essential. As the HR development director at McDonald's said, "It is not possible to build a successful business without cultivating a base of people who will able to manage the business and take over the operations in the future. One has to think long term."

Being flexible and willing to adapt to the Russian environment has been found to be a key success factor for operating in Russia. Margaret Jones, HR manager at Cadbury, explained that her firm initially set up very strict recruiting policies, requiring two years' work experience in a foreign company and specific education. However, the firm quickly realized that this was too stringent, and thus, Cadbury became more flexible.

Coca-Cola follows a general country-specific policy, and this is the case as it is in any other country in the world. Despite being an international company with an international image, Coca-Cola adjusts its operations to the conditions of the local environment. Coca-Cola has found that a good way to facilitate this local adaptation is to hire predominantly local personnel. Only 5 of Coca-Cola's 660 employees (as of 1999) in Moscow are expatriates. . . . A study of Russian HR practices revealed that having a good fixed salary is important to Russian workers, and companies with

PRACTICAL PERSPECTIVE 12-6 (Continued)

noncompetitive salaries will have difficulty attracting, motivating, and retaining workers. However, the study showed that the optimal compensation package combines bonuses and nonmonetary benefits as well. The study also revealed that most Russians value training and badly need some. As a result, effort should be placed on competence development. The benefits of using training as a tool for motivation and retention were also demonstrated. The study also highlights that while a competitive salary is important in retaining workers, probably the most important factor in retaining key personnel is having them believe that the firm is committed to Russia.

SOURCE: Excerpted and adapted form C. Fey, P. Engstrom, and I. Bjorkman, "Doing Business in Russia: Effective Human Resource Management Practices for Foreign Firms in Russia," Part 1 of 2 and Part 2 of 2, *Organizational Dynamics,* 28, no. 2 (Autumn 1999), pp. 69–80. Reprinted with permission of Elsevier Science.

needs are satisfied, they cease to be motivators. Subsequently, people are motivated by activities that can satisfy the next higher level, their social needs. Once the social needs are reasonably satisfied, individuals are motivated by activities that can satisfy their next level of needs, their esteem needs. And once these are reasonably satisfied, people then become motivated by activities that can satisfy their next level of needs, their self-actualization needs, which according to Maslow is the highest level of the needs hierarchy. Maslow also theorized that when a lower-level need is no longer present, it then again becomes the motivator.

Maslow's theory has not been empirically verified, however. In fact, it has been widely criticized. Terms such as *belonging* and *esteem* are vague. The meaning of *satisfaction* is unclear. For example, after a big meal, an individual would be full, and he or she, according to the theory, would not be motivated by food. However, this is not true in all cases—some individuals may still remain motivated by food because they have a memory and the ability to anticipate the future when hunger will occur again. Also, there is no evidence that satisfaction of one need activates the next higher need, and there is little support for the proposition that the level of satisfaction of a need diminishes its importance as a motivator.[32] In an international context, the hierarchy has been criticized as being based on Maslow's personal choice—American individualistic, middle-class values that put self-actualization and autonomy on top.[33] Furthermore, a study by the cross-cultural management researchers Haire, Ghiselli, and Porter concluded that workers in different cultures tend to have a different hierarchy of needs. For example, managers in the United States and Italy ranked security as being relatively less important than other needs (basic needs were omitted from the study); in India, Spain, and Germany, security ranked as relatively more important.[34] Maslow's individual-based theory thus does not have universal application. The ensuing section demonstrates how the theory has a different application in the Chinese culture.

I-Ching: Beyond Self-Actualization

Professors David V. Gibson and Francis Woomin Wu of the University of Texas at Austin and Fordham University, respectively, have used the *I-Ching* to form what they call the *social interaction paradigm of human cooperative behavior*. The *I-Ching* ("The Book of Change") was written by ancient Chinese philosophers and social leaders between 3000 and 1000 BCE and was interpreted by Confucius (551–479 BCE). (*I-Ching* has also been translated to mean "The Bible of Practicality.") The social interaction paradigm, which is used to explain the inherent cooperative culture behind the economic success of the Pacific Rim economies, extends the hierarchy of needs beyond the self-actualization need.[35] Gibson and Wu state,

> *Maslow's theory of human needs is not comprehensive enough to address the complexity of business and social communication required by increased human interaction and the emerging global economy. It does not provide a paradigm for social interaction in relation to real-world problems of the coming decades. Although Maslow's theory describes "love" as an important motivation, it refers mostly to "self-centered" social needs, or love receiving. "Society-based" social needs for undertaking cooperative tasks for the survival and prosperity of collectives from the level of groups to nations are not mentioned. Although these collectives are important in coordinating individual effort toward mutual benefit, the formation of social entities, such as organizations or communities, cannot be fully explained in terms of individual self-actualization or love and belongingness needs. . . . Instead, individual effort that is directed toward developing larger cooperative entities may result in the satisfaction of others' needs rather than just the needs of oneself. Collectives may actually restrain the individual from actualizing his or her own talent and power in order to facilitate intra- and interorganizational cooperation. When individuals act in ways that they perceive as rational in terms of pursuing their own goals, they may actually be disadvantaging themselves and others at the collective level. . . . Striving for high social needs without regard for immediate personal gain is symbiotic with the I-Ching philosophy, which emphasizes that as social beings, people must deal with social responsibilities throughout their lives. The greatest social welfare is achieved through the joint efforts of individuals creating better social and physical environments in which others can actualize their capacities. Greater value is placed on the ability to lead individuals and groups to cooperative output than on the actualization of one's own individual talent.*[36]

To help illustrate the above quotation, assume that a U.S. corporation's headquarters executive who monitors the activities of the firm's subsidiary in Japan notices that a young Japanese employee has strong capabilities and is highly productive. To reward the employee, the executive decides to promote him or her to a managerial position in charge of the group. This would be a mistake because it would demoralize both the capable employee and the group; it would disturb the group's *wa* (discussed in Chapter 10). The disruption of the group's harmony would result from the violation of the accepted Japanese practice of promoting elders and from the violation of the Japanese practice of rendering rewards to groups, not to an individual member of the group—even if his or her performance is outstanding. And individual members of the group do not want to be singled out for exceptional performance. In Japan, individuals adhere to the notion that "the nail that sticks out will be hammered down." (The corresponding Chinese saying is "The bigger trees catch the most wind.") This means that a group member who receives individual recognition will be ostracized and emotionally punished by the group.

The Chinese symbol of the *dragon*, which depicts the Eastern thought that the ultimate aim of the individual is to contribute to the larger collective, derives from the *I-Ching*.[37] The *dragon* symbolizes both individual freedom (it can fly) and the creation of shared social benefits (its flying through the clouds causes rain, which benefits all). Thus, as symbolized by the dragon, "individual self-actualization is not an end in itself, but merely a preparation for the more noble goal of contributing to the betterment of society."[38] Therefore, the social interaction paradigm of human cooperative behavior suggests that personal freedom is a necessary step toward social cooperation. New York City's current (2007) mayor Bloomberg is a multibillionaire who is working for the city for free. Does he fit this paradigm?

Gibson and Wu's addition of the stages of the social interaction paradigm of human cooperative behavior to Maslow's theory of human needs is depicted in Figure 12.2. The following discussion describes the additional stages.[39]

Stage 6: Social Awareness

The stage of social awareness, understanding human/social needs outside one's own individual-based ends, furnishes a base for interorganization cooperative behavior and for molding effective strategies to merge human endeavors to solve difficult problems. Confucian philosophy posits that the most effective leaders often possess humble origins, where they were exposed to basic human needs. Such origins equip leaders with the ability to recognize the needs of others.

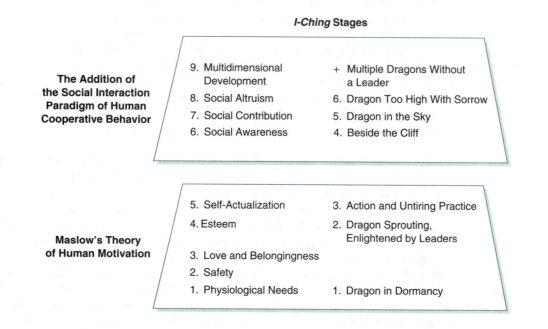

Figure 12.2   The Social Interaction Paradigm of Human Cooperation Behavior: An *I-Ching*–Based Expansion of Maslow's Individual Need Hierarchy

SOURCE: David V. Gibson and Francis Woomin Wu, "The Social Interaction Paradigm of Human Cooperative Behavior: Societal Motivation Beyond Maslow's Need Hierarchy," in *Proceedings of the Fourth International Conference on Comparative Management* (Kaohsiung, Taiwan: National Sun Yat-sen University, 1991). Reprinted with permission from Professor David V. Gibson. All rights reserved.

Stage 7: Social Contribution

Social contribution refers to the mixture of striving to fulfill other people's needs while simultaneously pursuing one's own personal growth and social power. At this stage, an individual searches for opportunities that benefit the collective. He or she looks for "win-win" situations.

Stage 8: Social Altruism

At this stage, an individual's major concern is the functioning of society. He or she acts to generate vital long-term benefits for others without wanting or needing to acquire rewards for himself or herself. Social altruism must be voluntary, and the individual must expect little overt appreciation because the beneficiaries are usually not aware of, or do not appreciate, the long-term benefits of his or her efforts. Social altruism requires the support of a wide range of people with influence. This support is generated in Stage 7, where the individual builds networks of organization and community ties, as well as a cooperative spirit.

Stage 9: Multidimensional Development

A key facet of multidimensional development is "stepping aside"—that is, leaving an important position and distributing political and economic power across public and private sectors. One downplays one's social power by helping others develop their leadership abilities and networks, so that many individuals, besides the dominant few, will have strong intra- and interorganizational connections and social power. This philosophy magnifies the effectiveness of cooperative action through intensified participation, and it stimulates the sharing of rewards. Consequently, a society's benefits are enhanced because more people contribute to the common good, and greater stability is attained because power and rewards are diffused and individuals network across multiple leaders and groups.

Earlier, it was suggested that the contributions of New York City's Mayor Bloomberg might fit the *I-Ching* framework, but the above suggests that he might have not yet reached Stage 9; however, it does suggest that the globally benevolent activities currently (2007) being carried out by the former U.S. president Jimmy Carter, and perhaps the former U.S. president Bill Clinton, as well as by some corporate leaders such as Bill Gates might fit Stage 9 activities. While in China, this author met some highly accomplished elder Chinese citizens who fit Stage 9.

As shown in Figure 12.2, *I-Ching* articulates the stages of leadership development by using the dragon as a metaphor:

1. *Dormant:* Dragon in dormancy

2. *Growth:* Dragon sprouting, enlightened by leaders

3. *Actualization:* Action and untiring practice

4. *Take-off:* Beside the cliff

5. *Service delivering:* Dragon in the sky

6. *Leading:* Dragon too high with sorrow, with a compensation strategy of multiple dragons capable of governing themselves

The I-Ching's dormant stage compares with the physiological and psychlogical stages of Maslow's theory; the *growth stage* compares with Maslow's love and esteem stages; and the *actualization stage* compares with Maslow's self-actualization stage. As indicated in Figure 12.2, the *I-Ching's* Stages 4, 5, and 6 are not captured by Maslow's theory.[40]

Gibson and Wu also develop their theory from the perspective of *Buddhism*. They divide Buddhism into two sects: *Hinayana*, which stresses the importance of self-restraint, and *Mahayana*, which stresses selfless devotion to society. Basically, *Hinayana* compares with self-actualization in Maslow's theory in the sense that it underscores the energy it takes to contain one's mind and to exercise one's full physical and mental strength. *Mahayana* compares with the *I-Ching's* later stages in the sense that it requires great initiative and compassion for others.[41]

The leadership motivation of the *I-Ching* contrasts with Western leadership motivation. Western leaders tend to be motivated by *the need for power*, while Asian leaders tend to be motivated more by a need resembling the Western *need for affiliation*.[42] The Asian leaders' "sorrow" (Stage 6) derives from their having to make decisions that affect others—Western leaders generally do not experience such "sorrow." In other words, leaders motivated by the philosophy of the *I-Ching* lack the arrogance typically demonstrated by Western leaders. Of course, there are exceptions in all cultures—not all Asian leaders adhere to the *I-Ching* philosophy, and not all Western leaders adhere to Western philosophy, such as the Western leaders mentioned above.

Cross-Cultural Behavior Modification

All organizations around the globe seek to attain organizational effectiveness. Effectiveness, however, may be defined differently across cultures. For example, in American organizations, effectiveness is often measured by profits, but in some cultures, profits are less important than other measures, such as quality of life (e.g., a clean, safe environment). One thing that is common around the globe, however, is that the attainment of organizational effectiveness requires employees to practice behavior desired by the organization. For instance, the export division of an international company requires certain staff to be present at certain times to process certain documents in a certain way. If the staff members decide not to be present at those times or decide to process the documents in their own way, organizational ineffectiveness may result. The company therefore needs to be assured that the staff members will be present when needed and that they will process the documents in the specified way. For example, it has been found that Saudis are unwilling to observe strict rules and regulations, while Iraqi managers show a strong tendency to follow rules and regulations.[43] The organization must then have programs in place to modify the behavior of employees— to develop employee behavior that conforms to the organization's needs.

All organizations attain the desired member behavior through reward and punishment techniques. But the importance level attached to the rewards and punishments varies across cultures. For example, giving money as a reward for desired behavior or not giving money because of undesired behavior may be a highly effective behavior modifier in some cultures but is not as effective in other cultures. In some cultures, the prospect of being rewarded with a big individual office may encourage an employee to work hard and to conform to the behavior desired by the organization. But in other cultures, it may not—for instance, American managers may work hard for such a reward, but Japanese managers are quite satisfied with a small individual office or simply sharing an office with other employees. In the same context, employees in some cultures are motivated by the prospect of being rewarded with challenging work and more job responsibility, while employees in other cultures may prefer job security. For instance, British workers may be motivated more by challenging work, and French workers may be motivated more by job security.

Total Quality Management and Empowerment

Relative to the awarding of challenging work as a reward, today's popular total quality management (TQM) concept advances the notion of empowering employees (usually in groups) as a means of improving organizational effectiveness.[44] Fundamentally, TQM calls for giving employees more challenging work. It is believed that employees must be given the responsibility for deciding the most effective and efficient way to service the organization's customers (both internal and external). However, individuals in some cultures are more receptive (or less receptive) to TQM/empowerment programs than individuals in other cultures.[45] For example, people in collectivistic (low individualism) societies are likely to work much better in groups than people in high-individualism societies, who tend be competitive and prefer to work on their own.

Michael K. Hui et al., using 57,561 adults in 42 nations, between 1990 and 1993, surveyed cross-cultural variations in empowerment effects on job autonomy and job satisfaction. Their study revealed that that empowerment has a stronger effect on job satisfaction in small power distance cultures than in strong power distance cultures and that job satisfaction and job autonomy tend to be higher in the more economically wealthy countries than in the less economically wealthy countries.[46] The results of their study are presented in Table 12.5.

Furthermore, TQM and empowerment theories assume that individuals will take the initiative in getting things done. However, individuals in strong uncertainty avoidance cultures are likely to take less initiative than individuals in weak uncertainty avoidance cultures, and vice versa. This is because taking the initiative normally means taking a risk, and people in weak uncertainty avoidance cultures tend to take greater risks than people in strong uncertainty avoidance cultures.[47] For instance, "industrial democracy" in Sweden, a weak uncertainty avoidance culture, was initiated in the form of local experiments and was subsequently given a legislative framework. But in Germany, a strong uncertainty avoidance culture, industrial democracy was initiated by a legislative framework first and then localized in organizations.[48] Also, individuals in some cultures tend to perceive managers' efforts to apply TQM/empowerment programs as efforts to manipulate them. (Practical Perspective 12.7 describes Motorola's efforts to implement TQM/empowerment programs in its Malaysia and Florida plants.)

Work Goals and Values Vary Across Cultures

In the industrialized world, the role of work in an individual's life is extremely important. What sort of work goals do people seek? Several decades ago, Frederick Herzberg,

TABLE 12.5 Effect of Empowerment and Job Satisfaction

Country	Job Satisfaction	Job Autonomy
France	6.78	6.41
Britain	7.42	6.98
W. Germany	7.17	6.18
Italy	7.29	6.74
Netherlands	7.48	7.16
Denmark	8.24	7.41
Belgium	7.79	7.05
Spain	6.99	6.37
Ireland	7.81	6.91
N. Ireland	7.85	6.78
United States	7.85	7.36
Canada	7.88	7.22
Japan	7.66	7.63
Mexico	7.66	6.87
S. Africa	7.45	6.88
Hungary	7.22	6.18
Norway	7.88	7.01
Sweden	8.08	7.72
Iceland	7.86	6.94
Argentina	7.63	7.56
Finland	7.56	7.18
S. Korea	6.51	6.85
Poland	8.25	7.69
Switzerland	8.40	7.66
Brazil	7.52	7.40
Nigeria	7.48	6.99
Chile	7.63	7.00
Belarus	6.10	5.06
India	7.03	6.54

TABLE 12.5 (Continued)

Country	Job Satisfaction	Job Autonomy
Czechoslovakia	6.78	5.69
E. Germany	6.75	6.00
Slovenia	7.21	6.01
Bulgaria	6.20	5.42
Romania	6.56	6.05
China	7.01	5.88
Portugal	7.42	6.95
Austria	6.63	6.65
Turkey	5.72	6.67
Lithuania	6.97	6.17
Latvia	6.45	6.01
Estonia	6.66	6.24
Russia	6.28	5.47

SOURCE: Adapted from M. K. Hui, K. Au, and H. Fock, "Empowerment Effects Across Cultures," *Journal of International Business Studies*, 35 (2004), p. 49.

NOTE: The respondents were asked to rate their degree of job satisfaction and their degree of job autonomy on a scale of 1 to 10.

PRACTICAL PERSPECTIVE 12-7

Importing Enthusiasm

Inside Motorola Inc.'s glistening walkie-talkie plant in Penang (Malaysia), the atmosphere resembles a high school sports department. Group shots of exuberant Malaysian production workers, charts with performance statistics, and morale-boosting slogans line the walls. A trophy case is filled with awards hauled back from quality competitions across the United States and Asia by teams with names such as "Orient Express" and "Road Runners." The messages are hammered home: We are a family. This is your company. This is a grand global experiment in plant management by one of the best-run American companies. The methods used to promote worker excellence at the Penang plant are a big part of Motorola's blueprint for developing a well-trained, motivated, and highly productive workforce, especially in emerging markets such as China and Vietnam.

This is potentially frightening news for American and even Japanese workers, who think they still have a lock on more demanding jobs. But in Motorola's case, the company is trying to allay that fear by improving the productivity and motivation of workers in its U.S. plants as well. And Motorola is using the lessons learned in Penang to boost the morale and involvement of workers back home. . . . The (Penang) plant's quality-control program . . . relies in part on the thousands of recommendations it receives from workers. Last year (1993), employees submitted 41,000 suggestions for improving operations, which resulted in $2 million in savings. "Here," says Managing Director Ko Soek King, "everyone marches in the same direction."

PRACTICAL PERSPECTIVE 12-7 (Continued)

The Motorola approach means a great deal in a developing country such as Malaysia, where workers are used to being treated by management as disposable robots. To the typical American worker, though, it may sound more like the usual corporate motivational pap. But the "I Recommend" program, so successful in Malaysia, is also part of Motorola's approach to boost quality in the United States. That's especially so at the company's 2,300-worker factory in Plantation, Florida, which makes products similar to those in Penang. The goal, pursued by Motorola worldwide, is to get employees at all levels to forget narrow job titles and work together in teams to identify and act on problems that hinder quality and productivity. The Plantation plant now displays lists of star employees, and managers hand out everything from "golden attitude" pins to cash bonuses for good ideas. New applicants are screened on the basis of their attitude toward "teamwork."

But getting them to match the Malaysians' enthusiasm hasn't been easy. "The whole plant in Penang had this craving for learning," said Jerry Mysliwiec, director of manufacturing in Plantation, who spent three years in Penang in the late 1980s. "People in the United States are less trusting and believing." And at first, many of the recommendations that came in weren't very helpful. Recalls Craig Kenyon, another manager in Plantation, "They were things like 'Move the garbage can from point A to point B.'" After a slow start, "empowerment" is starting to take hold in Florida, too. . . . The U.S. and Malaysian workers share one reason to stay on their toes: fear of losing their jobs. Not long ago, a quality team was assembled in Florida to examine a component production line whose workers' morale was at rock bottom. Hourly output was one third of the counterpart line in Penang. The Plantation team boosted output by nearly 150% by, among other things, reducing 18 work stations to 6 . . . (the) product change and a highly automated line were giving the team a new goal: to find new jobs for the workers no longer needed.

Malaysians also must stay alert. Just as the Penang plant had its origins as a source of cheap labor, the workers' fear is that Motorola someday could shift work to an even cheaper locale. So managers are trying to increase the plant's share of R&D and looking for ways to boost efficiency even further. Said Managing Director Ko, "I constantly tell them that we will lose out to other places if we aren't cost-competitive." Ko knew firsthand about the coming competition. Her next post is Tianjin, China, where she will be in charge of a new factory. "In China, we are starting with people with a higher level of technical training," she said. "I give them five years before they catch up with us." If that's an accurate prediction, workers in both the United States and Malaysia will have even more reason to keep hustling. For both production workers and engineers, staying competitive is the only real job guarantee in the global economy.

SOURCE: Excerpted and adapted from Peter Engardio and Gail DeGeorge, "Importing Enthusiasm," in "21st Century Capitalism," Special issue, *Business Week* (1994), pp. 122–123. Copyright © 1994, McGraw-Hill, New York. Used with permission.

an American researcher, identified numerous work goals, including salary, work conditions, security, supervision, achievement, and recognition, and the importance level individuals attach to them.[49] Herzberg's findings posit that factors such as an increase in pay, improvement in working conditions, more security, and improved supervision do not motivate employees to increase production, but they will demotivate employees and cause them to produce less when perceived as inadequate. What motivates employees, according to Herzberg's findings, is the presence of factors such as opportunity for personal growth, challenging work, and recognition, but the absence of these factors does not cause demotivation. It should be noted that his research subjects were professionally homogeneous Americans (accountants and engineers). Does the importance level employees attach to various work goals vary across countries?

Variation of Work Goals Across Cultures

To obtain an answer to the above question, Itzhak Harpaz, a researcher at the University of Haifa, Israel, surveyed employees from seven countries. The countries and the number of respondents from each country were as follows: Belgium (5,450), Great Britain (773), Germany (1,278), Israel (973), Japan (3,226), the Netherlands (996), and the United States (1,000). The employees were asked to rank 11 work goals.[50]

The results are shown in Table 12.6. As Table 12.6 shows, employees in Belgium, Great Britain, Israel, and the United States ranked "interesting work" as the most important facet of their work lives, and employees in Japan, the Netherlands, and Germany ranked it second or third. The Japanese employees ranked "match between person and job" as the most important facet of their work lives, employees in the Netherlands ranked "autonomy" as the most important, and German employees ranked "pay" as No. 1. "Pay" was ranked 2nd in Belgium, Great Britain, and the United

TABLE 12.6	**Mean Ranks and Intracountry Ranking of Work Goals**					
Work Goals	**Belgium**	**Britain**	**Germany**	**Israel**	**Japan**	**Netherlands**	**United States**
Opportunity to learn	5.80[a]	5.55	4.97	5.83	6.26	5.38	6.16
	7[b]	8	9	5	7	9	5
Interpersonal relations	6.34	6.33	6.43	6.67	6.39	7.19	6.08
	5	4	4	2	6	3	7
Opportunity for promotion	4.49	4.27	4.48	5.29	3.33	3.31	5.08
	10	11	10	8	11	11	10
Convenient work hours	4.71	6.11	5.71	5.53	5.46	5.59	5.25
	9	5	6	7	8	8	9
Variety	5.96	5.62	5.71	4.89	5.05	6.86	6.10
	6	7	6	11	9	4	6
Interesting work	8.25	8.02	7.26	6.75	7.38	7.59	7.41
	1	1	3	1	2	2	1
Job security	6.80	7.12	7.57	5.22	6.71	5.68	6.30
	3	3	2	10	4	7	3
Match between person and job	5.77	5.63	6.09	5.61	7.83	6.17	6.19
	8	6	5	6	1	6	4
Pay	7.13	7.80	7.73	6.60	6.56	6.27	6.82
	2	2	1	3	5	5	2
Working conditions	4.19	4.87	4.39	5.28	4.18	5.03	4.84
	11	9	11	9	10	10	11
Autonomy	6.56	4.69	5.66	6.00	6.89	7.61	5.79
	4	10	8	4	3	1	8

SOURCE: Itzhak Harpaz, "The Importance of Work Goals: An International Perspective," *Journal of International Business Studies,* 21, no. 1 (First Quarter 1990), p. 81. Copyright © 1990. Reprinted with permission.

a. Mean ranks are shown in the top line of each cell.

b. The rank of each work goal within a given country is shown in the bottom line of each cell. Rank 1 is the most important work goal for a country, and rank 11 is the least important.

States, 3rd in Israel, and 5th in Japan and the Netherlands. Thus, as Table 12.6 depicts, while the ranking of the "interesting work" value is fairly consistent across the seven nations, many of the other values are not. For example, while "autonomy" was ranked 1st in the Netherlands, it was 4th in Belgium and Israel, 8th in the United States, and 10th in Britain.

An interesting point in this study is that Japan was the only country Geert Hofstede classified as a collectivist (low individualism) society. People in these cultures value group harmony to a greater extent than do people in high-individualism societies. This would help explain why "match between person and job" was ranked the No. 1 work value by the Japanese employees—being in the right job helps maintain harmony. Israel and the Netherlands were the only countries classified by Hofstede as feminine societies; the others were classified as masculine societies. According to Hofstede, people in feminine cultures strongly value the maintenance of good interpersonal relations, and people in masculine cultures tend to need to perform and to assert themselves.[51] Israel and the Netherlands were the only two of the seven societies included in this study to rank the "good interpersonal relations" work value higher than the "pay" work value.

The results of the above study indicate that the importance people place on work goals tends to vary from culture to culture. It should be noted that the study included only advanced industrialized countries. Therefore, those work goals that match across cultures may be generalized only to advanced countries. Thus, the same study conducted in industrially less advanced countries is likely to produce different results—if people are not well fed or are relatively illiterate, they may not rank "interesting work" or "challenging work" very high and may rank money very highly. For example, the cross-cultural researchers Philip Hughes and Brian Sheehan interviewed Eastman Kodak employees in Australia and Thailand work sites to determine what they valued most about their work. Australian employees valued interesting and challenging work, and Thai employees valued work primarily for the friends with whom they worked.[52] (Practical Perspective 12.5, presented earlier, and Practical Perspective 12.8 illustrate how money is very important to Chinese workers.)

PRACTICAL PERSPECTIVE 12-8

In China, Firms Find Some Employees Just Keep Going and Going and Going

Chantelle Qian is bright, personable, and resourceful. Fluent in Mandarin, English, and Japanese, experienced in human-resources management and marketing, the 27-year-old (as of 1997) Shanghai native has put her skills to work.

A bit too well, some would say. Qian has held four executive positions in four years.

In China, thousands of highly skilled people made it a practice to hop from job to job, often within a matter of months. "The average turnover in China for many midlevel to senior-level executive posts is 8 to 12 months," said Polly Yip, the China division manager for KPMG Peat Marwick's human resources consulting service in Hong Kong. "The talent pool is small, job opportunities are numerous, and people are constantly looking for better career prospects."

High Turnover

Roughly 17% of the local managers working for joint ventures in Guangzhou switched jobs during the year ended February 1 (1997), according to a survey by the compensation consultant Watson Wyatt Worldwide. Turnover rates were marginally lower in Shanghai and Beijing—about 12%, down from roughly 15% last year.

The people most in demand, and most likely to job hop, are in finance and accounting and sales and marketing and include those filling general manger posts, according to Yip and Mona W. Chan, a director at Watson Wyatt in Hong Kong.

But times were changing. Recruitment and compensation consultants said that local professionals in China are holding on to jobs longer as joint-venture companies launch retention programs that often provide training, regular salary reviews, more executive benefits, and, most important, a clearly defined career path.

"When [markets in] China first opened" in the 1980s, "many people made job moves simply for money," recalled Chan. "For 20 percent more, they'd take a new job. Now, they're more concerned about career development than just monetary rewards," she said. "Job candidates were asking about training, promotions, housing, savings programs, and, recently, retirement benefits," she said.

Professionals Wanted

But this doesn't mean the days of frequent job-hopping were over. The pool of skilled professionals in China with overseas work experience or advanced degrees from abroad couldn't meet the demand, estimated by some experts as 10 jobs for every qualified person.

And demand was growing quickly. The need for executives among large corporations will increase by at least 400% during the next decade, according to a 1996 study by the human resource consultants Korn/Ferry International. "That estimate might even be conservative as the number and size of foreign-funded enterprises grew and state-operated enterprises tried to reform to be competitive," said Ng Sek-hong, an associate professor at the University of Hong Kong who studied employment issues in China.

"Part of the problem may be differing perceptions about what constitutes short-term and long-term employment," observed Nigel P. R. Isherwood, the human resources director at Nestlé (China) Investment Services in Beijing. "Many new hires can't see beyond six months to a year, while we see a minimum commitment of three to four years," Isherwood explained.

"After a year at Nestlé, people were itching for a promotion or a new job," Isherwood said. "But Nestlé, which employed 5,000 people in China and manufactured and sold instant coffee, tea, creamer, and milk products, found most executives aren't up to speed until their second year," he noted. "We look to the long term—a career," Isherwood explained. "We want people who will stick with us, who have management aspirations and potential."

Focus on Retention

To keep staff, Nestlé and other companies were hustling to install retention programs that met employee demands.

Qian, the Shanghai job-hopper, said that money used to be a prime motivator. Now her priorities have shifted. "Training and benefits are important," she said. "And it's important that the company provide career development."

Some companies offer training as an incentive. Motorola, Inc. had a full-blown internal university, teaching language and computer courses to support staff, technical courses to engineers, and management to its managers. Coca-Cola China Ltd., a unit of Coca-Cola Company, had a management school in China for its staff. And Ericsson China Ltd., a unit of Sweden's Telefon AB L.M. Ericsson, opened a Beijing training center in mid-1995 to hone employees' managerial and technical skills.

SOURCE: Excerpted and adapted from Hal Lipper, "In China Firms Find Some Employees Just Keep Going and Going and Going," *The Wall Street Journal* (December 5, 1997), p. B13A. Permission conveyed through Copyright Clearance Center, Inc.

The Full Appreciation of Work Done

The work values included in the above study are not all-inclusive—there are other work values. For example, Professor Colin P. Silverthorne of the University of San Francisco conducted a study to compare employee work motivation in the United States, Russia, and Taiwan. Silverthorne's study contained some work values that were not contained in Harpaz's study—for instance, "full appreciation of work done." The results of Silverthorne's study are included in Table 12.7.

Silverthorne asked managers in the three countries to rank the 10 work values based on how they believed their employees would rank them.[53] Their rankings are indicated by M in Table 12.7. The professor then asked the managers' employees to rank the same 10 values. Their rankings are indicated by E in Table 12.7. Note that American employees ranked "full appreciation of work done" as No. 1 and "interesting work" (ranked No. 1 in the Harpaz study) as No. 2. Note also that "full appreciation of work done" was ranked seventh by the Russian employees and fourth by the Taiwanese, and "interesting work" was ranked fifth by the Taiwanese. As illustrated in Table 12.7, American managers' and employees' rankings are far more closely matched than are the Russians' and the Taiwanese's. One explanation as to why U.S. managers' and employees' rankings are more closely matched may be that U.S. management theories and managerial development programs, which have been administered in Russia and Taiwan to a lesser extent, have in the past several decades sensitized American managers to the fact that organizational

---

TABLE 12.7   Rankings of Work Values in the United States, Russia, and Taiwan

	United States 1990–1991		Russia 1991		Taiwan 1990–1991	
	M	E	M	E	M	E
Full appreciation of work done	2	1	8	7	1	4
Feeling "in" on things	8	7	9	2	3	8
Sympathetic help on personal problems	9	10	1	8	8	6
Job security	1	3	5	6	6	1
Good wages	4	5	7	10	4	2
Work that keeps you interested	3	2	10	3	2	5
Promotion and growth in organization	5	4	6	1	7	3
Personal loyalty to workers	6	8	2	4	9	9
Good working conditions	7	6	3	9	5	7
Tactful disciplining	10	9	4	5	10	10

SOURCE: Adapted from Colin P. Silverthorne, "Work Motivation in the United States, Russia, and the Republic of China (Taiwan): A Comparison," *Journal of Applied Social Psychology*, 22, no. 20 (1992), p. 1634. Copyright © V. H. Winston & Son, Inc., 1992. Used with permission. All rights reserved.

NOTE: M = Rankings of the work goals as managers believed their employees would rank them. E = Rankings by the employees.

effectiveness depends on their being aware of motivating factors. Note also that the Russian employees rated "promotion and growth in the organization" as No. 1. This compares with the more recent findings discussed in Practical Perspective 12.6, wherein training programs were found to serve as a strong employee motivator in Russian organizations. This suggests that when international corporations hire locals to manage their foreign subsidiaries, their HR managers must make sure that the locals are put through the appropriate development programs; and they must ascertain the extent employees in the culture are motivated to learn, as well as their ability to learn.[54]

Work Values: A Study of a Chinese Factory

Addressing the problem of cross-cultural human resource management, Professors John C. Beck and Martha Nibley Beck conducted a study of a factory in China whose top management was experimenting with cross-cultural management.[55] The factory, located in southern China in the town of Zhongshan, was operated by a Hong Kong subsidiary of a Japanese corporation. One part of the plant was managed by local Chinese managers, another part by Hong Kong managers, and a third part by Japanese expatriates. The factory was originally built by the communist government to produce cardboard boxes. In the late 1970s, it was purchased by the Hong Kong Japanese subsidiary to manufacture small electronic consumer goods for foreign markets, such as the United States, Japan, and Europe. Due to rising costs at home, the Japanese firm began to use this factory more and more in the mid-1980s.

To produce "Japanese-quality" products, the Hong Kong subsidiary's top management decided to mix the managerial styles at the factory. Top management attempted to implement a mix of the Japanese, Hong Kong, American, and mainland Chinese styles. The factory was divided into three different sections. The first section, which consisted of the first and second floors of the plant's largest building, was managed by a supervisor from mainland China. The second section, which consisted of the third and fourth floors, was overseen by Hong Kong managers. And the third section, which consisted of the fifth floor, was overseen by two Japanese supervisors.

Before conducting their own study, Beck and Beck interviewed the Hong Kong subsidiary's top management. The researchers were informed that the section run by the mainland Chinese supervisors was sloppy and lazily managed. The section operated by the Hong Kong managers was highly productive but somewhat ramshackle and disorganized. And the section operated by the Japanese supervisors, "just like the Japanese," was clean, efficient, and highly coordinated. The professors thus concluded that the Hong Kong top management believed that the managers with superior skills that had proven effective in one culture could be applied effectively in another cultural setting. Beck and Beck subsequently studied the situation at the factory. Their findings and conclusions are described below.

Differences Between the Three Sections

Chinese Managers. The first section was managed by a mainland Chinese supervisor left over from the factory's cardboard box–producing days. This section contained the facilities for producing the plastic casings the firm uses in its radios and stereo headsets. The production technology was simple and required little labor from the eight workers in the section. The mainland Chinese manager was thus assigned to a section with very low production technology. The section, according to the professors, appeared to live up to its reputation of being similar to Chinese-managed factories,

458 PART VI ● CROSS-CULTURAL COORDINATION

which are usually unkempt and lackadaisically operated. The workers appeared to take little interest in their jobs.

Hong Kong Managers. The second section, operated by the Hong Kong managers, consisted of 180 floor workers. The majority of these employees spent their working hours arranged along two assembly lines, assembling small radios and portable cassette players. The Hong Kong managers were therefore assigned to a more advanced production technology. The professors observed that the emphasis in this section appeared to be on speed of production, and little attention was being paid to tidiness—there was debris of all types. There were shelves where workers were supposed to leave their shoes after replacing them with rubber slippers—which was mandatory. But most of the employees did not take off their shoes and did not put on the rubber slippers. The Hong Kong managers told the professors that it was "mandatory" but not "required" (organizations often have policies mandating certain behaviors that are not enforced by management, and employees practice a different behavior). The professors also observed that the managers publicly "scolded" the employees when they made mistakes.

Japanese Managers. The third section, managed by the Japanese expatriates, contained 103 line workers. They were responsible for producing polyvaricon capacitors, tiny coil-like components used in small audio electronic devices. The Japanese managers were thus assigned to a very advanced production technology. According to Beck and Beck, this section demonstrated a striking contrast to the first and second sections. The room was very clean and orderly. All employees were mandated, as well as required, to take off their shoes and put on their rubber slippers. There were no exceptions, and all the shoes were tidily arranged in the proper area. Unlike the Hong Kong managers, the Japanese managers did not apply rushed behavior or public scolding.

Which Sections Were the Most Successful?

Beck and Beck sought to determine which sections were the most effective. The professors omitted the first section from the analysis because it contained very few employees. Thus, only the second and third sections (Hong Kong and Japanese managers) were analyzed. They centered their analysis on determining worker satisfaction and disaggregating levels of dissatisfaction determined by the nature of the task and factors specifically related to managerial tactics on the part of the supervisors. Their investigation used in-depth interviews and broad-scale questionnaires.

The Second Section (Hong Kong Managers). According to the professors, the workers in the second section were "old" employees who had been well trained in all aspects relating to the line. The section was doing very well, quality standards were being met, and most days the workers produced more than their quotas.

The Third Section (Japanese Managers). The third section had a high employee turnover, which was very costly to the company. Thus, employees in the second section were more satisfied (or less dissatisfied) than the employees in the third section.

Differences Attributed to Management Styles

Beck and Beck attributed the differences to the leadership styles applied by the Hong Kong and Japanese managers. The employees in the second section were more satisfied with their leaders than were the employees in the third section. The styles used by top managers in the second and third sections differed. The leadership approach used by the managers in the second section adhered to local culture; the approach applied by the managers in the third section did not. For example, the Chinese and Japanese societies share the traditional value of removing one's shoes before entering a home and walking barefoot on the floor. However, in China the value is loosely followed, while in Japan it is rigidly followed. Thus, the professors found, the Japanese managers' rigid insistence that the employees in the third section follow this practice irritated them and led to resentment (dissatisfaction). As noted earlier, the Hong Kong managers in the second section did not enforce this value, so there was no employee resentment (no dissatisfaction).

Beck and Beck also concluded that whether managers practiced open criticism also affected employees' satisfaction level. The Japanese managers practiced quiet, nonaccusatory behavior, while the Hong Kong managers practiced open criticism. Culturally, the practice of public scolding (*ma ren*) is quite acceptable in China, while in Japan, such a practice is highly unacceptable. The Chinese view such a practice as open communication and view the practice of quiet, subtle criticism as "sneakiness" or lack of open communication. The Japanese managers' subtle approach thus contributed to employee dissatisfaction.

Somewhat related to the above practice, the management of a large department store in Xian, China, selects its 40 worst sales clerks each year and has them write self-criticisms and analyze their shortcomings. The managers then hang a plaque with a picture over their workplace.[56] This observation, as well as Beck and Beck's observation, took place in the 1980s. This author visited two model Chinese factories in Shanghai in June 1994. At each factory, there were large glass cases with large color pictures of individual employees (such as mechanical engineers who work alone) and of groups of employees being recognized as outstanding employees and groups of the month. This may mean that employees' work values in China are changing or that Chinese values differ from region to region.

Flexibility in Cross-Cultural Leadership and Motivation

As suggested above, there are no leadership and motivation theories with clearly global application. The following section discusses how leadership styles and motivation approaches differ in Germany, France, the Netherlands, and Chinese societies.[57] (How the leadership style differs between the United States and Japan was discussed earlier.)

Leadership and Motivation Approaches in Four Countries

Germany

In Germany, highly skilled and responsible workers do not necessarily require a manager to "motivate" them American-style. These workers expect their superiors, who generally possess an engineering background, to assign their tasks and to be the expert in solving technical problems. German workers thus require little supervision. This means that German organizations would require relatively fewer supervisors than would organizations in many other cultures. For example, a comparison of similar organizations in Germany, Britain, and France showed that Germans have the highest rate of personnel in productive roles and the lowest in both leadership and staff roles.

France

Unlike Americans, the French do not think in terms of managers versus nonmanagers. Rather, they think in terms of *cadres* versus *noncadres*. One becomes a member of a cadre by attending the right schools and remains a member for the rest of his or her life. Furthermore, regardless of task, cadres possess the privileges of a higher social class, and it is very rare for noncadres to cross the ranks.

The Netherlands

Leadership in the Netherlands is different from what it is in the United States. Leadership in the United States presupposes assertiveness, as opposed to consensus and modesty in the Netherlands. However, in the Netherlands there are time-consuming ritual consultations to conserve the appearance of consensus and modesty.

Chinese Societies

Chinese businesspeople living or operating in other than mainland China countries, such as Taiwan, Singapore, and formerly Hong Kong, tend to prefer economic activities in which large gains can be attained with few human resources. They employ few professional managers. They do employ their sons, and sometimes daughters, who have graduated from prestigious business schools, but they continue running the family business the Chinese way. (For an illustration of an exception, refer to Practical Perspective 12.9.) They keep their enterprises small because of their perception that nonfamily employees will not be loyal and, if they are competent, will start their own business. This type of view is found in the history of Chinese society, where there have been no formal laws, only formal networks of influential people steered by general principles of Confucian virtue. The authorities were often unreliable, thus no one could be trusted except one's family.[58]

The above suggests that international managers are confronted with an enormous challenge. They are faced with the complex task of having to determine the leadership

PRACTICAL PERSPECTIVE 12-9

First Pacific's Pearls

For all their money-making abilities, the ethnic Chinese business clans have a major weakness. They jealously keep decision making within the family. Only by marriage into the patriarch's clan can a nonfamily employee acquire real power within the group.... This reluctance to share power or wealth limits the ability of many Chinese-owned businesses to grow and ensures that many will suffer under inept heirs. The Indonesian multibillionaire Liem Sinoe Liong is a glaring exception to the rule. The Indonesian surname of the Liem family's Chinese name is Salim. Based in Jakarta, Liem/Salim's main business, Salim Group, has holdings in everything from cement to noodles.

In the late 1970s, Liem/Salim encouraged his son, Anthony Salim, to recruit nonfamily talent. Anthony Salim approached Manuel Pangilinan, a young investment banker then working for American Express Bank in Hong Kong. Pangilinan was a Filipino who was educated in Jesuit schools before receiving an M.B.A. from Wharton in 1968. Would Pangilinan set up a Hong Kong–based investment arm for the Liem family? He would. In 1981, at age 35, Pangilinan acquired for the Liem/Salims a tiny Hong Kong finance company for $1.5 million. From this seed sprouted Hong Kong–based First Pacific Co. Ltd., an emerging trans-Asia conglomerate. . . .

"The Salims are unique," said Pangilinan. "They are one of the few Chinese groups that's recognized the distinction between ownership and management." And profitably so. Their 35% holding in First Pacific is currently (1995) worth $400 million, and Manny Pangilinan is considered a member-in-very-good-standing of the extended Liem/Salim family.

SOURCE: Excerpted and adapted from Andrew Tanzer, "First Pacific's Pearls," *Forbes* (February 13, 1995), pp. 48, 50. Reprinted by permission of *Forbes Magazine*. © 1999.

style and the motivation preferred by different people in different cultures and adapt to them appropriately. This also suggests that effective international managers must be highly versatile; they must know how to manage in multicultural settings. (The development of these global managers was discussed in Chapter 8.)

The Impact of Information Technology on Changing Values Across Cultures

Much of the practical and academic media report that current information technology, such as the Internet, e-mail, e-commerce, movies, and television, is linking the many cultures around the globe, which is leading to the Westernization of the world, and thus to globalization. As an illustration, Practical Perspective 12.10 describes the changes taking place in India. But the changes that information technology is inducing may merely be the modernization of societies, neither Westernization nor globalization.[59] As nations modernize, they will still maintain their own deeply rooted cultures, some of which, such as in China, are thousands of years old. Thus, while the practical aspects (in technical matters) of a culture may change as a result of information technology, the value aspects of the culture will remain intact for at least several generations.

PRACTICAL PERSPECTIVE 12-10

India's Youth

Every day at 8 a.m., her straight black hair tied neatly in a braid, 16-year-old Neelam Aggarwal rides three miles to school in a horse-drawn buggy. She would like to be a doctor someday. But for a girl like Neelam, who lives in the dusty, impoverished village of Farah in India's northern state of Uttar Pradesh, such a vocation seems remote. For starters, her school—like most village schools in India—doesn't even offer science classes for girls.

PRACTICAL PERSPECTIVE 12-10 (*Continued*)

But Neelam, one of eight daughters of a sweet maker, has no intention of becoming a housewife even if she doesn't get that medical degree. "I want to make something of myself," she says. So each day, after school, Neelam operates what amounts to the village's only pubic telephone—a cellular phone owned by the Indian cellular operator Koshika. By charging her fellow villagers for making calls, Neelam can (in 1999) make as much as $25 on a really good day. She is saving the money for computer classes, which she hopes would lead to a good job.

Ten years earlier, few girls in India would have dared to be like Neelam. But today, she is the very embodiment of Indian youth—ambitious, technology oriented, and confident. Her generation is the product of the incredible sociological change wrought by eight years of economic liberalization in India, a period of painful transition from one-party, socialist rule to an economy where free markets play a much bigger role. Indian society also has been transformed by the Internet and cable television—forces young people were best equipped to exploit.

India's youth were already having an enormous impact on the economy, on companies hoping to sell them products, on the media, and on the culture. Unlike previous generations, youths were not obsessed with the ins and outs of politics. Thus, the election, which pitted the ruling Bharatiya Janata Party against the Congress Party, failed to ignite the passions of the young. "Today, even if Parliament blew up, no one from this generation would notice," says Rama Bijapurkar, a marketing consultant, "It has little relevance for them." Liberalization's children also differ from their conservative, insular parents in that they proudly mix Indian values with Western packaging. They enjoy wearing saris and still admire Mahatma Gandhi. But they also like wearing blue jeans, drinking fizzy sodas, and watching MTV.

How the Young Are Different

Older Generation

- Idealized Gandhi-style poverty, socialist theory
- Grew up amid famines
- Had only one state-run TV channel
- Mostly technophobic
- Tended to be avid savers
- Grew up with a stable government led by one party; upper-caste domination
- Favored medicine, engineering, or civil service as careers
- Average literacy levels of 30%
- Tastes tended toward tradition: drinking tea, eating at home

New Generation

- Wants to get rich, admires capitalism
- Grew up amid food surpluses
- Can watch 50 TV channels via cable and satellite TV
- Mostly technology savvy
- Tend to be guiltless consumers
- Grew up with constantly shaky coalitions; more voice for lower castes
- Favor computer-driven and other high-paying career choices
- Average literacy levels of 52%
- Tastes tend toward modern: Western food and sodas, eating out

SOURCE: Excerpted and adapted form Manjeet Kripalani, "India's Youth: Capitalist Generation," *Business Week* (October 11, 1999), pp. 128E2, 128E4. Reprinted with permission.

Summary

This chapter has proposed that the appropriate leadership style and the motivational incentives a cross-cultural manager applies are, for the most part, determined by the culture in which he or she is managing. But in some situations, as discussed in Chapter 11, other factors may supersede the cultural factors in importance as the determinants of the appropriate style and incentives. The chapter has also suggested that U.S.-based theories do not have cross-cultural application. And it concluded that culture also influences the degree of importance people place on work values.

KEY TERMS AND CONCEPTS

1. Cross-cultural leadership
2. American-based leadership and motivation theories
3. Respect-oriented leadership
4. The PM theory of leadership
5. Innovator, implementer, and pacifier leadership
6. Self-actualization
7. To better serve society/the group
8. Southeast Asian management
9. Theory T and Theory T+
10. Application of one approach on a worldwide basis
11. Social interaction paradigm of human cooperative behavior
12. *I-Ching*
13. The dragon
14. Social awareness, social contribution, and social altruism
16. Multidimensional development ("stepping aside")
15. Collective
17. "Dragon too high with sorrow"
18. Hinayana and Mahayana
19. Cross-cultural behavior modification
20. Total quality management and empowerment
21. Cultural conversion
22. Work goals vary across cultures
23. "Mandatory" but not "required"
24. Open criticism
25. Information technology and changing values

DISCUSSION QUESTIONS

1. What is the notion of Theory X and Theory Y and System 4 management with respect to leadership style? Do you agree? Why?
2. What is the impact of culture on empowerment?
3. How do Theories X and Y differ from Theories T and T+?
4. The assumptions on which Theories X and Y are based do not apply in Southeast Asia. Why not?

5. Maslow's hierarchy of needs theory does not have global application. Discuss this statement.

6. How does Maslow's hierarchy of needs theory differ from the social interaction paradigm of human cooperative behavior?

7. How are work goals affected by culture?

8. Discuss information technology and how it changes values across cultures.

EXERCISES

1. You are a cross-cultural training specialist. Your client is a global corporation that has employed you to train one of its home-country employees who is being prepared to manage the corporation's foreign subsidiary in the Philippines. At home, the employee has been an effective manager by applying a "relationship-oriented" leadership style. What would you tell the employee?

2. You are the HR manager assigned to recruit three top-level managers for three of the company's foreign subsidiaries. One of the subsidiaries is in the strategic planning stages and has not yet been started. The second subsidiary has recently been started amid much chaos. The third subsidiary has been established and is now operating under conditions of stability. For each subsidiary, describe the leadership characteristics each manager requires to be effective. Discuss why you chose those characteristics.

3. You are a cross-cultural training specialist. Your client is a global corporation that has employed you to train one of its home-country employees who is being prepared to manage the corporation's foreign subsidiary in mainland China. With respect to motivation and work values, what would you tell the employee?

4. You are a cross-cultural training specialist. Your client is a global corporation that has employed you to train one of its home-country employees who is being prepared to manage the corporation's foreign subsidiary in The Netherlands. With respect to motivation and work values, what would you tell the employee?

5. You are a cross-cultural training specialist. Your client is a global corporation that has employed you to train one of its home-country employees who is being prepared to manage the corporation's foreign subsidiary in France. With respect to motivation and work values, what would you tell the employee?

ASSIGNMENT

Contact a manager who has had experience managing an enterprise in a foreign country. Ask him or her to share his or her experience relative to leadership and motivation in that country. What were the differences he or she perceived? Prepare a brief report for presentation in class.

CASE 12-1

Putting on the Ritz

When Horst H. Schulze stood before the core staff of the Ritz-Carlton, Hong Kong, he gave his usual talk about team ownership and the need to correct "challenges" (a euphemism for problems) as soon as they occurred. After speaking animatedly for 50 minutes, the German-born Schulze asked a young man trained as a bellhop, "In what hotel did you work previously?" The young man smiled broadly and answered in perfect English, "My pleasure, Mr. Schulze." Reflects Schulze, 53, "In that culture, they want to say yes and are eager to please, but they didn't get what I was saying at all."

Shaking his head at the memory he added, "I knew at that moment I had seriously underestimated what it would take to operate in the Far East. I was used to a quick start: going in with a cross-trained team 10 days before opening and putting the finishing touches on the local staff and then leaving. I will never do that again." As President and COO of the Atlanta-based Ritz-Carlton Hotel Company, one of the world's most renowned hotel management companies, Schulze has high standards, yet he doesn't expect any more from his employees than he does from himself. Before the grand opening of a new luxury hotel or resort, Schulze flies in to conduct orientations personally. He dons blue jeans to work alongside his employees, ensuring that every detail is letter-perfect.

That drive for excellence helped the Ritz-Carlton became the first company to win the U.S. Commerce Department's Malcolm Baldrige National Quality Award . . . Schulze attributed much of the victory to the Ritz-Carlton's infusing its 14,000-employee organization with a team spirit and a sense of individual empowerment. For example, any employee was authorized to spend as much as $2,000 to satisfy a disgruntled guest. Although that award-winning management style brought the rapidly expanding company international kudos, Schulze learned only recently that it doesn't necessarily translate into ready acceptance. "Our first efforts in the international market were opening two hotels in Australia," he said. "Because we spoke the same language, in my mind it wasn't going to be any different than managing a hotel in California. In hindsight, however, the Australians viewed teams and total quality management with a great deal of skepticism. They have been won over to the Ritz-Carlton way, but it took about a year before they no longer thought of it as 'a bunch of American hype.'"

After his epiphany in Hong Kong, Schulze—a slim, elegant man who was decidedly passionate about the hotel business—was still firmly committed to hiring locals to run the hotel. "They have an understanding of the local culture that outsiders cannot possibly attain quickly enough," he said. However, to ensure that the Ritz-Carlton corporate culture isn't lost in the equation, the core staff of locals will now be hired a full year before the hotel is scheduled to open. "There is such a thing as a different culture," said Schulze, who began in the hotel business as a 17-year-old busboy in Germany and came to the United States in 1965 to work with Hilton. . . . "We knew that, yet we didn't fully appreciate the importance of it until Hong Kong. Now, we are being careful to teach the Ritz-Carlton culture while allowing the locals to combine it with their own so as to better relate it to their compatriots in their style."

Throughout most of the 1980s, Schulze had his hands more than full with expansion in the United States. Then, when the luxury hotel market took a major hit with the collapse of the real estate market, he began looking to export Ritz-Carlton's credo: "We are ladies and gentlemen

(Continued)

(Continued)

serving ladies and gentlemen." Besides the foreign properties in Hong Kong and Australia, the privately held company . . . operated a resort in Cancún, Mexico, and was scheduled to open the Hotel Arts Barcelona. The latter was the company's first property in Europe. (It didn't own the rights to the Ritz-Carlton name in France, England, Spain, or Canada.) And the Spaniards employed in Barcelona received a yearlong training within the organization.

Schulze was primarily focusing on expanding Ritz-Carlton's franchise in the Pacific Rim. "That's where most of our opportunity is because that's where the business traveler is going," he said. "We go to the strategic locations because we want to build loyalty with our existing customers. The Pacific Rim and Asia are the most dynamic regions in the global economy and represent the cornerstone for our second decade of development." The Ritz-Carlton broke ground in Osaka, Japan, in December 1993 and had agreements to provide technical service and support for properties in Tokyo, Jakarta, Nagoya, Singapore, Bangkok, Kuala Lumpur, Seoul, Auckland, and Bali. The company established a development office in Hong Kong and was negotiating to develop properties in Shanghai, Cheju Island, Guangzhou, Taipei, Melbourne, Pusan, and Manila and a second site in Tokyo, Beijing, Shenzhen, the Gold Coast, and Adelaide.

"The Ritz-Carlton's reputation . . . was one of its most precious assets. . . . Our guests expect a certain level of service and having demands met on time is one of the keys," says Schulze. "However, in Hong Kong, that same rapidity is viewed as rude and intrusive. It was hard to convince them that Europeans and Americans who sat in a restaurant for two or three hours for lunch would not be coming back." Overcoming such skepticism and suspicion was paramount to the company's overseas success. In this case, Schulze discovered that the Chinese have a great respect for written information. By showing Hong Kong employees the extensive surveys the company had done regarding guests' requirements, he was able to convince the staff that speed was paramount.

Among the most difficult hurdles he faced in Hong Kong was convincing the staff that management valued their input. Schulze always opened the orientation by declaring imperiously, "My name is Horst Schulze. I am president of this company, and I am very important." After a dramatic pause, he would add, "And so are you. You are equally important." In the United States, that statement was met with approval and nods. In Hong Kong, it was met with disbelief. "When I started setting silverware on the tables in the restaurant the day before orientation started, the Chinese supervisors said, 'Why are you doing that? The workers come tomorrow.'" Recalls Schulze, "They couldn't fathom the idea of leading by example—a management technique we take for granted in the United States. Understanding the idea of mutual respect was difficult, too. They were used to being the boss, period."

Companies that use management styles readily accepted in the United States must gird themselves for such battles. Schulze noticed that although the Hong Kong Chinese were clearly unconvinced that team management would work initially; they were loath to admit their disbelief. In Mexico, he knew immediately that the employees were dubious. "When I was working through the mission statement with the dishwashers, a practice I complete with each department, I asked if they had any questions," says Schulze. "The Mexicans were very open about their lack of faith in individual empowerment. They questioned everything, but they were also quicker to rally to our ways once they understood that we were sincere." In hindsight, Schulze believes that it took the Australians almost three years to get with the Ritz-Carlton program. "That was completely our fault. Because English was the language there, I took it for granted that they understood us."

Questions

1. What type of leader—an innovator, an implementer, a pacifier, or a combination of two or three—do you believe Schulze is? Which facts in the article led to your conclusion?

2. Do you believe that Schulze is an effective cross-cultural leader? Why?

3. Why did the Australians view teams and TQM with skepticism?

SOURCE: Exerpted and adapted from Echo Montgomery Garrett, "Putting on the Ritz," *World Trade* (April 1994), pp. 52–56. Copyright © 1994. *World Trade* magazine. Used with permission. All rights reserved.

CASE 12-2

The Rewarded Chinese Olympic Stars

For China's Olympic stars, the gold medals around their necks in Barcelona were just a foretaste of what was to come. As a symbol of China's invincibility in the swimming pool and on the ping-pong table, the athletes returned home to be showered with gold and cash to an estimated value of $182,000 each, tax-free.

In a country where the average annual income (in 1992) was under $400, it was perhaps inevitable that the awards provoked feelings of envy and claims from other professionals. Rocket scientists pointed out that the launch of a Long March rocket carrying an Australian communications satellite was also considered a patriotic victory. As a result, 20 rocket scientists have each been awarded 5,000 yuan (about $900).

Questions

1. Discuss the case within the context of the hierarchy of needs framework described in this chapter. How does the rocket scientists' behavior relate to the *I-Ching* philosophy?

2. Discuss the scientists' work values.

SOURCE: Excerpted from "China: New Rich," *The Economist* (October 10, 1992), p. 36. Reprinted with permission.

CASE 12-3

Volvo's Enriched Job Strategy

Volvo executives decided that one way to improve job conditions was through a job enrichment program. Volvo experimented with this idea by converting its Uddevalla, Sweden, plant to a job-enriched facility. Automobiles were built in small workshops by teams of approximately 12 autonomous workers. Each team member was trained to be capable of doing every job the team was responsible for in building the automobile. There were very few supervisors in the plant. Thus, members of the team learned and received feedback from the other members—not from supervisors. Volvo declared the experiment at Uddevalla a success and implemented it at its three other plants in Sweden. Volvo found the program motivational, efficient, and profitable.

Questions

1. Using a cultural perspective, why do you think the program worked so well at Volvo?

2. Do you believe the program would work as well with American employees at a U.S. car builder? Why?

SOURCE: Adapted from William E. Nothdurft, "How to Produce Work-Ready Workers," *Across the Board* (September 1990), pp. 47–52. Reprinted with permission.

NOTES

1. "Foreign Bodies," *CA Magazine* (November 1993), p. 21.

2. B. M. Bass, P. C. Burger, R. Duktor, and G. V. Barrett, *Assessment of Managers: An International Comparison* (New York: Free Press, 1979).

3. Ibid.

4. V. Terpstra, *The Cultural Environment of International Business* (Cincinnati, OH: South-Western Publishing, 1978).

5. P. T. Terry, "The English in Management," *Management Today,* 1, no. 11 (1979), pp. 90–97.

6. M. P. Mangaliso, N. A. Mangaliso, and J. H. Burton, "Management in Africa, or Africa in Management? The African Philosophical Thought on Organizational Discourse," Paper presented at the International Management Division, Academy of Management Annual Meeting, San Diego, CA (August 6, 1998), p. 21.

7. Douglas McGregor, *The Human Side of the Enterprise* (New York: McGraw-Hill, 1960); Rensis Likert, *The Human Organization: Its Management and Value* (New York: McGraw-Hill, 1961).

8. Robert R. Blake and Jane S. Mouton, *The Managerial Grid* (Houston, TX: Gulf Publishing, 1964).

9. Cited in Bernard M. Bass, *Bass & Stogdill's Handbook of Leadership: Theory, Research, & Managerial Applications,* 3rd ed. (New York: The Free Press, 1990), p. 796.

10. See Robert Westwood, "Harmony and Patriarchy: The Cultural Basis for 'Paternalistic Headship' Among Overseas Chinese," *Organization Studies,* 18, no. 3 (1997), pp. 445–480.

11. Bass, *Bass & Stogdill's Handbook,* op cit.

12. Claude Cellich, "When Cultures Collide: Managing Sussessfully Across Cultures," *International Journal of Conflict Management,* 8, no. 2 (April 1997), p. 176.

13. M. Bennett, "Testing Management Theories Culturally," *Journal of Applied Psychology,* 62 (1977), pp. 578–581.

14. J. M. Ivancevich, D. M. Schweiger, and J. W. Ragan, "Employee Stress, Health, and Attitudes: A Comparison of American, Indian, and Japanese Managers," Paper presented at the Annual Meeting of the Academy of Management, Chicago (1986).

15. "Companies With Happy Staff Have More Success," *Business Times (South Africa)* (May 2, 1999), Appointments section, p. 1.

16. See V. V. Baba and M. E. Ace, "Serendipity in Leadership: Initiating Structure and Consideration in the Classroom," *Human Relations,* 42 (June 1989), pp. 509–525.

17. L. R. Anderson, "Management of the Mixed-Cultural Work Group," *Organizational Behavior and Human Performance,* 31 (1983), pp. 303–330.

18. Bass et al., *Assessment of Managers,* op cit.

19. Cellich, "When Cultures Collide: Managing Successfully Across Cultures," op cit., p. 1.

20. Mark F. Peterson, "PM Theory in Japan and China: What's in It for the United States," *Organizational Dynamics* (Spring 1988), p. 22.

21. For a discussion on other characteristics managers require when entering a foreign market, see P. Herrmann and D. K. Datta, "CEO Successor Characteristics and the Choice of Foreign Market Entry Mode: An Empirical Study," *Journal of International Business Studies,* 33, no. 3 (2002), p. 556.

22. This discussion draws from C. A. Rodrigues, "Identifying the Right Leader for the Right Situation," *Personnel* (September 1988), pp. 43–46; C. A. Rodrigues, "The Situation and National Culture as Contingencies for Leadership Behavior: Two Conceptual Models," in S. B. Prasad (Ed.), *Advances in International Comparative Management,* 5 (Greenwich, CT: JAI Press, 1990); C. A. Rodrigues, "Developing Three-Dimensional Leaders," *Journal of Management Development,* 12, no. 3 (1993), pp. 4–11.

23. J. P. Wright, *On a Clear Day You Can See General Motors* (Grosse Pointe, MI: Wright Enterprises, 1979).

24. R. Mitchell, "Jack Welch: How Good a Manager?" *Business Week* (December 14, 1987), pp. 92–95.

25. Rodrigues, "Developing Three-Dimensional Leaders," op cit.

26. For a more complete discussion of this topic, see C. A. Rodrigues, "Application of High-Quality Leadership as an International Competitive Advantage," in A. J. Ali (Ed.), *How to Manage for International Competitiveness* (Binghampton, NY: The Haworth Press, 1992).

27. Cited in Geert Hofstede, "The Applicability of McGregor's Theories in Southeast Asia," *Journal of Management Development,* 6, no. 3 (1987), p. 16.

28. Ibid., pp. 16–18.

29. Ibid., p. 17.

30. Ibid., pp. 17–18.

31. Abraham H. Maslow, "Theory of Human Motivation," *Psychological Review,* 50 (July 1943), pp. 370–396.

32. J. C. Williams, *Human Behavior in Organizations* (Cincinnati, OH: South-Western Publishing, 1982), pp. 80–81.

33. Geert Hofstede, "The Cultural Relativity of the Quality of Life Concept," *Academy of Management Review,* 9, no. 3 (1984), p. 396.

34. M. Haire, E. E. Ghiselli, and L. W. Porter, *Managerial Thinking: An International Study* (New York: John Wiley & Sons, 1966).

35. David V. Gibson and Francis Woomin Wu, "The Social Interaction Paradigm of Human Cooperative Behavior: Societal Motivation Beyond Maslow's Need Hierarchy," in *Proceedings of the Fourth International Conference on Comparative Management* (Kaohsiung, Taiwan: National Sun Yat-sen University, 1991). Used with permission from professor David V. Gibson. All rights reserved.

36. Ibid., p. 99.

37. Ibid.

38. Ibid.

39. Ibid., pp. 100–101.

40. Ibid., p. 101.

41. Ibid.

42. For a discussion on the three learned motivation needs, the need for achievement, the need for power, and the need for affiliation, refer to David C. McClelland, *The Achieving Society* (Princeton, NJ: Van Nostrand Reinhold, 1961).

43. M. Alaki, *Business Administration in Saudi Arabia* (Jeddah, Saudi Arabia: Dar AlShorouq, 1979); Z. B. Al-Musavi, "The Administrative Staff on the Scale," *The Economist (Iraq)*, 35 (1973), p. 6670; A. Ali, "A Comparative Study Of Managerial Beliefs About Work in the Arab States," in R. Farmer (Ed.), *Advances in International Comparative Management* (Greenwich, CT: JAI Press, 1989), p. 4.

44. See Carl A. Rodrigues, "A Framework for Defining Total Quality Management," *Competitiveness Review*, 5, no. 2 (1995), pp. 32–47; Richard S. Johnson, *TQM: Leadership for Quality Transformation* (Milwaukee, WI: ASQC Quality Press, 1993).

45. See Carl A. Rodrigues, "Employee Participation and Empowerment Programs: Problems of Definition and Implementation," *Empowerment in Organizations: An International Journal*, 2, no. 1 (1994), pp. 29–40.

46. M. K. Hui, K. Au, and H. Fock, "Empowerment Effects Across Cultures," *Journal of International Business Studies*, 35 (2004), pp. 46–60.

47. See Bass et al., *Assessment of Managers*, op cit.; Geert Hofstede, *Culture's Consequence: International Differences in Work-Related Values* (Beverly Hills, CA: Sage Publications, 1980).

48. Geert Hofstede, "Motivation, Leadership, and Organization: Do American Theories Apply Abroad?" *Organizational Dynamics* (Summer 1990), p. 57.

49. Frederick Herzberg, "One More Time: How Do You Motivate Employees?" *Harvard Business Review*, 46 (January–February 1968), pp. 53–62.

50. Itzhak Harpaz, "The Importance of Work Goals: An International Perspective," *Journal of International Business Studies*, 21, no. 1 (First Quarter 1990), p. 81.

51. Hofstede, *Culture's Consequence*, op cit.

52. Philip Hughes and Brian Sheehan, "Business Across Cultures: The Comparison of Some Business Practices in Thailand and Australia," *Asian Review* (Bangkok, Thailand: Chulalongkorn University, Institute of Asian Studies, 1993), p. 263.

53. Colin P. Silverthorne, "Work Motivation in the United States, Russia, and the Republic of China (Taiwan): A Comparison," *Journal of Applied Social Psychology*, 22, no. 20 (1992), pp. 1631–1639.

54. See D. Minbaeva, T. Pedersen, I. Bjorkman, C. F. Frey, and H. Park, "MNC Knowledge Transfer, Subsidiary Absorptive Capacity, and HRM," *Journal of International Business Studies*, 34 (2003), pp. 586–599.

55. This discussion draws from John C. Beck and Martha Nibley Beck, "The Cultural Buffer: Managing Human Resources in a Chinese Factory," in G. R. Ferris (Ed.), *Research in Personnel and Human Resources Management* (Greenwich, CT: JAI Press, 1990), pp. 89–107.

56. Adi Ignatius, "Now if Ms. Wong Insults a Customer, She Gets an Award," *The Wall Street Journal* (January 24, 1989) p. 1.

57. This discussion draws from Geert Hofstede, "Cultural Constraints in Management Theories," *The Academy of Management Executive*, 7, no. 1 (1993), pp. 81–94.

58. See also Andrew Tanzer, "First Pacific's Pearl's," *Forbes* (February 13, 1995), pp. 48, 50.

59. See Hellmut Schutte, "Asian Cultures and the Global Consumer," *Mastering Marketing* (September 21, 1998), pp. 2–3.

Part VII

INTERNATIONAL CONTROL

The intention of the control process is to enable managers to compare actual activities with planned activities. Planning (discussed in Chapter 4) and controlling are thus closely linked. When the organization establishes tactical objectives (discussed in Chapter 4), management must establish feedback mechanisms to verify that those objectives are being attained. The question, however, is how much control. Part VII deals with the question of how much control is appropriate in a global context. When corporations establish subsidiaries in foreign countries, the managers at headquarters must decide how best to maintain control over foreign activities—that is, how to ensure that activities in foreign markets are being carried out as planned. These managers are therefore confronted with the task of deciding whether to give the subsidiaries autonomy (loose, decentralized control) or make decisions at home (rigid, centralized control) or, if both are ineffective, how to attain a balance between the two. Chapter 13 discusses this aspect of control.

HEADQUARTERS-FOREIGN SUBSIDIARY CONTROL RELATIONSHIPS

Multinational companies, like Phillips, Unilever, and ITT, have relied on a decentralized structure and a diversified strategy to be responsive to local conditions. Global companies, like Matsushita and Kao, are organized around a strong central headquarters and treat the world market as an integrated whole, where universal consumer demand outweighs local preferences. International companies, like General Electric and Procter & Gamble, are structured to adapt and transfer the parent company's knowledge to foreign markets and to allow national units to adapt products and ideas from the parent company to local markets.[1]

Learning Objectives of the Chapter

When businesses establish operating subsidiaries in foreign countries, their headquarters' managers must establish an effective headquarters–foreign subsidiary control relationship (HSR). According to the principles of traditional management, a relationship may be one of centralization, or it may be one of decentralization. The pros and cons of both centralized and decentralized controls are discussed below. According to the principles of contemporary management, the control relationship is expressed in terms of three basic headquarters–foreign subsidiary governance mechanisms: centralization, formalization, and normative integration. The appropriate control relationship is contingent on cultural and situational factors.

Irrespective of whether they may subscribe to the views of contemporary management or traditional management, headquarters managers of effective international business enterprises must establish the HSR that best attains the overall goals and objectives of the corporation. After studying this chapter, you should be able to do the following:

1. Discuss centralized and decentralized HSRs
2. Describe the factors that affect the decision of whether to establish a centralized or a decentralized relationship
3. Describe centralization, formalization, and normative integration relationships
4. Discuss the cultural and situational factors that influence the use of the three relationships
5. Discuss how a balanced relationship is accomplished

Global Controls: Centralization and Decentralization

To maintain proper control systems, an appropriate organizational structure (discussed in Chapter 6) is essential. Along with identifying the appropriate structure, headquarters management must decide whether the HSR should be centralized or decentralized. In a centralized system, most of the important decisions relative to local matters are made by the headquarters management. In a decentralized system, managers at the subsidiary are given the autonomy to make most of the important decisions relative to local matters.

There are advantages and disadvantages in both approaches. For example, it is difficult for the headquarters managers located in Paris, to know what type of benefits best meet the expectations of workers in a subsidiary located in Rio de Janeiro, Brazil. Local managers would know best. In other words, it is difficult to standardize tasks such as human resource management across cultures.[2] Joanne Webster, the human resource director for Gupta Corporation, a 260-employee (as of 1993; and as of 2007 it still employed more than 200 employees and is now called Keynote[3]) software company based in Menlo Park, California, stated that she has seen multiple kinds of organizational structures and now has her own ideal: "At my last company, Europe was operated like a separate company that mirrored the United States. When we were acquired, it all went into corporate in the United States, which had the responsibility for overseeing everything, even the salary surveys." Webster now finds herself leaning toward establishing human resource departments in geographic areas, with managers handling employee relations and training but reporting to her office. Webster does not believe that "we in the United States can develop the expertise in all the employment regulations. We would want to hire someone closer to the action. They would have that expertise and base their compensation and benefits on what works in Europe."[4] (Practical Perspective 13.1 presents a human resources director's view on decentralization.)

Also, foreign markets are now changing rapidly, and since local managers are closer to the market, they are able to keep abreast of local changes better than headquarters managers. Therefore, unduly centralized control can deprive global aspirants of vital contacts with foreign customers.[5] The case of AT&T illustrates this point:

AT&T employs about 54,000 [as of 1993] workers in foreign markets, of which about half are in AT&T's traditional lines of equipment and communication services and the rest in its NCR computer unit. But local management is spotty, and equipment and long-distance businesses report up through separate units based in Basking Ridge, New Jersey. Virtually all major decisions are made in the United States, requiring foreign proposals to snake their way up through myriad departments before getting approval. 'That's much too far from our customers to achieve on-site, rapid decision making,' said Victor Pelson, chief of AT&T Global Operations. 'The market is changing very rapidly.'[6]

(As of 2007, AT&T is the largest communications holding company in the United States and worldwide, employing 301,760 employees, and its revenues in 2006 were more than 117 billion.[7])

PRACTICAL PERSPECTIVE 13-1

Bridging Cultural Gaps

Deng Tao is Director of Human Resources for Greater China at Allied Signal and the winner of the *China STAFF* Beijing HR Manager of the Year Award 1998. His career path has moved from five years as a soldier of the People's Liberation Army (PLA) in Xinjiang province, northwest China, to five years in a state-owned enterprise (SOE), to a career as a Human Resources professional in multinational corporations. In 1984 he joined Hewlett-Packard, and then he moved to Mersk Shipping Company, before joining Allied Signal in 1997. Allied Signal, which produces automotive and aerospace equipment, has 12 legal entities in China, 6 of which are wholly foreign owned enterprises (WFOEs) and 6 are joint-ventures. The firm employs over 1,000 people in China.

[In an interview to the editor of] *China STAFF* [Deng Tao was asked,] "If a company decides to localize, how should they go about it? What is the role of training, development, and assessment?"

[Deng Tao responded,] "With a multinational doing business in China, we [local managers] are the people who have experience; we know China; we know how to run a company. We can bridge the difference between the corporate headquarters far away in the United States and how we run the business in China. Whenever there is an initiative from the corporate headquarters, we ask how can it be implemented successfully in China and in different cities (because development stages vary from city to city—Xian is quite different from Shanghai). It is challenging because Allied Signal is a very decentralized culture and diversified business. The challenge for me is how to tell the U.S. counterpart how to implement things in China. We have to make some changes [to their initiatives] because some initiatives are very complex. We try to make them simple, easy to use, easy to implement."

SOURCE: Excerpted from "The Long March From the PLA into HR Management," *China STAFF,* 5, no. 6 (May 1999), pp. 18–21. Reprinted with permission.

Decentralizing such decisions would therefore be advantageous. On the other hand, when decision making is decentralized, judgments made by local managers may sometimes have negative consequences for other subsidiaries and/or may not be the best decision when the overall firm's objectives are considered. For instance, a decision made by managers at the Rio de Janeiro subsidiary to pay generous benefits to their workers may demoralize workers in other subsidiaries if they perceive their benefits to be comparatively unfair. Centralized decision making would thus enable headquarters managers to consider the consequences of a decision on all the firm's subsidiaries. Centralization, in this respect, would be advantageous.

As another example, managers of a subsidiary with decision-making power may decide to expand their subsidiary's market. In their efforts, they may unknowingly (or knowingly) be competing with another of the firm's subsidiaries. For example, in the 1980s, top management at firms such as Ford, IBM, Digital Equipment, and Texas Instruments saw their increasingly important international operations become slow-moving clones of corporate headquarters. Little communication or coordination occurred among regions. Even worse, country organizations sometimes spent more energy competing with each other than they did fighting the competition.[8]

In the fiscal year ending March 1994, Japan's Matsushita realized nearly 50% of its $64.3 billion in sales in overseas markets, and its foreign factories supplied two thirds of the goods sold abroad. Matsushita, at the time, allowed its plants to set their own rules, fine-tuning manufacturing. Many of Matsushita's overseas plants began competing with the company's factories in Japan.[9] However, historically, some Japanese corporations have encouraged competition among its subsidiaries; the logic being that it encourages its subsidiaries to perform better than the others. The Chinese government, which owns the Chinese corporations, encourages the same competition among their subsidiaries as exists among the subsidiaries of the Japanese corporations. The French government, which several decades ago nationalized its key industries, also encouraged the same behavior.

Centralized control would have helped avert such a situation, and it would have been advantageous in this respect. On the other hand, centralized controls requiring local managers to obtain permission for practical application of their innovative ideas may actually inhibit local initiatives that would benefit the overall organization. The case of Japanese corporations' practices illustrates how centralization can be disadvantageous:

> Unwillingness to give foreigners much clout could put Japanese companies at a disadvantage. Even at Uniden, where 277 out of 10,000 employees work in Japan, Japanese executives run all the foreign subsidiaries, and most key decisions are made at headquarters. Overcentralized management compounds the problem. Taku Ogata, an advisor on China for Nomura Research Institute, Ltd. and author of a Japanese bestseller, The Secret of Success in China, thinks the unwillingness of Japanese companies to give authority to foreign executives is causing them to fall behind their Western competitors in China. Westerners hire Chinese managers, turn them loose, and reward them lavishly if they do well. By contrast, Japanese companies hesitate to hire Chinese at high levels, and Chinese prefer to work for Western companies because the pay is better.[10]

Headquarters managers are therefore often confronted with the problem of deciding whether to maintain central control over decisions relating to the firm's foreign subsidiaries or allow local managers to use their own discretion in decision making. Of course, when an organization adopts a certain approach, it does not adhere to it rigidly; it changes approaches when needed. For example, when an enterprise operating on a decentralized basis is confronted with the need to transform itself due to environmental changes, headquarters management will centralize decision making. But after the transformation has been accomplished, central management may again decentralize decision making to the local subsidiaries to enable them to establish a strong local presence. The case of Berkel illustrates this point:

Maatschappij Van Berkel's Patent N.V., a Dutch-based MNC supplier of weighing and food processing equipment, took action to meet competitive cost pressures by transforming itself into a sales and service firm. To manage the complicated process of rationalizing its manufacturing and engineering activities and phasing in an out-sourced product line, Berkel temporarily adopted a highly centralized decision-making structure. But once the transformation was accomplished, the headquarters loosened control over its national operating companies and resumed the more autonomous decision-making style that in the past had helped build a strong local presence.[11]

Some of the traditional factors used by top management to determine whether to centralize or decentralize are outlined in Table 13.1.[12]

Split Control. A solution to the issues outlined in Table 13–1 is the application of split control. Some functions work better when decisions are decentralized, while others work better when decisions are centralized.[13] Nevertheless, some degree of central oversight is required. (See Practical Perspectives 13.2 and 13.3.) The ensuing sections present contemporary thinking relative to HSR.[14]

TABLE 13.1	Traditional Determinants of Centralization and Decentralization
Industry	Firms in an industry that requires product consistency across many foreign markets (such as firms with a global strategy) tend to centralize control. On the other hand, firms in an industry that must produce to suit the needs of specific foreign markets (such as firms with a multidomestic strategy) tend to decentralize decision making. This is because the former needs much more central coordination than the latter.
Type of subsidiary	Foreign manufacturing subsidiaries are likely to be more controlled by headquarters managers than foreign marketing subsidiaries. This is because manufacturing technologies tend to be consistently applicable across foreign markets and can therefore be centrally coordinated. On the other hand, marketing technologies generally require a great deal of cross-cultural adaptation, which is generally best accomplished by local managers.
Function	International functions such as finance and accounting are likely to be more centrally controlled than functions such as hiring local workers. Top management generally likes to control "the purse" (money), and local managers would have a better grasp of the local labor market than would central headquarters managers.
Range of subsidiaries	Those foreign subsidiaries that provide a wide range of products for diverse markets tend to be less centrally controlled than those that provide uniform products for uniform markets. The latter is not too complicated for headquarters managers to control, while the former would be too complex for central managers to control, and local managers are best able to make the adaptations required by the diverse markets.
Number and size of subsidiaries in a market	Companies with a few large subsidiaries in a foreign area tend to decentralize more than firms with many small units. Many small units in a market would require more central coordination among the units than would a few large units, which can more easily coordinate in matters among themselves.
Ownership structure	Partially owned foreign subsidiaries—for example, joint ventures—are more likely to be less centrally controlled than wholly owned foreign subsidiaries. The expertise, such as knowledge of the local culture, markets, and legal systems, often lies in the foreign partner, while in the wholly owned subsidiary the expertise often lies in the home office.

TABLE 13.1	(Continued)
Date of acquisition	Newly acquired foreign subsidiaries that continue manufacturing their old product lines under the same managers tend to be less centrally controlled because the old managers possess the expertise. However, when the subsidiary subsequently grows and begins to expand into other products and markets, central control increases because central expertise and coordination is now needed.
Headquarters' interest and expertise	The greater the headquarters management's personal interest in the subsidiary and the greater the expertise in the subsidiary's business area, the greater central control over the foreign subsidiary it maintains. If management's personal interest is low and there is little expertise is little, central control will be lower. (For an illustration, refer to Practical Perspective 13.2.)
Distance	Distant foreign subsidiaries tend to be less centrally controlled—although, as indicated earlier, because of recent advances in global communications technologies distance no longer matters.
Environment	Subsidiaries located in countries with environments that are unfamiliar to headquarters management tend to be given greater autonomy than those that are located in familiar environments. Also, if the foreign subsidiary is located in a dynamic, changing local environment, the tendency is for headquarters management to decentralize. Local management is more familiar with the local environment and more in touch with the rapid changes that take place locally than headquarters management, and it is therefore better able to cope.
Corporate goals	If the goal of headquarters managers is to maintain maximum power, then more central control is applied. If it is to maximize local market share, however, control tends to be decentralized. Local managers are generally more familiar with the local market conditions and are therefore better equipped to carry the growth objective. (For an illustration, refer to Practical Perspective 13.3.)
Ownership	If the enterprise is owned and managed by a few individuals, these managers may maintain a closer watch over their foreign interests than would professional managers of an enterprise that is owned by a large number of stockholders. (Of course, the other factors must also be considered.)
Headquarters' confidence in subsidiaries and management	When confidence in the foreign subsidiary's managerial abilities increases, decision making tends to become more shared and less dictated by headquarters management. And, vice versa, when it decreases, the tendency is to apply more central control.
Success of the subsidiary	If the foreign subsidiary is perceived as being highly successful, headquarters control tends to lessen. But when things are not going well locally, headquarters management becomes more involved and centralist.
Intersubsidiary transactions	A firm with a substantial volume of intersubsidiary transactions tends to be centralized because when organizational effectiveness depends on several subunits, central coordination is usually required.
Importance of foreign market	Headquarters management may want to monitor an important foreign market very closely. Therefore, control over a foreign subsidiary in that market would be more centralized than it would be for subsidiaries located in markets that are of less importance.
Foreign laws	The government of the nation in which a foreign subsidiary is located may require that the subsidiary be managed by locals. Central control would thus be less.
Individuals	If managers of the foreign subsidiary require autonomy, the tendency is to apply less central control. Attempts to control these individuals from the headquarters would result in ineffectiveness. On the other hand, some individuals, culturally, prefer that decisions be centrally made.

PRACTICAL PERSPECTIVE 13-2

Managing Headquarters

Since the days of the East India Company, the country manager (CM) has been the eyes and ears of the multinational corporation in foreign markets. Despite the globalization of markets and the pressures on many MNCs in favor of greater headquarters coordination, studies confirm the continued importance of CMs with profit and loss responsibility as drivers of business growth, especially in emerging markets.

Here we [J. A. Quelch and C. M. Dinhtan] present the first country-specific study of CMs in an emerging market—in this case, Vietnam. From in-depth personal interviews with 14 CMs in Vietnam, representing MNCs across a diverse range of goods and services, our aim was to identify who the CMs were and why they had been selected, how they spent their time and how they expected to spend their time in the future, and what they regard as their principal challenges and how they dealt with them. Although we cannot claim that our findings are generalizable [Vietnam], we do believe they reflect the experiences of CMs in other transitional economies around the world....

Almost all the CMs in our study reported to a regional headquarters, typically located in Singapore. Six of the 14 CMs believed their required interactions with regional and world headquarters were more of a hindrance than a help. This was especially the case when no headquarters managers had Vietnamese experience or relevant experience from other emerging markets. Common complaints included the frequency and scope of financial reporting, often in formats that were inappropriate for emerging markets; numerous "parachute" visits from headquarters personnel, especially when the Vietnam operation had been accorded a high profile in the MNCs annual report; and a consequent impatience for quick results, including, for example, achieving break-even in the second year of operations.

The level and frequency of oversight from regional and world headquarters is a function not merely of the scope of operations but also of the MNC's experience in emerging markets (less experience implying more oversight) and the perceived competence of the CM. In our study, a typical reporting pattern required four face-to-face meetings per year with the CM's regional manager. However, the relatively inexperienced CM of one of the smallest operations we examined was required to visit regional headquarters twice a month.

Managing the Vietnamese opportunity successfully calls for decentralization to a highly competent, culturally sensitive CM whom government officials and joint venture partners can respect. The market is highly competitive, with many MNCs jockeying for position, and customers are savvy, often unwilling to accept anything less than the latest product technology. Such circumstances call for CMs with the power to respond quickly to the local environment. It is essential to success that MNCs invest in their selection processes and appoint CMs to whom they feel comfortable delegating authority.

SOURCE: Excerpted from John A. Quelch and Christine M. Dinh-Tan, "Country Managers in Transitional Economies: The Case of Vietnam," *Business Horizons* (July–August 1998), pp. 34–39. Reprinted with permission.

Headquarters–Foreign Subsidiary Governance Mechanisms

A contemporary idea on HSRs has been discussed by professors of business management, Sumantra Ghoshal of INSEAD, France, and Nitin Nohria of Harvard Business School. They described the relationships in terms of three basic HSRs: centralization, formalization, and normative integration.[15] According to them, centralization concerns the role of formal authority and hierarchical mechanisms in the company's

PRACTICAL PERSPECTIVE 13-3

China's Car Guy

Nearly two years ago Hu Mao Yuan, 48, the first president of Shanghai General Motors, found himself enduring a sleepless night at the Renaissance Center Hotel in Detroit, far from his home in China. A veteran manager of state-owned corporations, Hu was kept awake by fears that the $1.5 billion enterprise with GM—the largest U.S. joint venture in the People's Republic—would wind up "as an auto company that just produces quarrels" between its partners. He spent that night fretting over a set of cooperative principles that would stress the independence of the joint venture. As it turns out, Hu could have rested peacefully: The project has been a hit: The Buicks now rolling out of a state-of-the-art plant in Shanghai are the highest-quality cars of that model being produced anywhere in the world—and they are also selling.

Hu has drawn much of the credit for this promising start. Top officials at General Motors are quick to attribute the early success of this ambitious and risky investment to his leadership and his ability to bridge the gap between Western and Chinese business practices. Says Rudolph A. Schlais, Jr., president of General Motors Asia Pacific: "He's a businessman and hard-charger who understands the Chinese system." . . .

His performance has pleased not only GM but his Chinese bosses as well. In July, Hu was appointed president and chief executive of Shanghai Automotive Industry Corporation. (SAIC), the largest and most successful automotive manufacturer in China—and GM's partner. . . .

Selected by Shanghai government as one of the 100 most promising managers in the city, Hu was dispatched to Georgia Tech in 1995 to study business administration. Before leaving for Atlanta, he finished a master's thesis at Fudan University in Shanghai on zero defects in quality control at Hui Zhong, a producer of trucks and components that he had headed. Shanghai authorities pulled him out of Georgia Tech after three months to lead the Chinese team forming the GM joint venture. Recalls Hu: "Both parties had to overcome a lot of obstacles—differences in social, political, and legal systems. I wasn't surprised that we had difficulties." . . .

Later Hu tells *Fortune* how he has made a fifty-fifty joint venture work, which he says "is difficult anywhere in the world." A joint board sets broad policies, but the top SGM executives in Shanghai—two from each of the owners—make the company's operating decisions. Says Hu: "If you hand a problem to your boss, he may not think you are capable. I like to solve things myself." In doing so, Hu has helped fit GM's strategic goal of capturing a significant share of the Chinese market while operating in an environment in which government support is crucial to business success.

From the start, the joint venture partners agreed that GM would inject technology and management skill to support a world-class car company, complete with exclusive Chinese dealers and vigorous marketing. Making that happen in the People's Republic proved to be tougher than either partner expected. The Chinese government, for instance, still dictates what products automakers can build, as well as how many and at what price. Moreover, GM is required to use locally made components, 40 percent in terms of value this year [1999] and 60 percent next year. And while sharing its latest technology, GM is restricted by Chinese law to owning just half of the joint venture.

Hu notes, "GM naturally wanted control." Bitter disputes long bedeviled SGM, even though the two partners spent 17 months negotiating contracts that stack about a foot high. Remarks Hu: "They were just done to meet legal requirements, and we never had time to took at them afterward." Inside the joint venture, officially formed in March 1997, the arguments raged so intensely that Hu told his GM associates, "I think Ford and Volkswagen would be very happy to see us quarrel." Says Philip Murtaugh, 44, executive vice president and the senior GM manager in the joint venture: "We had a lot of shooting matches but finally established a level of trust." Murtaugh credits Hu with moving American and Chinese managers from confrontation, unavoidable in negotiations, to cooperation, and says, "He could run a company anywhere in the world."

Dealing with the egos of leaders of the biggest corporation on earth proved to be an enormous challenge for Hu, who says, "In many other places GM won't listen to its local partners. That made my job more creative. It's not easy to change the attitudes of GM people." Nonetheless, he broke through deadlocks by establishing great rapport with Murtaugh, a bright young charger himself.

SOURCE: Excerpted from Louis Kraar, "China's Car Guy," *Fortune* (October 11, 1999), pp. 238–244. Copyright © 1999 Time Inc. Reprinted by permission.

decision-making processes; formalization represents decision making through bureaucratic mechanisms such as formal systems, established rules, and prescribed procedures; and normative integration relies neither on direct headquarters involvement nor on impersonal rules but on the socialization of managers into a set of shared goals, values, and beliefs that then shape their perspectives and behavior.[16] (Organizations that adopt the matrix organizational structure, discussed in Chapter 6, also tend to adopt the normative integration approach.)

The ensuing sections present two schemes that identify factors to help determine the right HSR. The first scheme posits that national cultural dimensions affect the relationship. The second proposes that certain situational factors influence the relationship in all countries.

The National Culture Scheme

As discussed in Chapter 1, the cross-cultural researcher Geert Hofstede[17] proposed a paradigm to study the impact of national culture on individual behavior. He developed a typology consisting of four national cultural dimensions by which a society can be classified: power distance, individualism, uncertainty avoidance, and masculinity. He later added a fifth dimension—Confucianism. The following section indicates whether the HSR with subsidiaries located in these cultures leans toward low or high centralization (C), low or high formalization (F), or low or high normative integration (NI). (See Table 13.2.)

TABLE 13.2	**The National Culture Framework**
Cultural Determinants	**Headquarters–Foreign Subsidiary Control Relationship**
Large power distance	HC
Small power distance	LC, HF, or HNI
High individualism	HC or HF
Low individualism	LF, HNI
Strong uncertainty avoidance	HF or HC
Weak uncertainty avoidance	LC or HNI
Confucianism	LF, HC, HNI
High masculinity	HF
Low masculinity	LC, HNI

SOURCE: Carl A. Rodrigues, "Headquarters–Foreign Subsidiary Control Relationships: Three Conceptual Frameworks," *Empowerment in Organizations: An International Journal*, 3, no. 3 (1995), p. 26.

NOTE: H = high; L = low; C = centralization; F = formalization; NI = normative integration.

Power Distance

Moderate to Large Power Distance. Individuals in societies dominated by this dimension tend to accept centralized power and depend heavily on superiors for direction. Therefore, an HSR leaning toward high C probably would be preferred by subsidiary managers who are dominated by this cultural dimension.

Moderate to Small Power Distance. Individuals in societies dominated by this cultural dimension do not tolerate highly centralized power and expect to be consulted, at least, in decision making. Furthermore, Hofstede remarked that status differences in these countries are suspect. Thus, subsidiary managers who are dominated by this cultural dimension probably would favor an HSR leaning toward low C, high NI, or high F.

The research project previously discussed, including M.B.A. students from Germany, Great Britain (both small power distance societies), and France (a large power distance society),[18] provides some support for the conclusions about a country's power distance measure influencing HSR. The students were asked to write their own diagnosis of and solution to a case problem. The majority of the French referred the problem to the next higher authority—they sought direction (high C). The British handled the problem (low C or high NI), and the Germans attributed it to a lack of formal policy and proposed establishing one (high F). Decision making in many of the Latin American cultures, which generally measure high on the power distance dimension, tends to be centralized.[19]

Individualism

Moderate to High Individualism. Individuals in societies dominated by this dimension think in "me" terms and look after primarily their own interests. Since these individuals often consider their own objectives to be more important than the organization's, the HSR that evolves in subsidiaries managed by people influenced by this cultural dimension probably leans toward high C or high F.

Moderate to Low Individualism. Low-individualism societies are tightly integrated and individuals belong to "in-groups" from which they cannot detach themselves. People think in "we" as opposed to "me" terms and obtain satisfaction from a job well done by the group. Individuals in these societies are controlled mainly by the group's norms and values. These people would therefore require less formal structure than individuals who think in "me" terms. An HSR leaning toward high NI would thus fit these societies.

Findings by some researchers lend support to the above contentions. These researchers concluded that control systems in the United States (a high-individualism culture) are designed under the assumption that workers and management seek "primary control" over their work environments.[20] Primary control is manifested when employees with individualistic tendencies attempt to shape the existing social and behavioral factors surrounding them, including coworkers, specific events, or their environments, with the intention of increasing their rewards.[21] Thus, many employees exhibit behaviors and establish goals that may diverge from those desired by the organization. For these reasons, control systems consisting of rules, standards, and norms of behavior are established to guide, motivate, and evaluate employees' behavioral performance (high F).[22] On the other hand, organizations in Japan (a low-individualism culture) rely more on "secondary controls," controls that depend mostly on informal peer pressure (high NI).[23] And Japanese corporations with subsidiaries in the United States tend to give American managers working for them little or no authority.[24]

Uncertainty Avoidance

Moderate to Strong Uncertainty Avoidance. Individuals in these cultures feel uneasy in situations of uncertainty and ambiguity and prefer structure and direction. Therefore, because it tends to reduce uncertainty for individuals, managers of subsidiaries who are influenced by this cultural dimension probably would prefer an HSR leaning toward high F or high C. Hofstede has proposed that improving quality of life for employees in these societies implies offering more security and perhaps more task structure on the job (high F).

Moderate to Weak Uncertainty Avoidance. Hofstede found that in countries dominated by a moderate to weak uncertainty avoidance dimension, individuals tend to be relatively tolerant of uncertainty and ambiguity; they do not require as high C or high F as do people in strong uncertainty avoidance cultures. Thus, an HSR leaning toward low C or high NI probably would be preferred by managers of subsidiaries who are dominated by this cultural dimension, since it provides more challenge than does high C and high F.

For example, managers in Britain, a weak uncertainty avoidance culture, tend to value achievement and autonomy (low C or high NI behavior), and managers in France, a strong uncertainty avoidance society, value competent supervision, sound company policies, fringe benefits, security, and comfortable working conditions (high C and high F).[25] French managers do not believe that matrix organizations (discussed in Chapter 6), which tend to apply high-NI behavior, are feasible; they view them as violating the principle of unit of command.[26]

Confucianism

As pointed out in Chapter 1, individuals in East Asian cultures (the People's Republic of China, South Korea, Japan, Hong Kong, and Singapore) are also influenced by the Confucian cultural dimension. In essence, individuals in Confucian-based organizations are forced to adhere to rigid, informal group norms and values (high-NI relationship). Since individuals are so strictly bound to group norms, organizations based on the Confucian cultural dimension probably apply less formalization (low F) than do organizations in the West. This contention is partially supported by research findings that organizations in China, where the Confucian influence is still strong, tend to be far less formalized than Western organizations.[27] There is evidence that Confucian-based organizations apply high C. For example, South Korean managers demonstrate the Confucian virtues of loyalty and obedience to authorities, and they tend not to adopt systems of shared management and power equalization within organizations.[28] Chinese subordinates have been found to be passive, preferring that others make decisions for them (high C).[29]

Masculinity

Moderate to High Masculinity. Societies dominated by this dimension stress material success and assertiveness and assign different roles to males and females. To review, males are expected to carry out the competitive roles in society; females are expected to care for the nonmaterial quality of life. In strong-masculinity countries, where people perceive such behavior as being inequitable, an HSR leaning toward high F, emphasizing reduction of such social inequities would probably be preferred. One finds evidence of this in recent programs in the United States, a society with a moderate- to high-masculinity cultural dimension—the Equal Pay Act of 1963, Title VII of the Civil Rights Act of 1964, affirmative action and equal employment opportunity programs, and in Japan with its very high-masculinity culture—the Employment Opportunity Law of 1986.

Moderate to Low Masculinity. Hofstede also concluded that those nations dominated by a low-masculinity cultural dimension stress interpersonal relationships, a concern for others and the overall quality of life, and define relatively overlapping social roles for males and females. In these cultures, neither male nor female need be ambitious or competitive; both may aspire to a life that does not assign great importance to material success and believe in mutual respect for each other. According to Hofstede,[30] improved quality of work life for individuals in these societies means offering opportunities for developing relationships on the job, which is perhaps best accomplished through low-C or high-NI HSR. For example, people in Sweden, a low-masculinity society, generally prefer organic (low C, NI) organizational structures, and they like to be involved in the decision-making process.

The Situational Scheme

The above presented a national culture scheme as a means of determining HSRs. However, as pointed out in Chapter 11, the scheme serves mainly as a generalization—as a starting point for analysis, and many organizational theorists[31] have argued that, irrespective of a society's culture, individuals are forced to adapt attitudes and behaviors that comply with the imperatives of industrialization. This means that HSRs are affected more by situational factors than cultural factors. Thus, we arrive at the situational scheme. (See Table 13.3.)

The Subsidiary's Local Context

Ghoshal and Nohria believe that HSRs are not identical for all subsidiaries throughout the company, that each HSR can be governed by a different combination of the three mechanisms (C, F, NI), and that companies adopt different modes of governance to fit each subsidiary's local context. The local context, according to them, can vary in a number of ways, but two of the most important ways are environmental complexity (the level of technological dynamism and competitive intensity) and the amount of local resources available to the subsidiary.[32] Some subsidiaries may be managing advanced technologies (e.g., computers) in a very competitive market (high environmental complexity), while others may be managing older technologies (e.g., steel production) in a stable market (low environmental complexity). Some subsidiaries may have an abundance of resources, while others have scarce resources. Ghoshal and Nohria developed a scheme that matches HSR to subsidiary contexts. Their scheme is as follows:[33]

1. Low environment complexity and low levels of local resources indicate a high level of centralization and low levels of formalization and normative integration.

TABLE 13.3	The Situational Framework

Situational Determinants	Headquarters–Foreign Subsidiary Control Relationship
The subsidiary's local context	
Low complexity; low level of resources	HC, LF, LNI
Low complexity; high level of resources	LC, HF, HNI
High complexity; low level of resources	MC, LF, HNI
High complexity; high level of resources	LC, MF, HNI
The organization's size	
Large-scale organization	HF
Large-scale organization with global strategy	LC, HC, HNI
Large-scale organization with multidomestic strategy	LC, HF
Small-scale organization	HNI or HC
Organizational functions	
R&D-like functions	HNI, LC, LF
Production-like functions	
With multidomestic strategy	HF
With global strategy	HNI, MC
Cash management-like functions	HC, HF
Organization in crisis conditions	
In an environment of scarcity	HC or HF
In an environment of abundance	LC, HNI
Management's preference	
Likes to maintain strong control	HC
Likes to maintain stability	HF
Likes to maintain adaptability, flexibility	HNI
Information technology: communication costs	
Costs are high	LC
Costs fall	HC
Costs continue falling	HNI

SOURCE: Carl A. Rodrigues, "Headquarters-Foreign Subsidiary Control Relationships: Three Conceptual Frameworks," *Empowerment in Organizations: An International Journal*, 3, no. 3 (1995), p. 29.

NOTE: H = high; L = low; M = moderate; C = centralization; F = formalization; NI = normative integration.

2. Low environment complexity and high levels of resources indicate a low level of centralization and high levels of formalization and normative integration.

3. High environment complexity and low resource levels indicate a moderate level of centralization, a low level of formalization, and a high level of normative integration.

4. High environment complexity and high resource levels indicate a low level of centralization, a moderate level of formalization, and a high level of normative integration.

Size of the Organization

The size of the organization has been found to be a factor in determining HSRs. Large-scale organizations have tended to apply structural relationships leaning toward high F and small-scale organizations tend to apply a high NI or high C structural relationship.[34] However, this factor is influenced by the organization's strategy. Some international businesses establish a global strategy. The global corporation uses all its resources against its competitors in a very integrated fashion. All its foreign subsidiaries and divisions are highly interdependent in both operations and strategy. As an expert said,

> In a global business, management competes worldwide against a small number of other multinationals in the world market. Strategy is centralized, and various aspects of operations are decentralized or centralized as economics and effectiveness dictate. The company seeks to respond to particular local market needs, while avoiding a compromise of efficiency of the overall global system.[35]

Companies that apply the global strategy include IBM in computers; Caterpillar in large construction equipment; Timex, Seiko, and Citizen in watches; and General Electric, Siemens, and Mitsubishi in heavy electrical equipment. Many corporations that adopt the global strategy approach also adopt the matrix organizational structure. In the matrix structure, there is extensive cooperation among all the operating subsidiaries. Therefore, the global corporation relies on an HSR with a combination of low C, high C, and high NI.

Many international firms establish a multidomestic strategy. The multidomestic firm has a different strategy for each of its foreign markets. In this type of strategy,

> a company's management tries to operate effectively across a series of worldwide positions with diverse product requirements, growth rates, competitive environments, and political risks. The company prefers that local managers do what is necessary to succeed in R&D, production, marketing, and distribution but holds them responsible for results.[36]

In essence, this type of corporation competes with local companies on a market-by-market basis. A multitude of American corporations use this strategy—for example, Procter & Gamble in household products, Honeywell in controls, Alcoa in aluminum, and General Foods in consumer goods. Large organizations that adopt a multidomestic strategy tend to apply low C; but for accountability reasons, they also tend to rely on bureaucratic (high F) HSRs.

Type of Organizational Function

The internal aspects of the organization are also determinants of structural relationships.[37] Some subunits apply high-organic, NI relationships, while others in the same organization apply high-C or -F relationships. Thus, R&D subsidiaries, because their functional effectiveness often depends on an integration of numerous individuals' ideas, probably function more effectively with a relationship leaning toward low F, low C, and high NI. Subunits such as production, a function that usually requires high structure to ensure production efficiency, probably work best with a relationship leaning toward high F—this, however, may be more so for corporations with a multidomestic strategy than for companies with a global strategy. To ensure overall production efficiency, global corporations often integrate production across all subsidiaries by use of the matrix organization structure, thus applying a high NI with some degree of central coordination (moderate C). Functions such as cash management are usually centralized (high C) and formalized (high F). For example, Broken Hill Proprietary Company Ltd., a U.S.-based producer/distributor of minerals, petroleum, and steel, has centralized cash management in the corporation but has decentralized and localized the management of resource gathering, marketing, and distribution.[38] (Practical Perspective 13.4 illustrates how BICC Cables dealt with the need to decentralize certain functions while at the same time centralizing the information technology function.)

PRACTICAL PERSPECTIVE 13-4

Getting the "Hardware" Right: The Case of BICC Cables

One of the primary challenges in an organisation is to set up an IT function. How well the function is set up is a major factor in its effectiveness. Yet setting the functions up well requires highly effective IT management in the first place. And what constitutes a well-structured IT function can change over time with the strategic needs of the organisation and with the characteristics of IT.

For many years BICC Cables had allowed its worldwide operations great local decision-making authority. Customers usually made local purchasing decisions. The company believed that managers of local operating units would make the best business decisions if they had responsibility for all factors affecting profitability—including IT.

Two issues caused the company to rethink its IT management strategy. First, managers anticipated a shift toward customers purchasing globally—a trend that would require greater interdependence among local operations. Second, they became aware of developments in IT that seemed to require a different management approach. The company's capital budgeting committee found itself simultaneously considering requests from two different operating units to replace aging legacy information systems with an enterprise software package. The two had done a thorough evaluation to determine the best package for their needs—and had chosen two different packages.

Members of the committee asked themselves several questions. Didn't the two units do basically the same things? If so, how could two different packages both be best? How much would it cost to adopt different IT solutions in different parts of the company? And how would different IT solutions in different parts of the company hinder it from responding to likely future business trends? Preliminary investigations revealed that a corporate approach to acquiring enterprise software would yield major saving over a decentralised approach.

Of course, the committee's questions raised a number of red flags. How would local units react to any recentralisation of IT management? Would this seriously undermine the autonomy that operational managers needed to control profitability? These were clearly serious concerns, requiring careful handling.

The committee put both requests on hold pending further study of the need for common systems, and Andrew Cox, the company's chief financial officer, hired its first chief information officer, Alan Harrison. To combat fears of "IT empire-building," Harrison operated for several years as a "department of one." He convened a company-wide task force to chart the major business processes of one of the local operations. Each site was then asked to review the charts, noting local differences. The results were quite compelling: the commonalties in business processes across local operations were far greater than the differences. Thus it looked possible to select a single enterprise package representing what was best for the company as whole.

The next step was to form a company-wide software selection task force to evaluate several options, including the two first championed by local units. The evaluation criteria were rigorously defined in advance to forestall any criticism from the "losers." When the committee completed its selection, Harrison negotiated a very favourable corporate contract with the software vendor.

The corporate purchase agreement was not the last of the new IT management decisions raised by enterprise software. Still to be decided were which units would adopt the software, how much local autonomy there would be in software configuration, and how implementation and support would be managed. To ensure local commitment to implementing software successfully, units were still required to apply to the capital budget committee for funding. All were expected to justify their applications but they were granted freedom to justify their applications in locally relevant terms. Some cited business benefits such as inventory reductions; others emphasized IT cost savings.

To enable a coordinated response to customers in the future, BICC Cables decided to develop a common enterprise model. Local operations could request changes but these would be treated as changes to the core model rather than as changes in local implementations. On the other hand, local operations were expected to implement the software themselves with consulting support from the vendor and from the still small (but no longer one-man) IT function. Because enterprise software involves a long-term commitment to a vendor's product family (and therefore a series of future upgrades), the local units were thought to require the capacity to manage implementations locally.

The case of BICC Cables illustrates several points about improving the effectiveness of the IT function. First, decisions about the "hardware" of the IT function (its size; structure; mission; and tasks, including the activities to be outsourced) are critical. Second, these decisions must be revisited from time to time as changes occur in the nature of the business and in the opportunities and challenges posed by new information technologies. Third, these decisions will not be the same for all companies but will depend on such things as the industry in which a company operates; the company's specific business strategies; and its size, structure, and historical management culture.

SOURCE: Excerpted from "Organising a Better IT Function," *Financial Times* (London), Survey Edition 1 (February 15, 1999), p. 5. Reprinted with permission.

Organizations Under Crisis Conditions

Numerous studies have revealed that organizations confronted with crisis conditions—environmental hostility, turbulence, and financial adversity—tend to increase the formalization and standardization of procedures, place greater emphasis on previously established rules, and centralize and involve fewer people in the decision-making process.[39] (The case of Samsung in Practical Perspective 13.5 illustrates this point.) In other words, headquarters managers of organizations confronted with crisis conditions usually apply an HSR leaning toward high F or high C. It has been found, however, that this occurs more frequently when the organization exists in an environment of scarcity than when it exists in an environment of abundance.[40] Organizations confronted with crisis conditions in an environment of abundance tend to decentralize (low-C, high-NI behavior).

Management's Preference

Culturally, management would prefer to maintain strong control over activities (high C); strong organizational stability, and thus a bureaucratic system (high F); or a flexible, adaptable organization, and therefore an interactive approach (high NI). The U.S.-based giant Johnson & Johnson is an illustration of a company whose management has over the years developed a corporate culture that promotes decentralization but encourages managers to act in a global, concerted fashion when necessary.

PRACTICAL PERSPECTIVE 13-5

The Man Who Shook Up Samsung

Even in a year of remarkable recovery for Asia, some of the region's leading companies were foundering because of old bad habits. That wasn't the case with Samsung Electronics, whose CEO, Yun Jong Yong, used Asia's chaos to reinvent a company that seemed near death—a feat that has earned Yun Fortune's title of Asia's Businessman of the Year.

When Yun took command of Samsung, their earnings had largely evaporated because of a long decline in the prices of memory chips—then Samsung's main source of profit. And the company was losing money on its low-priced me-too models of TVs and microwave ovens. "There was a sense that this company could go down. It was that extreme," said Yun. So extreme, in fact, that Samsung's chairman authorized Yun, an electrical engineer, . . . to make changes shocking to most Koreans—chopping one third of the payroll and replacing half of the senior managers; selling off $1.9 billions in assets, from an executive jet to an entire semiconductor division; refusing to tolerate long presentations or reports; and welcoming a foreigner to the corporate board. Then Yun launched a slew of leading-edge products, including Internet music players, flat-panel displays, and a line of 5.5 oz. cell phones with both voice-activated dialing and Internet access. The result: . . . the company's stocks, listed in Korea and widely held internationally, rose 233%, to $227 a share, last year (1999).[a] Thus, compared with other major Korean companies, Samsung survived the Asian financial crisis of 1997–1998 relatively unharmed. . . . Considered a strong competitor by its rivals, Samsung Electronics expanded production dramatically to become the world's largest manufacturer of DRAM chips, refrigerators, flash memory, and optical storage drives, and it aims to become the top manufacturer of 20 products globally by 2010.[b]

SOURCES:

a. Excerpted and adapted from Louis Kraar, "Asia's Businessman of the Year," *Fortune* (January 24, 2000), p. 28. Copyright © 2000 Time Inc. Reprinted by permission. b. http://en.wikipedia.org/wiki/Samsung (May 7, 2007).

Johnson & Johnson is performing an incredible act that defies logic. Not only does it run no fewer than 33 major lines of business with an astounding 168 operating companies in 53 countries, but it also runs them well. Johnson & Johnson may have mastered the art of decentralized management better than any other company in the world. Long before the rest of corporate America made "empowerment" a management buzzword, J&J was practicing it. As early as the 1930s, its longtime chairman Robert Wood Johnson pushed the idea of decentralization. Believing that smaller, self-governing units were more manageable, quicker to react to their markets, and more accountable, the son of a Johnson & Johnson cofounder encouraged early mainstays such as Ethicon, Inc., a sutures maker, and Personal Products Company, the feminine-hygiene business, to operate independently.[41]

Government Involvement

The extent to which a government is involved in corporate-level governance—for example, in communist countries—affects the organization's performance. It has been found that the Chinese government's involvement in the management affairs of firms has led to negative economic effects at the firm level.[42]

Information Technology: Communication Costs

Current information technology, such as the Internet, the Web, and videoconferencing, is forcing many organizations to rethink and reengineer their organizational structures and their information systems. This chapter presents numerous factors that influence the type of organizational structures and controls managers adopt. Another factor that influences organizational structure and control is communication costs. As improvements in technology reduce communication and coordination costs, the preferred way to make decisions moves in three stages.[43]

In the first stage, when communication costs are high, the best way to make decisions is via independent decentralized decision makers (low C). As communication costs fall, it becomes more feasible in many decision-making situations to bring information from remote areas to a hub, where centralized decision makers (high C) can have a broad perspective of the whole organization and therefore can make better decisions than the isolated, local decision makers.

As communication costs continue to fall, many organizations will be more effective if connected, decentralized decision makers make the decisions (HNI). For example, Swisscom, one of Europe's leading telecommunications and networking companies, has installed a new workflow system supplied by CSE Systems Corporation, an Austrian document technology company. The primary objective is to accelerate the flow of information throughout the company, which (as of 1999) employed approximately 21,000 people. The system provides an intranet gateway for distribution of documents and data within the enterprise and to external parties.[44]

International Managers Must Consider Both Schemes

As pointed out in Chapter 11, both the cultural and the situational schemes are well supported by research. Therefore, when making a decision about the right HSR, international managers will have to consider both schemes. When international managers make a mistake and select the wrong HSR, it usually costs their company a great deal of money to rectify it, and there will be nonmonetary costs as well, such as low employee morale, and so on. Either extreme—too much centralization and too little decentralization or too little centralization and too much decentralization—eventually leads to managerial problems. Hence, international managers must seek a balance between centralized and decentralized HSR.

A Framework for Attaining a Balanced HSR

As Kenichi Ohmae, head of McKinsey's office in Tokyo, proposes,

The conditions in each market are too varied, the nuances of competition too complex, and the changes in climate too subtle and too rapid for long-distance management.

No matter how good they are, no matter how well supported analytically, the decision makers at the center are just too far removed from the intricacies of individual markets and the needs of local customers.[45]

But decentralizing key decisions creates its own problems, and no company can operate effectively for a long period of time through a totally centralized or a totally decentralized control relationship. In other words, as classical U.S. management principles indicate, there must be a balance between centralization and decentralization; Wal-Mart, for example, has learned this the hard way; it has learned at great cost that its centralized system doesn't work in many cultures.[46] (This means that Johnson & Johnson may not be as decentralized as the media make it out to be.) A major problem confronting headquarters' managers is how to attain an HSR with balanced centralization and decentralization: How to obtain assurance that decisions made by subsidiary managers are in tune with the enterprise's overall objectives and that decisions made by headquarters management are not sabotaged by subsidiary management. (Note that in Practical Perspective 13.3, General Motors attained this balance.) The ensuing section describes a framework for attaining a balanced HSR.

Due Process as a Means of Attaining Balanced HSRs

Historically, when headquarters managers made decisions (such as establishing strategic plans) that had to be executed by subsidiary managers, many managers relied on implementation control mechanisms such as incentive compensation, monitoring systems, and rewards and punishments. W. Chan Kim, an associate professor of strategy and international management, and Renee A. Mauborgne, a research associate of management and international business, both at INSEAD, France, conducted extensive research to ascertain what it takes for multinationals to successfully execute global strategies. The top managers of subsidiaries they interviewed indicated that these implementation control mechanisms alone were neither sufficient nor effective; that they were not particularly motivating, and that they were not foolproof.[47]

The subsidiary managers indicated that effective implementation requires that due process be exercised in global decision making. The due process is depicted in Figure 13.1.

Due process means that

1. the head office is familiar with subsidiaries' local situations,

2. two-way communication exists in the global strategy-making process,

3. the head office is relatively consistent in making decisions across subsidiary units,

4. subsidiary units can legitimately challenge the head office's strategic views and decisions, and

5. subsidiary units receive an explanation for the final decisions.[48]

This model means that organizations can attain a balance between centralization and decentralization if they apply extensive vertical and horizontal communication throughout the overall system. Application of the matrix organization structure (discussed in Chapter 6) can help attain this type of communication. More is needed, however. Practical Perspectives 13.6 and 13.7 suggest that the development of corporate global core values, which cut across all foreign subsidiaries, would help provide a balance.

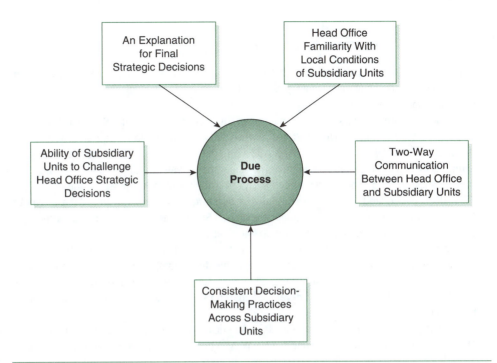

Figure 13.1   What Is Due Process in Global Strategic Decision Making?

SOURCE: W. Chan Kim and Renee A. Mauborgne, "Making Global Strategies Work," *Sloan Management Review* (Spring 1993), p. 12. By permission of the publisher. Copyright © 1993 by the Sloan Management Review Association. All rights reserved.

PRACTICAL PERSPECTIVE 13-6

Transplanting Corporate Cultures Globally

Asea Brown Boveri, Inc. (ABB), the electrical-engineering giant, is the quintessential global company. It has a clearly defined mission statement and a culture that supports the mission. . . . "We think about ABB as a company without any regard to national boundaries," said Richard P. Randazzo, who, as ABB's vice president of HR, works out of the company's Stamford, Connecticut, base and oversees the company's HR operations in the United States. "We just operate on a global basis. A lot of other companies see boundaries and barriers, but from a business standpoint, this company is intent on transcending those boundaries." Indeed, more than 50 percent of its sales are in Europe, 20 percent are in North America, 20 percent in Asia, and the rest are in South America and Africa. The official language is English; the official currency is the dollar. . . .

It's a highly decentralized business (the United States alone has 50 companies, each with its own president). Divisions treat each other as vendors and customers, invoicing one another and maintaining accounts payable and receivable from other divisions. Characterized by *Forbes* as a company that has no discernible national identity, ABB's corporate culture is one of its strong defining features. The company embodies the phrase think globally, act locally. According to Randazzo, ABB's culture is focused tightly on making money. Its personality profile is a hands-on, action-oriented, travel-to-the-opportunity kind of business. Each division acts locally in response to customers and employees.

PRACTICAL PERSPECTIVE 13-6 (Continued)

But managers are required to think globally about sourcing. For example, if the dollar is strong relative to the Swedish krona, then the company sources more from Sweden because goods and services are cheaper there. When that changes, sourcing also changes.

Corporate culture mixes with the culture of the country in which ABB operates. "There's no attempt by the corporation to tell us in the United States how we should behave relative to our customers or to our employees," said Randazzo. (Other HR executives oversee ABB's HR operations in its different business segments and the different countries in which the company operates.) The senior management team is composed largely of Europeans, so at times they give Randazzo quizzical looks when he says that they can't ask a person's age or marital status when recruiting. "They don't understand some of the affirmative-action targets we have, but they don't attempt to influence any of that. The rationale is that we know more about the United States marketplace than the Germans, the Swedes, or the Swiss will ever know, and therefore, we're better able to deal with it."

But cultures aren't static. They influence each other. For one, HR management plays a much more significant role in the United States than it does in Europe. According to Randazzo, this is the arena in which Americans have had significant influence on ABB's Europeans, addressing such issues as employee involvement, empowerment, and total quality. In fact, the U.S. HR staff developed materials for conducting management training, some of which were translated into German.

Likewise, the Europeans have influenced the Americans. They've brought a sense of business urgency to the company. They helped with downsizing, lowering the break-even point and getting the organization focused. Understanding local attitudes helps corporate cultures take root. Not all corporate cultures transplant well overseas. Companies that try to graft the Stars and Stripes forever in a foreign location will likely encounter resistance. Those that are sensitive to local attitudes and customs are bound to be more successful.[a]

The company's official name has been changed to ABB, headquartered in Zurick, Switzerland. It operates mainly in the power and industrial automation technology areas, operating in around 100 countries, with about 108,000 employees. Its 2006 revenue was US$ 24,412 million. Fred Kindle assumed the role of President and CEO on January 1, 2005.[b]

SOURCES:

a. Excerpted from Charlene M. Solomon, "Transplanting Corporate Cultures Globally," *Personnel Journal* (October 1993), pp. 80–81. Reprinted with the permission of Personnel Journal, ACC Communications, Inc., Cosa Mesa, CA. All rights reserved.

b. http://en.wikipedia.org/wiki/ASEA_Brown_Boveri (May 7, 2007).

PRACTICAL PERSPECTIVE 13-7

Global Vision and Core Values

In April 1992, Chairman Riley P. Bechtel issued the company's (Bechtel Corporation) new strategic plan called Toward 2001. In it, he articulated his global vision and core values, making a commitment to analyze and change the corporate culture within a global context. To be most effective, it was essential to learn about employees' beliefs and attitudes. Gaufin's HR staff issued a 102-question survey to 22,000 employees. Questions asked employees about communication, training and advancement opportunities, the work environment, and the importance of international and domestic field experience to professional development. The staff followed up with more than 200 focus groups at the firm's domestic and international locations.

In response to the results, each large office developed specific action plans to address employee concerns, which included communication between management and employees and the availability of training programs for people at field locations. . . .

"The survey is a way of listening to employees. It gives us ways to implement the corporate culture more effectively," said Gaufin. The 1992 survey is the baseline. Periodic surveys will provide means of measuring progress. "There are a lot of challenges when it comes to implementing some of the changes," said Gaufin. For example, different cultures perceive performance reviews in different ways. "We have to be sure that we're not going against accepted practices in other parts of the world," she said. Furthermore, part of the new strategic plan focuses on empowered teams. Gaufin said that will be a challenge, too. . . .

Of course, state-of-the-art telecommunications facilitate the cultural exchange. Many employees have considerable international phone contact with each other. Videoconferencing and in-person meetings with foreign colleagues build social relationships. The company also televises major company meetings to Europe.

These are key ways to convey corporate culture. In Bechtel's case, this is particularly important. As the speedy mobilization to help fight the Kuwait fires attests, employees sometimes are called on to move to another location on a few days' notice. A highly decentralized, flexible structure makes this rapid response possible. Work often is done with project teams. They form to accomplish specific tasks. U.S. expatriates, other expatriates, and local nationals do the job and then demobilize. This type of work arrangement, the speed at which the company can respond, and the company's flexibility also make it imperative that employees fully comprehend the company's mission.

"Obviously, you have to communicate the company's purpose and its objectives," said Morgan. "The culture provides guidance for the employee on how the company wants to achieve those objectives." . . . In addition, the HR staff . . . uses pre-employment interviews to communicate some of the company's culture, particularly when hiring managers. The issue of fit involves not only technical skills and qualifications but also the assurance that the employee will be comfortable with Bechtel's way of doing things. . . .

Training and development are other areas in which Bechtel communicates its goals and values. Morgan, who is Australian and has lived in a variety of off-shore settings, says that international training is heightened when you teach mixed groups of U.S. expatriates and local nationals. The training goes both ways. U.S. expatriates communicate the company's ideals and personality to local nationals, and the nationals transmit the host culture to the Americans.[a]

Bechtel Corporation (Bechtel Group) is currently (2007) the largest engineering company in the United States, ranked as the 6th largest privately owned company in the United States. With headquarters in San Francisco, Bechtel had 40,000 employees. As of 2005 working on projects in nearly 50 countries with $18.1 billion in revenue. Its CEO is Riley P. Bechtel.[b]

SOURCES:

a. Excerpted and adapted from Charlene M. Solomon, "Transplanting Corporate Cultures Globally," *Personnel Journal* (October 1993), pp. 80–81. Reprinted with permission of Personnel Journal, ACC Communications, Inc., Cosa Mesa, CA. All rights reserved.

b. http://en.wikipedia.org/wiki/Bechtel (May 7, 2007).

Global Corporate Culture and Core Values as a Means of Attaining Balance

As indicated in Chapter 1, cross-cultural researchers have broken down the meaning of corporate/organizational culture into symbols, heroes, and rituals, which they defined as organizational practice, and into values such as good/evil, beautiful/ugly, normal/ abnormal, and rational/irrational. These researchers contend that corporate/ organizational cultures "reflect nationality, demographics of employees and managers, industry, and market; they are related to organization structure and control systems; but all of these leave room for unique and idiosyncratic elements."[49] Among national cultures, comparing "otherwise similar people," these researchers found "considerable differences in values." Among corporate cultures, the opposite was the case; they found "considerable differences in practices for people who held about the same values."[50]

Therefore, according to these researchers, the value aspects of corporate culture are attributed to nationality, but the practice aspects are attributed to the corporation, and the corporation changes practices in response to environmental demands. Since the environment changes at different times for different organizations, the practice aspects will differ from corporation to corporation, even when the values remain relatively similar. This means that individuals in the same national culture may possess broad behavioral similarities but different practices, depending on the corporation they work for.

The development of global corporate core values—that is, values that cut across all subsidiaries located around the globe—would help provide a balance. For example, Asea Brown Boveri, Inc. (ABB), the electrical engineering giant, is the quintessential global company. It has a clearly defined mission statement and a culture that supports the mission. "We think about ABB as a company without any regard to national boundaries," says Richard P. Randazzo, who, as ABB's vice president of HR, works out of the company's Stamford, Connecticut, base and oversees the company's HR operations in the United States. "We just operate on a global basis. A lot of other companies see boundaries and barriers, but from a business standpoint, this company is intent on transcending those boundaries."[51]

In April 1992, Chairman Riley P. Bechtel issued Bechtel Corporation's new strategic plan called Toward 2001. In it, he articulated his global vision and core values, making a commitment to analyze and change the corporate culture within a global context: "The culture provides guidance for the employee on how the company wants to achieve those objectives."[52] "It's vitally important that the [transnational] company have a strong company culture," says Calvin Reynolds, senior fellow at the Wharton School of the University of Pennsylvania and senior counselor for the New York City-based Organization Resources Counselors. "If you don't have a strong set of cultural principles from which to function, when people get overseas, they're so lacking in clarity that no one knows where he or she is going."[53]

Nurturing Balance

The above suggests that a global corporation can develop a value system with global application, in which individual subsidiaries adapt practices suitable to the local situation. David Whitwam, CEO of Whirlpool Corporation, also supports this contention, stating,

> When we acquired Philips [a floundering European appliance business in [1989] . . . Wall Street analysts expected us to ship 500 people over to Europe, plug them into the plants and distribution systems, and give them six months or a year to turn the business around. They expected us to impose the "superior American way" of operating on the European organization. . . . If you try to gain control of an organization by simply subjugating it to your preconceptions, you can expect to pay for your short-term profits with long-term resistance and resentment. That's why we chose another course. During the first year, I think we had two people from the United States working in Europe, and neither was a senior manager. By the end of the second year, we had maybe a half a dozen U.S. managers there—again, none at the senior level. We listened and observed. We worked hard to communicate

the company's vision, objectives, and philosophy to the European workforce. Building a shared understanding takes time, and we had to learn how to do that in a multilingual, multinational environment. Today we have 15,000 employees in Europe with only 10 from U.S. operations. They all report to European bosses, with the exception of Hank Bowman, executive vice president of Whirlpool Europe.[54]

Gurcharan Das, formerly chairman and managing director of Procter & Gamble India, said the same thing:

Globalization does not mean imposing homogeneous solutions in a pluralistic world. It means having a global vision and strategy, but it also means cultivating roots and individual identities. It means nourishing local insights, but it also means reemploying communicable ideas in new geographies around the world.[55]

Practical Perspective 13.7 describes Bechtel Corporation's approach to changing corporate culture within a global context. Figure 13.2 depicts the framework for attaining a balance between centralization and decentralization, and therefore a balanced HSR.

Selling Issues

The above model suggests that to nourish a balanced HSR, management must sell corporate issues to the locals, which requires an understanding of the local culture.[56] Figure 13.3 presents a stage model of issue-selling intention and strategies, and Figure 13.4, the impact of national culture on issue-selling intention and strategy.

The above frameworks are practicable only if the top managers are able to understand them and are willing to apply them and if the locals understand them and are willing to participate.[57] This textbook would help students enhance and fortify the concepts of international business management in different cultures.

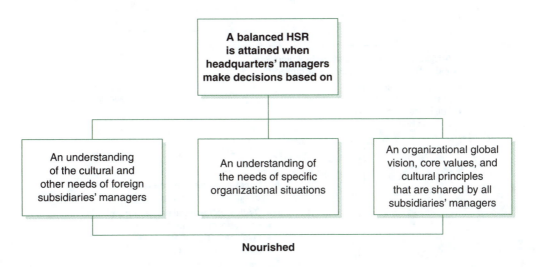

Figure 13.2 Attaining a Balanced Headquarters–Foreign Subsidiary Control Relationship (HSR)

SOURCE: Carl A. Rodrigues, "Headquarters–Foreign Subsidiary Control Relationships: Three Conceptual Frameworks," *Empowerment in Organizations: An International Journal*, 3, no. 3 (1995), pp. 33.

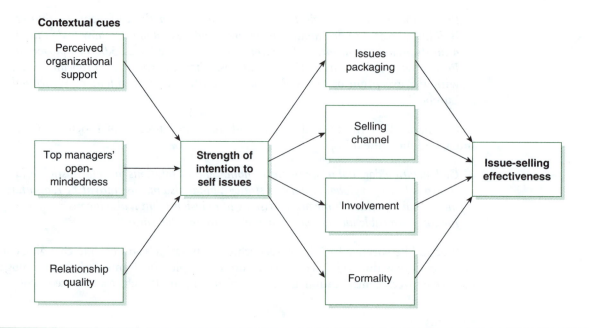

Figure 13.3 Stage Model of Issue-Selling Intention and Strategies

SOURCE: Y. Ling, S. W. Floyd, and D. C. Baldridge, "Toward a Model of Issue-Selling by Subsidiary Managers in Multinational Organizations," *Journal of International Business Studies*, 36 (2005), p. 639.

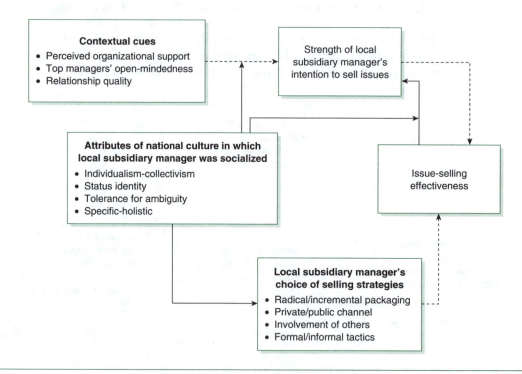

Figure 13.4 The Impact of National Culture on Issue-Selling Intention and Strategies

SOURCE: Y. Ling, S. W. Floyd, and D. C. Baldridge, "Toward a Model of Issue-Selling by Subsidiary Managers in Multinational Organizations," *Journal of International Business Studies,* 36 (2005), p. 641.

Summary

This chapter has addressed the topic of HSRs. It has presented the traditional concepts of centralized and decentralized HSRs as well as several factors that help headquarters managers determine the appropriate relationship. It has also addressed the contemporary concepts of centralization, formalization, and normative integration HSRs and presented cross-cultural and situational factors that help headquarters managers determine the appropriate relationship. It has proposed that effective global corporations need to establish a balanced HSR and that balance can be attained through the implementation of a global corporate culture and core values.

KEY TERMS AND CONCEPTS

1. Subsidiary

2. Headquarters–foreign subsidiary control relationships (HSRs)

3. Centralization; decentralization

4. Headquarters management's confidence in the foreign subsidiaries' management abilities

5. Local presence

6. Governance mechanisms

7. Formalization; normative integration

8. The national culture scheme

9. Cultural dimensions affect relationships

10. The situational scheme

11. The subsidiary's local context

12. Environmental complexity and amount of local resources

13. Size of the organization; type of organizational function; crisis conditions; management's preference; and communication costs

14. A balanced headquarters–foreign subsidiaries control relationship

15. Vertical and horizontal communication

16. Matrix structure

17. Practices and values

18. Adapting practices to local situation

19. Corporate core value system has global application

20. Global corporate culture and core values as a balance

21. Nurturing balance

DISCUSSION QUESTIONS

1. Describe the centralized and decentralized HSRs and some of the pros and cons of each.

2. Which types of HSRs are foreign manufacturing and foreign marketing subsidiaries likely to generate?

3. What kind of HSR is the function of recruiting and selecting personnel in foreign subsidiaries likely to generate?

4. Why are foreign subsidiaries that provide a wide range of products less centrally controlled than those that provide a narrow range of products?

5. Describe the centralization, formalization, and normative integration HSRs.

6. What type of HSR—centralization, formalization, or normative integration—fits low-individualism cultures? Why?

7. Managers of foreign subsidiaries who are dominated by a small power distance cultural dimension are likely to favor a normative integration or a formalization HSR. Do you agree or disagree? Why?

8. Describe the degrees of centralization, formalization, and normative integration in a HSR when the foreign subsidiary is confronted with a high environment of complexity and low level of local resources.

9. How does current information technology enable organizations to shift from a highly centralized control system to a high normative integration system?

10. How do global corporate cultures and core values help provide a balanced HSR?

EXERCISES

1. You are from the headquarters of a U.S.-based company. You are assigned to create subsidiaries in France. What type of HSRs—centralization, formalization, or normative integration—would you establish in each country? Why?

2. You are from the headquarters of a U.S.-based company. You are assigned to create subsidiaries in Britain. What type of HSRs—centralization, formalization, or normative integration—would you establish in each country? Why?

3. You are from the headquarters of a U.S.-based company. You are assigned to create subsidiaries in China. What type of HSRs—centralization, formalization, or normative integration—would you establish in each country? Why?

4. You are the headquarters executive responsible for the financial aspects of the overall corporation. What type of HSR—centralization, formalization, or normative integration—are you likely to establish? Why?

5. Top management of a global corporation that manufactures and distributes product Y has decided to divest its manufacturing operations and concentrate on its distribution operations. How is the transformation best approached? (Refer to Practical Perspective 13.6.) Which HSR is likely to emerge?

ASSIGNMENT

Contact a senior international executive of a corporation. Ask him or her to describe his or her company's foreign subsidiary control relationship. Write a short report for presentation in class.

CASE 13-1

Electrolux

Global business or product-division managers have one overriding responsibility: to further the company's global-scale efficiency and competitiveness. This task requires not only the perspective to recognize opportunities and risks across national and functional boundaries but also the skill to coordinate activities and link capabilities across those barriers. The global business manager's overall goal is to capture the full benefit of integrated worldwide operations.

To be effective, the three core roles a business manager must play are strategist for his or her organization, architect of its worldwide asset and resource configuration, and coordinator of transactions across national borders. Leif Johansson, now president of Electrolux, the Swedish-based company, played all three roles successfully in his earlier position as head of the household appliance division.

In 1983, when 32-year-old Johansson assumed responsibility for the division, he took over a business that had been built up through more than 100 acquisitions over the previous eight years. By the late 1980s, Electrolux's portfolio included more than 20 brands sold in some 40 countries, with acquisitions continuing throughout the decade. Zanussi, for example, the big Italian manufacturer acquired by Electrolux in 1984, had built a strong market presence based on its reputation for innovation in household and commercial appliances. In addition, Arthur Martin in France and Zoppas in Norway had strong local brand position but limited innovative capability. As a result of these acquisitions, Electrolux had accumulated a patchwork quilt of companies, each with a different product portfolio, market position, and competitive situation. Johansson soon recognized the need for an overall strategy to coordinate and integrate his dispersed operations.

Talks with national marketing managers quickly convinced him that dropping local brands and standardizing around a few high-volume regional and global products would be unwise. He agreed with the local managers that their national brands were vital to maintaining consumer loyalty, distribution leverage, and competitive flexibility in markets that they saw fragmenting into more and more segments. But Johansson also understood the views of his division staff members, who pointed to the many similarities in product characteristics and consumer needs in the various markets. The division staff was certain Electrolux could use this advantage to cut across markets and increase competitiveness.

Johansson led a strategy review with a task force of product-division staff and national marketing managers. While the task force confirmed the marketing managers' notion of growing segmentation, its broader perspective enabled Johansson to see a convergence of segments across national markets. Their closer analysis also refined management's understanding of local market needs, concluding that consumers perceived "localness" mainly in terms of how it was designed or what features it offered. From this analysis, Johansson fashioned a product-market strategy that identified two full-line regional brands to be promoted and supported in all European markets. He positioned the Electrolux brand to respond to the cross-market segment for high prestige (customers characterized as "conservatives"), while the Zanussi brand would fill the segment where innovative products were key (for "trendsetters").

The local brands were clustered in the other two market segments pinpointed in the analysis: "yuppies" ("young and aggressive" urban professionals) and "environmentalists" ("warm and friendly" people interested in basic-value products). The new strategy provided Electrolux with localized brands that responded to the needs of these consumer groups. At the same time, the

(Continued)

(Continued)

company captured the efficiencies possible by standardizing the basic chassis and components of these local-brand products, turning them out in high volume in specialized regional plants. So, by tracking product and market trends across borders, Leif Johansson captured valuable global-scale efficiencies while reaping the benefits of a flexible response to national market fragmentation. What's more, though he took on the leadership role as a strategist, Johansson never assumed he alone had the understanding or the ability to form a global appliance strategy; he relied heavily on both corporate and local managers. Indeed, Johansson continued to solicit guidance on strategy through a council of country managers called the 1992 Group and through a set of product councils made up of functional managers.

Newly developed business strategies obviously need coordination. In practice, the specialization of assets and resources swells the flow of products and components among national units, requiring a firm hand to synchronize and control that flow. For organizations whose operations have become more dispersed and specialized at the same time that their strategies have become more connected and integrated, coordination across borders is a tough challenge. Business managers must fashion a repertoire of approaches and tools, from simple centralized control to management of exceptions identified through formal policies to indirect management via informal communication channels. Leif Johansson coordinated product flow—across his 35 national sales units and 29 regional sourcing facilities—by establishing broad sourcing policies and transfer-pricing ranges that set limits but left negotiations to internal suppliers and customers. For instance, each sales unit could negotiate a transfer price with its internal source for a certain product in a set range that was usually valid for a year. If the negotiations moved outside that range, the companies had to check with headquarters. As a coordinator, Johansson led the deliberations that defined the logic and philosophy of the parameters, but he stepped back and let individual unit managers run their own organizations, except when a matter went beyond policy limits.

In contrast, coordination of business strategy in Johansson's division was managed through teams that cut across the formal hierarchy. Instead of centralizing, he relied on managers to share the responsibility for monitoring implementation and resolving problems through teams. To protect the image and positioning of his regional brands—Electrolux and Zanussi—he set up a brand-coordination group for each. Group members came from the sales companies in key countries, and the chairperson was a corporate marketing executive. Both groups were responsible for building a coherent, pan-European strategy for the brand they represented. To rationalize the various product strategies across Europe, Johansson created product-line boards to oversee these strategies and to exploit any synergies. Each product line had its own board made up of the corporate product-line manager, who was chair, and his or her product managers. The Quattro 500 refrigerator-freezer, which was designed in Italy, built in Finland, and marketed in Sweden, was one example of how these boards successfully integrated product strategy.

In addition, the 1992 Group periodically reviewed the division's overall results, kept an eye on its manufacturing and marketing infrastructure, and supervised major development programs and investment projects. Capturing the symbolic value of 1992 in its name, the group was chaired by Johansson himself and included business managers from Italy, the United Kingdom, Spain, the United States, France, Switzerland, and Sweden.

The building blocks for most worldwide companies are their national subsidiaries. If the global business manager's main objective is to achieve global-scale efficiency and competitiveness, the national subsidiary manager's is to be sensitive and responsive to the local market. Country managers play the pivotal role not only in meeting local customer needs but also in satisfying the host government's requirements and defending their company's market positions against local and external competitors.

The need for local flexibility often puts the country manager in conflict with the global business manager. But in a successful transnational like Electrolux, negotiation can resolve these differences. In this era of intense competition around the world, companies cannot afford to permit a subsidiary manager to defend parochial interests as "king of the country." Nor should headquarters allow national subsidiaries to become the battleground for corporate holy wars fought in the name of globalization.

Questions

1. What type of headquarters-subsidiary relationship did Johansson establish?

2. Did he nurture corporate culture across the firm's subsidiaries? If so, how?

3. Discuss the role information technology might play in Electrolux.

SOURCE: Reprinted by permission of *Harvard Business Review*. An excerpt from C. A. Barlett and S. Ghoshal, "What Is a Global Manager?" *Harvard Business Review* (September–October 1992), pp. 125–128. Copyright © 1992 by the President and Fellows of Harvard College. All rights reserved.

CASE 13-2

See Jack. See Jack Run Europe

You don't become head of General Electric by being scaredy-cat, but one thing frightens Jack Welch, even after 18 years in the job; the sheer size of the company. "Don't talk to me about how big this place is," he says, nearly shouting. "I hate it." Size means sloth, systems, and smugness rather than speed, simplicity, and self-confidence. Over and over, Welch urges people to "tear this place apart."

At the same time, of course, he has grown GE so much it's, well, scary. GE is the ninth-biggest and second most profitable company in the world. Since Welch took over in 1981, GE's sales have risen 3.7 times (from $27.2 billion to $100.5 billion), and profits have grown 5.7 times (from $1.6 to $9.2 billion). Size is a burden if you try to lug it around, but it's an advantage if you can make it work for you. "Jack always says, 'You can't manage a company the size of GE. You leverage it,'" says Claudio Santiago. Spanish-born Santiago, 42, works in Florence, Italy, as CEO of one of GE's bigger divisions, a $2.1 billion-in-sales compressor and turbine manufacturer, Nuovo Pignone.

Welcome to global GE. Businesses like Nuovo Pignone symbolize one of the biggest stories of Welch's storied career: how America's most admired company, and a very American one, has become a truly global corporation. It is the story of how GE leveraged its businesses to buy and build, in just over a decade, a European business nearly as large as all GE was when Welch became CEO, and now intends to do the same in Asia, only faster. It is the story of how GE leverages its intellectual capital—an incomparable management tool kit that has turned a bunch of state-run

(Continued)

(Continued)

sinecures and niche businesses into a powerhouse whose net income, now a fifth of the company's, is compounding at 34 percent a year. And it's the story of the lever itself, the reason this Gargantua can be as agile as Nijinksy: a leadership-development system that won't let GE stop improving.

Since 1990, GE has paid nearly $30 billion for 133 European acquisitions; some 90,000 people are on GE's payroll there, about as many as Euro-giant Axa and BP Amoco employ worldwide. Europe accounted for $24.4 billion of 1998 revenue, of which only $2.7 billion, or 11 percent, came from exports from America. Inflation-adjusted, that's less than at the start of the decade.

When you do a lot of deals—GE made 108 acquisitions worldwide last year—you get good at it. One secret is an "integration model" developed chiefly at deal-hungry GE Capital Services. It rests on an obvious fact, but one many companies fudge: There are no "mergers of equal" here; there are acquisitions. "If you won't want to change, don't be acquired," says Norris Woodruff, a general manager in Industrial Systems and an in-house expert on the subject. Sure, GE wants to inspire change rather than compel it, to learn as well as teach, but GE is boss.

A second key point: Integration begins before the deal, with a due-diligence team that's not just financial but includes human resources and general management. They draft a plan to take effect the instant the pens are capped. Says James Conheady, an unsentimental Irishman who runs HR for GE Power Controls, which makes circuit breakers and the like and is based in Barcelona, "You have to move very, very quickly. There's a window of opportunity—an expectation of change—so you must deliver it fast."

First to arrive is someone from finance who is expected, literally on day one, to take control of the books, with the general ledger set up in the format GE uses worldwide. An "integration manager" is a half-step behind—usually a high-potential youngster brevetted into the acquired company. The integration manager doesn't supplant the people running the business. He works full-time on integration; the general manager runs the shop and owns the P&L.

"There's nothing special about these changes except the speed with which GE does them. But they're worth two to eight percentage points of operating margin," says Joaquim Agut, the Catalonian CEO of GE Power Controls, an $800 million operation composed of ten acquisitions in eight countries, including his family-owned company, sold in 1993.

After generic change comes GEneric change. Agut ticks off a list of GE tools—CAP, CMS, MGPD, bullet trains, QMI, Six Sigma, and more—and says they're worth another eight points of margin. That's an astonishing number, but you can make the case: Ten businesses that today represent about half of GE's European revenues had a combined operating margin of 5 percent in their first year of GE ownership, vs. an expected 13 percent margin for 1999.

Says Welch: "These companies have nothing in common except leadership and best practices," but that's not chopped liver. In the view of Merrill Lynch analyst Jeanne Terrile, GE is not so much a collection of businesses as it is "a repository of information and expertise that can be leveraged over a huge installed base." The ability to leverage expertise is why GE's globalization works.

Among GE management tools, several are particularly powerful aids to globalization. One of them, Work-Out, is so fundamental that GE trademarked the term and in its values statement says, "GE leaders . . . are committed to Work-Out." Work-Outs, begun in 1989, are meetings that can be called by anybody to address any problem, from niggling to humongous, with no boss in the room. When the participants have a plan—kill that stupid form, replace that balky pump—the boss must say yes or no on the spot, no haggling, no waffling. Work-Outs have become so common that there's probably one every day in each sizable GE facility, without management's knowing about it till someone pops in saying, "We had a Work-Out and need to talk to you."

Its simplicity is deceptive. Piazzolla says, "We saw 'committed to Work-Out' and asked, 'What's Work-Out? A meeting? Why should we spend time in meetings?'" But Work-Out's few rules totally subvert traditional executive power, and that's radical, especially in Europe.

Says Welch: "Getting a company to be informal is a huge deal, and no one ever talks about it." Informality is the key to GE's in-your-face, just-do-it culture. It allows the other tools to work QMI, for example, is "quick market intelligence," a tool adapted from Wal-Mart. A regularly scheduled, intense meeting where managers, salespeople, and others pore over data and share anecdotes to get a pulse of the market, QMI can't succeed if people are afraid to tell the boss he's all wet. . . .

GE's European work force has taken to its style with surprising ease. Says Anneliese Monden, who runs GE's leadership development programs in Europe: "Respect for titles isn't what GE is about, and it's a little strange in the beginning. Once people understand it's safe to think, they love it." According to Kary Wright, an American who is site manager of the aircraft-engine repair facility in Wales, "Personal contact is the key. You need it to share best practices."

"GE is a language—it is a world—and at the beginning it is difficult," says Pier Luigi Ferrara, 62, Nuovo Pignone's chairman.

More and more, the language of GE is the language of Six Sigma, the quality initiative begun in late 1995. It has become central to GE's ability to operate as a global whole. "Six Sigma" refers to a standard of excellence defined as having no more than 3.4 defects per million—in anything, whether it's manufacturing, billing, or loan processing. GE says it will spend $500 million on Six Sigma projects this year and will get more than $2 billion in benefits.

A global company needs a common language. Six Sigma is it, more than English. The shared lexicon makes it easier to swap ideas around GE. Before, two plant managers, even making the same product, probably had different performance measures. Says Piet van Abeelen, vice president for Six Sigma,

without Six Sigma, if you run a plant and I run a plant, it's tough to understand your numbers. Then you can say, 'Your ideas won't work, because I'm different.' Well, cry me a river. The commonalties are what matter. If you make the metrics the same, we can talk.

And they talk: Never in business history have so many people talked so much to so many other people as they do at GE. In 1988, when GE started benchmarking other companies and sharing best practices internally, people embraced the notion, but with reluctance, as one might embrace a loved one who had come in from a hard run on a hot day.

It's obvious to anyone who spends time in GE that hesitation has turned to obsession. Says Welch: "This is all about moving intellectual capital—taking ideas and moving them around faster and faster and faster." There is no "GE Europe" per se—no Rome to which all roads lead; the businesses report in to Schenectady, Cincinnati, Milwaukee, Kansas City, etc. But there are dozens of councils: In Europe alone, a Corporate Executive Council for the pooh-bahs, a Marketing Council, Technical Council, Sourcing Council, Finance Council, Human Resources Council, Sales Council, Manufacturing Council, Quality Council, and more. Each business operates similar cross-business or cross-functional networks, which meet for a day or two every few months. Probably every professional in the company—tens of thousands of people—sits on at least one cross-business council. At meetings, everybody is expected to bring something—an idea that made a few bucks, a process that's quicker than the old one. "Go to the European Corporate Executives Council," says Larry Johnston, just named to head it, "and you see 30 people writing all day long."

GE's culture is both deeply competitive and furiously collaborative. It's a company joke that within minutes of Welch's leaving a site, the phone starts ringing as other businesses ask. "What's

(Continued)

(Continued)

this thing you told Jack about?" More and more best practices flow both ways across the Atlantic. A system for managing sales forces developed in Barcelona is spreading worldwide. In May 1998, in Florence, Welch heard how a Six Sigma team making turbine packages had cut the total cost by 30 percent. "Show me," Welch demanded, and spent an hour grilling the team so he could, when he left, tell everybody else in GE to call Nuovo Pignone.

Ultimately people, not money or tools, make the global GE work. From the beginning, Welch has poured money and energy into creating a massive iceberg of leadership ability. The tip is Crotonville, the company's spiffy executive development campus in New York State; it was a "hovel" when Welch took over, according to one GE executive. What's beneath Crotonville is more important—a passion for leadership development everywhere in the company. The heads of GE's European businesses, asked how much of their time is spent on HR subjects, give answers ranging from 30 to 50 percent.

There's nothing egalitarian about GE's HR philosophy. It finds the best and culls the rest—period. It can be a cultural shock. Says Tone Rongstand, 32, who has been promoted twice in 1999 and now heads risk management for GE Consumer Finance in Norway: "When I was young I went to a ski competition, and the winner was the one who went in the average time. This is not like GE!"

Leadership development ranks with Work-Out, Six Sigma, and idea swapping as GE's best tools for globalization. It starts with new hires—or people at newly acquired companies. Engineers might get into TLP, a tough, two-year technical leadership program that involves three eight-month projects interwoven with classroom work in project management, process-improvement methods, and so on. Similar courses exist in every functional discipline from finance to information management, as well as Six Sigma training leading to "black belt" and "master black belt" status. Still more courses are offered at intermediate and advanced levels, always with lots of time in the field.

Questions

1. Discuss GE's headquarters-subsidiary control relationship.

2. Compare and contrast this case with Practical Perspectives 13.6 and 13.7.

SOURCE: Excerpted from Thomas A. Stewart, "See Jack. See Jack Run Europe," *Fortune* (September 27, 1999), pp. 124–136. Copyright © 1999 Time Inc. Reprinted by permission.

NOTES

1. Ron Ashkenas, "Breaking Through the Global Boundaries," *Executive Excellence,* 16, no. 7 (July 1999).

2. D. Rouzies, M. Segalla, and B. A. Weitz, "Cultural Impact on European Staffing Decisions in Sales Management," *International Journal of Research in Marketing,* 20, no. 1 (March 2003), pp. 67–85.

3. www.keynote.com (April 2007).

4. Cited by Stephanie Overman, "Going Global," *HR Magazine* (September 1993), pp. 49–50.

5. Joann S. Lublin, "Too Much, Too Fast," *The Wall Street Journal* (September 26, 1996), p. R8.

6. John J. Keller, "AT&T to Give Foreign Units More Autonomy," *The Wall Street Journal* (December 13, 1993), p. A4.

7. www.att.com (April 5, 2007).

8. P. Dwyer et al., "Tearing up Today's Organization Chart," *Business Week: 21st Century Capitalism* (Special Issue, 1994), p. 81.

9. Brendan R. Schlender, "Matsushita Shows How to Go Global," *Fortune* (July 11, 1994), p. 162.

10. Dwyer et al., "Tearing up Today's Organization Chart," op cit., p. 90.

11. John Dupuy, "Learning to Manage World-Class Strategy," *Management Review* (October 1991), p. 40.

12. The factors contained in Table 13.1 are adapted from Richard D. Robinson, *Internationalization of Business: An Introduction* (New York: The Dryden Press, 1984), pp. 268–269.

13. See C.-B. Choi and P. W. Beamish, "Split Management Control and International Joint Venture Performance," *Journal of International Business Studies,* 35 (2004), pp. 201–215.

14. For recent studies on this aspect, see T. Buck and A. Shahrim, "The Translation of Corporate Governance Changes Across National Cultures: The Case of Germany," *Journal of International Business Studies,* 36 (2005), pp. 42–61; Y. Luo, "Market-Seeking MNEs in an Emerging Market: How Parent-Subsidiary Links Shape Overseas Success," *Journal of International Business Studies,* 34 (2003), pp. 290–309; D. A. Griffith and M. B. Myers, "The Performance Implications of Strategic Fit of Relational Norm Governance Strategies in Global Chain Relationships," *Journal of International Business Studies,* 36 (2005), pp. 254–269; A. Ferner, P. Almond, and T. Colling, "Institutional Theory and the Cross-National Transfer of Employment Policy: The Case of 'Workforce' Diversity in U.S. Multinationals, *Journal of International Business Studies,* 36 (2005), pp. 304–321; Y. Gong, O. Shenkar, Y. Luo, and M-K. Nyaw, "Human Resources and International Joint Venture Performance: A System Perspective, *Journal of International Business Studies,* 36 (2005), pp. 505–515; J. Q. Barden, H. K. Steensma, and M. A. Lyles, "The Influence of Parent Control Structure on Conflict in Vietnamese International Joint Ventures: An Organizational Justice-Based Contingency Approach," *Journal of International Business Studies,* 36 (2005), pp. 156–174; Shih-Fen S. Chen, "Extending Internalization Theory: A New Perspective on International Technology Transfer and Its Generalization," *Journal of International Business Studies,* 36 (2005), pp. 231–245; D. Minbaeva, T. Pedersen, I. Bjorkman, C. F. Fey, and H. J. Park, "MNC Knowledge Transfer, Subsidiary Absorptive Capacity, and HRM," *Journal of International Business Studies,* 34 (2003), pp. 586–599; P. J. Buckley and N. Hashai, "A Global System View of Firm Boundaries," *Journal of International Business Studies,* 35 (2004), pp. 33–45.

15. Sumantra Ghoshal and Nitin Nohria, "Horses for Courses: Organizational Forms for Multinational Corporations," *Sloan Management Review* (Winter 1993), p. 28.

16. Ibid.

17. Geert Hofstede, *Culture's Consequences: International Differences in Work-Related Values* (Beverly Hills, CA: Sage, 1980).

18. Cited by Geert Hofstede, "Motivation, Leadership, and Organization: Do American Theories Apply Abroad?" *Organizational Dynamics* (Summer 1980), p. 60.

19. J. S. Osland, S. DeFranco, and A. Osland, "Organizational Implications of Latin American Culture: Lessons From an Expatriate," *Journal of Management Inquiry,* 8, no. 2 (June 1999), pp. 219–234.

20. J. R. Weisz, F. M. Rothbaum, and T. C. Blackburn, "Standing out and Standing in: The Psychology of Control in America and Japan," *American Psychologist,* 39 (1984), pp. 955–969.

21. R. N. Bellah, R. Madsen, W. M. Sullivan, A. Swidler, and S. M. Tipton (Eds.), *Individualism and Commitment in American Life* (New York: Harper & Row, 1987).

22. W. G. Ouchi, "The Relationship Between Organizational Structure and Control," *Administrative Science Quarterly,* 22 (1987), pp. 95–113.

23. Weisz et al., "Standing out and Standing in," op cit.

24. Leah Nathans, "A Matter of Control," *Business Month* (September 1988), pp. 46–52.

25. R. N. Kannungo and R. W. Wright, "A Cross-Cultural Comparative Study of Managerial Job Attitudes," *Journal of International Business Studies,* 14, no. 2 (1983), pp. 115–129.

26. Cited by Hofstede, "Motivation, Leadership, and Organization," op cit., p. 60.

27. S. G. Redding and D. S. Pugh, "The Formal and the Informal: Japanese and Chinese Organizational Studies," in S. R. Clegg, D. C. Dunphy, and S. G. Redding (Eds.), *The Enterprise and Management in East Asia* (Hong Kong: Center for Asian Studies, 1986).

28. K. H. Chung, "A Comparative Study of Managerial Characteristics of Domestic, International, and Governmental Institutions in Korea," Paper presented at the Midwest Conference of Asian Affairs, Minneapolis, MN (1978); W. S. Nam, *The Traditional Pattern of Korean Industrial Management,* ILCORK Working Paper No. 14 (Manoa, HI: University of Hawaii, Social Science Research Institute, 1971); G. W. England and R. Lee, "Organizational Goals and Expected Behavior Among American, Japanese, and Korean Managers: A Comparative Study," *Academy of Management Journal,* 4 (1971), pp. 425–438; J. Harbron, "Korea's Executives Are Not Quite the New Japanese," *The Business Quarterly,* 44 (1979), pp. 16–19.

29. R. H. Solomon, *Mao's Revolution and Chinese Political Culture* (Berkeley: University of California Press, 1971).

30. Geert Hofstede, "The Cultural Relativity of the Quality of Life Concept," *Academy of Management Review,* 9, no. 3 (1984), pp. 389–398.

31. R. E. Caves, "Industrial Organization, Corporate Strategy and Structure," *Journal of Economic Literature,* 18 (1980), p. 64; M. Haire, E. Ghiselli, and L. W. Porter, *Managerial Thinking: An International Study* (New York: John Wiley & Sons, 1966); D. J. Hickson, C. R. Hinings, J. McMillan, and J. P Schwitter, "The Culture Free Context of Organization Structure: A Tri-National Comparison," *Sociology,* 8 (1974), pp. 59–80.

32. Ghoshal and Nohria, "Horses and Courses: Organizational Forms for Multinational Corporations," op cit.

33. Ibid.

34. H. Aldrich, *Organizations and Environments* (Englewood Cliffs, NJ: Prentice Hall, 1979); L. Greiner, "Evolution and Revolution as Organizations Grow," *Harvard Business Review* (July–August 1972), p. 41.

35. Thomas Hout, Michael E. Porter, and Eileen Rudden, "How Global Companies Win Out," *Harvard Business Review* (September–October 1982), p. 103.

36. Ibid.

37. Lawrence and J. W. Lorsch, *Organization and Environment: Managing Differentiation and Integration* (Cambridge, MA: Harvard University, Graduate School of Business Administration, Division of Research, 1967).

38. Decentralizing for Competitive Advantage," *Across the Board,* 31 (January 1994), p. 26.

39. R. E. Miles, C. C. Snow, and J. Pfeffer, "Organization Environment: Concepts and Issues," *Industrial Relations,* 13 (1974), pp. 244–264; K. Weick, *The Social Psychology of Organization* (Reading, MA: Addison-Wesley, 1969); R. F. Zammuto, "Growth, Stability, and Decline in American College and University Enrollments," *Educational Administration Quarterly,* 19, no. 1 (1983), pp. 83–89.

40. M. Yasai-Ardekani, "Effects of Environmental Scarcity and Munificence on the Relationship of Context to Organizational Structure," *Academy of Management Journal,* 32, no. 1 (1989), pp. 131–156.

41. Excerpted from Brian O'Reilly, "J&J Is on a Roll," *Fortune* (December 26, 1994), pp. 178–192; Joseph Weber, "A Big Company That Works," *Business Week* (May 4, 1992), p. 125.

42. See V. Nee, S. Opper, and S. Wong, "Developing State and Corporate Governance in China," *Management and Organization Review,* 3, no. 1 (March 2007), pp. 19–53.

43. This idea is drawn from Thomas W. Malone, "Is Empowerment Just a Fad? Control, Decision Making, and IT," *Sloan Management Review,* 38, no. 2 (Winter 1997), pp. 23–25.

44. David O. Stephens, "The Globalization of Information Technology in Multinational Corporations," *Information Management Journal,* 33, no. 3 (July 1999), pp. 66–71.

45. Kenichi Ohmae, "Planning for a Global Harvest," *Harvard Business Review* (July–August 1989), p. 136.

46. M. Landler and M. Barbaro, "Wal-Mart Discovers That Its Formula Doesn't Fit Every Culture," *The New York Times* (August 20, 2006), p. C1.

47. W. C. Kim and R. A. Mauborgne, "Making Global Strategies Work," *Sloan Management Review* (Spring 1993), p. 11.

48. Ibid.

49. G. Hofstede, B. Neuijen, D. D. Ohayv, G. Sanders, "Measuring Organizational Cultures: A Qualitative and Quantitative Study Across Twenty Cases," *Administrative Science Quarterly,* 35 (1990), pp. 286–316.

50. Ibid., p. 312.

51. Charlene M. Solomon, "Transplanting Corporate Cultures Globally," *Personnel Journal* (October 1993), pp. 80–81.

52. Ibid.

53. Ibid.

54. Regina Fazio Maruca, "The Right Way to Go Global: An Interview with Whirlpool CEO David Whitwam," *Harvard Business Review* (March–April 1994), p. 139.

55. Gurcharan Das, "Local Memoirs of a Global Manager," *Harvard Business Review* (March–April 1993), p. 38.

56. Y. Ling, S. W. Floyd, and D. C. Baldridge, "Toward a Model of Issue-Selling by Subsidiary Managers in Multinational Organizations," *Journal of International Business Studies,* 36 (2005), pp. 637–654.

57. See J. R. Brown, C. S. Dev, and Z. Zhou, "Broadening the Foreign Market Entry Mode Decision: Separating Ownership and Control," *Journal of International Business Studies,* 34 (2003), pp. 473–488; A. Madhok, "Cost, Value and Foreign Market Entry Mode: The Transaction and the Firm," *Strategic Management Journal,* 18 (1997), pp. 39–61.

Part VIII

OPTIONAL COURSE INTEGRATIVE ASSIGNMENT

This section presents suggested instructions for preparing a project aiming to integrate the entire textbook—a sort of mini course thesis.

Group or Individual Project

Ideally, groups of three or four students are formed to develop the project, but it can be done by a single individual.

(a) Select a domestic product(s) and/or service (real or fiction), and develop a 10-year timetable, first for national growth and then for international growth, showing the major growth activities, such as when and where it was started; domestic market expansion, such as acquisition(s), mergers, new products/services, where and when, and so on; and future expansion of the project.

(b) Or, similarly, select a domestic company (real or fiction), and develop a 10-year timetable for national growth and then international growth, showing the major activities, such as when and where it was started; its product(s)/service(s); domestic market expansion, such as acquisition(s), mergers, new products/services, where and when, and so on; and project future expansion.

(c) Or, alternatively, select an existing established international business company, and show both the company's nationalization and internationalization activities, such as when and where it was started; its product(s)/service(s); domestic market expansion, such as acquisition(s), mergers, new products/services, where and when, and so on; and future expansion of the project.

The project should be guided by the contents of the textbook, including the process, the anecdotes, the practical perspectives, and the cases.

Sources of information include

- The textbook
- Interviewing a knowledgeable executive or executives
- Books with stories about the business
- Articles appearing in the practical media about the business
- The Internet—many businesses post their history on their Web site.

To be able to do this project, students should have completed a thorough study of the textbook, the assigned readings, and the class discussions.

The group or individual should share the findings with the class. The project requires the instructor's approval.

A paper, typed double-spaced, should be submitted.

The grade should be based on the substance and the presentation mechanics of the written paper (criteria as suggested below).

Note: The objective of the project is more to acquire a functional understanding of the internationalization process than to acquire a hands-on understanding. In this context, students are often not able to obtain full corporate information, and thus they will sometimes have to "be creative" in preparing the project.

Some Suggested Guidelines for Preparing the Project

1. Business's domestic development history (issues to be addressed)
   - What is (or are) the product(s) and/or service(s) the business provides or will provide?
   - When was the company started or when will it be started? Where?
   - Historically, businesses start small in a local area and grow nationally slowly as they learn to manage larger organizations before they start internationalizing their operations.
   - How did the company grow nationally or how will it grow nationally?
   - Which organizational structure or structures were or are to be used? (Chapter 6)
   - How was or how will the operations be controlled? (Chapter 13)
   - What is the firm's domestic market competitive strength(s) or what will it (they) be? Is it its product/service, trademark/brand name, cultural identification, quality, price, management?
   - How was the competitive strength(s) developed (through media promotion, through word-of-mouth promotion, through quality, through pricing, through distribution, or through a combination?
   - What are the firm's domestic weaknesses, if any?
   - Who are the major domestic competitors?

2. Business's international development history (issues to be addressed)
   - Where did it or will it begin? Why? (e.g., similarity of cultures or attractive financial package offered by the country(s) and so on) (Chapters 3, 4)

As an illustration, New York City's Radio City Music Hall decided to internationalize its famous Christmas Spectacular Show. Its plan was to perform its first show in Detroit and

Myrtle Beach, South Carolina. After its management had acquired experience managing a larger organization, it would take its show to four additional U.S. cities, and subsequently to four more U.S. cities. After its management had learned how to manage an even larger organization, it would start internationalizing the show. To acquire international experience, it had plans to take the show to Tokyo and Paris and then expand further internationally (Radio City Musical Hall's management terminated its expansion program after entering several U.S. cities.)

Disney's theme park was opened in California, and then it opened in Florida, then in Japan, then in France, and recently in China.

Practical Perspective 4.4, Bury Thy Teacher, is a good illustration of how Chicago's 97-year-old Schwinn Bicycle Co. failed because it internationalized its operations without international management experience.

- In what way(s) did or will the company contribute to the foreign country's economic development objectives? That is, why did or would the country's government welcome the company? (Chapter 3)
- How did it or will it develop a good relationship with the foreign government? (Chapter 3)
- What is or what will be the company's international strength(s)/competitive advantages and/or weaknesses? Cultural cache? Reputation? Pricing? Quality? (Chapters 4 and 5)

    For example, Wal-Mart's strength is price. Coca Cola's and McDonald's major strength is the American cultural cache. Japanese corporations tend to use both price and quality as their major strength.

- How did it or will it deal with its international business weaknesses?

    For example, Disney entered Japan's market via joint ventures with experienced Japanese companies, but it floundered in its entry to France because it went at it alone without being familiar enough with the French culture (a weakness).

- How did or how will the company make itself known in the foreign market before entering it? Through promotion? Through free samples?
- What was or will be the firm's international pricing, promotion, and product/service strategy?
- How did it enter or how will it enter the foreign market? By exporting? By alliances with local companies that have international management experience or with experienced companies in the foreign market? (Chapters 4 and 5)
- If it formed or will form a partnership, what kind of partnership—for example, joint venture or strategic alliance? (Chapters 4 and 5). Why use that approach? Did or does the country's laws mandate that form of entry?
- If it entered via partnership or acquisition or merger, how did it deal with the differences in corporate cultures? (Chapter 8)
- How did it or how will it develop international business/management skills? By employing experienced executives? By forming an alliance with a company possessing international skills? By acquiring these skills by going through the internationalization process slowly—starting out with low dependence on foreign sales and gradually increasing dependence as it develops its skills? Why was that approach used or why will it be used?
- Is or will the company's staffing view be ethnocentric or polycentric? Why use that view? How does the nature of the company, service or manufacturing, influence the view? (Chapter 7)

- How does it or how will it attract high-caliber executives for foreign assignments? (Chapter 8).
- How does or how will the company attract or train high-caliber foreign-country executives? (Chapter 8)
- How did it or will it develop workers' skills in the foreign market? (Chapter 8)
- What kind of decision-making style worked or will work best in developing the foreign market? (Chapters 1 and 11)
- What kind of leadership style worked or will work best in developing the foreign market? (Chapters 1 and 12)
- What are or will be its international organizational structure? (Chapter 6)
- How was or how will the international operations be controlled? (Chapter 13)
- Did or will the company adopt a cross-national ethics and social responsibility code? Describe it. (Chapter 2)
- Discuss the overall impact of culture on international management.
- Discuss the role IT plays in the organization.

Some Suggested Criteria to Be Used for Evaluation of the Project: Class Presentation and Written Paper

A. Extent of coverage of historical development of domestic business, including domestic SWOT analysis

B. Extent of coverage of historical development of international business, including
   - why business was internationalized,
   - international SWOT analysis,
   - why the foreign market would welcome the product/service,
   - strategy for internationalizing home managers,
   - product/service strategy,
   - promotion strategy,
   - entry strategy,
   - pricing strategy,
   - strategy for training foreign managers,
   - strategy for training foreign employees,
   - strategy for cross-cultural training of expatriates and repatriates,
   - organizational structure/control mechanisms,
   - discussion of culture, and
   - discussion of the role of IT in managing the business enterprise

C. Flow of classroom presentation
   - Clarity of presentation
   - Use of visual aids
   - Liveliness of the presentation (without monotonous reading of notes)
   - Flow of written presentation
   - Clarity of written presentation

INDEX

ABOUT THE AUTHOR

Carl Rodrigues has been teaching international business management for 25 years. During this period, he has regularly published in academic journals and presented several papers on this subject at academic conferences. He also traveled extensively throughout the world. In the early 1990s, he lectured on contemporary Western management theory to professors and graduate students at two major universities in China. Prior to entering the academia, he worked for five years with an American Indian tribe in its modernization efforts under the U.S. Indian Self-Determination Act of 1974—this tribe was the first one to have undergone such a program.